LATIN AMERICA

ITS PROBLEMS AND ITS PROMISE

A Multidisciplinary Introduction

FIFTH EDITION

EDITED BY

Jan Knippers Black

Monterey Institute of International Studies

**WESTVIEW
PRESS**

A Member of the Perseus Books Group

*This fifth edition is dedicated to all of the
contributors to earlier editions—our esteemed colleagues
and my cherished friends—who are now deceased:*

E. Bradford Burns
Eldon (Bud) Kenworthy
John D. Martz
Brady Tyson
Rene A. Dreifuss

Westview Press books are available at special discounts for bulk purchases in the United
States by corporations, institutions, and other organizations. For more information, please
contact the Special Markets Department at the Perseus Books Group, 2300 Chestnut Street,
Suite 200, Philadelphia, PA 19103, or call (800) 810-4145, ext. 5000, or e-mail
special.markets@perseusbooks.com.

Library of Congress Cataloging-in-Publication Data
Latin America : its problems and its promise : a multidisciplinary introduction / edited by
Jan Knippers Black. — 5th ed.
   p. cm.
Includes bibliographical references and index.
ISBN 978-0-8133-4400-3 (alk. paper)
1. Latin America. I. Black, Jan Knippers, 1940-
F1406.7.L38 2010
980—dc22
                                        2010003420

10 9 8 7 6 5 4 3 2 1

Contents

PART THREE: ECONOMIC AND SOCIAL STRUCTURES

PART FOUR: POLITICAL PROCESSES AND TRENDS

PART FIVE: EXTERNAL RELATIONS

PART SIX: MEXICO AND CENTRAL AMERICA

Maps, Tables, and Figures

*(All photographs that introduce part openers
were taken by Jan Knippers Black)*

MAPS

TABLES

ix

FIGURES

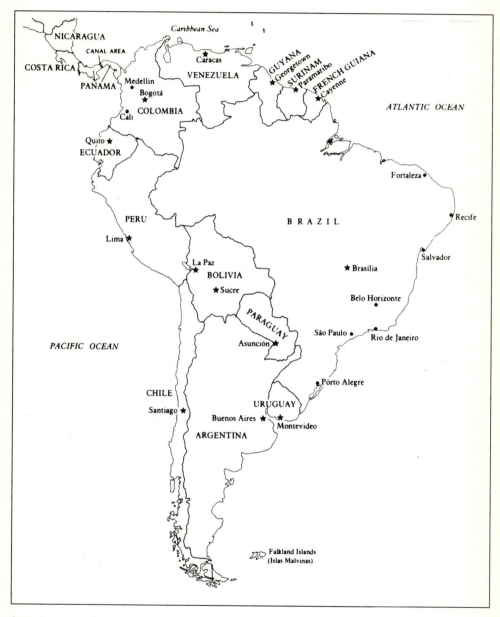

South America

Reprinted, with permission, from Howard J. Wiarda and Harvey F. Kline, eds., *Latin American Politics and Development*, Second Edition (Boulder, Colo.: Westview Press, 1985).

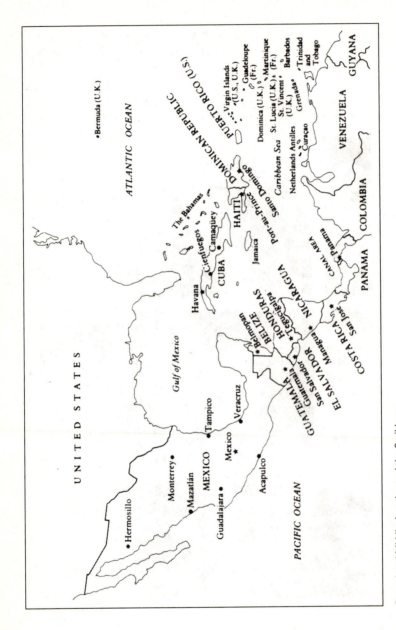

Central and Middle America and the Caribbean

Reprinted, with permission, from Howard J. Wiarda and Harvey F. Kline, eds., *Latin American Politics and Development*, Second Edition (Boulder, Colo.: Westview Press, 1985).

Chapter 1

INTRODUCTION

Latin America Leading the Learning Curve

JAN KNIPPERS BLACK

Latin Americans and Latin Americanists have become accustomed over many decades to hearing that "when the United States sneezes, Latin America catches pneumonia." But in the fall of 2008, the United States came down with a bad case of pneumonia—and Latin America sneezed.

This is a good time to be a Latin Americanist. Never more than now in the near half century since, as a founding generation Peace Corps volunteer, I first began to focus on Western Hemisphere affairs, have I sensed among Latin Americans— leaders and publics alike—a greater inclination to optimism and activism, self-confidence and social and regional solidarity. At the close of the first decade of the twenty-first century, most of the Latin American countries are moving in the direction of expanded popular participation in creditable elections and of public assertiveness with respect both to foreign policy and to domestic considerations in economic decision making. Trade patterns and partnerships are increasingly diversified, and a report released by the UN Economic Commission for Latin America and the Caribbean (UNECLAC) in 2009 indicated that between 2006 and 2008, except for Mexico, poverty had diminished across the region. The region did indeed sneeze in 2009 after exposure to the US crisis, but even the hardest hit, close-in neighbors approached 2010 with recovery prospects stronger than those of the United States.

The waves of hope and anticipation of change that were sweeping the region when I arrived in Chile in the early 1960s were soon to give way to tyranny and terror, in South America first in the 1960s and 1970s, and in Mesoamerica in the 1980s. The first edition of this book, appearing in 1984, had to report on ongoing struggles to emerge from a political and economic abyss and a pattern in Central America of insurgency and counterinsurgency without promise of resolution.

Shaky "democratic transitions" and sporadic "market emergence" in the 1990s brought relief for some, but upbeat major media storylines obscured the rumblings of discontent or desperation that lacked a forum and remained beneath the radar screen. Thus, in the first decade of the twenty-first century, it may have appeared from a distance that Latin America was emerging from a deep sleep, as

1

silent suffering acquired voice and became demand, and anomic protest became coherent, mobilized, focused pursuit of change, expressed in some cases in electoral outcomes and policy.

In the early 1960s the overriding concern in hemispheric affairs was whether or not a young and charismatic US president would be able to pressure each of the other Latin American governments to sever relations with Cuba. When Western Hemisphere presidents met in early 2009, the overriding issue was whether the Latin American governments, acting as one, would be able to pressure a young and charismatic US president to renew relations with Cuba.

This turn of events, accompanied by new expressions and manifestations of nationalism and regionalism, has been for the most vociferous of US pundits cause for alarm. Any metaphoric move toward the exit of the US backyard is by definition a move to the left, which in the absence of an all-defining cold war, has been relabeled terrorism. Cooler heads are inclined to see national self-assertion or opposition to US policy as evidence that the United States has not been paying enough attention to Latin America.

As US attention to Latin America has meant everything from stripping out the resources to sending in the marines, I'd be inclined to say that enough of the usual kind of attention is already too much. But there is indeed a sense in which we are paying far too little attention. US institutions have become accustomed over the past century to thinking in terms of what we should be *teaching* Latin Americans (on the basis, one presumes, of our vast experience in doing things right). In fact, we should be paying attention because we have so much to *learn* from Latin America—because, to misquote Pogo, "we have met the *suckers*, and they are us."

Some of the lessons we should be learning from Latin America (elaborated in the conclusion to this book) include humility and lessons in development as seen from the bottom up (Latin Americans turned to self-help because it was the only help available); lessons in electoral democracy from those who have understood that defending the right to vote without defending the right to creditable electoral processes and credible outcomes amounts to complicity in fraud; lessons in democratic transition, in the importance particularly of prosecuting rights abuse and corruption in order to reconstruct the rule of law and recover national self-respect; and lessons in security for the unarmed and unaffluent—on finding security, for example, in truth, in numbers, and in rejection of control by fear.

LESSONS FROM THE FRONT LINES

Latin America, as the first region of what is now called the Third World to be thoroughly subjugated by European colonialism and the first to throw off that subjugation, has long been the Third World's pacesetter and harbinger. It was first to adopt the trappings of a republic and first, in varying degrees and by varying means, to bring some reality to the rhetoric of popular participation.

Latin America was first to elaborate legal, institutional, and political bases in support of national economic sovereignty, and first to see those bases obliterated and constitutions shredded by military dictatorship. It was first then, particularly under the dictatorships of the Southern Cone, to be forced open for "free trade"—

in fact, very costly debt, deregulation and dependence—and first, along with Africa in the 1980s, to experience shock therapy and economic meltdown.

A trend to limited redemocratization and sporadic economic growth that raised hopes in the 1990s gave way early in the new millennium to widespread cynicism, anger, and desperation, as prices rose, wages fell, and income gaps widened. In the short term, new manifestations of social discontent kept governments enfeebled and economies off-balance. Ahead of the curve at that time was not a very comfortable place to be. By the end of the decade, however, such conditions had generated in response new parties and new categories of social movements that have since led to more meaningful participation.

Meanwhile, the hope for change that was palpable in the South began to reverberate in the North as well. The United States, while lagging, found itself in 2009 on the same trajectory as Latin America, riding a new wave of optimism and activism. It must be noted, though, that from pole to pole in the Western Hemisphere, increased political participation had failed to bring about acceptable levels of government accountability. The label of "violin governments" that many Chileans had assigned to their coalition governments of the 1930s and 1940s—so labeled as they were said to be held by the Left and played by the Right—seemed an apt characterization for many Hemisphere governments in the twenty-first century. Those governments were more or less elected and more or less civilian, but public sectors in most countries were still largely overwhelmed by private sectors— by the global concentration and mobility of money.

Moreover, while some governments had done a commendable job of resurrecting economies and raising employment and wages, income gaps almost everywhere had continued to grow. And gaps in the Western Hemisphere continued to exceed those in most other world regions. By mid-2009, the US economic meltdown of 2008 had led to contractions in most Latin American economies as well, but in most the long-term damage was not expected to be so far-reaching as in the United States; according to UNECLAC, recovery in Latin America was anticipated to be stronger and sooner than in the United States. From the booming Brazilian economy to the badly damaged Mexican one, quite respectable growth rates were expected for 2010. It should be noted, however, that as in the United States, the first markets to make a robust comeback were the financial markets.

SCHOLARS IN CONTEXT

The same pressures and perceptions faced by US and Latin American policymakers set the agenda and the parameters that govern academic discourse. Thus to the student who must launch his or her exploration of Latin America through the eyes and ears, the assumptions and perspectives, and the theoretical and ideological filters of others, it would be useful to know something of the intellectual paths that have been traveled by the specialists in the field. Those paths have circled, dead-ended, and U-turned, merged and diverged; they are now, as always, subject to turns in new directions. The attempt to understand social relations, especially in an area so diverse and complex as Latin America, can never be a simple matter of learning "the facts." There will always be many facts in dispute; answers depend on the nature of available data, on the interests of the sources consulted, and on how questions are asked. Confronted, as one must be in a multiauthored text with differing points of view and thus differing interpretations of the same historical and social data, the student may find it worthwhile to begin the study of Latin America with a study of Latin Americanists.

It is to be expected that interests and interpretations of social phenomena will vary from one discipline to another. The geographer may find, for example, that soil quality, climate, and topography determine settlement patterns and socioeconomic relations, which in turn configure political systems. The anthropologist may find explanation for social harmony or social conflict in ethnic and cultural patterns. The economist may find that political trends derive from economic ones, while the political scientist may see power relationships as overriding. In the study of Latin America, however, there has always been a unifying theme.

From the perspectives of US- and European-based scholars, as well as from those of Latin America's own creative and scholarly writers, the study of Latin America has been approached as the study of a problem, or set of problems. The problems might be capsulized as underdevelopment and political instability or, more simply, as poverty or inequality and the failure of democratic systems to take hold. The search for the roots, causes, and progenitors of these problems has generally led in one of three directions: to the Iberians—the conquistadores and the institutions, attitudes, and cultural traits they brought with them to the New World; to the Latin Americans themselves—the alleged greed of the elites, absence of entrepreneurship in the middle classes, or passivity of the masses; or to the United States and the international capitalist system it promotes and defends.

Long before US scholars began to direct their attention to Latin America's problems, the area's own intellectuals were absorbed by the question of where to place the blame. Domingo Faustino Sarmiento and other nineteenth-century intellectual and political leaders of cosmopolitan Buenos Aires blamed the cycles of anarchy and tyranny their newly independent country was suffering on Hispanic influences.[1] Sarmiento in later life directed his scorn toward Latin America's own "melting pot." Influenced by social Darwinism, he diagnosed "the decadent state" of Argentine society as deriving from its racial components of Spanish, mestizo, Indian, and Negro.

Turning the tables at the turn of the twentieth century, José Enrique Rodó, Uruguay's foremost literary figure, urged the youth of his country—in his masterpiece, *Ariel*—to shun the materialism of the United States and to cling to the spiritual and intellectual values of their Spanish heritage. A strong current of Latin American social thought, reflected in art and music as well as literature, that gained momentum a few decades into the twentieth century has touted the strengths of native American cultures and blamed both Hispanic and North American influences for the prevailing instability and social injustice. Likewise, in the Caribbean, the black power movements of the 1960s and 1970s called Europe and Anglo-America to task for the region's underdevelopment.

US Latin American studies as an interdisciplinary field in the United States and, by extension, the coming of age of analysis of Latin American social and political systems are clearly the illegitimate offspring of Fidel Castro. Prior to the Cuban revolution, historians, anthropologists, and literary scholars had generally pursued their studies of Latin American subjects in disciplinary isolation. Political analysis had been largely limited to formal legal studies, highlighting the fact that Latin American regimes rarely lived up to the standards, borrowed from France and the United States, embodied in their constitutions. Such studies generally drew their explanatory theses from the distinctive historical and cultural traditions of the United States of North America and the disunited states of Latin America and, in so doing, contributed to the mystification of the political process in both areas.[2] The Iberian heritage of feudalism, authoritarianism, and Catholicism was seen as the major obstacle to democratic and socioeconomic reforms.

The surge of interest in Latin America on the part of US politicians and academics (encouraged by newly available government-funded fellowships and contracts) that accompanied the Cuban revolution coincided with the acceleration of decolonization elsewhere and the expansion of attention to the Third World generally by the previously parochial disciplines of economics and political science. Thus, development and modernization theory, formulated to address change processes in other parts of the Third World, came to dominate the study of Latin America as well. Studies falling under these rubrics generally posited that either the economic and political systems of Latin America would increasingly approximate those of the United States and Western Europe or the area would be engulfed in violent revolution.

The invalidation of many of the assumptions of development and modernization theorists by the onrush of events—particularly by the fall of democratic regimes and their replacement by military dictatorships—resulted in a theoretical backlash as well as in long overdue attention to the work of Latin American theorists. The backlash was expressed in a reassertion of the tenacity of tradition, of the fundamentally conservative character of Latin American society. This perspective has been endowed with greater theoretical and conceptual sophistication in studies using the corporatist model. Corporatism stresses the hierarchical organization of modern institutions and the persistence of control from the top.

A large body of Latin American literature, dating back to "the black legend" of the cruelty and intolerance of Spanish colonial rule, supports the historical and cultural explanations for the failure of democracy. But the trends that had dominated the social sciences in the major Latin American countries were variations on the Marxist themes of class conflict and imperialism. One such body of thought, known as dependency theory, came to rival development and modernization theory for predominance among US and European specialists in Latin American studies. Dependency theory held that Latin American underdevelopment should be understood as a by-product of the international capitalist system.

With the end of the Cold War, that international capitalist system struck back with a force that suppressed all previously contending paradigms. Some Latin American theorists continued to urge attention to national and local markets, to social and economic democracy, and to a new kind of nationalism. But a triumphalist neoliberalism that stressed open markets, privatization, and elections-as-democracy and gave no quarter to social concerns came to dominate elite institutions throughout the hemisphere through the end of the century.

These theoretical trends and approaches have permeated all aspects of Latin American studies, because—to a far greater extent than in Europe or the United States—philosophy, literature, the arts, and other pursuits of the intelligentsia in

Latin America tend to reflect national or regional concerns. It could hardly be otherwise; the cataclysmic episodes of insurgency and repression, revolution and counterrevolution, leave no one untouched.

Blaming the Iberians: Corporatism and Culture

The historical-cultural approach to the study of Latin America and its problems draws attention to the persistence in contemporary Latin America of attitudes, institutions, and social relations that are said to have been characteristic of the Iberian Peninsula in medieval times.[3] According to this view, the Spanish conquistadores, crown officials, and Roman Catholic missionaries transplanted in the New World a social system firmly based on elitism, authoritarianism, and militarism.

The Portuguese legacy differed from that of Spain in its greater tolerance of racial and cultural diversity, but, like the Spanish, the Portuguese inculcated in their New World offspring a rigid sense of social, political, and cultural hierarchy. Public morality was an integral part of the political culture, and the Catholic Church, also hierarchical in structure, absolutist in doctrine, and authoritarian in practice, shared with the institutions of government the responsibility for the maintenance of the political and moral order.

During the early colonial period, a great debate raged among intellectuals and governmental and spiritual leaders in Spain and its colonies as to whether native Americans were fully human. It was finally concluded that the Church's Christianizing mission implied recognition of the fundamental human attributes of the Indians. But in much of the empire, the slaughter or enslavement of the Indians proceeded nevertheless, and it is clear that many contemporary Latin Americans continue to see the Indians as belonging to a lesser order of humanity.

Corporatism

The corporatist model, drawn primarily from medieval Catholic thought and observed, to some degree, in Spain under Franco and Portugal under Salazar, was found to "fit" midcentury Latin American politics to a greater degree than some of the models derived from development and modernization theory. The model, elaborated in works by Wiarda, Schmitter, Malloy, Erickson, and others, has called attention to the tendency to vertical, as opposed to horizontal, organization among politically active groups in Latin America.[4] Such groups, in corporatist systems, are controlled and manipulated by authoritarian governments so that communications and power flow from the top down rather than from the bottom up.

Few Latin Americanists would dispute the observation that vestiges of medieval Iberia are still to be found in Latin America. Nor is the existence of corporatist tendencies a subject of great controversy. The point at which many Latin Americanists depart from the findings of some scholars pursuing historical-cultural or corporatist approaches is the supposition that modern manifestations of elitism and authoritarianism are due primarily to colonization by Spain and Portugal.

Critics note, for example, that some countries that experienced fiercely authoritarian, military rule in the 1970s and 1980s (Chile and Uruguay, for example) had enjoyed constitutional and more or less democratic rule throughout most of the twentieth century. Furthermore, the Southern Cone (Argentina, Uruguay, and Chile) was among the areas least influenced by colonial Spain. In Argentina, descendants of Italian immigrants, who arrived in great waves around the turn of the twentieth century, now outnumber the descendants of Spanish settlers. Surely some common denominators of vintage more recent than the colonial period are needed to explain the resurgence of authoritarianism in Latin America in the late twentieth century. Moreover, the qualitative difference between traditional corporatism and the modern bureaucratic-technocratic variety has often been understated. By the end of the 1980s, the popularity of the corporatist paradigm appeared to be waning, and some of its former proponents, including Howard Wiarda, had turned to an emphasis on cultural causation.

Cultural Causation

The late 1980s saw a revival of interest in the explanatory power of culture as an independent variable. Samuel Huntington began to suggest that development and modernization may be distinctively Western goals. He alleged that aspirations to wealth, equity, democracy, stability, and autonomy emerge from Western, particularly Nordic, experience, and that other cultures may prefer simplicity, austerity, hierarchy, authoritarianism, discipline, and militarism.[5] This view represents a considerable retreat for a theorist who once believed Western-style modernization to be irresistible. Huntington had retreated even further by the turn of the century. In single-authored works and in *Culture Matters: How Values Shape Human Progress*, which he co-edited with Lawrence Harrison, one finds echoes of the late-occurring social Darwinism of Sarmiento.[6]

BLAMING THE LATIN AMERICANS: DEVELOPMENT AND MODERNIZATION THEORY

Whereas analyses of contemporary Latin America based on the traditional, or historical-cultural, approach tended to have a static quality, development and modernization theory introduced a new dynamism into the field. The new approach highlighted the facts that for better or worse, social change was indeed under way and that to a great extent, that change was in response or in reaction to the spread of the ideas and technologies of the more industrialized world, primarily the United States and Western Europe, to the Third World.

The body of thought that came to be known as development and/or modernization theory—terms often used interchangeably—was pioneered primarily by US scholars in the late 1950s and the first half of the 1960s. In economics, development theory presumed that with the infusion of capital and the acquisition of business skills, and with the advantage of not having to reinvent the wheel, the nations that had yet to experience their industrial revolutions would pass at an accelerated pace along paths already broken by Western Europe and the United States. Walt W. Rostow further assumed that economic development, at least beyond a stage he called "take-off," was irreversible.[7]

From the perspective of anthropologists and sociologists, "modernization" generally meant the ingestion of the supposedly Western attitudinal traits of rationalism, instrumentalism, achievement orientation, and the like. This approach stressed the felicitous consequences of the spread of modern communications media, of education in science and the liberal arts, and of technology transfer, and it implied that Third World societies could (and should) become developed through the accelerated absorption of individuals into the middle class or the modern industrial sector.

Political scientists borrowed liberally from the other social sciences, often without seeming to notice that in their extreme formulations these theories amounted to a virtual denial of the stuff of their own discipline: power relationships. Political scientists did, however, offer their own set of indices of development and/or modernization. Gabriel Almond, for example, stressed structural differentiation (the elaboration of economic and political roles), whereas Samuel Huntington stressed political institutions.[8] Other scholars focused on participation, egalitarianism, and governmental capability, assuming such attributes to be mutually reinforcing. Huntington, however, seeing expanding participation in the absence of institutionalization as destabilizing, prioritized stability. Martin C. Needler, perceiving the same contradiction, prioritized participation but noted that in the absence of steady economic growth it would have a destabilizing effect on systems of limited democracy, threatening the imposition of authoritarianism.[9]

These trends in the social sciences coincided with the Cuban revolution and thus with the Alliance for Progress and the emergence of interdisciplinary programs in Latin American studies. Development came to be one of the major goals of the Alliance for Progress; the other was security—the prevention of "another Cuba." The few critical voices, such as that of Albert O. Hirschman, who argued that such goals might be contradictory, were generally ignored.[10] The prevailing view, that "unrest" was an impediment to progress and had to be contained by strengthened security forces, won out in academic as well as in governmental circles until a wave of military takeovers forced a reevaluation.

Critics of development and modernization theory have pointed out that its adherents were inclined either to see what they wanted to see or to label whatever they saw as progress. Economists, for example, measured development by using aggregate data on the growth of gross national product or per capita income, data that were blind to the skewed distribution of income. While US economists lavished praise on Brazil's "economic miracle," Brazil's own dictator, General Emilio Garrastazú Médici, commented in 1970 that "the economy is doing fine, but the people aren't."[11]

A tendency common to much of the work based on development and modernization theory was a peculiar sort of ethnocentricity based on an idealized and class-delimited national or North Atlantic self-image. If Latin Americans and other peoples of the Third World had failed to achieve development or modernization, it was assumed to be because they lacked our industriousness and had failed to see their own problems as clearly as we saw them. In effect, the blame for poverty and powerlessness was placed squarely on the poor and powerless.

Scholars of the period were not necessarily in accord as to which of the indices of development and modernization were most relevant and useful. Nevertheless, distinctions between value-free and value-laden concepts were rarely well drawn. The behavioralist tendency in the social sciences, which was also coming into its own in the 1960s, sharpened the inclination of social scientists, attempting to be "scientific," to hold acknowledged bias in disdain. Thus, those scholars who argued that economic growth and stability were the most important indices of development and those who challenged that redistribution of wealth and the expansion of political participation were more important tended to maintain the pretense that they were arguing over facts rather than over values.

As military regimes swept the hemisphere in the 1960s and 1970s, replacing democratic ones, the development approach was discredited and superseded by newer theoretical trends, particularly dependency. Some of the theorists once attracted to the development paradigm became persuaded by the arguments of dependency theory. Others came to stress the interdependence of First and Third Worlds or to look for cultural causation in differing levels of development. Many of the attitudes and assumptions associated with development theory were revived in the 1990s through the currency of neoliberalism, but the latter also displayed striking differences.

BLAMING THE UNITED STATES: DEPENDENCY AND RELATED THEORIES

In his earlier ideological incarnation as one of the originators of dependency theory, Brazilian social scientist Fernando Henrique Cardoso responded to the question, "What is dependency?" by saying, "It's what you call imperialism if you don't want to lose your Ford Foundation grant." (Elected president of Brazil in 1994, Cardoso then began to call dependency theory his Frankenstein.) More precisely, as Susanne Bodenheimer Jonas has noted, dependency refers to the perspective from "below," whereas the Marxist theory of imperialism provides the perspective from "above."[12] As the Marxist theory of imperialism seeks to explain why and how the dominant classes of the dominant capitalist powers expand their spheres of exploitation and political control, dependency theory examines what this relationship of unequal bargaining and multilayered exploitation means to the dominated classes in the dominated countries.

The dependency approach, unabashedly normative, derived its impulse largely from the attempts of the United Nations Economic Commission for Latin America (ECLA) in the early 1960s, under the leadership of Argentine economist Raúl Prebisch, to understand and counteract such problems as the deterioration in the terms of trade for producers of primary (nonindustrial) products. A renewed awareness of economic exploitation and dependency followed upon disillusionment with industrialization through import substitution, Latin American economic integration, and other solutions proposed by ECLA. Thus, a number of Latin American political scientists and sociologists, including Brazilians Cardoso and Teotonio dos Santos and Chilean Osvaldo Sunkel, renewed their efforts to explain patterns of social class structure and predict the structural changes that are inherent in the process of capitalist development in a dependent state.

Among the assumptions that underpin dependency theory are the following. First, the distribution of power and status in national and international arenas is ultimately determined by economic relationships. Second, the causes of underdevelopment are not to be found in national systems alone but must be sought in the pattern of economic relations between hegemonic, or dominant, powers and their client states. The perpetuation of the pattern of inequality within client states is managed by a clientele class, which might be seen as the modern functional equivalent of a formal colonial apparatus. Third, both within and among states, the unfettered forces of the marketplace tend to exacerbate rather than to mitigate existing inequalities. That is, the dominant foreign power benefits at the expense of its client states, and the clientele class benefits at the expense of other classes.

Dependency theorists further held that development would not take place through the "trickle-down" of wealth nor through the gradual diffusion of modern attitudes and modern technology; that the upward mobility of individuals expressed by their gradual absorption into the modern sector is no solution to the problem of the impoverishment of the masses; and that stability is no virtue in a system of pronounced inequality. In fact, most dependency theorists, or, in Spanish, *dependentistas,* believed that only by breaking out of the international capitalist system and establishing socialist regimes would Latin American nations gain control over their own decision making and expand the options available to them.[13]

Whereas modernization and development theorists had seen foreign investment and foreign aid as critical to development in the Third World, *dependentistas* saw such investment and aid as means of extracting capital from client states. *Dependentistas* would probably agree with the observation of US congressman Dante Fascell (D-Florida) that aid is a means whereby the poor of the rich countries contribute to the rich of the poor countries. They might also add that aid is yet another means whereby the poor of the rich countries contribute to the rich of the *rich* countries.

Andre Gunder Frank, comparing the experiences of the Latin American states during World War I and the Depression of the 1930s with their experiences during periods when the links were stronger between those states and the industrialized West, concluded in 1970 that satellites, or client states, experience their greatest industrial development when their ties to the more developed states are weakest.[14] Other scholars, noting, for example, the industrial expansion of Brazil in the late 1960s and early 1970s, maintain that rapid industrial growth may take place under conditions of dependency. There is general agreement, however, that to the extent that economic growth takes place under conditions of dependency, it is a distorted pattern of growth that exacerbates existing inequalities among both classes and regions within client states.

Like development theory, dependency theory has been limited by an excessive reliance on aggregate data and a "black box" approach—which treats nations like black boxes, shedding no light on internal dynamics or relationships. Such an approach deals with the outcome of unequal relations between nations but fails to elaborate the political mechanisms whereby dependent relationships are perpetuated. Furthermore, in assigning primacy to economic relationships, *dependentistas* tend to give short shrift to other factors, such as the pursuit of institutional, or bureaucratic, interests, which may have an important bearing upon relations between dominant powers and client states and upon relations among political actors within client states.

Penetration Theory and Bureaucratic Authoritarianism

Other approaches that share many of the assumptions of dependency theory and serve to elaborate or refine our understanding of politics in dependent states include penetration theory and the model of bureaucratic authoritarianism. Penetration theory seeks to identify the means whereby a dominant foreign power influences policy in a client state not only directly, through diplomatic pressures, but also indirectly, through the manipulation of political competition within the client state.[15] Bureaucratic authoritarianism, according to Argentine political scientist Guillermo O'Donnell, who coined the phrase, is the likely outcome of social and economic modernization in the context of delayed, or dependent, development. Such impersonal, institutional dictatorship is not a vestige of the feudalistic rule imposed by Spain or Portugal but rather a response to a perceived threat to the capitalist system. According to O'Donnell, the levels of coercion and of economic orthodoxy that are imposed depend upon the level of perceived threat.[16]

The Center-Periphery Model

The relationships hypothesized or described by dependency theorists have been incorporated by Norwegian scholar Johan Galtung into a model of elegant simplicity.[17] According to the center-periphery model, elites of the center, or metropolis, draw bounty from the periphery of their own state system (through taxes, for example), which they devote to the nurture and support of co-opted elites of client or "peripheral" states. In turn, elites of those client states, dependent upon elites of the center for assistance in exploiting and suppressing their own peripheral, or nonelite, populations, have no choice but to allow center elites to participate in, or share in the product of, the exploitation of the peripheral peoples of the peripheral states.

World Systems Theory

World systems theory, pioneered by Immanuel Wallerstein, also views the world economy as segmented into core and periphery areas.[18] Rather than focusing on the interactions of governments, however, this approach calls attention to the transnational interactions of nonstate actors, particularly multinational corporations and banks. The international economy is said to be driven by the initiatives of economic elites, particularly of the developed capitalist states, whose governments normally do their bidding. The control centers of the world economy then are financial rather than political capitals. The farther one lives from such a center, the less the "trickle down" of its wealth will be experienced.

Wallerstein, who sees the ideas of *dependentistas* as falling within the world system perspective, takes issue with more traditional Marxists and liberals alike for what he calls a rigidly developmentalist approach. That is, both schools assume that each nation-state must pass through the same set of stages, or modes of extracting surplus, in the same order. As he sees it, the nation-state system, which came into being in part as a convenience to economic elites of an earlier era, has ceased to be the essential institutional base of the global economy. The contemporary struggle, then, is not between rich and poor states, but rather between rich and poor classes in a global society.

INTERESTS AT THE CORE OF THEORETICAL DIFFERENCE

The basic differences among the preceding approaches relate more to interest than to analysis and, in that regard, might best be posed as a dichotomy. For example, some might see a division of interests between the First World and the Third; but that fails to account for the fact that Third World elites, pursuing class as well as individual interests, often adopt First World perspectives. First World scholars and humanitarians often identify with the disadvantaged of the Third World. An elitist versus egalitarian, or concentrational versus redistributive bifurcation might avoid territorial and cultural implications and be more readily comprehensible; but it imputes values that are not generally acknowledged.

There is, however a more clear-cut means of dealing with dichotomy while avoiding unwelcome imputation; it is a dichotomy expressed as preference, and as perception of efficacy, of means. That is, the two approaches claim a common goal of progress or development for all in the long run, but differ in means seen as appropriate to achieving the goal. One approach sees the material interests of rich and poor nations and peoples as being in harmony and thus amenable to a single strategy. The other sees those interests as being directly in conflict—as in a zero-sum game.

Not surprisingly, the one size fits all strategy tends to be employed by the states or classes who own the pattern—those in a position to decide what that size will be. Colonial and neocolonial powers, for example, and their elite allies in client states might be expected to see the policies and undertakings that serve their interests as serving those also of the conquered and colonized. Such an assumption of *harmonic* interests is not likely to be shared, however, by the conquered and the colonized. The latter are more likely to see the interests of conquerors and conquered as *discordant*. This dichotomy will be seen more clearly in the theoretical monopolization, followed by theoretical polarization, that followed the deconstruction of the Cold War ideational framework.

SEEKING COMMON GROUND

Dichotomies and unacknowledged interests notwithstanding, none of the approaches, models, and theories applied to the study of Latin America wholly excludes the others. The differences among them are largely differences of perspective, emphasis, and value judgment. Adherents of development and modernization theory, like those of the historical-cultural approach, tend to focus on the attitudes of individuals and the behavior of institutions, though the former are more attuned to the indices of change whereas the latter more often stress continuity. Both pay tribute to the achievements of the modern West and deplore the antidemocratic influences of the Iberian tradition, but development and modernization theorists, more readily than historical-cultural analysts, see approximation to the Western model as a plausible solution.

Drawing explicitly on Marxist concepts, dependency theory looks to material interests and class conflict as well as to international patterns of trade, aid, and political control for explanations of political process at the national level. Thus, even when scholars of differing schools can agree as to what happened, they are likely to disagree as to why it happened. Whereas development and modernization theorists, for example, have generally viewed the public and private vehicles of US influence as forces for democratic and social reform, dependency theorists have viewed them as antidemocratic and antiegalitarian forces.

In the late 1980s, a number of scholars sought to resolve the debate between development and dependency theorists by seeking common ground or to supersede the debate by asking a different set of questions. One consequence was a new emphasis on "interdependence." Another was a wide-angle focus, reaching across disciplines and deep into the history of industrialization to explore, in particular, relationships between the state and the private sector, domestic and foreign. That approach was labeled the new international political economy.

Interdependence

Whereas scholars dealing with relations between developed states and the Third World tended to focus in the 1960s on the benefits of such relations for the Third World and, in the 1970s, on the detriment of such relations to the Third World, many scholars in the 1980s began to focus instead on complementary needs and common problems. Some noted, for example, an increasing vulnerability on the part of the industrialized states to economic problems in the Third World. The high interest rates of the early 1980s in the First World, particularly the United States, were devastating to Latin American economies. The consequent debt crisis in Latin America then threatened the solvency of US banks and closed markets for US manufactured goods.

International Political Economy

The international political economy (IPE) agenda recaptured the scope of nineteenth-century social concerns for the purpose of addressing contemporary policy issues. Thus, the assumptions and findings of IPE theorists tend to cut across, and perhaps defuse, the development-dependency debates. In addressing Third World issues, IPE theorists, like dependency theorists, seek explanation for means and levels of development in class conflict rather than in assumptions about attitudes. Like modernization and development theorists, however, they generally find a positive relationship between development and democracy. They accept, to a point, the *dependentista* assertion that Third World countries have been disadvantaged by their participation in the global economy, but hold that positive results have on occasion been achieved where Third World governments had the capacity to negotiate the conditions of their participation.

Like the world system school, the IPE school finds no preordained sequence of stages in development. IPE, however, faults the world system approach for underestimation of the role of the state in determining economic outcomes. Rejecting both the liberal preference for an unfettered market and the Marxist choice of state dominance of economic decision making, international political economy theorists contend that both state and market have important roles to play and that on occasion they are mutually reinforcing. Effective operation of the market may in fact be dependent upon the vigilance of a strong state, prepared to intervene where necessary.

Like dependency theorists, adherents of the IPE approach concern themselves with the contradiction between the territorial character of state power and the

transnational character of economic power, but IPE theorists argue that the penetration of foreign capital does not necessarily shrink the economic role of the state.
Studies of petrochemical and iron industries in Brazil by Peter Evans, of the oil industry in Venezuela by Franklin Tugwell, and of the copper industry in Chile by
Theodore Moran have shown that foreign-owned extractive sectors may stimulate
state entrepreneurial activity; that in itself, however, does not necessarily advance
living standards or other indices of development.[19]

THE POST–COLD WAR PARADIGMATIC SHIFT

Though the Cold War ended with a whimper rather than a bang, the postwar period has had much in common with the aftermath of other wars—shifting boundaries and trade patterns, new categories of the displaced and the deprived. The
winner in this case, however, was not a country or set of countries but an economic
system. That system was not just capitalism; it was a socially premodern version of
capitalism bulwarked by postmodern technology.

Spencerian capitalism, emerging triumphant, demanded unconditional surrender not just of socialism in its extreme forms but also of many experiments in state
planning and regulation, state-run enterprise and protected domestic industry, and
welfare provision—experiments that in Latin America, and particularly in the
most developed Latin American states, were survivals of several decades of political
development and economic nationalism. Such globalization of economic power
and planning meant also a level of hegemony in the realm of ideas unprecedented
perhaps since the era of scholasticism. That is not to say that there was no dissidence or heresy. So long as there have been spokesmen of the haves proclaiming
that trends and policies in their interest were in the interest also of the have-nots,
there have been defenders of the have-nots having the nerve to say "not so." But
one thing the have-nots have not in such times is a forum.

The kind of economic devastation that followed the final cataclysms of the Cold
War in the region of its epicenter got a long head start in Latin America. The debt
crisis of the early 1980s left Latin American leaders at the mercy of creditors and
currency speculators. The state itself, as a representative of a sovereign people, was
so weakened that any line of policy, or even rhetoric, that smacked of economic
nationalism threatened to set off a stampede of fleeing capital.

The surrender of economic policymaking seemed not to be a matter of choice,
but domestic constituencies nonetheless demanded explanation and justification,
which was scripted in neoliberal terms. Dependency theorists might claim that
this turn of events had validated their analysis of the problem; but in a globalized
economy—that is, without an alternative market or credit source—they were left
without politically feasible solutions.

Liberalism and Neoliberalism
Like persons and places and religions, theories that acquire celebrity status—and
thus usefulness to the powerful—become caricatures of themselves or their original versions; and liberalism was no exception. As elaborated in 1776 by Adam
Smith, it was a progressive proposition, designed to redistribute wealth and opportunity from opulent courts and colonizers monopolizing trade under a system

known as mercantilism to a new class of merchants and entrepreneurs whose interests and power were to be limited by competition. Smith, however, recognized the danger of the evolution of monopolies and advocated strict governmental regulation to prevent such a development.

As liberalism came to be championed by an expansive Great Britain in the nineteenth century and the United States in the twentieth century, its qualifiers faded and its progressive features were transformed. The surviving core of the theory held that states had a common interest in the free flow of goods, services, and capital across national borders. Smith's laissez-faire principle was reinforced by David Ricardo's theory of comparative advantage. That theory posited that states should take advantage of their raw materials, low labor costs, technologies, or other strengths in order to specialize in those goods they could produce most efficiently, while trading for goods in which other states had the advantage. In colonial and neocolonial systems, the advantage accrued, of course, to mother countries, not colonies.

Development and modernization theory was a legitimate offspring of liberalism, and like its sire it served to explain and legitimate the seemingly limitless opportunities and responsibilities of an imperial power at its peak. Like liberalism also it sought to promote social and political change in adversary or client states, within limits dictated by elite and hegemonic economic interest.

Though its power center does not reside in a state, neoliberalism shares those circumstances and attributes of its forebears; but whereas development theory sought to strengthen state institutions, neoliberalism as expressed in policy tends to eviscerate them. Governments in general are seen as wasteful and corrupt, their deficits inflationary, their budgets a drain on resources that might otherwise be directed to servicing debt and attracting investment. And privatization of government enterprises or services that might bring in a profit has commonly been a condition for the extension of credit. These and other measures that have come to be known collectively as "structural adjustment" are in the context of neoliberalism both policy prescriptions and factors in explanation and prediction of economic growth and stability or its absence. It is also assumed that an economy restructured along the lines prescribed is a prerequisite for a smoothly functioning electoral democracy. It has been conveniently forgotten that in general the "opening" of Latin American economies coincided with the shut-down of democratic systems in the 1970s rather than with their return.

What Was Left? Critics and Heretics

With the end of the Cold War, the right had lost its cover story, but the left had lost something harder to come by; it had lost its dream.

Criticism of neoliberalism as theory and as policy has exhibited little in the way of romanticism or radicalism. It was not in spite of the enormity of Latin America's problems and the pressures that private interests were able to bring to bear against the public interest but *because* of them that political strategies and policy alternatives from the left in the 1990s were measured and modest.

The *dependentista* school had not vanished, though some might argue—since Cardoso was elected president of Brazil as a born-again neoliberal—that it had gone under deep cover. Osvaldo Sunkel, in his influential book *Development from*

Within,[20] argued that while a strategy of export promotion may be unavoidable, a healthy economy, resistant to the effects of global market volatility, demands priority attention to the development of the domestic market. The late Andre Gunder Frank, who joined world systems scholars in the study of long cycles of history, found Latin America in the early 1990s to be increasingly marginalized from world trading systems. More important, he saw commerce centering once again in the twenty-first century in the Orient, and particularly China.

Mexican scholar and political columnist Jorge Castañeda, in *Utopia Unarmed,*[21] observed that the entire political spectrum shifted sharply to the right in the 1990s. In that context, he found the left alive and well and living in the center—or what used to be the center. He did not interpret such repositioning, however, as surrender or battle fatigue; rather, he saw it as the outcome of learning through painful experience to see politics as the art of the possible. Castañeda called for a revival of nationalism, but reformulated so as to promote transnational coalition building and to accommodate regional economic integration.

A Message from the Street

While the left in the ivory towers of academia, politics, and punditry may have been, at the turn of the twenty-first century, alive and well and living in the center, the disadvantaged people for whom they purported to speak had taken to the streets; and momentum with respect to the articulation and projection of their message had shifted to the street-level world of social activists and social movements.

Throughout the hemisphere, from Mexico to Argentina, those whose resources and livelihoods and safety nets had been usurped by the faceless corporate and institutional predators who came to be identified with neoliberal globalization found new means of organizing and making themselves heard. The Zapatistas of the Mexican state of Chiapas garnered support from around the world as the virtual version of their revolution was played out in poetry on the Internet. In Colombia, "peace communities" put up unarmed resistance to guerrillas and government-supported paramilitaries alike. In Ecuador and Bolivia, indigenous communities coalesced to bring down elite-based governments. In Argentina, barter clubs, co-op factories, and neighborhood support groups overcame anarchy when government collapsed. And in Brazil, landless workers, more than a million strong, helped to propel the leader of a genuine workers' party into the presidency.

All of this newly effective commotion in the streets and fields and forests provided a new focus for Latin Americanists. Sonia Alvarez was among the first to call attention to the potential of popular, grassroots movements in Latin America.[22] Such movements, in Latin America and elsewhere, have benefited greatly from the work of a multifaceted thicket of non-governmental organizations, operating at all levels from local to global. Henry Veltmeyer, James Petras, and Cristobal Kay are among the Latin Americanists who have dealt with this important development.[23]

Activists' Alternative Perspectives

The last decade of the twentieth century and the first decade of the twenty-first saw, in fact, the amassing of a great body of scholarly and popular literature inspired by addressing needs and interests that run counter to those advanced by neoliberalism. This intellectual flourishing, however, particularly on the part of environmentalists, feminists, and advocates of grassroots community development, was slow to generate a great debate, mainly because until recently economists, who enjoyed unchallenged disciplinary primacy in the business of theoretical legitimation, generally ignored it.

Between these concerns and neoliberalism as now advanced there is little common ground. From the perspective of environmentalism, the global village is being stripped of resources by a feeding frenzy set off by deregulation and the new openness of markets and fueled by hard-currency debt-service requirements. Globe-hopping investors deplete, despoil, and depart, leaving communities and ecosystems devastated.

Likewise, scholars engaging in gender analysis along with chroniclers and supporters of the international women's movement, have noted that the front-line victims of the economic restructuring now sweeping the global village are women. Shrinkage of the public sector has cost women their best professional jobs at the same time that loss of family services, pensions, and benefits has expanded their responsibilities. Even as women were scoring great advances in political roles, they were being squeezed out of the better-paying formal economy and drawn in ever greater numbers into exploitative informal-sector work. Jane Jaquette has done seminal work on the mobilization of women to confront social and political crises.[24] Mala Htun represents a new generation of women focusing not only on women in politics but on the politics of gender issues.[25]

As governments, bound first to distant creditors, defaulted on their obligations to their own citizens, the newly displaced and deprived were discovering what the long-suffering have always known—that the last bastion of security is a community organized and aware of the need for general commitment and mutual support. Theorists of grassroots development note that such awareness and commitment runs counter to the dog-eat-dog or all-eat-dog options suggested by neoliberal individualism. Moreover, globalization—the alienation or distancing of decision making about priorities and livelihoods—presents a dire threat to the ideal of individual and collective self-sufficiency, or "empowerment," that is the philosophical foundation of community development.

Globalizing Justice?

With increasing success, since the first major street demonstrations against the World Trade Organization (WTO) in Seattle in 1999, opponents of neoliberal globalization have broadened their constituencies, united diverse groups and causes, and made their voices heard. Since the Seattle meeting, massive demonstrations have regularly dogged the deliberations of international financial institutions and other global money movers, and after several years of covering the action, media analysts finally began to ask why. A new threshold was crossed at the WTO forum in Cancún in 2003, when for the first time NGOs had moved up from the street to work directly with delegations of Third World governments. Under Brazilian leadership, a coalition including China and India as well as Argentina and several other Latin American countries blocked the next round of the WTO's proposed reforms and derailed, at least temporarily, the proposed Free Trade Agreement of the Americas (FTAA).

Thus, the surge of events, prompted by bottom-up initiatives, seems finally to have broken the paradigmatic monopoly of neoliberalism. Though advocates and critics rarely engage each other in straightforward debate or in pursuit of theoretical synthesis, perspectives alternative to or critical of neoliberal globalization are gaining increasing attention in the media and in academia—even among Nobel laureates in economics—and laying the groundwork for a vibrant new dialogue on the fundamentals of democracy and development.[26]

Many of those concerned about the dark side of globalization point out that the issue is not globalization itself—global interaction or togetherness—but rather what is being globalized. They say that, in contrast to their intellectual detractors and political adversaries, they would advance the globalization of social justice, biological and cultural diversity, and respect for human rights. In fact, as anti-terrorism replaces anti-communism as the new all-purpose trump card of the powerful, Latin Americanists are once again edging into the forefront of social criticism. It could hardly be otherwise; the New American century declared by the Bush administration sounded to Latin Americans and Latin Americanists like a century with which we were already all too familiar.[27] Perhaps the second decade of this new century will imbue us with a new vision and give us a fresh start in a different direction.

ACADEMIC INTEGRATION ON A NEW BASIS

It may well be that the effects of neoliberal globalization on living standards for most in the Western Hemisphere, from Canada to the Southern Cone, have been negative. But globalization has also been expressed and felt in ways other than theft on a grander scale. And in terms of academic pursuits, it has promoted or enabled increasing collaboration and integration, or reintegration, of efforts among scholars from pole to pole. Gender, environmental, and human rights concentrations remain strong, and Latin and Anglo Americans alike are giving increasing attention to rural poverty and the indigenous, to issues of immigration and healthcare, to challenges facing youth, including the militarization of policing and control of street gangs, to the problem of jobless economic growth and, once again, to South American rather than North American approaches to economic integration.[28]

Much of this has been led or inspired by the diaspora communities. Canadian and European universities and social activist communities that welcomed exiles from Latin America in the 1970 and 1980s have been well positioned to help budding scholars and academic systems in reconstruction in Latin America to get beyond official histories and to learn and teach from their own experience. The United States has lagged in this regard, but US-based scholars are benefiting from the support and learning experiences of our colleagues elsewhere in the hemisphere to bring pressure to bear on our own government and academic institutions. Frustrated by seeing our invited colleagues from Cuba turned away at the border year after year, the Latin American Studies Association, born in the 1960s in the United States but now an international organization with some six thousand members, has resolved not to meet again in the United States until the US government sees fit to welcome our members regardless of states of origin or residence. There is still much good that might come from relearning the meaning of being a good neighbor.

N O T E S

1. Sarmiento's best-known work is *Facundo.* English translation: *Civilization and Barbarism: The Life of Juan Facundo Quiroga* (New York: Collier, 1961).

2. This author submits that one of the reasons that Latin American politics has been so poorly understood by North Americans is that North American politics is also poorly understood by them.

3. Among the Latin Americanists whose works have tended to be in this vein are Fredrick Pike, John Mander, Charles Wagley, Claudio Veliz, Ronald Newton, William S. Stokes, and William Lyle Schurz.

4. Works highlighting corporatism or employing corporatist models include Howard J. Wiarda, *Corporatism and Development: The Portuguese Experience* (Amherst: University of Massachusetts Press, 1977); Howard J. Wiarda, ed., *Politics and Social Change in Latin America: The Distinct Tradition* (Amherst: University of Massachusetts Press, 1974); Philippe C. Schmitter, *Interest Conflict and Political Change in Brazil* (Stanford, Calif.: Stanford University Press, 1971); James M. Malloy, ed., *Authoritarianism and Corporatism in Latin America* (Pittsburgh: University of Pittsburgh Press, 1977); and Kenneth Paul Erickson, *The Brazilian Corporative State: Working Class Politics* (Berkeley: University of California Press, 1977).

5. Samuel Huntington and Myron Weiner, eds., *Understanding Political Development* (Boston: Little, Brown, 1987), pp. 21–28.

6. Basic Books, 2000.

7. Walt W. Rostow, *The Stages of Economic Growth* (London: Cambridge University Press, 1960).

8. Gabriel Almond and G. Bingham Powell, *Comparative Politics: A Developmental Approach* (Boston: Little, Brown, 1966); and Samuel Huntington, *Political Order in Changing Societies* (New Haven, Conn: Yale University Press, 1968)

9. Martin C. Needler, *Political Development in Latin America: Instability, Violence, and Evolutionary Change* (New York: Random House, 1968). Other applications of development theory to the study of Latin America have included Charles W. Anderson, *Politics and Economic Change in Latin America* (Princeton: Van Nostrand, 1967); and Edward J. Williams and Freeman Wright, *Latin American Politics: A Developmenetal Approach* (Palo Alto, Calif.: Mayfield, 1975).

10. Albert O. Hirschman, *Journeys Toward Progress: Studies of Economic Policymaking in Latin America* (New York: Twentieth Century Fund, 1963).

11. Cited in Dan Griffin, "The Boom in Brazil: An Awful Lot of Everything," *Washington Post,* May 27, 1973.

12. Susanne Bodenheimer Jonas, "Dependency and Imperialism: The Roots of Latin American Development," *Politics and Society,* May 1977, pp. 327–357.

13. Richard Fagen, "Studying Latin American Politics: Some Implications of a Dependency Approach," *Latin American Research Review* 12, no. 2 (1977): 3–26.

14. Andre Gunder Frank, *Development and Underdevelopment in Latin America* (New York: Monthly Review Press, 1968).

15. For an elaboration and application of penetration theory, see Jan Knippers Black, *United States Penetration of Brazil* (Philadelphia: University of Pennsylvania Press, 1977), forthcoming in Portuguese edition from Fundacao Joaquim Nabuco, Editora Massangana, Recife.

16. Guillermo O'Donnell, *Modernization and Bureaucratic-Authoritarianism: Studies in South American Politics,* Politics of Modernization Series, no. 9 (Berkeley: Institute of International Studies, University of California, 1973).

17. Johan Galtung, "A Structural Theory of Imperialism," *Journal of Peace Research* 8, no. 2 (1972), pp. 81–117.

18. Immanuel Wallerstein, *The Modern World-System: Capitalist Agriculture and the Origins of the European World-Economy in the Sixteenth Century* (New York: Academic Press, 1974).

19. See Peter Evans, *Dependent Development: The Alliance of Multinational, State, and Local Capital in Brazil* (Princeton: Princeton University Press, 1979); Franklin Tugwell, *The Politics of Oil in Venezuela* (Stanford, Calif.: Stanford University Press, 1975); and Theodore H. Moran, *Multinational Corporations and the Politics of Dependence: Copper in Chile* (Princeton: Princeton University Press, 1975).

20. Osvaldo Sunkel, ed., *Development from Within: Toward a Neostructuralist Approach for Latin America* (Boulder, Colo.: Lynne Rienner, 1993).

21. Jorge B. Castañeda, *Utopia Unarmed: The Latin American Left After the Cold War* (New York: Knopf, 1993).

22. See Alvarez and Arturo Escobar, eds., *The Making of Social Movements in Latin America: Identity, Strategy, and Democracy* (Boulder: Westview, 1992).

23. Henry Veltmeyer, *On the Move: The Politics of Social Change in Latin America* (New York: Broadway Press, 2007); James Petras and Henry Veltmeyer, *What's Left in Latin America? Regime Change in New Times* (UK: Ashgate, 2009); Cristobal Kay and A. Haroon Akram-Lodhi, *Peasants and Globalization* (New York: Routledge, 2008).

24. Jane S. Jaquette, *The Women's Movement in Latin America* (Boston: Unwin Hyman, 1989).

25. Mala Htun, *Sex and the State: Abortion, Divorce, and the Family Under Latin American Dictatorships and Democracies* (Cambridge: Cambridge University Press, 2003).

26. See, for example, René Armand Dreifuss, *A Epoca Das Perplexidades* (Petropolis: Editora Voces, 1996); William Robinson, *Transnational Conflicts:Central America, Social Change, and Globalization* (London: Verso, 2003); and Jan Black, *Inequity in the Global Village: Recycled Rhetoric and Disposable People* (Westport, Conn.: Kumarian, 1999).

27. See Virginia Bouvier, ed., *The Globalization of US-Latin American Relations: Democracy, Intervention, and Human Rights* (Westport, Conn.: Praeger, 2002).

28. See William Robinson, *Latin America and Global Capitalism* (Baltimore: Johns Hopkins Press, 2008); Joseph Nevins, *Operation Gatekeeper* (New York: Routledge, 2002); and Jan Knippers Black, *The Politics of Human Rights Protection* (Boulder: Rowman & Littlefield, 2009).

PART I

THE LAND AND
THE PEOPLE

Chapter 2

LANDSCAPE AND SETTLEMENT PATTERNS

ALFONSO GONZALEZ

LATIN AMERICA IS AMONG the largest world culture regions, with an area of 20.5 million square kilometers (7.9 million square miles), more than double the size of the United States. It has the greatest latitudinal range of any world region, extending from 32 degrees north latitude to 56 degrees south latitude. The air distance from northwestern Mexico to northern South America is nearly 5,000 kilometers (more than 3,000 miles), and from there to Cape Horn, following the general curvature of the continent, is an additional 7,500 kilometers (more than 4,600 miles). As a consequence, the region has a highly diversified ecology. Although it is primarily tropical, it encompasses some midlatitude environments, and there is great variation in the physiography, climate, vegetation, soil types, and minerals that are encountered in the region.

OUTSTANDING PHYSICAL CHARACTERISTICS

Latin America has some unique physical characteristics. The Andes, for example, comprise the highest continuous mountain barrier on earth with a lineal extent of more than 7,000 kilometers (4,400 miles). The chain includes the highest summits outside of central Asia with at least three dozen peaks higher than Mount McKinley (6,194 meters; 20,320 feet), the highest summit in North America. Virtually every maximum or near-maximum elevation for most of the world's features (except summits) occurs in the Andes—the highest settlement, capital city, railroad, highway, mining activities, commercial airport, volcanoes, navigable lake, snowline, and so on. Furthermore, the steepest coastal gradient anywhere occurs in Colombia.

The Amazon is physically the world's greatest river. Although second to the Nile in length, it has the greatest discharge volume, drainage basin, and length of navigable waterways of any river on earth. The highest and most voluminous waterfalls are located in South America. Two or three of the world's highest falls occur in the Guiana highlands, and five of the seven greatest waterfalls in the world, in volume of flow, are in the Brazilian highlands. Although the waterpower potential of Latin

America is somewhat less than that of Asia, one-fifth of the world's potential hydroelectric power is found in Latin America.

Latin America is a unique faunal region, the neotropical zoogeographical realm, which covers all of Latin America except northern and central highland Mexico and the Bahamas. Although the diversity of mammalian animal life is somewhat greater in the African region, no world region has so many unique mammalian families. Furthermore, Latin America has the most diverse bird life and a highly varied and complex collection of lower animals.

Latin America has the highest proportion of any world region (nearly 50 percent) of its area in forests; Amazonia and the Guiana highlands represent the largest continuous tropical rain forest area on earth. Latin America also contains the greatest absolute area in forest, almost 25 percent of the world total, and the highest per capita forested area of any world region. Only a third of this forested area is both economically productive and accessible, unfortunately, making Latin America a net importer of forest-based products. Currently the forests are being reduced at an unprecedented rate. More than 400,000 square kilometers (over 150,000 square miles) of forested area were cleared for other uses during the 1990s in tropical South America and Mexico. This is approximately 50 percent of the world's net total loss of forests.

A number of extremes distinguish the climate of Latin America. Some of the coastal lowlands and island stations approach the world record of approximately 13 degrees C (23 degrees F) between the highest and lowest temperatures ever recorded. Probably the driest region on earth is the Peruvian-Atacama desert, especially in northern Chile. Nevertheless, southern Chile is one of the rainiest places on earth, receiving measurable precipitation for as many as 325 days a year. The wettest place in the Western Hemisphere is located in the western Colombian Andes, which receive more than 8.5 meters (335 inches) of rainfall annually.

Latin America is periodically beset by major natural disasters that destroy both lives and property; the area is second only to the Orient in major natural disasters. Earthquakes occur with great frequency along the western highland margin of the region. Two of the greatest quakes outside the Orient occurred in 1868 and in 1970 in highland Peru, each causing the loss of 50,000 to 70,000 lives. Devastating quakes occurred in 1972 at Managua, Nicaragua, in 1975 in central Guatemala, and in 1985 in Mexico City. There are fifty or more active volcanoes in the region (approximately 25 percent of the world total). The eruptions of Mount Pelée (Martinique) in 1902, which resulted in the deaths of at least 30,000 people, and Nevado del Ruiz (Colombia) in 1985, with more than 22,000 killed, rank among the greatest volcanic eruptions of modern times. Hurricanes occur regularly in the Caribbean basin and with less frequency on the Pacific coast of Mexico, often causing thousands of deaths. Perhaps the greatest avalanche ever recorded occurred in the Peruvian Andes.

OUTSTANDING POPULATION AND
SETTLEMENT CHARACTERISTICS

Latin America also has a distinctive pattern of population and settlement. In 2009 its population was approximately 570 million. More than 8 percent of the world's population now resides in Latin America, compared to less than 2 percent during the colonial period. It is the only world region that has consistently experienced population growth that is faster than the world average since the mid-eighteenth century. Latin America became the fastest growing region soon after World War I; it was overtaken by the Middle East and sub-Saharan Africa during the 1970s.

Latin America's rate of population growth has been gradually decreasing since the early 1960s, although recently the decline has been more significant. Nevertheless, the region's population continues to increase by more than 8 million annually. Soon after World War II, the average rate of growth was 2.7 to 2.9 percent per year. It is currently expanding at less than 2 percent annually. The greatest rates of growth occur in northern Central America and Andean South America. Traditionally, the slowest growth has occurred in Argentina and Uruguay, although more recently these countries have been joined by Chile, most of the Antilles, Brazil, and some smaller countries. The potential for further population growth remains in those few countries in which the death rate remains relatively high, notably Haiti. Family planning programs in the region became generally significant in the late 1960s.

The age structure of the population is characteristic of underdeveloped regions generally—a high proportion of younger people (32 percent 15 or younger) and a low proportion of older people (6 percent 65 years or older). Dependency ratios (proportions of the very young and very old in relation to the productive ages, 15–64) are somewhat high (but declining) in the region, placing an additional burden on the economy. Partially related to this situation is the fact that only about 40 percent of the population is economically active (compared with about 50 percent in developed regions). With falling mortality rates, growing numbers of people will be entering the labor force, currently more than 3 million annually, which will place heavy demands on employment opportunities, educational and health facilities, and housing.

In Latin America, infant mortality rates are the lowest of any underdeveloped region, and life expectancy is the longest. A subregion of the Orient, East Asia, however, now has rates that approximate the Latin American average. Mortality aside, there is still a significant gap between levels of living in Latin America and in the more developed regions.

The population density of Latin America averages approximately twenty-six inhabitants per square kilometer (more than 67 per square mile), which is only slightly more than half the world average and is comparable to several other world regions. Most of the countries of Latin America are, therefore, below the world average in density; exceptions include the Antilles, El Salvador, Guatemala, Costa Rica, and more recently Honduras and Mexico. Partly as a consequence of relatively low crop yields, population pressure on available cropland is greater in Latin America than in any developed world region, but such pressure is lower than in any other underdeveloped area.

The pattern of population distribution in Latin America includes a concentration on the periphery, especially in South America and on the Pacific margins of Central America. Population is also concentrated in the highlands within the tropics, with one-half to three-quarters of the national populations in the upland areas. Major exceptions are the Antilles, Nicaragua, Panama, Belize, and the Guianas.

FIGURE 2.1 Latin America: Natural Regions

Latin America has a larger population in the highlands than any other world region does.

The region has a nucleated pattern of settlement, with semi-isolated population clusters and national population cores. Population clusters have been detached, although this is diminishing with population growth and improved transportation. Generally 10 to 25 percent of the national area of a Latin American country contains 50 percent or more of the national population. As a result, most countries include large, sparsely settled areas—50 percent of the area of Latin America contains only about 5 percent of the region's total population. The population pattern demonstrates that the effective area of settlement in most countries is still a small segment of the total national territory, but many outlying areas are growing faster than the overall growth rate.

Rapid urbanization has characterized Latin America, especially since World War II, making it the most highly urbanized underdeveloped region. Its population was one-half urban by 1965 and is now about three-quarters urban, the result of both natural increase (excess of births over deaths) and internal migration, with probably 3–4 million migrants recently moving into the urban centers. The causes of rapid urbanization include rural poverty (the "push" factor—expulsion from the countryside); the fast rate of natural increase in the rural areas; the scarcity of available arable land, especially in the traditional areas of settlement; the land tenure system (*latifundia,* the predominance of large estates, and *minifundia,* the prevalence of many small landholdings); limited rural employment opportunities and low wages. Restricted social services provide an undesirable rural habitat over most of the region. The attractions of the city (the "pull" factor—employment, higher wages, and improved social services) make the cities, especially the capitals, appealing to impoverished rural residents.

The largest city of each country (the capital, except in Brazil, Ecuador, Belize, and also now possibly Bolivia) tends to dominate the life of the country and is generally much larger than the second largest city. This degree of primacy is more accentuated in Latin America than in any other world region. Some countries are highly urbanized, notably Venezuela and the Southern Cone countries of South America, while the most rural areas are Central America, Haiti, and the Guianas.

Natural Regions

Latin America may be subdivided into thirteen natural regions (see Figure 2.1). Although based fundamentally on physiographic characteristics, these areas also possess unifying characteristics of climate, natural vegetation, and soils. Since these natural regions present differing sets of problems for human settlement and economic development, the human patterns are often largely a response to locational and physical factors. Crude approximations of the areas, populations, and densities for the natural regions of Latin America are presented in Table 2.1.

Gulf-Caribbean Coastal Lowlands

The Gulf-Caribbean coastal lowlands are a continuation of the Atlantic-Gulf coastal lowlands of the United States, but south of the Rio Grande (Rio Bravo to the Mexicans) the coastal plain is narrower and interrupted. In the northernmost section, in the Mexican state of Tamaulipas, the climate is mostly subhumid (low-latitude steppe). This section is relatively sparsely settled, although the lower Rio Grande Valley has dense settlement because of agriculture and the newly developed gas fields. South of Tamaulipas, the coastal lowland is tropical in climate, vegetation, and soils.

The coastal plain becomes very narrow in portions of Veracruz and along sections of Central America; it is broadest in Yucatán and is fairly broad in Nicaragua and

TABLE 2.1   Natural Regions of Latin America

	Area (thousand km²)	Population (thousand) 2002	Percent Annual Growth 1995–2002	Density (per km²)	Percent of Total Area	Percent of Total Population 2002
Gulf-Caribbean Coastal Lowlands	763	35134	2.94	38.6	3.7	6.7
Pacific Littoral	487	24102	1.32	49.5	2.4	4.6
Cordilleran Highlands	3234	167173	1.42	51.7	15.7	31.7
Antilles	234	37393	0.81	159.6	1.1	7.1
Llanos (Orinoco)	641	5985	3.71	9.3	3.1	1.1
Guiana Highlands	1103	2889	1.89	2.6	5.4	0.5
Amazonia	4956	16630	3.19	3.4	24.1	3.2
Brazilian Highlands	4335	160363	1.51	37.0	21.1	30.5
Peruvian–Atacama Desert	402	14546	2.67	36.2	2.0	2.8
Middle Chile	255	13640	0.78	53.5	1.2	2.6
South Chile	241	239	-0.03	1.0	1.2	0.05
La Plata–Parana Basin	2356	40441	1.46	17.2	11.5	7.7
Northwest Argentina–Patagonia	1538	8099	1.51	5.3	7.5	1.5
Total Latin America	20544	526634	2.51	25.6	100.0	100.0

Note: Figures are estimates and totals may not coincide with above data or with other data for Latin America because of changing boundaries, estimates, and rounding.

adjoining sections of Honduras and Costa Rica. Many portions of the coastal plain are characterized by poor drainage, resulting in swamps and marshes. Precipitation occurs throughout the year, but it is concentrated in the warmer months and is often twice as great as on the Pacific littoral. Many parts of the coastal lowlands are subject to violent tropical storms, especially from August through November. These hurricanes sometimes cause great loss of life and extensive property damage.

The soils generally are not highly productive under continuous tillage. These lowland areas have traditionally had only scattered areas of settlement, frequently associated with commercial plantation agriculture, especially bananas, and with fishing and logging. However, in recent decades, the lowlands have seen an influx of migrants.

The Yucatán peninsula, a platform of coral rock with limestone beds, is characterized by shallow, dry rendzina soil, with many sinkholes (*cenotes*) and few surface streams. The eastern and southern sections of the Mexican portion of the peninsula, Belize, and the northern third of Guatemala (the Petén) comprise one of the most sparsely settled areas of the coastal lowlands. Nevertheless, in pre-Columbian times, this area was the cultural hearth of the Mayan civilization, with population densities significantly above current levels.

The older petroleum fields of Mexico were centered in northern Veracruz. Reduced production continues from fields near Tampico, Tuxpan, and Poza Rica, but the great petroleum and natural gas fields were opened in the 1970s in southern Veracruz, Tabasco, adjacent Campeche, and on the offshore banks. Agricultural expansion in this region predates the development of the petroleum and natural gas industries.

The Gulf-Caribbean coastal lowlands extend into neighboring Colombia and Venezuela in South America. There they mainly comprise the Atrato and Magdalena valleys of Colombia and the Maracaibo basin of Venezuela, which contains Latin America's largest lake. These areas have been attracting migration from the more traditional highland centers of settlement because of the production of bananas and other tropical crops in Colombia and the great petroleum production in the Maracaibo district of Venezuela.

Antilles (West Indies)

The Antilles form one of the world's most important archipelagoes. The total area of the islands is only 238,000 square kilometers (92,000 square miles), approximately the size of Oregon. Cuba alone makes up one-half of the area; the Greater Antilles—Hispaniola, Jamaica, and Puerto Rico—comprise most of the remainder. The islands enclose one of the world's largest seas, the Caribbean, on the north and east.

The Greater Antilles are a complex folded and block-faulted mountain system that is mostly submerged. They consist of two ridges separated by a deep trough. The Lesser Antilles, extending from east of Puerto Rico to the Netherlands Antilles off the coast of South America, consist of several small islands with an arcuate shape, convex toward the Atlantic Ocean, and structurally connected with the highlands of Venezuela. The northern section, the Leeward Islands, extend from the Virgin Islands to north of Guadeloupe, or possibly as far south as Martinique. The southern islands are the Windwards. The total area of the Lesser Antilles is less than 13,000 square kilometers (5,019 square miles), about the size of Connecticut. The Antilles region, like the northern mainland of Central America and most of Mexico, is regularly exposed to hurricanes. The climate throughout the Antilles gives rise to either tropical rain forest or tropical savanna.

The Antilles, except for the Bahamas and the Turks and Caicos, are more densely settled than any other area of Latin America. The inhabitants are of predominantly African descent. The geographic location, combined with an equable climate and productive soils, gave rise to the earliest plantation economies of the New World. These were based primarily on sugar, although later bananas, coffee, and other crops were added.

The plantation agricultural economy has declined recently, especially on the smaller islands. Other economic activities, including tourism, subsistence agriculture, and commerce, have generally proved inadequate to support the dense populations. Mineral wealth in this region overall is minor but has importance for eastern Cuba, Jamaica, and Trinidad. Relatively rapid population growth in the post–World War II period without compensating socioeconomic development caused a large exodus to the United States, the United Kingdom, France, the Netherlands, and Canada.

Pacific Littoral: Coastal Plains and Valleys

The Pacific margins of Middle America and the northern section of South America represent a narrow zone of diverse physical landscapes. The peninsula of Baja (Lower) California, in Mexico, represents the southern extension of the Pacific mountain system of North America and consists of a long series of blocks tilted toward the Pacific Ocean with a steep fault scarp to the east on the Gulf of California side. This arid, shrub-covered region has been, with parts of Yucatán, the most sparsely settled and isolated area of Mexico. In 1972 a paved highway was opened that runs the length of the peninsula, nearly 1,900 kilometers (1,180 miles).

Across the Gulf of California lies the almost equally arid Sonoran desert, the southward extension of the basin-and-range topography of the United States. Although the population is greater toward the more humid south, many of the river valleys of southern Sonora and northern Sinaloa are densely settled and intensively utilized due to the irrigation projects developed since the revolution.

From approximately Mazatlán southward, the remainder of the coastal margin of Mexico, Central America, Colombia, and Ecuador is generally narrow; in places it disappears completely as the highlands reach the shore. The population along the Mexican section of this coastal zone is relatively sparse but increasing. The Pacific coastal margins of Central America tend to have greater population settlements than the Caribbean coasts, except in Honduras, but the coastal lowlands on both sides of the isthmus are undergoing a rapid increase in settlement. Most of Panama's population is located in the Pacific lowlands, whereas Nicaragua's is in the lake district lowlands close to the Pacific.

The extremely humid Pacific coastal margins of Colombia are sparsely settled and relatively isolated from the country's national settlement core. However, the growing commercial importance of the port of Buenaventura has stimulated population migration into this heavily forested area. The coastal margins and Guayas lowlands of Ecuador contain approximately half of that country's population and constitute a rapidly expanding area of development. Since World War II the cultivation of tropical products, especially bananas, has encouraged settlement in this region, where the ports and the largest city (Guayaquil) of the country are located.

CORDILLERAN RANGES: INTERMONTANE BASINS AND PLATEAUS

The highland spine of the American Cordillera extends the length of Latin America near the Pacific margin of the region. This is the most extensive natural region, more than 12,000 kilometers (7,458 miles) as the crow flies; it is also one of the most populous, with about 170 million inhabitants. From Mexico to Bolivia, this highland zone contains from about half to more than three-quarters of the population of every country except Belize, Nicaragua, and Panama.

The Cordillera is a young, complex mountain system with diverse features, rock types, and geologic structures. Peaks attain elevations of nearly 7,000 meters (22,966 feet). Aconcagua, rising 6,960 meters (22,835 feet) on the Chilean-Argentine border just north of Santiago, is the highest summit in the world outside of central Asia. The passes are extremely high in the Andes, and throughout most of the Cordillera the high elevations, steep slopes, and rugged terrain present serious obstacles to transportation. Glacier and ice fields occur throughout much of the mountain system, even at the equator, and reach sea level in southern Chile. There are snowcapped peaks in the highland zones of Mexico and every country of South America within the Cordilleran system.

Within Latin America, the Cordillera attains its greatest width in northern Mexico (1,000 kilometers; more than 600 miles) and Bolivia (800 kilometers; 500

miles). It becomes very narrow in southern Central America and again in Chile. There are four major topographic breaks in this formidable barrier: (1) the Isthmus of Tehuantepec in Mexico; (2) the Nicaraguan graben lowlands, which run from the San Juan River in the Caribbean coastal zone through the lake district northwest to the Gulf of Fonseca (part of this route was considered an alternate for a canal during the last century); (3) the Panamanian isthmus, where the canal is located; and (4) the Atrato–San Juan river valleys across northwestern Colombia.

The mountain system also contains numerous intermontane basins and plateaus, the largest being those of northern and central Mexico and the Altiplano of Peru and Bolivia. These plateaus are the major population zones of Mexico and Bolivia. The system contains some fifty active volcanoes—the greatest concentration in the world outside the Orient—concentrated in five zones: (1) the volcanic axis of Mexico, along the southern margin of the Mexican plateau; (2) the Central American Pacific volcanic belt, extending from just inside the Mexican border to Costa Rica; (3) southern Colombia and Ecuador, including the Galápagos Islands; (4) central and southern Peru; and (5) Chile, where the two highest active volcanoes in the world are found. The only volcanic activity in Latin America outside the Cordilleran system occurs on three of the Lesser Antilles. Throughout its length, except in northern Mexico, the Cordilleran region is one of the most earthquake-prone regions on earth. Strong quakes occur regularly and cause considerable loss of life.

Most of the population in the western Cordilleran highlands of Latin America is found in the tropical zone or on its margins, where there is a considerable range of climate. Climate and vegetation vary in accordance with altitude and temperature. The altitudinal boundaries of the climatic zones vary among localities because of latitude, windward/leeward location, exposure, precipitation, and humidity. In the highlands, although the seasonal range of temperature is comparable to that in the adjacent lowlands, the diurnal range is usually greater, especially during the dry season. Table 2.2 gives a general overview of the major altitudinal zones in Latin America.

Throughout the Cordilleran highlands, the more productive basins have numerous urban communities and high rural densities. Increasing population pressure and the land tenure system have stimulated a massive rural-to-urban migration and, to a lesser degree, agricultural colonization of the sparsely settled lowlands. The region has great mineral wealth, but it is concentrated in northern and central Mexico and in Peru and Bolivia.

The higher zones have a greater proportion of Amerindians, especially in Guatemala and the central Andean counties. Populations of African descent are concentrated in the *tierra caliente* zone, especially the Caribbean lowlands of Central America, the lowlands of Colombia, and to a lesser degree, the coastal zones of Venezuela and Ecuador.

ORINOCO LLANOS

The Llanos ("plains") lie between the Venezuelan-Colombian Andes and the Guiana highlands and are drained by the Orinoco River system. This basin, divided almost evenly between Venezuela and Colombia, is the third largest in Latin

America, accommodating the third greatest river discharge in the region. In size, the Llanos region approximates the state of Texas; it is one of the five very sparsely settled natural regions of Latin America.

Petroleum and iron ore have been exploited for some time in the eastern Llanos of Venezuela, but the most widespread activity is cattle ranching. Recent decades have witnessed migration in both countries from the densely settled highlands to the forested margins and the open grassland districts of these lowlands. Settlers have reportedly encountered resistance from a few nomadic Amerindian tribes in the area.

Guiana Highlands

The Guiana highlands, including the associated coastal lowlands, are 60 percent larger than the Llanos but have even fewer people, making the Guiana region, Amazonia, and South Chile the most sparsely settled regions in Latin America. A narrow coastal lowland along the Guianas contains 90 percent of the population of those countries. There is also a narrow riverine lowland between the Guiana highlands and the Orinoco River. It contains the greater part of the population and economic activity of the Guiana highlands of Venezuela, nearly one-half of the area of that country.

Much of the upland surface has been dissected by streams, and the world's highest waterfalls are located near the Venezuelan-Guyanan border. This highland massif and the Brazilian highlands comprise remnants of the oldest rocks on the continent—primarily a granitic base partially capped by a resistant sedimentary layer. Bauxite, iron ore, and manganese are the most important mineral deposits of the area; gold and diamonds are also found there.

Amazonia

The Amazon basin is the largest natural region of Latin America and one of the most homogeneous. Although nearly three-quarters of the basin lies within Brazil, portions of the region extend into Peru, Bolivia, Colombia, and Ecuador. Despite the basin's immense area, its population is extremely sparse. Only about 3 percent of the population of Latin America resides in this largest river basin on earth.

The Amazon River is the greatest river on earth in volume, although it is slightly shorter than the longest river, the Nile. The Amazon accounts for nearly one-fifth of the total world river discharge into the oceans. The outlet of the river is more than 300 kilometers (186 miles) wide and contains an island the size of southern New England. It is the most navigable river system on earth. There is no bridge across the Amazon in its entire lowland traverse of the continent. Despite the river's immense silt discharge, the delta has undergone little development because of coastal subsidence and coastal currents. Few places on earth can match Amazonia with regard to the diversity of life forms that inhabit it.

The Amazon basin can be generally divided into two major parts: the low-lying, level alluvial lowlands, or floodplain, and the upland plains. The floodplain is of varying width and comprises approximately one-tenth of the basin's area. This zone consists of a series of broad, disconnected swamps with natural levees. Much

TABLE 2.2 Altitudinal Zonation of Climates in Latin America

Lower Altitudinal Limit	Zone	Average Monthly Temperature	Major Agricultural Commodities
4,500 m (14,000 ft)	permanent snowfields (*nevados*)	<0°C (<32°F)	
3,000/3,500 m (10,000/ 11,500 ft)	alpine meadows (*tierra helada, páramos*)	6°–10°C (43°–54°F)	livestock grazing (especially sheep and goats, with llamas and alpacas in the central Andes) (above treeline and general crop cultivation)
2,000 m (6,000/ 6,500 ft)	temperate (*tierra fría*)	10°–17°C (54°–65°F)	midlatitude crops: wheat, barley, white potatoes, apples, and other deciduous fruits
600/1,000 m (2,000/ 3,000 ft)	subtropical (*tierra templada*)	17°–24°C (65°–75°F)	coffee, maize, cotton, rice, citrus, sugarcane
Sea level	tropical (*tierra caliente*)	24°–28°C (75°–83°F)	bananas, cacao, rubber, palms (coconut, oil), pineapples, mangoes (crops of subtropical zone also, except for coffee)

Note: Metric and English measure figures are rounded so conversion is not exact.

of the area is inundated at various times of the year. The most fertile soils, replenished by river silt, constitute the best agricultural land, and by far the greater part of the settlements lie within this zone. The upland plains are generally above the periodic river flooding and contain the highly leached and laterized soils typical of many tropical environments. The population in this zone is extremely sparse. Recently deforestation has accelerated to alarming proportions as increasing areas are being devoted to crop cultivation and cattle ranching. An extensive highway network, begun in the 1970s, is being constructed along with hydroelectric dam projects. Considerable mineral wealth has been discovered and is being exploited, especially iron, ferro alloys, bauxite, gold, and petroleum. The destruction of the habitat is of serious concern for the aboriginal Amerinds; soil erosion, the loss of wildlife and plant species, and the alteration of regional and global climates are also sources of global concern.

Brazilian Highlands

The dissected Brazilian plateau and its associated coastal lowlands make up the second largest natural region of Latin America and, with the Cordilleran highlands, have the largest population of the entire region. Nearly one-third of Latin America's population resides in this natural region, which accounts for half of Brazil's area and almost all of its population.

The diverse Brazilian highlands consist of (1) a prominent seaward escarpment, the Serra do Mar of the southern section, which acted as a transportation handicap and barrier to early penetration of the interior; (2) the rolling, dissected plateau of the interior of this highland zone, which is inclined away from the ocean so that drainage is generally toward the interior before it eventually reaches the ocean; and (3) the old, eroded, and rounded mountain ranges that are found in different sections of the uplands. The east-central section of this Brazilian shield, notably in the state of Minas Gerais (General Mines), is highly mineralized with significant deposits of iron, ferro alloys, diamonds, and gold.

The narrow and discontinuous coastal plain accounts for only 5 to 10 percent of the area of Brazil but about a third of the population, including five of the largest cities—Rio de Janeiro, Recife, Salvador, Fortaleza, and Porto Alegre. The coastal lowlands have a tropical rain forest, or monsoon, climate and broadleaf evergreen forests. Tropical savanna occurs along much of the northeastern coast and the northern and central portions of the interior highlands. However, the interior northeastern section is a comparatively subhumid region. Its periodic droughts have had devastating effects on the nearly 30 percent of the national population residing in the nine poverty-stricken states of this section. This has been a zone of out-migration, primarily to the coastal plantation zone and the industrial and commercial centers in the south and southeast.

The southern highland section has a humid subtropical climate and, on the Paraná plateau, soil hospitable to coffee. Population growth is somewhat faster in São Paulo—which, combined with the three southern states, contain nearly two-fifths of the national population—than in the other eastern sections of the country. The interior plateau is also undergoing in-migration and rapid growth and development, although the region is still sparsely settled.

PERUVIAN-ATACAMA DESERT

The Peruvian-Atacama desert region consists of a narrow coastal zone that extends 3,000 to 3,500 kilometers (approximately 1,800 to 2,000 miles) from near the Ecuadoran-Peruvian border to Coquimbo, Chile. The coastal plain is extremely narrow or absent, and the coastline generally lacks enclosed, protected harbors. Isolated blocks and low coastal hills also characterize parts of the zone, and in places there are low but steep escarpments behind the shore. There are few perennial streams, especially toward the south.

The combination of the Pacific anticyclone, the cool Humboldt current, and winds that parallel the coast makes this coastal zone perhaps the driest on earth. Arica, Chile, at the border with Peru, has the lowest average annual precipitation (0.5 millimeters; 0.02 inches) of any weather station on earth. Another station, Iquique, less than 200 kilometers (more than 100 miles) to the south, has gone fourteen years without measurable precipitation. However, the El Niño phenomenon occurs occasionally and brings heavy rains and floods. Atmospheric and oceanic disturbances displace the cool Humboldt (or Peru) current farther offshore, permitting warmer water from the equatorial region to move southward off the coast of Ecuador and Peru. The loss of fisheries and marine birds can also be catastrophic.

The great mineral wealth in what is now Chile, first of nitrates and later of copper, opened sections of the arid north of that country to development. However, this one-third of the country contains less than one-tenth of the national population. Significant iron ore is exploited in southern Peru and the extreme south of the Atacama in Chile. In Peru, as in Chile, many stretches are barren both of vegetation and habitation, but fairly dense settlement occurs in the irrigated narrow coastal valleys, especially from Lima north.

MIDDLE CHILE

The relatively small middle Chile region, lying between Coquimbo and Puerto Montt, comprises only one-third of the national area but contains slightly more than nine-tenths of the country's population, most of the agricultural land and industrial production, and much of the mineral wealth.

The northernmost section of this region is desert/steppe, a transition to the arid region of the Atacama. Most of northern middle Chile, however, has a Mediterranean climate. In this sector, the summers remain dry; the mild winter is the season of precipitation. In some places irrigation is necessary during the summer. This sector, which includes the capital, Santiago, contains more than 70 percent of Chile's population. The remainder of middle Chile, south of Concepción, is less densely settled. Precipitation is greater in this area and occurs throughout the year. Southern middle Chile is the most important forest-producing region of the country. The major mineral resource is copper.

SOUTH CHILE

South Chile, another small natural region, has a very sparse population. The coastal range is partially submerged to form an archipelago, and much of the longitudinal valley is drowned. Andean glaciers reach sea level in this region, which is one of the four major fjorded coasts on earth. The region is rugged and isolated, cold, rainy, and dreary. There are no road or rail extensions south of Puerto Montt.

Only 2 percent of Chile's population resides in this third of the country. Most of those people are concentrated in the northern sector, on Chiloé Island—where forest quality and soils are relatively good—and in the Atlantic portion of Chile. There, in the rain shadow of the low Andean chain along the Strait of Magellan, the main economic activities are sheep raising, forestry, and the production of coal and petroleum.

Northwest Argentina and Patagonia

Patagonia and northwest Argentina compose one of the larger of the natural regions of Latin America and lie entirely within Argentina. The northwest is larger and more populous than Patagonia, yet the two subregions contain less than a quarter of the country's population in more than half the national territory. In addition to sparse settlement, aridity and uplands characterize this natural region.

Northwest Argentina is characterized by a series of pre-Cordilleran and pampan ranges that attain their greatest breadth at 30–35 degrees south latitude and extend into the provinces of San Luis and western Córdoba. Most of the settlement and irrigated agriculture occur in the basin oases of the foothills.

The desert and steppe area of Patagonia is the only midlatitude arid climate in the Southern Hemisphere and the only major arid region on the east coast of a continent. The soils of Patagonia and part of Tierra del Fuego, like those of arid northern Mexico, are typical desert soils—productive when irrigated—and important agricultural output, especially fruit, is obtained from the densely settled and intensively cultivated oases. There are some mining communities in northwest Argentina. Petroleum is produced in both coastal Patagonia and the Andean foothills of the northwest. Much of the region, however, is sparsely settled and devoted to livestock ranching.

La Plata-Paraná Basin

The La Plata-Paraná basin, the third largest in the Western Hemisphere, after the Amazon and the Mississippi, encompasses the La Plata estuary, the master stream—the Paraná—and its tributaries, notably the Paraguay and Uruguay rivers. The basin lies mostly within northeastern Argentina but also includes all of Uruguay and Paraguay and a portion of southeastern Bolivia. (A significant portion of Brazil is also drained by this river system, but most of that region of Brazil is included in the Brazilian highlands natural region.) The La Plata-Paraná basin is also one of the most populous of the natural regions and contains the Argentine nucleus of settlement.

This natural region has several subregions: the Gran Chaco (west of the Paraná and Paraguay rivers from 29 degrees to 30 degrees south latitude northward to Bolivia), eastern Paraguay (east of the Paraguay River), Mesopotamia (Argentina between the Paraná–Alto Paraná and Uruguay rivers), the pampas (grasslands radiating outward from Buenos Aires for more than 600 kilometers [400 miles]), and Uruguay. The soils over much of the area are mollisols, deep and dark with organic matter and minerals, that develop near the humid-dry climatic boundary in the midlatitudes. These are the richest soils in Latin America and among the best in the world. The pampa is the major food surplus–producing region of Latin America. However, soil quality deteriorates toward the drier Northwest and Patagonia, especially northward into the humid tropics. The prevailing climate over most of the region is humid subtropical, comparable to the southeastern United States, with hot, rainy summers and mild winters.

Conclusion

The natural environments of Latin America are diverse and display varying degrees of settlement and development. The three largest regions—Amazonia, the Brazilian highlands, and the Cordilleran system—comprise nearly two-thirds of the total area of Latin America. The Cordilleran highlands are very rugged, presenting enormous problems for cultivation and transport, but this has been the traditional area of settlement since pre-Columbian times for most of the countries that lie within the region. The Cordilleran and Brazilian highlands contain 65 percent of Latin America's population. At the other extreme, five regions—Amazonia, Guiana highlands, northwest Argentina and Patagonia, Llanos, and South Chile—comprise more than 40 percent of Latin America but contain about 6 percent of the population. Rates of population growth in these sparsely settled areas, however, are rapid (except in the midlatitudes), as pressure on land and resources in the traditional settlement areas stimulates internal migration. Despite this significant movement, the great migration within Latin America funnels people into the major urban centers. This rural-urban migration is many times greater than the migration into sparsely settled regions.

Suggested Readings

Physical Geography

Blouet, Brian W. "The Environment." In Brian W. Blouet and Olwyn M. Blouet, eds., *Latin America and the Caribbean: A Systematic and Regional Survey.* 4th ed. Wiley, 2002. Chapter 2.

Clawson, David L. *Latin America and the Caribbean: Lands and Peoples.* 3rd ed. McGraw-Hill, 2004. Chapters 2–4.

Handbook of Middle American Indians. Vol. 1, *Natural Environment and Early Cultures.* Edited by Robert C. West. University of Texas Press, 1964. Eight of the chapters provide detailed study of the different aspects of the physical environment of Middle America. Probably the best overview of the physical geography of this part of Latin America.

Handbook of South American Indians. Vol. 6, *Physical Anthropology, Linguistics, and Cultural Geography of South American Indians.* Reprint. Cooper Square, 1963. The section by Carl O. Sauer, "Geography of South America" (pp. 319–344), pertains to the physical landscape of the continent and can serve as a companion piece (although not as detailed) to the *Handbook of Middle American Indians* to complete the coverage of all of Latin America.

Kendrew, Wilfrid George. *The Climates of the Continents.* 5th ed. Clarendon, 1961. Part 6, "South America, Central America, Mexico, the West Indies," pp. 464–527. Probably one of the best accounts, although perhaps too detailed, of meteorological and climatic conditions in Latin America.

Robinson, H. *Latin America.* 4th ed. MacDonald & Evans, 1977. Chapter 1.

Verdoorn, Frans, ed. *Plants and Plant Science in Latin America.* Ronald Press, 1945. This older work is still an informative source for the phytogeography and agriculture of the region, as well as for other aspects of the physical environment.

Population

Blouet, Brian W. "Population: Growth, Distribution, and Migration." In Brian W. Blouet and Olwyn M. Blouet, eds., *Latin America and the Caribbean: A Systematic and Regional Survey.* 4th ed. Wiley, 2002. Chapter 5.

Gonzalez, Alfonso. "Latin America: Population and Settlement." In Richard G. Boehm and Sent Visser, eds., *Latin America: Case Studies.* Kendall Hunt, 1984. Chapter 6.

Merrick, Thos. W., et al. "Population Pressures in Latin America." *Population Bulletin* 41, no. 3 (1986).

Sánchez-Albornoz, Nicolás. *Population of Latin America: A History.* University of California Press, 1974. This volume presents a thorough study of the growth and development of Latin America's population (chapters 1–4) and includes chapters (6–8) that deal with recent trends and prospects.

Sargent, Charles S. "The Latin American City." In Brian W. Blouet and Olwyn M. Blouet, eds., *Latin America and the Caribbean: A Systematic and Regional Survey.* 4th ed. Wiley, 2002. Chapter 6.

Chapter 3

The Indian Populations
of Latin America

Karl H. Schwerin

In order to understand the contemporary character and distribution of Indian populations in Latin America, it is necessary to know something about the nature of indigenous societies at the time of European discovery. The native inhabitants of the New World represented a great range of cultural development, from simple hunting and gathering bands to complex, literate civilizations. Within the area of present-day Latin America, the great majority of peoples had reached levels of significant cultural achievement. Most societies were food producers, and in many respects the region from central Mexico southward was more advanced than the area that became northern Mexico, the United States, and Canada. In fact, North America is the only major world region where the majority of the aboriginal peoples relied on gathering, hunting, and fishing for their subsistence. By contrast, South America was inhabited by predominantly agricultural societies.[1]

Nonetheless, a full range of cultural variability also existed in the Latin American region. Although specialists might want to differentiate a great number of categories, it is more instructive for our purposes to treat the early Indian societies as belonging to one of three major types. Marginal hunters and gatherers were restricted for the most part to Argentina, Uruguay, and parts of coastal Brazil. They were also predominant on the northern frontier of the Spanish empire, the arid deserts of northern Mexico. Lowland extensive agriculturists were much more widespread, ranging from central Chile throughout most of interior Brazil to the whole of the Amazon basin, including those portions now within the territorial borders of Bolivia, Peru, Ecuador, Colombia, Venezuela, and the Guianas. They also occupied the rest of Colombia and Venezuela and ranged northward through the whole of Central America and the Antilles. The third principal type was the highland intensive agriculturists, many of whom achieved state-level societies in the mountains and plateaus of Mexico, Guatemala, Ecuador, Peru, and Bolivia.

During the latter part of the twentieth century, a vigorous debate raged among historical demographers concerning the aboriginal population of the Americas at the time of European discovery. Estimates range from 13 million to more than 100 million. For the Latin American region, however, an estimate of 80 million seems

39

likely. Sixty million of these people belonged to the civilized states of Middle America and the central Andes. Most of the remaining, numbering about 18 million, were lowland agriculturists in the interior of South America, the northern coastal region, the Caribbean, and Central America. Hunting and gathering peoples accounted for no more than 2 million persons, and the figure was probably closer to 1 million.

European conquest radically disturbed the aboriginal societies. Perhaps the most drastic effect was a rapid and massive population decline, characterized by modern investigators as a "demographic disaster." The principal cause of the disaster was the introduction of several new diseases that decimated the native populations through repeated epidemic outbreaks. The wars of conquest also took their toll, as did slavery and other abuses of Indian labor, and there were ecological repercussions because of interference with the seasonal rhythm of native agriculture (by removing native labor for Spanish needs at critical periods in the agricultural calendar) and the introduction of livestock (which competed with natives for land and invaded their planted fields).

Estimates of the rate of depopulation differ, but the best calculations suggest an average decline of 95 percent in 130 years, leaving only about 4 million Indians south of what is now the United States in 1650. It must be remembered, however, that an unknown portion of this decline is represented by the mestizo offspring of European or African fathers and Indian mothers, who were treated as a class or caste apart from their parents and often sought to "pass" into the higher-status European category.

The Caribbean population, which was conquered first, was wiped out in less than fifty years. African slaves were introduced to replace the Caribbean Indians as a labor force. Most of the continental hunters and gatherers have also become extinct. The lowland agriculturists declined drastically, with many groups becoming extinct (some continue to disappear today); others, however, have survived and are today increasing in number. In the areas of highland civilization, there was also a drastic population decline, but the population reached its low of perhaps 3 million to 5 million around 1650. Thereafter it grew slowly until the beginning of the nineteenth century. Since that time, the Indian population of Middle America and the central Andes has been growing at an increasingly rapid rate.

PRECONQUEST SOCIETIES

A moment's reflection about the areas occupied by these three major culture types suggests that these regions are still characterized by distinctive populations today. Elman Service has dubbed these areas Euro-America, Mestizo-America, and Indo-America, respectively.[2] Why are such differences of aboriginal culture type reflected in differences among the modern populations? Commonly, this is explained as resulting from differences in administrative policies of the European colonial powers. Not only did such policies differ among Spain, Portugal, and Great Britain, but there were differences in the way the policies were implemented in various parts of the colonial empires. Thus it is frequently maintained that colonial policies were enforced more rigorously in the Antilles, Mexico, and Peru and that greater control was exerted over the colonists in those areas, both because these colonies were more valuable and because they contained greater numbers of colonists. In contrast, there was less interest in colonies like Venezuela and Buenos Aires, and consequently crown control was more lax in those areas.

Another way of responding to the question of contemporary differences begins by looking at the diversity of aboriginal cultures encountered by the white man and recognizing that the Europeans were forced to adjust differently in accordance with the basic differences in native cultures.[3]

The object of European conquest was to profit from the newly discovered areas. The conquerors assessed tribute from the native populations (by means of the *encomienda* and the *corregimiento*) or exploited native labor in profit-making enterprises (through forced labor projects, or the *repartimiento*) such as construction, mining, ranching, and later textiles.

In the highland areas of Mexico and Guatemala and in the central Andes, native societies had achieved a high level of cultural development, with complex state organization. The native peoples were integrally involved with complex economic, social, and political institutions and depended on them to maintain their traditional way of life. They would not have found it easy to survive if cut off from these state-level institutions. In addition, most of them had no easily accessible refuge from Spanish domination. Given the existence of well-defined state institutions in which the native populations were accustomed to functioning, it was relatively easy for the European conquistadores to take over these institutions and control the population from the top, much as the native elite had. This method was effective because of the system of indirect administration that was worked out. Only minor modifications were made in most native institutions (except for religious ones), especially on the lower levels where native intermediaries continued to be employed in governing the mass of the population.[4]

Throughout the colonial period, there was a fair amount of racial mixture, and the native elites were gradually absorbed into the dominant Spanish ruling class. Among Indian commoners, local community and familial institutions remained strong in spite of racial mixture with the Spanish overlords and their African slaves. To this day, many Indian languages continue to be spoken throughout these areas, many rural communities have maintained their identification as Indian, and many aboriginal and/or ethnically distinct customs have been retained as central features of the local cultures. These are the areas Service characterizes as Indo-America.[5]

Lowland areas were occupied mostly by extensive agriculturists who were organized principally as independent localized tribes or villages.[6] Here there were no large organized communities or state-level institutions. Gaining control of these small independent groups was difficult, for conquest of one did not include authority over its neighbor. The European strategy was to capture single families and individuals and force them to become household servants or work as agricultural slaves. The intimacy that existed between masters and household slaves or small numbers of agricultural slaves led to a rapid mestization of the native groups. Mestizos tended to identify with the dominant European population and be absorbed into its lower levels. Thus there was a continuing need to acquire additional slaves from the native groups. The *bandeirantes* of São Paulo are the best-known example of this type of exploitation. Their periodic expeditions ranged far and wide throughout the interior to capture Indian slaves. This type of

exploitative relationship between the European colonists and native societies led to
the breakdown of the more accessible Indian communities. Many fled to remote
refuge areas where they might avoid the depredations of slavers. Some have survived to the present day in these isolated locations, particularly in southern Chile,
parts of Amazonia, the interior of Venezuela, parts of Central America, and the extremely rugged and isolated regions of northern Mexico. These are the areas that
Service identifies as Mestizo-America.[7]

Plantation agriculture required large numbers of laborers. The social and physical separation between owners and field laborers meant that the workers were
treated impersonally. Indian slaves often fled to the interior, since they were familiar with the environment and knew how to survive there. Even if they were unable
to return to their own community, they could plug into other, similar native communities and social systems. The very serious problem of runaway Indian slaves led
plantation owners to import African slaves, who were easier to control. The
Africans were in a wholly unfamiliar environment—an alien terrain filled with unknown plants and animals. They could not speak the native languages, they did
not know how to participate in the aboriginal social systems, and consequently
they were unable to flee.

Plantation agriculture developed principally in coastal Brazil, the Caribbean,
and coastal Peru. In most of these areas, the African racial type remains predominant today, and I would therefore characterize them as Afro-Americans.

Where the European intruders found it impossible to control or enslave the native population, they attempted to exterminate the natives or to drive them out of
the areas of settlement. Hunters and gatherers lived a simple life, unburdened with
numerous possessions or a complex technology. They were more or less nomadic
and could readily flee European control. Some survived on the margins of European settlement; a few actually developed a highly successful adaptive strategy of
attacking and living off the European settlements. Among such groups were the
Tehuelche and Puelche of Argentina; the Pehuenche of Chile; the Argentine Arau-
canians; the Abipón, Mbayá, and other Guaicuruan tribes of the Gran Chaco in
Paraguay; and the Charrúa of Uruguay. At the northern limits of the Spanish
colonies in northern Mexico, New Mexico, and Texas, similar groups developed.
Apache, Ute, and Comanche raiders preyed on Spanish settlements for several
hundred years, resulting in chronic warfare between native groups and the Spanish
colonists. The Spanish settlements grew gradually over time, and eventually the
Spanish were able to exterminate the native raiders. The areas where the native
populations have been wholly eliminated are what Service calls Euro-America, and
they include Argentina, Uruguay, and Costa Rica.[8]

One other point is worth emphasizing in this analysis of differential relations
between the conquering Europeans and native societies. European culture was
structurally complex, representing a state level of organization. In this sense, it was
most like the cultures of the highland state-organized peoples, less like those of the
lowland agriculturists, and most distinct from the cultures of the marginal hunters
and gatherers. There was a more or less direct correlation between the cultural
complexity of a native society and its survival after European conquest. It thus appears that the more alike the conquerors and the conquered, the easier the adjustment to conquest; the less difficult and disruptive the adjustment, the more likely

TABLE 3.1   Amerindian Population of Latin America, c. 2000

Country	Total Population	Indian Population	Indian Percent of Total
Euro-America (approx. 1 percent)	44,529,000	511,870	1.1
Argentina, Uruguay, Costa Rica			
Afro-America (< 1 percent)	185,058,000	489,066	0.26
Coastal Brazil	138,914,000	96,780	<0.1
Guianas	1,324,000	80,286	6.1
Coastal Colombia (est.)	7,095,000	306,700	4.3
Antilles	37,725,000	5,300	—
Mestizo-America (< 5 percent)	183,977,634	3,204,679	1.7
Northern Mexico	39,501,629	415,518	0.1
Central America (excl. Costa Rica)	21,229,469	1,063,000	5.0
Highland and Eastern Colombia (est.)	35,905,000	431,000	1.2
Venezuela (est.)	23,900,000	382,400	1.6
Braz. Amazonia	43,119,000	373,587	0.9
Paraguay	5,206,101	85,674	1.6
Chile	15,116,435	453,500	3.0
Indo-America (>10 percent)	108,433,219	27,798,844	25.6
Central and Southern Mexico	57,981,783	6,862,484	11.8
Belize	232,111	24,501	10.6
Guatemala	9,133,000	4,000,000	43.8
Ecuador	10,508,000	3,111,900	29.6
Peru	22,304,000	9,100,000	40.8
Bolivia	8,274,325	4,700,000	56.8

the conquered people were to survive and preserve at least the local basis of their native social organization and cultural forms.

Contemporary Latin America

Euro-America and Afro-America

Table 3.1 gives the current distribution of the Amerindian population in Latin America according to the latest more or less complete data readily available, which range from 2000 to 2007.[9] In Euro-America and Afro-America, the indigenous population generally accounts for 1 percent or less of the total population. In Euro-America, it is slightly more than 1 percent, and in Afro-America it actually averages much less than that.

The principal exception is in the three Guianas, where population is sparse and total population numbers are low. Because the population is limited and intrusive groups are concentrated along the coast, the indigenous groups that occupy the interior of those countries have not faced as much direct competition as in Brazil or the Antilles. This situation is now changing because since independence, the Guianas have increasingly looked to the development of the interior as integral to national economic development, although as the nonrenewable resources are depleted, the perceived usefulness of the indigenous population likely will diminish at the same time. In the case of Guyana, development of the interior is also a means of asserting and consolidating rights to territory claimed also by neighboring Venezuela.[10]

In Euro-America population growth has been slow, although the indigenous population has increased by more than 150,000 in the last decade, a growth rate of nearly 30 percent, compared to only 4.2 percent in the general population. Indigenous activism in Argentina led to legal recognition in 1989. Subsequently indigenous people were granted land titles, and indigenous rights were recognized in the constitution of 1994.[11] In Afro-America the indigenous population has increased by more than 300,000 in the same time period but still represents no more than 0.4 percent of the total population. Significant changes in coastal Brazil (from 61,485 in 1990 to 96,780 in 2000) and northern Colombia (from an estimated 139,596 in 1980 to an estimated 596,000 in 2005) probably represent differences in defining what constitutes an Indian, as well as different methods of enumeration. Only modest change has occurred in the Guianas. There is increasing evidence, however, of significant numbers of people with indigenous ancestry who are systematically excluded from census enumeration and denied recognition as "real Indians" for reasons of national pride and discrimination. Costa Rica, for example, considers itself European, while campaigns of ethnocide have occurred in El Salvador and Guatemala. In Brazil it's felt that identification of Indians hinders development of the interior. There may be a half million or more Indians in the Antilles and Central America alone.[12]

Mestizo-America

Most of the surviving indigenous populations of this region live in distinct communities, where they retain their aboriginal culture and their identity as members of a traditional community that is not integrated into national society. They continue to function as members of distinct cultures within the modern state, thus leading some authorities to characterize them as "Fourth World" societies. But numerous native groups in this region are currently in the process of acculturating to the dominant national cultures, with significant numbers migrating to the cities.

There are nearly 4 million Indians out of a total population of nearly 180 million. It is worth noting that the indigenous population of this region has increased by nearly 650,000 since 2000, an increase of 20 percent. While the population as a whole has remained more or less stable, the Indians have increased from 1.7 percent to 2.5 percent of the total. On a country-by-country basis, the Indians represent less than 1 percent to just under 6 percent of the total population (see Table 3.1). Where up-to-date information is available, their numbers show a modest population growth.

In northern Mexico, the principal group is the Tarahumara—subsistence farmers widely scattered throughout their rugged mountain homeland. In Central America, interior Venezuela, and the vast Amazon basin, the aboriginal populations were less dense at the time of European contact than in the Andean states. Disease, slavery, and European warfare against these highly divided groups led to their decimation and extinction in many localities. Nonetheless, a number of ethnically distinct groups persist in more isolated localities or on reserves protected by missionaries or national governments. Most of these populations are found in the lowland tropical areas.

The economy of these lowland villages is based on subsistence slash-and-burn farming of tropical crops. The most important staples are manioc, bananas, and yams, but these are supplemented by a variety of other crops. Some groups, like the Karinya of Venezuela, cultivate nearly a hundred different crops. Fishing is also an important subsistence activity, providing the principal source of dietary protein. Hunting is generally less important, and even this activity is often oriented toward riverine and aquatic species (turtle, caiman, ducks, manatee, and so on). In some groups that lack ready access to the rivers—such as the Jivaro and the Yanomamö—hunting assumes greater importance. By exploiting the diverse resources of agriculture, fishing, and hunting, most of these groups have maintained a nutritionally balanced diet. Their crafts are generally simple, although many groups make excellent baskets and some, like the Jívaro, are known for their fine pottery.

Villages are politically independent, and ethnic identity is recognized only as a consequence of sharing a common language, common customs, and a mutual ethnic consciousness. Settlements generally number fewer than 300 inhabitants, although they may occasionally range up to as many as 1,000 to 2,000. Traditionally these groups resided in communal houses, with one or more located in each settlement. Sociopolitical organization is based on kinship ties. Marriage tends to be endogamous within the local group. The headman or chief has limited authority over the group; he usually enjoys few, if any, special privileges. His influence is based on personal prestige and does not extend beyond the local village. The division of labor is based strictly on age and sex. With the exception of the shaman, there is no full-time specialization. Recent research has, however, uncovered evidence of earlier widespread multiethnic regional networks linking groups in trading and ritual exchanges.[13]

Warfare is frequent and often bitter, but it is never pursued for purposes of conquering territory or exacting tribute. Usually it is justified in terms of revenge, or sometimes to gain prestige or to acquire trophies that have supernatural power. Many anthropologists subscribe to an ecological explanation for warfare among these communities—seeing it as a mechanism for acquiring and maintaining access to scarce resources, such as rivers, with their abundance of fish and game; good farmland, also mostly along the rivers; and, among the Yanomamö, women. Warfare may also serve to keep populations dispersed so as not to overexploit the limited resources of the tropical environment.

Except for marriage, which tends to be treated in a matter-of-fact way, life crisis rites are strongly emphasized among these peoples. Shamanism is important and highly developed. The shaman works to cure illness, affect the weather, and ensure success in warfare. Often he organizes group religious festivals and dances as well. He is generally the guardian of community religious tradition. The shaman may also practice witchcraft and sorcery, though he rarely admits to doing so unless it is directed against enemy groups. Shamans (as well as all adult men) use a wide variety of narcotics in curing and in other religious ceremonies. Although the concept of a high god may exist, it is relatively unimportant in religious belief and ritual. Instead, religion centers on culture heroes who made the world what it is today, and on nature spirits who are closely associated with subsistence concerns, particularly fishing and hunting.

The Mapuche of southern Chile are somewhat distinct, since they have adopted European crops and farming techniques and participate, to a certain extent, in the national society. They sell crop surpluses in the regional market, their children receive formal schooling, and they participate, at least marginally, in national political, legal, and judicial institutions. Under the Pinochet regime, however, they suffered severe discrimination and many communities lost their land.

All of the groups in Mestizo-America are under increasing pressure from national societies because the isolated areas they occupy are being opened up by highway construction, spontaneous colonization by peasant farmers, national development programs, and projects for the exploitation of natural resources by numerous multinational corporations. In Central America, the native groups seem to be holding their own so far, although there are concerns for the future. In Nicaragua the revolutionary Sandinista government was startled to find the 120,000 Miskito Indians living in the Caribbean lowlands resisting efforts to absorb them into national society. After several years of tense relations, the Mosquitía region was formally recognized as an autonomous region within the Nicaraguan state.

During the 1990s, the Venezuelan government attempted to protect Indian lands through legal action. The constitution of 1999 officially recognized indigenous languages and cultures and guaranteed their inalienable rights to occupy ancestral lands, maintain their ethnic identity and cultural traditions, and receive an education appropriate to their sociocultural traditions. Intellectual property rights are also guaranteed and protected.[14] Authorities in Colombia, Bolivia, and Paraguay have generally ignored the problems of the natives, but in Colombia indigenous peoples have suffered high levels of violence perpetrated by security forces, drug traffickers, leftist guerrillas, and paramilitary groups, as well as severe poverty. Efforts to legislate more rigorous paternalistic control over indigenous groups were defeated. Instead, indigenous groups helped write a new constitution in the late 1980s that recognizes indigenous peoples as Colombian citizens with full rights. Indigenous representatives have also been elected to the Colombian congress.[15]

Brazil has vacillated between looking the other way while natives are pushed out or exterminated and attempting to resettle them on reserves. Brazil continues to have one of the worst human rights records with respect to its Indian population.[16] When pressured by development interests, responsible officials have generally allowed these reserves to be fragmented or whittled down. For example, in spite of a vociferous international outcry, Brazil made no concerted effort to keep thousands of prospectors, miners, and traders from intruding on Yanomamö territory. The democratic constitution of 1988 includes a chapter on indigenous peoples that revises relations between them and the state, terminating five centuries of integrationist policy. On paper it increased the rights of Indians, recognizing their right to land and the existence of collective (community) Indian rights. But Brazilian practice continues to be integrationist, while state and local governments ignore abuse of constitutionally guaranteed Indian rights.

Although most of these Indians have remained in distinct, small-scale communities, increasing numbers have followed the general demographic trend in Latin

America of rural-to-urban migration. Many Indians are known to reside in Latin American cities, but obtaining a reliable estimate of their numbers is nearly impossible. To judge from the available figures, more than 200,000 Indians are probably urban dwellers in Mestizo-America.

These traditional peoples cannot be ignored as human beings. Certainly they are just as important as any other identifiable group in the countries of Mestizo-America. Many of their current difficulties arise from the fact that in terms of their numbers and the economic or political impact that they exercise, they represent a very small segment of the modern population.

Indo-America

The most significant indigenous populations, in terms of numbers and their place in national society, are the modern Indian types found in Indo-America, comprising most of Mexico, Guatemala, and the central Andean countries of Ecuador, Peru, and Bolivia. These Indians, who tend to live in the highland regions of those countries, must be included in any consideration of modern Latin America. Although their way of life differs from that of the non-Indians in the countries where they live, they share many patterns and institutions, mainly of European origin, with the other citizens. Numerically, they are an important segment of the population, constituting more than 10 percent in almost all of these countries. In some countries, such as Peru, Guatemala, and Bolivia, they make up from 40 to 60 percent of the population, respectively (see Table 3.1).

Taking Indo-America as a whole, the indigenous population amounts to more than 30 million, or 26.7 percent of the total population. This represents an increase of more than 3 million, or nearly 11 percent, during the first decade of the twenty-first century. Compare this to the growth in the general population of just over 7 million, or about 6.5 percent. Clearly the indigenous population continues to grow more rapidly than the general population.

During the colonial period, the Indians of these countries were taught Catholicism and often were concentrated into Spanish-type villages, where European forms of community organization were forced on them. They borrowed freely from the European culture of the sixteenth and seventeenth centuries—a culture that in many respects contained as many "folk features" as their own. By the beginning of the eighteenth century, the fusion of the aboriginal and colonial Spanish patterns had formed a new culture among these peoples. This culture persists today, unchanged in its main outlines, and constitutes an important variant of national patterns in these highland countries. Because this culture is relatively unchanged from colonial times, it contrasts markedly with modern cultural patterns and is sometimes erroneously believed to represent a survival of aboriginal cultural practices.

Modern Indians in these countries generally speak an aboriginal language, although many speak Spanish as well. Community cohesion tends to persist at a high level despite the encroaching power of the national states. The Indians of each community generally think of themselves as ethnic units, separate from other Indian groups and from non-Indian nationals of the country in which they reside. They are people of the village or town rather than Mexicans, Guatemalans, or Peruvians. Frequently they wear a distinctive costume that identifies them as members of a particular pueblo. At the beginning of the twenty-first century, however, the global costume of Nikes, T-shirts, and blue jeans is favored by Indians and non-Indians alike.

Community structure is characteristically of the type known as the closed corporate peasant community—an organized communal structure with clearly defined social boundaries; it is very clear who does and who does not belong to the community. The community generally does not identify with the nation; its members find their personal and social satisfaction within the community by adhering to its traditional value system. The corporate peasant community is held together not by ties of kinship but by coownership of a landholding corporation. Members are not allowed to sell or rent land to outsiders, and this taboo severely limits the degree to which factors outside the community can affect the structure of private property or the development of class differences within the community. This is one of the most important ways of promoting and maintaining community integration.

In another common pattern, especially in the central Andes, the Indians are clustered as peons on large hacienda estates. They have no secure rights to property but work the land belonging to a non-Indian owner. In exchange they receive a plot of land on which to build a house and grow subsistence crops. Although a small wage may be paid, the plot of land serves in lieu of most wage income. The hacienda owner discourages community organization and tries to establish personal ties between himself and each laborer, thereby exercising greater control over his labor force. At the same time, by encouraging maintenance of the peons' native language and distinctive ethnic identity, with its own traditional customs, he ensures that the peonage community will remain isolated from the larger society.

These peasant communities depend on agriculture as their principal means of subsistence. Most of the land that the peasants possess for their own use is of marginal productivity. It is exploited by means of traditional technology, which involves continuous physical effort and manual labor. Peasants rely on both the hoe and the plow drawn by draft animals and make little use of modern machinery. Their staple crops include the principal cereal grains (corn, wheat, barley), a variety of legumes (beans, broad beans, lentils, garbanzos, peas), chili peppers, and in the Andes, a variety of root crops, including potatoes. Most agriculture follows a short fallow cycle, with fields being rested for one year after several years of cropping. Fertilizers are expensive and seldom used, although insecticides have become popular in recent years. In some areas irrigation is important.

Crafts are highly developed. The manufacture of textiles, pottery, baskets, wood carvings, jewelry, and toys often achieves a high degree of aesthetic creativity. The economy of the closed corporate community is closely linked to a peculiar sort of regional marketing system. Different villages specialize in different commodities, and these are brought together and exchanged in the market. For the same reason, the market brings together a much larger supply of articles than merchants in any one community could afford to keep continuously in their stores. Thus there is much wider access to the products of each community. A shortage of money requires that sales and purchases in the market be small. The producer typically offers his or her goods for sale in order to obtain small amounts of cash in order to purchase other goods. In recent years, increasing quantities of cheap manufactured goods have been introduced into the regional market system and sometimes provide stiff competition for locally produced handicrafts. Another source of cash income is seasonal migration to work on plantations and *fincas* that produce sugar, coffee, or other goods for export. Typically this migration involves movement from highland peasant communities to lowland areas. In Mexico increasing numbers of indigenous peasants are traveling to the northern part of the country or even into the United States as documented or undocumented migrant workers employed by agribusiness, food processing, textiles, or other industrial enterprises. Some may come from Guatemala or Central America.

The basic social unit of these communities is the nuclear family. Households average about six persons. Marriage may be consecrated through formal religious ceremonies, but a high incidence of marriages result from elopement or abduction. Marriage is usually with an unrelated person, but it is preferentially endogamous within the village. This preference serves as another mechanism for local community integration. Fertility is high among these people, and although the infant mortality has also been high, the mortality rate has declined over the past several decades, leading to rapid population growth. The institution of *compadrazgo*, which establishes a special relationship between the parents and godparents of a child, is another important mechanism for social integration and mutual support.

Settlement patterns vary considerably. In some areas, such as central Mexico, residence is concentrated in a compact village. In others, such as southern Mexico or highland Ecuador, residences are scattered throughout the community's territory. In the organization of the local community, traditional native officials are often maintained alongside representatives of the national bureaucracy. The community's system of power embraces the male members of the society and makes achievement of power a matter of group decision rather than one of individually achieved status. This system of power is tied into a religious system or a series of interlocking religious systems. The politico-religious system as a whole tends to define the boundaries of the local group and acts as a symbol of collective unity. Prestige within the community is largely related to rising from office to office within this system. Conspicuous consumption, principally by putting on elaborate fiesta celebrations, is geared to this communally approved system of power and religion, and it serves to level differences of wealth within the community. The system thus avoids class divisions that might undermine the corporate structure of the community. Various psychic mechanisms of control, such as institutionalized envy and the concept of "limited good," also help maintain the traditional values and way of life.[17]

Modern Indians are nominally Catholic, but their religious practices incorporate aboriginal beliefs as well. In addition, Catholic saints are endowed with local characteristics and powers. Fiestas are held to honor the patron saint and other locally important saints, and *cargos,* or religious offices, as well as magical practices, are assumed to preserve and promote these saint cults. Traditional fiestas and associated ceremonies and celebrations are an important part of the traditional culture and help preserve a distinctive local identity. Some communities maintain folk priests—cantors, for example—who have contributed to the survival of folk beliefs and practices in the absence (sometimes for several generations) of Catholic priests. During the past couple of decades, however, evangelical Protestant sects have successfully recruited large numbers of indigenous adherents, particularly in Mexico and Guatemala. This often creates conflict between new converts and traditional segments of the community. *Evangélicos* typically abjure alcohol and dancing, refuse to participate in the traditional fiesta system, and tend to withdraw from customary practices of community reciprocity, thus creating factionalism and undermining community integration. In southern Mexico many supporters of the Zapatista movement were Protestants who moved out of the traditional communities and often were in conflict with the established indigenous leadership, which remained Roman Catholic.

Illness and disease are explained as resulting from an imbalance in the hot and cold humors that occur in the body, in the foods consumed, and in objects that the individual encounters. Certain psychological disorders are also explained as a result of *susto* or *espanto* ("fright"), in which the individual is frightened by an encounter with a supernatural entity, sometimes resulting in loss of the soul. The curing of these disorders is usually in the hands of local *curanderos* ("folk doctors") who may attempt to restore the hot-cold imbalance, call upon aboriginal spirits or Christian saints, or apply herbal remedies. Ethnographic reports suggest that many of the empirical remedies of these *curanderos* are effective and that their treatments are largely successful. Family members who can afford to do so may try to hedge the probabilities of a successful cure by also consulting a medical doctor.

Adherence to the traditional culture validates membership in an existing society and acts as a passport to participation in the life of the community. The typical peasant can amass enough wealth to acquire the prestige symbols of the Indian system, and thus the individual is encouraged to maintain his identification with that system. The particular traits held by an Indian help him remain within the equilibrium of relationships that maintain the community. On the other hand, non-Indians must attempt to gain wealth within the national system, where it is impossible to accumulate enough wealth through hard work to permit access to the prestige symbols of the upper sector. The non-Indian peasant is thus perpetually frustrated in his attempt to achieve meaningful goals.

These modern Indian populations are important elements of the national societies. Numerically, they represent a significant proportion of the total population. They participate, if only marginally, in the economic, political, and religious institutions of the nation, and they represent a large, inexpensive pool of labor that can be recruited whenever unskilled labor is required. There is a slow but constant interchange of ideas between the Indian subcultures on the one hand and the national culture on the other.

The first decade of the twenty-first century has been marked by increasing Indian activism and political participation. There has been a renaissance in indigenous languages and cultures, and indigenous organizations have sought to maintain or reassert control over traditional lands and resources. The Zapatista uprising of January 1994 in Chiapas is perhaps the most widely reported. It was motivated by limited access to land, the threat of increased economic disadvantage with the implementation of the North American Free Trade Agreement (NAFTA), long-standing abuse of the indigenous population by the dominant mestizo inhabitants, and government inaction in addressing these problems. Negotiations to resolve these complaints have continued so long that one wonders how willing the Mexican government really is to deal with them.

In Guatemala the genocidal policies of the government in the 1970s and early 1980s were directed against suspected Mayan subversion. Over 400 villages were destroyed and their inhabitants massacred. By the late 1980s massive oppression had abated, with new protections for "indigenous communities" being written into the 1985 constitution. Still, considerable tension exists between Maya and Ladino (non-Indian) in that country. The Maya community continues to be fragmented, but a new intellectual leadership is emerging, new forms of organization are being developed, and Mayan towns are defending themselves from government abuse. At the same time, human rights activists who seek to address past and present abuses continue to be threatened. That the Maya themselves are taking an active role in defining their own identity may give hope for eventual development of a plurinational state in Guatemala.

Similar developments may be seen in growing Indian political participation in Bolivia, where the Aymara leader Víctor Hugo Cárdenas was elected vice president in 1993. Indigenous farmers have long demonstrated against programs encouraged by the United States to control coca production. Then in 2003 the government's proposal to sell Bolivia's gas reserves to an American company provoked massive demonstrations led by Aymara union leader Evo Morales. In the end the government abandoned the proposal and President Gonzalo Sánchez de Lozada resigned. In the 2005 national election Evo Morales was elected president of the country, the first Aymara head of state since the Spanish conquest. His administration has acted to promote a variety of indigenous interests.

Peru has long been the most conservative Andean nation, with strong biases against the 40 percent of the population that is indigenous. Yet in 2001 Alejandro Toledo, a man of Indian descent whose parents were Quechua speakers, was elected president, albeit by a slim margin. To a considerable extent his electoral success was realized by his open identification with the Indian heritage of Peru.

In Ecuador the indigenous movement has created a strong organizational base that is now an important actor in the national political arena. It has organized indigenous communities, established bilingual education, and resisted neoliberal economic policies. It has created a place in the political agenda where indigenous people are not merely subjects, but also active members of civil society. The cultural demands of the indigenous movement have allowed them to create a political force that came as a surprise to both the state and the left in Ecuador. Indigenous people were a major element in forcing the resignation of Ecuadorian President Jamil Mahuad in 2000.

With modernization, education, and improved communication, as well as other developments, Indian interaction with the national culture is increasing all the time. The worldwide process of globalization is profoundly affecting the Indians of Latin America, just as it is nonindigenous populations. Continuing population growth and resultant pressures on the land have led to a large-scale migration to the cities. Today there are probably 5 million Indians or more living in the towns and cities of Indo-America. Once they arrive in the cities there is rapid acculturation to urban life. But at the same time, they maintain their ties to and identification with the home community. Urban residents frequently return to visit their relatives or to attend major fiestas. There is also evidence that with increased incomes and greater sophistication, traditional customs and practices are being revived and even intensified in many of these communities. Thus, in spite of modernizing influences, there are indications that for the foreseeable future, many of these contemporary Indian communities will retain their ethnically distinctive subcultures, while the activism cited above may produce newer forms of nationwide indigenous identity.

NOTES

1. Herbert Barry III, "Regional and Worldwide Variations in Culture," *Ethnology* 7, no. 2 (1968): 207–217; and George Peter Murdock, "Ethnographic Atlas," *Ethnology* 6, no. 2 (1967).

2. Elman R. Service, "Indian-European Relations in Colonial Latin America," *American Anthropologist* 57 (1955): 411–412.

3. Ibid., p. 411.

4. Ibid., p. 418.

5. Ibid., pp. 411–412.

6. Some lowland societies were organized as chiefdoms—small, weakly centralized societies that were transitional between independent villages and strongly centralized states; in fact, they generally integrated a number of dependent villages. Chiefdoms were typically unstable, and with European conquest removal of the ruler usually resulted in social disintegration. The constituent villages then reverted to the level of independent communities. Karl H. Schwerin. "The Anthropological Antecedents: Caciques, Cacicazgos, and Caciquismo," in *The Caciques: Oligarchical Politics and the System of Caciquismo in the Luso-Hispano World*, ed. Robert Kern and Ronald Dolkart (Albuquerque: University of New Mexico Press, 1973), pp. 5–17.

7. Service, "Indian-European Relations," pp. 411–412, 418.

8. Ibid., pp. 411–412, 420.

9. Population figures are somewhat disparate. A few countries have not conducted a recent census or have not separated out their indigenous population. In these cases I have estimated the indigenous population by using recent World Bank estimates for total population, and assuming the same rate of growth since 2000 for the indigenous groups. In other cases indigenous populations were either enumerated or estimated for the late 1990s or since 2000. In several cases, not only has there been a recent census of indigenous populations, but the data is available on the Internet. See, for example, www.joshuaproject.net/countries.php?rog3=AR; www.inegi.gob.mx/est/contenidos/espanol/tematicos/mediano/med.asp?t=mlen01&c=3325; http://abyayala.nativeweb.org/ecuador/pueblos.php; www.dgeec.gov.py/Publicaciones/censo_indigena/Paraguay.pdf; venezuelanindian.blogspot.com/2006/03/ethnic-groups-in-venezuela-according.html.

10. William Heningsgaard and Jason Clay, "The Upper Mazaruni Dam," *Cultural Survival Newsletter* 4, no. 3 (1980): 103.

11. Gastón Gordillo and Silvia Hirsch, "Indigenous Struggles and Contested Identities in Argentina," *Journal of Latin American Anthropology* 8, no. 3 (2003): 4–30.

12. *Cultural Survival Quarterly* 13, no. 3 (1989); for 1980 population figures, see Table 3.1 in my chapter in Jan Knippers Black, *Latin America: Its Problems and Its Promise*, 2d ed. (Boulder: Westview, 1991). Population figures for 1990 may be found in Table 3.1 of the 3rd ed. (1998). Figures for 2000 are presented in Table 3.1 of the 4th ed. (2005) and on p. 43 of the present edition.

13. Nelly Arvelo-Jimenéz and Horacio Biord Castillo, "The Impact of Conquest on Contemporary Indigenous Peoples of the Guiana Shield: The System of Orinoco Re-

gional Interdependence," in *Amazonian Indians from Prehistory to the Present: Anthropological Perspectives*, ed. Anna Roosevelt (Tucson: University of Arizona Press, 1994), pp. 55–78; Silvia M. Vidal, "Kuwé Duwákalumi: The Arawak Sacred Routes of Migration, Trade, and Resistance," *Ethnohistory* 47, no. 3–4 (2000): 635–667; Karl H. Schwerin, "Carib Warfare and Slaving," *Antropológica* 99–100 (2003): 45–72.

14. See Sánchez P. Domingo, *A New Reality for Venezuela's Indigenous Peoples*, Venezuelan National Foundation for Indigenous Studies, www.centrelink.org/Sanchez English.html.

15. Donna Lee Van Cott, ed., *Indigenous Peoples and Democracy in Latin America* (New York: St. Martin's, 1994).

16. Amnesty International, *Brazil: "We Are the Land": Indigenous People's Struggle for Human Rights* (New York: Amnesty International, 1992).

17. George M. Foster, *Tzintzuntzan: Mexican Peasants in a Changing World*, rev. ed. (New York: Elsevier, 1979), pp. 122–166.

SUGGESTED READINGS

Allen, Catherine J. *The Hold Life Has: Coca and Cultural Identity in an Andean Community*. Washington, DC: Smithsonian Institution, 1988. Discusses the social and ceremonial life of a highland community, emphasizing the ritual importance of mountain peaks and the socially and ceremonially integrative functions of coca use.

Amnesty International. *Brazil: "We Are the Land": Indigenous People's Struggle for Human Rights*. New York: Amnesty International, 1992. Details abuses of indigenous human rights in Brazil.

Barry, Herbert, III. "Regional and Worldwide Variations in Culture." *Ethnology* 7, no. 2 (1968): 207–217. A cross-cultural statistical analysis, based on the *Ethnographic Atlas* (see Murdock 1967), of the distribution worldwide, and by continents, of the major types of subsistence economy, family customs, and social structure.

Brown, Michael F. *Tsewa's Gift: Magic and Meaning in an Amazonian Society*. Washington, DC: Smithsonian Institution Press, 1985. Explores how Aguaruna magical practices mold their transactions with nature as well as practical activities such as hunting, gardening, and romantic relations.

Buechler, Hans C., and Judith-Maria Buechler. *The Bolivian Aymara*. Case Studies in Cultural Anthropology. New York: Holt, Rinehart & Winston, 1971. One of the few complete ethnographic descriptions of an Aymara community and the best short study available.

Cancian, Frank. *Economics and Prestige in a Maya Community: The Religious Cargo System in Zinacantan*. Stanford: Stanford University Press, 1965. Offers a thorough analysis of a typical religious cargo system and shows how traditional practices have been modified and elaborated in response to population growth and increasing wealth differentiation within the community.

Chagnon, Napoleon A. *Yanomamö: The Fierce People*. 5th ed. Case Studies in Cultural Anthropology. New York: Holt, Rinehart & Winston, 1995. The classic study of a warlike people who inhabit an isolated area in the northern Amazon basin.

Davis, Shelton H. *Victims of the Miracle: Development and the Indians of Brazil*. Cambridge: Cambridge University Press, 1977. Attempts to document the disruptive impact that Amazon development programs have on the native peoples of the tropical forest.

Denevan, William M., ed. *The Native Population of the Americas in 1492*. Madison: University of Wisconsin Press, 1976. An edited volume that treats the historical demography of the Americas. Each chapter considers some aspect of the basic disagreement about the relative size of the aboriginal population of the New World.

Faron, Louis C. *The Mapuche Indians of Chile.* Case Studies in Cultural Anthropology. New York: Holt, Rinehart & Winston, 1968. An excellent summary of contemporary culture among the peasant Araucanian farmers of southern Chile.

Foster, George M. *Tzintzuntzan: Mexican Peasants in a Changing World.* Rev. ed. New York: Elsevier, 1979. The best general account of peasant society and worldview in Latin America. Although most inhabitants of Tzintzuntzan are mestizo, they share many characteristics with modern Indians or the closed corporate peasant communities of Indo-America.

Gregor, Thomas. *Mehinaku: The Drama of Daily Life in a Brazilian Indian Village.* Chicago: University of Chicago Press, 1977. The peaceful Mehinaku, who live in the southern Amazon basin, contrast strikingly with the warlike Yanomamö (Chagnon 1968).

Heningsgaard, William, and Jason Clay. "The Upper Mazaruni Dam." *Cultural Survival Newsletter* 4, no. 3 (1980): 103. A brief account of the economic and political factors behind the construction of the dam and how this project is depriving the Akawaio of their land.

Hill, Jonathan D., ed. *Rethinking History and Myth: Indigenous South American Perspectives on the Past.* Urbana: University of Illinois Press, 1988. Documents how South American indigenous peoples, in the highlands as well as the lowlands, have utilized both myth and history to develop dynamic interpretations of past and present interaction with colonial and national societies.

Isbell, Billie Jean. *To Defend Ourselves: Ecology and Ritual in an Andean Village.* Austin: University of Texas, 1978. Good analysis of a typical Andean community that treats both traditional culture and the processes of accommodating to a changing nation.

Murdock, George Peter. "Ethnographic Atlas." *Ethnology* 6, no. 2 (1967). The culmination of Murdock's lifelong interest in tabulating the occurrence of cultural traits on a worldwide basis.

Murphy, Yolanda, and Robert F. Murphy. *Women of the Forest.* New York: Columbia University Press, 1974. An excellent account of a typical Amazonian society with an emphasis on the role of women and the woman's point of view.

Overing, Joanna, and Alan Passes, eds. *The Anthropology of Love and Anger: The Aesthetics of Conviviality in Native Amazonia.* London: Routledge, 2001. Reveals that indigenous South American thought and practice are fundamentally dissimilar from Western patterns. Conviviality or "sociality" is attained only through negotiation of the negative features of communal living to achieve positive harmony and sociability.

Schwerin, Karl H. "The Anthropological Antecedents: Caciques, Cacicazgos, and Caciquismo." In *The Caciques: Oligarchical Politics and the System of Caciquismo in the Luso-Hispano World,* ed. Robert Kern and Ronald Dolkart, pp. 5–17. Albuquerque: University of New Mexico Press, 1973. A summary statement on the general nature of chiefdoms, or *cacicazgos,* in pre-Columbian Latin America with discussion of their distribution and principal social and cultural characteristics.

——. *Oil and Steel: Processes of Karinya Culture Change in Response to Industrial Development.* Latin American Studies 4. Los Angeles: UCLA Press, 1966. A comparison of social and cultural characteristics in two Venezuelan Indian communities with a theoretical analysis of the processes of culture change that occurred there during the twentieth century.

Service, Elman R. "Indian-European Relations in Colonial Latin America." *American Anthropologist* 57 (1955): 411–425. Presents the thesis that major differences in the character of modern Latin American states can be traced to European responses to differences in aboriginal cultural patterns, especially in relation to subsistence and sociopolitical complexity.

Stephen, Lynn. *Zapotec Women.* Austin: University of Texas Press, 1991. Explores how commercial weaving for export has altered the lives of Zapotec women in recent decades. Class, ethnicity, and gender determine women's roles and standing in the community. Although the expansion of capitalism has produced class differentiation, it has also reinforced kin-based institutions supporting local ethnic identity.

Urban, Greg, and Joel Sherzer, eds. *Nation-states and Indians in Latin America.* Austin: University of Texas Press, 1991. Looks at the interaction between Amerindian cultures and the European-origin nation-states of Latin America.

Van Cott, Donna Lee, ed. *Indigenous Peoples and Democracy in Latin America.* New York: St. Martin's, 1994. Analyzes, within a broader theoretical framework, indigenous movements in eight Latin American countries: Bolivia, Colombia, Peru, and Ecuador; Mexico and Guatemala; Brazil and Paraguay.

Vogt, Evon Z. *The Zinacantecos of Mexico: A Modern Maya Way of Life.* Case Studies in Cultural Anthropology. New York: Holt, Rinehart & Winston, 1970. Since 1955, Vogt directed the Harvard Chiapas Project in the *municipio* of Zinacantán in southern Mexico. This project has been dedicated to continuous observation and study in the same community in order to better understand the directional processes at work in social and cultural systems.

Warren, Kay B., and Jean E. Jackson, eds. *Indigenous Movements, Self-representation, and the State in Latin America.* Austin: University of Texas Press, 2002. How indigenous movements in Latin America attempt to influence national agendas when governments articulate ambivalent attitudes about encouraging ethnic diversity.

Chapter 4

HARMONIZING AND DISHARMONIZING HUMAN AND NATURAL ENVIRONMENTS

DAVID STEA AND G. SHANE LEWIS

IDENTIFICATION AND prioritization of specific environmental issues varies widely around Latin America. "Environment" is much more than physical surrounds, and it cannot be dissociated from politics, poverty, insecure land tenure, human rights, and gender issues. North Americans and many Latin Americans alike share bits of conventional wisdom, popularly held myths concerning the root causes of environmental problems. While containing certain partial truths, all are in the balance largely false, and this chapter attempts implicitly to debunk them. The discussion begins with some basic issues; proceeds to case studies; continues with an update of current environmental issues related to western Amazonia, Plan Panamá-Pacífico, and Plan Colombia; and concludes with a critique of a few suggested solutions. In this relatively brief treatment, neither all nations nor all possible environmental issues can be considered, nor can we devote more than a few lines to the Caribbean islands, whose environmental problems, exacerbated by poverty and widening gaps between rich and poor, include deforestation, water pollution, and loss of fisheries. For the same reason, specific citations are provided only for direct quotes.

BASIC ISSUES

The issues basic to defining and describing Latin American environmental problems, shared with the rest of the developing world, include the relationship of economic development to so-called *sustainable* development. Both forms of development imply efficiency.[1] The efficiency involved in sustainability, in particular, must exist in order that the present use of important resources not endanger the availability of such resources to future generations. In this, as mentioned above, environmental issues are entwined not just with relative availability of natural resources but with human beings—viewed as resources—with the social, cultural, and political issues which are, in turn, intimately interrelated with economic development.

Economic development is a prime issue of the southern tier, and environmental conservation is stressed by the North. While viewed as opposed by many participants in the 1992 Rio Declaration, these concerns—economy and environment, in terms of both concern and action—must be mutually reinforcing. The usual measure of economic development—standard of living, as indexed by GNP—cannot be opposed to quality of life, including environment, difficult to index quantitatively. Truly *sustainable* development cannot take place unless socioeconomic development and environmental improvement proceed together, catalyzed by political action and will. Thus of importance here is "political ecology" or, more inclusively, "sociopolitical ecology."

Central to the concerns of—and protest against—the 2002 World Summit on Sustainable Development were the prospects for and implementation of "globalization." One effect of globalization to date, in the opinion of many, has been to *increase* negative externalities (Franko 2003) and, often, to impact developing countries disproportionately, and especially the poor of such countries. An outstanding example of so-called free trade agreements affecting Latin America is NAFTA, the North American Free Trade Agreement. Regardless of what it has done to or for the three national economies involved (Canada, Mexico, and the United States), there is substantial disagreement concerning whether NAFTA has contributed to worsening labor conditions (especially in Mexico) and to environmental degradation.

In sum, there is no single Latin American environmental problem; rather, there are multiple environmental problems:

> There is a broad array of environmental issues in the region that vary in importance based upon who you are, where you live, and what economic resources are available to you. The priority list depends on whether you are rich or poor, urban or rural, male or female. A middle-class resident of Santiago, Chile, is likely to complain most about air quality, while someone living in a shack in São Paolo might be most affected by problems of water sanitation. A rubber tapper might ally with an international rain forest activist in arguing that tropical deforestation is the most pressing issue, but for very different reasons. Problems in maintaining fishing stocks off the coast of Argentina might seem a long way from the concerns of the Indians in Peru's Altiplano. Women might worry about the ways communities struggle to overcome deficits with water or sewage. (Franko 2003, 444–445)

Socioeconomic levels are intimately linked with levels of environmental quality, since poverty is both a cause and an effect of environmental degradation. In the absence of secure land tenure, the rural poor act rationally, in the short term, when they seek to extract as much from the land as possible. When excluded from the establishment and management of reserves, as in the case of the Monarch Butterfly Reserve in the Mexican states of México and Michoacán, neighboring farmers understandably began to nibble at the edges of the reserve. Land tenure is an issue in urban areas as well, where irregular settlements, or "squatments," occupy precarious terrain such as denuded hillsides. These squatments represent a rational solution to the otherwise intractable problem of ultra low-cost housing. Land tenure involves not just private *minifundia* or urban lots, but an understanding of how common areas are to be regulated to avoid the so-called tragedy of the commons.

URBANIZATION

Degrees of urbanization do not differentiate Latin American countries from the United States. Just over 77 percent of the US population lived in cities in 2000, while almost 80 percent lived in cities in Latin America. Five Latin American countries are more than 81 percent urbanized: Argentina, Brazil, Chile, Uruguay, and Venezuela. In Uruguay over 91 percent of the population lives in metropolitan areas. Recent estimates suggest that by the year 2025, Latin America will be the most urbanized of the world's continents, with 85 percent of its population living in cities. Any differences in environmental problems of Latin America and the industrialized world, therefore, are not related to *degree* of urbanization, but rather (1) to the *nature* of that urbanization and (2) to the lifestyle of rural peoples. Of the more than 20 percent of the US population who live in rural areas, less than 1 percent is actively engaged in agriculture. Rural dwellers of Latin America are mostly farmers with the vast majority living in poverty, and some using technology unchanged in hundreds of years. As demonstrated by the NAFTA-facilitated importation of hybrid US corn by the cradle of corn—Mexico—rural dwellers cannot compete in the market with expanding international agribusiness.

In contrast to the United States, where over 100 million people are spread over forty cities of a million or more inhabitants each, in all but one country of Latin America a single megacity dwarfs all others.[2] Since the 1950s these megalopolises have attracted immigrants from increasingly impoverished rural areas. Many move initially to intermediate towns and then to the primate city, occupying land belonging to the government or the Church, or left undeveloped by private landowners. Such areas of irregular settlement, characterizing primate cities in Asia and Africa as well, often represent 20 percent or more of the urban population. For these people, the most pressing problems are water and sanitation. Due to the absence of sanitary facilities, fecal matter remains on the ground. When it becomes desiccated during the dry season, as in the case of Mexico City, it is carried as windblown dust from the periphery into the center.

The proportion of urbanized space devoted to green areas—parks, plazas, and so on—has decreased markedly over the past half century. This is important not only because it reduces opportunities for outdoor recreation, but also because trees and green plants reduce certain forms of pollution. Mexico City, once renowned for its parks, is now, as a result of unregulated sprawl, among the cities with the smallest proportion of green space.

Each urban socioeconomic group perceives its problems from its own perspective, blames the others, and sees different solutions, mostly to be mediated by passively awaited governmental action. For those who dwell in irregular settlements, the most pressing problem is usually insecure land tenure; urban environmental problems are perceived as the absence of piped drinkable water and sewage disposal. People can and do upgrade their homes, but even with organization cannot provide the requisite infrastructure on their own. There are, however, hopeful signs. In Mexico's Colonia Miguel Hidalgo and Venezuela's Casalta II, two predominantly low-income neighborhoods with many irregularities, the residents, with the cooperation of faculty and students from neighboring universities, took environmental improvement into their own hands. Residents of Casalta II organized their work with the aid of donated computers, while residents of Colonia Miguel Hidalgo solved the problem of dirt streets that flooded during the rainy season by buying their own asphalt and threatening to do their own paving.[3]

The urban middle class perceives the most pressing environmental problems to be air pollution and choking traffic, whose solution is left to governmental entities. The wealthier perceive similar problems but fail to understand them and usually assign blame to the ignorance of the poor (Roberts 1994). Bypassing this circle of blame, Jaime Lerner, then mayor of Curitiba, Brazil (population nearly 2 million), pursued an integrative approach to solving his city's environmental problems, relieving floods by diverting rain water into park lakes, developing a trash-for-food/transport exchange system for squatters, designing a metro-like bus system, planning 150 kilometers of bicycle paths, and initiating tax breaks for green areas development. Results included a decrease of 30 percent in gas consumption and an equivalent reduction in private car usage.

Deforestation and Associated Issues

With regard to true rain forests, Costa Rica is frequently cited for exemplary conservation, with Brazil at the apex of deforestation. The reality, however, is more complex. Brazil today has only 63 percent of the principal preconquest ecosystems intact, having lost 93 percent of the Atlantic forest, 50 percent of the *cerrado*, and 15 percent of its Amazonian forest. The Amazon river basin contains 20 percent of the world's fresh water. The Amazon forest is estimated to be the habitat of 50 percent of the world's species, and between 0.25 and 1.25 million indigenous persons. The current rate of destruction of the Brazilian Amazon ranges from 0.5 percent to 1.2 percent annually and represented a mean loss of *at least* 3 million hectares a year during the fifteen years between 1980 and 1995. Such land use conversion has often been aided by loans received from the World Bank and other international organizations.

While Amazonia represents the greatest loss in forest *area*, the fastest *rate* of deforestation is in Central America. Tiny Costa Rica lost about 50,000 hectares annually between 1980 and 1995. Although constituting no more than one-sixtieth of the *area* of deforestation in Amazonia, the *rate* of loss is at least 2.5 times that of the Brazilian Amazon over the same fifteen-year period, and one of the highest in Latin America.

What accounts for the paradox of the most environmentally conscious nation of Central America, a nation that has stressed low-impact ecotourism as a sustainable road to development, also exhibiting a high rate of deforestation? Among the causes of deforestation in Latin America as a whole are, in order of importance, conversion of land use for agriculture, logging on a commercial scale, firewood gathering, and cattle raising. Cattle raising has received the most attention in the United States with the so-called hamburger thesis or hamburger connection.

The hamburger thesis holds that forests are cleared for pasture to provide beef for US fast food chains. However, and not just in the case of Costa Rica, this thesis is only a partial explanation, in two senses. First, it represents just 8 percent of forest clearing, overall. Second, from the mid-1970s to the 1990s, US consumption of Costa Rican beef decreased, while Costa Rican consumption increased. The Costa Rican cattle business experienced a severe crisis in the 1980s, as export taxes and interest rates increased while beef prices dropped in the 1980s to 1950–1960 levels. As less affluent ranchers are forced to move farther out, clearing still more forest, predatory animals, especially pumas, begin to take their toll on cattle, and this increases costs. Ranching may seem a relatively low-maintenance economic activity. However, all these factors taken together make ranching land degrading and not necessarily profitable.

With regard to beef production, export, and consumption, what has changed is domestic demand. In the United States, a preference for tender steaks implies feedlot cattle; thus Central American beef, tougher but tastier, is deemed suitable only for hamburgers. In much of Latin America, however, *carne asada* is the standard food product of range-fed cattle, and increasingly so. In traditional beef-exporting countries such as Brazil, El Salvador, Guatemala, Nicaragua, and Panama, domestic demand by the 1980s was growing faster than that for export production.

> Domestic demand has received insufficient attention in the "hamburger connection" literature, something that is particularly unfortunate in a period when it is of much greater weight as a stimulus to cattle production in Central America, Brazil, and elsewhere. It has long been recognized that meat is a product with a very high income elasticity of demand . . . small increases in income levels produce proportionately greater increases in demand . . . population growth and urbanization are still producing rapidly rising demand for beef. (Edelman 1995)

Lester Brown's *Who Will Feed China?* proposes that increased affluence, as in the case of China's billion and a half people, inevitably produces rising domestic demand for beef.

In quantitative terms, conversion of forest to agricultural use is even more important. Some of this forest clearing is accomplished by peasant farmers, many encouraged by ill considered national subsidies for land clearing, such as those offered in Brazil to settlers in Amazonia to reduce concentrations of the poor in other parts of the country. In lowland tropical rain forests, soil is generally nutrient poor while elsewhere, deforestation leads to loss of fertile topsoil. As increased ranching in other parts of Latin America forces small-scale farmers to move into more precarious and less fertile areas such as steep hillsides, deforestation and reduction or elimination of fallowing lead to further loss of soil fertility (and of topsoil itself), reducing farm productivity and further impoverishing farmers.

Of even greater importance in deforestation is monocrop export agribusiness, such as melon raising in Honduras. Such agriculture involves intensive irrigation and uses large quantities of herbicides, pesticides, and chemical fertilizers.[4] Because the lower-level toxic chemicals formerly used left residues that impeded the importation of such products into the United States, producers switched to chemicals with a short half-life but which were more toxic when used. The impact of their use has fallen mainly on agricultural workers, especially in Mexico. Further, such toxic chemicals find their way into streams and rivers and eventually fish and even cattle, which graze on land once used for agriculture.

With the North emphasizing the interception of drug traffic and industrialized countries increasingly demanding high-quality timber, attention has been drawn to the impact of Andean coca cultivation and lumbering on land use and deforestation. National and multinational lumber companies use heavy equipment to cut wide roads into forests to extract massive mahogany tree trunks. These roads provide access for local timber cutters to extract wood of lower value, and later for colonists to enter the ravaged forest, clearing the area for cultivation. Farmers burn the remainder to prepare for cultivation. Where the soil is too exhausted to support agriculture, burning by ranchers allows grasses to grow that later feed cattle. In years past, smoke clouds that covered nearby towns and obscured the sun were visible from outer space.

Older logging roads also enable coca farmers to gain access to potential new garden plots deep within forested areas. Coca production in Peru has deforested 700,000 hectares over the past three decades, and since 1900 it has accounted for 10 percent of deforestation in Amazonian Peru. Coca is the primary, most profitable crop in certain areas, such as Bolivia's Chapare, but it is not the only crop, for several reasons:

> Coca leaf is the most difficult crop to accommodate within a production system based on family labor because the labor requirements are very high in comparison to other crops . . . Farmers do not grow coca leaf because it is particularly attractive; they grow it because . . . it is the only crop for which they know they will have a buyer. (Painter 1995, 156–158)

As indicated above regarding legal agribusiness, the use of insecticides by an overwhelming majority of Andean coca farmers takes its toll in terms of toxic runoff and further contamination of waterways already degraded by deforestation-produced erosion.

Insecure land tenure means indifferent land stewardship. It is not economically rational to expend much energy caring for land that may be taken away without warning. In the Amazon basin of Peru, the rate of deforestation by squatters is twice that of legal tenants, for two possible reasons. First, squatters are likely to be more recent arrivals and therefore less familiar with the local ecology. Second, with insecure tenure it makes better sense to plant annual rather than perennial crops. This argues as well, ironically, for longer-term timber concessions, such as those now favored by the World Bank as well as by Conservation International. Such concessions encourage replanting trees that mature over relatively short periods of time but not mahogany, which requires eighty to one hundred years for maturity. Market unpredictability also affects the acceptability of long-term concessions.

ENERGY, EXTRACTIVE INDUSTRIES,
AND ENVIRONMENT

Energy resource extraction and energy resource consumption, which vary greatly across Latin America, both produce environmental impacts. Mexico's energy consumption level was 15 percent, and Guatemala's just 6 percent, of the US level in 2000. Examining *changes* in energy consumption levels, however, reveals a different picture. While per capita energy consumption increased 7 percent in the United States between 1970 and 2000, Brazil's and Mexico's more than doubled, Guatemala's more than tripled, and Paraguay's increased by almost 600 percent.

Latin American energy consumption is increasing because of the following: growing urbanization with concomitant substitution of fossil fuel energy for biomass energy, automobile acquisition and use, and expanded energy-intensive agribusiness (chemical fertilizers, heavy equipment, etc.). Energy efficiency has, as a rule, been poor. A combination of subsidized energy pricing in countries such as Mexico and a profit orientation elsewhere means that electrical appliances marketed in Brazil are only half as efficient as their US equivalents. In fact, energy efficiency has decreased. In 2000 a unit of output required 7 percent more energy input than the same unit of output in 1980.

Along with energy consumption, air pollution has also grown proportionately. Carbon dioxide emission was more than a third higher in 2000 than in 1980, the five years from 1995 to 2000 accounting for more than half this growth in Latin America. As a whole, Latin America produces just over 5 percent of the world's greenhouse gas emissions. While Mexico and Brazil account for more than half of this, the emissions of these two countries taken together are only 12 percent of US emissions, the lower per capita energy consumption reflecting lower mean incomes in the Latin American countries. But as income inequality is greater in Latin America than anywhere else in the world, so is per capita energy consumption. The consumption rates of the wealthy in Mexico and Brazil are greater than those of the same class in the United States, itself no paragon of conservation.

Electric power is generated by fossil fuels in some areas and by hydroelectric facilities in others. Hydroelectric dams are the largest and most expensive construction projects in the world. Construction costs are so high that large loans from transnational banks, such as the World Bank, are required. In the 1980s Brazil's 2010 Plan proposed nearly eighty dams along the Amazon tributaries. Of these, some had already been completed, while others were under construction. This monumental set of projects was intended to provide electric power for the distant megacities of Sao Paolo and Rio de Janeiro. Environmental impacts, however, would fall on rural Amazonia, including the flooding of farmland, loss of fertile silt, loss of species, and disease proliferation. Further, the useful lifespan of such megadams as energy generators, often overestimated, is limited by eventual siltation.

Oil is a major extractive industry, and its impacts on western Amazonia are treated in the update section of this chapter. Refinery development on Mexico's gulf coast, spurred by drilling into massive offshore deposits, has completely changed the ecology of the state of Tabasco. Further, impacts of the petroleum industry are not limited to areas of sparse population. In Mexico, for example, the environment of Coatzacoalcos, Tabasco, has suffered greatly, while in Guadalajara a mid-1990s Pemex gas pipeline explosion killed 250 people along a seven-mile stretch of poor communities.

Other extractive industries include tin mines in Bolivia and gold mines in Brazil. Rich silver mines in Guanajuato, Mexico, and Potosi, Bolivia, funded European wars of the eighteenth and nineteenth centuries. Potosi's silver-rich mountain acquired a twin: a hill of slag. The long-term cumulative impacts of mercury used in silver refining in Guanajuato's *haciendas de beneficio* are still unknown.

IMPACTS ON INDIGENOUS PEOPLES:
ANOTHER HUMAN DIMENSION

Some people criticize deforestation for the consequent loss of plant species whose curative properties are as yet undiscovered (by Western industrialized nations) and for the loss as well of ethnomedical knowledge among displaced indigenous forest dwellers. Further, the environmental impacts of urban development in Latin America often fall disproportionately on the urban poor, and the impacts of rural development often fall disproportionately on the rural poor. A case in point is the Mexican state of Chiapas.

On New Year's Day 1994, the Zapatista Army of Liberation rose in revolt against the federal and state governments. The rebels occupied a number of *municipios* and several major towns in the eastern part of Chiapas on the Guatemalan border, a part of Mexico untouched by the land reforms of the early-twentieth-century revolution. Although many Mayan inhabitants of Chiapas came from other parts of Mexico or fled from Guatemala's genocidal civil war, others had developed sustainable agricultural practices over centuries.

But the mestizo colonists dominated, and deforestation progressed until over 95 percent of Chiapas's tropical and montane rain forests had disappeared. In 1978, then-president José López Portillo created the Montes Azules Biosphere Reserve in an attempt to preserve 1,250 square miles of the Lacandón forest, the first internal ecological reserve in Mexico. Inhabitants of the area, excluded from decision making about the reserve, were forcibly evicted. Relocated outside the reserve, they felt free to take advantage of lax enforcement of the reserve's status (few funds were allotted to patrolling the area), moving boundary posts at night when no one was looking.

In prior years, as elsewhere in Mexico, the male members of many Chiapaneco families had become accustomed to spending part of each year elsewhere, such as the United States, as laborers. Other Mayan farmers continued to suffer under the same regime that had brought about the revolution, many as landless peasants subsisting marginally under the yoke of exploitative ranchers and landlords. This, together with the end of land reform, additional population pressures from the 22,000 or more Guatemalan refugees who remained in Chiapas, and the threat of NAFTA-style free trade impacting coffee and corn production, contributed to the Zapatista uprising and its short-lived success.[5]

CLASS, GENDER, AND TRANSNATIONAL IMPACTS

First is the issue of gender impacts. "Women hold up half the sky," it is said, but they till more than half the earth. They also haul water and firewood, tasks that consume increasing amounts of their time as they go greater distances each year in search of these two vital resources. As poverty grows, women are left to tend village gardens as men go to the cities (or to the United States) in search of wage labor. They live at a subsistence level with the aid of remittances sent from far away. In Mexico's *maquiladora* industries, women were, until recently, the principal employees. Forced by inadequate income to seek barely habitable housing near the plants in which they worked, they became the unwilling recipients of pollution and toxic wastes.

Second, women and children tend to be hit hardest by natural hazards, which also have unnatural, human-induced dimensions. It has been suggested, for example, that enormous reservoirs have the capacity to trigger earthquakes in seismic areas. Further, the impacts of these hazards often fall disproportionately upon the poor. Mexico, Central America, and the Andean countries are earthquake prone, and in several Latin American countries *terremotos* (earthquakes) are called *clasemotos*. The authorities' often callous and classist response exacerbates popular distrust of governments. Sometimes, paradoxically, this produces results favorable to reinforcing community. When the federal government refused outside aid following the horrific 1985 Mexico City earthquake, urban communities formed their own relief teams. Any reduction in loss of life from this disaster can be attributed largely to these informal groups. The government did act, however, when Mexico's volcano Popocatépetl resumed activity several years ago. The mountain peasants who were evacuated later returned to find their houses empty and sacked of all possessions. When Popo again spewed ash a year later, these same people, understandably, refused to move.

Third, the relief efforts that follow environmental disasters produce their own effects. In some cases disaster relief is almost as damaging as the disaster itself. Outside "experts" who arrive expecting all the comforts and conveniences of home occasionally contribute more to the confusion than to the solution. When the call goes out for earthquake relief from abroad, well-meaning people likely send powdered milk (water supplies are much more likely to be disrupted than the cattle) and canned food (but no can openers). Monetary contributions are as likely to end up in the hands of corrupt government officials as in the hands of disaster victims.

Fourth, complementing environmental impacts of agriculture are the impacts of mariculture, the cultivation of marine organisms for food on the sea and its shores. The cultivation of shrimp for export in such countries as Honduras is a case in point. To increase access to the shrimp, a quick-result strategy is decimation of the coastal mangroves.[6] The short-term productivity of the shrimp fisheries increases temporarily along with long-term environmental degradation, which includes increased flooding, and eventual long-term loss of seafood productivity. Further, the mangroves, which provide nurseries for fish and shellfish, as well as protecting the shoreline from storms and flooding, do not regenerate easily. Other approaches to improving shrimp fisheries are not environmentally damaging, such as a project to assist the movement of shrimp from ocean to lagoon in coastal Oaxaca, Mexico.

Finally, some environmental problems straddle international borders. Latin American countries do not correspond to bioregions or ecoregions, and twentieth-century border wars have been ecological disasters. Amazonia, although usually identified with Brazil, actually extends into all the countries bordering Brazil to the north and west. Thus the conservation of Amazonia, or at least the amelioration of damage to the region, is a matter of international cooperation. The US–Mexican border region is more than 3,000 kilometers long, the largest part of it consisting of the Rio Grande/Rio Bravo. A mere trickle after making its way around the Big Bend, it is replenished by the Pecos River on the US side and the Rio Conchos on the Mexican side. From Laredo/Nuevo Laredo on down, the lower Rio Grande is so depleted that it dies on the beach before reaching the Gulf of Mexico. *Maquiladoras* taking advantage of lax enforcement of Mexico's stringent environmental laws use the river as a sewer for the disposal of toxic wastes, damaging the health of the poor who inhabit both sides of the river. Pollution does not respect international boundaries, and jurisdictional confusion exacerbates the problem, in spite of the International Boundary and Water Commission.

SOLUTIONS . . . OR ARE THEY?

Debt-for-Nature Swaps

Conservation organizations have come up with what some consider to be a perfect partial solution to environmental degradation: the polluter involved offers to pay a part of the national debt of the country involved in return for a pledge from that country to spend an equivalent in national currency to establish, say, a national park. Another view is that the impact of debt-for-nature swaps on either debts or nature as minimal. Ultimately the question is, Who benefits and who pays?

There have been more than twenty debt-for-nature swaps worldwide. Latin American countries involved in such swaps include Bolivia, Costa Rica, and Ecuador. In Bolivia, Conservation International (CI) arranged the first debt-for-nature swap in the Americas in 1987. The arrangement was rushed (perhaps CI was in too much of a hurry to be the first to broker such a swap) as neither CI nor government agencies could exercise much control over rapacious lumber companies:

> The logic of debt relief in exchange for conservation is flawed in Bolivia. This is because the poor bear the debt burden, not the political and economic elite, who contracted the debt in the first place. The elite feel no "relief," only an economic threat. They value debt-for-nature swaps only for the international respectability—and money—swaps attract. (Jones 1995, p. 202)

The experiences of the World Wildlife Fund in Costa Rica and Fundación Natura in Ecuador are similar. In the latter case, funds were adequate to acquire land areas in Andean and Amazonian Ecuador and the Galápagos Islands, but not to protect these areas from poachers and illegal loggers.

Ecotourism

Ecotourism can be defined as "responsible travel to natural areas, which conserves the environment and sustains the well-being of local people" (Anonymous 2003). Ecotourism, low-impact tourism, and other alternative forms of tourism represent the largest areas of economic growth in much of the world, including Latin America. Ecotourism promises to bring money and jobs into impoverished communities and ecologically or culturally sensitive areas, assuming that local residents can then develop their economies along lines that help protect resources that attract tourists.

National and regional tourism promotion agencies tend to view tourism as a panacea. Environmental protection agencies are generally more guarded in their view, since the link between bringing additional people into a sensitive area and establishing greater protections for that area can be tenuous and indirect. The problems of alternative tourism development serve as examples of the broader conflicts and paradoxes present in all efforts at sustainable development. There are costs and benefits to different groups that should be—but rarely are—balanced.

Even small, isolated communities have begun to view ecotourism and alternative tourism as preferred development paths. Over the past decade, the managers of protected natural areas have begun seeking more input from locals over use of area resources. This is a critical step because, unlike the norm in the United States, many protected natural areas of Latin America already have long-established, if isolated, communities of residents. Cultural shifts are often required to make natural areas viable ecotourism destinations. Without consensus building and a broad appreciation of how such industry could benefit the community, these changes can be impossible. State and local governments seldom have the political will or the personnel to enforce restrictions in designated park areas when these conflict with local needs or values. El Cielo Biosphere Reserve in the Mexican state of Tamaulipas is a positive example. There, women have established cooperatives dedicated to providing assistance to and making provisions for ecotourism (Lewitsky 2002).

Advantages of ecotourism include providing rural employment opportunities that enable people to remain on their ancestral lands and maintaining urban water quality and quantity through preservation of natural areas. People living in rural areas of Latin America see tourism as attracting increased government services, such as paved roads, water, sewage treatment, electricity, and so on. Some of these services do increase the human carrying capacity of an area. Ecotourism can also assist local organizations in the direction of better land stewardship, for example, less random garbage disposal in areas with an economic interest in ecotourism.

Disadvantages and challenges of ecotourism include problems incident to the creation of parks and reserves: poaching, fire suppression, managing exotic flora and fauna, and plant epidemics. Lack of resources for enforcement has led to problems with fires, wildlife, and facilities theft. Wilderness reserves are frequently administered under a confusing patchwork of jurisdictions, characterized by gaps and overlapping spheres of governmental responsibility; all are chronically underfunded.

Residents of reserves, if not included in reserve management, may conflict with "free-ranging" tourists who disrupt traditional agriculture practices and livestock. Auto traffic degrades the natural environment that originally attracted tourists and causes additional erosion and associated damage, especially in fragile desert ecosystems. Commitment to ecotourism may imply cyclical livelihood, potentially subject to wild swings and possibly ending in obsolescence. Crime warnings promulgated by the US Department of State can impact an entire region economically.

CONTEMPORARY THREATS AND CHALLENGES

Oil and Western Amazonia

While issues of rain forest loss in Brazilian Amazonia are by now relatively well-known, environmental problems of western Amazonia, specifically Ecuador, Peru, Colombia, Bolivia, and Venezuela, have been less visible until quite recently. The majority have involved the negative impacts of oil exploration and extraction on the environment of indigenous peoples and on indigenous peoples themselves.

Exploration, drilling, and transportation of fossil fuels is of special concern in the major oil-producing nations of Latin America, which together supplied almost a third of US oil imports in 2007 (Kurlanzick 2008). Petroleum exploration has proceeded with little concern for the environment, whether carried out by national oil companies such as Mexico's Pemex or Ecuador's Petroecuador or multinationals such as Texaco and Conoco. Inadequate or absent monitoring of leaks has resulted in massive pollution of rivers and streams in Ecuador and Peru. Toxic wastes discharged into waterways, including arsenic, lead, oil, and sulfates, kill fish and cattle that come to drink.

In both Peru and Ecuador, displacement of indigenous populations and environmental contamination have sparked uprisings in rural areas, but the governments have responded in different ways. In Ecuador, liberal president Rafael Correa has sided with indigenous plaintiffs in their court case against Chevron, which acquired the original offender, Texaco, in 2001. But when tribespeople clashed with police near the towns of Bagua Grande and Bagua Chica on June 5, 2009, Peru's conservative president, Alan García, blamed the resulting carnage entirely on the indigenes. In Peru, communities with no springs must drink polluted river water. Firms from other countries are involved, such as Argentina's Pluspetrol, which plans to cut a pipeline through indigenous lands. Clashes between security forces and Amazon tribes have become so violent that on June 17, 2009, Yehude Simón, Peru's prime minister, announced his resignation (Carroll 2009).

In Ecuador, lawyers for the plaintiffs claim that Texaco's toxic dumping exceeds the crude spilled in the Exxon Valdez disaster in 1989 (Llana 2009) by a factor of thirty. Petroecuador assumed Texaco's operations in 1992, prior to its acquisition by Chevron, but the damage had been done. Texaco had dumped over 18 billion gallons of toxic waste and filled more than 900 waste pits with toxic sludge. Chevron claims that it cleaned up the damage caused by Texaco. But, besides claiming irreparable ecological damage, the plaintiffs claim that over 1,000 cancer deaths resulted; the defendants respond that determining the cause or causes of these cancer cases is impossible (Llana 2009; Vidal 2009).

Plan Colombia

Plan Colombia is a $3 billion program financed by the United States intended to eradicate cannabis, coca, and poppy crops by means of herbicides sprayed aerially in Colombia and other Andean countries. In fact, the spraying has gone on since the 1970s, resulting in environmental, social, and economic damage beyond the eradication of drug-producing plants. A large number of corn plants, basic to rural nutrition in Colombia, have been destroyed. Soil has been damaged and erosion has increased as a result of pesticide overuse (Ballve 2009).

In the Ecuadorian Amazon herbicides identical to those used in Colombia have killed valuable trees and destroyed manioc, a staple of many indigenous Amazonian people, reportedly resulting in illness and death ("Justice or Extortion?" 2009). The Colombian military has been using, among other chemical weapons, fusarium oxysporum, a transgenic fungus favored by Washington but condemned by scientists and environmentalists worldwide because of the dangers it poses to the biodiversity of the Amazon region. The fungus has the capacity to mutate and scatter, perhaps affecting such coastal crops as coffee, citrus, and plantains. The Biological and Toxic Weapons Convention has characterized this transgenic fungus as "a biological agent for war" that cannot be withdrawn from the environment and has unpredictable effects. These effects could spread from Colombia to Ecuador, Peru, and even Brazil.

There is currently further concern that Colombians, displaced by the toxic fumigations and escalation of armed conflicts among government forces, guerrillas, and paramilitaries, may start pouring across the border into Ecuador.

Plan Puebla Panamá

Plan Puebla Panamá (PPP), also known as the Mesoamerican Integration and Development Project, or Mesoamerican Project, was announced by Mexican president Vicente Fox in 2001 to integrate the region that stretches from Mexico's nine southern states through Central America to Colombia, along five development corridors. More than 85 percent of its funding was intended for transportation and transport infrastructure. Protests were mounted by farmers opposing a planned airport and by Zapatista Subcomandante Marcos. Concerned about political and environmental impacts, he stated that Zapatistas would not permit implementation of the PPP in the areas under their control. These conflicts, compounded by funding problems, forced a moratorium on PPP, which was not launched again until early 2004 (Pickard 2004).

The two best-known PPP projects are the Electrical Integration System for Central America, with much of the electricity generated being targeted for the United States, and the Mesoamerican Transport Integration Initiative. The PPP, following the models of such Latin American free trade agreements as NAFTA, includes among its goals privatization of land, water, and public services. It is derived from a neoliberal model of development, favoring interests of multinational enterprises despite possible environmental damage and facilitating access, through its physical infrastructure, to natural resources.

The transportation initiative includes the trans-Texas corridor, Mesoamerican highway and rail system from the United States to South America, opening up vast areas to development and associated environmental impacts. It is also intended, via sea links, to facilitate trade with China. Rail lines will connect Kansas City to the Mexican port of Lazaro Cardenas in Michoacan. There are plans for expansion at Punto Colonet on the Pacific coast of Baja California, currently an *ejido* of less than 3,000 residents, near a pristine stretch of coastal beach. The huge port, along with 300 kilometer rail line connecting it with the US border, will be completed through the investment of US$5 billion. The port is designed to facilitate trade between the United States and Asia, to provide an alternative to US ports at Long Beach and Los Angeles, currently operating at close to maximum capacity, and to bypass the high union wages paid at US ports.

Conclusion

Recent improvements in preserving Latin American environments include innovative use of alternative energy sources; popular movements for forest preservation; and creative involvement of the private sector. Universities have initiated environmental engineering programs, and primary schools give environmental education classes to young children. However, environmental engineering has invariably focused on remedial rather than preventative action and omitted sociocultural considerations, while the effect of environmental education programs is that adults depend largely on their children to teach them about the environment.

There are larger factors. External forces included the World Bank and regional development bank lending policies, the actions of multinational corporations, and the interests of industrialized countries. Banks' preference for ultralarge development projects (which vastly increase national debt) and neoliberal structural readjustment programs, for GNP and technological increments, have ensured that economic development and environmental concerns will conflict. Another factor involves internal divisions within the Latin American countries themselves: the gap between incredible wealth and incredible poverty; between whites and mestizos on the one hand, and indigenous peoples on the other; between urban modernity and rural traditionalism; and between female subservience and male hegemony. More democratic political regimes, recently elected in some Latin America countries, hold out promise in a number of realms. It is to be hoped that social and physical aspects of environmental preservation will be among them.[7]

Notes

1. "Efficiency," as used here, has no scale implications. There are as many diseconomies of scale as economies of scale (Schumacher 1973; Hawken 1993).

2. The sole exception's are Brazil, whose twin megacities, Rio de Janeiro and Sao Paulo, are among the world's most populous, and Ecuador, where Quito and Quayaquil are comparable in size.

3. This was a threat to the reigning party, the PRI, which had traditionally manipulated votes and voters by (later unfulfilled) promises of community improvement.

4. The rate of increase in chemical fertilizer use in Latin America was eight times as high in 1990–1999 as it was in 1980–1989.

5. In 1992, the much publicized reform to Article 27 of the Mexican constitution of 1917 ended land reform policies that had shaped the relationship between government and peasants for three-quarters of a century.

6. Such coastal areas are called "wetlands" by those who appreciate their value, "swamps" by those who don't.

7. Sincere appreciation is extended to Silvia Elguea for comments and suggestions. Any errors of fact or interpretation are the sole responsibility of the authors.

RECOMMENDED READINGS

Cummings, B. J. *Dam the Rivers, Damn the People: Development and Resistance in Amazonian Brazil.* London: Earthscan, 1990.

Dogse, P., and B. van Droste. *Debt-for-Nature Exchanges and Biosphere Reserves: Experiences and Potential.* Paris: UNESCO, 1990.

Ganster, P. *The U.S.–Mexico Border Environment: A Road Map to a Sustainable 2020.* San Diego: San Diego State University Press, 2000.

Johnston, B. R., ed. *Who Pays the Price? The Sociocultural Context of Environmental Crisis.* Washington, D.C.: Island Press, 1994.

———. *Life and Death Matters: Human Rights and the Environment at the End of the Millennium.* Walnut Creek, CA.: Altamira, 1997.

"Justice or Extortion?" *The Economist* 391, no. 8632 (2009): 42.

Painter, M., and W. H. Durham, eds. *The Social Causes of Environmental Destruction in Latin America.* Ann Arbor: University of Michigan Press, 1995.

Pickard, M. *The Plan Puebla-Panama Revived: Looking Back to See What's Ahead.* Interhemispheric Resource Center, 2004.

Punta, Colonet. "Tenders Called." *Railway Gazette International*, September 9, 2008.

Roberts, Bryan R. "Urbanization and the Environment in Developing Countries: Latin America in Comparative Perspective." In L. Arizpe, M. P. Stone, and D. C. Major, eds., *Population and Environment: Rethinking the Debate* (Boulder: Westview, 1994).

Simon, Joel. *Endangered Mexico: An Environment on the Edge.* San Francisco: Sierra Book Club, 1997.

Westerhoff, P. *The U.S.–Mexican Border Environment: Water Issues Along the U.S.–Mexican Border.* San Diego: San Diego State University Press, 2000.

BIBLIOGRAPHY

Adams, G. "Images Reveal True Horror of Amazon's Tiananmen." *Independent*, June 19, 2009.

Ballve, T. "The Dark Side of Plan Colombia." *Nation*, May 27, 2009.

Bedoya Garland, E. "The Social and Economic Causes of Deforestation in the Peruvian Amazon Basin: Natives and Colonists." In M. Painter and W. H. Durham, eds., *The Social Causes of Environmental Destruction in Latin America*. Ann Arbor: University of Michigan Press, 1995.

Brown, L. R. *Who Will Feed China? Wake-up Call for a Small Planet.* New York: Norton, 1995.

Carroll, R. "Peru's Prime Minister to Step Down." *Guardian*, June 17, 2009.

Cronon, W. *Changes in the Land.* New York: Hill & Wang, 1983.

Clark, J. G. "Economic Development Versus Sustainable Societies: Reflections on the Players in a Crucial Context." *Annual Review of Ecology and Systematics* 26 (1995): 225–248.

Cunningham, A. B. "Indigenous Knowledge and Biodiversity." In S. E. Place, ed., *Tropical Rainforests: Latin American Nature and Society in Transition*. Wilmington: Scholarly Resources, 1993.

Collett, M. "Bolivia Blazes Trail . . . to Where?" *Christian Science Monitor*, July 10, 1989.

Czitrom Baus, S. *Sistema de Bombeo por Energía de Oleaje*. Mexico, D.F.: Videoservicios Profesionales, 2000. Video.

Díaz Romero, P. *Huicholes y pesticidas*. Mexico, D.F.: Red de Acción sobre Plaguicidas y Alternativas en México, 1994. Video.

Dourojeanni, M. "Impactos ambientales de la coca y la producción de cocaína en la amazonia peruana." In F. Leonard and R. Castro, eds., *Pasta Basica de Cocaina*, pp. 281–299. Lima, Peru: Centro de Información y Educación del Abuso de Drogas, 1989.

Edelman, M. "Rethinking the Hamburger Thesis: Deforestation and the Crisis of Central Americas's Beef." In M. Painter and W. H. Durham, eds., *The Social Causes of Environmental Destruction in Latin America*. Ann Arbor: University of Michigan Press, 1995.

Elguea Vejar, S. *La ética ecológica desde una perspectiva ecofeminista*. Master's thesis, Universidad Nacional Autónoma de México, 2001.

———. "Revisión sobre algunos aspectos que involucrán sustancias tóxicas." *Sociotam* 10, no. 1 (2000): 165–174.

Franko, P. *The Puzzle of Latin American Economic Development*. New York: Rowman & Littlefield, 2003.

Gebara, I. "Ecofeminism: A Latin American Perspective." *Crosscurrents*, Spring 2003, 93–103.

Gedicks, A. *Resource Rebels: Native Challenges to Mining and Oil Corporations*. Cambridge, MA: South End, 2001.

Guillet, D. "Toward a Cultural Ecology of Mountains: The Central Andes and the Himalayas Compared." *Current Anthropology* 24, no. 5 (1983): 561–574.

Hardin, G. "The Tragedy of the Commons." *Science* 16, no. 2 (1968): 1242–1248.

Harrington, T. "Tourism Damages Amazon Region." In S. E. Place, ed., *Tropical Rainforests: Latin American Nature and Society in Transition*, pp. 185–193. Wilmington: Scholarly Resources, 1993.

Hawken, P. *The Ecology of Commerce*. New York: HarperCollins, 1993.

Holl, K. D., G. C. Daily, and P. R. Ehrlich. "Knowledge and Perceptions in Costa Rica Regarding Environment, Population, and Biodiversity Issues." *Conservation Biology* 9, no. 6 (1995): 1548–1558.

International Boundary and Water Commission. *Regional Assessment of Water Quality in the Rio Grande Basin*. IBWC, 2003.

Jarvis, L. S. *Livestock Development in Latin America*. Washington, D.C.: World Bank, 1986.

Jones, J. C. "Environmental Destruction, Ethnic Discrimination, and International Aid in Bolivia." In M. Painter and W. H. Durham, eds., *The Social Causes of Environmental Destruction in Latin America*. Ann Arbor: University of Michigan Press, 1995.

"Justice or Extortion?" *The Economist* 391, no. 8632 (2009): 42

Kenworthy, E. "Nature in Latin America: Images and Issues." In J. K. Black, ed., *Latin America: Its Problems and Its Promises*. 3rd ed. Boulder: Westview.

Kurlantzick, J. "Put a Tyrant in Your Tank." *Mother Jones*, May-June 2008, 38–42.

Landa, R., J. Meave, and J. Carabias. "Environmental Deterioration in Rural Mexico: An Examination of the Concept." *Ecological Applications*, February 1997, 316–329.

Lewitsky, M. "Characteristics of a Successful Community Cooperative: A Case Study in the Community of Alta Cimas, El Cielo Biosphere, Tamaulipas, Mexico." Master's thesis, Southwest Texas State University, 2002.

Llana, S. M. "Chevron Fights Massive Lawsuit in Ecuador." *Christian Science Monitor*, May 29, 2009.

López, R. "The Policy Roots of Socioeconomic Stagnation and Environmental Implosion: Latin America, 1950–2000." *World Development* 31, no. 2 (2003): 259–280.

Mahoney, R. "Debt-for-Nature Swaps: Who Really Benefits?" In S. E. Place, ed., *Tropical Rainforests: Latin American Nature and Society in Transition*, pp. 185–193. Wilmington: Scholarly Resources, 1993.

Meadows, D. "The City of First Priorities." *Whole Earth Review*, Spring 1995.

Painter, M. "Anthropological Perspectives on Environmental Destruction." In M. Painter and W. H. Durham, eds., *The Social Causes of Environmental Destruction in Latin America*. Ann Arbor: University of Michigan Press, 1995.

———. "Upland-Lowland Production Linkages and Land Degradation in Bolivia." In M. Painter and W. H. Durham, eds., *The Social Causes of Environmental Destruction in Latin America*. Ann Arbor: University of Michigan Press, 1995.

Pastor, R. "NAFTA's Green Opportunity." *Issues in Science and Technology*, Summer 1993, 47–54.

Pickard, M. *The Plan Puebla-Panamá Revived: Looking Back to See What's Ahead.* Interhemispheric Resource Center, 2004.

Price, D. *Before the Bulldozer*. Washington, D.C.: Seven Locks, 1989.

Punta, Colonet. "Tenders Called." *Railway Gazette International*, September 9, 2008.

Rabinovitch, J., and J. Leitman. "Urban Planning in Curitiba." *Scientific American,* March 1996.

Sanchez, E., K. Cronick, and E. Wiesenfeld. "Psychological Variables in Participation: A Case Study." In D. Canter, M. Krampen, and D. Stea, eds., *New Directions in Environmenal Participation*. Aldershot, UK: Gower, 1988.

Sanderson, S. E. "Mexico's Environmental Future." *Current History*, February 1993.

Schumacher, E. F. *Small Is Beautiful: Economics as if People Mattered*. New York: Harper & Row, 1973.

Schwartz, N. B. "Colonization, Development, and Deforestation in Peten, Northern Guatemala." In M. Painter and W. H. Durham, eds., *The Social Causes of Environmental Destruction in Latin America*. Ann Arbor: University of Michigan Press, 1995.

Snell, M. B. "A Fine Balance: Cultivating Smaller Families and Healthier Farms in Ecuador's Highlands." *Sierra*, January-February 2004, 27–29.

Stanley, D. "Demystifying the Tragedy of the Commons: The Resin Tappers of Honduras." In S. E. Place, ed., *Tropical Rainforests: Latin American Nature and Society in Transition*, pp. 185–193. Wilmington: Scholarly Resources, 1993.

Stea, D. "Debunking the Myths: Indigenous Settlements in Tropical Forests." In *Proceedings of the Seventh Annual Peter van Dresser Workshop on Village Development*. Albuquerque: Public Service Co. of New Mexico, 1994.

———. "Human and Cultural Resources in the New World Tropics." *Proceedings, New Jersey Academy of Sciences*. New Brunswick: Rutgers University, 1993.

Stea, D., and V. Coreno. "Acción comunitaria, participación pública, y planificación ambiental en una colonia mexicana." In D. M. Connor, ed., *Participación Pública: Un Manual*. Victoria, B.C.: CDS, 1997.

Stea, D., S. Elguea, and C. Perez Bustillo. "Environment, Development, and Indigenous Revolution in Chiapas." In B. R. Johnston, ed., *Life and Death Matters: Human Rights and the Environment at the End of the Millennium*, pp. 213–237. Walnut Creek, CA: Altamira, 1997.

Stone, D., and C. Major, eds. *Population and Environment: Rethinking the Debate*. Boulder: Westview, 1994.

Stonich, S. "Producing Food for Export: Environmental Quality and Social Justice Implications of Shrimp Mariculture in Honduras." In B. R. Johnston, ed., *Who Pays the Price? The Sociocultural Context of Environmental Crisis.* Washington, D.C.: Island Press, 1994.

Stonich, S. C. "Development, Rural Impoverishment, and Environmental Destruction in Honduras." In M. Painter and W. H. Durham, eds., *The Social Causes of Environmental Destruction in Latin America.* Ann Arbor: University of Michigan Press, 1995.

Swinton, S., G. Escobar, and T. Reardon. "Poverty and Environment in Latin America." *World Development* 31, no. 11 (2003): 1865–1872.

Tropical Forest Management Trust. *Promising Approaches to Natural Forest Management in Latin America.* Gainesville, FL: Tropical Forest Management Trust, 1991. Video.

Vidal, J. "We Are Fighting for Our Lives and Our Dignity." *The Guardian*, June 13, 2009.

Wasserman, E. "Environment, Health, and Gender in Latin America: Trends and Research Issues." *Environmental Research Section* 8 (1999): 253–273.

Williams, M. "Land Invasions Rising in Brazil." *Austin American-Statesman*, November 15, 2003, A21–A22.

World Bank. *Energy Efficiency and Conservation in the Developing World: The World Bank's Role.* Washington, D.C.: World Bank, 1993.

PART II

HISTORICAL SETTING

Chapter 5

COLONIAL LATIN AMERICA

PETER BAKEWELL

THE COLONIAL PERIOD in Latin America lasted just over 300 years and would be impossible to describe even broadly in a few pages. So this chapter does not try to give a summary of events in colonial times. Rather, it aims to examine two broad themes: (1) What, in a quite practical way, is meant by "colonialism" in Latin America in the 1500s, 1600s, and 1700s? (2) What features and influences of colonial times have carried over into, and helped to form, the Latin America of today?

CONQUEST AND SETTLEMENT

Let's begin with some basic dates and geographical data. The colonial period of Latin America began when Columbus sailed across the Atlantic from Spain in 1492 and claimed the lands he touched for Spain. They were, on that first voyage of 1492–1493, the islands of Cuba and, as the Spaniards came to call it, Hispaniola (now divided between the Dominican Republic and Haiti). It is illogical to say that Columbus "discovered" the Americas because obviously the true discoverers were the people who first entered and settled them. And people from Asia had done those things many tens of thousands of years before Columbus arrived, becoming in the course of time what are now referred to as native Americans. From the point of view of Spain and Europe in general, however, Columbus did find the Americas, and more importantly, his "discovery" led to the establishment of a permanent link between the two sides of the Atlantic—something that the Norse expeditions to North America from Greenland, around AD 1000, had failed to do.

As soon as Columbus reported the existence of Cuba and Hispaniola to the Spanish crown, Spain claimed the right to settle and govern those islands and other lands that might be found in the same direction. The pope of the day, Alexander VI, who was a Spaniard, confirmed the claim. His confirmation was sought because, as the chief representative of God on earth, he was the highest authority in the world known to Christian rulers. In any case, no other European state, with the possible exception of Portugal, was strong enough to challenge Spain's claim to possess and govern the lands Columbus had found.

The Portuguese had been exploring westward and southward in the Atlantic for many decades before 1492 and were understandably disturbed by Spain's claim to all land on the west side of the Atlantic. Conflict was averted, however, by an agreement (the Treaty of Tordesillas) drawn up in 1494 that divided the tasks of exploring and settling the world between the two countries. To the west of an imaginary north-south line in the Atlantic, Spain should explore and settle, and to the east of that line, Portugal should do so. Although unanticipated at the time, that agreement would give Portugal a large section of eastern South America since, as defined in the treaty, the line passed down through the mouth of the Amazon, leaving the coastline again at about 30 degrees south latitude. Hence, the eastern bulge of South America, once it was discovered in 1500, became Portuguese territory, forming the basis of modern Brazil.

The colonial history of Spanish America, having begun in 1492 with Columbus, ended in the years 1810–1825 as the various Spanish colonies in the Americas, with two exceptions, fought for and gained their independence. The exceptions were Cuba and Puerto Rico, which did not become free of Spain until 1898. Brazil broke from Portugal in 1822. So, in both the Spanish and Portuguese cases, the colonial period was long—almost twice as long as the time that has elapsed between independence and the present.

Colonial Spanish America was much larger than Portuguese America. Even though the Portuguese gradually pushed westward beyond the Tordesillas line, Spanish America still covered a greater area, extending ultimately from the southern tip of South America to well within the present limits of the United States. In the 1700s, Spain had settlements as far north as San Francisco in California, southern Arizona, most of New Mexico, and much of Texas—as well as in a substantial part of Florida. And all territory, with a few exceptions—most notably Brazil—between that northern frontier and the far tip of South America was Spanish. Spain also held the larger Caribbean islands and some of the smaller ones. The empire in the Americas—Las Indias (the Indies), as the Spanish called their possessions—was truly vast: some 9,000 miles (almost 14,500 kilometers) from north to south.

COLONIAL GOVERNMENTS AND ECONOMIES

What made these great areas explored and settled by Spain and Portugal colonies? First, certainly, is the fact that the two home countries governed them. One of the remarkable features of Latin American colonial history is that governments were set up and actually worked, despite forbidding difficulties. For one thing, distances were enormous, not only within the Americas but also between the Americas and Europe. The colonial period was a time of sailing ships, which were slow and unreliable. (Ships improved technically with time, but not until the 1700s were they good enough to sail regularly around Cape Horn to the colonies on the west coast of South America. Before then, travelers from Spain reached the west coast by crossing the Atlantic to the Isthmus of Panama, crossing the isthmus by barge and mule, and taking Pacific ships to the various west coast ports.) Travel within the colonies was beset by difficulties such as mountains, deserts, forests, and temperature extremes. One basic necessity of effective government—communication—was therefore difficult to achieve from the start. Nevertheless, governments were installed, and their authority was extended even into remarkably remote areas.

The Spanish had the greater problems because of the size of their colonies and the distance from Spain. (Brazil was quite easily reached by sea from Portugal.) The Spanish home government saw, once the size of the Americas began to be appreciated, that it would have to delegate responsibility to administrators in the colonies, since making all the necessary decisions in Spain would be impossible. So two powerful positions—viceroys who would live in Mexico City and Lima—were created. The officeholders were usually Spanish noblemen of much experience who acted in place of the king (which is precisely the meaning of the word "viceroy"). They had authority to make all but the largest of decisions, and each was ultimately responsible for everything that happened in the area under his command. The first viceroy appointed to Mexico City arrived in 1535. As the area of Spanish exploration expanded, this viceroy came to have control over Mexico, the Spanish islands of the Caribbean, and all of Central America except Panama. This area of authority, or jurisdiction, was known as the viceroyalty of New Spain. The first viceroy in South America reached Lima in 1544. This territory eventually included everything from Panama in the north to Tierra del Fuego in the south, excluding, of course, Portuguese America. The jurisdiction centered on Lima was known as the viceroyalty of Peru. In the 1700s, for closer control, two further viceroyalties were created in South America: New Granada (corresponding roughly to modern Colombia) in 1739 and River Plate (roughly speaking, modern Argentina) in 1776.

Obviously it would have been impossible for individuals to run these vast viceroyalties unassisted. So in the 1500s the Spanish government at home created a series of councils to assist the viceroys and carry their authority far from the two viceregal capitals of that time. These councils were called *audiencias*. Besides advising the viceroys and making executive decisions themselves, these councils functioned as regional courts of appeal. By 1570 there were ten *audiencias,* each with authority over a large subarea. At a lower administrative level than the *audiencias* were local governors, some administering large frontier regions and others, of lesser rank, towns and villages.

By modern administrative standards, this system was clumsy and corrupt. Many officials, for example, paid more attention to preventing other officials from intruding on their powers than they did to implementing the king's law. And nearly all officials, in the general manner of the times in Europe, saw their position as a means of enriching themselves far beyond their salaries, which were often low. In view of the difficulties, it is a near miracle that the system worked at all. Also surprising is the speedy construction of the system. Generally speaking, within a few years of the conquest of a given region, there were royal administrators in place to enforce laws, collect taxes, and send reports home. Although Spanish America was a vast and rough place, the king's men made their presence felt throughout most of it, and they commanded respect.

The Portuguese set up a similar system in Brazil centered on Bahia (until Rio de Janeiro became the capital in the mid-1700s) but never achieved quite such a powerful grip on their colony as Spain did. There were various reasons for this difference. Portugal simply did not have the money or manpower to create a powerful administrative machine like the one Spain built in the Americas. For many decades after founding Brazil, Portugal paid far more attention to its spice-yielding colonies in the Far East than to the apparently rather poorly endowed coast of Brazil.

The first outstanding feature of colonization, therefore, was government. The second was the extraction of wealth from the Americas. The Spanish freely admitted that they had conquered the Americas for the sake of gold and God. One of the main tasks of the colonial governments was to ensure that Spain and Portugal received as large an income as possible from the colonies. The main type of wealth that Spain received from its colonies was silver. We tend to think of Spanish gold, sunk perhaps in galleons off the coast of Florida, and the conquerors did find large amounts of gold. But in the long run, silver proved to be more plentiful. One of the main reasons for Spain's very rapid exploration and settlement of the Americas (and hence for the quick expansion of government) was that the conquerors ranged far and wide in search of mines. In a surprisingly large number of places, they found them, especially in the highlands of Mexico and what is now Bolivia. These mines were the greatest sources of silver in the world throughout the Latin American colonial period, and they made Spain the envy of its neighbors in Europe. Other profitable goods that Spain took from the Americas were red and blue dyes, chocolate beans, hides, sugar, and some spices.

The Portuguese also did well from their colony in Brazil. Before 1560 or so, the main export was a wood that yielded a red dye. From then until about 1700, a far more profitable export predominated: sugar, which the colonists produced on large plantations. For fifty years thereafter, gold and diamonds were the most spectacular products of the Brazilian economy, stimulating substantial population of the interior for the first time and increased immigration from Portugal. Finally, in the last half century or so of colonial times, the sugar trade recovered and the cultivation of other crops, such as chocolate and rice, grew.

The term "exploitation" is often applied to the extraction of wealth by Spain and Portugal from their American colonies. It signifies an unjust and greedy grasping by the colonizing powers of the natural riches of Latin America—a process that had the result, among others, of leaving the states of Latin America considerably poorer than they otherwise would have been after independence. But an unqualified charge of exploitation against the Spanish and Portuguese is too crude to be convincing. In some cases, the valuable export product was something that the colonizers had introduced into the Americas: sugar, for instance, in the case of Brazil, or hides from cattle introduced into Mexico by the Spanish. And even where the exported wealth was something already existing in the Americas, such as silver, that wealth was not merely lying on the ground waiting to be picked up and sent back to Europe. In all cases, and especially in that of mining, successful extraction of the product was the result of the application of new techniques, investment of capital, and use of freighting methods not known in the Americas before the Spanish and Portuguese arrived. The wealth of the Americas was great, but it did not come for nothing, even to the greatest of the conquerors or the most fortunate of settlers.

EXPLOITATION OF LABOR

That said, it cannot be denied that the term "exploitation" describes how the Spaniards and Portuguese used native Americans for labor. Within a few years of the conquest, the idea became firmly rooted among settlers, and even among some theologians and government officials, that native Americans were by nature inferior to Europeans. It seemed, therefore, quite natural to the colonists and both governments that the natives, once conquered, should work for their conquerors. Some enlightened Spaniards and Portuguese opposed this reasoning, but their views were far outweighed by Iberian public opinion. So the American native peoples were forced in one way or another to work for the colonists. Sometimes they were enslaved. This was common in both Spanish and Portuguese America between the conquest and the mid-1500s. Also in the 1500s, many natives were distributed among Spanish settlers in a system called *encomienda* ("entrustment"). The people who had been "entrusted" were to work for the settler or supply a tribute in goods or cash in return for being taught Christianity and the Spanish way of life in general. Settlers were also charged with protecting the people entrusted to them from enemies. On paper, this *encomienda* arrangement had strengths. The natives were not legally slaves of the settlers but free people. In return for services rendered, they were to receive physical security and what was for the Spanish, at least, the highest spiritual gift imaginable: Christianity. In fact, however, few Spaniards fulfilled their part of the bargain, and the *encomienda* often became an oppressive means of making the native people work for the settlers.

Because of its damaging effects and because it tended to direct disproportionate amounts of native tribute and labor toward the conquerors and early settlers at the expense of later Spanish immigrants, the *encomienda* soon ceased to be the home government's preferred arrangement for the supply of native labor to the colonists. Indeed, from the 1540s on, the home government actively opposed the *encomienda* and tried to take native people away from those settlers to whom they had been entrusted—much to the settlers' anger. From the 1550s on, draft labor was introduced in many places. A small proportion of the adult men from each Indian town would be assigned each year for a period of time—between a week and a month, generally—to a Spanish employer. The assignments were made by a Spanish official, and, at least in principle, workers were directed to tasks of public utility: agriculture, road and bridge building, and mining (because it was a central economic activity).

When the system began, draft labor was probably less of a burden on the natives than *encomienda* had been. It also probably made more effective use of native labor because the draft spread the available workers more evenly among Spanish employers. During the second half of the 1500s, however, the number of settlers wanting workers increased while the native population decreased, with the result that draft work soon became a very great burden for the native people. Consequently they offered themselves for hire to individual Spanish settlers, evading the draft as best they could. Since many employers were in great need of workers, the native volunteers could obtain much higher wages than they were paid under the draft system. Paying wages to volunteer workers was first practiced by settlers who were short of labor and had the means to pay, in silver mining, for example. By 1600, for example, three-quarters of all mining workers in Mexico were native people who had been drawn by the high pay. After 1600, wage labor became increasingly common in many occupations in Spanish America. Broadly speaking, it gave the workers more freedom and better conditions than the previous labor arrangements had done. So it is generally true that the 1500s were the years of harshest exploitation of native workers by the Spanish.

When there was a shortage of native people to work for the Europeans, black slaves were imported from Africa. Exactly how many slaves were brought across the Atlantic in colonial times to Latin America is not known, but the number was certainly in excess of 3 million, with the main importing regions being Brazil and the Spanish Caribbean. Both regions produced sugar on plantations—strenuous labor that blacks tolerated better than native Americans did. In the Spanish Caribbean, most of the native populations of the large islands perished in the sixteenth century due to maltreatment, enslavement, and, above all, disease. In Brazil, the natives survived in larger numbers, but they were unable to adapt to plantation labor. The importation of blacks into Brazil was simplified and cheapened by Brazil's proximity to the West African coast, which was the source of most slaves in colonial times. In addition, Portugal had several small colonies and bases on that coast where slaves were traded.

Increasing numbers of black slaves were needed after the Spanish and Portuguese conquests in the Americas because the native populations declined dramatically. There were several reasons for this decline. Some natives were killed in the battles of the conquest. More serious, however, were the aftereffects of conquest: the seizure of good agricultural land by the Europeans; the disruption of native families resulting from the imposition of labor burdens; and a falling birthrate among native peoples as a result of poor nutrition, social dislocation, and, above all, discouragement at finding themselves, their beliefs, and their gods so easily overcome.

Even more damaging to the native populations, however, were the sicknesses that the Europeans unwittingly brought with them. Many diseases common in Europe, Africa, and Asia were unknown in the Americas because of the geographical separation of the continents. Consequently, the American native peoples suffered severely from seemingly minor infections such as the common cold and measles. Other diseases that are still considered dangerous were also transmitted to the Americas by the conquest: plague and, most damaging of all, smallpox. These sicknesses cut great swaths through the natives in conquered areas in the 1500s. In most regions settled by the Spanish, native populations had dropped by the end of the 1500s to 10 percent or less of what they had been just before the conquest, perhaps less in Brazil. Many native people there fled to the interior forests, so it is not clear how many fled and how many died.

The terrible destruction of the native populations is one of the striking features of the social history of colonial Latin America, and its effects were equally striking. It meant that far more black slaves were imported than would otherwise have been the case. It made the fate of the surviving Indians considerably harder since they were forced to do the work of those who had died (although some survivors received higher wages for their work if they chose to become wage laborers), and it reduced the difference in numbers between the native population and the white population, thus accelerating the rate of racial mixing between whites and natives. As a result, the present-day populations of Latin America are notably whiter and more European in culture than they would have been if the natives had survived in their original numbers.

Roman Catholic Evangelism

In view of the work burden and harsh treatment to which native Americans were subjected by the conquerors, it might seem contradictory that Roman Catholic evangelism was one of the two main motives for the conquest and settlement of Latin America. But it was indeed so, especially for the Spanish. Spain was the most powerful Christian country in the world when Columbus crossed the Atlantic, and it continued to be strong for a century thereafter. The Spaniards were sure, for a variety of reasons, that it was not a matter of chance that their expedition, led by Columbus, had established the link between Europe and the Americas. They felt that Spain, as the leading Christian nation of the time, had been singled out by God to conquer and settle the Americas and to carry the Christian faith (for them, of course, the only true faith) to the native peoples of that region. Some Spaniards believed in certain biblical prophecies that once the whole world had been converted to Christianity, Christ would return and rule in justice and peace for a thousand years (the Millennium). Clearly the Americas made up a large part of the world, and the Millennium could not begin until Christians converted its peoples. In apparently entrusting the Christianization of the Americas to Spain, God had given it a central part to play in the history of the world. Spain's work in spreading the true faith was to be a large and direct contribution to the second coming of Christ. Only a small minority of Spaniards, mainly some mystically inclined Franciscan friars, truly believed in this prophecy, but the fact that even a few priests could see Spain's mission in the Americas as having such cosmic importance is some indication of Spanish religious zeal.

That zeal resulted in great efforts to convert American native peoples during the first fifty years or so after the conquest in various regions of the Americas. Many remarkably tough and intelligent missionaries—drawn mainly from the Franciscan, Dominican, and Augustinian orders—set to work in Spain's expanding colonies. Their efforts were especially vigorous in Mexico, as manifested by the many church buildings that have survived from the 1500s. Millions of native people were baptized. Most of them did not understand Christianity very well and ended up mixing elements of their preconquest religion with elements of Christianity. The friars, however, generally took the view that it was better to convert many people partially than a few thoroughly.

After the mid-1500s, Spain's missionary zeal waned for many reasons. One was an understandable fatigue among the missionaries after many years of effort and after the newness of the challenge had gone. Another reason was that by then, many native people in the central areas of Spanish settlement had been converted up to a point and could be entrusted to the more humdrum care of parish priests. Missionary activity continued in remote frontier areas where there were peoples yet to be converted. Among the best-known and enduring of these later missionary enterprises were those of the Franciscans in New Mexico and the Jesuits in Paraguay.

The Portuguese were, on the whole, less concerned than the Spanish with making natives into Christians. From the start, the Portuguese had less religious zeal than the Spaniards, and possessing colonies in Africa and Asia, as well as in the Americas, meant that their effort was spread rather thin. Precisely because of this lack of interest, however, the Jesuits found an open field for mission activity in Brazil from about 1550 onward. They dominated the religious history of colonial Brazil as no single order managed to do in Spanish America. The spread of Jesuit missionary villages into the interior became one of the means by which Portuguese America advanced westward beyond the Tordesillas line in the 1600s and 1700s.

Conclusion

Some of the main features of colonization by Spain and Portugal in the Americas included rapid exploration and settlement (particularly by the Spanish), rapid installation of government (again more noticeable in the case of the Spanish than the Portuguese), economic employment of the settled lands for the profit of individual colonists as well as the home governments, exploitation of native labor, importation of black slaves, and the spread of Christianity. Some of the processes took place only in the 1500s, though their influence persisted long after that time. Others—the utilization of land and other resources and the exploitation of native and black workers—continued through colonial times. They persisted in changing forms; for example, by the progression from slavery and *encomienda* to draft labor and finally to wage labor.

Similarly, there were changes, as time passed, in the strength of colonial governments. The rapid formation of an administrative apparatus in Spanish America in the 1500s was a strenuous business, and the system was relaxed somewhat once it had been built. This tendency was increased by Spain's growing problems in Europe in the late 1500s, which distracted the home government's attention from the colonies. As a result of these and other influences, colonial governments were less effective and disciplined in the 1600s than in the previous century. In the 1700s, Spain attempted, with some success, to remedy this weakness. The creation of two new viceroyalties was part of this effort (New Granada in 1739 and River Plate in 1776), and many other administrative reforms were also introduced. Consequently the force of Spanish government was felt by colonists in areas where it had never been strongly present before, and Spain's income from colonial taxes increased several times over. But many colonists resented the increasing pressure of government and taxation felt in the late 1700s and turned their thoughts toward greater self-determination and, in the end, toward outright independence from Spain.

Suggested Readings

Bakewell, Peter. *A History of Latin America*. 2nd ed. Oxford: Blackwell, 2003.

Bethell, Leslie. *The Cambridge History of Latin America*. Vols. 1–2. Cambridge: Cambridge University Press, 1984.

Chevalier, François. *Land and Society in Colonial Mexico*. Berkeley: University of California Press, 1963.

Gibson, Charles. *The Aztecs Under Spanish Rule: A History of the Indians of the Valley of Mexico*. Stanford: Stanford University Press, 1964.

Haring, Clarence H. *The Spanish Empire in America*. New York: Oxford University Press, 1947.

Hemming, John. *The Conquest of the Incas*. New York: Harcourt, Brace, Jovanovich, 1970.

Lockhart, James, and Enrique Otte, eds. *Letters and People of the Spanish Indies: The Sixteenth Century.* Cambridge: Cambridge University Press, 1976.

Lockhart, James, and Stuart B. Schwartz. *Early Latin America: A History of Colonial Spanish America and Brazil.* Cambridge: Cambridge University Press, 1983.

Lynch, John. *Spain Under the Hapsburgs.* 2 vols. Oxford: Oxford University Press, 1964–1969.

———. *The Spanish-American Revolutions, 1808–1826.* New York: Norton, 1973.

Maclachlan, Colin M., and Jaime E. Rodríguez. *The Forging of the Cosmic Race: A Reinterpretation of Colonial Mexico.* Berkeley: University of California Press, 1980.

Parry, John H. *The Spanish Seaborne Empire.* New York: Knopf, 1966.

Phelan, John L. *The Kingdom of Quito in the Seventeenth Century: Bureaucratic Politics in the Spanish Empire.* Madison: University of Wisconsin Press, 1967.

Schwartz, Stuart B. *Sovereignty and Society in Colonial Brazil: The High Court of Bahia and Its Judges, 1609–1745.* Berkeley: University of California Press, 1973.

———. *Sugar Plantations in the Formation of Brazilian Society: Bahia, 1550–1835.* Cambridge: Cambridge University Press, 1985.

Chapter 6

LATIN AMERICA
SINCE INDEPENDENCE

An Overview

MICHAEL CONNIFF

IN THE PAST TWO centuries, the region we know as Latin America has experienced immense changes, generally following the patterns of the rest of the Western world. These changes include the shift from colonial status to independence; from monarchy to democracy; from agricultural, pastoral, and mining economies to industrial ones; from rural to urban residency; from traditional cultures to multifaceted ones; and from simple to complex societies. Historians usually emphasize continuities over long periods, but in the case of modern Latin America, the changes clearly overwhelmed lingering inheritances from the past.

This change has been all the more extraordinary because of the enormous diversity of peoples, geographies, resources, and ruling structures the region inherited from colonial times. The founders of new countries in this era faced greater difficulties in building institutions, citizenries, and national identities than their counterparts in North America and Europe. Travel was difficult and costly. Large numbers, often majorities, of their people did not speak the national languages nor identify with their leaders. Huge segments of some economies relied on labor imported from abroad, mostly African slaves but also coerced workers from other parts of the world. Ethnically, religiously, culturally, the countries that emerged from independence were segmented, even disjointed.

Today Latin America consists of nearly a half billion persons in over thirty countries, ranging from the Brazilian powerhouse to tiny island nations in the Caribbean. A few colonies persist—the Dutch and French territories—but they are mere reminders of a distant past. Most Latin American countries are democracies, largely presidential but with a few parliamentary systems, especially the former British dependencies. A rough tally shows that some 200 million persons participated in elections since the year 2000, a turnout rate that surpasses those of the United States and of many Western European countries. The economies of the larger countries, moreover, have become industrialized and sophisticated, and their workforces have organized into powerful unions and federations. Latin American women, who sometimes played exceptional leadership roles in the nineteenth century, have become respected actors in the political, economic, cultural, and social realms in the twenty-first.

These trends—generally, the "westernization" of Latin America—seem about to give way to global forces that would sweep these people into a worldwide system of economic transactions, migration flows, power blocs or centers, climatic and meteorological vectors, and cultural transformations. Latin Americans themselves, however, show signs of rejecting such globalization, which would threaten their identity and perhaps undermine their control over their own destiny.

POLITICAL GENERATIONS

For reasons not fully understood, leadership patterns in Latin America seemed to run in generations during the past 200 years. Similar domestic situations, external pressures, foreign models, geographical determinants, broad economic cycles, and other factors probably brought about this patterned evolution.

The first identifiable generation of leaders in modern Latin America was made up of the precursors of independence, the men and women who struggled against European rule in the Americas and the status deprivation brought on by colonialism. Most were socially well-to-do, though born in the New World and hence Creoles, and most had good educations for the period. Most also had personal as well as political grievances against the colonial authorities and distant monarchies that ruled their lives. These leaders included Antonio Nariño, the Colombian firebrand; Tiradentes, the Brazilian revolutionary; Francisco Miranda, the Venezuelan adventurer; and Toussaint L'Ouverture, the African prince who began the overthrow of the French slave regime of St. Domingue, today Haiti. The precursors sacrificed their material well-being and eventually their lives, becoming martyrs to independence.

The next generation comprised the heroes of independence, those who overthrew European rule in the Americas during the 1810s and 1820s. Most were born in the 1780s and grew up with Enlightenment ideals. They tended to come from propertied families whose interests diverged from those of the colonial regime. The foremost hero of independence was Simón Bolívar, known as the Liberator of South America, followed closely by José de San Martín, who helped consolidate Argentina's independence and drove the Spanish from Chile and portions of Peru. Bernardo O'Higgins of Chile also figures in this group.

Several pseudoheroes emerged in the era of independence, leaders who took advantage of the struggles of others and declared separation from Europe, but without the sacrifices and courage of the true heroes. This group includes General Agustín Iturbide of Mexico, Emperor Pedro I of Brazil, and President Francisco de Paula Santander of Colombia.

The conclusion of the wars of independence coincided with the onset of depression in Europe, bringing on a period of falling trade, prices, and incomes around the world. Latin Americans defaulted on loans and sought refuge in protectionism for domestic producers. The next leadership generation, the caudillos, rose to power in this setting. These leaders dominated the stage until the mid-nineteenth century and guided their young nations through perilous times. Foremost among the caudillos were José Antonio de Santa Anna of Mexico, Juan Manuel de Rosas of Argentina, Diego Portales of Chile, and José Antonio Páez of Venezuela. Caudillos are often referred to as men on horseback, and indeed most were mounted while commanding troops. Yet their strength and authority also came from personal qualities such as fairness, intelligence, courage, rectitude, and respect for hierarchy. They gathered followers and troops loyal to themselves and believed deeply in their legitimacy, regardless of existing constitutions. They cared for order and command, not for rule of law. Caudillos gave the outside world a negative impression of the region, yet they held their countries together, avoided warfare, reduced crime, and preserved a subsistence level of economic activity.

In the mid-nineteenth century, more principled leaders rose to power across the region, usually inspired by the promise of liberalism as practiced in Europe. These autocratic modernizers paid attention to constitutions and legislatures, enacted laws providing more freedom and equality for citizens, and tried to diminish the privileges of traditional institutions like the military, the Church, and landowners. Most of the reforms they introduced were aimed at unleashing the economic potential of land and labor, and at attracting foreign investment and technology. The best examples of the autocratic modernizer are Emperor Pedro II of Brazil, Benito Juárez of Mexico, and Bartolomé Mitre of Argentina. A second generation arose somewhat later, exemplified by Justo Rufino Barrios of Guatemala, Julio Roca of Argentina, Porfirio Díaz of Mexico, and Antonio Guzmán Blanco of Venezuela. The stability and incentives provided by these two generations led to construction of railroads and port facilities, urban modernization, distribution of public lands, growing efficiency in mining, ranching, agriculture, and industry, and booming export trade. For this reason, the second half of the nineteenth century is often called the era of the export economies.

After the turn of the twentieth century, fresh breezes blew over South America and awakened a different sort of leader, the early populist. This generation was also principled but shifted goals from economic to social and political progress. Their economies boomed but their peoples suffered. Constitutional provisions for elections and representation languished. And the well-being of the workers and peasants, male and female, declined due to killing labor regimes and lack of protections. The three outstanding examples of early populists were José Batlle y Ordóñez in Uruguay, Hipólito Yrigoyen in Argentina, and Arturo Alessandri in Chile. These leaders championed workers' rights, public benefit over private privilege, restrictions on foreign capital, and open, clean elections. They campaigned among the common people and promised to defend their interests. And most of the early populists were reasonably honest and successful in fulfilling their campaign pledges. The appearance of this generation marked the beginning of democracy in the region.

Another generation arose at the turn of the century, the dictators of the Caribbean basin. What they lacked in principles they made up for in greed and self-indulgence. Guaranteed power by corrupt military forces, the dictators went about the usual business of governing (building public works and utilities, hosting foreign corporations, expanding native enterprises, collecting taxes) but never consulted the common people nor concerned themselves with the general welfare.

They enriched themselves obscenely at public expense. Among the best examples of this generation were Manuel Estrada Cabrera of Guatemala and Mario García Menocal and Gerardo Machado of Cuba. Since their economies depended heavily on US markets and Wall Street banks, the dictators maintained close relations with Washington, DC. When necessary, they were capable of horrific violence and repression to protect the wealth and position they and their families enjoyed.

Not all leaders sought power at the ballot box to institute needed reforms. Almost simultaneously a generation of revolutionaries arose and led rebel armies against dictators and entrenched interests in government. Mexico's revolution of 1910–1920 is the best known of these uprisings, led by infamous *guerrilleros* like Pancho Villa and Emiliano Zapata, but there were others too in this period. Luís Carlos Prestes of Brazil pulled together several thousand rebel officers and recruits who had first protested in 1922 and led them on a great march through the backlands of his country. And in Nicaragua, Augusto Sandino mounted a guerrilla action that stymied his own country's forces as well as US Marines sent to capture him. Few of these revolutionaries lived to take power and carry out their programs, but their courage and tactics inspired a later generation of revolutionaries that would be more successful.

A classic generation of dictators of the Caribbean basin arose during and after the Great Depression of the 1930s. As vain, corrupt, power-hungry, and venal as its predecessor, this generation differed in its relation to and dependence on the United States. Because of a policy change during President Franklin Roosevelt's administration, the United States eschewed military intervention into Latin American countries. In the case of Cuba, Nicaragua, the Dominican Republic, and several other countries, however, instability led the United States to continue encouraging the formation of effective national guards, which could maintain order and protect US interests. In each case, the commander of the national guard gravitated to the presidency of his country and assumed dictatorial powers, with the blessing of the United States. The best known of these classic dictators of the Caribbean basin were Anastasio Somoza of Nicaragua, Fulgencio Batista of Cuba, and Rafael Trujillo of the Dominican Republic. They ruled for decades or passed along power to their children and cronies.

After World War II ended, a new generation of populists appeared in Latin America, no longer limited to the Southern Cone. The return of peace and the victory of the Western democracies strengthened the demands, internal as well as foreign, for elected governments in the region. The United States pressured dictators to step aside in favor of duly-elected representatives. The mid–twentieth century classic populists, as they are called, revolutionized political campaigns, elections, media, and behavior. The best examples are Juan and Evita Perón of Argentina, Getúlio Vargas of Brazil (after 1945), José María Velasco Ibarra of Ecuador, and Rómulo Betancourt of Venezuela. The classic populists posed as men of the people, protectors of the poor, defenders of the nation, and enemies of traditional corrupt politicians. Beyond that, they appealed to popular culture and used the print and electronic media expertly. They promised better lives for workers and farmers, a helping hand and the vote to women, prosperity for business owners— something for practically everyone. They also traveled widely by car, bus, train, airplane, and even horseback to visit every possible constituent. They were indefatigable campaigners, tireless speakers. They strove to create the impression of a personal connection to each and every voter.

The classic populists came from varied backgrounds and defy easy classification as to ideology. Their generation was defined more by how they got power—in competitive elections—than what they did in office. Some flirted with major structural changes in society; others drifted with little in the way of a program. Some are remembered for major accomplishments; others were removed for incompetence or worse. One change they introduced across the board, however: the demand that direct, honest elections with the largest possible participation be the sole method of gaining high office. From World War II until the early twenty-first century, voter participation rose from under 20 million to over 200 million. Along the way populists and others extended the franchise to women, illiterates, immigrants, sixteen-year-olds, and soldiers in most countries. The advent of mass politics dates to the rise of the populists in midcentury.

A new generation of revolutionaries appeared in mid-twentieth century as well, inspiring other rebel chieftains, both urban and rural. These leaders, exemplified by Fidel Castro and Ernesto "Ché" Guevara in Cuba and Daniel Ortega in Nicaragua, practiced an ancient form of warfare in contemporary settings—among the urban poor or in peasant regions. Just as importantly, they established revolutionary regimes in the context of the Cold War between the United States and the Soviet Union, thereby posing a security threat to the former. Latin America suddenly became a more dangerous, complex region in world affairs after Castro's success.

The new revolutionaries demonstrated that small bands of *guerrilleros* with the right strategy could defeat vastly larger armed forces. They also showed that propaganda and psychological tactics play an important part in revolutionary struggles. Finally, they proved that a relatively small country can defy the will of the United States and survive. Once in power, the revolutionaries carried out major structural changes of a socialist nature, leading to a huge exodus of propertied and professional families. They nationalized most major enterprises and hence cut themselves off from trade and investment from the capitalist world and most international financial institutions. Throughout the region young leaders aspired to repeat the achievements of Fidel Castro in Cuba, who remains one of the last communist heroes in the world today.

In the mid-1960s, a spate of right-wing coups brought to power a generation never before in the limelight, the military high command. At one point, a majority of the South American population lived under these military regimes. Unlike the earlier dictators, some of whom were military but took power as individuals, this generation of officers assumed control as institutional leaders who saw it as their duty to save their countries and clean up their politics and economies. Their regimes, sometimes characterized as the national security states, acted on the premise that the leaders who preceded them—populists perhaps, or incompetents—could not be trusted with power. They would open their nations to leftist agitation or at least to collapse and disorder. In either case, the military leaders saw it as their institutional mission to prevent disintegration of public order and likely communist revolution. These leaders, best exemplified by Jorge Videla in Argentina, Humberto Castello Branco in Brazil, and Augusto Pinochet in Chile, believed that the internal cohesion and competence of the military corps would save the nation, generate economic development, strengthen international ties, and bring about citizen solidarity. Of course they could also fight internal or external battles if necessary.

As the 1970s and 1980s wore on, many of the aims and promises of the military regimes failed to materialize, and they grew unpopular and sometimes teetered on the brink of disaster. In order to extricate themselves from government, the military leaders found ways, sometimes gradual and other times abrupt, to return power to civilians. This process, at first called *apertura*, later *transition* and *democratization*, took place at various times in the 1980s. The last to exit power was Pinochet, who stepped down in 1990, ironically after losing a national plebiscite.

The generation of leaders that assumed control after the departure of the military proved heterogeneous. Veteran politicians like Fernando Belaúnde Terry in Peru, Raúl Alfonsín in Argentina, and José Sarney in Brazil generally failed to bring consensus and mission to their administrations. Insoluble economic and social problems plagued them, as well as generalized recessionary conditions. None was able to build a viable governing party.

A last identifiable generation in contemporary Latin America was made up of the neopopulists, dating from the 1990s. Like their predecessors, they strove to create loyalty and electoral participation among followers by appealing to nationalism and by promising improvements for the common people. They were unusually adept at using media, public relations, and polling tools. The biggest difference between this generation and the earlier populists was their abandonment of economic nationalism and pro-labor policies in favor of neoliberal reforms such as lower tariffs, privatization, and a pro-business stance. The most prominent neopopulists have been Fernando Collor de Melo in Brazil, Alberto Fujimori in Peru, and Carlos Menem in Argentina. Collor stumbled badly in office and was impeached, but Fujimori and Menem had successful terms and were reelected.

The preceding account of the many generations of leaders in Latin America does not include all countries, of course; instead, it suggests broad political trends throughout the region. Mexico has not followed this progression since the revolution of 1910–1920 because of the enormous impact of that event on virtually all aspects of Mexican life. For one thing, the military generals, especially Álvaro Obregón, Plutarco Elías Calles, and Lázaro Cárdenas, dominated politics for twenty years and left in place an official party, the Partido Revolucionario Institucional (PRI), which governed the country for the next seventy years. Beginning with Miguel Alemán, elected in 1946, a long succession of party leaders trained in the law occupied the presidency.

In 1982, however, partly in response to the economic crisis generated by a world recession, the PRI chose an economist, Miguel de la Madrid, as president. The next two presidents were also economists, which reflected the high priority the PRI placed on growth in GNP and jobs. In 1994 the economist presidents took a huge gamble by joining the United States and Canada in a North American Free Trade Agreement, or NAFTA. Mexico's economy stabilized in the 1990s, due largely to the economic prosperity of its northern trade partner. Still, the results of NAFTA were not positive enough to keep most Mexicans loyal to the party. In 2000 they rebelled and elected an opposition president, Vicente Fox of the Partido de Acción Nacional (PAN), in a veritable political earthquake. A former businessman and state governor, Fox continued to emphasize the economy and tried to establish friendlier relations with the United States, in order to regularize the status of millions of Mexicans illegally living and working in the north. His efforts bore little fruit, however, because the terrorist attacks of September 11, 2001, caused the United States to harden its security along the border and turn away from constructive relations with Mexico.

In the 2006 presidential election, the public was offered a dramatic choice between a little-known PAN leader, Felipe Calderón, a spirited but flawed PRI candidate, and a flamboyant populist from the leftist Partido Revolucionario Democrático (PRD), Andrés Manuel López Obrador. The election came down to a virtual tie between Calderón and López Obrador, and the vote counting dragged on for weeks. The election tribunal eventually decided for Calderón, an outcome that elicited protests that lasted months. As controversial as this was, it also demonstrated that Mexico's political system had evolved into a competitive and unpredictable one in a relatively short time.

ECONOMIC CYCLES

Similar to the generational succession in politics, the economic history of Latin America followed a series of global business cycles, with superimposed waves of imported technology, immigration, and economic theory. Major expansions occurred in the periods 1816–1828, 1840–1869, 1880–1891, 1898–1914, 1920–1929, 1946–1972, and 1990–2000. By the same token, major recessions or depressions occurred in the 1830s, 1870s, 1890s, 1930s, 1980s, and the early years of the twenty-first century. These expansions and retreats affected the quality of life and sociopolitical interactions of the people.

The earliest economic boom in Latin America coincided with the last round of fighting for independence, and it was not experienced uniformly throughout the hemisphere. Countries that depended on silver exports, especially Mexico and Bolivia, experienced major disruptions and spent their early years of nationhood struggling to subsist. Countries where fighting was less intense and production could revive found 1820s markets extremely favorable for raw materials. This was especially true for Brazil's exports of sugar, cotton, coffee, and hides and skins. The boom was assisted by a general round of loans from British banks and by exuberant European and US trading missions to the region. This cycle ended in a general North Atlantic depression in the 1830s.

By the 1840s Mexican silver production began to grow, and Brazil's new crops, coffee and cacao, found thirsty markets in Europe and the United States. Venezuela, Colombia, and Costa Rica expanded their coffee production, and Venezuela and Ecuador increased exports of cacao. Argentina began diversifying its exports to include wool produced by immigrant shepherds. Cuba, although still a Spanish colony, became the first Latin American country to employ the workhorses of the industrial revolution: railroads, steam engines, and iron milling equipment. Sadly, this decade also saw historic numbers of African slaves imported to Cuba and Brazil. This iniquitous trade would not end altogether until the 1860s.

The rise of the autocratic modernizers in the 1850s reinforced this expansion by improving corporate law, inviting foreign investors, welcoming immigrants, and subsidizing transportation infrastructure. Chilean exports surged with the advent of a new market in California and the revival of copper prices after midcentury. To a considerable degree, this economic growth was fueled by the second wave of industrialization in Europe and the occupation of the US Midwest by millions of immigrants. Staples like sugar, coffee, cocoa, rum, cereals, and dried beef continued to enjoy high prices for the rest of the century. Huge amounts of guano from Peru and nitrates from Chile fertilized the farms of Europe and the East Coast of the United States. Meanwhile, industries in the north consumed growing inputs of hardwood, nonprecious metal ores, cotton, hides, and nitrates.

Downturns in the Atlantic economies stifled demand for Latin American products in the 1870s and again in the 1890s, but the overall trend line sloped sharply upward. Argentina and Uruguay experienced a veritable revolution on the pampas, with the advent of meatpacking plants, grain exports, and wool production. Steam threshers and harvesters multiplied the land under cultivation. To the north, no matter how fast Brazilians expanded coffee plantings, they could not satisfy world demand until the 1890s. European companies built railroads across South America, while US firms did so in Mexico. Port facilities were improved to accommodate a new generation of iron-hulled transatlantic steamers. Millions of Europeans flocked to South America, especially Argentina and Brazil, to participate in the agricultural revolution under way. So despite down cycles, the golden age of the export economies in Latin America did not really end until the 1920s.

Although exports of raw materials and food commodities dominated Latin America's economies during this period, considerable industrial expansion also took place. Food and beverage processing led the way, followed by clothing and textiles, building materials, and consumer goods. Many of these manufacturing firms were owned by European and US immigrants, who joined the national elites through partnerships and marriages. In some advanced economies—Mexico, Brazil, and Argentina especially—capital was increasingly transferred from primary production to industry as a way to hedge against declines in prices and demand. Moreover, some primary exports were processed before shipping (e.g., refined sugar, cured tobacco leaf, rum, rope fibers, semirefined metal ore, dried and cured cacao, and nitrates).

New and exotic products joined the flood of exports around the turn of the twentieth century. Bananas grown in Jamaica and later Central America were shipped under refrigeration for ripening in foreign markets. Rubber from the Amazon became a ubiquitous material in the age of electric appliances, bicycles, and automobiles. Copra from coconut palms cultivated on tropical beaches rendered comestible oil for northern food industries. Chicle from southern Mexico became chewing gum. Herbs, spices, and flavorings from tropical regions delighted the palates of northern consumers.

By the 1920s most of Latin America was fully integrated into global trade and production systems. European and US investors underwrote much of the heavy industrial growth, while native capital financed light industry. The technology and immigrants also came from abroad. Between 1880 and 1930, some 20 million foreigners moved to Latin America, literally changing the complexion of whole cities and regions.

World War I tentatively cut Latin America off from capital and markets, and the Great Depression did so more definitively. By 1945 the region's economies had changed in remarkable ways due to two world wars and the worst depression in modern times. Banking and finance had developed to the point that the economies no longer relied on foreign investment as before. From their earliest efforts in the 1860s and 1870s, native and immigrant families developed banks and insurance firms capable of managing most local business. In the larger countries, manufacturers supplied a large proportion of the consumer goods and considerable amount of capital goods required. In some instances, immigrants actually developed new technologies in their shops and labs. Perhaps most strikingly, Latin Americans' willingness to believe orthodox economic theory from Europe virtually ended.

Throughout the nineteenth century, two theories to guide economic behavior prevailed, traditional Spanish capitalism and classic liberalism derived from Enlightenment writers like David Ricardo and Adam Smith. The former valued capital in the form of land, machinery, animals, buildings, and cash that could be made to produce goods through the application of labor. Ownership of fixed assets and the ability to coerce labor were critical in the traditional economy. So too was the power to protect capital, create legislation, secure markets, and provide an orderly setting for business. Most successful nineteenth-century businesses followed this traditional family-based pattern.

The newer ideas of liberalism found adherents from the generation of the precursors onward, until it became broadly accepted by the autocratic modernizers. In this view, the factors of production (land, labor, and capital—which came bundled with technology) had to be brought together in creative ways for profitable business. The government should do as little as possible to restrict the entrepreneurial efforts of its citizens, a policy known as laissez-faire capitalism. Liberalism also held that each country should pursue its competitive advantage in world markets, the so-called international division of labor. If Europe produced cheap and reliable manufactures, Latin America ought to focus on tropical agriculture and mining. The terms of trade would reward both sides in their transactions.

If a limited number of powerful families or institutions monopolized land, labor, and political power, the vast majority of the population could never aspire to become productive citizens. In the case of Latin America, liberals saw obstacles to economic growth in the vast expanses of land held by the state, Amerindian reservations, and the Church; the prevalence of coerced labor (especially African and Amerindian) unavailable to new businesses; high tariffs; social and religious barriers against immigration; and restrictions on natural resource exploitation. Advocates of removing these obstacles undertook huge reform programs that awakened the wrath of those whose power was being diminished, especially the army and the Church. Benito Juárez carried out the boldest changes, collectively known as La Reforma, but others did so as well: Mariano Gálvez of Guatemala, the so-called Liberal Oligarchy in Venezuela, and General José Hilario López of Colombia. These programs provoked opposition and even civil war—known as the War of the Reform in Mexico—but in the end the liberals prevailed. Without these reforms, the economic boom that followed would likely not have occurred.

The liberal theories that prevailed after about the 1870s became dogma and reigned until the Great Depression. They stressed low tariffs, private over public enterprise, international division of labor, protection of property rights, stable currencies (preferably tied to gold), borders open to foreign immigration and investment, and weak labor organization. As noted above, this arrangement did not prevent Latin Americans from founding important industries in this era, either with tariff protection or because of costly international freight charges. And in Mexico and Brazil, government leaders often showed favoritism toward native producers while paying lip service to liberal ideals. They did this through subsidized transport systems, commodity price supports, tax advantages, low-cost credit, and protectionist tariffs.

The isolation of Latin America from the North Atlantic economies during World War I, and the sheer horror of death and destruction wrought by the fighting, shook Latin Americans' faith in European philosophies and models. True, in the 1920s many countries returned to trading in conventional products with traditional partners, but now the United States made a bid for economic leadership in the hemisphere. Communications, shipping, and finance also tended to shift toward the United States.

The Great Depression further eroded faith in the nineteenth-century liberal economic model. Trading broke down, nations defaulted on loans, businesses failed, currencies collapsed, and the entire economic system seemed to crumble. National leaders looked for new ways to do business, like barter deals and cartelization of commodities. It was a dog-eat-dog situation that might one day lapse into world war again. John Maynard Keynes had already proposed major revisions to classic liberalism that promised recovery from the ravages of depression. Franklin Roosevelt reversed US policy and used federal money for public works and foreign aid and held bilateral trade talks to promote economic recovery and job creation.

Latin American leaders took unusual and sometimes creative steps to ameliorate the impact of the Depression in their nations. Mexico sped up the resettlement of Indians and peasants on communal lands, or *ejidos,* where they could at least subsist. Brazil experimented with alcohol-fueled engines and withheld coffee from the world market. Argentina struck a deal with England for preferential trade treatment. Chile created a national investment bank to promote economic development. Everywhere in the hemisphere domestic manufacturers moved boldly into consumer markets that had previously been served by imports. It was the end of an era.

After the war Latin Americans increasingly embraced an alternative theory of economics, with major domestic and external implications. This theory sprang from research conducted at the newly founded UN Economic Commission for Latin America (ECLA), based in Santiago, Chile. The basic tenet of this institute was that since the beginning of the twentieth century primary commodities had suffered declining terms of trade vis-à-vis manufactured goods. This meant that Latin America had to ship increasing amounts of goods to Europe and the United States to maintain the same level of import consumption. Further, they argued that adverse terms of trade would always favor the industrial countries, due to economies of scale, elasticity of demand for manufactures, oligopolistic pricing, and productivity gains from technological advances. The only way for Latin America to catch up was to industrialize also.

The strategy ECLA proposed was called import substitution industrialization (ISI). In this model, a country used tariffs to protect new industries until they could compete against imports. Eventually they would be as efficient as their competitors. Second, ECLA argued that the region's most valuable assets—land, labor, capital, natural resources—were tied up in unproductive arrangements, much as the liberals had claimed in the mid-nineteenth century. Structural reforms were needed to unleash their potential: land reform, housing, worker education, tax reform, health improvements, and so forth. Finally, ECLA proposed unorthodox ways to finance economic growth, through deficit spending and market-expanding customs unions. Remarkably, this new theory became an orthodoxy of its own and even served as the inspiration for John Kennedy's Alliance for Progress in the 1960s!

Most of the generation of the populists after World War II followed ECLA strategies to industrialize and gain a degree of economic independence from the industrialized world. They adopted ISI, carried out land and tax reform, set up programs for literacy and public health, and invested in education at all levels. Deficit spending, carried too far, often led to chronic inflation. For a time customs unions forged ahead (e.g., the Central American Common Market, the Latin American Free Trade Area, the Andean Pact, the Caribbean CARICOM), but in the long run they accomplished little.

The military regimes of the 1960s–1980s tended to adopt neoliberal policies as a way to clean up excesses of the populist era, yet circumstances did not favor their success. Only in Chile did a frankly laissez-faire approach work, led by economists associated with the University of Chicago. In Brazil, Argentina, and Uruguay, early experiments with neoliberalism gave way to frenzied attempts to promote growth, deal with balance of payments crises, shore up currencies, and create jobs for the masses of young people joining the workforce each year. Neoliberalism simply took too long to produce results. What emerged was called heterodoxy, or a jumble of whatever policies seemed capable of solving the problems of the moment. Nowhere was heterodoxy so pronounced as in Brazil during the ascendancy of finance minister Delfim Netto. In the end, failures of economic management contributed heavily to the military's decision to return to the barracks.

The 1980s found most of Latin America in such financial trouble that it is often called the "lost decade." Stagflation and hyperinflation, energy crises, unemployment, debt defaults and serial rollovers, failed protectionism, capital flight, and general mismanagement plagued the region. Oil-rich countries like Mexico, Venezuela, and Ecuador found themselves unable to use their resources effectively. Those without oil resorted to extremes like alcohol fuel, nuclear plants, charcoal, and huge hydroelectric projects. In the end, the region did not emerge from the doldrums until the Atlantic economy began its recovery in the early 1990s.

Since that time, neoliberal policies have become the new orthodoxy in much of the region. Chile was taken as a model for export-led growth in the 1980s. The US-trained economist-presidents of Mexico, and certainly Vicente Fox, followed this line, as did the finance ministers of Argentina, Brazil, and Peru. For a time, Argentina and Brazil pegged their currencies to the US dollar to gain price stability. El Salvador and Ecuador actually adopted the US dollar as currency, joining Panama. Even Cuba, which lost its subsidy when the Soviet Union collapsed, moved to attract investment and the US dollar. The rest of the neoliberal recipe has been tried out in most countries: tariff reduction, direct foreign investment, elimination of subsidies and price controls, privatization, ending deficit spending, and curbing overly generous benefits for public employees. The pace of neoliberalization slowed in the early 2000s due to the recession, and several countries led by Brazil killed the US drive to create a free trade area in the hemisphere. More and more Latin American leaders are voicing reluctance to follow the old neoliberal model, but there is little agreement about what will replace it.

CONCLUSION

Latin America entered the twenty-first century by confronting global challenges, no longer using the hemisphere or the West as a frame of reference. These challenges include trade competition against fierce rivals in Asia, first the so-called Tigers, and now China. They also include an energy system groaning under the demands of the First World while trying to accommodate the development needs of the Third World. The superpower United States conducts business all around the globe, so Latin Americans need to be aware of developments on that scale. The threat from international terrorism, world crime and drug networks, war, epidemic diseases, and the inevitable economic crises must be monitored daily by Latin American leaders. Hemispheric organizations like the OAS, the School of the Americas (now renamed WHINSEC), the Inter-American Defense Board, and the Pan American Health Organization are largely obsolete today. Latin Americans must operate in the rarefied atmosphere of the United Nations, the World Bank, the International Monetary Fund, the World Trade Organization, and other global entities.

Apart from these political and security challenges, Latin Americans must survive economically in a multipolar world that becomes more integrated with each passing year. The region's best and brightest minds are devising their integration into this global economy, running some of the biggest companies in the world—petroleum, aviation, mining, manufacturing, entertainment, food, telecommunications, and services—gambling that multinational corporate management is here to stay. How will individual workers and farmers operate in an informed way in this sort of world? The answer will perhaps dictate the success or failure of the integration process.

Less dramatic yet perhaps just as threatening in the long run will be the challenges of cultural erosion and the loss of social cohesion under the onslaught of global media. At the moment the media are dominated by US, European, and Japanese companies, which project leisure programming to the rest of the world—cinema, drama, music, games, sports, and news. Whether Latin Americans can domesticate or Latinize this programming remains to be seen. By the same token, Spanish and Portuguese language media, originating primarily in the United States but also coming from Mexico, Brazil, and Spain, are a growing presence in US markets. The future of the arts, family life, spiritual worship, leisure activities, individual and group creativity, and the very core of Latin American-ness are at stake in this confrontation of cultures.

REFERENCES

Bulmer-Thomas, Victor. *The Economic History of Latin America Since Independence.* Cambridge: Cambridge University Press, 1994.

Bushnell, David, and Neill Macaulay. *The Emergence of Latin America in the Nineteenth Century*. New York: Oxford University Press, 1988.

Clayton, Lawrence, and Michael L. Conniff. *A History of Modern Latin America*. 2nd ed. Florence, KY: Thompson-Wadsworth, 2004.

Conniff, Michael L., ed. *Populism in Latin America*. Tuscaloosa: University of Alabama Press, 1999.

Haber, Stephen, ed. *How Latin America Fell Behind*. Stanford: Stanford University Press, 1997.

PART III

ECONOMIC AND
SOCIAL STRUCTURES

Chapter 7

Latin American Economies Restructure, Again

William P. Glade

Recent years have brought a lively interest in Latin American economic restructuring. What this means, in practice, is far from easy to ascertain, given the complexity and variety that characterize the Latin American economies. They range from economically dynamic Brazil, now firmly ensconced among the BRIC economies (Brazil, Russia, India, China—emerging powers of real economic significance) to tiny, deeply impoverished Haiti, one of poorest nations of the world. Just about every combination of size, income level, and structure of national production can be found in between—along with a complicated medley of geographical and climatic conditions. Nevertheless, with the exception of Haiti, Honduras, and Nicaragua, the countries of the region have at least made it out of the poorest category in the World Bank's four-category classification scheme and are more or less firmly ensconced in the lower middle income and upper middle income categories.[1]

Performance, historically, has been no less varied, though all of Latin America has, since the 1970s, been outdistanced by the Asian "tigers" old and new. Since the baroque narrative of Latin America's development and backwardness comes from an accumulation of institutional overlays from five consecutive episodes of systemic reorganization, a quick romp through the centuries may help us understand the problems that nowadays beset the region and tell us whether, in today's unexpectedly severe global economic context, the region settled into a permanent policy mode with the dramatic economic restructuring of the 1980s and 1990s or is poised on the cusp of yet another macro-systemic change.[2]

The policy episode that began in the 1980s, which the Inter-American Development Bank rightly labeled a silent revolution in economic policy, is only the latest of five restructurings that have been visited on the region since the arrival of Columbus and his crew. Something remains of each of these in the contemporary economic landscape, and from the second restructuring onward, those advocating new policies have thoughtfully left us a diagnostic interpretation of what went before. Taken together, these edited versions of economic history are immensely helpful in piecing together a record of how the region got to where it is today.

What lies ahead, however, is at this point beclouded by the recrudescence of long-discredited economic populisms in Argentina, Bolivia, Venezuela, Ecuador, and Nicaragua, and the lingering death of the decrepit socialism of Cuba. Above all, however, the policy future is fraught with deep uncertainty owing to the crisis in the world financial system that took such ruthless shape in 2008.

There is no little irony in the conjuncture of circumstances in the region. In the fifth restructuring, as we shall see, Latin American countries were counseled to make their economies more transparent, to deregulate (and in some instances to develop new regulations), inter alia, and to address the seemingly intractable problems of huge disparities in the distribution of income. They were urged to engage more broadly and competitively with the world market. Yet the present economic slump has affected most severely the countries most closely integrated with the US economy, the wellspring of the crisis. Income disparities in the United States have reached levels not seen since 1929. The capital markets of this pivotal country in world capitalism have become so opaque that even major financial institutions were caught unawares and unprepared for the global financial crisis that hit the world in 2008. What is more, for all the talk of refining the regulatory systems of Latin America, it soon became painfully clear that inadequate regulation and even deregulation in critical areas of the US economy played a major role in precipitating the crisis. Latin Americans can certainly be pardoned for thinking "Physician, heal thyself."

THE PARADE OF RESTRUCTURINGS

The first "structural adjustment" began when the Spanish replaced sundry indigenous economic systems with one that was more in accord with imperial aspirations and European norms.[3] So transformative and sweeping was this project that it far surpasses in magnitude and scope any restructuring since attempted. Institutions, technology, and relations with the rest of the world, or even among the regions of the Americas, were altered profoundly and irrevocably. Veritable revolutions occurred in the technology of transport, agriculture, animal husbandry, and mining, and wholly new elements of a money economy were introduced, along with an administratively managed economic interaction with Europe and, to a much lesser extent, with Asia. Within the overseas kingdoms of Spain, interregional commerce took place on an unprecedented scale. What emerged was a bureaucratically administered and intricately regulated system that brought under royal direction an ensemble of new local and regional economies, dispersed over a territory more vast and more challenging than any European monarchy had yet tried to govern. It was in effect an integrated trading territory larger than anything cobbled together until quite recent times in Latin America. As for Brazil, given its primitive development prior to Portuguese settlement, the leap forward was even greater. This vast area became essentially a slave-based export platform for the Portuguese monarchy, centering on sugar at first but diversifying into gemstones and other minerals in the eighteenth century in a move that also reduced the relative importance of slave labor.

Agriculturally based, the Spanish American economy was in time organized by a growing latifundism that defied stated royal objectives and was expanded by demographic and other factors. For example, the native population declined steeply as a result of exposure to European diseases, which vacated much land traditionally worked by the indigenous peoples. Peoples were relocated for ease of governance and partial acculturation (vacating customary land occupation). There was a fundamental incompatibility between pre-Columbian land claims and those based on European custom. Spanish settlements needed to devote considerable acreage to the production of food crops and pasturage for the draft animals on which the colonial transport system rested. Then too, settlers persistently attempted to lay hold of the huge expanse of land claimed by the crown but poorly defended by the royal bureaucracy. Private estates of considerable size eventually became the basic unit in agriculture, displacing many of the community-held lands the crown had reassigned to the indigenous population. Over the centuries church institutions also acquired extensive landholdings, often the best managed in the colonies. Inasmuch as land was the fundamental productive resource in an agrarian economy and the source of livelihood for the overwhelming majority of the labor force, the evolution of this pattern of land tenure established systematic inequality that persists in some ways to the present day.[4]

Trade, among the urban centers in Spain's overseas colonies and between the colonies and Spain, was a major activity, closely supervised by the crown to ensure the collection of the taxes that formed the structure of public finance. A considerable number of artisan manufactures grew up, based on both indigenous and Spanish craft technologies. These too were generally regulated by royal and municipal ordinances and, in the case of the nonindigenous craftsmen, by guild regulations—except where larger workshops, known as *obrajes,* developed. Capital for settlement and other purposes was supplied by the public sector, merchant financiers, and, above all, ecclesiastical institutions that supplied mortgage loans at relatively low interest rates. The technological stagnation that was perpetuated in agriculture, mining, and manufacture by this imperially sheltered system of production had its institutional counterpart in the stunted development of the financial sector, which included nothing remotely resembling contemporary European developments. This left the region singularly ill equipped to establish a competitive capitalist economic organization when Spain's empire came to an end.

The ambitious imperial enterprise was punctuated by the development of important mining centers that supplied treasure for the Spanish crown and its never-ending dynastic wars in Europe. It nourished an administrative machinery that grew in size and complexity as the centuries passed and salted huge amounts of bullion among the European suppliers who furnished the New World with luxury imports. The New World economy's resources continued to be invested in the construction of urban centers and costly transport networks to link them, so that Spanish government, society, and culture—all of which could be considered analytically as produced public goods—could take root and prosper in the American setting.

A quadruple legacy, therefore, was bequeathed to Latin America from the colonial period. Local political organization was arrested by Spanish bureaucratic centralism; the insurgents who threw off Spanish rule had no real experience in self-government to draw on as they set about devising their new republics. Technological backwardness was pervasive, shielded as Spanish America had been from the exchanges of goods, services, and technologies that had propelled contemporary European economies toward modernity. Organizational or social capital remained little changed from the sixteenth and seventeenth centuries—at a time when the commercial revolution was reshaping the institutional architecture of Europe (and North America). Perhaps most nefarious of all, the foundational systems of inequality inherited from pre-Columbian times were modified and continued with the European overlay, so that a pronounced inequality in the distribution of wealth and income (and access to the opportunity structure) has been a dominant characteristic of Latin America ever since. To be sure, recent research has pointed out that the degree of inequality in Latin America then, and even through the first half of the nineteenth century, was by no means exceptional in relation to other parts of the world in those days.[5] But cultural cleavages, interethnic differences in social and human capital, and strikingly differential access to power over land and other resources, including a voice in public policy, provided a setting in which subsequent developments spurred by rapidly expanding exports and foreign capital inflows would generate increasing disparities in income and wealth, not to mention in effective political power.

The second restructuring was launched in the eighteenth century by the Bourbons. It sought a modest liberalization of trade, a revivification of the American production system (especially in mining), some fiscal reforms, and greater efficiency in the administration of the imperial enterprise—objectives not too distant from those that are motivating today's structural adjustment programs. Formal or de jure trade flows were moderately liberalized and informal or de facto trade flows (smuggling, contraband) also increased considerably by all accounts. What is mainly interesting for our purposes, however, is that this second restructuring occasioned considerable analytical reflection on the conditions then prevailing in Spain's overseas kingdoms, both to diagnose ills and prescribe remedies. Indeed, from the economic writings of the Spanish mercantilists, who had an impressively sophisticated understanding of economic processes, and the commissioned reports of special reconnaissance missions, of which the tour by Alexander von Humboldt may be the best known, we catch more than a passing glimpse of what needed to be done to remedy the accumulated weaknesses of the colonial economy.[6] Though the second restructuring program was only partially implemented, it had a generally positive impact, as revealed by the quickening tempo of economic life as the eighteenth century drew to a close. The institutional architecture laid down by the first restructuring, however, remained in place, save in the field of governance when independence came. Worse, the gains achieved by the second restructuring were largely wasted in the half century of political and administrative disorder that gripped most of Latin America after independence. Only Brazil, Chile, and Cuba (still under Spanish rule) were exempted from this protracted economic disruption.

Of more than passing interest was the divergent growth path taken by Brazil, which from the outset was conceived by the Portuguese as a commercial venture, supplementing the trading opportunities their earlier voyages along and around the African coast to Asia had opened up. No traded goods were ready for the picking, however, and establishing commercial viability required the Portuguese to transfer the sugar plantation technology they had developed on islands in the eastern Atlantic to northeastern Brazil. When native labor proved insufficient (the indigenous population was quite sparse compared with Mexico, Guatemala, and the Andean highlands), slaves from Africa were imported to run the enterprise. The high initial fixed costs this entailed ensured that earning a return on the investment in labor supply would motivate plantation owners to extract an exportable surplus for sale to European markets.

Apart from northeastern Brazil, where the colonial capital was located, the rest of the colony served mainly to supply the plantation economy with a simple range of commodities. The eighteenth century brought a mining boom in east central Brazil and pulled population southward, giving an additional impetus to growth in regions previously quite marginal, making Rio an important port and shifting the labor regime away from slave labor. The mining boom reinforced the export orientation of the Brazilian economy and consolidated its trading ties with the commercial network the Portuguese had constructed in Europe, including with Portugal's ally Great Britain, a rapidly growing market.

The third restructuring, a more ambitious enterprise than the second, arrived after a half century hiatus in which economic dislocation plagued the region with the arrival of independence. As noted above, Brazil, Chile, and Cuba were the principal exceptions. The aftermath of independence included considerable economic wreckage—most artisan manufactures were replaced by cheap factory-made imports from Europe, public investment in infrastructure was neglected, there were repeated defaults on external debt (both public and private), the enfeebled fiscal systems were plundered by political adventurers, royal and clerical safeguards against exploitation of the indigenous population were removed, the public domain was raped, and the policy framework was plagued by instability. This scenario was very different from what the fighters for independence said they had in mind when they chased out Spanish bureaucrats. Public finances were a shambles, high risk levels undermined the investment environment, and a region now hitching its fortunes to the increasingly vibrant international economy did so bereft of even the rudimentary banking institutions needed to mobilize and allocate resources in the increasingly monetized capitalist system that was spreading out of Europe. In a sense, the third restructuring, launched when the political picture finally settled down a bit, was a bold remediation for this half century of failure.

The middle decades of the nineteenth century worked out much better in Brazil and Chile. Both provided a favorable climate for the germination of the new economic system that in time spread over the whole of Latin America, albeit unevenly. Chile attained a reasonable degree of political stability and was able to build a favorable investment climate for domestic as well as foreign capitalists, segueing quickly into an export-based expansion. Owing to circumstances in Europe, the Portuguese court moved to Brazil. When it finally returned to Lisbon, it left behind an emperor to take charge of an independent Brazil that was governed from Rio, the city to which the court had fled under British protection. Thanks to the close commercial and political ties the new country inherited from its metropole with the center of the industrial revolution and to the effortless way it attained independence, Brazil was spared the turmoil that proved so costly elsewhere on the continent. And with the climate for economic modernization undisturbed by political change, the way was laid for a third dramatic export boom.[7] This time the product was coffee and the location was in the south of the country, so that the rapid spread of coffee cultivation on Brazilian-owned plantations around São Paulo triggered an explosion of economic expansion in this previously frontier region, based on a free labor force, the attraction of substantial capital and immigration from Europe, and the stimulation of capitalistic development throughout the south of the country.

From around 1870 to 1930, the third restructuring, which centered on the development of export economies, came to Spanish America and paid off handsomely for those not trapped by the inequality systems that developed after 1492. As in Brazil for the whole of the nineteenth century, two engines of growth—the production and sale to world markets of a growing variety of primary commodities and the influx of foreign capital that made the export production system possible—propelled Latin America into the modern economic arena and transformed the economic dynamics of the region. Even more than the second restructuring, this project anticipated some of the main features of the so-called Washington Consensus, the chief difference being that there was no stable of deficit-generating public enterprises to privatize.[8] Trade liberalization and the creation of a climate favorable to investment, both domestic and foreign, buttressed the new economic order, though here and there cautious interventionary measures were employed to stimulate early manufacturing development.

The third restructuring was an institution-building period par excellence as most of the organizational accoutrements of modern capitalism appeared in all the principal urban centers, moving in some cases beyond by the vectors of modern transportation and communications systems. Commercial banks, shipping companies, accounting firms, engineering firms, port works, new railway, street railway, and telecommunications companies, smelters, capitalistically organized mining companies, insurance companies, plantations using narrow-gauge railways and steam-powered refineries, and a slew of other enterprises provided the social and organizational capital Latin America needed to belatedly join the modern economy of the West and attract the human capital needed to keep the ensemble in operation. Harbingers of a new age of factory production also sprang up here and there, following the needs of export-fed markets and new structures of production. Most new manufacturers produced consumer goods, but foundries, smelters, and machine shops were indicative of the possibilities for industrial deepening, and around the turn of the century the first integrated iron- and steelworks appeared in Monterrey, Mexico.

Over much of the region, these new developments occurred in scattered enclaves; growth was markedly uneven. Interregional disparities were greater than ever before, setting the stage for the notoriously uneven development that characterizes most of Latin America today. Much of the area and population was thus left behind by the modernizing forces of international capitalism and its domestic offshoots, including substantial numbers of people trapped in subsistence cultivation.[9] Shorn of their communal holdings and proletarianized by the unrestricted expansion of large landholdings, the indigenous peoples seemed destined for cultural obliteration in the liberal project that most governments pursued.[10] At the northern end of Latin America, these contradictions were particularly notable in Mexico, but they were in greater or lesser measure shared by most of Latin America. In the south of Brazil and the Rio de la Plata, however, the new economic in-

fluences spread untrammeled by colonial residues or sizable indigenous populations, with a transformative power that brought into being a region that today
constitutes the economic heartland of South America (and the Mercosur, the
southern Common Market). Argentina even managed to reach the end of this era
as one of the world's most prosperous economies, so that "rich as an Argentine"
gained currency in Europe to describe vast wealth.[11] Between the two, Uruguay,
which also was notably progressive in its political order, even came to be known as
the Switzerland of Latin America.

This restructuring, like the second one, stimulated an abundance of new writing, this time mostly in the vein of the classical/neoclassical school of political
economy and positivism, to reinterpret the past for its diagnostic value and prescribe ingredients for the policy armamentarium the governments of the day were
putting together to ensure continued growth and even progress, a term still in
vogue in that pre-postmodern intellectual ambiance. It would be stretching a point
to call this an age of unbridled laissez-faire, but it most certainly was one filled to
overflowing with capitalist sentiments and language.

But beyond the Rio de la Plata and broad swatches of Chile and central and
southern Brazil, the spottiness of the transformation made for glaring inequalities
and a plethora of organizational and cultural disparities—contradictions of such
severity as to delight the heart of a Marxist. In Mexico, as already noted, these were
particularly acute, so that only a decade into the century, the ancien régime, as the
nouveau régime soon came to be perceived, was cast aside and a kind of anticipa-
tory glimpse of the next restructuring hove into view: one that would use a kind of
economic nationalism to accelerate the process of industrialization. In Mexico, almost uniquely until the Bolivian revolution of the 1950s, agrarian reform was at
first the dominant policy priority. But when the fourth restructuring set in during
the late 1930s and 1940s, manufacturing called the tune.

ISI: THE FOURTH RESTRUCTURING

During the closing decades of the nineteenth century, the first modern factories
appeared here and there in Latin America: in Argentina, Chile, Brazil, and Mexico
especially but scattered elsewhere as well. Population growth, modest urbanization,
the enrichment of the area's human resources by immigration (entrepreneurs as
well as skilled labor), and rising income, together with integrated railways and
telecommunication lines, gradually expanded domestic markets and with them the
number of local manufacturing establishments. As the twentieth century unfolded,
these market-based trends further widened the industrial base—spurred on,
briefly, by the interruption of European imports during World War I. As we interpret the record of growth in more recent decades, we need to remember that several of these factors—population growth, rapid urbanization, the national
infrastructure development, and rising per capita income—have continued to support manufacturing development, both broadening and deepening the industrial
structure independently of the effects of policy.

When the Great Depression hit and export earnings collapsed, the depreciation
of Latin American currencies favored the further expansion of domestic industry
to replace the unavailable imports, while by this time tariffs originally designed for

revenue had gradually been raised to levels according a measure of protection for competing local products. And while depression thus knocked out one of the props of the age of export-led expansion, the other engine of the region's third-restructuring growth, foreign investment, was likewise rendered *hors de combat* by the massive disorganization of capital markets in the centers of capitalism.[12] Import supplies and capital imports continued to be disrupted when World War II began, and while domestic manufacturing was spreading to meet the gap between domestic aggregate demand and imports, governments increasingly questioned the wisdom of continuing to rely on the external sector as the mainstay of economic growth. Such conditioning circumstances lasted into the postwar era while traditional sources of import supplies continued to be choked back by reconstruction priorities. This effort also absorbed most of the capital Europe could generate and the United States could export.

It remained for the new UN Economic Commission for Latin America (ECLA), based in Santiago, Chile, to fashion out of these circumstances a rationale for systematic promotion, under state leadership, of accelerated industrial development.[13] Thereafter, until the debt crisis struck in 1982, the policies that had evolved by ad hoc adaptation to circumstances in the 1930s and 1940s were reshaped into a well-articulated development program that called for a variety of interventionary measures and in time spawned the movement toward regional integration as an expedient to preserve the momentum of industrialization. Protective tariffs, fiscal incentives, exchange-rate controls, parastatal financial and industrial enterprises, and a host of other policy instruments were deployed to push industrial development forward and, from the early 1960s, to promote such schemes as the Central American Common Market, the larger Latin American Free Trade Area, and the smaller Caribbean Free Trade Area—to which were added the Andean Pact and the Caribbean Common Market. None of these regional associations lived up to initial expectations, but in most there was a significant growth of intraregional trade—and, most likely, equally significant trade diversion effects.

Amid these changes there were also notable shifts in inter-American economic relations. The 1930s had brought the reciprocal trade agreements to build preferential commercial ties between the United States and Latin America, and the inauguration of the Export-Import Bank introduced government financing into the web of economic relationships. Technical assistance and additional intergovernmental financing for capital projects began during World War II, when the United States had need of increased Latin American production capacity. A trickle of economic aid of these types, especially technical assistance, continued through the 1950s, when the World Bank became a significant external source of development financing and the Organization of American States a modest supplier of economic counsel and technical assistance through such entities as the Pan American Health Organization.[14] While the regional integration movement was reaching its heyday, the Inter-American Development Bank was instituted at the end of the 1950s as a multilateral regional supplier of development finance (and technical counsel). Soon thereafter the Alliance for Progress, sometimes misleadingly equated with the Marshall Plan, was introduced to mobilize public resources on a large scale for a concerted regional development push.[15] By the 1970s, however, these initiatives were playing out.

Baptized "import-substituting industrialization" (ISI), the strategy came to be administered carelessly, distorted from the pristine ECLA vision by rent seeking interest groups and populist policies that were characterized as macroeconomic populism.[16] Bedecked also with some of the trappings of the modern welfare state to placate the crucial urban constituencies, the public sector came to exemplify a concept of the state as the great piñata. Inflation was rampant, balance-of-payments crises were frequent, agricultural and traditional export sectors were undermined, and in time the policy environment turned increasingly hostile to foreign direct investment.[17] To cap the mounting list of problems, Latin America's export market share was generally eroded in favor of other Third World exporters, and fiscal profligacy and excessive bureaucratization combined with the discouragement of foreign investment and the need to cover growing trade imbalances to produce an increasing reliance on commercial loans from money-center banks. Meanwhile domestic savings rates were depressed by adverse policies and capital flight was unintentionally stimulated. The industrialization that had been designed to replace imports had in fact made Latin America more dependent on imports than ever before.

The jig was up when the oil shocks of the 1970s worked their effects, and (on top of all the external-sector adjustments) the industrialized countries more or less simultaneously undertook to put an end to accelerating inflation, causing export prices and earnings to drop precipitously. The repercussions in Latin America produced the debt crisis, which struck all the countries save Colombia in the early 1980s and effectively ended the half century of accelerated industrialization and the policy framework that had sustained and nurtured it.[18] The longer-term effect of the crisis was to usher in yet another major shift in economic policy that gradually spread over the continent.[19]

THE FIFTH RESTRUCTURING AND WHAT IT REVEALS

Chile, Mexico, Argentina, and latterly Peru were at the forefront of the new policy agenda, which promoted macroeconomic stabilization, the ending of financial repression (the freeing of interest rates to find market-determined levels), and the removal of most exchange rate controls so that the prices in the foreign exchange market would be anchored in supply-demand relationships. The deregulation of other prices and the withdrawal of subsidies also furthered the marketization of economic decision making. Trade liberalization widened the scope of contestable markets and intensified competitive pressures, bringing about greater productive and allocative efficiency while aligning domestic price structures with those prevailing in the world market. In greater or lesser measure, deregulation was also used to create a more favorable climate for capital formation, both domestic and foreign.

Privatization, once the most controversial of the new policies, was employed for a variety of objectives: to strengthen the fiscal system by removing deficit-generating enterprises from the public portfolio and using the sales proceeds to reduce national debt; to link local production facilities more securely into the globalized production, financing, and marketing networks; to tap the more ample supplies of capital available in the private sector; and to pave the way for continuing technological upgrading. Secondary objectives included the reduction of labor redundancy and making national capital markets more robust, both by spreading the ownership of shares and by enriching the options available to investors for portfolio diversification.

The 1994–1995 peso crisis and its repercussions aside, the benefits of structural adjustment were swifter to materialize than might have been expected, given all that had been said about the distortions and other shortcomings of the previous policy era, in which so many canons of economic orthodoxy were violated. No doubt it was the flagrant character of these "violations" that led many to interpret the debt crisis as a well-deserved day of reckoning, in which policy sins of omission and commission alike would finally be paid for. Yet just as the three preceding restructuring episodes were the occasions for retrospective diagnoses of the economic frailties that led into the restructurings, so also the present turnabout affords a useful vantage point from which to reflect on what legacy the twentieth century has left for the Latin American economies. A summing up of sorts, in other words, is plainly in order—not only to assess the policies of the neoliberal model that critics called the great restoration of capitalism but also to interpret the costs and benefits of the two most recent eras that have brought Latin America to this point.

Clearly the foundations of growth were established in the 1870–1930 era, which, while it lasted, did much to bring substantial parts of Latin America into the modern age, filling in institutional deficits left over from the colonial age and repairing the damage inflicted in the first decades of independence. Amid the new organizational infrastructure through which Latin America was increasingly engaged with the world market, incipient industrialization appeared as the harbinger of the more sweeping changes that redrew the economic map of the region after 1930.

Notwithstanding the obvious costs of the ISI policies that followed in the wake of the Great Depression and World War II, considerable strength was nevertheless added to the Latin American resource base, expanding the array of production options and creating the basis for more production versatility than the region exhibited in, say, 1929. The structure of production was totally transformed, and along with it the distribution of the labor force. But compared with the state of the region's economy at the close of the era of export-led growth, the Latin America of 1997 was richer by far in human resources and in the organizational or social capital on which everything in the last analysis rests. The feverish pace of institution building that has characterized Latin America since the 1930s has been deeply flawed and often haphazard. Protectionism run riot contributed to both misallocations of resources among sectors and industries and suboptimal efficiency at the microlevel, just as it made rent seeking pervasive and spread the opportunities for a socially corrosive corruption. Both no doubt contributed to the lopsided distribution of income for which Latin America has become notorious.

Yet real factor productivity has nonetheless chalked up impressive advances in most of the region, and there has been an enormous amount of learning by doing, in both public and private sectors. For all the problems and setbacks, per capita income for an awesomely larger population has reached levels far above those that prevailed before market-induced industrialization was joined by policy-induced industrialization.

In country after country, comparative advantages based on natural endowments have been supplanted by comparative advantages derived from organizational growth and the accumulation of human capital. For example, Brazil, noted as late as the mid-1960s for its overwhelming export dependence on coffee, became, thanks to policy adaptations that began in the latter part of that decade, a country whose exports have consisted primarily of manufactures, including a range of sophisticated exports (to highly competitive markets) that extends from *telenovelas* and oil field services to aircraft and automobiles, in addition to an increasingly diversified primary commodity base. Colombia, another coffee country, has learned to export coal, petroleum, flowers, and a variety of other products. Chile has moved away from a lopsided dependence on copper into a varied basket of higher-value products, and Mexican industrial products are eating into the commanding lead acquired in the 1970s by petroleum exports.[20]

The Chilean case is particularly instructive. Given the disruptive policy shifts introduced by the Allende regime of the early 1970s and the Pinochet regime that followed, the Chilean industrial sector might have been expected to vanish in the face of rapid trade liberalization and a deliberately overvalued currency, policies adopted as the cornerstones of restructuring—especially when the banking system, which was ruined under Allende, collapsed a second time in the midst of the restructuring. Nevertheless, the manufacturing sector managed to survive and grow stronger, in organizational capacity and efficiency if not in scale, and the economy as a whole eventually turned in a stellar performance year after year.

In short, behind the debt and peso crises and all the *Sturm und Drang* of the restructuring controversies, the evidence is unmistakable that the three consecutive policy regimes that began around 1870 have enabled the current restructuring to be carried out with considerable success. The new climate has also made the Mercosur, North American Free Trade Agreement (NAFTA), and the general economic opening effective catalysts for economic revival and renewal. In this, the reborn regional integration movement offers a notable contrast to the various experiments that characterized the 1960s: the Central American Common Market (CACM), the Latin American Free Trade Agreement (LAFTA), the Caribbean Free Trade Agreement (CARIFTA), and the Andean Pact, all of which petered out after their initial momentum—victims of economic nationalism, contradictory policies, feckless bureaucrats, and faulty design. Today the Mercosur (which comprises Brazil, Argentina, Uruguay, and Paraguay) has emerged as the largest and most successful example of regional economic cooperation in the Third World, and NAFTA, for all its stresses and strains, represents a bold attempt to meld economies more disparate than any of those brought together in the European Union.[21]

To be sure, a number of troubling accounts payable remain on the national ledger sheets—the so-called social deficit. Environmental conditions have deteriorated over much of the continent, and the cities have patently exceeded the carrying capacity of their infrastructure, with consequent decay in the living conditions for all, even the rich. Their walled compounds admit increasingly polluted air, and from time to time they must sally forth to confront growing congestion and social disorder.[22]

Huge numbers of people and much of the rural sector have been left on the sidelines in the sweeping renovation effort, and the disparities among regions and income classes are greater than ever before.[23] Compared with the high-performance Asian economies, the most unequal Asian income distributions are more equitable than the least unequal of the Latin American cases. And the people Columbus encountered on his voyages mostly live still in a state of economic and cultural anorexia, as powerless politically as they are deprived of assets and purchasing power in the economic arena.[24]

Much remains to be done to make the current national projects credible as a path for general progress.[25] But for all its ills, Latin America has more resources today than it has ever had before to enlist in the needed cleanup and social rectification efforts, which cannot be postponed much longer, and more social capability and institutional capacity as well. Considering that these assets too are products of development (albeit nonmeasured public goods components that are not conventionally reckoned in the national accounts) and considering as well that they contribute importantly to the future capacity to produce, one could reasonably conclude that the recorded growth figures for much of the last century, high as they were, have actually understated the rate of change—though a full and balanced accounting would have to tally the accumulated social costs as a major offset to this record of achievement. In Argentina, the legacy costs, politically speaking, seem insurmountable, at least for the time being, and the same is true for the other populist countries. Mexico, with a greater productive potential than ever before, has suffered for the time being from the US recession as well as from the appalling political and social costs associated with the illegal narcotics industry and the violence it has visited on the country. While the US economic recovery will take care of the former problem, no resolution is as yet in sight for the latter, and the costs may continue to mount. No country shares Brazil's enviable position: its remarkable adroitness in policy design and implementation, together with its ever growing resource base, seems to ensure continued expansion and moderation of inequality for as far as the eye can see. Perhaps only the outcomes in the current century will enable us to judge with some assurance of accuracy the net asset or liability position of the region as a whole and its constituent economies. Whether a sixth restructuring will be needed or a refinement of the last one will suffice will constitute the economic drama of the years immediately ahead.

NOTES

1. The World Bank groups economies into four categories. Low-income countries, mostly in Africa and Asia, include the large majority of the world's population. Most of Latin America has climbed into the lower-middle-income or upper-middle-income category, alongside Turkey, the central and eastern European countries, and the ex-Soviet republics, as well as the high-performance Asian economies.

2. The literature on Latin American economic history is enormous. Readers interested in it can conveniently begin with relevant volumes in Leslie Bethell, ed., *The Cambridge History of Latin America* (New York: Cambridge University Press, 1984); or William Glade, *The Latin American Economies: A Study of Their Institutional Evolution* (New York: American Book Company, 1969). See also B. R. Mitchell, *International Historical Statistics: The Americas and Australasia, 1750–1988* (Detroit: Gale, 1983).

3. Large city-state empires run by Aztecs (in Mexico) and Incas (in Peru, Ecuador, and Bolivia) at the time of the conquest were agriculturally based and boasted extensive trade routes within them, partly to collect tribute and sacrificial victims from subjugated peoples. The Maya were by then in an advanced state of decline. Apart from a few others, such as the Chibcha in Colombia, the remaining Amerindian groupings were still in the

hunting and fishing stage of technological development—with scattered regions of sedentary agriculture. Long-distance traffic was moved by human bearers over footpaths, there being no wheeled carts or draft animals (other than the llamas used as pack animals). Thus two immense adjustments had to occur with European colonization: the shift of cropland to pasturage to fuel the new transport technology based on pack and draft animals and a massive dedication of resources to road and bridge construction, an undertaking made immensely costly by the topography and distances involved.

4. The latifundiary foundations of Spanish America were not part of the original aims of the crown, which in principle was also committed to protection of the native population. A voluminous corpus of decrees, partly administered by royal officials and partly overseen by a parallel ecclesiastical bureaucracy, was designed to safeguard the social blueprint on which the empire was theoretically constructed. But the chronic hunger of the royal treasury had to be fed by all kinds of expedients, ranging from the sale of lower-level offices to payments by which land claims, even illegal ones, could be regularized, and problems of communication and bureaucratic oversight reduced the efficiency (and integrity) of administration. Thus the collision between metropolitan ideals and New World realities left a deposit of institutions that shaped social relations in ways that were unintended but were foundational for what came afterward. Brazil, in contrast, was based explicitly on large-scale plantation agriculture for export, utilizing imported slave labor, almost from the beginning, and its administrative overlay was much less complex than in Spanish America.

5. Jeffrey G. Williamson, *Five Centuries of Latin American Inequality*, NBER Working Paper 15305, August 2009.

6. Had these economists had a better address, say, in England or France, they would undoubtedly have been credited with great contributions to the embryonic science of economics. But in Spain they worked beyond the intellectual pale defined by the upcoming liberal modernization movements of the Enlightenment and hence never figured much in any citation index of the day.

7. Neither the ending of the empire in exchange for republican government nor the abolition of slavery, both of which events came at the dawning of the belle époque (1890–1914), occasioned serious conflict in Brazil.

8. The term refers to the standard policy package recommended by the IMF and the World Bank for countries in need of economic resuscitation: macroeconomic stabilization programs, trade liberalization, deregulation of prices (including interest rates) and general business activity (including foreign investment), market-based exchange-rate policies, and privatization, inter alia.

9. For a path into the huge literature on agrarian development, see Robert G. Keith, *Haciendas and Plantations in Latin American History* (New York: Holmes & Meier, 1977).

10. The spread of latifundism to dimensions unimagined even by the end of the colonial age was fostered by factors both political and technological. In the political realm, the ownership of government was held by the class most interested in expanding its landholdings, and liberal ideology provided a cloak for self-aggrandizement. In the technology realm, the spread of railways and telecommunications conferred value on parts of the public domain that had formerly held no interest for anyone save the native population that lived there.

11. In this region, where a relatively gentle topography and temperate climate facilitated agriculture and ranching, the cheap construction of roads and railways, supplemented by South America's most important inland waterway, spurred development and heightened the productivity of the immense amount of human capital that arrived through mass immigration from Europe.

12. The period is well covered in Rosemary Thorp, ed., *Latin America in the 1930s: The Role of the Periphery in World Crisis* (New York: St. Martin's, 1984).

13. The ECLA became in effect a graduate school for training a new generation of Latin American economists, the principal source of doctrinal inspiration for national industrial policies, a major purveyor of technical assistance for project and program planning, and the generator of a systematic strategy of development that was widely borrowed in other less developed parts of the world. See Sebastian Edwards, *Forty Years of Latin America's Economic Development: From the Alliance for Progress to the Washington Consensus,* NBER Working Paper 15190, July 2009, for a generally critical assessment of what occurred in the phase of import substituting industrialization and how such internal contradictions as endemic inflation and balance of payments problems, to name only two, brought the process to an end.

14. The International Labour Organization, the Food and Agriculture Organization, and various other UN-related entities also came onto the Latin American stage in this era.

15. Smaller but important inter-American contributions, especially in institution building, were made by the Peace Corps and the Inter-American Development Foundation, and by private US foundations such as Kellogg, Rockefeller, and Ford. The private foundations, however, had in some instances begun their Latin American programs before the 1960s, and by the end of that decade they were drawing back in favor of new programs in the United States. Significant advances in building Latin American intellectual capital resulted from their efforts as well as from the investments of others such as the Tinker Foundation, the Latin American Scholarship Program of American Universities, the US Agency for International Development, a variety of church-related undertakings, and the Fulbright program.

16. Extremely effective analysis of the destabilizing patterns of policy that developed is contained in Rudiger Dornbusch and Sebastian Edwards, *The Macroeconomics of Populism in Latin America* (Chicago: University of Chicago Press, 1991).

17. An ever-increasing overburden of regulation was applied to foreign direct investment, and restrictive regulation was also applied to technology transfers. A culmination of sorts was reached in the Andean Pact countries in the form of provisions to accelerate foreign disinvestment.

18. A different set of events had brought the Chilean economy to collapse in 1973, with the result that the fifth restructuring began there as a pioneering experiment in the mid-1970s, a decade before similar policies were introduced elsewhere in the region. For the Chilean case, see Dominique Hachette and Rolf Luders-Schwarzenburg, *Privatization in Chile: An Economic Appraisal* (San Francisco: ICSS Press, 1993); and Barry Bosworth, Rudiger Dornbush, and Raúl Laban, eds., *The Chilean Economy: Policy Lessons and Challenges* (Washington, DC: Brookings Institution, 1994). For the debt crisis, see S. Griffith-Jones and Osvaldo Sunkel, *Debt and Development Crises in Latin America: The End of an Illusion* (New York: Oxford University Press, 1986); and Robert Devlin, *Debt and Crisis in Latin America: The Supply Side of the Story* (Princeton: Princeton University Press, 1994).

19. Sebastian Edwards, *Crisis and Reform in Latin America: From Despair to Hope* (New York: Oxford University Press, 1995), provides a masterful review of the reform measures and their impacts.

20. Montague Lord, "Manufacturing Exports," in *Economic and Social Progress in Latin America, 1992* (Washington, DC: Inter-American Development Bank, 1992).

21. Greece and Portugal, the poorest members, were much smaller than Mexico and also relatively closer to European levels in per capita income—and therefore more readily "digestible." The closer counterpart to the NAFTA combination would have been the ad-

mission of Turkey into the European Community, a challenge the Europeans prudently declined.

22. Gordon J. MacDonald, Daniel L. Nielson, and Marc A. Stern, eds., *Latin American Environmental Policy in International Perspective* (Boulder: Westview, 1997); Michael Painter and William H. Durham, eds., *The Social Causes of Environmental Destruction in Latin America* (Ann Arbor: University of Michigan Press, 1995).

23. Samuel A. Morley, *Poverty and Inequality in Latin America* (Baltimore: Johns Hopkins University Press, 1995); William Thiesenhusen, *Broken Promises: Agrarian Reform and the Latin American Campesino* (Boulder: Westview, 1995).

24. George Psacharaopoulos and Harry A. Patrinos, eds., *Indigenous People and Poverty in Latin America* (Washington, DC: World Bank, 1994); and Donna Lee Van Cott, ed., *Indigenous Peoples and Democracy in Latin America* (New York: St. Martin's, 1994).

25. Dagmar Raczynski, ed., *Strategies to Combat Poverty in Latin America* (Washington, DC: Inter-American Development Bank, 1996).

SUGGESTED READINGS

Agosin, Manuel R., ed. *Foreign Direct Investment in Latin America*. Washington, DC: Inter-American Development Bank, 1995. With its focus on the revival of capital inflows into a restructured region, this book is well paired with another book from the same publisher, Jose Antonio Ocampo and Roberto Steiner, eds., *Foreign Capital in Latin America* (1994). Both are strongly technical in their analysis.

Baer, Werner. *The Brazilian Economy: Growth and Development*. 6th ed. New York: Praeger, 2001. It is not hard to understand why this masterful analysis of Latin America's largest economy has gone through so many editions.

Bethell, Leslie, ed. *The Cambridge History of Latin America*. New York: Cambridge University Press, 1984. This landmark work has chapters on economic aspects scattered among its multiple volumes.

Bresser Pereira, Luiz Carlos. *Economic Crisis and State Reform in Brazil: Toward a New Interpretation of Latin America*. Boulder: Lynne Rienner, 1996. A noted specialist who grew to professional maturity under ISI speaks his piece on what has come to pass with the structural adjustment reforms, though Brazil has lagged notably on making many of them.

Glade, William. *The Latin American Economies: A Study of Their Institutional Evolution*. New York: American Book Company, 1969.

Gordon, Wendell. *The Political Economy of Latin America*. New York: Columbia University Press, 1966. One of the best of the several textbooks written in the 1960s and 1970s on Latin American development.

Hachette, Dominique, and Rolf Luders-Schwarzenberg. *Privatization in Chile: An Economic Appraisal*. San Francisco: ICS Publishers, 1993. A magisterial analysis of this controversial policy in Latin America's trailblazing country.

Huber, Evelyn, and Frank Safford, eds. *Agrarian Structure and Political Power: Landlord and Peasant in the Making of Latin America*. Pittsburgh: University of Pittsburgh Press, 1995.

Inter-American Development Bank. *Economic and Social Progress in Latin America*. An annual report containing current economic information on the different countries, a useful set of time series data, and an extended analytical treatment of particular aspects of Latin American development, such as fiscal decentralization, social security reform, manufacturing exports, and so on. Earlier volumes have titles that vary slightly from the latest volumes.

Maddison, Angus, et al. *The Political Economy of Poverty, Equity, and Growth: Brazil and Mexico*. New York: Oxford University Press, 1992. One of a series of paired country studies by World Bank specialists, this one provides an intimate look at the two most important Latin American economies that for all their historical differences have gone through many of the same development policy hoops in recent years.

Almeida, Ozorio de, Anna Luiza, and João S. Campari. *Sustainable Settlement in the Brazilian Amazon*. New York: Oxford University Press, 1995. A well-reasoned and well-documented analytical foray into a controversial facet of Latin American development; the problem explored extends beyond Brazil. See also Charles H. Wood and Marianne Schmink, *Contested Frontiers in Amazonia* (New York: Columbia University Press, 1992), for an authoritative treatment of the demographic forces in environmental degradation.

Prebisch, Raúl. *Change and Development: Latin America's Great Task*. New York: Praeger, 1971. A rethinking of the Latin American predicament on the eve of the great borrowing spree and the oil shocks by the man who, more than any other, shaped Latin American economic policy in the postwar period. The classical statement of the prevailing diagnosis of Latin American conditions and the policy that flowed from it is found in ECLA, *The Economic Development of Latin America and Its Principal Problems* (Santíago: United Nations Economic Commission for Latin America, 1950). ECLA, *Development Problems of Latin America* (Austin: University of Texas Press, 1970), is a handy compilation of documents from the UN Economic Commission for Latin America that define the guiding vision of ISI policies.

Story, Dale. *Industry, the State, and Public Policy in Mexico*. Austin: University of Texas Press, 1986. For Mexico, see Roderic Ai Camp, *Entrepreneurs and Politics in Twentieth-Century Mexico* (New York: Oxford University Press, 1989). For an equivalent glimpse of the policy process in Brazil, see Ben Ross Schneider, *Politics Within the State: Elite Bureaucrats and Industrial Policy in Authoritarian Brazil* (Pittsburgh: University of Pittsburgh Press, 1991). These three books afford an insight into the dynamics that generated the economic outcomes analyzed by Maddison and colleagues. Although the neoliberal model has slightly altered the institutional arrangements that these three studies examined, we would be rash to assume that the old order has altogether vanished in policy determination. In Latin America, as in the United States, policymakers listen selectively.

Thiesenhusen, William C. *Broken Promises: Agrarian Reform and the Latin American Campesino*. Boulder: Westview, 1995. An important retrospective assessment by one who has followed the vagaries of agricultural policy for many years.

Tokman, Victor. *Beyond Regulation: The Informal Economy in Latin America*. Boulder: Lynne Rienner, 1992. Although the so-called informal sector was first spotted in Africa by ILO researchers, its Latin American twin has inspired a huge volume of studies, of which this is a good example. Hernando de Soto, *The Other Path: The Invisible Revolution in the Third World* (New York: Harper & Row, 1989), did much, in its earlier Spanish-language version, to stimulate scholarship on the Latin American phenomenon, though housing studies in squatter settlements during the early 1960s were perhaps the first to note the rise of the informal sector or the underground economy.

Urrutia, Miguel, ed. *Long-term Trends in Latin American Economic Development*. Washington, DC: Inter-American Development Bank, 1991. See especially chapters 1–2.

Weeks, John. *The Economies of Central America*. New York: Holmes & Meier, 1985. Though written before this troubled region began to settle down, the survey is nonetheless useful for understanding what democratic governments will have to deal with today.

Chapter 8

Social Structure and Change in Latin America

Henry Veltmeyer and James Petras

For close to three decades, from the 1950s to the end of the 1970s, Latin America experienced historically unprecedented high rates of economic growth—around 5 percent in the aggregate and 2.5 percent on a per capita basis. This growth, together with associated developments, was based on a model of state-led development characterized by (1) government intervention in the economy, including regulation of private activity and restrictions on foreign investment; (2) an inward orientation of production, producing for the domestic rather than the world market; (3) import substitution, protecting and encouraging the growth of domestic industry; and (4) growth with equity, social reform to improve access of small producers to the means of production (land, capital, and technology) and the share of working-class families in the national income.

In the 1970s, this process of development was arrested and reversed by governments in Chile and Argentina, both military dictatorships, acting in the interest of the economically dominant propertied class, which was deeply concerned about the mounting claims made by a restive working class and landless peasantry against their property. In the 1980s, under conditions of a region-wide debt crisis and a democratization process (the return to state power by elected regimes and the rule of law), a solution was found to both the growing power of the working class and the widespread economic imbalances. The structural adjustment program (SAP), as it was called at the time, was a series of economic stabilization measures and structural reforms designed by the economists at the World Bank on the basis of a Washington Consensus on the policies needed to bring about a new world order of neoliberal globalization in which the "forces of freedom" would be liberated from the shackles and regulatory constraints of the welfare development state, promoting free market capitalist development on a global scale.[1]

Pioneered by Chile's military regime under Augusto Pinochet but eventually adopted by or imposed on the other governments in the region, the SAP provides a standard recipe for curing a country's ills: (1) stabilization of the currency (adoption of a "realistic" exchange rate, i.e., devaluation); (2) liberalization of trade and capital flows, eliminating or reducing trade barriers and favorable treatment of domestic capital; (3) reorientation of production toward the world market and opening up the economy to foreign competition; (4) deregulation of private activity; (5) privatization of public enterprises and all means of social production; (6) downsizing the state, reducing the scale and scope of its market intervention, eliminating subsidies and control of prices; and (7) fiscal austerity—a policy of fiscal discipline and balanced budgets. After two and a half decades of such policies based on a neoliberal model of economic development,[2] Latin America today is a very different place from what it was in the 1970s and what it was becoming. In the process, a revolution—or rather a counterrevolution—has been wrought in the social structure of Latin American society and the distribution of the social product.

It is of critical importance to understand the nature of this social structure. For one thing, the capacity for people to change this structure and thereby to improve the conditions of their social existence to some extent depends on this understanding. For another, it is not possible to understand the development of Latin American society in its critical dimensions (economic, social, political) without a solid grasp of the social structure that underlies this development.

THE SOCIAL STRUCTURE OF LATIN AMERICA

There are three basic levels to social analysis. One is in terms of the distribution or composition of a population's social characteristics. At this level, we can identify a number of ascribed or socially constructed features such as gender, age, race/ethnicity, and achieved characteristics such as level of education. A second form of analysis operates at a different (structural) level, identifying sets of positions occupied by groups of people and the social and economic conditions associated with these positions. Arguably, this is the most critical level of social analysis, requiring a combination of theoretical abstraction and empirical analysis. A third type of social analysis is based on the subjective and political conditions of people's behavior and experience, identifying the forms of their social awareness and action associated with their shared position. In practice, the problem is how and where to combine these three forms of social analysis—to make the appropriate or necessary connections.

At the structural level, a number of critical factors and defining characteristics can be identified. One is spatial distribution and location. In these terms, Table 8.1 distinguishes between two groups of the population, one located in the region's urban centers and the other in the countryside, in the smaller communities and farms of rural society. The table also points toward a fundamental change in the urban-rural distribution of the population as well as in the gender composition of the labor force since the 1970s.

Table 8.1 identifies significant country-by-country variations in the urban-rural distribution of the population. It highlights major changes in the structure of this distribution over the past two and a half decades, which many economists and sociologists associate with what might be termed the "great transformation": the transformation of a traditional, agrarian and precapitalist form of society and economy into a modern industrial capitalist system. Behind this transformation (driving the forces of change, as it were) is a process of capitalist development and proletarianization (the separation of the direct producers from their means of pro-

TABLE 8.1   The Population of Latin America: Some Basic Distributions, Selected Countries, 1975–2008

	Population (2010)[a] Millions	% Urban[b] '75	% Urban[b] '00	Labor Participation Rate[c] F/M '75	Labor Participation Rate[c] F/M '06/07	Labor Participation Rate[c] % F/M '06/07
Argentina	40.5	78	90	30/69	50/75	47
Bolivia	10.4	41	65	62/82	48/68	58
Brazil	199.9	56	80	36/76	58/80	52
Chile	17.1	75	86	43/73	38/66	49
Colombia	47.9	57	75	29/64	52/80	61
Ecuador	14.2	45	63	21/70	54/81	39
Mexico	110.1	59	75	26/71	48/82	48
Uruguay	3.4	82	93	25/67	54/75	67
Venezuela	28.8	72	87	25/67	50/79	54
Central America/Cuba	56.8	42	56			
Caribbean, English Speaking	42.3	49	67			
Latin America + Caribbean	593.7					

Sources: (a-b) ECLAC, Statistical Yearbook, 2002; ECLAC, Demographic Bulletin, No. 69. Latin America and the Caribbean: Population Estimates and Projections, 2002.

duction and the transformation of small-scale or peasant agricultural producers into a proletariat). However, the tangible feature of structural change that many analysts fix on is *urbanization*—the shift of the "economically active population" (to use a concept favored by economists) from the rural areas or countryside to the cities and urban centers. Indeed, as Table 8.2 makes evident, Latin America has witnessed a rapid process of urbanization over the past three decades of capitalist development, although this development has not proceeded according to the dominant theory—the surplus labor released from the countryside in the migration of the rural poor would be absorbed by modern capitalist industry, providing ample opportunities for wage-labor and social mobility.[3] What has developed instead is the growth of an enormous sub- and semiproletariat of street workers and what Mike Davis (2006) has described as a "planet of slums" in a burgeoning urban sprawl.

Table 8.2 shows that, in most cases, the population shift toward urban centers involves a change of at least ten percentage points. Table 8.2 also identifies a trend toward the feminization of the labor force. This trend, identified in the relative shift of women and men in labor force participation from 1975 to 2005, has accelerated over the past three decades of capitalist development, even though the participation rate of women in the urban labor force is still below that of men as well as that of women in other parts of the world. More significant, however, is that relative to men, women are generally integrated into the urban economy under conditions of sexist discrimination and a higher rate of exploitation. This is reflected in the fact that most employment growth over the past two decades has been in a sector characterized by low pay, poor working conditions, and irregularity; and women are disproportionately represented in jobs with these forms of employment and working conditions. Another indicator of sexism in the labor force can be found in the male/female ratio of average earned income by job in the urban labor force, which in economies as diverse as Bolivia, Chile, Mexico, and Venezuela ranges from .38 to .45 (UNDP 2003, Table 23). In many parts of the world over the past two decades women's participation rate has begun to approach men's, and the gender ratio of earned income is more in the range of .65 to .70. Clearly women in these situations still have a long way to go in their protracted struggle for equality. But it is just as clear that in many Latin American societies and economies they have an even greater distance to travel in this struggle, which, it could be added, is an important part of a wider class struggle.

Even a preliminary and limited demographic analysis identifies patterns in these variations in socioeconomic and working conditions that correspond to differences in a broader social structure. To some degree this is reflected in other elements of this structure, such as the distribution of economic activities (Table 8.2) and the associated pattern of income distribution (Table 8.3). A cursory examination of these patterns indicates that the corresponding "structures" (institutionalized patterns or ways of doing things) are interconnected and form a system. An individual's economic activity and share of society's productive resources or wealth, as well as the income derived from ownership of or access to this wealth, is directly related to his or her position within the social structure.

Within the economic and social system in place throughout Latin America and elsewhere, income is a critically important determinant of an individual and each household's "life chances" (to use a term coined by Max Weber). Most people require money or income for meeting their basic needs, and the major source of this income is work, either for wages or a salary (employment) or on one's own account (self-employment) or commodity production (the direct production of goods and services for sale). Latin American society, with the exception of Cuba, includes a class of individuals who receive income in the form of rent or profit derived from their ownership of property in the means of social production. Most people, however, have to work for a living—they are part of the working class, dispossessed of land or any other means of production and thus dependent on the sale of their labor power. Table 8.4 provides a graphic, if theoretical, representation of the class structure of Latin American society and of the position of workers and producers in the popular sector of this structure.

THE LATIN AMERICAN SOCIAL STRUCTURE

To gauge the social and political forces generated in support or in resistance to the neoliberal (market-oriented) economic reforms implemented in the 1980s, it is important to examine the underlying social structure. Changes in this structure over the past two decades of forces of change and policy reforms have had a significant impact on the politics of change—on the forces that have been mobilized in support of or opposition to the neoliberal model. The neoliberal reforms implemented under the Washington Consensus have also produced changes in class

TABLE 8.2 The Structure of Economic Activity: Selected Countries Listed in Reverse Order of GDP per Capita, 2000-2007

	GDP per capita[a] ($ US 2006/2007)	% Share of Total Production (2005)[b]		
		Agriculture	Industry	Services
Bolivia	1,090	22	28	68
Ecuador	1,628	11	15	63
Peru	2,751	8	27	65
Colombia	2,861	13	30	57
Brazil	4,183	8	36	56
Venezuela	5,787	5	50	45
Chile	6,127	11	34	56
Mexico	7,094	4	27	69
Uruguay	7,255	6	27	67
Argentina	9,397	5	28	68

Source: (a) *ECLAC, Statistical Yearbook for Latin America and the Caribbean, 2008,* A.1. (b) World Bank, World Development Report (2006), pp. 238-39.

TABLE 8.3 Shares of National Income by Poorest/Richest Groups: % Poor Households: Selected Countries Ranked by Level of HD in 2007

HDI Rank[1]		Poorest 40% (2006/07)	Richest 10% (2006/07)	Poor Households % (2006/07)	
34	Argentina	15.4	34.1	23.7	21.0
40	Uruguay	21.1	27.5	17.9	18.1
43	Chile	14.6	37.2	38.5	13.9
55	Mexico	16.9	32.9	42.1	26.8
64	Colombia	12.2	41.0	52.7	45.4
65	Brazil	12.7	42.1	41.2	26.9
69	Venezuela	18.4	25.7	38.6	-
97	Ecuador	15.4	35.5	62.1	38.8
114	Bolivia	11.2	35.5	52.6	42.4

Sources: World Bank, *World Development Report,* 2003; ECLAC, *Statistical Yearbook for Latin America and the Caribbean,* 2008, A.6.

1. The UNDP in its annual report (2002) ranks 175 countries according to their level of 'human development,' an index (HDI) that aggregates and weights the score of each country on (i) GDP (national income) per capita, measured in terms of 'purchasing power parity' (PPP) rather than official currency exchange rates; (ii) longevity, measured in terms of life expectancy; and (iii) level and quality of education, an indicator of a person's capacity of choice in their life.

TABLE 8.4   The Latin American Class Structure (Estimated Distribution of the Population by Social Class)

	Urban	*Rural*
Capitalist Class	4	2
Middle Class		
Management/Professional (UM)	5	2
Business operators/entrepreneurs (M)	10	4
Service providers, technicians, etc.	11	7
Family farmers (medium-sized) (M)		10
Working Class (proletariat)		
Formal (factories, offices, mines)	21	10
Informal /semi-proletariat (street, land)	49	35
Agricultural Producers (popular sector)		
Small-scale commodity producers		10
Peasant farmers		20

Source: These very rough estimates of the class distribution of the population in Latin America are based on official laborforce data provided by ECLAC in its annual *Statistical Yearbook* (2008) and its *Social Panorama of Latin America*, Statistical Annex (2008). Also see the ILO's *World Employment Report* (2006). It is not possible to accurately gauge the class structure because official laborforce data distribute the population on the basis of an industrial and occupational classification that does not correspond to the structure of class relations. The above estimates are based on simple averages of statistics provided for the eight largest countries in the region that account for over 90% of the total population. For example, regarding the figure of 49% for the urban laborforce that is in the unstructured 'informal' sector, statistics vary from a high of 65% in Peru and 65% in Bolivia to an estimated 31% in Chile, and 42% in Argentina and Brazil. 49% represents an unweighted average for the eight countries in South America.

relations and associated conditions, mobilizing the social forces of resistance and change in the popular sector.

The major element of the social structure in Latin American societies is the relationship of capital to labor, which encompasses both those who own the means of production and those who have been dispossessed of all means of production, left only with their labor power, which they have to exchange for a wage. In addition to these two basic classes, there are several classes of individuals who occupy a position somewhere in between or located entirely outside the structure of the wage-labor relation. The most important of these is composed of individuals who own some means of production, physical and tangible or mental and intangible, but are not in a position to purchase the labor power of the direct producers. These individuals are generally viewed as part of the traditional middle class, sharing this position with intellectuals, professionals, and low-level managers of capitalist or public enterprises.

The Capitalist Class

Members of the capitalist class are easy enough to identify by the size of their capital (big, medium, small) and by functional criteria (industrial, commercial, financial, rentier), as well as by the perquisites of their position, such as wealth and power. Estimates as to the size of the capitalist class range from a low of 3 percent in countries like Bolivia to 5–6 percent for Argentina, Brazil, Chile, and Mexico, and with a weighted regional average of under 5 percent of the economically active population (EAP). The employer category in Table 8.4 provides a rough (and admittedly poor) proxy measure of this class, assuming that the capitalist sector is about two-thirds of all employers and that the vast majority of these employers dispose of very little capital. In actual fact, the core of the capitalist class is composed of people who derive most of their income from investment. The population census lists these individuals—making up less than 1 percent of most national populations—in the category of financiers.

The core of this class is composed of individuals connected to the "big economic groups," a complex of banking, industrial, and agro-export conglomerates. In each country a small group of such conglomerates (big economic groups) can be identified, in addition to larger groupings (the new bourgeoisie) formed with the free market reforms implemented since the 1980s. It is possible in each country to identify various factions and groupings within the dominant capitalist class in terms of the source as well as size of their capital. For example, in Mexico and to various lesser degrees in other countries, there is a large and politically significant bureaucratic class formed on the basis of privileged access to state resources and its regulatory and other powers. This part of the Mexican bourgeoisie is internally divided into different factions and connected through ties of common interest to other factions of the capitalist class such as the industrialists, financiers, and bankers. In addition to these capitalists, there are groups of individuals who serve as CEOs of the transnational corporations that operate in each country or are connected to institutions such as the International Monetary Fund (IMF). They form a powerful faction of the capitalist class as a whole, with resources and connections that constitute a significant factor in the internal and political dynamics of the class struggle.

Policies instituted in the 1980s created several other elements of the dominant capitalist class. Of particular significance here is the large-scale privatization of public enterprises undertaken by many regimes. In the case of Mexico, the privatization of over a thousand state enterprises under the administration of Carlos Salinas from 1989 to 1994 spawned a number of enormous private fortunes, which are reflected in the identification by *Forbes* in 1993 of twenty-four billionaires in Mexico, more than the number identified for all of Latin America just two years earlier. These billionaires, who include Carlos Slim, currently ranked by *Forbes* as the richest man in the world, together with their not quite so wealthy associates (the thousands of mere millionaires created in the economic reform process), form the core of the region's new bourgeoisie, a propertied and entrepreneurial class that is well connected to the local political establishments as well as to the international financial institutions (IFIs) and multinational corporations (MNCs) that dominate the global economy. This bourgeoisie forms a part—albeit subordinate—of what the sociologist Leslie Sklair (1997) has termed the "transnational capitalist class" and the authors the "global ruling class."

The Middle Class

Important components of the middle class include those who hold land for the purpose of agricultural production and those who operate small businesses, mostly in the urban centers. Although these two components vary significantly by country and have been subject to forces that have tended to decimate them, they remain numerically—and politically—important in most countries. The expansion of corporate capital has had a negative impact on the conditions of existence and survival of both the independent smallholders of land and urban-centered businesses. The specific impact of the government's economic policies on their enterprises and activities is more difficult to gauge. In every country a large number of small businesses and landholdings—over 50 percent in many cases—involve marginal economic operations, microenterprises, whose owners are barely able to survive in the so-called informal sector. In this connection it is possible to distinguish between the formal petite bourgeoisie (the traditional middle class) and an informal petite bourgeoisie (mostly a highly indebted group of family farmers), which comprises an estimated 10 percent of the region's EAP.

Another key element of the middle class is often identified as professionals—individuals who provide a broad range of intellectual services, from the semiprofessional services of teachers, technicians, social workers, bureaucrats, and office managers to the professional and high-level management and business services provided by the legion of well-paid functionaries (of capital as well as government). A number of sociologists view these high-level functionaries and managers of capitalist and state enterprise as a distinct (professional management) class that constitutes an estimated 4–5 percent of the EAP in most countries. This is probably a fair estimate if restricted to the upper stratum of paid functionaries and distinguished from the two other major and much larger elements of the middle class—small proprietors (independent producers and business operators) and lower-level paid functionaries (salaried employees in public and private enterprises, semiprofessionals, and intellectuals).

The size of this social category (the middle class) in different societies is difficult to measure, largely because of the ambiguity of its position in the class structure. In countries like Argentina it is very large—perhaps as much as 30 percent of the economically active population. In other countries, such as Bolivia and Ecuador, with a sizable multiethnic or plurinational population, it is much smaller. As salaried employees, they can also be regarded as part of the working class—a white-collar element concerned with some form of mental or nonphysical labor. In any case, whether viewed as a stratum of the middle class or the working class, these individuals probably make up 10–15 percent of the EAP. In Table 8.4 they are subsumed under the formal working class, with no attempt to differentiate among different categories of stratification or possible political divisions—manual and mental, waged and salaried, urban and rural, private and public sector, male and female, organized and unorganized.

Whether or not these categories relate to differences in political orientation or response is hard to say, a matter of empirical analysis. A cursory look at the political responses to the neoliberal policies implemented in the 1980s and 1990s suggests that there is a strong element of resistance and opposition from groups tied to the education system, state enterprises, and the bureaucracy. This is because individuals and groups in this public sector have been seriously affected by policies of privatization and the cutback of the state apparatus. To a considerable but varying degree in different countries, neoliberal policies have produced a bifurcation of this class, with some elements doing well and accommodated to the neoliberal agenda and other elements doing poorly and disposed toward resistance. In a number of contexts like Argentina and Mexico, this class constitutes an important if not critical factor in the dynamics of social change.

The Working Class

The working class comprises the vast majority of the population but takes diverse forms. In many countries it has been substantially restructured as a result of policy-induced economic and political conditions associated with SAPs. Today's working class differs from that of the 1980s. Back then most workers worked in the private sector of capitalist and small businesses and in the public sector—in factories, industrial plants, mines, and offices. Today, however, most workers in many countries work "on their own account" or for miserable wages under precarious conditions and without benefits or social security—on the streets or in the service and retail sectors. In rural society most workers labor seasonally for low wages or mix subsistence farming with off-farm wage labor. A sharp distinction thus has to be made between an industrial proletariat and traditional wage laborers (only a small part of the working class today) and those who work in the streets and on their own account, or without pay (housewives and unpaid family members). In the context of developments since the 1980s, the latter has assumed a growing proportion of the working class in all countries (see Table 8.3).

(i) The Formal Sector. Together with the big and the petite bourgeoisie, these workers make up the so-called modern or capitalist sector of the economy, which accounts for an estimated 30 percent of the regional EAP. Estimates as to the size of this class fluctuate widely but essentially define three categories of countries: the Southern Cone (Argentina, Chile, Uruguay), where the formal proletariat represents a clear majority of the EAP; an intermediate grouping of countries (Brazil, Costa Rica, Panama, Peru) in which this class amounts to at least 25 percent of the EAP; and the rest of Latin America, where it represents on average barely 10 percent of the population.

In the 1960s and 1970s, these workers formed the social base of organized labor—the union movement that in each country led the struggle against capital for better wages and working conditions. And in the 1970s, in the context of a region-wide (indeed worldwide) counteroffensive by capital, this class was also the chief target of state repression, of the "dirty war" against subversives waged by the national security military regimes that took state power all over the region. In the 1980s context of a regional debt crisis, the institution of market-friendly reforms, and a redemocratization process, the formal proletariat also bore the brunt of efforts to restructure the economy and the society. In this process, the industrial proletariat in the private sector, the backbone of the labor movement, was severely retrenched and in some cases decimated. From 1988 to 1992, these industries lost 1.3 million workers, a process that continued to unfold throughout the 1990s. As a result of these developments, the industrial proletariat was reduced to a shadow of what it had once been—decimated numerically, weakened organizationally, and everywhere on the defensive, with a weak leadership accommodated to tripartite or corporatist arrangements, unable to mount an effective campaign or mobilize the significant potential political forces of labor against capital.

By the end of the 1980s public sector employees and workers constituted an important part of both the working class and the labor movement. This was the result of a decades-long process of state-led development in infrastructure and social services as well as the nationalization of enterprises in strategic industries such as oil. However, a key element of the new economic model of structural adjustment to the requirements of a single global economy (globalization) was a policy of privatization—turning over (or returning) public enterprises to the private sector (profit making). Carlos Salinas de Gortari, president of Mexico from 1988 to 1994, turned over 1,100 public enterprises to the private sector, effectively privatizing all public enterprises in the key sectors of the economy—with the exception of electric power generation and the extraction and processing of oil. In the 1990s the other political regimes in the region, notably in Argentina and Brazil, the two other biggest economies in the region (with Mexico, accounting up to 75 percent of the gross regional product), followed suit. By the end of the decade the privatization agenda had weakened the public sector of the labor movement both numerically and politically.

(ii) **The Informal Sector.** The largest component of the working class, representing in many countries over half of the labor force and as much as 65 percent of workers (in the case of Bolivia and Peru), the informal proletariat is characterized by a diverse mix of production relations: irregular and nonstandard forms of wage labor for operators of small and unstable enterprises; part-time or casual labor without the protection of a legal contract (at least 54 percent of all workers); wage labor for subcontractors; self-employment (the operation of unregulated microenterprises producing or selling goods and services in the home, in makeshift workplaces, and in the streets); domestic services to middle-class and bourgeois households; and an array of illegal activities ranging from petty thievery, burglary, and smuggling to the manufacture, distribution, and sale of drugs. By all accounts the size of this class, combined with the small-firm sector, has been on the rise, increasing its share of the EAP from less than a third in the early 1980s to over half of the occupied labor force in the late 1990s. According to Alejandro Portes and colleagues (1989) and studies by the International Labor Organization, in a number of countries the informal sector accounted for up to 90 percent of job and employment growth over the past decade and a half.

The Peasantry and the Rural Proletariat

As a region Latin America is overly urbanized in relation to the capacity of industry to absorb the large numbers of individuals dispossessed of productive land or otherwise led to migrate to the rapidly growing towns and cities. In the postwar period, a large part of the rural population was pushed into the towns and cities, converted an urban proletariat. This process also led to the formation of a huge sector of informal enterprises and activities. In some cities (e.g., El Alto, a peri-urban center on the outskirts of Bolivia's capital city La Paz, with a predominantly indigenous population of rural migrants), a majority of workers live and work in the city during the week and return to the countryside on weekends, combining agricultural activity (subsistence production) with informal (unstructured) work relations and conditions, and urban-rural living, making it difficult for statisticians to mark inhabitants as either urban or rural.

In the countryside an even more complex structure of economic activities and relations of production evolved. This sector incorporated various classes of producers and workers, including both middle-class and capitalist operators of farms and businesses; a rural proletariat composed of wage workers in these sectors; a large class of smallholders, composed of individuals and households involved in farming or work under diverse relations of subsistence, independent commodity production, sharecropping, and other forms of tenancy (including, as in the case of indigenous communities in Bolivia, Ecuador, Guatemala and Mexico, various forms of communal tenure); the semiproletariat, who make up the majority of direct producers in most countries; and large numbers of landless or near-landless rural workers, in the case of Brazil totaling millions of families.

Although the EAP includes large numbers of children under working age, elders, retirees, the disabled, and other dependents, it also includes an equally large number of individuals, mostly women, whose contribution to domestic and social production is not accounted for and whose labor is not remunerated at all. The majority of rural households have at least one member in this position, accounting for a significant number—perhaps 25 percent of the rural population.

The expansion of capitalism in the countryside has resulted in variations of this class structure. In addition, it has generated various processes of change within this structure: the transformation of the hacienda system of tenant farming into capitalist farming and agribusiness—what the Inter-American Development Bank (IDB) defines as the entrepreneurial sector of commercial enterprises; the growth of temporary, casual, and seasonal forms of wage labor; the feminization of rural wage labor; and the urbanization of this labor.

THE SOCIAL IMPACT OF NEOLIBERAL REFORMS

In the summer of 1982 the Mexican government announced that it was unable to pay the interest on its accumulated external debt, sending shock waves throughout the international finance community. Under widespread structural conditions of extraordinarily high interest rates and plummeting export commodity prices, Mexico would not be alone, threatening the entire fabric of global capital. However, the IFIs, under the guardianship of the IMF, rallied in defense of the system.

The solution, imposed on or adopted by country after country in the region (most often as a condition of renegotiating debt or accessing new capital in the form of loans, aid, or investment), was a program of market-oriented economic reforms or structural adjustments. The stated goal of this program was growth and macroeconomic equilibrium (restoration of growth in the total output of goods and services under conditions of balanced budgets, the control of price inflation). There are, however, major unstated goals of these sweeping reforms, which include making sure of the capacity of countries in the region to service (make payments on) their external debts. But the major internal adjustment has been a restructuring of labor, particularly in regard to its share of national income and increased flexibility. As to labor's share of national income (as opposed to the share that goes to capital—is invested rather than consumed or used to purchase goods and services), most countries in the region have experienced a significant reduction—from 30 percent and greater (up to 40 percent in some cases) down to 20 percent and lower. These declines in the share of labor in national income signify a corresponding increase in the share given to or appropriated by capital—presumably in the interest of increasing the rate of national investment, deemed to be the most critical factor in a process of economic activation.

The social cost of this process of structural adjustment has been a deepening and extension of poverty, the conditions of which (unemployment, informalization of work relations and conditions, economic insecurity, falling wages, low income, homelessness, malnutrition, disease, illiteracy) have been borne mainly by the working class. A large part of this class has been impoverished in the process, as has a part of the middle class. In addition there are significant gender as well as class and national ethnic dimensions to poverty and other conditions of structural adjustment. In terms of the basic indicators of social development, Cuba, the one Latin American country that has pursued a socialist rather than a capitalist path, stands out as a striking anomaly, with levels of education, health, and welfare comparable to the most industrially developed countries in the world. The UNDP *Human Development Report* for both 2003 and 2006 provides a clear testament to this.

By the early 1980s, after three and a half decades of sustained economic and social change, the material conditions of social existence for the majority of the population had substantially improved. In the 1980s, however, under conditions of a widespread debt crisis and structural adjustment, these gains were wiped out. With a fall of up to 60 percent in the value of wages or purchasing power in a matter of just a few years in the 1980s, the life situation of most people in the region seriously deteriorated.

Despite a minimal and fragile recovery after close to a decade of sweeping economic reforms, in many countries the average level of income and standard of living in the 1990s was lower than it was in 1970. Under conditions that include growth in unemployment, informalization of labor relations, a drastic decline in the value of wages, and cutbacks in government services and social programs, the process of structural adjustment to which the economies in the region were subjected led to a substantial worsening in the distribution of wealth and income, already among the most unequal and inequitable in the world. The income gap between the poorest households and the richest widened and deepened, in some cases dramatically. Today in every country in the region the top decile of income earners receive over 30 percent of the national income—48 percent in the case of Brazil, which, according to the World Bank exhibits one of the most skewed income distributions in the world. Worldwide only Sierra Leone is disgraced by a greater maldistribution of income, although unlike Brazil (Petras and Veltmeyer 2003), it cannot hold government policies under the Washington Consensus responsible. Also, the decline in both the share of labor in national income and the purchasing power of workers' wages over the years, as well as the loss of employment opportunities in most countries, had a strong impact on those at the bottom of the income pyramid and class structure. The overall result has been a significant increase in income inequality for most countries in the region.

These inequalities have produced striking differences in social situations for different groups and classes of the population. At one extreme they have spawned a small number of billionaires, whose combined wealth exceeds that of half of the population and whose conditions of social existence are almost unimaginable and certainly obscene. At the other extreme, the grossly unequal distribution of wealth and income is reflected in widening and deepening poverty. The population living in poverty substantially increased during the 1980s, declined somewhat in the early 1990s, but has moved steadily upward as of 1995, with the beginnings of another decade lost to development. By the end of the decade, according to some estimates (see Table 8.3 above), over a third of all households (58 percent in Ecuador) were impoverished to the point of being unable to meet their basic needs. Most of these households are located in the urban centers, although the incidence of poverty is higher in the rural areas, home to the landless and near landless, masses of marginal small landholders and producers, and most indigenous peoples who form 10 percent or so of the population in the region (up to and more than 50 percent in countries like Ecuador, Bolivia, and Guatemala). Typically, this element of the population suffers the most blatant forms of exploitation and oppression and the resulting conditions of abject poverty.

By official accounts (CEPAL 2008), poverty rates in Latin America have been falling—or were until the current global financial crisis, which has had serious repercussions in the real economy of most societies, particularly in Mexico, the economy most integrated into the US economy at the epicenter of the crisis. It is calculated that with a decline of up to 10 percent in national production in 2009, at least 750,000 jobs have disappeared and the ranks of the poor have undoubtedly thickened. According to official statistics the poverty rate, especially as regards destitution or extreme poverty, regionwide has fallen by 25 to 30 percent over the past decade. What is unclear, however, is the explanation. For one thing, it appears that at least a part of the success in meeting a major milestone in the first new millennium goal of halving the rate of extreme poverty by 2015 is the result of statistical fiat—defining the poor away. Also, it is evident that a large part of the relative success in alleviating extreme poverty has a lot more to do with actions taken by the poor, especially migration and remittances of earned income to their communities and family members, than government policies. Where policy measures, fiscal expenditures, and antipoverty programs have been a factor, as in Chile and Brazil, then the credit can be given to a post–Washington Consensus on the need for a more socially inclusive form of neoliberalism as well as popular pressures on the government.

THE DYNAMICS OF CLASS STRUGGLE: POLITICAL RESPONSES TO NEOLIBERAL REFORM AND CRISIS

Over the years, there has been a recurring debate as to the social base and political dynamics of social movements for change in the region. However, the policies and conditions of structural adjustment have recast some of the issues involved, especially as relates to the popular sector of civil society. But two important questions remain. One is whether the objective and subjective conditions of struggle, resistance, and protest are structural and class based or based on localized struggles for and the politics of identity, defined by gender, ethnicity, and other culturally specific struggles. A second contested area has to do with the specific structural source of the conditions that have given rise to social movements and the politics of resistance and social protest.

Apart from the problem of determining how relations of exploitation and social exclusion fit in the social structure of Latin American societies, the political conditions of these relations—the social and political forces that have been generated—are not clear. Forms of popular resistance and political protest and the conditions that produced them need further study. Some preliminary results of such a study are briefly summarized below.

Living in Slums and Working the Streets on One's Own Account
The dramatic growth of the informal sector reflects decisions made by members of income-poor households (often recent rural emigrants) in the failed search for income-generating employment. These "decisions" are generally shaped by conditions over which their agents have absolutely no control and provide few if any options. In other words, to the degree that there is agency involved in these decisions and actions, it represents a survival strategy, a defensive response to the economic and social conditions of poverty—the deprivation of basic needs. As such, it represents a form of self-exploitation by household members who are generally constrained to provide labor power, or the products of their self-organized labor, at a level of remuneration well below its value. As for the women in these households, their rate of exploitation tends to be considerably higher than that for men, given their general responsibility for household and reproductive labor, which, when added to their social production, often leads to working days of twelve to sixteen hours, or seventy- to eighty-hour workweeks.

However, as a household strategy, self-exploitative informal economic activities, even with all members participating, have not enabled many households to meet the basic needs of its members for food, nutrition, shelter, clothing, education—and human development (expansion of choice). As a result, in the context of deepening economic crisis and adjustment, the female heads of some of these income-poor urban households in the 1980s came together to pool their limited resources and cooperate in the provision for these needs. Such interhousehold forms of cooperation and association can be found in most shantytowns in cities such as Lima, Mexico City, São Paulo, Rio de Janeiro, Santiago, and Guayaquil. According to some theorists, these households have created a new form of economy—a "social economy" that does not rely on (or make use of) money but on barter, free labor, and relations of solidarity.

The Popular Economy: Community-Based Cooperation
and Local Development
In Lima, Peru, as early as 1979 a number of *comedores populares* (popular canteens/dining halls/soup kitchens) were set up and cooperatively run by a group of around fifty women from income-poor shantytown households. By 1982 there were already an estimated 1,500 such organizations, in addition to 6,500 or so "glass of milk" committees that brought together and serviced over 100,000 households. In Santiago similar forms of popular economic organization (PEO), the *ol-*

las comunales (communal soup pots) and community soup kitchens, were formed on the basis of various associations of women in *las poblaciones,* as they are called in Chile (each country describes them in the same way but in different words—ranchos, favelas, villas de miseria, etc.), the shantytowns that surrounded the city. Such associations existed in Chile in the early 1970s, but under conditions created by the sweeping free market reforms of the Pinochet regime and the worst economic crisis in the region, they proliferated. In 1982, when the country was in the throes of another economic crisis, there were thirty-four *ollas comunales* in Santiago; by 1988, fifteen years into the Pinochet regime, there were 232 of them. By the 1980s, entire networks of such popular organizations, based on associations of women, were formed throughout the shantytowns. In addition to the *ollas comunales*, they included self-help groups, production workshops (small units with three to fifteen people producing and selling goods and services such as bread, clothing, laundry, carpentry, etc.), organizations for the unemployed, housing committees, committees for the homeless, and organizations related to housing problems such as water and electricity.

Similar women's organizations of the urban poor were formed in Brazil, Mexico, and other countries at the time subject to the same conditions of crisis and adjustment, or austerity measures. By taking charge in this manner, the women of poor working-class households came to feel empowered—collectively stronger and more self-reliant, capacitated to act in their own collective interest. In a number of cases, embryonic civil society organizations (CSOs) also provided a grassroots base for mobilizing resistance to the austerity and repressive policies of military regimes in the 1970s and the equally repressive economic policies of many neoliberal governments in the 1980s and 1990s. In this context, these CSOs represented the transition made by some associations of the urban poor from community action to collective protest. However, they also formed the social base of an alternative to collective protest and the formation of social movements, made available and presented to the poor by the overseas development associations (ODAs) and governments.[4] The option was participatory development in the form of local development—projects implemented in the community by a growing army of nongovernmental organizations (NGOs) enlisted in the cause of turning popular organizations away from a confrontational politics (direct action) to a new politics of dialogue, consultation, and participation in public policy.

From Community Development to Street Protest

Distinguishing between forms of community-based cooperative actions and collective forms of resistance and seeing where the former end and the latter begin is difficult. But in the context of spreading reforms, worsening socioeconomic conditions, and military rule, the urban poor took to the streets and moved from collective community action to collective forms of protest, including rioting and demonstrations. There is no question about the effectiveness and political impact of these collective acts of protest. In the outburst of political protest from 1983 to 1986, the urban poor were center stage, and working women were among the first to protest the regressive and repressive free market policies. Unionized workers, in contrast, were slow to respond and took their cue from the urban poor. And the intellectuals and politicos associated with the traditional parties were even slower to react and were manifestly ineffective in attempts to direct the self-mobilized forces of the urban poor, who in specific situations were joined in their struggles by unionized workers, students, teachers, public employees, shopkeepers, and other elements of an impoverished middle class.

A widely documented form of overt resistance and protest against neoliberal policies of stabilization and structural adjustment is the *riot*—the spontaneous outbreak of street protests against publicly announced increases in the price of food, gasoline, kerosene, or means of transportation. In the contemporary context of debt and adjustment, the first recorded street riots occurred as early as 1976 in Peru. In subsequent years there were sporadic outbreaks in various countries and a veritable wave of riots in 1982–1983 in Argentina, Bolivia, Brazil, Chile, Ecuador, and Panama. The forty-nine recorded riots in these years (fifty-two if we add the riots of 1984 in the Dominican Republic) represented more than one-third of all recorded riots worldwide at the time. A second wave of rioting hit the region in 1985–1986, followed by a series of riots in Venezuela in 1989 that left over 300 dead. This uprising of the urban poor was the first of four major uprisings that would take place in the subsequent decades of neoliberalism in Latin America. The other uprisings included the gas wars in the highlands of Bolivia, which in 2000 initiated a five-year period of revolutionary insurrection in the country that ended with the death of eighty indigenous rebels and the rise of Evo Morales, leader of a social movement of coca-producing indigenous peasants. The third uprising, also of indigenous peasants, occurred in Ecuador with the ousters of President Abdalá Bucaram in 1997 and of the neoliberal President Jamil Mahuad in 2000. The fourth uprising took place in December 2001 in Argentina under conditions of deep economic crisis. In this case the actor in the uprising was a social movement of urban unemployed workers called *piqueteros* because of their tactic of setting up pickets at highway blockades, used in the 1990s by the popular movement of indigenous peasants in the region.

The immediate trigger of these riots and uprisings in the late 1980s and then more generally in the 1990s and the new millennium is beyond dispute. They were a response to policy measures attributed to the IMF, often the symbolic if not immediate target of protest. In this connection, rioters and protesters were manifestly unsympathetic to the concern of Latin American governments to get prices right by cutting or eliminating subsidies and price controls or other such austerity measures. In some countries like Ecuador (January 2001) and Argentina (December 2001) rioting and protests against such policies have brought down governments; other governments were forced to retreat from a neoliberal agenda, which includes both austerity measures (eliminating subsidies, cutting social programs), liberalization of trade (opening up local markets to overseas competitors), and the privatization of public enterprises.

Riots are but one of a number of politically overt forms of resistance and acts of street protest against austerity measures. They have often been combined with other tactics such as mass demonstrations, marches on public buildings, encampments, land occupations, roadblocks, hunger strikes, boycotts, work stoppages, nonattendance at work or school, labor strikes (the traditional tactic of organized labor), as well as civic strikes. A most effective tactic used by indigenous peasant farmers in Bolivia and Ecuador, and more recently by unemployed workers in Argentina, has been *cortas de ruta*—cutting off and barricading highway and other transportation access to economic activity.

These acts of resistance and protest bring together diverse groups and classes in the popular sector and lead to concerted action. For example, in 1994 in Ecuador, an association of urban women, the Federation of Trade Unions, and the National Association of Indigenous Peoples took to the streets in a carefully orchestrated and scheduled series of marches, mass demonstrations, and strikes. Similar associations were formed in other countries in response to the same conditions. For example, after the peso was devalued in December 1994, more than 1,200 demonstrations and 550 marches—a daily average of five acts of protest—were organized in Mexico City in the space of a year. On one day alone (March 10, 1995), there were over 100 separate acts of protest. This wave of street protests was followed by the formation of a huge coalition of diverse social movements and organizations of farmers, peasants, independent business operators, workers, and nongovernmental organizations (NGOs) that came together to reject the government's economic model, which has generated only misery and unemployment. For the past five years in Argentina the streets in popular neighborhoods have been veritable cauldrons of protest, bringing together families of unemployed workers with other workers and groups in the popular sector in a common struggle against the source of their oppression—most often neoliberal policies of structural adjustment and globalization.

Workplace Protest and Resistance

In the context of widespread economic restructuring, the Latin American working class is not what it once was. A traditional stratum of full-time workers remains in place, strategically situated in various expanding industries, organized to defend and advance their collective interests, able to negotiate collective contracts with managers of capitalist enterprises and to engage in effective workplace strike action. However, in the 1990s, such workers were in the minority. They tended to be on the defensive, with a weakened capacity for collective action in an inhospitable if not hostile environment and an accommodating and compromised leadership, disposed to engage in tripartite pacts with business and government.

Under these conditions, the politics of resistance by workers in the formal sector of capitalist firms, public institutions, and remaining state enterprises tends to take different forms than before. Class struggle still involves strikes and electoral activity, but resistance to and protest against government policies of structural adjustment are now more likely to take the form of street demonstrations, mass rallies, and marches on government buildings, as well as takeover of factories. Currently up to 200 factories have been occupied and taken over by the workers in the industrial cities of Argentina.

Many workers remain opposed to the neoliberal agenda, as evident in the mass actions of workers all across the region throughout the 1990s. In Bolivia, almost every year since 1995, public sector workers and other workers organized by the powerful Workers Central, the Central de Obreros de Bolivia (COB), have orchestrated multiple mass actions, including declarations of a general strike, with the *cocaleros* and other indigenous peasant organizations, with major popular mobilizations against efforts of the political class to extend the privatization agenda.

Despite the understanding reached between the COB and the government in 1995, that led among other things to the end of a fifty-day teachers' strike, organizations of affiliated workers affirmed their commitment to continue the struggle against neoliberal policies. In the same year a similar commitment was expressed by over 150,000 workers in Mexico City on May Day in a massive rally against the government's privatization policy as well as an announced 50 percent increase in the value-added tax (VAT) and other elements of the government's neoliberal program. If anything, protest actions by workers and direct producers in different sectors over the years in Bolivia, Ecuador, Mexico and elsewhere have increased in number if not in intensity. The Confederation of Indigenous Nationalities of Ecuador (CONAIE) conducted in January 2004 a massive mobilization of the most diverse social and political forces of resistance against the government's neoliberal policies. Key sectors of organized labor were involved in this exercise in popular democracy.

No government in the region adopted the neoliberal program of policy reforms with such avidity as Carlos Menem's regime in Argentina in the 1990s. By 1998, however, Menem's policies, regarded by the World Bank as a model for other countries in the region to follow, brought about an economic crisis of momentous proportions, reflected in the official unemployment rate that grew from under 7 percent early in the decade to over 20 percent in 2002—up to 60 percent in some areas. Another consequence of the crisis was the impoverishment not only of the working class but of half of what had once been the most powerful middle class in Latin America—"the new poor." On December 19–20, 2001, the growing economic crisis exploded, bringing together a growing movement of unemployed workers and the pot-banging impoverished middle-class employees, service professionals and paraprofessionals, and business operators. In a matter of weeks up to four governments were brought down, workers occupied hundreds of factories, and unemployed workers and their families increased the pace of their *cortas de ruta,* cutting off and blockading major transportation routes in an effort to force the governments to institute short-term work projects and deal with a variety of demands by an increasingly restive population. The country was caught up in what could be seen as a prerevolutionary situation—somewhere between the worst recession in Argentina's history and the rapid growth and mobilization of a new community-based movement of unemployed workers.

Protest and Resistance in the Countryside
The penetration of capitalism into the countryside has been associated with a number of developments, including the transformation of the hacienda system of tenant labor into a wage labor–based system of agro-export production; a crisis in peasant agriculture based on communal forms of land tenure; the expulsion of proletarianized producers from the land, leading to a massive migration from the countryside to the urban centers; and a marked increase in temporary and seasonal forms of wage labor in the agricultural sector, with a significant gender dimension.

These combined developments have had a decided impact on the political capacity of workers and producers in the countryside and on the form of their organized resistance. For one thing, changes in employment practices toward more casual, precarious, and feminized forms of "flexible" labor have tended to increase the control of capital and the bargaining power of employers vis-à-vis labor. For another, the casualization of rural labor has contributed to the fracturing of a well established and at times militant peasant movement. Although seasonal and casual laborers can be highly militant, they are notoriously difficult to organize in part because of their mixed composition and shifting residence. As for the mass of land-less workers that has been generated, the pressure to migrate and the possibility of doing so have also undercut their capacity to organize and fight in the countryside.

Throughout the countryside conditions of capital accumulation and policies of structural adjustment have spawned numerous associations of producers and work-ers, organized with the objective of resistance and political protest. The central issue for these organizations has been to agree on a form of struggle that is appropriate to their condition and can generate resources and cross-class support. The lengthy de-bates on this issue were relatively inconsequential until the January 1994 outbreak of armed insurrection in Chiapas, Mexico. Among the highland peoples in the area, such uprisings have not been unusual; this one had been in the works since the early 1980s. In Chiapas on January 1, 1994, a number of distinct but interrelated processes led to the formation of the Zapatista Army of National Liberation.

The demands of the Zapatistas relate to conditions generated by economic and political structures that are deeply embedded in the history of the state's indige-nous peoples, but a subsequent declaration by Subcomandante Marcos, the official spokesperson for the Clandestine Revolutionary Indigenous Committee, points to the right of rebellion against the inhumane and unjust policies of neoliberalism. In this declaration, the Zapatistas threatened to march on Mexico City to press their demands, a similar approach to that taken by indigenous peoples in both Bolivia and Ecuador. In Bolivia the blockade of highways and mass marches on La Paz in 1993 and again in 1995 came in response to the call by the federation of organized urban workers for support of their struggle. However, in Mexico, as in Ecuador, there was no such call. It was the action of indigenous peoples that provoked the response of urban workers, leading to widespread mobilization and the creation of a social movement in solidarity with the Zapatista struggle in Chiapas and with similar struggles waged by indigenous peoples and peasant producers elsewhere. In January 2001 the indigenous uprising in Ecuador not only brought down the gov-ernment but managed to take it over, holding all the reins of state power via a tri-umvirate that represented the rebellious indigenous peasants of the country, a coalition of organized workers and social groups led by the state oil workers, and the armed forces. This popular government lasted for a matter of hours, but the message resounded throughout the corridors of political power across Latin Amer-ica: workers and peasants in the popular sector were on the march—a long march toward liberation, democracy, and state power.

STRATEGIC AND POLITICAL RESPONSES TO THE CRISIS IN THE POPULAR SECTOR

Capitalism has an inherent propensity toward crisis, as is evident in the recurrent pattern of financial and production crises over the years in the region. These crises take multiple forms and by all accounts induce a process of creative destruction—including of capital itself (e.g., in the ongoing crisis transmitted from its epicenter in the United States up to 40 percent of financial capital, it is estimated, has simply disappeared since the onset of the crisis in 2008), in the process undermining the existing structure of production (economic and social) relations among different classes and groups of individuals, and inducing a restructuring designed to reactivate the accumulation of capital.

The powers that be (the guardians of the neoliberal and imperial world order) have responded to the crisis by tightening the rules on rampant speculation, making enormous fortunes without contributing in any way to production, and reestablishing some sort of regulatory control (global governance) over highly mobile and ballooning forms of financial capital that has no productive function, serving only to enrich speculators looking for a quick profit. Most of the governments in Latin America have followed suit, viewing the crisis as essentially financial in character, requiring only a regulatory fix and anticyclical measures using the fiscal and monetary policy tools at their disposal. However, in the popular sector, especially when it comes to the social movements, it is increasingly evident that the crisis is not merely financial and amenable to a policy fix. The crisis is systemic: it is a crisis of the neoliberal model that is used by most governments to guide policy. What is required, and what the social movements in the popular sector (i.e., on the left) are demanding is structural change, an abandonment of neoliberal policies. This means going beyond the palliative measures and mild reforms proposed by the political class—even in countries such as Argentina, Brazil, and Chile where the left (or more accurately the center left) has achieved or gained access to state power.[5]

CONCLUSION

The social structure of Latin American society is fraught with problems that bear most heavily on the working class. The nature of these problems are best understood in terms of economic policies that governments in the region have instituted at the behest of capital—a US-dominated and imperial transnational capitalist class. These policies, packaged and presented as the structural adjustment program, relate to an agenda of this class to create a single global capitalist economy and to integrate countries across the world into it.

Widespread implementation of this agenda over the past two decades and a half has brought about a radically different Latin America from one that had been in the works. The resulting society is characterized by class divisions that need to be analyzed in both economic and in political terms. In economic terms we can identify conditions of economic exploitation and social exclusion that have led to a serious regression in the life chances of most people. At issue in these life chances is the growth of poverty and deepening social inequality in access to society's productive resources and in the distribution of the income generated by these resources.

However, the same process that generated these conditions has also generated forces of opposition and resistance to the agenda of the dominant and ruling class. In political terms it is possible to discern the emergence of social movements designed to mobilize the forces of opposition and resistance. These movements take diverse forms and require further study. However, it is clear enough that their political dynamics derive from conditions of class relations and not from the localized politics of gender and ethnic identity, as some would argue. In the context of these conditions found in most countries in Latin America, the widespread and multiform politics of protest and social movements of opposition and resistance relate to the social costs of structural adjustment, the conditions of which have been catastrophic for the majority of the working population. This is clear enough. However, the dynamics of political opposition to these conditions—the dynamics of class struggle—need further study. This is where sociology comes in. Or should.

Notes

1. On the policy—and political—dynamics of this development, which at the time was new but now (after twenty-five years) is a decaying neoliberal world order, see Petras and Veltmeyer 2001.

2. On this development, see Petras and Veltmeyer 2001; and Veltmeyer and Petras 2000.

3. A recent restatement of this theory can be found in the World Bank's 2008 world development report *Agriculture for Development*. For a critique of this theory, see Veltmeyer 2009.

4. On this, see Petras and Veltmeyer 2001, chap. 8 ("NGOs in the Service of Imperialism").

5. On these political developments, see Petras and Veltmeyer 2009.

Suggested Readings

ECLA. 2008. *Statistical Yearbook of Latin America and the Caribbean*. Santiago.

Petras, James, and Henry Veltmeyer. 2001. *Globalization Unmasked: Imperialism in the 21st Century*. London: Zed.

———. 2009. *What's Left in Latin America*. UK: Ashgate.

Portes, Alejandro, et al., eds. 1989. *The Informal Economy: Studies in Advanced and Less Developed Countries,* Baltimore: John Hopkins University Press.

UNDP. 2006. *Human Development Report*. New York: Oxford University Press.

Veltmeyer, Henry. 2009. "The World Bank on Agriculture for Development: A Failure of Imagination or the Power of Ideology?" *Journal of Peasant Studies* 36, no. 2: 393–410.

Veltmeyer, Henry, and James Petras. 2000. *The Dynamics of Social Change in Latin America*. London: Macmillan.

World Bank. 2008. *World Development Report: Agriculture for Development*. New York: Oxford University Press.

Chapter 9

STRATEGIES AND TRENDS IN LATIN AMERICAN ACTIVISM

WENDY MUSE SINEK

LATIN AMERICA HAS often been a site of vibrant grassroots activism, and this has never been more evident than within recent years. Since 2000, social movements in Brazil and Venezuela have been instrumental in electing leftist presidents to office, while presidents in Peru, Ecuador, Argentina, and Bolivia were unseated in part due to massive outpourings of popular discontent. Yet despite increased activism, traditional structures that facilitate political participation, most notably unions and labor-based parties, have weakened in recent decades. Some analysts claim this erosion demonstrates that ordinary people are alienated from the political process. Others take a different view, contending that community associations and social movements are becoming important actors in the political arena.

This chapter will expand on the latter perspective, introducing the reader to some emerging trends in Latin American activism between 2000 and 2010. After briefly differentiating social movement activity from broader forms of collective action, the chapter discusses how changes in the region's economic models have weakened traditional structures of interest intermediation. These dynamics have created political space that some grassroots activists have attempted to fill. Four issue areas—unemployment, housing rights, affordable municipal services, and urban violence—are discussed in detail. Finally, the chapter presents some strategic predicaments that activist organizations face as they evolve, and discusses their implications for future political engagement.

WHAT IS A SOCIAL MOVEMENT?

Collective action appears in many forms. From protests and picket lines to boycotts and flash mobs, collective action arguably exists whenever people do something together. Social movements constitute a specific type of collective action. Drawing from Tarrow's 1998 definition, a social movement is a group of ordinary people, possibly joined by more influential citizens, that engages in sustained confrontations with authority in order to achieve social change.

Social movements are organized but not institutionalized. When compared to other groups in civil society, such as NGOs, interest groups, and political parties, social movements are the least organizationally defined. They often have no formal charter or membership requirements, and they tend to be decentralized. Decision-making procedures may exist, but grassroots members tend to have a greater voice in these areas than in parties or interest associations. It is not unusual for decisions to be taken on an ad hoc basis, especially if protests arise spontaneously. Similarly, movements vary with respect to leadership. Some are directed by skillful political entrepreneurs while others are headed by volunteer members; some resist identifying a leader entirely.

However, there must be some minimal level of organization. Isolated, spontaneous action such as a riot may form part of a social movement or spark the emergence of one, but by itself does not constitute a movement. At the same time, action must be partially extrainstitutional. If all of the group's activity is directed by an organization such as an NGO or a political party, then these collective actions are not yet a social movement. At least some activity must take place outside established institutional channels.

Similarly, movements are collective efforts that extend over time. If many people decide to engage in the same action but are not coordinated in their effort, then the aggregate effect is a social trend, not a movement. Along the same lines, movements engage in activity that is ongoing. The time frame of the action can be short, but it must extend beyond a one-time event.

Finally, social movements are comprised of people who cannot access mainstream channels of power. This does not mean that participants must be poor or lower-class—though they often are. For example, movements in Latin America that arose to resist authoritarian rule were often formed by middle-class individuals; during that period, even those with economic resources lacked access to channels of political influence. The key point is that while citizens with access to power might ally with a movement, the majority of movement participants are those who are excluded from traditional power structures.

Economic Changes and Grassroots Reactions

Social movements tend to form around issues that have not yet been taken up by those with mainstream access to power. Movement members act collectively to place these issues of concern onto the public agenda. In Latin America, many emerging social movements find their roots in economic developments.

The question of popular representation arose in the twentieth century in Latin America as the new working classes sought to make their voices heard in the political arena. Two new institutions were created as a means of incorporating labor into the political system: unions and union-affiliated populist parties.[1] Albeit imperfectly, the working classes were able to express their demands through these structures. However, Latin America's economic context has changed markedly since the 1970s, and this has engendered profound social and political changes. Many of these effects are discussed elsewhere in this volume; here, I draw out the implications of these changes for social movements in Latin America. Essentially, links among unions, populist parties, and the lower classes do not function as well as they used to in representing interests within the political sphere.

After World War II, many countries in Latin America followed an import substitution industrialization (ISI) economic model. The economy was oriented toward producing goods for the domestic market to reduce dependence on foreign imports. In this model, the goals of creating economic growth and meeting the demands of labor were not in conflict. Because workers were also consumers, it was in the interest of both labor and business to raise wages. As a result, there was space for class compromise; labor-based parties, as well as business interests, were successful in gaining political and economic concessions from the state.

However, the onset of the debt crisis, along with problems inherent in this model of production, made ISI difficult to sustain. In 1973 members of OPEC (Organization of Petroleum-Exporting Countries) increased the price of oil fourfold and deposited their rapidly expanding revenues in Western banks. In turn, the banks made numerous loans with extremely low interest rates to developing countries, especially those in Latin America, a region considered to be a low investment risk with great potential for future growth. For their part, Latin American countries borrowed heavily—not only to invest in domestic development projects but also to fuel the ISI model with capital. When OPEC raised oil prices again during the 1980s, borrowing increased even more, since countries needed to purchase oil as well as make payments on their debt. Yet as the demand for loans increased, creditors became more cautious, and banks began making shorter-term loans at higher interest rates. By 1982 this cycle of debt had snowballed into a crisis situation, and when Mexico announced in August that it could not meet the payments on its debt, lending throughout Latin America came to an abrupt halt.

As developing countries with debt burdens struggled to manage them, international lending institutions often demanded liberal economic reforms, such as open markets, increased exports, and privatization in exchange for debt restructuring. These economic transformations in Latin America have had some positive results: short-term capital flows to the region have increased, competition is prevalent, and both production and consumption have become more efficient. Concurrently, aggregate measures of income have also increased. Efforts to reduce poverty in the region have seen some recent success; from 2002 to 2008, the percentage of people living in poverty dropped by almost ten percentage points.[2]

Yet this wealth has not been widely shared. Overall, Latin America features the most unequal distribution of wealth and income in the world, with the wealthiest 10 percent receiving, on average, incomes that are seventeen times greater than the poorest 40 percent. In some countries, such as Colombia and Brazil, the disparity is closer to 25 to 1. Moreover, while overall poverty rates in the region have decreased, the number of people living in absolute poverty—the poorest of the poor—is on the rise. Economic growth may be creating new jobs, but many of these are in the informal labor sector, which lack social benefits such as pensions and health care. Finally, the International Labor Organization predicts that the 2008 financial crisis and corresponding worldwide economic slowdown is likely to bring job growth in Latin America to a halt, and unemployment is predicted to rise significantly.

One outcome of this economic shift has been the erosion of populist coalitions and union influence. When a nation's customers are located in the international arena instead of the domestic market, the state no longer needs to strengthen its national consumer base to facilitate economic growth. Moreover, international lending organizations encourage states to become fiscally responsible by curtailing social spending, which diminishes their capacity to implement and expand domestic benefits. As a result, the state no longer has the same incentives—or the same financial ability—to make concessions that benefit working-class interests. As for the unions, a side effect of increased production efficiency has been a decrease in the number of workers employed within the formal labor sector. Since the potential membership pool for unions has diminished, their effectiveness has become similarly limited in representing the interests of the working class.

EMERGING CONTENTIOUS ISSUES IN LATIN AMERICA

Latin America has been home to some of the most vibrant social movements in recent history. The emergence of the labor movement around the world in the nineteenth century also found expression in Latin America, as have the feminist, black consciousness, and gay rights movements. Peasant struggles for land, as well as indigenous advocates for cultural autonomy, have also become important actors within the political arena. These movements, as well as many other civil society groups, were instrumental in pushing forward recent transitions to democracy in many Latin American countries, and continue to hold governments responsible for past human rights abuses. Each movement has a rich history worth exploring; the reader is referred to the "Additional Resources" section for more detail.

The focus of this chapter, however, is on emerging trends in Latin American collective action. As mentioned above, recent economic changes have engendered particular social dislocations, leaving labor-based political parties and unions less effective as interest intermediators. Organizations that traditionally represented popular interests in Latin America hold less influence today, yet marginalized groups still want their concerns addressed. The working classes, the unemployed, and the poor arguably have more grievances than ever, and they want influence over economic and social policies that affect their lives. Some have taken matters into their own hands, and a resurgence of collective action has been the result. This section provides an overview of four issues around which grassroots activism has emerged: unemployment, housing rights, affordable municipal services, and urban violence.

Unemployment

As the formal labor sector has shrunk in Latin America, the issue of persistent unemployment has affected the lives of many. Argentina has arguably suffered the brunt of this current trend, and the *piqueteros* (picketing unemployed workers) have become an increasingly influential social movement with a growing political voice.

Although Argentina's economy had been relatively stable throughout the twentieth century (the annual unemployment rate had rarely surpassed 4 percent), it underwent substantial restructuring during the 1990s. [3] Deindustrialization led to a marked decrease in the number of workers employed in the formal sector, and unemployment increased, reaching 18.5 percent by the middle of the decade. At the same time, Argentina lacked a "social safety net" for unemployed persons, and as government support for education, health care, and pension plans declined, the ranks of the informal labor sector and the poor swelled. Unable to rely on unions, these workers turned to neighborhood associations to advance their interests, and the unemployed workers' movement began at the local level.

One of the first labor actions took place in the province of Neuquen, an oil-producing enclave that had been privatized in 1991, resulting in massive layoffs. Over 7,000 unemployed workers set up roadblocks with sticks to prevent vehicles from entering or leaving the area. The police attempted to clear the roads, but the unemployed stood their ground. The conflict was resolved when the provincial governor offered the protesters work through the Plan Trabajar. In the following months, unemployed workers began organizing in different communities around the country, especially greater Buenos Aires, Mar del Plata, and Cordoba. They became known as *piqueteros* due to their primary tactic of setting up roadblocks to press for their demands. These include not only increased jobs and labor programs, but also widespread national reforms to address poverty and hardship in the provinces.

In this way, collective action against poverty in Argentina has become centered within local, community-based organizations instead of traditional workplace-based unions. This sentiment is expressed in one of the *piquetero* movement's main slogans, "The new factory is the territory," calling for unemployed workers to come together in their own neighborhoods, just as they did in the factories, to establish social links and become relevant political actors. Although unemployment and poverty remain major issues of concern, the *piquetero* movement has succeeded in many endeavors, sparking the creation of new labor programs or preventing their subsequent retrenchment. Most notably, however, the unemployed are now recognized as a significant political actor in Argentina. Local communities have become a space in which the popular sectors have been able to organize and articulate their interests, and the issue of providing jobs for all who want to work has been placed on the national agenda.

Homelessness and Housing Rights

Collective action is also coalescing around the right to affordable basic housing. The wave of migration from rural areas to cities that could not support the population influx has led to hundreds of thousands of people settling in shantytowns on the edges of urban areas. At the same time, governments have often been persuaded to reduce domestic spending in order to meet their financial obligations to lending institutions. In response to these problems, grassroots activists have pressured governments at all levels to improve the quality of life in urban communities.

One social movement attempting to address these issues is the Homeless Workers Movement (Movimento dos Trabalhadores Sem Teto, MTST) in Brazil. The members, nearly 300,000 poor urban families and growing, state on the MTST website that they are "unemployed, homeless, and hungry, but most of all, we are excluded from political decisions that determine the course of our lives." The MTST asserts that about 74 million Brazilians, or 43 percent of the population, are either homeless or living in buildings that lack running water, electricity, and sanitation. However, Brazil's National Institute of Geography and Statistics lists over 540,000 empty apartments in greater São Paulo alone. These buildings stand vacant due to land speculation and exorbitantly high rents, and it is this disjuncture between homeless families and potential housing solutions that the MTST seeks to confront.

To demonstrate the need for affordable housing and city services, the MTST occupies abandoned buildings. During the summer of 2003, MTST occupations took place throughout the country. In Recife, a former children's hospital was turned into makeshift apartments for 80 families, and in the state of São Paulo, 3,500 individuals created a shantytown in a vacant lot owned by Volkswagen.[4] Although police in riot gear and sharpshooters in helicopters forced the homeless to evacuate, international media attention provoked anger in Germany and put MTST's concerns on the international agenda. Two years later, the movement occupied land in Taboão da Serra, São Paulo, that had been vacant for over twenty-five years. After eight months of struggle, the governor agreed to subsidize building material for 600 homes. The MTST continues to call attention to the problem of affordable public housing, and activists have been invited to participate in negotiations with the Brazilian government on the federal level to find solutions to urban homelessness.

A similar movement exists in Peru and, to a lesser extent, Ecuador and Venezuela. Though they lack a formal unifying organization like the MTST, many poor families in the Andes have illegally seized land on the outskirts of major cities since the 1950s. Thousands of people might invade a site in the middle of the night, using scrap metal, lumber, and cardboard to build shelters and create a "squatter settlement" community. The following day, local authorities often bulldoze the settlement and evict the squatters, but determined families persist in setting up camp night after night until municipal governments finally capitulate. Over time, residents make improvements to their homes and employ a variety of strategies to pressure the municipal government to supply city services, such as running water, garbage collection, and electricity to their community.

Paul Dosh (2010) describes the success of the United Front of the Peoples of Peru (Frente Unitario de los Pueblos del Perú, or FUPP). Shantytown residents in southern Lima were frustrated with the government's inability to provide their community with basic city services, such as running water and electricity. Residents took matters into their own hands and obtained services for themselves, but this put hundreds of families in debt. Recognizing that the state had failed to uphold its obligations to these citizens, the Peruvian government agreed to cancel their debts. However, when successive administrations reneged on this promise, residents created the FUPP. At present, residents have paid twenty years' worth of interest on their loans, yet have made little progress in reducing the principal on the debt, and may face foreclosure if they cannot keep up with the payments. The FUPP draws members from fifteen districts throughout Lima, and continues to advocate for affordable housing and public services for Lima's poor.

Affordable Public Services

In a similar vein, massive urban protests have erupted over the high cost of public services. Latin American states are striving to become fiscally responsible, but these constraints have affected the availability of public services. In many Latin American cities, water supplies are erratic, sewage treatment is nonexistent, roads are in poor condition, and access to public health care services is severely restricted. In some cases, states have privatized public services, but the resulting cost increases are a catalyst for public protest.

One of the most dramatic examples of this dynamic occurred in Bolivia. As a condition of debt relief, the IMF required that the country privatize municipal water systems, and Bechtel Corporation purchased the water monopoly. Within weeks this action tripled consumer prices for water. In January 2000, the city of Cochabamba was completely shut down—schools and businesses closed, protesters blocked the main highways and shut down the airport, essentially cutting off all transportation alternatives. Residents occupied the main central plaza, set up organizing headquarters, and hung a banner that proclaimed "El Agua es Nuestra, Carajo!" (The water is ours, dammit). For over four months, similar actions took place across the country. The government agreed to review the water contract with Bechtel, but no further actions were taken. People refused to pay their water bills, and in return Bechtel threatened to cut off the city's water supply.

Public support for the protesters increased once the Bechtel contract was made public. Sympathetic members of congress leaked the contract to the protesters, revealing that Bechtel had provided no up-front investment in Bolivia and was guaranteed to earn at least a 16 percent profit. This new information caused the people to demand that the government lower water rates and restore control of the water supply to the Bolivian state. After four months of sustained collective action, culminating in an indefinite strike and highway blockade, the Bolivian government finally agreed to cancel Bechtel's contract in April 2000. Despite subsequent challenges, including a lawsuit demanding US$50 million from the Bolivian people for canceling the water contract, the "water warriors" movement remains a powerful social force in Bolivia.[5]

Violence and Police Brutality

Public safety is also a concern in Latin America. The United Nations Development Program reported in 2008 that Central America had become the most violent region in the world in terms of nonpolitical crime. The murder rate is three times greater than the global average, and illegal firearms circulate freely. Early 2009 data also indicated an increase in violent crime for Venezuela, Colombia, Argentina, and Brazil. Finally, Rio de Janeiro is arguably the city that is most affected by urban violence. The annual homicide rate is 50 per 100,000 people, nearly twice that of Central America's average.

Some Brazilian NGOs are attempting to address this problem. For example, Viva Rio has been at the forefront of combating trafficking in small arms and improving urban life for all of Rio's residents. In August 2003, members of Viva Rio organized a public destruction of over 4,000 firearms confiscated from criminals, crushing some with a steamroller and destroying others in a pyre, termed the

"Flame of Peace." Actions continued throughout the next two months, as tens of thousands of people held demonstrations in major Brazilian cities to show their support for a nationwide disarmament statute to create strong restrictions on firearms ownership. The statute was approved by the Brazilian legislature in December 2003.

Some of the most effective checks on urban violence have come from social movements founded by those who have been directly affected by police brutality. Juliana Farias (2005) describes the emergence of the Posso me Identificar? (Can I identify myself?) movement. On April 17, 2003, four young men were shot dead by military police in Borel, a community located in the northern part of Rio de Janeiro. Police claimed that the men were drug dealers and that the police had invaded the area in order to combat drug trafficking. However, official autopsies indicated that the men were killed by shots to the back of the head, not in a self-defense shootout as the police had claimed. Moreover, the four young men were not connected with drug gangs at all. One was a taxi driver, one was a student, one was a painter and bricklayer, and one was a mechanic. They had been waiting outside a barbershop when the police incursion began, and initially they attempted to identify themselves to the police to prove that they were not criminals. However, the police refused to look at their identification papers or even let them speak in their defense, and all of the young men were shot.

In response to the "slaughter of Borel," families and neighbors began to organize. Through sustained public demonstrations, they pressured the city government to investigate the killings. Marching through some of the wealthiest areas of Rio, mothers carried photos of their murdered sons alongside posters that read "Posso me identificar?" to call attention to the fact that the youths were killed without being given the opportunity to identify themselves to the police and demonstrate their innocence. This slogan eventually became associated with the Borel residents' campaign for justice, and it caught the attention of Amnesty International, which took up the issue. After almost a year had passed, Rio's city government agreed to investigate the incident. Despite the fact that the crime scene had been compromised by the time the investigations took place, five police officers were charged and two convicted of murder.

However, the campaign did not end there. Given that police brutality occurs in neighborhoods across Rio de Janeiro, the residents of Borel joined with relatives of victims in other communities to help them seek justice. The movement is now known as the Rede de Comunidades e Movimentos Contra a Violência (Network of Communities and Movements Against Violence). This grassroots social movement empowers the marginalized poor of Rio de Janeiro to denounce violence and human rights violations wherever they occur.

COMMON PREDICAMENTS: STRATEGIC CHOICES FOR SUCCESS

The four areas just discussed—unemployment, housing rights, affordable public services, and urban violence—are prominent issues around which collective action has coalesced in Latin America. As events unfold, how will these movements respond to the challenges that will undoubtedly arise? Each movement has its own individual characteristics, and will necessarily undergo change in ways that are unique in some respects. Nevertheless, by considering some general dynamics of social movement organizations and identifying common patterns, we can gain insight into decisions taken by movement leaders and activists. In the course of its life cycle, a social movement experiences certain defining moments at which it must make particular choices with respect to achieving its goals. These "common predicaments" represent a similar set of decision-making areas, basic questions such as, Who are we? What do we want? How are we going to get it?

Who Are We? Selecting Movement Members

Movements do not usually confront each predicament at the same time; there are particular instances at which each becomes important. One of the first choices for emerging movements centers on questions of membership: determining who can qualify as a movement participant. One dimension of this decision revolves around clarifying how *narrow verses broad* the organization should be in its outreach efforts. If the movement is open to all who sympathize with the group's goals, even if they are not part of the movement's targeted beneficiaries, this can result in a larger organization. The benefits of this are clear: additional members may give the movement more power to voice its concerns as well as expanded public recognition. Yet at the same time, there is power to be gained through limiting membership to certain individuals or groups.

Paul Dosh (2010) describes a salient example of this common predicament. In 1995 a group of 300 Ecuadorian families, the Cooperative of San Juan Bosco, organized an illegal land invasion of Itchimbía Park in metropolitan Quito, which had become a dumping ground for refuse and waste.[6] The cooperative defined itself in environmental terms and, beyond settling in the park, intended to act as its ecological custodian. However, when 3,000 additional squatters arrived the night after the invasion, the cooperative had to make a choice: either allow the newcomers to join, and possibly gain political strength in numbers, or refuse to admit them, restricting membership to those with a proven commitment to environmental conservation. The group decided on the latter course of action, and by January 2004, the settlers of San Juan Bosco had legally built high-quality condominiums and initiated the task of park management.

In selecting movement members, leaders also need to clarify whether membership should be primarily *identity-based or goal-based*. In other words, must supporters share a common identity as well as common goals? While no movement organization is solely based on identity, movements generally focus on substantive issues to a greater or lesser degree. Defining a movement's identity is also important because the way the movement sees itself, and wants to be seen by others, affects what it will do to achieve its goals. For example, if a movement's goal centers on winning *acknowledgment* of a particular cultural identity and preserving its uniqueness, as in the case of pan-Mayan indigenous movements, it may be most practical to limit membership to those who share this identity. However, if the movement emphasizes gaining *rights* for a particular identity, as indigenous activists in Ecuador do in their effort to expand bilingual education, then the movement may be strengthened by allowing all ideological sympathizers to join, even if they do not share the identity of the group in question.

What Do We Want? Determining Movement Goals

Social movements also face the task of deciding what they hope to achieve through collective action. This is an ongoing predicament. It is a concern in the initial stages of movement formation, and it can arise repeatedly if limited goals are realized, or if more expansive goals prove too difficult to attain.

First, it is necessary to clarify the movement's scope; whether to pursue a *narrow agenda* or a *broader one*. If a movement decides to focus on fewer issues, it may succeed in attracting a unified base of supporters who have a common vision, as well as minimizing internal conflict. However, limited goals may also narrow the range of potential participants, and defining a movement's aims too specifically risks leaving some aspects of the movement's agenda unaddressed. Conversely, there may be "something for everyone" in a movement with a wide array of goals, and this variety has the potential to attract a larger base of supporters. Yet an inclusive agenda is likely to attract a more diverse membership with conflicting priorities. This variation can render overall consensus difficult to attain, and the movement may find itself fragmenting into contradictory factions.

The Brazilian Movimento Sem Terra (Landless Rural Workers Movement, or MST) is currently struggling with this predicament. During the 1990s, the movement's goals expanded to encompass broader social and economic issues, such as the international campaign against genetically modified food and opposing the creation of a Free Trade Area of the Americas. However, there is an incipient disconnect between these ideological goals and those of local grassroots activists, especially among new urban entrants who are eager to obtain land for themselves and their families. Since the movement's leaders do not want to narrow the current agenda, they are attempting to make these broader concerns relevant to their newest members.

A second aspect of determining movement goals includes clarifying the degree to which the movement aims for *overall systemic or more delimited change*. The movement may choose a limited approach if it seeks to implement or revoke specific laws, procedures, and policies within the current system. At the other end of the spectrum, a movement may opt for overhauling existing institutional structures if it seeks comprehensive systemic change. Actions oriented toward limited change may earn greater public legitimacy and generate relatively less social conflict. However, the movement must navigate within existing institutional structures, which may or may not be well suited to implementing the movement's agenda. Successful systemic change, on the other hand, allows institutions to be crafted in a way that meets the group's goals over the long term. Yet achieving systemic change is often fraught with risk and social upheaval, since efforts to transform entrenched institutions often meet with a great deal of resistance.

The decision to aim for limited or systemic change is closely tied to the distinction between narrow and broad goals mentioned above. Narrower goals can often be achieved by changing specific parts of the existing system, while broader goals may require transforming social, economic, and political institutions. However, this relationship does not always hold. A narrow goal, such as land redistribution or wage increases, may threaten powerful entrenched interests within the system,

and therefore have little chance of being implemented unless systemic change occurs. Conversely, a broader goal, such as societal recognition of indigenous rights,
may be addressed within the scope of the current system, such as through enactment of a constitutional amendment.

Finally, movements also need to determine if their goals, once achieved, will be
collective or *private:* will the benefits extend to everyone in society, or will they be
limited in some way? If the benefits are available to everyone, this raises the free-
rider dilemma that Mancur Olson (1965) described: there will be little incentive
for individuals to work in support of the movement's goals if the benefits are not
contingent on participation. Olson's solution to the collective action problem is to
provide selective incentives that are linked to participation in the movement. This
strategy has been successfully employed by many organizations; for example, it
was arguably one important factor that allowed the MST to expand rapidly.
Shortly after the organization was officially formed in 1984, a group of landless
families that had been encamped at Erval Seco finally gained official title to a
nearby government-owned farm. Families who initially joined the occupation but
left during the ensuing months received nothing, but those who endured until the
end acquired land of their own. This provided a powerful selective incentive for individual landless workers to join the MST and remain on the encampments despite years of hardship, and the number and size of occupations grew throughout
Brazil over the next few years.

At the same time, selective incentives are not always necessary for high levels of
participation. The desire to collaborate with friends, rectify an injustice, and/or
overcome hardship in pursuit of a collective goal are just a few of the factors that
can motivate individuals to participate in collective endeavors even when individual gain is unlikely. Also, translating a movement's goals into private benefits can
be difficult. Some intangible goals, such as expanded political and social rights,
may be nearly impossible to privatize. What is more, exclusive benefits are often
contrary to the movement's underlying ideological framework. Consider the various movements that aim to recognize the rights of the indigenous by formally
amending the constitution. It would be antithetical to the movement's purpose, as
well as impractical, to prevent indigenous persons who had not participated in the
movement from enjoying equal and expanded rights if they are achieved. While offering private goods to participants can be a powerful tool for member recruitment
and retention, such an approach can be difficult to implement in practice, and
may not always be necessary in order to attract movement participants.

How Are We Going to Get It? Choosing Movement Strategies
Once a movement determines who can qualify as a member and clarifies the nature of its goals, the question of strategy becomes salient: what should the movement actually do to achieve its ends? One important strategic dimension involves
coalitional choice—the extent to which the movement forms alliances with other
organizations or pursues an autonomous course. The question of *autonomy versus
alliances* is a recurring, long-term predicament that social movements face
throughout their life cycle.

A coalitional strategy based on alliances occurs when a social movement partners
with outside actors in order to combine resources, knowledge, and capabilities. Al-

lies can provide an infusion of resources, both financial and organizational, and this can be especially welcome during the process of movement formation. Grassroots movements comprised primarily of poor and working-class individuals often find that networks, skilled leadership, and financial assistance provided by alliance partners can help the movement address its goals more effectively.

However, external organizations often have their own interests and agenda in mind. Groups that contribute resources may believe that doing so gives them authority to drive the local movement's ideological and tactical agendas. If the degree of difference between the movement's goals and its allies' agenda is small, this is not a significant drawback. When a large discrepancy exists, however, grassroots members may not be included in leadership and decision-making roles. Conversely, a movement that chooses an autonomous course is free to determine its own agenda and priorities without external influence. An important trade-off is that an autonomous movement depends solely on its own resources to organize and implement collective action.

The Argentine *piquetero* movement has recently faced this predicament. Delamata (2003) claims that since 1999, clientelistic ties between the movement and political parties have eroded, as subsidies have gone directly to unemployed individuals instead of local party bosses. This new autonomy enabled the movement to respond more directly to its members' needs and gave leaders increased freedom to choose their own strategies.

However, by the beginning of 2000, the Alianza administration allowed labor programs to expire and reduced federal funding for new initiatives. Garay (2007) argues that this new policy direction, combined with sharply increasing poverty, strengthened alliances between the *piqueteros* and one of the main Argentine labor confederations, the CTA. As a result, the *piquetero* movement expanded geographically and its demands on the national government gained strength. The election of the leftist president Nestor Kirchner in 2003 provided an additional political opportunity, and the *piquetero* movement forged an alliance with the governing coalition. The movement supported Kirchner's policies, and in return the *piqueteros* gained some leverage over policymaking. At present, the unemployed workers movement is attempting to navigate this coalitional choice. The movement is attaining its policy goals through its alliance with the governing coalition, but it is challenged with retaining its autonomy as a result.

Another dimension of strategy involves determining whether the movement should pursue its goals through *legal* or *extralegal means*. This question arises less frequently than others presented here, but when it does, it can be intense. Most movements find that employing legal methods works well when pursuing narrowly defined goals within a context of limited change. However, after legal strategies have been undertaken for an extended period without success, movements may consider resorting to extralegal means to advance their cause. These methods can encompass nonviolent, passive resistance strategies of refusing to comply with existing laws, as well as acts of civil disobedience such as sit-ins, protest marches, and boycotts. At another level, violence may or may not be present if movement participants engage in strikes, roadblocks, building takeovers, and land invasions in order to make their voices heard. In extreme form, extralegal methods can also include strategies centered on violence, such as mass riots and armed rebellion.

The Zapatistas in Mexico provide a classic example of this strategic choice. Contemporary indigenous activism in Chiapas is rooted in various peasant union organizations that were created during the 1970s and 1980s. These organizations protested the dismantling of the traditional *ejido* system of land tenure, corruption of public officials, widespread poverty in the countryside, and general lack of indigenous political representation. In some instances the Mexican authorities ignored their demands, while in other cases they pledged reforms, but implemented them minimally, if at all. Finally, when peaceful protests were met with violent repression, many indigenous activists took up arms in resistance.

On January 1, 1994, the Zapatistas occupied municipal buildings and town centers in seven cities, released prisoners, and took over radio stations to get their message out to the people. One communiqué explained their actions: "We let the world know of our decision to fight for our most elementary rights in the only way that the governmental authorities have left us: armed struggle." [7] However, by 1996, two years after their initial uprising, the Zapatistas were expressing an eagerness to revert to legal methods. The *Fourth Declaration of the Lacandon Jungle* outlines a thirteen-point plan to transform into a national grassroots opposition movement that "does not struggle to take political power, but for a democracy where those who govern, govern by obeying."[8] Ten years later, the Zapatistas implemented this plan through The Other Campaign, a series of community meetings held throughout Mexico. The Zapatista leaders met with not only peasant supporters but also factory workers, students, gay and lesbian groups, intellectuals, and environmental activists. Their goal was to galvanize public support for a constitutional convention that would revise the Mexican constitution along socialist lines. These actions indicate that the Zapatistas' strategy is now based on working within the system. Instead of attempting to overthrow the regime, they seek to change the constitution through legal means. Although they have declined to participate in electoral politics, the Zapatistas apparently have rejected extralegal methods and have made a strong commitment to peaceful resistance.

FUTURE DIRECTIONS IN LATIN AMERICAN ACTIVISM

As economic transformations across the region have rendered political parties and unions less effective advocates for the working classes, people have turned to social movements and grassroots activism to express their interests within the political sphere. While collective action is not a new phenomenon in Latin America, initial evidence indicates that contemporary contention differs from earlier protest in significant ways. This final section draws some implications for future political engagement from these differences.

Multiple Overlapping Goals

First, movements in Latin America increasingly focus on multiple overlapping goals. In Mexico, protest against economic policy has merged with demands for democratic and honest governance (Wada 2005). Bolivia's "water warriors" not only resist the privatization of natural resources but also advocate for ethnic, indigenous, and general human rights protection (Shultz 2005). Struggles for land reform in Brazil now intersect with urban demands for housing, and to some extent the women's movement and the rights of the indigenous in the Amazon (Wolford 2003).

Emerging social movements appear receptive to expanded goals. In September 2009, the MTST decided to go beyond demands for urban housing and protest against Brazil's extreme social and economic inequality by occupying an exclusive São Paulo shopping mall, Parque Dom Pedro. Only a small percentage of Brazilians can afford the high-priced goods on sale, and armed guards stationed at the entrance keep out "undesirables." Yet on Brazil's Independence Day, over 20,000 people joined the MTST in a parade through the streets, culminating in a rally inside the mall. One movement leader stated that "the minimum wage in Brazil is three times less than what a family needs to survive, and yet corrupt politicians earn high salaries and spend over $20 USD on a cup of coffee. What kind of independence is this? We call for our elected leaders to work for the people and defend our interests."[9] In this way, the MTST is an example of a movement that has expanded its goals beyond obtaining benefits for individual members. Latin American activists are increasingly blurring the boundaries of their contentious action in order to focus public attention on the root economic and cultural causes of unemployment, homelessness, and urban violence.

Transnational Contention

Increasing global integration and advances in information technology mean that contentious politics is less likely to be contained within national boundaries. In Latin America, groups of activists are connecting across national borders in order to share information, strategies, and tactics. A classic example is the movement for agrarian reform. Many national peasant organizations also participate in two international groups, the Latin American Coordinating Body of Peasant Organizations (CLOC) and Vía Campesina. These organizations provide a structure through which activists can exchange ideas and coordinate activities. For example, the United Nations declared October 16 as International World Food Day. In 2009 Via Campesina capitalized on this occasion to organize protests all over the world against genetically modified food. Latin American peasant and indigenous groups worked with environmental activists in India, Europe, and the United States to coordinate demonstrations outside the headquarters of Monsanto and other multinational corporations across the globe.

Moreover, transnational contention was arguably crucial in the ability of Bolivia's "water warriors" to resist Bechtel's lawsuit in response to canceling their water contract. The Bolivian movement coordinated with a sympathetic local NGO, the Democracy Center, which in turn helped organize a worldwide media campaign to publicize the issue. Environmental activists and other sympathizers in the United States occupied the lobby of Bechtel's headquarters in protest, and an online petition in support of the Bolivian people was endorsed by citizens from over forty countries. In light of sustained negative publicity, Bechtel eventually settled the lawsuit for a symbolic sum of thirty cents in January 2006. These examples illustrate some of the ways in which protest is spreading outside national borders and is becoming more effective as a result.

Interest Action

Finally, in some areas of Latin America, the targets of collective action are not always political actors. Traditionally, social movements have developed their goals, strategies, and tactics around how to pressure governments to address their interests. As we have seen, many organizations continue to do this, and rightly so; ideally, Latin American states would provide education, health care, security, and basic municipal services to all of their citizens.

However, as O'Donnell (1993) argues, the state may have low capacity for action in some parts of Latin America. Grassroots organizations have interests, but if the state is not capable of addressing their needs, then it makes little sense to rely on the state for services that it cannot provide. In other cases, the state has high capacity, but political officials have few incentives to address the needs of marginalized communities.

For example, the city of Rio de Janeiro, Brazil, has fifty city council seats to represent its 12 million residents. However, the city is not divided into electoral districts, so candidates are not tied to any particular geographic area. This means that politicians have no incentive to respond to the needs of any particular group. A candidate may promise improvements to a given urban area, but if he does not deliver once elected, he does not need to convince the residents of that area to vote for him again. He can seek votes from pensioners, or youth, or a different neighborhood entirely. In practice, this dynamic allows political officials to ignore many urban areas and yet be repeatedly elected to office.

In cases like these, when political officials are unresponsive or representative channels are blocked, people are organizing to address their needs on their own. They are turning to grassroots organizations not for intermediation but for *action*. The strategies these organizations choose are similar to those that Collier and Handlin (2009) describe as "self-provisioning"—pooling their internal skills and resources to craft their own solutions. However, initial evidence indicates that some organizations are going beyond material "provisioning" in their efforts to transform their communities.

For example, in Rocinha, arguably Rio's largest urban slum, the grassroots group Viramundo created a short film about the neighborhood's main problems: the growing rat infestation, the spread of tuberculosis, and increasing teen pregnancy rates. The intended audience was mainly their fellow friends and neighbors, focusing on what the neighborhood can do to protect their own health, regardless of government intervention. The film and its corresponding photos have been shown not only throughout the community but also in neighboring areas, Brazilian and foreign universities, and at the 2009 World Social Forum. However, Viramundo's work, while focused on improving the community's public health, looks beyond this immediate local goal. Through music and social events, this creative organization brings middle- and upper-class residents together with poor urban neighborhoods in order to reduce prejudice and collaborate on shared public health concerns.

In another poor urban community located in Rio's northern zone, parents created CIACAC (the Centro Integrado de Apoio as Crianças e Adolescentes de Comunidades, or the Integrated Community Center Supporting Children and Adolescents) to provide children with educational after-school activities. Each activity has a dual purpose: not only to provide academic reinforcement but also to teach cooperation, self-esteem, and how to speak up for one's rights. CIACAC also builds connections within and outside of their local community. Children who regularly attend are eligible to participate in field trips to visit museums, concerts, plays, and other events within Rio's city center. The organization works with parents and neighbors to raise funds, find chaperones, arrange transportation, and create a collaborative plan for each trip. In this way, parents become more involved both in their children's lives and in the neighborhood, creating a sense of solidarity and community engagement.

Finally, Catalytic Communities (CatComm) was founded in 2000 to help community activists in Rio connect with each other. The idea was to give innovative social projects, such as the two described above, a way to share solutions, information, and best practices. From this simple idea, the project has developed a Community Solutions Database that has documented the efforts of over 250 grassroots neighborhood projects in twenty-one countries.

These organizations do not have direct political action as a primary goal. But at the same time, neither are they concerned with meeting the material interests of their local communities alone. Each project incorporates broad human rights-based goals within its local mission, and strives to connect with allies wherever they are—in the wealthy neighborhood next door or across the globe.

Although these organizations were not created with political action in mind, they are ideally poised to confront political officials should the opportunity arise. Neighborhood residents become habituated to working together, collaborating across social classes, and using technology to connect with like-minded international allies. When crises occur, these skills are essential for undertaking political action.

For example, in October 2009, Rio de Janeiro was selected as the site of the 2016 Olympic Games. Within weeks of the announcement, city officials proposed a plan to demolish the poor urban communities located at the site of the future Olympic Village. However, these are some of the few neighborhoods in Rio that have no involvement in drug trafficking, and the city council did not offer residents an opportunity for public comment.

In response, community leaders organized against the plan to remove their peaceful, legal neighborhoods. Social projects across the city have been able to connect with each other through CatComm for years, and in November 2009, they developed the ROAR project (Rio Olympics Accountability Reporters) to train local leaders in the creative use of social media for political engagement. Funds for this training program are being raised both domestically and internationally through social networking sites such as Facebook Causes.

Although these organizations may not fit the traditional definition of a social movement, they clearly have political potential. Their day-to-day activities build important civic skills, and communities can leverage these skills to advocate for their interests in the political arena, as well as bring international attention to their cause.

Conclusion

Individuals at the grassroots level are engaging in collective action with renewed vitality in Latin America, and this chapter has introduced some of the emerging organizations that are channeling their demands. As economic transformations across the region have rendered political parties and unions less effective advocates for the working classes, social movements and local neighborhood organizations have become additional vehicles through which ordinary people can express their interests within the political sphere. Additionally, while some emerging grassroots organizations do not focus on political action, evidence—at least in the case of Rio de Janeiro—indicates that the civic skills they foster can be valuable resources for future political engagement. As long as parties and unions remain flawed in their ability to accurately express the public will, it is reasonable to expect that Latin Americans will continue to voice their concerns through collective action.

Notes

1. Ruth Berins Collier and David Collier, *Shaping the Political Arena* (Princeton: Princeton University Press, 1991).

2. ECLAC, Social Panorama of Latin America 2008, December 10, 2008.

3. This discussion primarily draws from the research of Gabriela Delamata, "The Organizations of Unemployed Workers in Greater Buenos Aires: The Erosion of Clientelistic Practices," a working paper presented at the UC-Berkeley Center for Latin American Studies, October 2003; and Candelaria Garay, "Social Policy and Collective Action: Unemployed Workers, Community Associations, and Protest in Argentina," *Politics and Society* 35, no. 2 (2007): 301–328.

4. *O Globo*, August 8, 2003; *Correio da Bahía*, August 9, 2003; *O País*, August 10, 2003.

5. In January 2006, arguably resulting from negative publicity, Bechtel settled its lawsuit against the Bolivian people for the symbolic sum of thirty cents. For more details, see Jim Schultz and Melissa Crane Draper, eds., *Dignity and Defiance: Stories from Bolivia's Challenge to Globalization* (Berkeley: University of California Press, 2009).

6. Paul Dosh, *Demanding the Land: Urban Popular Movements in Peru and Ecuador, 1990–2005* (University Park: Pennsylvania State University Press, 2010).

7. Fiona Jeffries, "Zapatismo and the Intergalactic Age," in *Globalization and Postmodern Politics*, ed. Roger Burbach (London: Pluto, 2001).

8. EZLN, *Fourth Declaration of the Lacandon Jungle*, January 1, 1996, http://flag.blackened.net/revolt/mexico/ezln/jung4.html.

9. "Contra a farsa na politica e por nossos direitos!" MTST update, September 9, 2009, www.mtst.info/?q=node/992.

Suggested Readings

Collier, Ruth Berins. 2002. "Political Participation in the Age of Neoliberalism." *Center for Latin American Studies Newsletter*. Winter.

Collier, Ruth Berins, and David Collier. 1991. *Shaping the Political Arena*. Princeton: Princeton University Press.

Domínguez, Jorge I., ed. 1994. *Social Movements in Latin America: The Experience of Peasants, Workers, Women, the Urban Poor, and the Middle Sectors.* New York: Garland.

Dosh, Paul. 2010. *Demanding the Land: Urban Popular Movements in Peru and Ecuador, 1990–2005.* University Park: Pennsylvania State University Press.

Eckstein, Susan Eva, and Timothy P. Wickham-Crowley, eds. 2003. *Struggles for Social Rights in Latin America.* New York: Routledge.

———, eds. 2003. *What Justice? Whose Justice? Fighting for Fairness in Latin America.* Berkeley: University of California Press.

Farias Mello, Juliana. 2005. "Movimento 'Posso me Identificar?' De objetos da violência a sujeitos da política." Thesis, UERJ.

Garay, Candelaria. 2007. "Social Policy and Collective Action: Unemployed Workers, Community Associations, and Protest in Argentina." *Politics and Society* 35, no. 2: 301–328.

González, Victoria, and Karen Kampwirth, eds. 2001. *Radical Women in Latin America: Left and Right.* University Park: Pennsylvania State University Press.

Harvey, Neil. 1998. *The Chiapas Rebellion: The Struggle for Land and Democracy.* Durham, NC: Duke University Press.

Kapiszewski, Diana. 2009. "Targeting State and Society: The Strategic Repertoires of Associations." In Ruth Berins Collier and Samuel P. Handlin, eds., *Reorganizing Popular Politics: Participation and the New Interest Regime in Latin America.* State College: Pennsylvanian State University Press.

Keck, Margaret E., and Kathryn Sikkink. 1998. *Activists Beyond Borders: Advocacy Networks in International Politics.* Ithaca, NY: Cornell University Press.

O'Donnell, Guillermo. 1993. "On the State, Democratization, and Some Conceptual Problems: A Latin American View with Glances at Some Postcommunist Countries." *World Development* 21, no. 8.

Schultz, Jim, and Melissa Crane Draper, eds. 2009. *Dignity and Defiance: Stories from Bolivia's Challenge to Globalization.* Berkeley: University of California Press.

Sinclair, Minor, ed. 1995. *The New Politics of Survival: Grassroots Movements in Central America.* Washington, DC: EPICA/Monthly Review Press.

Smith, Jackie, Charles Chatfield, and Ron Pagnucco, eds. 1997. *Transnational Social Movements and Global Politics: Solidarity Beyond the State.* Syracuse, NY: Syracuse University Press.

Tarrow, Sidney. 1998. *Power in Movement: Social Movements and Contentious Politics.* New York: Cambridge University Press.

Warren, Kay B., and Jean E. Jackson, eds. 2002. *Indigenous Movements, Self-Representation, and the State in Latin America.* Austin: University of Texas Press.

Wright, Angus, and Wendy Wolford. 2003. *To Inherit the Earth: The Landless Movement and the Struggle for a New Brazil.* Oakland, CA: Food First Books.

Suggested Internet Resources

Some of the emerging movements discussed in this chapter have their own websites; those that present information in English are listed below.

CIACAC (Integrated Community Center Supporting Children and Adolescents)
www.ciacac.org

Contains photos, videos, and information about this social project as well as life in one of Rio de Janeiro's poor urban communities. The site is in Portuguese, but an English translation is expected to be available in 2010. CIACAC also has a Facebook group with information in English: www.facebook.com/group.php?v=info&ref=ts&gid=115 659635258

"Can I Identify Myself?" Network of Communities Against Violence
www.redecontraviolencia.org/Home
News and information about the movement against urban violence. Currently in Portuguese, with an English translation expected in 2010.

Catalytic Communities
www.catcomm.org/en
This site contains information in English about the organization's work in Rio de Janeiro, including the ROAR project, as well as the Community Solutions Database, which contains data on successful community initiatives from neighborhoods around the world.

The Democracy Center
http://democracyctr.org
Based in Cochabamba, Bolivia, and San Francisco, California, the Democracy Center advocates for social justice around the world, with a particular focus on the economic effects of globalization.

Food First: Institute for Food and Development Policy
www.foodfirst.org/index.html
Food First is a nonprofit think tank that investigates solutions to worldwide hunger and poverty, and advocates for establishing the right to sustenance as a fundamental human right.

Homeless Workers Movement (Movimento dos Trabalhadores Sem Teto, MTST)
www.mtst.org
Official site of the MTST; mostly in Portuguese but with some resources in English.

Landless Workers Movement (Movimento do Trabalhadores Rurais Sem Terra, MST)
www.mst.org.br
Official site of the MST. Contains almost daily updates on the movement's activities in Portuguese; most resources are translated into English.

Viramundo
http://web.me.com/viramundo/ViramundoEnglish/Home.html
This site contains extensive information in English about Viramundo's projects, including photos and films. The video mentioned in this chapter is available at: http://web.me.com/viramundo/ViramundoEnglish/Photogalleries/Photogalleries.html

Viva Rio
www.vivario.org.br/
Official site for Viva Rioate. Updated weekly in Portuguese, monthly in English.

PART IV

POLITICAL PROCESSES
AND TRENDS

Chapter 10

PARTICIPATION AND POLITICAL PROCESS

The Collapsible Pyramid

JAN KNIPPERS BLACK

ALL POLITICAL SYSTEMS are systems of limited participation. Even the societies we might call primitive—societies in which essential tasks and rewards are shared more or less equally among families—generally limit participation on the basis of sex and age; that is, women and minors are excluded. Such systems of exclusion may enjoy "legitimacy," or acceptance, even by the excluded, but they are ultimately based on physical prowess. Exclusion in more complex societies, like the modern nation-state, typically follows the lines of class, often reinforced by racial or ethnic divisions. Exclusion may also be based on political ideology.

In the United States, for example, the franchise was generally limited to property-holding white males until the 1830s, when the populist movement headed by Andrew Jackson led to the elimination of property-holding requirements. The franchise was extended to women in 1920 only after years of struggle on the part of the suffragettes. Suffrage for blacks in the South did not become effective until the issue was forced by the civil rights movement, led by Dr. Martin Luther King in the early 1960s. It was only after university students were mobilized in opposition to the Vietnam War that the voting age was lowered from twenty-one to eighteen. In parts of the country, poor blacks or Hispanics are still turned away from the polls by one device or another.

Furthermore, as suffrage has been extended, the vote, which is only one of many forms of political participation, has become devalued as a consequence of the preponderant role of money in the US electoral system. As campaigns have become outrageously costly media events, the candidate or elected official has become far more attentive to the wishes of major campaign contributors than to those of an amorphous electorate. The low level of voter turnout in the United States suggests, among other things, that a great many eligible voters see campaign promises as hollow and electoral choices as meaningless.

Likewise in Latin America, participation takes many forms, and effective participation is by no means automatic. For all but the wealthiest it must be earned or
won, often through protracted struggle and great sacrifice.

INEQUALITY AND THE BID FOR PARTICIPATION

Most complex, highly stratified social and political systems can be traced to armed
conquest, and the national systems of Latin America as we know them today are
no exception. The subjugation upon which contemporary social inequality in
Latin America is based included not only the conquest and enslavement by
Spaniards, Portuguese, and other Europeans of native American populations, but
also the kidnapping, by European merchants of flesh, of Africans and their subsequent enslavement in the New World.

The preponderance of brute force thus led to wealth, as the conquistadores acquired land and slaves or serfs and passed them on to their legitimate offspring.
Over time, this system of exploitation acquired a measure of legitimacy, as it was
moderated and condoned by the religious system imposed by the conquerors. In
Latin America as elsewhere, the violent roots of such systems of inequality have
been progressively obscured from subsequent generations of the conquered populations, and the myth has been established that differential reward and punishment
and limitations of access to wealth and power rest somehow on divine purpose or
merit. Those who would challenge that interpretation of the social reality are
branded subversive and dealt with accordingly.

Through miscegenation, immigration, and an increase in the categories of tasks
to be performed, classes of intermediate social and economic rank—between the
masters and the "slaves"—have come into being. It is quite possible, as social and
political systems become more complex, for individuals, through accepting the social myth and incorporating the values of the conquering class, to rise above the
status of their birth. The masters, however, do not voluntarily relinquish a share of
their authority to a lower stratum on the social pyramid. Such a sharing of power
across class lines comes about only when organization and the potential for the use
of force on the part of a lower social stratum are such that the masters conclude
that they must share their wealth and power or risk losing it all.

The great political theorists, at least since Aristotle, have noted that power systems and the distribution of wealth and opportunity are interdependent. Thus the
concepts of social class and class struggle introduced by Karl Marx are crucial to an
understanding of the political process in its broadest implications. These concepts
are, however, abstractions. Social classes do not compete as such. Individual competitors for political power act through or on behalf of groups, which in turn represent more or less limited sectors of society. Such groups may represent one or
more social classes, or a sector within a single class. They may act on behalf of one
class at one time and on behalf of another at a later date. They may act on behalf
of narrowly construed organizational or institutional interests, which only indirectly impinge on the class struggle. They may represent interests fundamentally
alien to their own societies. Or they may represent a combination of national and
foreign, class and institutional interests.

Political parties constitute only one of many categories of group actors in politics. The alignment of groups that participate or seek to participate in political competition in a particular national system depends to a large extent on the level of differentiation, or complexity, of the socioeconomic system. In any system based on marked inequality, those in power will maintain armed bodies (vigilante squads, police, and/or military units) to keep the have-nots from going after what the haves have and to ensure that the labor force fulfills the role to which it has been assigned.

A ruling class cannot perpetually maintain its position through the use or threat of brute force alone, however. Thus it will seek to fortify itself by propagating a religion or ideology that sanctions the existing order. The groups or institutions that provide force (e.g., the military) and legitimacy (e.g., the Church), since they are essential to maintaining the power position of the ruling class, will soon acquire a measure of power in their own right. In fact, at any level of development ruling elites must stabilize their own power positions by balancing the enforcers, or wielders of force, against the bestowers of legitimacy.

In an international system characterized by colonialism or hegemony (dominance by a foreign power), the ruling class of a colony or client state may be highly dependent on a foreign power. In most of Latin America, the conquering class remained Spanish or Portuguese, protected and legitimized by Spanish or Portuguese troops and clergymen for some 300 years.

Typically, in Latin America, participants in the political system at the time independence was achieved were the *hacendados,* or members of the landowning class, the military, and the Roman Catholic Church. The hegemony that had been exercised by Spain and Portugal during the colonial period was soon assumed by the United States in Mexico, Central America, and the Caribbean and by Great Britain (with lesser participation by other European powers) in South America. The United States gave strong competition to the British and other European powers in South America during the first half of the twentieth century and, by the end of World War II, had consolidated its position of dominance over the whole of Latin America.

The pace and order of the admission of new groups and classes to political participation have varied from country to country, having proceeded most rapidly in the Southern Cone countries and most slowly in the Andean and Central American highlands. In general, a commercial sector, associated with export-import operations, was admitted during the last half of the nineteenth century, and industrial elites and middle classes began participating in the first decades of the twentieth century. By the 1920s and 1930s, labor was organizing and making its bid, but in few countries was it admitted to participation before the 1940s and 1950s. The admission of peasants, by nonrevolutionary means, was scarcely even at issue until the 1960s, and it was not until 1979 in Ecuador and 1980 in Peru that new constitutions gave illiterates—the Indian peasants—the vote for the first time in those countries. Peasant participation has been rare and tenuous, and the peasants' gains, like those of organized labor, were reversed in several countries in the 1960s and 1970s through counterrevolution. In politics, there is no "final analysis"; as far as we know, participation and its perquisites may be won and lost and won again ad infinitum.

POLITICAL ACTORS AND ARENAS

The means of seeking entry into, or control of, a political system depends on the strength of the particular group, or political actor, and the openness of the system. In general, however, elections and other processes associated with the democratic system become available to groups previously excluded only *after* they have become organized and have demonstrated, through illegal or extralegal means, their ability to disrupt the system and threaten the interests of the power elite. Furthermore, as Charles Anderson has noted, election results are by no means considered sacred by all participants; elections are but one of the many means of garnering and demonstrating power.[1]

Anderson has pointed out that there are certain resources, or "power capabilities," without which governments would find it difficult or even impossible to function. These resources include, for example, a cooperative labor force, agricultural or industrial production, control over the use of armed force, moral sanction, popular support, and the support of a dominant foreign power. In order to secure participation in or control over the political process, political groups, or "power contenders," must demonstrate control of a power capability.

In most contemporary Latin American countries, these power contenders would include landowners, industrial and commercial elites, religious leaders, military factions, labor unions, political parties, students and intellectual leaders, foreign corporations, and agencies of foreign governments. In distinguishing between power contenders and power capabilities, Anderson notes that within the military establishment, the business community, the labor movement, or even the Catholic Church, there are generally various factions seeking to speak for the institution or the community. (Even agencies of the US government have been seen marching to different drummers. Civilian politicians in several countries have found, to their dismay, that the support of the US ambassador did not assure the support of the Pentagon and the CIA as well.) In order to be "taken into account" by the groups that are already participants in the system, a new power contender must flex its muscles. A military faction might demonstrate control of a power capability without firing a shot by establishing a credible claim to the loyalty of a few important garrisons. A labor federation might demonstrate such control by calling a successful general strike; a peasant group, by seizing a significant amount of land; a student group, by amassing a large turnout for a march; a political party, by receiving a sizable vote. Traditional participants, feeling threatened, might in turn demonstrate their own capabilities; disinvestment and capital flight are among the many ways economic elites may respond to threat.

When a new power contender demonstrates its capabilities, the power elite must decide whether the greater risk lies in admitting the new group to participation in the system or in attempting to suppress it. The new group may be admitted if the risk of suppression appears to be as great as the risk of recognition, and if groups that are already participating believe that the new group will be willing to abide by the rules of the game—that is, to respect the perquisites of the other players. Thus what Anderson calls the normal rule of Latin American political change, and what I call the defining principle of the evolutionary process, is that new power contenders may be added to the system but old ones may not be eliminated.

Political conflict, as Martin C. Needler notes, takes place simultaneously in various "arenas," differing in accessibility to social groups, in methods or "weapons" of competition, and in visibility to the public.[2] In the least developed political systems, the dominant arena is the private one, where family pressures, personal contacts, bribery, blackmail, and graft determine the outcome of political conflict. In the most highly developed polities, decisions are reached through popular election, parliamentary debate, and judicial review. Between the development levels of court intrigue and constitutional mediation of conflict is a level in which conflict takes place in the streets—in which demonstrations, strikes, and riots determine the outcome of the conflict.

Merging the models of Needler and Anderson, we might say that the "street arena" holds sway while the political elite is unwilling to admit new participants to the system but is unable to repress them fully. The street arena is employed not only by nonelites on the way up but by elites who fear that they are on the way down. When elites in a more highly developed constitutional system begin to feel that their interests are threatened by electoral and other constitutional processes, they will use the street arena—the provocation of highly visible "instability"— along with other arenas in preparing the way for counterrevolution.

SOCIAL CHANGE AND POLITICAL PROCESS

What factors, then, determine when and how participation will be won or lost by various groups and classes of Latin American societies? Many of the factors that contribute to pressure for social change fall into the category Karl Deutsch has labeled "social mobilization"—urbanization, education, and mass communication and the consequent "revolution of rising expectations."[3] The transistor radio has been called the greatest force for change in the twentieth century.

The circulation of new ideas or ideologies imported from other societies (Liberalism at the turn of the nineteenth century, Marxism at the turn of the twentieth) or revived from earlier eras of preconquest or national experience (Mexican and Andean *indigenismo* or "nativism," Nicaraguan *sandinismo*) may give momentum and a sense of direction to otherwise sporadic or unfocused social unrest. Likewise, hope may be aroused and organization promoted by the appearance of agents of change. These agents may be foreigners with new ideas and ambitions, such as labor leaders who emigrated from Europe at the turn of the twentieth century or representatives of foreign or international development agencies who have descended on Latin America since the 1960s. Or they may be Latin Americans associated with new institutions or with old institutions that are assuming new roles. Students, for example, became agents of change after national universities came into being in the early twentieth century, and Catholic clergymen and nuns, inspired by liberation theology, became powerful agents of change in the 1970s and 1980s. Pressure for change may also be generated by natural or man-made disasters, such as earthquakes or wars, by an abrupt downturn in the economy, or by a particularly greedy or brutal move by the ruling classes—a paranoid overreaction, for example, to some minor incident of protest or insubordination.

The factors that contribute to pressure for social change do not, however, in themselves predetermine what the nature of that change will be. The nature of the

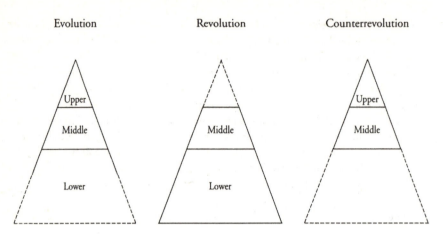

FIGURE 10.1   Political Participation by Social Strata: The Collapsible Pyramid

change that comes in response to social mobilization is a product of the interaction of the forces of change and the forces of resistance. If the political elite is willing and able to share power, incorporating new groups into the polity, change will follow the evolutionary pattern. If the elite is unwilling to share, determined instead to repress would-be participants, change may take the form of revolution, of counterrevolution, or of a holding operation (indecisive cycles of insurrection and repression) I call "boundary maintenance." The outcome will depend largely on the relative strength, unity, and determination of the opposing forces.

Thus the major political processes that may flow from social change or pressure for additional social change will be labeled, for the purposes of a model that can be called "the collapsible pyramid," as evolution, revolution, and counterrevolution (Figure 10.1). Political evolution implies the incorporation of new political actors, representing previously unrepresented social strata, without the displacement of previous participants in the system. Revolution is defined as the displacement or disestablishment of groups representing one or more strata from the upper reaches of the social pyramid. My definition of counterrevolution is implied in that of revolution. It is the displacement, or elimination from effective participation, of groups representing strata from the base of the social pyramid.

Evolution

The experiences of Latin American countries suggest that limitations on a client state's links to the dominant foreign power and racial or ethnic homogeneity are among the factors that make it more likely that change will follow the evolutionary pattern. Each of these two factors has independent explanatory power, but in Latin America, the two are also related historically.

Limitations on colonial or neocolonial control may be a consequence of, among other things, physical distance, competition among prospective hegemonic powers, or the relative absence of strategic or material assets. The political significance of such limitations is that, unable to rely on the backing of the dominant foreign power, the political elite may find it necessary to come to terms with new groups seeking participation. The first Latin American states in which the middle class, and to a lesser extent the working class, gained access to political power were those of the Southern Cone—Argentina, Uruguay, and, somewhat later, Chile. This area, which offered neither the gold and silver nor the exploitable Indian civilizations of the Andean and Middle American highlands, was of little interest to the Spanish crown. The Rio de la Plata basin was among the last areas of the New World to be settled by Europeans and among the first to declare and win independence.

Relative to the rigid hierarchical systems of Mexico, Peru, and other early centers of royal domination, the social systems of the Southern Cone were loosely stratified, and their political systems were fluid. The nomadic Indians of the pampas were gradually exterminated, while those across the Andes in Chile—fewer than 100,000 in the late nineteenth century—were confined on reservations. Most of the African captives who were delivered to the Rio de la Plata basin were subsequently transshipped north to zones where plantations were dominant. Argentina and Uruguay, predominantly mestizo at the time of independence, became overwhelmingly European as a consequence of large-scale immigration in the late nineteenth century. Chile's predominantly mestizo population was also relatively homogeneous. Thus the social distance to be bridged in those countries in the incorporation of new groups into the polity was not nearly so great as in the countries of predominant Indian population, presided over by a tiny Hispanic elite.

From the late colonial period until the end of World War II, the Southern Cone countries were subjects of competition among hegemonic powers. Great Britain had competed very successfully with Spain for dominance in matters of trade even before the struggle for independence was undertaken. Britain then remained the dominant, though not unchallenged, foreign power in the area until World War II. The rise of the middle class and the beginnings of labor organization occurred long before the United States acquired dominance over the area.

Other areas that have experienced evolutionary change have displayed some of the same characteristics. Venezuela and Costa Rica, for example, had sparse native American populations and were of little interest to the Spanish. Both have relatively homogeneous populations. Both were among the last areas to be settled by Europeans, and Venezuela, along with Argentina, was one of the first settlement areas to develop important trade ties with Britain and to rise in revolt against Spain. Representative government has been the rule rather than the exception in Costa Rica since the 1880s. In abolishing its army in 1948, Costa Rica eliminated a major threat to participation.[4]

The bid of the middle classes for participation has generally come about in conjunction with urbanization and the expansion of national institutions and government services. Spearheaded by merchants, bureaucrats, or students and intellectuals, middle-class movements have often led to the organization of new parties advocating social reform and appealing to incipient labor organizations. Victory at the ballot box, however, has generally been the confirmation, rather than the means, of middle-class ascent. The strength of the movement or party has had to be demonstrated first in the street arena, and its initial assumption of power has often been assisted by "young Turks" within the military.

As middle-class parties have generally needed the support of organized labor and to a lesser extent of peasants in order to confront the traditional political elite, the assumption of power by such parties has meant at least limited participation for the working classes as well—participation expressed, for example, in the right of collective bargaining as well as in the vote. Working-class groups may also be admitted prematurely to the political system, before their capabilities for disruption are fully developed, through the initiatives of one sector of the political elite that is seeking to enhance its position over another or by power holders seeking to maintain some degree of control over the development of labor's capabilities. Brazilian caudillo Getúlio Vargas cultivated labor as a counterpoise to the economic elite, but he kept it under the firm control of the labor ministry. In Colombia, the preemptive admission of organized labor and its incorporation into the pyramidal structures of the traditional parties delayed labor organization along horizontal lines of class interest.

The redistribution of power implied in the evolutionary process should be reflected in the long term in a redistribution of goods and services toward the newly participant groups. But this does not necessarily imply a redistribution toward all disadvantaged classes. For example, the economic position of a participating organized labor force may be enhanced while that of unorganized peasants or of unemployed and underemployed urban workers deteriorates. In Venezuela, the middle-class parties gained admittance to the system by incorporating the strength of organized labor into their own. Nevertheless, while organized labor has reaped the benefits of political participation, there is a large and growing class of unorganized poor in Venezuela for whom the resultant inflation has only made things worse.

Effective working-class participation and thoroughgoing redistribution have been known to come about, even in Latin America, through the evolutionary process. In the early twentieth century, Uruguay, without suffering the devastation of social revolution, came to enjoy one of the most fully democratic systems and most highly developed welfare states in the world. In 1973, however, Uruguay's social and political advantages were erased by a brutal counterrevolution that brought the military to power until 1984.

While economies were expanding (in Uruguay, for example, from early to mid twentieth century), the demands of newly participant social strata, such as urban labor, could be met without undue threat to the perquisites of traditional elites and middle classes; a concession to one pressure group was not necessarily at the expense of another. Moreover, the illusion of economic expansion could be maintained for a while by artificial means such as inflation or foreign borrowing. But when economies began to decline, the upper and middle classes came to fear that the gains of labor could only be at their expense. Moreover, in highly dependent economies, like those of Latin America, foreign businesses that feel threatened may appeal to their home governments and to public and private lending institutions to initiate measures, such as credit freezes and trade embargoes, that damage all economic interests in the client state.

Thus the economic elites, both foreign and domestic, with substantial middle-class support, backed by the dominant foreign power and fronted by the armed forces, move to silence lower-class demands and to regain control of the processes whereby wealth and power are allocated. Such was the fate of Brazil and the Southern Cone.

Costa Rica and Venezuela, the countries that most successfully maintained their evolutionary systems through the 1970s, were blessed with relatively healthy economies. But Costa Rica's economy, disabled by a drop in coffee prices, took a nosedive in the early 1980s. That country's democratic system was made more vulnerable by the efforts of the Reagan administration to transform its nonprofessional civil guard into a professional military establishment, and its social welfare system was stripped in the 1990s to meet the conditions of creditors.

Petrodollars have freed the Venezuelan government to meet the most urgent demands of the lower and middle classes without seriously taxing the rich. But petroleum wealth has not been converted into agricultural development and industrial diversification fast enough to alleviate the effects of oil-induced inflation and to bridge the gap between rich and poor. Rather, its social welfare system was stripped in the 1990s to meet the conditions of creditors; the oil bonanza has served, for the most part, to bloat the bureaucracy. The global oil glut of the 1980s, coupled with the foreign debt and the austerity measures imposed by creditors, has brought social tensions closer to the surface. Those tensions erupted in early 1989 in a popular rampage that left more than 300 dead and demonstrated the fragility of Venezuela's democracy.

Revolution

The displacement of a social stratum through revolution does not necessarily mean the physical elimination of individuals or the blocking of their participation, as individuals, in the political system. Rather, it means the removal of the resources (material or institutional) that have enabled them to exercise power as a class.

The revolutionary process is likely to involve violence both in the initial phase of insurgency and repression and in the secondary phase of struggle among insurgent groups. If the redistributional phase is delayed, renewed violence is likely to accompany that phase as well. But politics is the process whereby power relationships are established, so violence—or the threat of it—is implicit in all political processes. The violence accompanying revolution is not necessarily greater than that which accompanies other political processes.

The Cuban revolution claimed several thousand lives, but considerably fewer than the Argentine counterrevolution, which claimed some 10,000 to 30,000. About 50,000 people were killed in the course of the Nicaraguan revolution, and another 30,000 or so were killed in postrevolutionary struggles against the US-sponsored Contras, or counterrevolutionary forces, but an even greater number of Guatemalans have been killed, mainly by vigilantes and official security forces, in the "boundary maintenance" effort—the effort, essentially, to keep the Indians "in their place"—that characterized Guatemalan politics from 1954 at least until 1997. The Colombian *violencia*, suggestive of the pattern whereby elites maintain their position while nonelites fight only among themselves, claimed more than 200,000 lives over more than a decade (mainly 1948 to 1958) of sporadic, non-purposeful fighting. Revolution is only one—and perhaps the least likely—of many possible outcomes of violent confrontation.

The term "revolution" has been used very loosely, especially since the success of the Cuban revolution in 1959 spread hope or fear, depending on one's point of view, throughout the Americas. It has been used as a synonym for violence, for social change, or for regime change; it has even been appropriated by rightist military rulers, like those who seized the Brazilian government in 1964, in vain attempts to legitimize their own counterrevolutions. In fact, however, successful revolutions are most rare.

In the Western Hemisphere, Haiti was the only society to dismantle an entire ruling class (the French planters) in the process of ousting the colonial power. Haiti was not only the first Latin American country to gain independence (1804) and to undergo a successful revolution, but the first state in the modern world to be born of a slave revolt.

The other Latin American countries that have experienced successful revolutions are Mexico (1911), Bolivia (1952), Cuba (1959), and Nicaragua (1979). Insurrectionary forces showed great strength in El Salvador in the 1980s and remarkable tenacity, at least, in Guatemala, but counterrevolutionary forces, backed by the United States, also remained strong, as conflict surged and ebbed and surged again without resolution (see Chapter 16).

Facilitating Factors. Reams have been written on the causes of revolution in Latin America. Most of the causal factors cited fall into the category I have labeled "social mobilization." Such factors may rightly be viewed as causing pressure for political change, but in themselves they do not cause violent revolution. A necessary, though not sufficient, cause of violent revolution is the violent arrest of the nonviolent pursuit of change—the blocking of the evolutionary process.

Factors that have facilitated or contributed to the perpetual blockage of the evolutionary process, and thus to the maintenance of a low level of political participation, have included great social distance between elites and masses and proximity to the hegemonic power. The importance of the social distance factor lies in part in paranoia. The small elites of European origin who preside over a different racial group with an alien culture tend to feel vulnerable and fear that the slightest break in the traditional system of authority will unleash the contained wrath of centuries. Rather than welcoming the development of an incipient middle class that might serve a brokerage role and accepting the marginal political changes that might allow "things to go on as they are," the elites systematically eradicate would-be political brokers and strive to maintain a vacuum in the political center. This pattern has been particularly clear in recent decades in El Salvador and Guatemala.

The significance of close ties between dominant and client states has several facets. Bulwarked by the might of the colonial or hegemonic power, colonial or client-state oligarchies are under little pressure to offer incremental concessions to middle or lower classes. But, as previously noted, there is also a historical connection between the factors of social distance and external control. European civilization in the New World was built quite literally on the ruins of Indian ones, and figuratively on the backs of Indians and transplanted Africans. So it is no coincidence that the areas of earliest and deepest penetration by the colonial powers are also the areas of least racial homogeneity and greatest social distance. Those are also the areas in which landed aristocracies, with the long-term backing of colonial military, religious, and bureaucratic authority, became most firmly entrenched.

Even after routing the Spanish, the supposedly free states of Middle America and the Caribbean had little respite from foreign domination. After seizing half of

Mexico's territory, the United States, devastated by its own civil war, had to suffer competition from the French in Mexico and from the British in Central America in the latter half of the nineteenth century. But by the turn of the twentieth century, US control over that area was virtually complete. In the Dominican Republic, Hispanic elites, frightened by Haiti's successful slave revolt and a subsequent period of Haitian occupation of their end of the island, scrambled to exchange national sovereignty for security under the flag of some stronger country. They succeeded in persuading the Spanish to return for a brief sojourn. Cuba, after the Spanish-American War, merely exchanged one foreign master for another.

Thus there was rarely a time when middle-class pretenders, sporting reformist ideas, could pose a credible threat to ruling aristocracies. As major US corporations became an integral part of the power elite of those countries, the US government signaled that it would intervene militarily, if necessary, to protect the economic order from the greed and depredations of hungry natives. In fact, the United States did intervene extensively in the area and established constabularies in several countries that eventually replaced the original landholding oligarchy at the pinnacle of power.

Finally, the greater the economic and political dominance or penetration of a foreign power, the fewer will be the nationals with a major stake in the old order. By the mid-twentieth century, the extent of US economic holdings in much of Middle America and the Caribbean, and the fact that ruling constabularies answered to the United States rather than to any sector of local society, meant that relatively few families had extensive economic interests to protect and fewer still had a stake in the political order. Furthermore, the crudeness of US power plays enhanced the importance of nationalism as a unifying theme. All of these factors facilitated the construction of a multiclass alliance in opposition to the ruling groups, particularly in Cuba and Nicaragua and to varying extents in Mexico, Guatemala, and the Dominican Republic. In the last two countries, reformist, potentially revolutionary movements were crushed in 1954 and 1965, respectively, by US military intervention.

Another social phenomenon that has correlated with insurgency and, in some cases, with successful revolution in Latin America has been the physical uprooting of subject populations. In the case of the Chaco War between Bolivia and Paraguay (1932–1935), peasants on both sides of the border, mobilized for the war, were not prepared to be demobilized when the fighting was over. In Paraguay, they contributed to the rise of a new party, which seized power in 1936. In Bolivia, they organized other Indian peasants, who ultimately seized the land and disestablished the Hispanic landholding aristocracy.

Throughout Middle America in the late nineteenth and early twentieth centuries, Indians were driven from their traditional communally held lands by Hispanic planters or US corporations intent upon cashing in on the expanding market for export crops, particularly coffee. Many of the peasant uprisings of the period, including that led by Zapata in Mexico, represented efforts to take back land that had been seized.

In Central America, the cycle of planter encroachment, peasant uprising, and government reprisal that gave rise, for example, to El Salvador's notorious *matanza* of 1932—the massacre of some 30,000 Indian peasants—has continued up to the present. The creeping uprootedness of Salvadorans was exacerbated suddenly in 1969 when the Soccer War, fought against Honduras, resulted in the displacement of some 300,000 Salvadoran peasants who had settled on uncrowded land across the Honduran border. These peasants were thrust back upon a rural society in which a majority of the peasants were already landless migrants in desperate competition for seasonal labor at meager wages. In northern Guatemala, the seizure of Indian land by non-Indians was accelerated in the 1970s when oil was discovered in the region.

The Phases of Revolution. The phases of a successful revolution that runs its full course—without falling prey to counterrevolution—may be described as (1) power transfer, (2) redistribution, (3) institutionalization, and (4) reconcentration.

Power Transfer. The political, or power transfer, phase is a twofold one, comprising the toppling of the offending regime and the consolidation of the new power structure. The first step of a revolution, the displacement of the old regime, calls for the launching of insurrectionary movements on different social levels, either independently or in coalition. Intra-elite political conflict is not in itself revolutionary. On the other hand, worker and peasant uprisings stand little chance of success unless there are important pockets of alienation in the middle class as well or unless the ruling class is sharply divided.

The dethroning, however, is only the beginning of the reallocation of political power. The affluent and the indigent, who may agree on the kind of government they do not want, cannot be expected to agree on the kind they want in its place. The struggle then continues within the coalition itself. As has often been noted, revolutions consume many of their authors.

In Mexico, after the demise of the Porfirio Díaz dictatorship in 1911, armed struggle continued intermittently for another ten years; yet another decade was to pass before power was consolidated in a predominantly middle-class party representing predominantly middle-class interests. In Bolivia, the middle-class party, the National Revolutionary Movement (MNR), which took power in 1952, chose to embrace the rampaging Indian peasants rather than attempt to suppress them. Nevertheless, the brevity of the tenure of the Bolivian revolution may be attributed in part to the facts that the competing interests of the three elements of the revolutionary triad—the MNR, the miners, and the peasants—were never reconciled and that no element of the triad was able to gain control over the others.

In the Cuban case, the consolidation of power in the hands of Castro and his rebel army, who favored, in particular, the rural poor, was facilitated by the mass exodus of middle- and upper-class Cubans to the United States. In Nicaragua the multiclass coalition that strained to project unity when Somoza fled with the national treasury in 1979 began to unravel within the year. Anti-Somoza businessmen, overwhelmed in their bid for power by the workers and peasants mobilized in support of the Sandinistas, turned to subversion in league with exiled national guardsmen and the US government.

Class Demolition and Redistribution. The fate of the various upper-level social strata, and the organizations and institutions representing them in political competition in the aftermath of revolution, has varied greatly from country to country. In general, however, a successful revolution requires the displacement of the colonial or hegemonic power that has backed the ruling elite and underwritten the old order. Such displacement does not imply that the external power is stripped of influence over the client state; rather, it means that that power is deprived of some of its prerevolutionary points of access or of its means of participating directly and overtly in domestic power struggles and policymaking. (It is not uncommon, for example, in Latin American countries that have not undergone revolution, for US officials to exercise a veto over presidential candidacies or cabinet appointments.)

In Haiti, the colonial power and the landowning aristocracy were one and the same. French officials and planters were expelled (or killed) in the course of the fighting, along with the military and religious institutions that protected and legitimized the rejected social order. Fifty years were to pass before Catholic priests again appeared on the scene.

In Mexico, the revolution disestablished the landowning aristocracy and the Church, which, until the reforms of the late 1860s, had itself been a major landowner. The revolution also displaced the sector of the business elite whose wealth and power were based on export-import operations and other external ties and weakened the ability of the United States to manipulate domestic power relationships. The national industrial sector was not a casualty of the revolution but rather a product of it; that sector was nurtured by the strengthened postrevolutionary state while the state itself began to fill the vacuum left by the displacement of foreign business interests from infrastructure (e.g., transportation and utilities) and the primary production sector.

Bolivia's landowning aristocracy was displaced in 1952 along with the private interests controlling the country's major industry, the tin mines. The Church, which had never been strong in Bolivia, was relatively unaffected, but the military officer corps was purged of the protectors of the prerevolutionary order. Although it had previously sought to suppress the MNR, the United States had little visibility in Bolivia and thus was not a major target of the revolutionary process. Consequently, the new MNR government accepted US economic and military assistance under conditions that contributed to the disintegration of the revolutionary coalition, the nurturing of a new military elite, and, ultimately, to counterrevolution. Hernán Siles Suazo, president from 1956 to 1960, commenting later on the strings attached to US assistance, said that the United States had given him just enough rope to hang himself.

Prerevolutionary Cuba was so thoroughly penetrated by US businesses that its patriarchal landholding elite and its nationally oriented industrialist class were relatively small and weak. Thus the most important displacements of the revolution were those of the hegemonic power (the United States) and the military establishment that served it and of the businesses based in or linked to the United States. Ultimately, however, almost all owners of income-producing property were deprived, as the economy was thoroughly socialized.

The initial targets of the Nicaraguan revolution were the Somocistas—the dictator, his relatives and cronies, and the National Guard that propped up the Somoza dynasty on the local level—and the United States, which had been the ultimate benefactor and protector of the dynasty. The removal of the Somocistas

provided the first fruits of victory for the purpose of redistribution. The economic
squeeze imposed by the United States and the counterrevolutionary stance adopted
by much of the remaining commercial elite led to some additional nationaliza-
tions. Nevertheless, some 60 percent of the economy remained in private hands.

The role of the Catholic Church in the Nicaraguan revolution represents a first.
Whereas in revolutions past the stance of the Church had ranged from moderate
opposition to outright hostility to insurrectionary groups and revolutionary goals,
the Nicaraguan church was among the most potent and committed elements of
the revolutionary coalition. In the aftermath of the revolution, however, while
most parish-level priests and nuns continued to support the Sandinista leadership,
the bishops withdrew their support or made it highly conditional.

Just as there has been considerable variation in the extent of displacement and
deprivation suffered by the upper classes in the aftermath of revolution, there has
been great variation in the extent of redistribution of wealth and power and in the
actual benefits reaped by lower social strata. The revolutionary process may be a
protracted one. In the case of the Mexican revolution, the constitution that set
forth the principles of the new social order did not appear until six years after the
overthrow of Porfirio Díaz in 1911, and the participation of workers and peasants
was not reflected in significant redistribution until the 1920s, under the presidency
of Alvaro Obregón. It was not until the administration of Lázaro Cárdenas
(1934–1940) that the most far-reaching redistribution was undertaken. During
that period, some 20 million hectares (49 million acres) of land were distributed to
peasant communities (*ejidos*), workers' rights were expanded and wages raised, and
the very important petroleum industry was nationalized.

The extent of redistribution and thus the success of a revolution depend in large
part on how much wealth there is to redistribute. Cuba, at the time of its revolution, was a relatively prosperous country as measured in GDP or per capita income. Redistribution primarily took the form of extended services, and within a
few years, Cuba's public health and educational systems were among the most
comprehensive in the hemisphere. In Bolivia and Nicaragua, by contrast, there was
relatively little wealth to redistribute. Haiti, where prerevolutionary wealth evaporated with the abolition of slavery, presents the starkest proof that successful revolution does not necessarily mean living happily ever after.

Institutionalization. The process of institutionalizing a revolution includes the creation of an entirely new set of political support groups as well as new constitutions,
laws, and behavior patterns. The process is complete when a mechanism for regulating succession to power is functioning more or less smoothly. The most important umbrella organization for the new support groups is usually a political party.
The Mexican revolutionary party took shape in 1929. It was reorganized in the
1930s and again in the 1940s, when it was renamed the Institutional Revolutionary
Party (PRI). Presidential elections take place every six years, and the PRI did not acknowledge defeat until 2000, though the 1988 margin was hotly contested.

The institutionalizing vehicle of the Bolivian revolution was to have been the
MNR. The MNR's first president, Víctor Paz Estenssoro, attributed the survival of
the revolution in its early years to the creation of armed peasant militias.[5] But the
party did not succeed in fully incorporating or coopting the miners or in institu-

tionalizing succession by prohibiting reelection; thus, the uninstitutionalized revolution succumbed to counterrevolution within twelve years.

In the Cuban case, the dominant vehicles of institutionalization on the national level have been the Communist Party and the Revolutionary Armed Forces. However, the levers of power in both organizations have remained in the hands of Castro and his rebels of the Sierra Maestra campaign. The national political superstructure is built on an extensive base of popular organizations. Although the mechanisms for succession at the pinnacle of power remain untested, local representation has been regulated by direct election since 1975 and members of the national legislative assembly have been chosen by direct election since 1992.

In Nicaragua, the Sandinista National Liberation Front (FSLN), which began in 1959 as a tiny insurrectionary group composed largely of university students, was already in a clearly dominant position at the time of the triumph of the revolution. Groups mobilized for fighting Somoza and his National Guard were quickly expanded and converted into vehicles for reconstruction and political support. Prerevolutionary political parties continued to operate after the revolution, but without numerical significance.

In the first elections of the postrevolutionary period, in November 1984, the Sandinistas won 67 percent of the vote. Under pressure from the United States, a coalition of prerevolutionary parties and factions withdrew from the race; but several other small parties participated and claimed seats in the National Assembly. Elections were held again in February 1990. This time, after a decade of suffering economic strangulation and proxy war mounted by the United States, the Sandinistas succumbed to defeat. The National Opposition Union (UNO), a US-funded coalition of fourteen organizations, won about 55 percent of the vote. Elements of the same coalition prevailed again in 1996, though the Sandinistas, as before, remained the largest party in the National Assembly, with about 40 percent of the seats, and regained the presidency in 2006.

Reconcentration. Thomas Jefferson once quipped that every country needs a revolution every twenty years. There is no "happily ever after" in politics. Revolutions, like other secular readjustments of power relationships, are impermanent. Wealth and power tend to reconcentrate.

Reconcentration is akin to evolution in reverse. It refers to a gradual weakening of the power and income positions of political participants from the lower echelons of the social pyramid. If a revolution is not subsequently undermined by counterrevolution, a period of reconcentration may be expected to follow the institutionalization of the revolution.

Revolutionary leaders may themselves become a "new class"—an economic as well as a power elite, as happened in Mexico. Or the new class may derive from the bureaucrats who inherit power when the revolutionary generation passes from the scene. In the Cuban case, although Castro and his rebel cohorts have conspicuously avoided the material trappings of elite status, rank differentiation, with accompanying privileges, has already crept into what was once a "people's" army.

Nevertheless, countries that have undergone successful revolutions tend to be far more stable than those in which progressive movements have been thwarted. And countries in which revolutions have been aborted, or reversed by counterrevolution, are the least stable of all. The redistribution that generally takes place within the first few years following the consolidation of a revolution gives most citizens a stake in the new government. That loyalty is likely to last at least for a couple of decades, until the passing of the revolutionary generation, and may, in fact, last long after the redistributional phase has given way to the reconcentration of wealth and power in a new class. On the other hand, where reform has been thwarted or revolution aborted, a vicious cycle of insurgency and repression generally sets in, a cycle that likewise may last for several decades.

Counterrevolution

Counterrevolution has been defined, for the purposes of this model, as the displacement of one or more strata of political participants from the base of the social pyramid. It may take place in response to an incomplete revolution or to rational or irrational fear of revolution. But it may reflect simply the recognition by economic elites that the logical long-term consequence of a political process that allows for the effective participation of nonelites will be redistribution of wealth as well as of power. In fact, since counterrevolution requires a military and paramilitary establishment at the service of an elite and/or of foreign interests, it is more likely to take place in countries in which political development has been evolutionary than in countries that have undergone successful revolution. It is precisely because the power bases of the economic elites and the connections of those elites with the military and the dominant foreign power have remained intact that a minority is able to override the apparent will of the majority—as imperfectly expressed, for example, in elections—and reverse the tide of redistribution. (The crushing of a political order through direct foreign occupation is not encompassed in this concept of counterrevolution.)

Although dictatorship has been the rule rather than the exception in the history of most Latin American countries, counterrevolution is largely a phenomenon of the latter half of the twentieth century; in earlier eras, there were rarely "participant" lower classes to be displaced. Among the first clear cases of counterrevolution was the overthrow of Guatemala's President Jacobo Arbenz in 1954, followed by the withdrawal of rights recently won by labor and the recovery by non-Indian *hacendados* of land that had been distributed to Indian peasants. Both Brazil and Bolivia underwent counterrevolution beginning in 1964, as did Chile and Uruguay in 1973. Argentina has experienced counterrevolutionary episodes periodically since 1930, the most dramatic having been those accompanying the military coups of 1966 and 1976.

Facilitating Factors. Deterioration of an economy, expressed particularly by runaway inflation, is among the most obvious factors that contribute to counterrevolution. In the face of a shrinking economic pie, middle-class elements, generally dependent and insecure, begin to see the demands of the working classes as a threat to their own precarious position. Thus a major portion of the middle class, anxious perhaps because of popular agitation and/or elite-inspired scare propaganda, aligns itself with the upper classes in a bid to reverse the trend toward redistribution.

Since the proponents of counterrevolution are a minority element of the population (were they not in a minority, their interests would not be threatened by democratic processes), counterrevolution can be successful only if that minority can rely on military and paramilitary forces that are alienated from the majority of the population. Furthermore, as the military role is central, the ultimate provocation leading to the overthrow of a reformist president and his replacement by a military government—typically, the first overt step of a counterrevolution—is often a threat to the military itself: rank-and-file insubordination, a military budget cut, or a threat of suspension of foreign military aid.

Even so, national economic elites and military establishments are not likely to undertake counterrevolution unless they can rely on the help, or at least the benign neutrality, of the dominant foreign power. With the possible exception of some of Argentina's counterrevolutionary episodes, all successful counterrevolutions in Latin America since the middle of the twentieth century have had the direct or indirect support of the United States. In some cases, economic deterioration, military alienation, middle-class fear, and other facilitating factors have been intentionally exacerbated by the actions of US government agencies. The complicity of the United States was particularly apparent in the Guatemalan, Brazilian, and Chilean cases.

The Phases of Counterrevolution. The initial phases of counterrevolution are related to those of revolution in that the struggle between proponents and opponents of counterrevolution is immediately followed by struggle among the counterrevolutionary conspirators themselves. Counterrevolution, like revolution, calls for a multiclass alliance—in this case, of upper and middle classes. It also requires a coalition of military and civilian elements. Even within the military, there are various factions with differing perspectives and objectives. In the Chilean case, the counterrevolution began with a bloody purge of the military itself.

The initial agreement among military conspirators to topple the incumbent president and to assume power in the name of the armed forces by no means assures agreement on longer-term objectives. Thus, simultaneously with the process of demobilizing the nonelites—the disarming of opponents in the street and constitutional arenas—the conspirators engage in fierce competition among themselves in the private arena. In general, power is first consolidated in the hands of the military faction favored by the dominant foreign power, though rivalry within the military is perpetual and the balance of power among factions may shift over time. Meanwhile, civilian parties and political leaders who expected to profit from the demise of their civilian opponents soon find themselves stripped of their power bases and vulnerable to the whims of the new military authorities.

Political Demobilization. The most immediate and dramatic manifestations of counterrevolution are political. The street arena is the first to be closed down. Laborers, peasants, and student leaders, for example, are killed or arrested, and their organizations are dissolved or "intervened" (taken over) by the new government. The constitutional arena is the next victim. Congress is dissolved or its less malleable members are purged. Courts and local governments are purged of uncooperative individuals. Some or all political parties are dissolved, and government ministries, university faculties, and communications media that might be obstructive or critical are purged and brought under government control. The political process moves back into the private arena, which is now centered in the military establishment but continues to embrace economic elites and representatives of the dominant foreign power.

The extent of violence involved and of government control required is dependent, of course, upon the country's level of political development: the greater the proportion of the population that had come to participate in the political system, the greater the violence required, at least initially, to demobilize it. In the cases of Argentina, Uruguay, Chile, and to a lesser extent, of Brazil and Bolivia, counterrevolution called for overt executions; disappearances (usually unacknowledged executions); the establishment of concentration camps; and systematic, highly modern, and sophisticated techniques of torture. In the case of less-developed Guatemala, counterrevolution was manifested in a reversion, so to speak, to the campaign of conquest and the Indian wars.

Although the Catholic Church, like most middle-class or nonclass national institutions, is subject to marked factionalism in the face of either revolution or counterrevolution, the severity of the violation of human rights in the course of modern counterrevolution has made the Church the primary bastion against the excesses of counterrevolutionary regimes. As the only national institution that cannot be crushed outright by military authorities, the Church becomes the refuge of last resort for the dissident and the devastated.

Once power has been consolidated in a dominant military faction and effective opposition to counterrevolution has been crushed, authorities are free to move ahead with the transformation of the economy.

Economic Transformation. Counterrevolutions do not merely freeze socioeconomic relationships or maintain the status quo. The expulsion of lower social strata (e.g., workers and peasants) from the political arena results in redistribution of wealth from the bottom up. This may be accomplished through a combination of tax, tariff, budget, wage, and land tenure policies. Land reform measures may be revoked or squatters may be expelled. Graduated personal and corporate income taxes may be diminished or abandoned in favor of regressive taxes. Social services may be cut, and wages may be frozen in the face of inflation.

The central role of the military and paramilitary forces dictates that their budgets will be expanded. The involvement of the hegemonic power and/or the requirement of external aid and investment dictate acceleration of the denationalization of resources and the adoption of policies that favor foreign enterprises over national ones. Thus the national industrialist class, which supported counterrevolution as a means of containing the demands of labor, finds itself crippled by tariff and credit policies and foreign competition. And the middle class, having lost free expression and political participation, suffers also the shrinkage of its economic mainstay—government employment.

Institutionalization. Institutionalization does not come easily to counterrevolutionary regimes, partly because of the difficulty of achieving legitimacy. Establishing procedures to routinize policymaking and the succession to power in a manner that does not threaten the power position of the ruling faction or of the counterrevolutionary elite also proves difficult.

Counterrevolutionary regimes have often sought the support, or at least the acceptance, of certain sectors or institutions by labeling themselves "revolutionary" or "Christian." Such regimes in Bolivia were able to court, or at least to neutralize, most peasant groups for the better part of the decade by waving the revolutionary banner while crushing the miners and other elements of organized labor. The revolutionary label adopted by Brazil's military rulers in 1964, however, did not appear to impress anyone.

Regimes claiming to be bastions of "Western Christian values confronting atheistic communism" often succeeded initially in attracting support from some element of the Church hierarchy. But as the oppressed tend to cast their lot with any institution that dares to speak for them, the weight of the Church's influence has shifted to those members of the hierarchy who have defied the government. In defending the poor and other victims of government oppression, the Church itself becomes liable to government reprisal. Once clergymen and nuns have been added to the ranks of those subjected to imprisonment, torture, and execution, it becomes more difficult for any element of the Church hierarchy to continue to serve as apologist for the regime. Thus appeals to the pious soon lose their credibility, and counterrevolutionary regimes fall back on the slogans of "national security" and "free enterprise" that appeal to their own limited constituencies.

Counterrevolutionary regimes, like other ruling elites, have sometimes attempted to coopt or to establish political movements or parties on the supposition that such movements or parties could be controlled from the top and grassroots initiatives could be blocked. But they have generally found that organizational initiatives carry unwarranted risks and may prove counterproductive.

Military governments are not necessarily counterrevolutionary, but counterrevolutionary governments are necessarily military, generally with considerable paramilitary support (police, vigilantes, "death squads," etc.) as well, since the abrupt reconcentration of wealth and power can be carried out only by armed force. Such regimes have begun their tenure as institutional ones, or what I will call "militocracies." Power is seized and exercised in the name of the armed forces as such, rather than by a caudillo, and the military establishment as a whole becomes the first-line political base of the government. The nominal president may be civilian, as was the case in Uruguay from 1973 to 1981, and a congress may be allowed to convene, as was usually the case in Brazil between 1964 and 1985, but such officials hold their posts for the convenience and at the sufferance of the military. Elections and plebiscites, held with varying degrees of regularity and under varying degrees and techniques of control, are the rule rather than the exception.

The failure of such regimes to achieve legitimacy may be compensated for by the maintenance of a high level of repression and coercion, but the failure to routinize succession to power means continual instability and vulnerability. The process whereby the most powerful position, be it the presidency or the highest military or army post, changes hands among individuals and factions is generally one or another form of palace coup, although it may be bloodless and may be sanctified by "elections."

In the Brazilian case, probably the most successful institutionalization of a counterrevolutionary regime, the succession process generally involved an "election" or polling process carried out among the highest-ranking officers (e.g., four-star generals). The victor of that process was then "nominated" by the official party and duly elected by an electoral college including members of the national congress and representatives of state legislative assemblies. Military elections—formal or informal polling among upper-echelon officers—are not simulations of democratic process; rather, they are simulated battles, as votes are weighted in accordance with command of firepower.

Decompression. Decompression (in Portuguese, *distensão*) is a term used by Brazilians in reference to the process that got under way in their country about 1978. In this discussion the term refers to the process in other countries as well—a process of attenuation of the power and control of the military and other counterrevolutionary forces, resulting in a lessening of repression and an increase in political participation, particularly by the middle class.

The factors that tend to weaken the grip of a counterrevolutionary elite are not unlike those that undermine other elites and other systems. They include division within the ruling group or between that group and its constituencies, economic stress, and external pressure. Commonly, all of these factors come into play simultaneously and reinforce each other.

The headiness of power and the spoils of office, not to mention the occasionally genuine conflicts of ideologies, are just as conducive to competition within a military caste as within a ruling civilian elite. If power becomes highly concentrated in the hands of an individual or a clique, other factions that have ceased to profit adequately from military rule may garner support from civilian groups in order to unseat the offending individual or clique. The price of civilian support will be a commitment to some degree of political opening.

Economic stress is likely to exacerbate divisions within the military as well as to alienate some elements of its constituency. The support of the dominant foreign power may be weakened or even withdrawn as a consequence of the regime's economic mismanagement. Also the level of repression may reach such proportions as to embarrass the hegemonic power. Such was the case in the mid-1970s when human rights policies adopted by the US Congress and highlighted briefly by the Carter administration served to weaken, at least temporarily, some of Latin America's counterrevolutionary regimes.

In the Brazilian case, all of these factors were apparent in the 1970s. But Brazil's decompression gained additional impetus as the façade of democracy—the apparatus of parties, elections, and representative bodies that had served the regime well in the process of institutionalization—blossomed into a reality beyond the facile control of the still dominant military. In Bolivia, neither revolution nor counterrevolution has gained any semblance of institutionalization; instability has reigned supreme. When the military abandoned power in 1982 to the government of Hernán Siles Suazo—elected but suppressed in 1980—it was primarily because the economy had collapsed under the weight of military corruption. Economic collapse was also a major factor in the disintegration of the Argentine regime that occurred in early 1983, but the disintegration had been accelerated by humiliating defeat in the Falklands/Malvinas war of 1982.

From Aristocracy to Militocracy

In general, the constitutional and legal systems of Latin American countries were borrowed from France and the United States and, at least until the twentieth century, served merely to legitimize political arrangements that had been reached in private—in the smoke-filled rooms of men's clubs and other gathering places of the wealthy. In such arenas, competition among landholding families, and later between landholders and representatives of new wealth based on international commerce and industry, could be regulated. Such competition was not necessarily peaceful; it often led to clashes among armed hirelings of families or sectors of the economic elite. But electoral and parliamentary systems were little more than a ritualistic adjunct to a process based on wealth, force, and interpersonal intrigue.

It was only with the successful bid for participation by the middle classes that electoral and parliamentary systems came to have a serious function. In general, however, Latin America's middle classes have not constituted an intermediate level of property holders. Nor have they represented other independent sources of wealth. Rather, they have been a salaried class, derived from and dependent on the expansion of commerce and government. Their bid for effective participation, beginning in the late nineteenth century in Argentina and continuing into the late twentieth century in Central America and the Andean highlands, could not (and cannot) rest on their own numbers and resources alone. They found it necessary to incorporate the numbers and the potential disruptiveness of lower social strata, particularly the incipient labor movement, into their power bases. Middle-class bids for political power have generally been spearheaded by university students and intellectuals and carried to fruition by political parties, but they have rarely been successful unless they were believed to have the backing of organized labor. Thus the effectiveness of the ballot box has been preceded by an effective demonstration of power on the streets and in the factories.

Where, for reasons of social distance based on racial and ethnic difference, the original postconquest aristocracy has concluded that it *dare* not expand political participation, and/or, for reasons of powerful external support, the economic elite has concluded that it *need* not expand political participation, the upshot has been either revolution or "boundary maintenance" depending on the relative strengths of contending forces.

Where aristocracies have felt constrained to give in to middle-class demands for effective political participation, democratic processes have acquired substance—for a time and to a point. But middle-class leaders have generally proved unable or unwilling to extend fully effective participation, through the electoral system, to urban workers and peasants, particularly when economic decline has sharpened competition between middle and lower classes.

Uruguay's felicitous early experience with the evolutionary process does not seem likely to be repeated in Latin America in the near future. Although a middle class may rise to the full exercise of political power through the evolutionary process, recent developments in Latin America suggest that, at least for the time being, there is a high threshold of participation that manual workers and peasants will not be allowed to cross.

Once middle-class parties and labor organizations have been incorporated into the system, political conflict may come to be centered in the constitutional arena. But at least in Latin America and perhaps in most dependent states, limited participatory democracy contains the seeds of its own destruction. The greater the level of effective participation and the longer the unbroken tenure of constitutional rule, the more policy will incline toward nationalism, nonalignment, and egalitarianism. Thus the middle class, dependent on salaries from the government or the property-holding upper class and insecure in its status, begins to align itself with the upper class. These classes, seeing their power slipping away and their economic interests threatened, abandon the constitutional arena. They enlist the military establishment and the United States in their defense against the perceived threat—until recently "the menace of communism." Thus counterrevolution is most likely and most violent precisely in those systems that have achieved the highest levels of political development through the evolutionary process.

The destabilized constitutional system is then replaced by a militocracy—a system in which the military establishment as a whole serves as a ruling elite. Competition for power within this system assumes the form of simulated battles, as command of firepower confers political power. Civilian instigators and supporters of counterrevolution soon find that military rulers are not content to become their pawns. Although economic policy initially reflects the interests of the counterrevolutionary coalition, over time it increasingly reflects the institutional and personal interests of military officers themselves.

Counterrevolutionary systems, like evolutionary and revolutionary ones, and the political and economic gains and losses they represent, are impermanent. But the praetorianism, or militarism, that facilitates counterrevolution and is in turn strengthened by it appears more durable. The Argentine military has often withdrawn in the period since the overthrow of Perón in 1955, but never to a safe enough distance to allow labor a free rein. Even though the military establishments of Chile and Uruguay withdraw from the direct exercise of power, it was not possible for those countries to return until after the turn of the century to the free-wheeling democracies that flourished before the counterrevolutions of the 1970s. Even if elections are unfettered, it will remain clear that full powers are not vested in the electorate. The experiences of Latin American countries suggest that nothing short of revolution would be likely to bring those military establishments fully under civilian control. And as Bolivia can attest, even revolution offers no long-term guarantees against militarism. At any rate, in countries having acquired a large middle class, revolution is no longer an option. And in the post–Cold War global village, where economic policymaking is centrally controlled by a creditor cartel, conquest of the state would no longer be much of a prize.

Transitions and Illusions

The end of the Cold War, and with it the end of the dialogue as to optimal and feasible means of organizing a new order, coincided with the end of militocracy in Latin America and the spread of democracy—at least the input, or electoral, side of it—over much of the globe. This welcome development may have become possible, however, precisely because those whose interests would be most threatened by egalitarianism did not feel threatened by the US-marketed election-as-spectacle approach to democracy, with its soaring costs and sinking value.

By the end of the 1980s—particularly after the elections in Paraguay and Chile in 1989—all of the South American countries had acquired a façade, at least, of civilian, constitutional rule. The "redemocratization" of Central America responded to a somewhat different set of pressures and dynamics, including greater sensitivity to the peculiarities of foreign policy decision making in Washington. The Reagan administration, seeking to roll back the revolution in Nicaragua and to crush rebellion in El Salvador and Guatemala, had found that scheduling elections throughout the region would persuade a recalcitrant Democratic Congress to continue appropriating military assistance. It was only in the 1990s, when US interests and priorities changed, that the process of pacific settlement, initiated by Latin American leaders and supported by the United Nations, bore fruit and elections acquired a meaningful role in the political process. Even then, however, elected leaders generally operated within parameters narrowly drawn by military and paramilitary bodies and domestic and foreign economic elites.

Redemocratization was accompanied early on by increasing indebtedness and surrender of economic sovereignty, the discrediting of reformist leaders and programs, and a return to economic elitism, albeit buffered by parties and parliaments and the ritual of elections. Civilian leaders sometimes appeared to be virtual prisoners in their own presidential palaces, and violence, particularly against the poor, continued unabated. A Brazilian social worker commented that the military dictatorship had "democratized" the violation of human rights in the sense that many among the usually untouchable rich were also abused. The subsequent redemocratization has meant that violations have once again been restricted to the poor, who have always been vulnerable.

In the first few years of the twenty-first century, as in the early 1960s, most Latin American governments were considered democratic because elections had taken place. In both instances, there was less to such democracy than met the eye. The obstacles and deceits were, however, of a different order. In the early 1960s, "democracy" was being discredited in Central America and the Caribbean by fraud, in the Southern Cone by vulnerability to military intervention. In the early years of the twenty-first century democracy was being discredited by irrelevance— by the absence of options and expectations. The democracy of the 1960s was unstable precisely because there was hope—hope that political democracy might lead in the direction of economic democracy. The democracy of the early 2000s was more nearly stable because there was little such hope (and consequently little fear). More than ever, electoral politics had become the moral equivalent of sport. Military force was no longer required to hold the line. The politically articulate were kept in check by the lack of options—and the lack of an alternate theoretical paradigm; and the desperate were distanced from the comfortable by gated communities and new categories of police.

CHALLENGES FOR A NEW MILLENNIUM

The problems now facing the continent's old and new democratic regimes are staggering, but they are not the same problems that most preoccupied national leaders during the last interlude of civilian rule a generation ago. That earlier generation of civilian leaders sought means of modernizing their economies at minimal cost to traditional and marginal sectors. As it happened, the cost has been scandalous, but modernization has indeed taken place. The overriding problems now are not those associated with traditionalism but rather with the flotsam of modernization: inflation and unemployment, urbanization and population growth, migration and displaced persons, crumbling cities, crime, pollution, and dwindling resources.

In the 1990s and into the new century, those Latin Americans who had dared to hope that the end of militocracy would bring economic development and social justice were sadly disillusioned. In fact, security forces still hovered. And inequitable socioeconomic systems were reinforced by the demands of foreign creditors and international financial institutions. Civilian elites who could no longer blame the military for policies that serve to line their own pockets at the expense of the impoverished masses could pass the buck to the seemingly omnipotent International Monetary Fund.

The resurgence of electoral politics from the 1980s into the twenty-first century came about in part because both military and civilian elites had come to recognize the need for an institutional buffer zone between management and labor, or between haves and have-nots. That is, elites had become willing to share their power—or at least their stage—so long as their new partners also shared the blame for inequitable policies. Even so, in many cases Latin America's return to democracy was instigated in large part by genuinely popular movements, parties, and leaders. Particularly in those cases, however, organization charts notwithstanding, the elected leaders lacked the full powers normally associated with the office: most important, control over military and paramilitary forces, including the police, and over resource allocation.

Potemkin Democracy

After a run of just over a dozen years, the redemocratization trend in Latin America began to be challenged. The overthrow in September 1991 of Haiti's civilian president, Father Jean-Bertrand Aristide, elected in 1990 by an impressive 68 percent majority, unleashed a savage assault on the Haitian people and prompted an exodus of refugees to an unwelcoming United States. Less than a year later, in April 1992, Peru's elected president, Alberto Fujimori, in league with the country's military high command, staged a coup of his own, dissolving the congress and detaining many of its members, particularly leaders of the dominant party, APRA.

In Venezuela, characterized for more than three decades by high per capita income and stable civilian rule, the debt crisis of the late 1980s forced incoming president Carlos Andrés Pérez of the social democratic party, Acción Democrática, to adopt extreme austerity measures. The upshot was rioting and police countermeasures that resulted in some 300 deaths by official count, 1,000 or more by unofficial count. The instability and discontent that followed generated a climate propitious for military conspiracy, which expressed itself in two abortive coup attempts in 1992.

Much of Latin America seemed be settling once again for a system relatively open but heavily compromised, a midpoint on the spectrum of political possibilities long known as *dictablanda* or *democradura* (soft dictatorship or hard democracy). New forms of authoritarianism had not been widely recognized as such, however, because in most cases repression had been selective or subtle, and elections, complete with hoopla and foreign observers, continued to take place regularly. In that regard, the Peruvian case appeared to be a harbinger. New elections several months after the 1992 coup restored credit and international respectability even though they were boycotted by the major parties.

Staging regular elections in Latin America without eliminating fraud or expanding effective participation also served to legitimate older authoritarian systems, thus giving them a new lease on life. The Paraguayan elections of May 9, 1993, for example, aroused international interest in that they offered the prospect that after almost a half century of military dictatorship Paraguay might at last undergo a transition to democracy. Paraguay had indeed come a long way since the corrupt and brutal thirty-five-year rule of General Alfredo Stoessner was ended by a coup d'état in 1989. But in 1993 the ruling triad of military, bureaucracy, and official party (the Colorados) still controlled most of the money, all of the weapons, and all of the electoral machinery. Even so, a new generation mobilized to force a democratic opening. Freedom of expression and of assembly gradually came to be generally respected; and the electoral process, flawed as it was, gave the opposition a leverage point from which to extract concessions. By 1996, the judiciary and the electoral tribunal had undergone major reform.

Meanwhile, in the 1990s, elections in Mexico were becoming more competitive in partisan terms, as the business-oriented National Action Party (PAN) and the left-leaning Revolutionary Democratic Party (PRD) wrested major provincial and municipal posts as well as congressional seats from the control of the PRI, seriously weakened by assassination, increasingly blatant corruption, and ever bolder narco-traffickers. A presidential victory for the PAN's Vicente Fox in 2000 was widely seen as a democratic breakthrough. However, Mexico's economy, now linked with those of the United States and Canada in the North American Free Trade Agreement (NAFTA), remained a crap game for the high rollers and a downward escalator for the majority, whose frustrations were expressed in strikes and demonstrations as well as in a rash of new guerrilla movements.

Renewed or continuing momentum toward redemocratization in the late 1990s took the form of US intervention in Haiti to restore civilian rule; the ratification of accords ending a struggle of more than thirty years between the Guatemalan government and the Guatemalan National Revolutionary Unity (URNG), a rebel coalition that has sought to represent the Mayan community; and serious attempts by the Honduran government to prosecute military and intelligence agents accused of human rights abuse.

On the other hand, even Haiti, one of the world's poorest countries, responded to creditors' demands for austerity measures; and availability of the weapons used so freely by political adversaries in Central America in the 1980s gave rise in the 1990s to a rash of routine street muggings. By 2004, Haiti's President Aristide, reelected in 2000, had once again been overthrown by many of the same military and paramilitary operatives who removed him in 1991. And the political climate in Guatemala had become increasingly tense. Meanwhile, guerrilla activity, along with narco-trafficking, continued in Peru and Colombia, provoking extralegal and often brutal military and paramilitary responses.

The bad news in Ecuador in early 1997 was that the imposition of austerity measures generated a crisis that deposed a president and left the country at one time with three claimants to the office. The good news was that the crisis did not—at least in the short term—give rise to a direct military takeover. The colonel soon to assume the presidency did so by election—elected, in fact, as a populist and nationalist. For the most part, contemporary manifestations of authoritarianism take the form of police power, its relevance to politics shrouded as unrest degenerates into anomic street crime and economic problems giving rise to it become increasingly untreatable at the national level. Still, those who saw democracy as failing to live up to its promise were not prepared to give up on it.

Getting out of Control

At the turn of the twentieth century, in some of the most populous and rapidly modernizing countries—Brazil, Argentina, and Mexico, for example—spurts of export-driven growth gave rise to illusions of economic progress. But the wealth so accumulated did not trickle down. And hard-working people tired of waiting to be trickled on. They also tired of waiting for the nonperforming seeds of democracy to take root. The upshot in Brazil was a halting but relatively peaceful and ultimately successful independence movement. In Argentina, it was a breakthrough from oligarchic to middle-class rule, underpinned by a broad-based political party. In Mexico, the upshot was all-consuming revolution that for a time brought peasants and workers to the bargaining table and that enabled a party of egalitarian roots to rule for some three-quarters of a century.

As before in Latin America, at the turn of the twenty-first century, spurts of economic growth bouncing from country to country, generated now by the draw of a broader range of resources, including cheap labor, offered the illusion of economic recovery. Economists' number crunching captured the tide of globalized free market successes but failed to record the gathering of a powerful undertow of anger and desperation. Likewise, as before, the illusion of democracy heightened frustration and opened crevices in carefully crafted control systems, giving rise to open agitation for the real thing.

What came to be seen as a new phase of Latin American populism was heralded by the election to the presidency of Venezuela in 1998 of Hugo Chávez. The election, by a strong margin, of the colonel who had led the first of two abortive coup attempts in the 1990s was generally viewed as a strong repudiation of the country's political establishment. Chávez's election on a nationalist, populist platform was to be followed in 2002 by that of Ecuador's Colonel Lucio Gutiérrez, leader of the military-indigenous rebellion of 2000.

As will be elaborated in succeeding chapters, the undertow of nationalism and populism, deriving from new deprivations and expressed in new forms of organization and of street theater or direct action, has unseated more or less elected governments in Peru, Ecuador, Argentina, and Bolivia. The same kinds of organizations, lacking the ambitions of revolutionary movements and the elaborated ideologies or programs of political parties but strong in numbers, in solidarity, and in determination, have underwritten governments in Venezuela, Argentina, and Brazil.

The Brazilian government of Luiz Inacio da Silva, universally known as Lula, elected in 2002, was based on the extraordinarily strong and broadly based Workers Party (PT), which grew out of the struggle against dictatorship. In Mexico and in Uruguay by 2004 new leftist parties—in Mexico, the Revolutionary Democratic Party (PRD) and in Uruguay, the Frente Amplio, or Broad Front—were making a strong showing in opinion polls, and the Socialist Party heading Chile's governing coalition was showing surprising strength.

The appearance that Latin America was getting out of control had become a source of some consternation to the Bush administration. It had intervened openly and unapologetically, through "diplomatic" threats and assertions, to influence the outcome of elections in Nicaragua, El Salvador, and Bolivia, as well as through poorly disguised attempts (successful in Haiti, unsuccessful in Venezuela) to bring about regime change by other old-fashioned means. Of greater concern to democratic leaders in the more developed states was the enhanced leverage available to those who would squelch any move toward expanded political participation and enhanced accountability through promoting market jitters and capital flight as well as through manipulation of electoral processes.

Other sources of unease in Latin America were new US funding agencies, like the Endowment for Democracy, for political operations, new technological exports, like voting machines of dubious security, and new means of information gathering. The Mexican government had opened an investigation into the collection of extensive and intimate data on its citizens by the US Department of Justice through a long-term contract with the same company that in 2000 overhauled Florida's voter registration records so as to erroneously disenfranchise thousands of mainly black voters in a presidential election decided by a few hundred votes.

Confronted by demands from Latin America's disadvantaged masses for greater participation, US leaders, speaking fervently of promoting democracy in Latin America, pulled ever tighter the leash of hemispheric hegemony. In so doing, those US leaders made it ever more clear to Latin Americans that achieving democracy must mean "getting out of control," that there could be no democracy without national sovereignty.

Twenty-First-Century Populism

The trend to populism, or center-left nationalism, deepened as the first decade of the twenty-first century wore on. Lula's victory in Brazil was followed in 2004 by the election in Uruguay of Tabare Vasquez, leader of the center-left Frente Amplio, the "broad front" of opposition to the old guard elite that had facilitated, or gone along with, the awful era of counterrevolution. After a period of upheaval in which the Hispanic elite was finding its role under constant challenge, Bolivia in 2005 elected Evo Morales, who was not only the country's first indigenous president but also leader of the union of *cocaleros*—the coca growing peasants who were the frontline targets of the US drug war. Liberal Party candidate Manuel ("Mel") Zelaya, elected president of Honduras that year, turned out to be a committed populist as well, enacting, for example, a major increase in the minimum wage.

The trend continued into 2006. René Préval of Haiti, Oscar Arias of Costa Rica, and Alan García of Peru had edged toward the center since their earlier heydays of nationalist leadership, but Michelle Bachelet represented a breakthrough in Chile, not only as an immediate survivor of Pinochet's cruelty but also as the country's first female president. Rafael Correa, whose popularity derived from the organization of major demonstrations, took a nationalist stance from the beginning in opposition to the encroachment of multinational corporations on the fragile habitats of indigenous Ecuadoreans and the intrusion on Ecuadorean territory of the Colombian military. Sandinista leader Daniel Ortega was elected again to the presidency of Nicaragua in 2006, in spite of, or because of, open opposition from the Bush administration.

The presidency of Argentina saw an electoral turnover in 2007 from the popular Peronist president Nestor Kirchner, who had bested the International Monetary Fund in the country's comeback from economic meltdown, to his wife, Cristina Kirchner, who as a senator had enjoyed a popular following of her own. Guatemala also elected a president from the center-left that year, Alvaro Colom, despite still dangerous fallout from that country's many years of race and class warfare. The Dominican Republic, in 2008, chose Leonel Fernandez, of the Dominican Liberation Party (PLD), founded by democratic and nationalist crusader Juan Bosch. Paraguay's presidential choice that year, Father Fernando Lugo, pulled the country away from the quagmire of the traditional party system, placing it on a more nearly nationalist and populist track. Moreover, suggesting belated validation of historic struggles, 2009 saw the election for the first time of a president representing El Salvador's revolutionary struggle, Mauricio Funes of the Farabundo Martí National Liberation Front (FMLN) and a president for Uruguay, José Mújica of the Frente Amplio, whose initiation to political activism had come through the young rebels known as the Tupamaros.

Strong trajectories threatening to the interests of old and new money are bound to generate countertrends, of course. One such election, in 2009, was that of Conservative Party candidate Ricardo Martinelli to the presidency of Panama. More consequential, however, have been the elections of 2006 in Mexico and Colombia. In Mexico, the lead apparently enjoyed in the final count by PRD candidate Manuel López Obrador, disappeared after a computer malfunction. When the count resumed, candidate Felipe Calderon of the more conservative incumbent Party of National Action (PAN) had a narrow lead that allowed him to claim victory. The outcome was challenged by the PRD. The demonstrations that followed, however, were peaceful and eventually fizzled out. But Mexico's compounding crises of drug mafia violence and economic disaster suggest that political contention will continue to be tense.

In Colombia, neither President Alvaro Uribe's reelection in 2006 nor the constitutional revision that allowed him to serve another term aroused serious open contention. The matter under contention there continues to be the central government's control of the territory it claims. The government's US-assisted war against the Revolutionary Armed Forces of Colombia (FARC) and the peasants who live in the territory more or less dominated by the FARC—at one time up to 40 to 60 percent of the national territory—has become a matter of overriding concern to Colombia's neighbors and, by extension to most of Latin America.

Adding to these matters of concern for the newly nationalistic and regionally better organized Latin American governments has been the military overthrow, in June, 2009, of Honduran president Zelaya, and his replacement in November by center-Right National party candidate Porfirio Lobo, through an election of dubious legitimacy. The contemporary generation of Latin American leaders remembers all too well what became of an earlier trend toward the deepening of democracy when elected populist governments began to fall victim to military coups. The outcome of that most recent Honduran election has been recognized by few governments—in the Western Hemisphere only four, but one of those four is that of the United States. This, along with a new US pact with Colombia that offers the US armed forces use of seven military bases around the perimeters of that country, has put the new Obama administration at odds with almost all of the Latin American countries. This is sad and ironic, given that the new US president was probably even more popular in Latin America than in the United States at the time he was elected. Latin Americans would not likely imagine that any US president would or could implant a flourishing democracy in their midst; but they continue to hold out hope for one who might stand back and allow it to happen.

NOTES

1. Charles W. Anderson, *Politics and Economic Change in Latin America* (Princeton, N.J.: Van Nostrand, 1967).

2. Martin C. Needler, *An Introduction to Latin American Politics: The Structure of Conflict* (Englewood Cliffs, N.J.: Prentice-Hall, 1977).

3. Karl Deutsch, "Social Mobilization and Political Development," *American Political Science Review*, September 1961.

4. Some scholars have viewed the outcome of Costa Rica's civil strife of 1948 as revolutionary. Others have viewed it as counterrevolutionary. The outcome, in this author's view, was mixed, with gains and losses for elements of both upper and lower social strata, but one that did not fundamentally alter the evolutionary course of change.

5. Conversations with Paz Estenssoro, Albuquerque, spring 1978. Paz told of a visit during his presidency by a delegation of peasants from a village on the Altiplano. They had come to plead for a telephone for the village and for a bridge to connect the village with a road leading to La Paz. Paz Estenssoro responded that the demands on his administration were enormous and the treasury was bare. The spokesman of the delegation then replied, "Mr. President, I'm sure you remember that an angry mob hanged former president Villarroel from a lamppost. When the counterrevolutionaries come for you, you can call us on our telephone and we'll come running across our bridge and save you!" Paz said they got their telephone and their bridge.

SUGGESTED READINGS

From the perspective of development theory, Charles W. Anderson, *Politics and Economic Change in Latin America* (Princeton, N.J.: Van Nostrand, 1967), has provided a useful model of political actors—who they are and how they go about seeking participation and power. Martin C. Needler, *Political Development in Latin America: Instability, Violence, and Evolutionary Change* (New York: Random House, 1968), foreshadowed more recent work on the relationships between economic and political development.

The paradigm that has had greatest currency for dealing with the counterrevolutionary trends of the 1970s was provided by Guillermo O'Donnell in *Modernization and Bureaucratic-Authoritarianism: Studies in South American Politics* (Berkeley: Institute of International Studies, University of California, 1973). Penny Lernoux, *Cry of the People* (New York: Doubleday, 1980), depicts the changing role of the Church in the face of revolution and counterrevolution. The roles of Latin America's modern military establishments are treated in Philippe C. Schmitter, ed., *Military Rule in Latin America: Function, Consequences, and Perspectives* (Beverly Hills, Calif.: Sage, 1973). Military withdrawal and the trend to "redemocratization" during the 1980s are covered in James M. Malloy and Mitchell A. Seligson, eds., *Authoritarians and Democrats: Regime Transition in Latin America* (Pittsburgh: University of Pittsburgh Press, 1987); Larry Diamond, Juan J. Linz, and Seymour Martin Lipset, eds., *Democracy in Developing Countries*, vol. 4, *Latin America* (Boulder: Lynne Rienner, 1989); and Robert A. Pastor, ed., with a foreword by Jimmy Carter and Raul Alfonsin, *Democracy in the Americas: Stopping the Pendulum* (New York: Holmes & Meier, 1989).

Cole Blasier, *The Hovering Giant: US Responses to Revolutionary Change in Latin America* (Pittsburgh: University of Pittsburgh Press, 1976), deals with the US stance vis-à-vis revolution, and Jan Knippers Black, *United States Penetration of Brazil* (Philadelphia: University of Pennsylvania Press, 1977), outlines the US role in destabilizing democratic governments and promoting counterrevolution. More general coverage of US involvement in the politics of Latin American and other Third World countries is found in Noam Chomsky and Edward S. Herman, *The Political Economy of Human Rights,* vol. 1, *The Washington Connection and Third World Fascism* (Boston: South End, 1979).

Among the many noteworthy books on mature and fledgling revolutionary regimes are Martin C. Needler, *Mexican Politics: The Containment of Conflict,* 3d ed. (New York: Praeger, 1995); Jorge Domínguez, *Cuba* (New Haven: Yale University Press, 1979); and Thomas W. Walker, *Nicaragua: The Land of Sandino* (Boulder: Westview, 1981). Late-developing Andean countries receive good coverage in David Scott Palmer, *Peru: The Authoritarian Tradition* (New York: Praeger, 1981); and Osvaldo Hurtado, *Political Power in Ecuador,* trans. Nick Mills (Albuquerque: University of New Mexico Press, 1980). The twenty-first-century populism of Venezuela's Hugo Chávez is addressed in Steve Ellner's 2009 book, *Rethinking Venezuelan Politics.*

Roots and branches of counterrevolutionary regimes are covered in Alfred Stepan, ed., *Authoritarian Brazil: Origins, Policies, and Future* (New Haven: Yale University Press, 1973); Arturo Valenzuela, *The Breakdown of Democracy in Chile* (Baltimore: Johns Hopkins University Press, 1978); and Peter G. Snow, *Political Forces in Argentina* (New York: Praeger, 1979). Previously classified documents on the period of military rule in Chile are laid out and interpreted by Peter Kornbluh in *The Pinochet File: A Declassified Dossier on Atrocity and Accountability* (New York: New Press, 2003).

Among the many outstanding books on tumultuous Central America are Stephen Schlesinger and Stephen Kinzer, *Bitter Fruit: The Untold Story of the American Coup in Guatemala* (New York: Doubleday, 1982); Cynthia Arnson, *El Salvador: A Revolution Confronts the United States* (Washington, D.C.: Institute for Policy Studies, 1982); Peter Calvert, ed., *The Central American Security System: North-South or East-West?* (Cambridge: Cambridge University Press, 1988); Peter Kornbluh and Malcolm Byrne, *The Iran-Contra Scandal: The Declassified History* (New York: New Press, 1993).

More recent assessments of the political potential of the military are found in Alfred Stepan, *Rethinking Military Politics: Brazil and the Southern Cone* (Princeton, N.J.: Princeton University Press, 1988); and Brian Loveman and Thomas M. Davies Jr., eds., *The Politics of Antipolitics: The Military in Latin America,* 3d ed. (Wilmington, Del.: Scholarly Resources, 1996).

Post–Cold War works on the Caribbean and Central America include Anthony Payne and Paul Sutton, *Modern Caribbean Politics* (Baltimore: Johns Hopkins University Press, 1993); and Thomas W. Walker, ed., *Nicaragua Without Illusions: Regime Transi-*

tion and Structural Adjustment in the 1990s (Wilmington, Del.: Scholarly Resources, 1997).

Valuable overviews of Western Hemisphere politics in the 20th century are found in Lars Schoultz, *Beneath the United States*, Cambridge: Harvard University Press, 1998, and Paul Drake, *Between Tyranny and Anarchy: A History of Democracy in Latin America*, Palo Alto, CA: Stanford University Press, 2009.

Chapter 11

WOMEN AND LATIN
AMERICAN POLITICS

Participation, Citizenship, and Democracy

JANE S. JAQUETTE

WOMEN'S POLITICAL PARTICIPATION—as women's movements, voters, and authors of new forms of political action as well as new legislation—has become a significant factor in Latin American politics. This chapter focuses on the changing patterns of women's political participation and their impact on a range of issues. It examines women's politicization using three different frames. The first is a *historical* frame. Against the conventional view that women have been oppressed by machismo and the Church, it argues that women have long been politically and economically active—during the colonial period, as fighters in the independence movements of the early nineteenth century, and as forces for social and political change during the twentieth century.

The second is the *social movement* frame. The period from the mid-1970s to the late 1980s saw a dramatic rise in women's movements, partly sparked by the UN Decade for Women, which was launched in Mexico City in 1975. Others were inspired by the Madres of the Plaza de Mayo, mothers whose children "disappeared" under Argentina's military dictatorship, and formed human rights movements in opposition to repressive military regimes. Popular women's groups came together in the urban peripheries to address survival needs during the regional economic crisis of the 1980s. During this period, marked by civil wars in Central America and resistance to military dictatorships in the Southern Cone and Peru, women gained recognition as political actors in their own right, demanding space for women's issues in the democratic governments that emerged in the 1980s and 1990s.

As democratization changed the rules of the game, however, social movements weakened and movement solidarity gave way to debates over *political representation*. The third section examines the successes and failures of two strategies: state feminism, which called for the establishment of women's ministries to institutionalize a women's perspective within the executive, and the adoption of gender quotas to ensure greater women's representation in national legislatures.

A wide range of factors have produced a cultural sea change regarding women's roles and rights in Latin America, which affects women's daily lives as well as their public roles and has made it possible to legislate reforms in family law, greater recognition of women's economic, political and reproductive rights, and laws criminalizing violence against women. All Latin American states have signed and ratified the UN Convention on the Elimination of Discrimination Against Women (CEDAW) and the regional convention on violence against women (Belém do Pará).

The conclusion assesses how women's political activism and debates among feminists over goals and strategies are relevant to the ways in which democracy is evolving in the region. The 1990s assumption that the political and economic systems of Latin America were converging around principles of representative democracy and market-oriented economic policies has been challenged by the rise of a new group of leaders on the left, united by their rejection of "neoliberal" economic policies. The feminist embrace of pluralism is being tested by the growing strength of indigenous identity politics which, I argue, has given contemporary populism new political content and legitimacy, but does not consistently support women's demands for equality.

These new developments do not diminish the remarkable successes Latin American women's movements have had over the last thirty years, nor can they reverse the ongoing processes of political mobilization that have given women more control over their own lives. But they are creating new issues for women and new challenges to feminist agendas.

THE HISTORICAL FRAME

Women can be excluded from politics more easily when their history of political activism is forgotten. Contemporary women's movements and feminist scholarship have greatly increased our knowledge of women's public and private lives from the precolonial period to the present. Francesca Miller demonstrates that women have been an integral part of the wider struggle for social justice in Latin America.[1] From the "encounter" between indigenous groups and their European conquerors to the wars of independence, women were significant and sometimes controversial figures. La Malinche, for example, who was both translator and lover to Hernan Cortes, is widely seen be seen as *la vendida* who sold out her people, as Octavio Paz portrays her. But Tzvetan Todorov casts her in a different light when he uses Doña Marina (as the Spanish called her) to argue that language and culture, not horses and guns, were critical weapons in the Spanish victory over the Aztecs.[2]

Miller draws on several accounts to recast our stereotype that European women in the New World were simply pampered elites. The slave trade brought women from Africa, bringing another component to the complex mix of races that has characterized Latin America since the colonial period. Indigenous and Afro-Latin American women actively participated in the resistance to slavery and Spanish rule.

Perhaps the brightest star of colonial intellectual life was a nun, Sor Juana de la Cruz (1648–1695). A great lyric poet and a favorite of the viceregal court in Mexico City, Sor Juana "transform[ed] her convent into a literary and intellectual salon."[3] Disciplined by the Church for her public role, Sor Juana retreated to a life of self-abnegation and died caring for fellow nuns stricken by an epidemic. Some have argued that Sor Juana's life exemplifies the patriarchal power of the family (as women faced the choice of marriage or convent) and the Church. But, as Miller suggests, it is hard to generalize. A woman's power in the colonial period depended on a number of factors, including wealth, race, marital status, education, and urban or rural residence.[4]

Accounts of the wars of independence in the first quarter of the nineteenth century are filled with heroic women who inspired revolutionary armies and became nationalist icons. Perhaps the most famous example is Policarpa Salavarrieta ("La Pola") of Colombia, who was publicly executed by the Spanish as a rebel in 1817, at the age of twenty. Over time, however, this image of the heroines of independence lost its revolutionary edge. Women were cast as "quintessential victims of war," whose most important patriotic duty was to send their sons to battle.[5] Simón Bolívar recognized the valor of women "Amazons" who fought side by side with men, but this did not alter his view that women "should not mix in public business" and that a woman's "family and her domestic duties are her first obligation." Nonetheless, Miller concludes, women revolutionaries were "inscribed women in history" and can be considered "precursors of latter-day female political activists."[6]

During much of the nineteenth century, Elizabeth Dore contends, women were increasingly displaced by capitalist property relations and disadvantaged by secularization because the Church had defended their property rights and officially advocated "sexual equality within marriage."[7] From her study of Diriomo, an Indian community in Nicaragua, Dore concludes that during the nineteenth century local governments modernized patriarchy by using their "ample powers of regulation and surveillance" to "regulate matters of domestic life."[8]

At the turn of the twentieth century, Latin American women began to organize. The first International Feminist Congress was held in 1910, and in 1916 North American and Latin American women joined together to form what became the Pan-American Women's International Committee and later the Pan-American League for the Advancement of Women (1922), which campaigned to put woman suffrage on the agenda of the League of Nations.[9]

Although these efforts did not receive widespread support at home, where conservative attitudes about women's roles prevailed, Latin American women leaders drew on their international networks and continued to press for reform. Their strategies anticipated the mutually reinforcing connections between the "local" and the "global" which have contributed to the success of many contemporary social movements.[10] Latin American women continued to take leadership roles in international forums. Women from Brazil, the Dominican Republic, and Mexico are responsible for the inclusion of the words "equal rights for men *and women*" in the first paragraph of the UN Charter.

In the twentieth century, women's participation in social and revolutionary movements challenged the confluence of capitalism, patriarchy, and state power. Women were involved in the Mexican revolution of 1910 but had little impact on the Mexican constitution of 1917. By contrast, women's visible roles in the Cuban (1959) and Nicaraguan (1979) revolutions meant that women had a visible role in the revolutionary governments and their new constitutions adopted a range of women's rights. These issues were also addressed in the platforms of guerrilla movements from El Salvador to Chiapas, reinforced by the Marxist ideological commitment to women's equality.[11]

WOMEN'S MOVEMENTS IN THE TRANSITIONS TO DEMOCRACY

Initially Latin Americans were dismissive toward the second wave feminism sweeping the United States and Western Europe. Feminists were described as "hedonistic" and "selfish," hostile to men and the family. The left saw feminism as a "diversion" from the necessary focus on class, while the right rejected feminism as an attack on women's "natural" roles as wives and mothers. Critics on both left and right labeled feminism a form of cultural imperialism. At the Tribune, the parallel meeting of NGO representatives to the first UN Conference on Women in Mexico City in 1975, many Latin American women argued forcefully that northern feminists were blind to the fact that the main cause of women's oppression was not patriarchy but "dependency"—economic exploitation of the South by the rich, industrialized North. Northern feminists in turn saw Latin American women as victims of "false consciousness" who refused to admit their oppression as women. Neither side gave much ground.

Feminist movements had already begun to emerge in several Latin American countries, however. During the late 1970s and the 1980s, they and other nonfeminist women's organizations began to play increasingly visible roles in the growing opposition to military dictatorships in Peru and the Southern Cone. Over time, feminist issues such as women's economic marginalization, violence against women, and women's legal and reproductive rights became salient issues in the national debates over what kind of democracies would emerge from the transitions in South, and later Central, America.

The women's movements of the 1980s were loosely knit coalitions of women's groups drawn from different classes and having different agendas, brought together by their shared opposition to authoritarian military governments. Urban poor women had organized for decades in response to specific needs—clinics, day care centers, and urban services—or to mount consumer boycotts. The economic decline that began after the first oil shock of 1973 and deepened into the lost decade of the 1980s increased women's neighborhood organizing, and in turn injected grassroots energy into the struggle for democracy.

Sonia Alvarez has described this process in Brazil, where the Mexico City conference inspired women concerned with issues of gender inequality to organize for the first time. Their meetings in turn gave the left-wing opposition, still barred from politics, a new forum for political action. Brazilian feminists saw themselves as a vanguard who would lead a "united, cross-class, mass based women's movement."[12] Although the women of popular or mass based organizations never thought of themselves as feminist, in meeting together they found common problems in their personal lives that brought them closer to the issues being voiced by feminists. For their part, many feminists, especially those who had been active on the left, were torn between their growing commitment to women's movements and their ties to political parties. In Brazil, as elsewhere in the region, they opted for "double militancy," trying to maintain their activism on both fronts and cooperating with other women across party lines, while trade union women began agitating for more attention to women's issues within their unions.

Women's human rights groups soon gained international attention. In Argentina in 1977 (a year after the military coup), fourteen women began to march silently in front of the presidential palace, demanding the return of their children who had been "disappeared"—killed or imprisoned and tortured—by the junta. [13] The Madres of the Plaza de Mayo were notable not only because of their cause and their courage, but also because of the implications of their politicization for feminist theory and action. The Madres were housewives who used their traditional roles as mothers to confront the military. As Marguerite Bouvard writes, the Madres, by denying that motherhood meant passivity and submission, "challenged the cynicism and militarization of Argentine society" and created an organization "based upon equality, ties of affection, and the promotion of radical goals."[14]

Women's popular organizations were also experimenting with new forms of organization. In Peru and Chile, they organized communal kitchens that were critical to family survival in the urban shantytowns hit hard by the debt crisis. In 1986 the municipal Vaso de Leche program distributed milk every day to a million children in Lima, and by 1988 there were about 600 communal dining halls organized by poor women in Lima's periphery. These initiatives provided women with skills in economic management and political organizing, with support from municipal governments, nongovernmental organizations, and the Church.[15]

Inspired by the Madres and the communal kitchens, women's movements in Latin America also served as real-world examples to feminist theorists in the North who were beginning to argue that "difference" rather than "equality" should be at the core of feminist theory and practice. Women should be wary of the male biases of the liberal tradition, they argued, which was based on a definition of citizenship biased in favor of male traits like individualism and competition, and a view of power based on violence.[16] "Militant motherhood" made it possible for women to mobilize in support of the family, rather than in opposition to it as early second wave feminists had done in the North.[17] It took issues like "reproduction, domestic tasks, the socialization of children . . . and sexuality" out of the realm of the natural into the world of the political. The Madres showed that women could enter politics in ways that emphasized solidarity over self-interest, while bringing about broad political change through nonviolence in the tradition of Gandhi and Martin Luther King Jr.[18]

These ideas were not accepted uncritically, however. Maruja Barrig observed that the communal kitchens "did not succeed in changing the way women valued their potential as citizens or as dynamic agents of change in their own communities," adding that the lack of "consistent links" to the public sphere meant that the "political dimension of everyday life remained separate from local and municipal politics . . . further accentuat[ing] false [gender] dichotomies."[19] And María del Carmen Feijoó, acknowledging that the example of the Madres had enabled more women to become politically active, expressed concern that the Madres also provided a modern and secular rationale for the patriarchal gender division of labor, which had formerly received its strongest ideological support from the conservative Catholic Church.[20]

Victoria Rodríguez explored the relationship between women's political mobilization, cultural change, and women's economic roles in her study of women and politics during the long process of democratic transition in Mexico during the 1980s and 1990s.[21] The debt crisis and structural adjustment policies of the 1980s pushed more women into the Mexican labor force, where they worked in *maquiladoras* (which preferred female labor) and the informal sector. Although they often lacked the benefits associated with formal sector and unionized jobs, earned only half of what men earned, and often returned to the household when economic conditions improved, Rodríguez argued that women's gains were "irreversible" because men had been "exposed to female decision-making and household democracy, and women have come to demand the more powerful household role that accompanies this more democratic environment."[22]

Another trend in the region was the rising number of households headed by women. Against the conventional view that they are an indicator of economic failure, Sylvia Chant found positive effects. Female-headed households have more options: daughters who work are more likely to send money back to their families when they are headed by women; and women spend more of their income on their families than men do, improving their children's nutrition and increasing their educational opportunities. In Chant's view, female-headed households thus subvert patriarchal definitions of the family.[23]

During the 1970s and 1980s, women's movements became recognized for their active role in the growing opposition to military rule, and this in turn gave them some leverage to put women's and feminist issues on the agendas of the new democratic governments. As governments geared up to present reports on the status of women in their countries at three UN conferences held during the Decade for Women, governments, UN agencies, and many nongovernmental organizations (NGOs) funded studies that produced a wealth of new sex-disaggregated data. These studies showed not only the degree to which women were disadvantaged economically and politically compared to men, but also the dramatic class differences among women in their access to resources and social services.[24]

The NGO conferences, held in tandem with the UN official meetings, connected women's groups regionally and globally to share information and strategies and thus spurred women's organizing. The three official conferences held during the decade and a fourth conference that took place in Beijing in 1995 established new international norms through their platforms of action and through the Convention on the Elimination of All Forms of Discrimination Against Women (CEDAW), signed in 1979 and eventually ratified by all Latin American states. [25]

DEMOCRACY AND REPRESENTATION

With the return to democracy, political parties displaced social movements from center stage. Women's movements had some early successes, participating actively in constitutional conventions and engaging in national debates over what the priorities of the new democratic governments should be. In Brazil, for example, the "lipstick lobby" convinced the constitutional assembly to adopt dozens of amendments addressing women's issues. In several countries, women's ministries were either established or given more resources and broader mandates.

But women's movements struggled as male-dominated political parties marginalized women's issues, and structural adjustment policies limited the resources states could allocate to social programs. Their difficulties were heightened by institutional weaknesses in the region's democracies, which were permeated by persistent authoritarian tendencies, corruption, growing personal insecurity, and compromised judicial systems.

Social movements arise during crises and often disappear after the crisis is over. Once the military returned to the barracks, it became clear how deeply women were divided by class and race and by their degree of commitment to feminist goals. Although environmental and human rights movements also lost leverage during the 1990s, women were at a greater disadvantage. Women are dispersed geographically, unable to use the bloc voting strategies based on residence that have empowered ethnic and indigenous groups. Proportional representation, common in Latin America, allows voters to choose among several parties according to their platforms, but there is no equivalent for women's movements of the green environmental parties. Women's agendas did not lend themselves to strategies such as truth commissions that had enabled human rights groups to pursue their goals.

Feminists, who were committed to addressing issues like divorce and women's reproductive rights, were also divided between those who called themselves "autonomous" and refused to be "coopted" by the governments and parties with which they often disagreed, and those willing to work within the system. In addition, many feminist organizations and women's groups were dependent on international funders that had their own agendas and required groups to follow accounting procedures and other guidelines which favored established NGOs over grassroots organizations. NGOs became increasingly professionalized and geared to providing services rather than engaging in advocacy, further accentuating race and class differences between NGO leaders and grassroots women. Sonia Alvarez called this process "NGOization," and the label stuck.[26]

In response to these changes, feminists and women's groups tried various strategies to ensure continued attention to women's issues. Two, state feminism and gender quotas for national legislatures, have made an important impact.

State Feminism

Brazilian feminists were innovators in seeking representation in the state. Women of the opposition PMDB (Brazilian Democratic Movement Party) were experimenting with the idea of a "Council on Woman's Condition" when their party won control of the state of São Paulo in 1982. When the council was established in 1983, it had no executive or implementation powers and no independent budget, but it "remobilized" the women's movement.[27] Fear that the government (still under military control at the national level) might institute a top-down policy of population control led to another form of state feminism: cooperation between the São Paulo Women's Health Organization and the state health department in the administration of contraceptive programs, while the council pressured the health ministry to create a commission on reproductive rights.[28] In 1985 the Council's Commission on Violence Against Women convinced the state of São Paulo to establish the first *delegacia da mulher,* a women's police station to deal with cases of violence against women. *Delegacias* were later established in other cities in Brazil and were widely imitated by other countries in Latin America and elsewhere.

The São Paulo council was a model for a National Council on Women's Rights (CNDM), which was established in the justice ministry in 1985. The CNDM had considerable policy influence from 1985 to 1988, and was able to work with independent women's group to get several amendments into the 1988 constitution.[29] In 1989, however, noted feminist Jacqueline Pitanguy, head of the CNDM, resigned in protest along with several others when the government cut the council's funds. The new council members appointed by the president did not come from the feminist movement. Although the next government did appoint women with feminist credentials, the ties between the council and the movement were never fully restored. Instead, NGOs, women's studies centers in universities, and journals became platforms for influencing public policy from outside, rather than within, the state.[30] Among the lessons many took from Brazil was that the state feminist strategy provided no guarantee that women's interests would be institutionalized within the state. Gender units like the CNDM served at the pleasure of the president and were highly vulnerable to shifts in the political winds.

In 1988 the women's movement in Chile, which took an active and visible role in the coalition that opposed the military regime of Augusto Pinochet, called for the new democratic government to attend to a list of feminist demands, including the establishment of a women's ministry with cabinet status. When the center-left coalition (the Concertación) came to power in 1990, it created Chile's Servicio Nacional de la Mujer (SERNAM).[31] From the beginning, however, SERNAM was caught between the demands of its feminist constituencies and resistance from the Christian Democratic Party within the ruling coalition as well as from social conservatives on the right.

Chilean politics were highly polarized. As Lisa Baldez notes, most of the women from the popular classes had strongly supported Salvador Allende, the socialist president elected in 1970 who died when the military attacked the presidential palace in the 1973 coup. In Chile, "Conservatives tend to view the women's movement, and feminism in particular, as a cultural cover for the traditional Marxist-Leninist left," and therefore as "an unacceptable threat to the social order."[32]

To maintain harmony, the Concertación appointed a director to head SERNAM who did not come from the feminist movement, and many concluded that the government did not intend to make feminist issues a priority. SERNAM was able to get a five-year equal opportunity plan for women through Congress, as well as legislation to recognize the rights of children born out of wedlock and of single mothers. But campaigns to pass an equal rights amendment failed twice, and the Chilean legislature did not pass a law legalizing divorce until 2004.[33] The issue of therapeutic abortion was not raised in congress until after the election of Michelle Bachelet (a socialist, atheist, physician, and single mother) in 2005.

As the women's movement weakened during the 1990s, SERNAM became the main conduit between women's organizations and the state. SERNAM supported specific programs (many funded by international donors) to educate women on their rights, address teenage pregnancy and women in poverty, and advocate legal reforms.[34] María Elena Valenzuela, who served on the staff of SERNAM, argues that as the women's movement fragmented in the 1990s, SERNAM's capacity to negotiate effectively was reduced. As "women lost the pluralist ideological space in which they had been working out their own issues," SERNAM was forced to play a "de facto leadership role by default."[35] Victoria Schild puts the blame on SER-NAM, however, charging that it weakened the women's movement by competing with independent groups. And by failing to challenge the economic policies of the Concertación, it turned activist women into docile "neoliberal citizens."[36]

Gender Quotas

Argentina led the way in experimenting with gender quotas by passing a law in 1991 which required all parties to nominate women to at least a third of the positions on their party lists (in proportional representation systems, parties gain a share of seats in the legislature according to the percentage of votes they win) and to put women in winnable positions on those lists. The number of women in the Argentine congress rose from 6 percent in the Chamber of Deputies and 8 percent in the Senate to nearly 36 percent in the Chamber and 42 percent in the Senate in the 2005–2007 legislative session.[37] Following the example of Argentina, as well as Spain and the Nordic countries, eleven other Latin American countries subsequently adopted electoral quotas. These laws vary widely and most have not been fully implemented, but they have on average doubled women's representation in national legislatures.[38]

Supporters of quota legislation used both equality and difference arguments in support of the legislation, justifying quotas on the egalitarian grounds that they would increase the number of women in elected positions, and on the difference grounds that women would bring different perspectives into policymaking. In most cases, electoral quotas did not result from activism by feminists, however, but from pressure by women party members and from international influences, including European political parties and the 1995 UN women's conference in Beijing.[39] Quotas can be advantageous to political leaders, especially those on the left who are under pressure from women members, because they allow parties to "do something" without committing themselves to controversial feminist positions that might cost them votes.

Quotas have their critics, however. Some predicted they would create policy "ghettos." Others warned that women would act only as proxies for others, such as husbands who were barred by term limits or corruption scandals from running for office themselves. Feminists worried that increasing the numbers of women elected would not necessarily produce legislation that was more sensitive to women or address feminist concerns. As Virginia Vargas put it, commenting on the large number of women in the administration of President Alberto Fujimori (1990–2000), "authoritarian women do not represent [me] any better than authoritarian men."[40]

Quota laws differ markedly in their effects. Only Costa Rica has come close to meeting the Argentine level of about 40 percent female representation. A study by Jutta Marx, Jutta Borner, and Mariana Caminotti comparing the effectiveness of quota legislation in Argentina and Brazil suggests some of the reasons why. Argentina's electoral system has proportional representation with "closed" party lists, meaning that the party decides who will be listed and the order in which they will appear. A decision by the Inter-American Commission on Human Rights in 1999 required Argentina clarify its quota law to ensure that women were in fact assigned to "winnable positions" on party lists. Under Decree 1246, if parties failed to follow the law, judges could decide where women candidates would be placed.[41]

By contrast, Brazil's electoral system has "open" lists, allowing voters to support individuals, so that women may not remain in "winnable" positions, even if the party puts them there. Parties are under little pressure to do so, however, as loopholes in the law allow them to expand their lists, effectively "cheating" on the percentages, and there are no serious sanctions for noncompliance.[42] These conditions are common elsewhere in the region. Like Brazil, many Latin American countries have electoral systems that allow votes for alternates, and women nominated for these positions can be counted toward meeting the party's quota.

In addition to assessing whether quota laws actually increase the number of women elected, there is the issue of whether electing more women makes a difference in terms of legislative outcomes. There is considerable evidence from Europe and North America that it does, but there is little research yet on Latin America. The Argentine case suggests that the same factors that have dramatically increased the percentage of women in congress can also be barriers to formulating and passing feminist legislation. The electoral process ensures that women deputies are dependent on the party leaders who nominate them, making it very difficult for them to cross party lines to develop woman-friendly legislation. There is a women's caucus in Brazil's legislature, but not in Argentina's. The quota in and of itself makes it more difficult for women deputies to be taken seriously by their male colleagues, reducing their leverage.

Leslie Schwindt-Beyer has studied whether the increased presence of women in national legislatures translates into legislative power, as measured by women's presence in leadership positions and their representation on committees dealing with the economy and security. She concludes that women are largely excluded from those positions, regardless of their numbers.[43] This reinforces Marx, Borner, and Caminotti's concern that, after more than fifteen years of quotas, women in Argentina and Brazil are still absent from their party's nominating process, which remains under the control of male party leaders.

Meanwhile, many "autonomous" feminists, women from the urban periphery, and rural women have been drawn to a new kind of opposition politics. They have joined organizations and voted for candidates that reject neoliberalism and capitalist globalization, which are viewed as having been forced on the region by US power and as serving US interests, not the interests of Latin America's poor. Antiglobalization groups have helped elect leftist leaders like Hugo Chávez in Venezuela, Evo Morales in Bolivia, Rafael Correa in Ecuador, and Daniel Ortega in Nicaragua, and have supported antisystem candidates who came close to victory in elections in Peru and Mexico. But these movements and parties rarely prioritize women's issues and in some cases are actively hostile to feminist agendas. For example, Nicaragua passed the most restrictive abortion law in the hemisphere soon after Ortega resumed the presidency. They represent a new set of challenges to women and women's movements in the region.

Feminist Encuentros

A series of regional feminist *encuentros,* held every three years since 1981, reflected the evolving discussions among Latin American feminists on the relationship between feminism, women's movements, and the state.[44] The first conference, held in Bogotá, drew two hundred feminists from fifty organizations and eleven countries;

in 1983 in Peru, there were three times as many participants. At the 1985 meeting in Brazil, a conflict emerged when the organizers refused to allow a busload of poor women from a Rio *favela* to participate in the meeting, a poignant illustration of ongoing class issues. The issue of autonomy versus working within the system, which arose at the first *encuentro,* continues to be sharply debated.

The fourth *encuentro* in 1987 in Taxco, Mexico, marked the first time a significant number of women from Central America and from organizations of the urban poor attended, which provoked discussions about what kinds of goals and organizations could truly be called feminist. Were women's groups who worked on survival issues interested only in practical outcomes for women (e.g., in health, education, housing, social services) and not in strategic challenges to patriarchy?[45] Should the issues of addressing urban poverty be left to the popular women's organizations while feminists concentrate on legal issues like women's human and reproductive rights?

These divisions arose from regional as well as class differences. The women's movements in Central America had formed during the civil wars of the 1980s, in a very different context from the transitions to democracy that had shaped the South American movements. Few of the Central American participants considered themselves "feminist." Most had come to discuss the issues arising from their activism within revolutionary movements, political parties, unions, and peasant and human rights organizations.[46] In the end, however, the Taxco *encuentro* opened the way for greater inclusivity and a pluralist understanding of feminism.

Race was an important focus of the fifth *encuentro,* held in Argentina in 1990, with 3,000 women attending; new networks were formed for black women and indigenous women, who met separately for the first time. The next meeting, scheduled to be held in El Salvador, was nearly shut down on the grounds that organizers had close ties with the radical opposition,[47] and because the meeting invited the open participation of lesbians. Although the organizers received death threats, the meeting was held as scheduled with 1,300 in attendance. The eleventh *encuentro* held in March 2009 in Mexico City drew 1,000 participants.[48]

FEMINISM, POPULISM, AND INDIGENOUS POLITICS

The past three decades of women's mobilization have greatly advanced women's legal, economic, and cultural status in the region, but have left the women's movements at odds with themselves and without a coherent vision of the future. The political dynamics in the region have not produced the economic growth or convergence many anticipated when the Berlin Wall fell. On the contrary, Latin American democracies, even those on the left, are increasingly diverse. The failure of liberal democratic governments and pro-market economic policies to address economic inequality has led to a crisis of democratic legitimacy and a search for alternatives that will address these issues more effectively.

Some leftist governments, such as those in Brazil, Uruguay, and Chile, can be classified as social democratic. The more radical governments on the left stop short of calling for state control of the economy, which has been recognized as a failure, but are experimenting with policies that are familiar from past Marxist and dependency critiques: a greater economic role for the state, nationalization of critical national resources (in effect, renegotiating contracts with oil and gas companies, often owned by multinational corporations), and an emphasis on redistribution over growth. They are developing domestic markets and reinstituting price and export controls.

These regimes are also radical in a political sense. Francisco Panizza describes the government of Hugo Chávez (since followed by Morales, Correa, and Ortega and others) as returning to the Latin American populist tradition. Populist democracy "strongly stresses notions of popular sovereignty . . . over the rights of the individual" and "majoritarianism over checks and balances," preferring plebiscites and referendums to political contestation and debate. Populist democracy, Panizza writes, "mistrusts political parties . . . as instruments of corrupt parties and entrenched oligarchic interests," and privileges the unmediated identification of "the people" and their political leader.[49]

The rise of indigenous politics, particularly in Bolivia and Ecuador (and potentially in Peru, Mexico, and Guatemala), has added a new dimension to populism. Through much of the twentieth century, the Marxist left opposed populism, regarding it as an opiate that drew workers and peasants toward demagogic leaders and away from revolutionary politics. But the appeal of "indigeneity" as an antidote to "savage" capitalism (on the grounds that indigenous traditions favor communal solidarity and are willing to protest governments and multinationals bent on exploiting natural resources, which are often located in indigenous territories) has given populism a new legitimacy on the left.

Several aspects of indigenous identity politics reinforce populist tendencies, creating a new hybrid form of politics. Populism favors a Manichean discourse that pits the moral purity of the people against the evil of their enemies. In the past, this was directed against the white oligarchy and the United States, but indigenous politics extends Manichean rhetoric to race, contrasting indigenous purity with the moral corruption of mestizos as well as whites and foreigners. Populism thinks of democracy in terms of "crowd action," protests and *piqueteros*, not liberal democratic norms and procedures, [50] Carlos de la Torre observes, and indigenous groups have gained power and popularity in Bolivia and Ecuador by blocking highways, occupying plazas, and holding mayors prisoner—tactics that are becoming more common in Peru as well. The populist leader portrays himself as the savior of the people, the "true nation," with whom he creates a bond that transcends mere institutions. Indigenous politics are not about party competition or checks and balances, but emphasize consensus. Dissent and opposition to the populist leader are unwelcome, even traitorous.

But de la Torre also points out that, in contrast to the Western pattern of political inclusion by the progressive extension of citizenship rights, Latin American populism recognizes that the citizenship rights of the "common people" are rarely respected or enforced under conditions of extreme inequality. What populist leaders offer that other political parties do not is "dignity and self-worth to those who are constantly discriminated against in their daily lives," and these, not material gains, are the most important source of political support.[51] Indigenous peoples have been subjected to extreme forms of racial as well as class discrimination. This helps explain the symbolic alliance between Evo Morales and Hugo Chávez, who often identifies himself with the indigenous, despite the fact that indigenous people make up only about 2.1 percent of Venezuela's population.

The convergence of populism and indigenous politics has drawn support from many who are seeking a new alternative on the left. This does not bode well for women's rights, however. The indigenous ideal of gender relations in the Andes is male-female complementarity, which is presented as a morally preferable alternative to gender equality. Researchers who compare the ideal of complementarity to the reality of life for Andean women offer a sobering list of ways in which the ideal is not matched in practice: these include physical and psychological abuse, forced marriage, women's confinement to the home and lack of voice in community affairs, and high levels of illiteracy and infant and maternal mortality. As indigenous identity becomes a political asset, women are charged with maintaining cultural purity in dress, language, and behavior, often with harsh sanctions against those who do not comply. Women can become indigenous leaders, but they cannot challenge the community's construction of gender relations.[52]

Populist/indigenous politics has been well received in antiglobalization circles and on the intellectual left in Latin America and abroad. These groups have often marginalized feminists and rejected feminist goals, and many activists appear to accept or even celebrate the challenges this new brand of politics represents to the principles of representation, contestation, and individual rights, which are fundamental to liberal democracy.

Feminism cannot escape its stake in these basic principles, and in forms of democracy that recognize and build on them. In a recent essay on civil society in Mexico, Mariclaire Acosta writes that Latin Americans are facing a choice between two paradigms, one that "attempts to facilitate the accumulation of social forces under the leadership of the popular sectors, represented by a party, a *caudillo,* or a revolutionary vanguard, in order to produce structural change," and another that produces change within a democratic framework "by utilizing and perfecting its institutional mechanisms."[53] Feminists and women's movements in Latin America also face this choice. Which one will they choose?

NOTES

1. Francesca Miller, *Latin American Women and the Search for Social Justice* (Hanover, NH: University Press of New England, 1991).

2. Compare Carmén Ramos Escandón, "Reading Gender in History," in *Gender Politics in Latin America: Debates in Theory and Practice,* ed. Elizabeth Dore (New York: Monthly Review Press, 1997) to Tzvetan Todorov, *The Conquest of America: The Question of the Other* (New York: Harper & Row, 1984). Cherrie Moraga and Gloria Anzaldúa analyze La Malinche as a cultural figure used to discipline chicana sexuality.

3. Octavio Paz, quoted in Miller, *Latin American Women,* 26.

4. See, for example, Asunción Lavrin, ed., *Sexuality and Marriage in Colonial Latin America* (Lincoln: University of Nebraska Press, 1989) and also her edited collection, *Latin American Women: Historical Perspectives* (Westport, CT: Greenwood, 1978).

5. Rebecca Earle, "Rape and the Anxious Public: Revolutionary Colombia, 1810–1830," in *Hidden Histories of Gender and the State in Latin America,* ed. Elizabeth Dore and Maxine Molyneux (Durham, NC: Duke University Press, 2000), 139–140.

6. Miller, *Latin American Women,* 32–34.

7. Elizabeth Dore, "One Step Forward, Two Steps Back: Gender and the State in the Long Nineteenth Century," In *Hidden Histories,* 16–17.

8. Elizabeth Dore, "Property, Households, and the Public Regulation of Domestic Life," in *Hidden Histories*, 166.

9. Miller, *Latin American Women*, chap. 4.

10. See Margaret Keck and Katherine Sikkink, *Activists Beyond Borders* (Ithaca, NY: Cornell University Press, 1998).

11. See Jane S. Jaquette, "Women's Role in Revolutionary Movements in Latin America," *Journal of Marriage and the Family*, 1973; on the Zapatistas, see Lynn Stephen, *Women and Social Movements in Latin America* (Austin: University of Texas Press, 1997). According to *Women in the Americas*, a 1995 report by the Inter-American Development Bank, Cuba's 1975 Family Code was "ground-breaking." In addition, "the Cuban state implemented policies to provide women with birth control, daycare, education and job training" (Inter-American Development Bank, *Women in the Americas*, 1995, 105). For recent assessments, see Maxine Molyneux, "State, Gender, and Institutional Change: The Federación de Mujeres Cubanas," in *Hidden Histories*, 291–321; and Margaret Randall, *Sandino's Daughters Revisited* (New Brunswick, NJ: Rutgers University Press, 1994).

12. Sonia Alvarez, "The (Trans)formation of Feminism(s) and Gender Politics in Democratizing Brazil," in *The Women's Movement in Latin America: Participation and Democracy*, ed. Jane S. Jaquette (Boulder: Westview, 1994), 21–23.

13. Marguerite Guzmán Bouvard, *Revolutionizing Motherhood: The Mothers of the Plaza de Mayo* (Wilmington, DE: Scholarly Resources, 1994), 69.

14. Ibid., 15.

15. Maruja Barrig, "The Difficult Equilibrium Between Bread and Roses: Women's Organizations and Democracy in Peru," in *Women's Movement in Latin America*, 164–165.

16. See, for example, Jean Bethke Elshtain, *Public Man, Private Woman* (Princeton, NJ: Princeton University Press, 1981); and "The Mothers of the Disappeared: An Encounter with Antigone's Daughters," in *Finding a New Feminism*, ed. Pamela Grande Jensen (Lanham, MD: Roman & Littlefield, 1996), 129–148. Carole Pateman's influential book, *The Sexual Contract* (Stanford, CA: Stanford University Press, 1988), makes a feminist socialist argument that liberal social contract theory excludes women.

17. See, for example, Betty Friedan, *The Feminine Mystique* (1963); and Shulamith Firestone, *The Dialectic of Sex* (1970).

18. Gloria Bonder, "The Study of Politics from the Standpoint of Women," quoted in Jaquette, conclusion to *Women's Movement in Latin America*, 224.

19. Barrig, "Difficult Equilibrium," 155.

20. María del Carmen Feijoó and Marcela María Alejandra Nari, "Women and Democracy in Argentina," in *Women's Movement in Latin America*, 115.

21. Victoria E. Rodríguez, *Women in Contemporary Mexican Politics* (Austin: University of Texas Press, 2003), chap. 2.

22. Ibid., 58.

23. Sylvia Chant, "Gender, Families, and Households" and conclusion, in Sylvia Chant and Nikki Craske, *Gender in Latin America* (New Brunswick, NJ: Rutgers University Press, 2003).

24. See "Latin American Women in Numbers," compiled by Teresa Valdés and colleagues for the UN conference in Beijing. Valdés also organized a project to equip women to monitor whether their countries were fulfilling the commitments they made under CEDAW and in Cairo (UN Conference on Population, 1994) and Beijing (Fourth International Conference on Women, 1995), the ICC, or Indice de Compromisos Cumplidos. Valdés describes the ICC project in an article cowritten with Alina Donoso, "Social Accountability and Citizen Participation," in *Feminist Agendas and*

Democracy in Latin America, ed. Jane S. Jaquette (Durham, NC: Duke University Press, 2009), 165–185.

25. On the advances made in UN conferences toward progressive international norms for women, see Mary K. Meyer and Elisabeth Prugl, eds., *Gender Politics and Global Governance* (Lanham, MD: Rowman & Littlefield, 1999); and essays in Anne Winslow, ed., *Women, Politics, and the United Nations* (Westport, CT: Greenwood, 1995).

26. Sonia Alvarez, "Advocating Feminism: The Latin American NGO "Boom," *International Feminist Journal of Politics* 1, no. 2 (1999): 181–209.

27. Alvarez, "(Trans)formation," 35. See also Alvarez, "Contradictions of a Woman's Space in a Male-Dominant State: The Political Role of the Commissions on the Status of Women in Postauthoritarian Brazil," in *Women, International Development, and Politics: The Bureaucratic Mire,* ed. Kathleen Staudt (Philadelphia: Temple University Press, 1990), 37–78.

28. Alvarez, "(Trans)formation," 40. Alvarez notes that although women's groups did not succeed in legalizing abortion, they did prevent a statement that protected life "beginning at conception" from being added to the constitution. "(Trans)formation," 66.

29. Teresa P. R. Caldeira, "Justice and Individual Rights: Challenges for Women's Movements and Democratization in Brazil," in *Women and Democracy: Latin America and Central and Eastern Europe,* ed. Jane S. Jaquette and Sharon L. Wolchik (Baltimore: Johns Hopkins Press, 1998), 93.

30. Caldeira, "Justice and Individual Rights," 78. On the positive effects of decentralization of state feminism during the presidency of Fernando Henrique Cardoso, see Fiona Macaulay, "Difundiéndose hacia arriba, hacia abajo y hacia dos lados: Políticas de género y oportunidades políticas en Brasil," in *De lo privado a lo public: Treinta años de lucha ciudadana en América Latina,"* ed. Nathalie Lebon and Elizabeth Meier (Mexico City: Siglo Veintiuno, 2006); forthcoming in English from Rutgers University Press, 2010.

31. This account draws on María Elena Valenzuela, "Women and the Democratization Process in Chile," *Women and Democracy: Latin America and Central and Eastern Europe,* 47–73.

32. Lisa Baldez (2002) notes that most of the women from the grassroots organizations had supported the leftist government of Salvador Allende (1970–1973); Baldez, *Why Women Protest: Women's Movements in Chile* (Cambridge: Cambridge University Press, 2002), 193–194.

33. For a detailed examination of the history of family law, divorce, and abortion in Argentina, Chile, and Brazil, see Mala Htun, *Sex and the State: Abortion, Divorce, and the Family under Latin American Dictatorships* (Cambridge: Cambridge University Press, 2003).

34. See Susan Franceschet, *Women and Politics in Chile* (Boulder: Lynne Rienner, 2006).

35. Valenzuela, "Women and Democratization in Chile," 59.

36. Veronica Schild, "New Subjects of Rights? Women's Movements and the Construction of Citizenship in the New Democracies," in *Cultures of Politics/Politics of Cultures: Revisioning Latin American Social Movements,* ed. Sonia E. Alvarez, Evelina Dagnino, and Arturo Escobar (Boulder: Westview, 1998), 105.

37. Jutta Marx, Jutta Borner, and Mariana Caminotti, "Gender Quotas, Candidate Selection, and Electoral Quotas: Comparing Argentina and Brazil," in *Feminist Agendas and Democracy in Latin America,* 50.

38. For up-to-date data on women in legislatures worldwide, see the website of the Inter-Parliamentary Union (www.ipu.org). On attitudes of women legislators in Central America, see Michelle A. Saint-Germain and Cynthia Chávez Metoyer, *Women Legislators in Latin America: Politics, Democracy, and Policy* (Austin: University of Texas Press, 2008). See also the excellent regional analyses from the International Institute for Democracy and Electoral Assistance (IDEA).

39. On the quota debates, see Craske, *Women in Politics in Latin America,* 22; Ilja A. Luciak, *After the Revolution: Gender and Democracy in El Salvador, Nicaragua, and Guatemala* (Baltimore: Johns Hopkins University Press, 2001); and Elizabeth Jelin, "Igualdad y diferencia: Dilemas de la ciudadanía de las mujeres en América Latina," *Cuadernos de estudios políticos* 7 (1997).

40. Quoted in Craske, *Women and Politics in Latin America* (New Brunswick, NJ: Rutgers University Press, 1999), 21.

41. Marx, Borner, and Caminotti, "Gender Quotas," 49.

42. Ibid., 52.

43. Leslie Schwindt-Beyer, "Women on the Sidelines: Women and Representation on Committees in Latin American Legislatures," *American Journal of Political Science* 49 (2005), 420–436.

44. In the following I draw on Nancy Saporta Sternbach et al., "Feminisms in Latin America: From Bogotá to San Bernardo," *Sogns* 27, no. 2 (1992); and summaries in Nikki Craske, *Women in the Americas* (Washington, DC: Inter-American Development Bank, 1995).

45. The term is from Maxine Molyneux's analysis of the programs for women in Nicaragua in the 1980s, "Mobilization Without Emancipation? Women's Interests, State, and Revolution in Nicaragua," *Feminist Studies* 11, no. 2 (1985).

46. See Miller, 235–237.

47. The Farabundo Martí Liberation Front or FMLN, the political party formed by the FMLN after the civil war ended. The FMLN candidate was elected president in 2009.

48. The theme was the impact of fundamentalism on women's lives, a term that covers all rigid ideological positions that are conceived of as different forms of patriarchy, not only the resurgence of Islam and socially conservative Catholicism, but also economic ideologies from Marxism to neoliberalism. See Vargas, "International Feminisms: The World Social Forum," in *Feminist Agendas and Democracy in Latin America,* 145–146.

49. Francisco Panizza, "Unarmed Utopia Revisited: The Resurgence of Left-of-Centre Politics in Latin America," *Political Studies* 53 (2005): 721–722.

50. Carlos de la Torre, *Populist Seduction in Latin America: The Ecuadorian Experience* (Athens: Ohio University Center for International Studies, 2000), 140–141.

51. Ibid., 142.

52. For detailed analysis of gender issues in Andean indigenous communities, see Maruja Barrig, "What Is Justice? Andean Women in Andean Development Projects," in *Women and Gender Equity in Development Theory and Practice,* ed. Jane S. Jaquette and Gale Summerfield (Durham, NC: Duke University Press, 2006), 107–134; and Manuela Lavinas Picq, "Gender Within Ethnicity: Human Rights and Politics in Ecuador," in *New Voices in the Study of Democracy in Latin America,* ed. Guillermo O'Donnell, Joseph S. Tulchin, and Augusto Varas (Washington, DC: Woodrow Wilson Center, 2000), 273–309.

53. In a book to be published by the Wilson Center Latin American Program (Washington, DC).

Suggested Readings

Chant, Sylvia, with Nikki Craske. *Gender in Latin America.* New Brunswick, NJ: Rutgers University Press, 2003.

Dore, Elizabeth, and Maxine Molyneux, eds. *Hidden Histories of Gender and the State in Latin America.* Durham, NC: Duke University Press, 2000.

Htun, Mala. *Sex and the State: Abortion, Divorce, and the Family Under Latin American Dictatorships and Democracy.* Cambridge: Cambridge University Press, 2003.

Jaquette, Jane S., ed. *Feminist Agendas and Democracy in Latin America.* Durham, NC: Duke University Press, 2009.

Kampworth, Karen, ed. *Gender and Populism in Latin America.* University Park: Pennsylvania State University Press, 2010.

Lebon, Nathalie, and Elizabeth Meier, eds. *De lo privado a lo público: Treinta años de lucha ciudadana en América Latina.* Mexico, DF: Siglo Veinteúno, 2006. Forthcoming in English from Rutgers University Press.

Miller, Francesca. *Latin American Women and the Search for Social Justice.* Hanover, NH: University Press of New England, 1991.

Saint-Germain, Michelle A., and Cynthia Chávez Metoyer. *Women Legislators in Latin America: Politics, Democracy, and Policy.* Austin: University of Texas Press, 2008.

Speed, Shannon, R. Aída Hernández Castillo, and Lynn M. Stephen, eds. *Dissident Women: Gender and Cultural Politics in Chiapas.* Austin: University of Texas Press, 2007.

Chapter 12

GLOBALIZATION, INSECURITY, AND CRISIS IN THE AMERICAS

JORGE NEF

SETTING THE STAGE: INSECURITY IN THE AMERICAS

BY MOST STATISTICAL accounts and with the few apparent exceptions of Haiti, Honduras, Bolivia, and Nicaragua, Latin America seems to occupy the upper layer of the other world. Unlike the Middle East, Africa, and especially Asia, the balance and diversity of resources to population looks quite promising. In this sense, Latin America and the Caribbean, other than by virtue of their proximity to the overdeveloped northern tier, made of the United States and the Dominion of Canada, show indicators suggesting that they have overcome critical poverty.

Until the 2008 global meltdown, business confidence among Western elites and their peripheral associates had been exuberantly high, fueling occasionally bullish waves of declamatory optimism. This mood reflected a steady recovery (3.3 percent average growth throughout the 1990s and nearly 6 percent in 2000 to 2007) that made investments profitable again, especially in contrast with the lost decade of the 1980s to the 1990s. However, underneath this façade of growth, distributional inequity, rooted in powerlessness and exclusion, not only remained but became more pronounced than in other regions of the world.[1] Most Latin Americans live under precarious and vulnerable circumstances. Even when economic recovery is factored in, the overall income levels for the first decade of the twenty-first century were below those of 1980.[2] As is the case throughout the globe, slow economic improvement has failed to translate into effective employment and social well-being.

Despite the fact that revolution looks unlikely for the moment, the long and deep social antagonisms under the formally democratic veneer have not vanished. Rather, they have resurfaced in the familiar spiral of poverty and institutional, repressive, criminal, and insurgent violence. The weak civilian governments that replaced the military dictatorships of the past and the few election-based regimes that survived the authoritarian 1970s have been paralyzed by ineffectiveness and low legitimacy. A careful look at the emerging literature and the mass of statistical and qualitative data renders a view that is far from optimistic. The proclaimed business and official confidence has little to do with social equity, political democracy, or even the state of real economic well-being; nor with actual security for the region's inhabitants. It rests, rather, on the ideological illusion that a felicitous correspondence between market politics and market economics has finally emerged, preventing turbulent social change from below.

Mutual Vulnerability

Two central propositions are advanced in this chapter. First, the repressive military regimes of the 1970s and the limited, "low-intensity" democracies that succeeded them exhibit a greater degree of continuity than the proponents of transition theory and the establishment media suggest. Despite the normalization supposedly taking place, persistent violence and political turmoil are not things of the past. The underlying social, economic, and international forces that have enjoyed extraterritorial power and privilege still prevail. Contrary to myth, the Americas as a whole, with few and reversible exceptions, have not undergone real social revolution. Their social and economic systems are mostly conservative and elitist. Regime stability has been maintained with significant levels of exclusion and systemic violence. Second, this kind of stability in the long run has hampered sustainable, equitable, and democratic development. In fact, the current style of modernization hinders real democracy and increases, rather than decreases, poverty and insecurity for most people in the hemisphere. As the current style of unipolar, imperial globalization[3] persists, so do de-democratization, widespread insecurity, and mutual vulnerability.

THE ROOTS OF UNDERDEVELOPMENT

Since the sixteenth century, the region has been subordinated to one or another more developed part of the world. The patterns of production, trade, and finance have reflected an enduring satellite-metropolis international division of labor. The insertion of Latin America and the Caribbean in the global economy, with their boom and bust cycles, was firmly established by the latter part of the nineteenth century. The export economy was based on raw materials shipped overseas, the import of manufactures, and the superexploitation of labor. The "modernization" of these commodity (and rentier) states has been largely antidevelopmental, as endogenous development has been conditioned and distorted by external factors, and has been undermined by flights of local capital, resulting in the marginalization and exclusion of most the population. Two centuries after formal independence, structural underdevelopment persists.

Under these conditions, social inequities have predictably endured, creating conditions favorable to the perpetuation of outward-looking and parasitic commercial elites, facilitating the emergence of a patrimonial system of labor relations based on indenture, paternalism, and servitude. Class and racial barriers have been intertwined in hierarchical, rigid, and exploitative social structures. The very existence of privilege has been largely a function of elites' linkages with external constituencies. Local oligarchies have objectively benefited from social inequities and foreign domination. These structural factors have become embedded in the national states and the system of inter-American relations, bringing about a vicious cycle: the key function of the regional and local political systems has been largely the maintenance of a hemispheric socioeconomic order based on inequality and de-development.

After decades of civil strife following independence, the prosperity brought about by increased demand for raw materials in industrial economies facilitated intra-elite compromise and the cessation of intra-elite conflict. Toward the end of the century most countries had evolved into various forms of stable oligarchic rule: "gentlemen politics." Generally, for as long as there was enough surplus to distribute among the elites, the danger of regional fracturing and civil wars remained low. Meanwhile, repression, by the newly professionalized military and police forces, was effectively directed against the lower strata. The transformation of a peasantry into a working class was also a by-product of the modernization and internationalization of the economy. While the military establishment acted as an insurance policy against popular challenges to the status quo, intra-elite consensus was maintained by regulating and facilitating private accumulation during export bonanzas. In a few instances (Uruguay, Argentina, Chile, Costa Rica, Mexico), the process of economic modernization gave rise to a greater degree of social differentiation, above and beyond the "butler" strata of officers and patrimonial clients on the public payroll. Instead, a middle class of sorts, constituted by professionals, employees, schoolteachers, bureaucrats, small retailers and the like, emerged as a buffer between the oligarchy and the mass of workers and peasants.

The Great Depression of the 1930s shattered the old oligarchic arrangement. With the collapse of markets, the tenuous system of accommodation that had sustained the republics crumbled. As intra-elite tensions increased, so did the challenges to the existing order coming from labor, the peasantry, and the dispossessed. In the aftermath of economic collapse, the "dictator of the thirties" became a dominant feature practically everywhere.[4] Yet, depending on the previous modality of socioeconomic development and institutional consolidation, the long-term effects of the crisis varied from country to country. In the relatively more industrialized South American nations and in Mexico, where middle-class reformism had evolved in the previous decades and where republican practices had become institutionalized, import substitution industrialization (ISI) with populism became the dominant form. Under the leadership of a middle class–controlled state, an uneasy alliance between national entrepreneurs and unionized labor was constructed. Their program was one of reactivation, employment creation, and national development. In the lesser developed societies in Central America and the Caribbean, which, with the exception of Costa Rica, lack a constitutional order or a meaningful professional and bureaucratic middle class, the populist alternative was impossible. The political pattern there was one of strict exclusion of the nonelite sectors. For the next thirty or forty years dictatorial rule with US support became entrenched.

Both patterns of conflict management began to fall apart between the mid-1940s and early 1950s. Riots, revolts, and generalized political turmoil exploded in Colombia, Costa Rica, Guatemala, El Salvador, Argentina, Venezuela, Peru, Bolivia, Cuba, and Puerto Rico. US administrations, mesmerized by the Cold War, the Truman Doctrine, a newly established Rio Treaty for the collective defense of the Americas (1947), and the hysteria of McCarthyism at home, responded to these domestic events in their backyard as threats to *American* national security. Local oligarchies, besieged by social unrest and vulnerable to popular mobilization and pressures for democratization, took advantage of the new international environment by playing with the anticommunist fears of their extraterritorial allies. Entangling transnational alliances between northern and southern business, political and military elites were built. The East-West conflict created the conditions for both a new North-South and elite-mass confrontation. It also marked the return of an active interventionism reminiscent of the "big stick" and "gunboat diplomacy" of Theodore Roosevelt and William Taft that preceded the 1934 Good Neighbor Policy of President Franklin D. Roosevelt. The rationale for interventionism was justified by a new and compelling ideological motif: the struggle between the free world and communism.

The CIA-orchestrated overthrow of the elected government of Guatemala in 1954 was paradigmatic of the new mood. The long-term effects of interventionism were destructive for the region's institutional and democratic development. Washington became the principal force preserving oppressive regimes and was an unabashed supporter of military dictatorships. Yet even this support proved insufficient to prevent the popular uprisings that precipitated a crisis of domination in Venezuela and Cuba in the late 1950s. In the 1960s Cuba appeared as the vanguard of a wave of national revolutionary movements backed by a wide array of popular forces. Its revolution was one of the most significant developments in the region since the Mexican revolution four decades earlier. It set into motion a fateful chain of events involving a confrontational escalation and a growing internationalization of domestic conflicts. Attempts to destabilize and subsequently overthrow Castro and reverse the revolution culminated in both the calamitous effort to undo the regime and President Kennedy's Alliance for Progress, launched in 1961. Washington's main purpose was to prevent another Cuba by encouraging mild social and economic reforms in the region. Economic and social development was perceived as the antidote to insurgency.[5] It was to be accomplished by propping up middle-class, progressive reformist and democratic governments. But the Alliance failed. Import substitution industrialization had already come to a dead end, populism had run its course, social tensions were mounting, and a profound fiscal crisis had set in. The inability of the reformist governments to deliver and quell social unrest rendered the initiative virtually useless.

Though ineffectual for the region's long-run democratic development, the other side of the alliance as a containment strategy[6] met with verifiable success. It involved the isolation of Cuba as well as a massive effort to give the collective defense of the Americas encoded in the Rio Treaty a new meaning: the introduction of counterinsurgency and civic action as the central preoccupation of the region's security forces.[7] A radical reorganization of the Latin American military ensued. The change in military mission and doctrine from the defense of territorial security (external aggression) by conventional forces to fighting the "internal enemy" by Special Forces was a blow to the already precarious sovereignty of the Latin American countries. It transformed the US security establishment into the head of a vertically integrated regional counterrevolutionary system, giving the local military a self-justifying and professional mission: fighting "subversion," however loosely defined.[8] In a relatively brief period and irrespective of declared intentions, the local military and police forces (the latter through public safety programs) had been turned into the dominant internal linkage groups, as "sentinels of empire" operating the lower rungs of the hemispheric security regime.[9] With the reformist and preventive side of the Alliance marred by internal and external inconsistencies, the counterinsurgency and containment elements took precedence over democratic concerns. This reorientation became manifest as early as 1964, with the Johnson administration's encouragement and promotion of the Brazilian coup and counterrevolution of 1964.

In the more institutionalized democracies, the exhaustion of import substitution and populism led to a breakdown of consensus and civic confidence. ISI with national populism failed to bring long-term sustainable development and political stability. In the 1960s wage and price spirals had become a muted and protracted form of civil strife in many countries. Political deadlock eroded both the legitimacy and the effectiveness of these regimes. Labor practices inherited from the populist years reproduced and accelerated the "push-up" effect of institutionalized social conflict. The rules of the pluralistic game weakened in the midst of rapid mass mobilization. The existing socioeconomic order, both domestic and international, ended up being maintained by resorting to naked yet highly bureaucratized repression under a new political alliance. The latter involved a coalition between the externally linked business elites, which gave content to a conservative economic package, and the security establishments, transnationalized by the ideological "professionalism" of the Cold War. The military, representing an externally trained, indoctrinated, and financed fraction of the middle class, provided the force required for keeping the population at bay. Its ideological-professional software was—and continues to be—the national security doctrine.[10]

Authoritarian Capitalism and the Repressive State

The national security doctrine, referred to as "Pentagonism" by Juan Bosch,[11] was constructed on three notions: an internal and external enemy ("subversion"), an external "friend" (the US-dominated regional security regime), and ideological frontiers. Its effect was to erode the national character of the local military institutions and decisively transnationalize the state. The explicit articulation of this strategic posture was the Nixon Doctrine, outlined in the Rockefeller report of 1969. The document clearly showed a shift in the normative ideal of political development, from democracy and participation to authoritarianism and order. Between 1969 and 1973, with a few notable exceptions,[12] the number of military dictatorships steadily climbed: ten in 1969, twelve in 1970, fourteen in 1972, and fifteen in 1973.

The liberal-authoritarian projects that unfolded in the 1970s rejected the nationalist and protectionist premises of import substitution and other induced development policies. Instead, economic growth was seen as a function of a reinsertion of the countries' economies into the international division of labor as exporters of raw materials: a return to a widened export economy. With the exception of Brazil in the late 1960s and the 1970s, economic modernization, far from "deepening industrialization" meant increased reliance on both the natural resource sector and heavy borrowing. The aggregate foreign debt, which in 1960 amounted to about

one-third of the regional annual exports, had grown by 1970 to 1.7 times the total value of exports. Just before the oil crisis in 1973, it had climbed to 1.9 times
that value. By 1993 the gap had grown to over 2.7 times,[13] and became stable at
about 1.8 times in 2002.[14] The strategy of hyperaccumulation also involved the
creation of favorable conditions, through deregulation, denationalization, and the
disarticulation of labor organizations, for domestic and transnational elites to increase their share of profits.

The era of national security was notable for persistent abuses of human rights;
the early neoliberal design of its economic strategies implied dismantling the welfare state, import substitution industrialization policies, and social safety nets developed since the 1930s. Authoritarian capitalism rejected the demand-side
implications of the early Cold War liberalism of the Alliance for Progress and was
more concerned with direct containment and the protection of the status quo than
with development.[15] Other than offering "economic miracles" financed by illusory
foreign investment, the orthodox policies imposed monetarism (later identified
with the Chicago School) over the structuralist, Keynesian doctrine of the UN
Economic Commission for Latin America (ECLA). These deflationary measures
were far more effective as a shock therapy—by atomizing labor, freezing wages, let-
ting prices float to world levels, and privatizing the economies—than in raising living standards. They were much more effective in the short run as weapons in a
social war, defining "friends" and "foes," than as instruments of national development. On the contrary, the long-term socioeconomic consequences of these policies were, by and large, disastrous and persistent for the region. So were their
social, environmental, and financial implications. In fact, far from generating stability and bringing prosperity, the combination of dictatorial rule with unrestricted
free market policies created a serious governability problem. The formula of authoritarian politics with free markets also set the conditions for the subsequent
debt crisis and recession of the 1980s.

The bureaucratic-authoritarian states that emerged in South America, patterned
on the example of post-1964 Brazil, were attempts at modernization from the top,
with strong external inducement. The benefits of this new order accrued to a small
alliance of domestic entrepreneurs and speculators supported by a technocratic-
military middle class and their business, political, and military associates in the imperial center. Its narrow base generated a persistent crisis of legitimacy that was
managed by three instruments. One was military force, through strengthening the
alliance between officers and the domestic socioeconomic elites. The other was the
inclusion of external constituencies—military, business, political, and diplomatic—
to compensate for lost internal support. The third was the demobilization and exclusion of the bulk of the population. Dictatorship became an intrinsic component
of economic freedom.[16] The social cost for the majorities was enormous, since overall living conditions declined and the gap between haves and have-nots widened.
Nor did these regimes succeed in unleashing real counterrevolutions. At best the national security regimes provided a repressive brake against social mobilization, economic nationalism, regional integration, and a perceived threat from the left. The
effective operation of their neoliberal policies required large amounts of external financing, which was facilitated in the 1970s and early 1980s by massive deposits of
recycled petrodollars in private Western banks.

Foreign Debt and Regime Crisis

Indebtedness fueled by the illusion of prosperity ensued. As both the governments and the private sector in the region increased their financial obligations, the failure of production and exports to keep pace with borrowing, and most importantly with soaring interest rates, resulted in huge debt burdens. Despite diverse ideological discourses, the hard-line military regimes in Brazil, Argentina, Chile, Uruguay, and Bolivia did not behave very differently from the more populist ones in Peru, Panama, or Ecuador, or those in civilian-controlled oil-producing countries (Mexico and Venezuela), or in the microstates of the Caribbean. The policies may have had different declared intentions, yet their effects were similar: unmanageable indebtedness and de-development throughout the region.

The crisis of dictatorship in Brazil, Argentina, Uruguay, and Chile involved the erosion of the political alliances that had permitted the implementation of the repressive socioeconomic projects. More inclusive military regimes like those of Peru, Ecuador, and Panama quietly faded away. The main political limitations of the national security regimes were threefold. (1) Government by force was ultimately untenable; (2) the pretended security was based on the insecurity of most of the population; and (3) national security was not national. The Nicaraguan uprising of 1979 and the protracted civil wars in El Salvador and Guatemala signaled another form of transition: popular, radical, and potentially antiliberal. From an imperial perspective, these endogenous developments posed a more serious threat to the maintenance of the hemispheric order than the erosion of bureaucratic authoritarianism in South America. The combined impact of economic crises, a growing inability to manage conflict among internal factions, and a new post-Watergate political coalition in Washington concerned about the long-run effects of authoritarian solutions created the conditions for military withdrawal. The Linowitz Report outlined a transitional strategy in 1975.[17] This document was heavily influenced by the views of the Trilateral Commission[18] and was critical of the previous "Pentagonist" policy toward Latin America. It constituted the blueprint for President Carter's initiative on democratization, and its subsequent implementation under the Reagan administration.

Intra-elite Alliances and "Democratic Transition"[19]

Democratic transition for most of Latin America was largely the result of intra-elite negotiations superintended by external actors. Rather than regime transition, this meant the consolidation of a nondemocratic socioeconomic order under a formally democratic façade. The orderly retreat of the national security regimes preserved many authoritarian traits. In this the reemerging democracies shared some of the political characteristics of older "managed democracies" such as Colombia, Venezuela, or Mexico, which did not experience direct military rule. Such closely watched transition to democracy had strict limits. Although authoritarian capitalism proved to be largely a developmental failure, the radical restructuring of the economies along free market lines by means of political repression had been profound enough to prevent a return to economic nationalism. Likewise, the restructuring and transnationalization of the security establishment made the pursuit of nationalist and nonaligned foreign policies impossible. In this sense, the political arrangements that emerged in Latin America as a result of redemocratization, while possessing the formal trappings of sovereignty and democracy, were neither truly democratic nor sovereign. They produced precariously balanced civilian regimes based on pacts of elites, with exclusionary political agendas and narrow internal support. In these, the popular sectors were effectively maintained outside the political arena, while external actors, both economic and military, enjoyed de facto veto power over the state. In addition, the countries remained saddled with cumbersome, in some cases unmanageable foreign debt, not to mention the debt management conditions of IMF-inspired structural adjustment policies (SAPs).

The ultimate effects of these policies have been the hegemonic perpetuation of dependence and underdevelopment. These traits express themselves in a vicious cycle of built-in vulnerability to external economic and political influence, requiring ever increasing doses of external supports. This vulnerability is dramatically illustrated by the inability of the countries to extricate themselves from chronic indebtedness: the debt trap.[20] Debt management became the number one political concern in the regional agenda in the early 1980s. The service, both principal and interest, grew from slightly over 40 percent of the total value of annual exports in 1979, to over 65 percent in 1983. The total indebtedness figure for 1988 was over $400 billion with the higher sums being incurred by Brazil, Mexico, Argentina, Chile, Venezuela, and Peru. Despite the fact that about half of the countries reduced their liabilities by 1990–1991, the overall debt grew to $421 billion: a 3.5 percent annual increase. By 2001 it reached $787 billion, expanding at an average annual rate of 8.7 percent. Out of the seventeen most indebted countries in the world in the 1990s, twelve were in the Latin American region. On average the annual interest rate payments fell from 33 percent of all exports in 1987 to 22 percent in 1991 as the lost decade came to an end. Between 1992 and 1999, the burden was reduced even further. Countries like Brazil and Mexico decelerated their rate of indebtedness respectively from staggering annual rates of 223 percent to 60 percent, and 206 to 156. These figures are unsustainable by any stretch of imagination. In the thirty years between 1970 and 2000 Argentina accelerated its already huge rate of indebtedness from a fifteen-year average annual growth of 178 percent to a rate of 256 percent annually. Venezuela, in turn, went from a yearly increase of 320 percent between 1970 and 1985 to a whopping 465 percent in the 1970 to 2000 period. If the debt problem is measured as inability to pay, an analysis of the ratio between exports and debt service shows figures that are equally dramatic. For instance, the ratio of debt service to exports for Argentina moved from an already high 34 percent in 1990 to over 71 percent in 2000. For Brazil, the jump was from 23 to nearly 91 percent. So far, and despite economic disasters in Mexico (1994), Ecuador (1999), Argentina (2001), Brazil (2002), and Bolivia (2003), most countries in the region did not default on their debt or resort to a strategy of debtors cartels. This policy of fiscal responsibility has been hard for the civil society, which had to absorb its full impact, especially after a number of governments "nationalized" corporate debt at taxpayer expense.

The end of the cycle of national security in the 1980s was a direct consequence of the insoluble contradictions between and within the reactionary coalitions in power and the centrality of external support for the authoritarian regime. Given limited resources, there was a long-run impossibility of reconciling the interests of the national security bureaucracies with those of domestic and foreign business. An additional problem emerged from the countries' extreme vulnerability to external factors (e.g., the unmanageable debt burden, deteriorating terms of trade) and constituencies. As power conflicts intensified in Washington in the post-Nixon era, opposition from liberal political sectors against authoritarian regimes grew. Furthermore, the shrinkage of crucial support from international business compounded the internal erosion of power suffered by the Latin American dictatorships. Democratic transition became the alternative to popular revolt. The conversion from dictatorship to limited democracy has to be seen in the context of the previous transition to national security, both in the bureaucratic-authoritarian context of the Southern Cone and in the less institutionalized setting of Central America. Growing participation and dependent development could coexist only under conditions of economic expansion and for as long as such participation did not threaten the perceived interests of the local and regional elites.

The Nature of the Receiver State

In the mid-1980s the mounting debt crisis set the parameters for the emergence throughout the Americas of a new political formula: a "receiver state" blending limited democracy and neoliberal economics. The result was a weak, highly transnationalized state, acting in partnership with foreign creditors and international financial institutions as manager, executor, and liquidator of national bankruptcy. The central function of this arrangement has been the administration of the debt combined with the implementation of structural adjustment policies geared to massive privatization and de-nationalization of the economy. This state reflects the nature of the transnationalized political alliances and the narrow spaces for political participation, where economic and fiscal policies have been effectively left out of the political debate. Yet these policies define the rules of the game and set the limits for social policies.

Pacts of Elites and Exclusionary Socioeconomic Agendas

The various national incarnations of receivership exhibit important differences. These depend on the nature of the transition processes, as well as the particular coloration of the civilian management to appear in the postauthoritarian period and the early adjustment phase. At close scrutiny, irrespective of the elected nature of the government in charge, the economic agenda has a striking resemblance with that imposed under authoritarian rule. These arrangements are not a mere transitional phase from elite domination to genuine democracy: free and participatory politics with effective popular control. Rather, the repressive state of the 1970s and the receiver state of the 1990s and 2000s are two different manifestations of a similar cluster of elite interests.

The receiver state expresses the consensus of a mostly transnational and conservative coalition, though at times managed by tamed center-left governments. Limited democracies, with narrow mobility opportunities and exclusionary agendas, have provided a thin cushion to confront the deep structural problems once controlled by repression. The current modality of conflict management, while reducing the most blatant human rights abuses, has left the most pressing and fundamental socioeconomic and political problems largely unresolved. The combination of the transnational integration of the domestic elites (economic, military, technocratic, and bureaucratic) with the demobilization and marginalization of the popular sectors does not provide a formula for stable governance, let alone democracy. In the absence of tangible rewards to buy legitimacy, insurgent, repressive, institutionalized (as well as criminal) violence has become a common expression. State failure—as in Ecuador in 1999, Argentina in 2001, and Colombia or Mexico in 2009—has also emerged as a distinct possibility.

Despite the phasing out of the old national security regimes, contemporary Latin America is not undergoing a change toward substantial democratization. Formal demilitarization and return to limited democracy are not synonymous with an alteration of the status quo. Nor is democracy nowadays any more "real" in those countries in the hemisphere where civilian governments have remained in control. On the contrary, the prevailing discourse on democracy among the official intelligentsia throughout the Americas involves a juxtaposition of a substantially domesticated democracy with neoliberal economics.[21] The above model amounts to a plutocracy with popular support, occasionally resorting to electoral rituals. While this "low-intensity democracy"[22] may appeal to the consumption-intensive, high-income core groups in the hemisphere, it is not really majority, let alone popular, rule. It is basically the same elitist formula articulated by the Trilateral Commission in the mid-1970s that considered the root cause of the crisis of democracy to be democracy itself. Under a legal façade, this mode of conflict management entrenches a corporatist pact of elites representing basically the same economic, social, and political alliances that sustained the antidemocratic regimes: the power elite at the core, the military, the local bourgeoisie, and upper segments of the middle classes. Democratic development, with the qualified exception of Costa Rica, is weak and fragile at best throughout the hemisphere.

The regressive socioeconomic policies implemented under authoritarian rule have been enshrined both in the pacts of transition and in ad hoc constitutional mechanisms. The re-democratized regimes are constrained by other factors too. One is the weakness of the governing political alliances, since the transition arrangements effectively excluded most left of center and populist political forces from holding power. Another is the crucial autonomous role played by the transnationalized security forces, as a parallel state to maintain the status quo and prevent exposure of past and present human rights abuses. Then there are the odious massive debt obligations incurred mostly under the previous repressive regimes. They severely limit the rendering of services to those in need, while fiscal austerity inevitably leads to confrontation and increasingly repressive governmental responses. The impact of the debt service on already exiguous fiscal resources is compounded by the strict conditions imposed by the international financial institutions (the IMF, the World Bank, the IDB, and private banks). Structural adjustments resulting from such conditions have gravitated against demands for reform, equity, and social justice, already frozen by the previous dictatorships.

The Biophysical and Environmental Effects of Public Policies

Since the 1980s, the Latin American and Caribbean countries have experienced an expanding and converging set of problems, whose common denominator is a fiscal crisis of the state. These affect employment, purchasing power, housing, safe drinking water, the quality of sanitation, the growing incidence of old and new diseases of epidemic proportions, a deteriorating ecosystem, and a profound inability to meet challenges. A regional health crisis is unfolding as life-threatening ailments that were considered eradicated (such as malaria, Chagas disease, tuberculosis) are making a dramatic comeback, and new morbidity and mortality factors (like HVI/AIDS or swine flu) are on the rise. This has happened at a time when social safety nets and health delivery mechanisms are collapsing as a consequence of structural adjustment policies. The 1990 cholera epidemic was paradigmatic of extreme mutual vulnerability. The combination of a poverty-driven disease, multiplied by the dismantling of the institutional mechanisms for disease containment and treatment, had the effect of multiplying generalized insecurity across class and national boundaries.

Environmental threats are another example of policy-driven dysfunction. These include sewage, waste, and air pollution, but also encompass a broader complexity of and multiplicity of reciprocating issues. In an earlier study Robles and I sketched a calamitous situation in which retro-feeding and destructive processes create a vicious cycle of vulnerability.[23] Current industrial, mining, and agricultural practices, mixed with uncontrolled urbanization, create an interwoven pattern of biophysical and social stress on the ecosystem and human populations.[24] For instance, deforestation, with its sequel of health-related effects, accounts annually for over 40 percent of the global loss of forests. On a per capita basis, this makes Latin America the number one contributor to green depletion and loss of biodiversity. Furthermore, in the midst of an expansion of agricultural production for export, food insecurity still remains a major threat to large segments of the population, even in the statistically "rich" countries. Once again, the pressure to manage the debt and its conditions put a premium on cash crops and the merciless exploitation of natural and human resources.

Structural Poverty and Inequality

Since 1980, those living below the poverty line in Latin America and the Caribbean *increased* from above 120 million to over 200 million and from 41 to 46 percent of the population.[25] The most affected have been those already vulnerable: women, children, the elderly, ethnic minorities. Though poverty and indigence have gone down to 1996 levels in most countries, overall deprivation is still higher than two decades ago, and rural poverty has increased steadily. Central America has been the most seriously affected by the double impact of concentration of wealth and the spread of poverty: at the verge of the twenty-first century, reportedly nearly 80 percent of its inhabitants were unable to access a basic food basket and half of these were destitute. According to the same report, between 1977 and 1994, Guatemala witnessed an accelerated concentration of wealth and resources with fewer than 2 percent of the landowners owning now more than 65 percent of the total farmland.[26] Between 1990 and 1993, after just two years of structural adjustment, the poverty rate in Honduras increased from 68 percent of the total population to 78 percent. In Nicaragua, as a result of the Contra war and the implementation of the postwar austerity package, 71.3 percent of the economically active population was either effectively unemployed or underemployed. Illiteracy, which had been effectively reduced to 12 percent between 1979 and 1989, actually *increased* in 1993 in absolute and relative terms. The same was the case with infant mortality, from 50 per 1,000 in the 1980s to 71 per 1,000 in 1991 and 83 per 1,000 in 1993. Although the acuteness of these figures has been less pronounced in recent years, the legacy of catastrophic decade of man-made and natural catastrophes has left a deep imprint.

Even the widely hailed economic "miracles" have not produced lasting development. The combination of entrenched elite interests, extreme free market agendas, and structural adjustment policies left a lasting burden of poverty and despair. The areas of health, education, and community development have suffered continuously, impacting precisely those who need the most. Since the end of the boom of the 1970s, Brazil's only enduring feature has been the most unequal income distribution in the Western Hemisphere, and one of the worst in the world. Chile's "success story" does not fare any better under close scrutiny. Between 1970 and 1987, the proportion of Chileans defined as poor increased by an average yearly rate of 7.2 percent. Meanwhile, real income per capita grew at an annual average rate of 0.3 percent. Since 1990, with a democratic government and despite the fact that the speed of impoverishment has been arrested, widespread privation persists. Despite impressive GNP annual growth rates between 4.5 and 10 percent, Chile has dismal pattern of income distribution.

Pauperization and expanding inequity are not limited to the cases mentioned above. They are present all over the hemisphere: throughout the Caribbean, in Argentina, Uruguay, Paraguay, Venezuela, Colombia, Peru, Bolivia, Ecuador, Panama, Costa Rica, the Dominican Republic, Haiti, and particularly Mexico. As mentioned, the most affected are the rural and urban poor, but white-collar, middle-class sectors have seen their economic opportunities and social safety nets dramatically eroded as well. In Latin America, as in Canada and the United States today, the middle classes are disintegrating in the growing gap between the extremes of wealth and poverty (Wolff 2003). [27]

Civil-Military Relations

Beneath the civilian mantle, praetorianism has a lingering presence. Given the polarized and violent nature of political conflicts, militarization has been a longstanding feature of the Latin American state. It has also been a constant in the United States. With few exceptions, the military establishment has played a disproportionately large role in most of the countries, whether under civilian executives or not. Even in the supposedly exceptional cases, careful examination reveals that direct military rule or militarized repression has always been present. This is abundantly clear in the deepening conflict in Colombia. Since the end of the Cold War, the military has been less conspicuously present in politics, but closer scrutiny reveals a more complex picture. The end of the civil conflicts in El Salvador and Nicaragua, declining insurgent threats in Peru, as well as the effects of structural adjustment packages on defense budgets, suggest a trend toward demilitarization.[28] Yet overall budget reductions have not been matched by personnel reductions. Rather, a small increase in personnel has taken place. But average figures are deceiving: downturns in countries with large establishments, such as Argentina (-39.8 percent), Chile (-9.1 percent), Nicaragua (-76.6 percent), and Peru (-12.5

percent), mask the incidence of significant upturns in most other countries. Twelve out of twenty of the countries actually increased the size of their defense forces between 1985 and 1991. Colombia topped the list with 76.7 percent, followed by Venezuela (53.1 percent), Guatemala (40.7 percent), and Mexico (35.6 percent). The largest establishment, Brazil's, with nearly 270,000, grew 7 percent between 1988 and 1993 (IISS 1087–1992).

Though in comparison with the G8 nations and the Middle East, the size of the Latin American forces is relatively modest, the impact, influence, and transnationalization of the security establishment, especially of its officer corps, remain extensive. Not including some 760,000 paramilitary and an indeterminate number of reservists, Latin America has over 1.3 million individuals under arms and spends close to $9 billion in defense. Given its economic base, Latin America remains overly militarized; the externally controlled security sector is still a voracious competitor for the scarce resources needed for development. It constitutes a persistent obstacle to the sovereignty of, and the cooperation among, nations and continues to be the single most serious threat to political stability, integration, sustainable democracy, and human rights.

With the end of the Cold War and a declining threat of regional insurgency, a fundamental security issue in the Americas is not so much how to protect society from external and internal enemies but how to safeguard the population in most countries from their security forces. In this context, we must reconsider civil-military relations and the nature of the prevailing civil-military regimes in the emerging inter-American order, especially in light of new strategic factors. One is the persistent conservative, interventionist, and apocalyptic mood in American politics, and the extensive post-9/11 resurgence of Pentagonism; a proclivity that the Obama administration will be hard-pressed to maintain. Another is lingering border tensions, exemplified by flare-ups like the 1995 Ecuadorian-Peruvian war. A third factor is the growing militarization of social conflicts, as in Mexico, or in the vertical and horizontal expansion of Colombia's civil strife, narco-wars in the Andean region and recently in Mexico, the ongoing confrontation between Venezuela and Colombia and Colombia and Ecuador and the involvement—both mercenary and otherwise—of Latin American forces in the Middle East conflict. Underpinning this dysfunctional militarization is the close and dependent association between the Latin American and US military establishments.

Limited Democracy and Elected Plutocracies

Current political developments in Latin America, while conveying a less repressive picture, especially by contrast with a somber record of the 1970s, present at best mixed signals. On the positive side, most of the region is ruled nowadays by governments generated through formally free and competitive elections: what Guyana's former prime minister Cheddi Jagan sarcastically called "5-minute democracy."[29] In various instances, some sort of consolidation has taken place, as a second and even a third generation of elected governments have been inaugurated. There have also been sporadic yet significant attempts to hold governments accountable to the electorate. Most importantly, as relations between Latin America and the United States deteriorated during the George W. Bush administration, center-left governments have been elected throughout the Americas between 2006 and

2009, including Nicaragua, Guatemala, El Salvador, Bolivia, Ecuador, Argentina, Paraguay, and even the United States. Instances of torture, disappearances, and blatant state terrorism, with notable exceptions such as Colombia, have become less frequent. However, there are also disturbing signs. One is the persistence, and even revival, of authoritarian and oligarchic traditions. Power remains highly concentrated. Other less tangible but basic values, such as respect for human life, honest government, and the reduction of discrimination and official abuse, are not widely adhered to. Corruption in both parts of the hemisphere is widespread, deep, and fast growing. The United States and Canada have not been exempt from scandal, bribery, and other forms of dishonest management in the councils of power.

Limited democracies based on pacts among elites are distinctively exclusionary. Until recently electoral processes, though a common sight throughout the Americas, have been void of choice and even meaning. Fraud and manipulation have been a common feature. Voters can cast the ballot but the menus and policy options are roughly the same. The socioeconomic and institutional pillars of the former national security regimes (landowners, business, foreign investors, and authoritarian preserves within the military, the judiciary, and the technocracy) are also those of the new democratic orchestrations. A majority of those who perpetrated crimes against humanity are still at large. Thus it is hardly surprising that public apathy and cynicism throughout the hemisphere are high, while government legitimacy is low. Despite the unfolding of formally contested elections during the 1990s in all of the countries and apparently normal constitutional reforms in a good number of others, these processes failed to provide real alternatives. The alienation of the population from the political process noted above has resulted until recently in extremely high rates of electoral abstention.[30] For instance, 84 percent abstained in the Guatemalan referendum of 1994 and 50 percent in El Salvador's general election of March 1994. In the Colombian parliamentary elections of 1994, over 70 percent did not vote, while in the Ecuadorian congressional competition the same year, spoiled ballots received the second largest plurality. Colombia tops the list of electoral abstention, with roughly 40 percent of the voters casing their ballots in 2000, and it is followed closely by the United States.[31] In addition, many of these contests have been tainted with serious irregularities. Yet the abovementioned tide of center-left shifts in presidential elections over the past three to four years indicates a changing pattern, though not yet a definitive trend.

Beyond ceremonial transfers of offices by electoral means and the absence of direct military rule, democracy in the Americas was not consolidated in the 1990–2000 decade. Transition remains incomplete and in some cases de-democratization has been the predominant trend. Oligarchies throughout the continent, despite the historical watershed of the Obama election in 2008, have shown a remarkable continuity. The old practice of executive *continuismo* and dynastic-type succession (the elimination of which was central to the region's past democratic agenda) has resurfaced. There is also a remarkable continuity of policy. Neoliberal recipes have become entrenched in the conditions attached to debt alleviation, regional trade agreements (such as NAFTA or MERCOSUR), and the so-called macroeconomic equilibrium policies that effectively remove fiscal, monetary, and credit matters from national political debate. In addition, the "new" Cold War in the context of unipolarism, with its pseudo moralistic and messianic discourse, has debilitated democracy, development, and security.

Conclusion: The Fires Within

A profound structural contradiction has emerged in the region's governance. If elected governments stressed *democracy*, equity, majority rule, and the interests of the public (the civil society), they would face relentless opposition and sabotage from domestic and international elites, leading to eventual ineffectiveness, if not outright destabilization. Thus the more common course is to stress *liberalism* and ignore the civil society and rule on behalf of the profit sector. This is what in the North American context Ralph Nader has labeled a *plutocracy.* The political cost of this option is very high in the long run: loss of legitimacy, sovereignty, and an erosion of the trust between elected officials and the electorate, a central tenet of both governance and pluralist institutionalization.

Given the level of political alienation, it is not surprising that popular insurrections have arisen among angry communities confronting threats to their livelihood: Chiapas (1993), Quito (2000), Buenos Aires (2001), and La Paz (2003). The mobilizations and insurrections mentioned above have had broad domestic and international implications. They are a specific Latin American expression of the antiglobalization (and anti-neoliberal) movement, recreating a civil society, where popular organizations had been crushed by the double squeeze of military rule in the 1970s and economic restructuring in the 1990s. These developments suggest that popular movements and rebellions are present in the new globalized regional order.[32] They have reemerged as political options, and we may witness more such manifestations in the near future. Instability, even under the illusion of the NAFTA and FTAA umbrella, is more than skin deep. On the other hand, by challenging the legitimacy of the new intra-elite and transnational arrangements, the new modes of resistance reveal the intrinsic weakness of the low-intensity democracies.

Thus from a long-range structural perspective, massive upheavals have not withered away altogether in the region, although their manifestations have changed. In a way, the social movements and broad coalitions that have opened prospects for democratic change in most of the Americas in recent years have built on the early protest mobilizations of the 1990s and early 2000s. Our analysis strongly suggests that the politics of limited democratization with neoliberal economics, while an improvement over the human rights record of the military dictatorships, imposes built-in constraints on the realization of a truly stable and sustainable democratic project for and by the bulk of the population. Nor is the combination of limited democracy with neoliberalism a guarantee against expanding corruption or popular alienation. In fact, the opposite seems to be the case. If economic recovery fails to produce a better standard of living for the majorities or if the structural economic crisis deepens, these weak and "pragmatic" civilian regimes may be overturned by equally weak, yet violently repressive civil-military regimes. After all, the national security doctrine is still the ideological "software" (or culture) of the security establishments and a regular staple in the training of Special Forces in the hemisphere. The "communist" subversion of yore is being replaced by a new definition of the internal enemy: "terrorism," "anarchy," "war on drugs," or more broadly anything that threatens the investment climate or the interests of the core elites. Growing military and US involvement, as in the case of Plan Colombia or Plan Mérida, or the expansion of the role of the US Southern Command, is a case in point. Certainly the post-9/11 atmosphere may have a destabilizing effect by reviving a hard "counterterrorist" posture to justify elite rule.

As the entire region becomes more closely integrated, a potentially dysfunctional system of mutual vulnerability has taken shape. Its impact on the life of millions throughout the Americas can be catastrophic. The present course points toward scenarios where unemployment, poverty, violence, criminality, health hazards, addiction, forced migration, massive population displacements, repression, and environmental decay feed on each other. The drug-trading regime is a dramatic illustration of this interconnectedness. The ties that link the drug trade begin with peasant producers in the depressed Andean region, and continue with crime syndicates in both producing and importing areas, corrupt officials (as well as rabid "patriots"), retailers, and users, ranging from the destitute to those in high social standing. Being an essentially consumer-driven market, and operating on pure market logic, its containment requires addressing its social-psychological and economic causes—including the roots of addiction—rather than exclusively its tactical symptoms.

Under these circumstances, the dysfunctional linkages of mutual vulnerability between North and South, and their multiple accelerators, create a spiraling lose-lose situation: a negative-score game. Without profound changes in both the South and the North of the hemisphere, the possibility of arresting or reversing serious threats to human security will remain doubtful. Short of a radical reorganization of the pattern of governance throughout the Americas, including decision making, accountability, and regional cooperation (e.g., the largely dysfunctional Inter-American system), multiple and critical dysfunctions are likely to increase.[33]

Regional security cannot be equated with short-term business confidence or with a messianic vision of Manifest Destiny, or "wars" on terrorism or drugs, or more recently, fending off the "Hispanic threat."[34] A breakdown of democratic development, prosperity, and equity, and rising tension in the more volatile countries of the region would have a direct and deleterious effect on the well-being and security of both Americas. The weakness of democratic institutions and their inability to move from democratic transition and elected plutocracies to consolidation of popular rule is a critical structural flaw in the security of the hemisphere. It is becoming painfully obvious that the end of the Cold War did not automatically translate into a Fukuyama-type scenario of the "end of history," with global prosperity, peace, and democracy.[35] The over two-decade-old democratic transition in the region cannot be made synonymous with either the entrenchment of participatory practices or with responsible government, let alone the enhancement of human dignity. The "safe," "limited," "low-intensity," and meaningless democracy, peddled by transition theorists and the neoauthoritarians, impedes more than facilitates the emergence of a sustainable security community in the Americas. So does the persistence of economic dogmatism and the rebirth of national security doctrines designed to fight elusive and perpetual global conflicts. Regime change throughout the hemisphere, particularly in the Northern tier, is a necessary condition for hemispheric human security.

NOTES

1. CEPAL, *Panorama Social de América Latina 2004* (online version, October 24, 2005). p. 1; also United Nations, Department of Economic and Social Affairs, *Report on the World Social Situation 2005: The Inequality Predicament*, August 25, 2005, p. 1.

2. United Nations, *World Economic and Social Survey 1994* (New York: United Nations), p. 42.

3. Terry-Lynn Karl and Richard Fagen, "The Logic of Hegemony: The United States as a Superpower in Central America," in Jan Triska, ed., *Dominant Powers and Subordinate States: The United States in Latin America and the Soviet Union in Eastern Europe* (Durham, NC: Duke University Press, 1986), pp. 218–238.

4. These include General Uriburu in Argentina, General Ibáñez in Chile, Getulio Vargas in Brazil, President Terra in Uruguay, General Somoza in Nicaragua, General Hernádez-Martínez in El Salvador, General Trujillo in the Dominican Republic, General Carías in Honduras, General Ubico in Guatemala, General Sánchez-Cerro in Peru, and Colonel Busch in Bolivia.

5. Eugene Stanley, *The Future of Underdeveloped Countries: Political Implications of Economic Development* (New York: Praeger, 1961), pp. 3–4.

6. US Senate Committee on Foreign Relations, Subcommittee on Western Hemisphere Affairs, Hearing (June 24–July 8, 1969), pp. 62–64, 57–61; also Yale Ferguson, "The Departments of Defense and State and Governor Rockefeller on US Military Policies and Programs in Latin America," in *Contemporary Inter-American Relations: A Reader in Theory and Issues*, (Englewood Cliffs: Prentice-Hall, 1972), pp. 327–328.

7. John Lovell, "Military-dominated Regimes and Political Development: A Critique of Some Prominent Views," in Monte Palmer and Larry Stern, eds., *Political Development in Changing Societies: An Analysis of Modernization* (Lexington: Heath Lexington, 1971), pp. 159–179.

8. Charles D. Corbett, *The Latin American Military as a Socio-Political Force: Case Studies of Bolivia and Argentina*, Monographs in International Affairs (Center for Advanced International Studies, University of Miami, 1972), pp. 13–19; also see "Appendix F: Précis of the Counterinsurgency Course (1963), the Special Warfare School Fort Bragg, North Carolina," in Willard Barber and Neale Ronning, *Internal Security and Military Power: Counterinsurgency and Civic Action in Latin America* (Ohio: Ohio State University Press, 1966), pp. 275–276, 217–245; US Army Special Warfare School, *Counterinsurgency Planning Guide*, Special Text no. 31–176 (1964).

9. Jan Knippers Black, *Sentinels of Empire: United States and Latin American Militarism*, Contributions in Political Science (Westport, CT: Greenwood, 1986), passim.

10. Jean-Louis Weil, Joseph Comblin, and Judge Senese, "The Repressive State: The Brazilian National Security Doctrine and Latin America," *LARU Studies*, no. 3 (Toronto: LARU, 1979), pp. 36–73; also see Robinson Rojas, "Notes on the Doctrine of National Security," 2003, www.rrojasdatabank.org/natsec1.

11. Juan Bosch, *El Pentagonismo sustituto del imperialismo*, 3rd ed. (Santo Domingo: Editora Alfa y Omega, 2000), pp. 5–14.

12. Mexico, Venezuela, Colombia, Costa Rica, and communist Cuba.

13. Our calculation is based on ECLA *Anuario Estadístico* data between 1970 and 1985.

14. According to ECLAC, *Anuario Estadístico 2001*, the figures for disbursed foreign debt were US$22,256,000 (1980) and US$739,930,000 (2000).

15. For a direct view of the "developmental deontology" of counterinsurgency, see US Army Special Warfare School, *Counterinsurgency Planning Guide*, Special Text no. 31–176 (1964).

16. Orlando Letelier, "The 'Chicago Boys' in Chile: Economic Freedom's Awful Toll," *The Nation*, August 28, 1976, pp. 138, 142.

17. Sol Linowitz, *The Americas in a Changing World* (New York: Quadrangle, 1975).

18. Holly Sklar, "Managing Dependence and Democracy: An Overview," in *Trilateralism: The Trilateral Commission and Elite Planning for World Management* (Montreal: Black Rose, 1980), pp. 1–55.

19. Arturo Siat and Gregorio Iriarte, "De la Seguridad Nacional al Trilateralismo," *Cuadernos de Cristianismo y Sociedad*, May 1979, pp. 23–24.

20. Osvaldo Martínez, "Debt and Foreign Capital: The Origins of the Crisis," *Latin American Perspectives*, Winter 1992, p. 65; World Bank, *World Development Report*, 1990, 1991 and 1992, and 1994, pp. 206–207; and *World Debt Tables: External Debt of Developing Countries*, 1987–1988, 1989–1990, and 1991–1992, vol. 2, *Country Tables* (Washington, D.C:. World Bank, 1988, 1989, 1992).

21. Verónica Montecinos and John Markoff, "Democrats and Technocrats: Professional Economists and Regime Transition in Latin America," *Canadian Journal of Development Studies* 14, no. 1 (1993): 7–22.

22. Barry Gills and Joel Rocamora, "Low-Intensity Democracy," *Third World Quarterly* 13, no. 3 (1992):501.

23. Jorge Nef and Wilder Robles, "Environmental Issues, Politics, and Administration in Latin America: An Overview," in Joseph Jabbra and Onkar Dwivedi, eds., *Governmental Response to Environmental Challenges in Global Perspective* (Amsterdam: IOS Press, 1998), pp. 42–62.

24. Urban population has expanded exponentially in the region, at nearly twice the average rate of population growth. While in 1950, only one city (Buenos Aires) ranked eighth among the ten most populated cities in the world (with 5 million), by 2000 there were three cities among the world's largest, respectively ranking second, fourth, and tenth: Mexico City (18.5 million), São Paulo (17.8 million), and Buenos Aires (12.6 million). While this expansion of megalopolis has been dramatic, even more pronounced is the growth of large metropolitan (Santiago, Bogota, Caracas, Lima) and secondary cities (Medellín, Curitiba, Córdoba, Concepción, Guadalajara, etc.). This phenomenon is the tip of the iceberg of a looming urban crisis, resulting from migration rooted in rural poverty. It has been estimated that by 2050 Latin America will be double the population of North America.

25. William Robinson, "Central America: Which Way After the Cold War?" *NotiSur*, February 25, 1994, pp. 1–9, esp. p. 5; also Oscar Altimir, "Income Distribution and Poverty Through Crisis and Adjustment," *CEPAL Review*, April 1994, passim.

26. *NotiSur*, January 14, 1994, p. 9.

27. William Robinson, citing the 1993 UNDP *Human Development Report*, notes that the wealthiest 20 percent of humanity receives 82.7 percent of the world's income. They also control 80 percent of world trade, 95 percent of all loans, 80 percent of all domestic savings, 80.5 percent of world investments. They consume 70 percent of world energy, 75 percent of all metals, 85 percent of its timber and 60 percent of its food supplies. He noted that in this context the middle classes are shrinking considerably, since the 20 percent of what could be called the world's middle class receives only 11.7 percent of the world's wealth. *NotiSur*, February 18, 1994, p. 7. A US study by the Levy Institute, based on the 1998 Federal Reserve's *Survey of Consumer Finances*, indicated that while the top 1 percent of the population controlled 38 percent of the country's net worth, the poorest 40 percent controlled 0.26 percent of it. In the period between 1983 and 1998,

the net worth of that top 1 percent increased 42.3 percent, while the bottom 40 percent of the population was 76.5 percent worse off. See Edward Wolff, "Recent Trends in Wealth Ownership, 1983–1998," Levy Institute Working Paper no. 300, Tables 2–3 (2003). All indications are that income concentration has worsened since 1998.

28. Between 1985 and 1991, the region's defense budgets declined on the average 24.6 percent, or 4.1 percent per year, and twelve out of twenty countries cut defense expenditures ranging between 59 percent (Chile) and 4.8 percent (Honduras). On the other hand, two rather large countries, Venezuela and Colombia, dramatically increased such expenditures: respectively 23 percent and 275 percent. When the number of troops is examined, the overall trend is a seemingly modest increase of 4.2 percent for the region, or 0.7 percent per year.

29. Cheddy Jagan, "Sustainable Development in the Americas," keynote address to the twenty-seventh annual Congress of the Canadian Association of Latin American and Caribbean Studies, York University, October 31, 1996.

30. *NotiSur*, February 1994, p. 8.

31. For purposes of comparison, the rate in the United States for 2002 was 46.6 percent and about 55 percent in Canada (2000). An examination of voting turnout in parliamentary elections held in both Latin and North America in the decade between 1988 and 1991 and 1998 and 2001 shows a declining trend in half of the countries and also low voting turnout in nearly half of the nations, by comparison to most European democracies.

32. *Latin America Weekly Report*, January 13, 1994, p. 2; February 17, 1994, p. 62; and February 17, 1994, 62.

33. Until the 2005 election of José Miguel Insulza to the general secretariat of the OAS, all secretaries-general had been supported by the United States; those denied Washington's support have been defeated.

34. Samuel Huntington, "The Hispanic Threat," *Foreign Policy*, March-April 2004, www.keepmedia.com/pubs/ForeignPolicy/2004/03/01/387925.

35. Francis Fukuyama, "The End of History?" *National Interest*, Summer 1989, pp. 3–18.

STATISTICAL SOURCES

World Bank. *World Development Report*, 1990, 1991 and 1992, passim; and 1994, pp. 206–207. Figures come from the International Bank of Reconstruction and Development/World Bank, *World Development Report 1989* and *World Development Report 1992. Development and the Environment* (New York: Oxford University Press, 1989, 1992). Data include total external debt; total external debt ratios, population growth and projections. The 1990 GNP figure for Nicaragua was estimated on the basis of the 1987 figure and an average decline of 2.5 percent per year. 2000 figures came from the United Nations Development Program, *Human Development Report 2002*, 203–205.

Altimir, Oscar. "Income Distribution and Poverty Through Crisis and Adjustment." *CEPAL Review*, April 1994, p. 12.

IISS. *The Military Balance*, several issues 1989–2003; *World Resources*, 1994–1995; *SIPRI Yearbook 1993*

International Institute for Democracy and Electoral Assistance (IDEA). *Voter Turnout from 1945 to Date*. Stockholm, Sweden, 2003. www.idea.int/vt/analysis.

TABLE 12.1   Twenty-First Century Trends in Latin American Presidential Elections

LEFT OF CENTER

Year	Country[1]	President	Party	Tendency	Share
1998	Venezuela	Hugo Chávez	PSUV[2]	Socialist	62.8%
2003	Brazil	Lula Da Silva	PT	Social democrat	48.6%
2004	Uruguay	Tabaré Vázquez	Broad Front	Center-left	51.6%
2005	Bolivia	Evo Morales	MAS[3]	Socialist	54.0%
2005	Honduras	Manuel Zelaya	PL	Liberal	49.9%
2006	Costa Rica	Oscar Arias	PLN	Social democrat	40.6%
2006	Haiti	Rene Preval	Lespwa	Left populist	51.1%
2006	Peru	Alan Garcia	APRA	Social democrat	52.6%
2006	Chile	Michelle Bachelet	PS	Social democrat	53/0%
2006	Ecuador	Rafael Correa	PAIS[4]	Christian humanist	57.0%
2006	Nicaragua	Daniel Ortega	FSNL[5]	Socialist	38/0%
2007	Argentina	Cristina Kirchner	PJ	Peronist	45.2%
2007	Guatemala	Álvaro Colom	UNE[6]	Center-left	53/0%
2008	Dominican Rep.	Leonel Fernández	PLD	Social democrat	53.8%
2008	Paraguay	Fernando Lugo	PDC[7]	Christian democrat	37.0%
2009	El Salvador	Mauricio Funes	FMLN[8]	Social democrat	52.0%

RIGHT OF CENTER

Year	Country	President	Party	Tendency	Share
2006	Columbia	Álvaro Uribe	PC[9]	conservative	62.0%
2006	Mexico	Felipe Calderón	PAN[10]	Conservative	35.9%
2009	Panama	Ricardo Martinelli	CD[11]	Conservative	60.6%

1. Note: We have not included here the English-speaking Commonwealth Caribbean countries (e.g., Jamaica, Trinidad Tobago, the Bahamas, and other island-states), nor Belize or Guyana in this list.

2. PSUV = United Socialist Party of Venezuela (2007), evolved from the 1980s Fifth Republic Movement.

3. MAS = Movimiento al Socialisml: Movement towards Socialism

4. PAIS = Patria Altiva y Soberana (Proud and Sovereign Motherland)

5. Sandinista = Left-leaning Socialist/Social Democrat: Sandinista From for National Liberation

6. UNE = Unión Nacionalde la Esperanza (National Unity for Hope)

7. PDC = Partido Demócrata Cristiano (Christian Democratic Party)

8. FMLN = Farabundo Martí para la Liberación Nacional: Farabundo Martí National Liberation Front

9. Primero Columbia: instrumental right-wing coalition

10. PAN = National Action Party

11. CD = Cambio Democratico: right-wing, neoliberal, breaking a left-wing trend in the region in 2009.

PART V

EXTERNAL RELATIONS

INTERNATIONAL RELATIONS IN LATIN AMERICA

Conflict and Cooperation

JAMES LEE RAY

THE BATTLE OF AYACUCHO in 1824 traditionally marks the end of Spanish rule in South America; Brazil broke its ties with Portugal a couple of years earlier. This chapter will focus on the relationships among the states that emerged from the ruins of Spanish and Portuguese empires in Latin America. The United States has played an important role in those relationships, of course, but the foreign policy of the United States vis-à-vis its southern neighbors will be treated only tangentially (US policy in Latin America is dealt with in Chapter 15). The United States will enter the discussion here, however, to the extent that it has presented challenges and problems that Latin American states have tried to address in their foreign policies and in their dealings with each other.

DREAMS OF UNITY, REALITIES OF STRIFE

The Early Years

The Spanish colonies achieved their independence in three more or less separate movements. The first movement originated in Mexico and was joined by Central America. Mexico emerged as an empire under Agustín de Iturbide, who annexed Central America. But that empire lasted only briefly. Central America went its own way in 1823, and by 1824 Iturbide had been kicked out of Mexico by General Antonio López de Santa Anna. Mexico, of course, evolved into a single independent nation, but the United Provinces of Central America had fallen apart by 1838, with Guatemala, Honduras, El Salvador, Nicaragua, and Costa Rica emerging as independent nations.

Simón Bolívar led the campaign for independence in the northern part of Spanish America while José de San Martín fought against the Spanish colonialists in the southern part of the continent. The two revolutionary leaders met in 1822 and discussed the possible coordination of their liberation efforts. For reasons that to this day are rather mysterious, they parted company without an agreement.

Consequently this early step toward the unification of Spanish America met the same fate as the numerous succeeding ones to date. It failed.

When Buenos Aires revolted against Spain, the leaders of that movement tried to bring the territory that became known as Paraguay along with them. But a Paraguayan army defeated troops from Buenos Aires who aimed to persuade Paraguayan leaders of the wisdom of unity against the Spanish. Buenos Aires, of course, provided the core of what became Argentina. Chile and Argentina, one can reasonably surmise, were fated to emerge as two countries because of the Andes Mountains, which separate them.

If Simón Bolívar had gotten his way, the territory that obtained freedom under his leadership would have emerged as two large republics. But Upper Peru, led by Antonio José de Sucre, wanted freedom from both Spain and Peru, and the first great republic of Bolívar's dreams was split into the independent countries of Bolivia and Peru. Bolívar did manage to bring the republic of Gran Colombia into the world in 1819, but by 1830, this republic had also fallen prey to geographical barriers, regional antagonisms, and the ambitions of quarreling political leaders. Gran Colombia dissolved ultimately into the separate countries of Venezuela, Colombia, and Ecuador. Bolívar died soon after "his" republic did. Shortly before his death, he mourned the demise of his dreams: "America is ungovernable. Those who have served the revolution have plowed the sea."

Nineteenth-Century Conflicts

Nineteenth-century relations among the newly independent countries in Latin America involved a series of important conflicts and wars, and the impact of those struggles continued into the twentieth century. Conflicts between Brazil and Argentina, for example, elicited the mediation of Great Britain, which managed to arrange the creation of the buffer state of Uruguay in 1830. Peru and Colombia agreed to settle a dispute between them in a process that resulted in the birth of another buffer state at about the same time—Ecuador. By 1835, General Andrés de Santa Cruz in Bolivia established the Peru-Bolivia Confederation as part of an effort to enlarge his domain. Both Chile and Argentina objected to this confederation because it represented a concentration of power that was dangerous to their continued independence. Although Argentina declared war against the confederation, Chilean intervention effectively brought about its dissolution in 1838.

The 1840s and 1850s were marked by subtle, more or less independent balance-of-power maneuverings among two sets of states: Chile and the other western states comprised the first set; Argentina, Uruguay, Paraguay, and Brazil on the eastern half of the continent made up the second. Major warfare was avoided until a bloody conflict occurred among the latter states beginning in 1864, with Uruguay serving as the pawn over which the other states fought. Both Brazil and Argentina had repeatedly attempted to influence the frequently violent political conflict in Uruguay in ways that would benefit their interests. Left to their own devices, Brazil and Argentina might have gone to war against each other over Uruguay. But Paraguay managed to get all three of these states into a war against it.

Until the 1860s, Paraguay had been rather isolated, ruled by dictators since the days of liberation. The second of these, Carlos Antonio López, relieved this isolation somewhat. Perhaps his most fateful decision was to put his son, Francisco

Solano López, in charge of Paraguay's army. In that role, the younger López traveled to England, France, Germany, Italy, and Spain in the early 1850s, picking up a large amount of arms and ammunition, ideas of grandeur from Napoleon III in France, and an Irish mistress, Elisa Lynch (whom he met in Paris), along the way.[1] Solano López became president of Paraguay in 1862 after his father died. In the ensuing years, he grew increasingly suspicious of the motives of both Brazilian and Argentine leaders with respect to Uruguay. In 1864, feeling certain of Brazil's imperialistic ambitions vis-à-vis Uruguay, he decided to thwart them forcefully. (Of course, Solano López had imperialistic ambitions of his own.) However, when he requested permission for his troops to cross part of Argentina en route to Uruguay, he was refused but sent his troops into Argentina anyway. Soon he found himself at war with Brazil, Argentina, and Uruguay.

Whether little Paraguay had any chance of winning the war is an interesting historical question. During the war, the provisions of a secret treaty signed by Brazil, Uruguay, and Argentina became known; it was obvious that Brazil and Argentina meant to destroy the government of Paraguay and help themselves to ample slices of Paraguayan territory. It is commonly asserted in standard historical sources that the Paraguayans fought so desperately that something on the order of nine out of ten males, or roughly half the population of the country, perished in the struggle. However, at least one contemporary historical-demographic analysis indicates that "the War of the Triple Alliance actually cost Paraguay between 8.7 and 19.5 percent of its prewar population. . . . The evidence demonstrates that the Paraguayan population casualties due to the war have been enormously exaggerated."[2]

Interestingly, both during and after the war, the nations of western Latin America objected to Brazilian and Argentine plans to dismember Paraguay and limit its sovereignty. This was an important step toward the integration of the two more or less independent balance-of-power systems on the continent.[3] That process was reinforced by rivalries among the western states that were to culminate in the War of the Pacific between Chile on one side and Bolivia and Peru on the other. They fought over the bleak Atacama desert and the rich nitrates it contained. By 1870 Chileans, Peruvians, and Bolivians were all exploiting the mineral resources of the area. The Chileans were the most energetic and successful in these ventures. Unfortunately, from their point of view, many of their successes occurred in territories that belonged to Bolivia or Peru. When the Bolivians tried to increase taxes on Chilean operations in their territory and the Peruvians nationalized Chilean nitrate works in theirs, the Chilean government decided to resist these steps by military means.

Chile was eminently successful in this war, which began in February 1879. By 1883 Chile had won, taking over Antofagasta from Bolivia and the provinces of Tarapacá, Tacna, and Arica from Peru. With the addition of that territory, "Chile entered . . . upon an era of unequaled prosperity from the sale of nitrates, copper and other minerals."[4] Bolivia and Peru, on the other hand, got nothing from the war but grievances, which survived for decades. Bolivia lost its only seaport at Antofagasta, and despite consistent efforts for the past 120 years, has yet to regain it. Chile promised Peru that a plebiscite would be held ten years after the war in the provinces of Tacna and Arica to determine their permanent status, but that plebiscite was continually postponed. The dispute was finally resolved in 1929 with the help of the US government. As a result of the Washington Protocol of that year, Chile retained Arica while Peru reclaimed Tacna.

THE CHANGING OF THE GUARD

The United States Edges Out Great Britain

The remainder of the nineteenth century in Latin America was most notable, perhaps, for the culmination of a long-term trend. The United States had issued its Monroe Doctrine in 1823, warning other states to refrain from colonizing efforts in the Western Hemisphere. It is widely agreed that the United States lacked the power to enforce the doctrine through most of the nineteenth century. Latin America was not, however, subjected to serious or sustained colonizing efforts for most of that century because Great Britain, in effect, enforced the Monroe Doctrine for the United States. (The most obvious exception to this rule occurred when France installed Maximilian as emperor of Mexico from 1864 to 1867.) Throughout most of the nineteenth century, Great Britain and the United States shared a common interest in keeping other powers out of Latin America. Long-range US ambitions to replace Great Britain as the most influential power in the Western Hemisphere added a measure of conflict to the relationship. In fact, "from the War of 1812 to the Venezuela boundary crisis of 1895, there was scarcely an administration or a decade in which the United States and Great Britain did not face a crisis or war scare in their tense and turbulent relations."[5]

In 1895 a crisis resulted from the culmination of a dispute between Great Britain and Venezuela over the boundary of British Guiana. President Grover Cleveland insisted on arbitration, and the British ultimately gave in, partly because they were more concerned at the time about the apparent inclination of the German kaiser to stir up trouble for them in South Africa.

Thus in 1895 the United States seriously began to challenge British hegemony in South America. Further indications of this "changing of the guard" were soon to follow. For example, in 1850, the United States and Great Britain had signed the Clayton-Bulwer Treaty, in which both agreed that neither would attempt to build or exclusively control any canal through Central America. But in 1901 the Clayton-Bulwer Treaty was superseded by the Hay-Pauncefote Treaty, which gave the United States exclusive rights to build and control an interoceanic canal.

The Era of US Military Intervention

In between the boundary dispute involving Great Britain and Venezuela and the Hay-Pauncefote Treaty, of course, the United States took on and defeated Spain in the Spanish-American War of 1898, acquiring Cuba, Puerto Rico, and the Philippines. By 1903, the United States had helped arrange Panama's independence from Colombia and had signed a treaty with the new Panamanian republic granting to the United States, in perpetuity, a zone in which a canal was to be built across the isthmus. A year later, Theodore Roosevelt proclaimed his famous corollary to the Monroe Doctrine, in which he claimed the right to intervene in the internal affairs of other nations in the Western Hemisphere that through "flagrant . . . wrongdoing or impotence" give rise to a need for an "international police power." The United States used this corollary as a rationale for a lengthy series of armed interventions in the ensuing years. For example, the United States militarily occupied Haiti from 1915 to 1934, the Dominican Republic from 1916 to 1924, and Nicaragua from 1912 to 1925 and again from 1927 to 1932. Since these were only the most prolonged examples among a longer list of interventions, it is not surprising that for the first decades of the twentieth century, one of the primary foreign policy concerns of the Latin American states was to restrain "the colossus of the North."

It is, perhaps, a revealing indication of the desperate and vulnerable position in which the Latin American states found themselves vis-à-vis the United States that the first line of defense to which they resorted was international law. As early as 1868, the Argentine jurist Carlos Calvo had argued that intervention by foreign governments to enforce claims of their citizens residing abroad was illegal because it violated the principle of national sovereignty. In 1902, when Venezuela was the target of a blockade by Britain, Germany, and Italy, the Argentine foreign minister, Luís Drago, argued that it was also illegal for foreign governments to intervene in attempts to collect public debts (which is what Britain, Germany, and Italy were doing).

The Calvo Doctrine and the Drago Doctrine were originally designed to counter interventions by European states, but the "Roosevelt Corollary . . . and the subsequent US interventions in the Caribbean area based on it, definitely shifted Latin American fears from Europe to the United States."[6] For the first three decades of the twentieth century, Latin American states tried repeatedly, and unsuccessfully, to get the United States to accept the international principle of nonintervention embodied in the doctrines espoused by Calvo and Drago.

Latin American states were only tangentially involved in World War I. Eight declared war, but only Brazil and Cuba played an active role in it. Five other states severed diplomatic relations with Germany, while such important states as Argentina, Chile, and Mexico remained neutral. Since the war cut off Latin American countries from major trading partners in Europe, it dramatically reinforced the paramount role of the United States in the Western Hemisphere, and US political pretensions were further reinforced by a burgeoning economic ascendancy. This made the Latin American states even more anxious, of course, to curb the interventionist tendencies of the US government, and many thought they had found a useful instrument in the League of Nations. That organization emphasized the principle of nonintervention and might have provided allies for the Latin American states against any interventionist moves by the United States. It is not surprising, then, that most Latin American countries were disappointed when the United States refused to join the League, even though its covenant explicitly recognized the legitimacy of the Monroe Doctrine.

Since the Latin American states had not succeeded in restraining the United States within the framework of the League of Nations, they pressed even harder to construct such restraints within the inter-American system. The Pan-American movement had begun with a meeting in Washington in 1889. From that year to 1928, there were six international conferences of American states. Those meetings adhered to a definite pattern. The United States was primarily interested in measures that would facilitate international trade, while the Latin American states sought measures that would secure them against intervention by the United States.

The official attitude of the US government began to change perceptibly in 1929. The new president, Herbert Hoover, ordered a study of the Monroe Doctrine in that year, and by 1930 he had publicly endorsed the results of that study in a move that amounted to a rejection of the Roosevelt Corollary. Franklin D. Roosevelt, of course, adopted the Good Neighbor Policy toward Latin America, the highlight of which was a nonintervention pledge made tentatively at the Seventh Inter-American Conference in Montevideo in 1933 and reaffirmed, with significantly smaller loopholes, at the Inter-American Conference for the Maintenance of Peace at Buenos Aires in 1936. The Roosevelt administration's sincerity was tested when Bolivia nationalized foreign oil companies in that country in 1937 and Mexico nationalized its oil industry in 1938. Roosevelt resisted pressures to intervene in both cases.

TERRITORIAL CONFLICT IN SOUTH AMERICA

The Chaco War

As the Latin American states were in the midst of their successful effort (albeit only temporarily) to deal with US interventionism, two of those states fought each other in the only major war between Latin American states in this century. This war was fought between the two big losers of the most important South American wars in the nineteenth century, perhaps not coincidentally. After Bolivia lost its outlet to the sea during the War of the Pacific, some historians argue, its leaders began to look to the Rio de la Plata system and possible ports on the Atlantic. This meant that Bolivia needed access to the Paraguay River, and early in the twentieth century, Bolivia began building forts in the area of that river in order to ensure access to it. Paraguay, in the meantime, according to several accounts, was looking for some way to recover its national honor after its humiliating defeat in the war against Brazil, Uruguay, and Argentina. The emotions evoked in this manner soon focused on the Chaco Boreal, a desolate area near the border between Paraguay and Bolivia. Both countries had made claims to this area as early as the mid-1500s, during the colonial era, and border clashes between the two states occurred as early as 1927. Then rumors of vast oil deposits in the Chaco added fuel to the controversy, so to speak. War finally broke out in 1932.

Bolivia's population at the time was roughly three times that of Paraguay, but Bolivia suffered disadvantages that, in the end, turned out to be more important. Perhaps the most important was the composition of its army. Most Bolivian soldiers were Indians who had been drafted into the army off the two-mile-high (3 kilometer) plain known as the Altiplano. They were not accustomed to the tropical heat of the Chaco and had no understanding of the conflict (which is not to say that they would have been enthusiastic if they *had* understood the reasons for the war). Paraguayan soldiers, in contrast, were more comfortable in the climate of the area and felt they were defending their homeland.

Even so, the war dragged on for three years, with both sides suffering heavy losses. Estimates of these losses vary widely. One apparently authoritative source concludes that 50,000 Paraguayan soldiers died in the conflict while 80,000 Bolivian soldiers met the same fate.[7] A truce was finally arranged in 1938. In the treaty, Paraguay was awarded most of the disputed Chaco area; Bolivia's reward was further frustration in its quest for an outlet to the sea.

Further Disputes

Two serious border disputes between Latin American states surfaced during the 1930s and 1940s. Both involved Peru. Peruvian troops seized the Amazon River town of Leticia in 1932. Since that town had been awarded to Colombia in 1930, the Colombian government sent troops to Leticia to make its objections known. There was some brief but bloody fighting. After a change of government in Peru, serious negotiations began. It took two years, but an amicable settlement was achieved, with Colombia retaining its hold on Leticia.

Peru was more successful in a dispute with Ecuador, which reached a crisis stage in 1941. Peruvian troops occupied territory claimed by Ecuador north of the Marañón River, which allows access to the Amazon River. The dispute escalated into actual military combat, with each side losing several hundred troops, but a wider war was averted, probably, by the Japanese attack on Pearl Harbor in December 1941. That catastrophe made the United States unwilling to let its neighbors engage in such disruptive activities. So the United States, in cooperation with Argentina, Brazil, and Chile, imposed peace through the Rio Protocol of 1942. The protocol forced Ecuador to relinquish control over the disputed territory, some 77,000 square miles (199,000 square kilometers), to Peru. Ecuador has never been happy with this solution, and in 1960 the Ecuadorian senate renounced the Rio Protocol. Open border clashes between Ecuador and Peru occurred in 1981, and a serious military conflict broke out between Ecuador and Peru in early 1995.

World War II and Its Aftermath

Latin American countries played a minor role in World War II. With the onset of the conflict, the United States tried to get the Western Hemisphere organized but met with more problems than might have been anticipated. Argentina was least enthusiastic about unifying against the Axis powers. The government of Argentina did not break relations with Germany until 1944 and did not declare war until 1945. Brazil, on the other hand, sent a significant number of troops to Italy, while Mexican troops served in the Pacific theater. Generally speaking, the effect of World War II on inter-American relations was to reinforce trends set in motion by World War I. Once again, the Latin American states were cut off from the world outside the Western Hemisphere and became more closely tied to the United States. The United States, of course, emerged from World War II as the most powerful state in the world, regardless of how power is defined or measured.

In the years after the war, a controversy about the agenda of relations between the United States and Latin American countries surfaced in a shape that was to remain consistent in the postwar decades. For the United States, the primary issue was communist subversion; the Latin American states, on the other hand, were almost always more interested in policies and strategies that would foster their economic development.

One of the first indications of concern about international economic issues on the part of Latin American states was their proposal to form the Economic Commission for Latin America (ECLA) as a part of the new United Nations organization. The United States was opposed to the idea, but ECLA was created in 1948 anyway. In the early 1950s, ECLA proposed the creation of a new inter-American bank and a Latin American common market (the Inter-American Development Bank was established in 1959). The United States was more interested in a collective defense treaty—the Inter-American Treaty of Reciprocal Assistance (Rio Treaty) signed on September 2, 1947—and the establishment of the Organization of American States (OAS) in 1948. Latin Americans preferred that economic issues be dealt with in ECLA, but "for years, the United States favored the OAS Inter-American Economic and Social Council and regarded the efforts of the competitor ECLA with political disapproval as well as deep distrust."[8]

REGIONAL APPROACHES TO DEVELOPMENT

Economic Integration as a Tool

One of the proposed solutions to the problems of underdevelopment seized on by ECLA and several Latin American economists was economic integration.[9] Integration might provide markets sufficiently large, for example, to make it feasible for Latin American states to manufacture their own capital goods, thus reducing their dependence imports. Large markets created by the elimination of intraregional tariff barriers, and the construction of common external tariffs that would be part of the economic integration processes, might also allow industries to benefit from economies of scale, which in turn could evoke efficiency at levels competitive on the world market.

With these ideas in mind, ECLA and national officials worked toward the creation of two regional integration organizations: the Central American Common Market (CACM) and the Latin American Free Trade Association (LAFTA). The former organization was launched in 1960 with Guatemala, El Salvador, Honduras, Nicaragua, and later Costa Rica as its members. Ten South American countries, later joined by Mexico, formed LAFTA in the same year. Both organizations were inspired to some extent by the success of the European Economic Community (EEC) and both were based on a philosophy of economic integration similar to that utilized in Europe. That is, CACM and LAFTA both sought economic integration on the basis of the functional (or neofunctional) theory of integration. According to that theory, the benefits that accrue to the member states as a result of the activities of the central organization of the integration organization mean that the member states, little by little, become willing to allow that central organization broader authority until someday (in theory), it is running virtually everything.[10]

Such ideas had seemed to work reasonably well in Europe, and they seemed to work for a time in Latin America. The CACM promoted a marked increase in intraregional trade, and the rate of economic growth of the Central American countries increased. Similarly, the members of LAFTA managed to negotiate numerous reductions of tariffs, and intraregional trade increased 100 percent from 1961 to 1968.[11] But the two organizations soon ran into problems, at least one of which plagued both.

That problem involved the distribution of the benefits of integration among the member states. The founders of both the CACM and LAFTA had anticipated this problem by initially giving special concessions to the poorer member states. The CACM, for example, adopted special incentives in order to lure new industries into the relatively poor states (i.e., Honduras and Nicaragua). Members of LAFTA divided themselves into three categories according to levels of development and size of domestic markets. The countries in the lower categories were given trade concessions and the right to protect some infant industries from competition with similar industries in such relatively developed countries as Brazil, Argentina, and Mexico. Nevertheless, by the end of the 1960s, both organizations were showing signs of strain resulting in part from suspicions among less developed members that they were not sharing equally in the benefits of integration.

Problems for CACM and LAFTA

In 1969 the CACM was plagued by an even more dramatic problem. Two of its member states, Honduras and El Salvador, fought a war against each other. El Salvador is densely populated, whereas Honduras is relatively underpopulated. Throughout the 1960s, unemployed workers from El Salvador poured into the empty fertile valleys in Honduras. By 1969 the military government of Honduras was facing considerable internal unrest and responded with a land reform program that, not accidentally, deprived many Salvadoran squatters of their recently acquired property.

The government of El Salvador responded with a surprise attack in July 1969. The attack failed, and a bloody stalemate resulted. The OAS managed to arrange a truce, which was broken in January 1970. A prolonged "cold war" between Honduras and El Salvador ensued. They stopped trading, and Honduras put an embargo on trade between El Salvador on the one hand and Nicaragua and Costa Rica on the other. All in all, the war was a devastating blow to the CACM.

In the process of resolving the conflict between Honduras and El Salvador, CACM officials and government leaders discovered other fissures in the organization that threatened its existence. Honduras had been dissatisfied with the Common Market in any case, for the eminently predictable reason. Honduras, along with Nicaragua the least developed country in that area, felt itself the victim of unfair competition. Relief from the burdens of such competition was difficult to arrange in the face of continued antagonism between El Salvador and Honduras. By the end of the 1970s, of course, the CACM faced a new set of problems. The overthrow of Somoza in Nicaragua and serious civil unrest elsewhere, especially in El Salvador, threatened to destroy what was left of the organization.

In the late 1960s, LAFTA also began to fall apart. Bolivia, Chile, Colombia, Ecuador, and Peru made plans to form a common market that excluded Argentina, Brazil, and Mexico. These five countries, later joined by Venezuela, formed what became known as the Andean Common Market (ANCOM). The members of ANCOM hoped to achieve enough economic strength to compete successfully with the larger, more economically developed countries in LAFTA. Then, according to the plan, the ANCOM countries would rejoin LAFTA and share more equally in the benefits of economic integration provided by that organization.

ANCOM aroused a lot of interest in the Third World because of its approach to foreign investment. By the late 1960s, the evidence arising out of the experience of the European Common Market made it obvious that multinational corporations (particularly US-based ones) could benefit enormously from the new, enlarged, and protected markets resulting from the process of economic integration. Some feared that integration among Latin American states might make them even more vulnerable to penetration and domination by foreign investors than they had been in the past. It was this fear, in part, that led ANCOM to adopt regulations aimed at controlling foreign investment within the boundaries of its member states.

There were rules, for example, concerning which sectors of the economies were open to investors. There were limits on the amount of capital that could be repatriated. Parent companies were forbidden to restrict exports by their subsidiaries. Provisions were also made to ensure that subsidiaries of foreign corporations would become locally owned in time. "Foreign enterprises already established in the Andean region must within three years of the code's adoption work out gradual divestment plans that would give local investors . . . majority control (51%) of the total shares within 15 years. New foreign investors must adopt similar 15-year fade-out schedules two years after production begins."[12]

How well these rules aimed at controlling foreign investments worked is a controversial question. Some corporations managed to obtain exceptions to them in important cases. And there are ways in which these kinds of rules can be subverted even if they are ostensibly enforced.[13] Furthermore, there were obvious differences in the manner in which the rules were enforced by the members. Chile provided the most spectacular example of these differences. Under Allende, of course, the Chilean government enthusiastically supported strict controls on foreign investment. The post-Allende government, however, was so desperate to attract foreign investment that it pushed hard for a relaxation of those controls. Even though the other members of ANCOM gave Chile much of what it wanted in this regard, the Pinochet regime withdrew Chile from the organization in 1976.

Peru, in the meantime, underwent a political transformation of its own. The Peruvian "revolution" in 1968 inspired many of the innovations adopted by ANCOM with respect to foreign investment. But the new regime experienced a series of economic disasters that helped bring about a change of government and a change of attitude about foreign investment. As a result of this transition, Peru became less enthusiastic toward some of the innovations adopted by ANCOM. This increased skepticism about the extent to which rules on paper were being enforced in fact. As the end of the 1970s approached, ANCOM could hardly be written off as a failure, but even sympathetic observers admitted that its future was uncertain.[14]

INTER-AMERICAN RELATIONS IN THE TWENTY-FIRST CENTURY: ECONOMIC DISLOCATIONS AND A "PINK TIDE"

Emerging from the end of the Cold War in the early 1990s, Latin America appeared to be poised on the threshold of an era of unprecedented political progress, stability, and democracy, as well as economic growth based on free trade and foreign investment, along with domestic economic policies based on market principles. In 1991, for example, an important economic integration organization, MERCOSUR, was formed by Argentina, Brazil, Paraguay, and Uruguay. By 1994, the *New York Times* declared that "on Rio's bay, two huge Brazilian cannons have been waiting for Argentine warships for decades, monuments to the long enmity between South America's two regional powers. But today the guns are frozen with rust, visited by tourists, many of them Argentines." The story goes on to attribute easing tensions between Brazil and Argentina, as well as similar improvements in bilateral relationships around the South American continent, to increased interdependence among these countries, primarily in the form of international trade.[15] As economic integration made important strides in the southern part of the Western Hemisphere in the early 1990s, it also enjoyed substantial progress in the northern part. The North American Free Trade Agreement (NAFTA) was launched in 1994.

In the meantime, traditional political instability reasserted itself when the democratically elected president of Haiti was ousted in an old-fashioned military coup in 1991 and the United States once again intervened militarily in Haiti's internal affairs in 1994. There were important differences between this intervention, however, and dozens of American military interventions that had preceded it in the previous decades not only in Haiti but in the rest of the Caribbean and Central America. For one thing, the intervention resulted in a democratically elected leader being restored to power. For another, this intervention was sanctioned by both the Organization of American States (OAS) and the Security Council of the United Nations. By 1994 democracy seemed more firmly entrenched throughout the Western hemisphere than ever before in its history; economic integration, economic growth, democracy, and political stability also seemed quite firmly in place.

But appearances were deceiving. In retrospect, 1994 seems a high-water mark in the inter-American system for democracy, economic integration, and progress, as well as interstate relations based on respect for international law and regional international organizations such as the OAS. Then, it seems, things began to fall apart.

For example, the launching of NAFTA coincided with the onset of a rebellion in the Mexican province of Chiapas, and an "economic shock, the Tequila crisis of 1994–95. Huge capital inflows into the country in the early 1990s were followed by rapid outflows towards the end of 1994, causing the peso to plunge."[16] NAFTA was associated with significantly increased trade among its members during the 1990s. And it may even have had something to do with the first peaceful transition of executive power in Mexico since the revolution from one independent political party to another, with the election of Vicente Fox in 2000. But by 2004, "politically, the skeptics, ten years on, can fairly claim victory. NAFTA is unpopular in all three countries."[17]

Furthermore, Mexico has encountered economic problems that threaten to tear it, and perhaps its political system, apart. In 2009 a widespread outbreak of swine flu threatened to devastate its crucial tourism industry. Then the global economic collapse seemingly sparked by a crisis in the US housing market seriously restricted Mexico's most important export market. And to top off this story of economic downturn and political misery, Mexico fell prey to vicious battles among "narco-gangs," or criminal cartels that export illegal drugs into the United States. [18]

In spite of all these economic and political problems, Mexico has so far not been engulfed in the "pink tide" bringing leftist regimes to power throughout much of Latin America, even though it came close during the election of 2006. Clearly at the vanguard of this pink tide has been Hugo Chávez in Venezuela. He orchestrated a failed coup in 1992, but since then has been elected president of Venezuela in 1998, 2000, and 2006. He was the target of a coup attempt in 2002. "Washington's initial enthusiasm for the short-lived April 2002 coup against the freely elected Chávez government raised questions in virtually every country in

Latin America about the sincerity of the Bush administration's commitment to democracy."[19]

By the end of the Bush administration, leftist or ostensibly socialist governments were in power in Brazil, Bolivia, Chile, Ecuador, and Argentina. Perhaps most ironically, in Central America, where the United States devoted vigorous Cold War era efforts to depose the Sandinistas in Nicaragua and to prevent the leftist Farabundo Martí National Liberation Front (FMLN) from coming to power in El Salvador, longtime Sandinista leader Daniel Ortega was elected president of Nicaragua in 2006, and Mauricio Funes of the FMLN was elected president of El Salvador in 2009.

What accounts for this widespread success of "socialist" and sometimes anti-US governments spread across such a wide swath of Latin America? Francis Fukuyama argues that the region's long-standing economic inequality promotes the creation of governments suspicious of market forces and the United States. "This high level of inequality has had enormous consequences for the region's long-term economic growth and political stability. Inequality delegitimizes the political system, gives rise to antisystemic social movements and political actors, and sets the stage for bitterly polarized social conflict."[20] In addition, however, the globally unpopular policies of the Bush administration may well have provided effective ammunition for forces inclined to be suspicious of the United States.[21] If one is to believe Oliver Stone's documentary movie *South of the Border,* Hugo Chávez is a socialist hero bringing stunning improvement to the lives of Veneuzelans and inspiring emulation throughout Latin America of a socialist vision that will establish a permanent gulf between Latin America and the United States.

How can this be happening after the demise of the Cold War, which seemed to discredit socialist, antimarket ideologies and theoretical principles? For one thing, the basic idea that governments should protect people from the negative impacts of market forces predates not only the Cold War but even Karl Marx. Which Chinese political leader asserted that "the state should take the entire management of commerce, industry, and agriculture into its own hands, with a view toward succoring the working classes and preventing them from being ground into the dust by the rich"? Mao Zedong? In fact, it was Chinese premier Wang An-shih, who "undertook a pervasive governmental domination of the Chinese economy" from 1068 to 1085.[22] In the United States, civil rights, consumer protection, and environmental protection laws give detailed instructions to automakers regarding how to run their affairs, and the government bails them out of economic difficulties with billions of dollars of subsidies. Consequently US citizens should not be so surprised if their neighbors to the south exhibit similar inclinations to avail themselves of political protections against deleterious economic developments or forces.

Furthermore, Latin America is a long way from being dominated by socialist paragons of leftist virtue that are unrelentingly opposed to the United States. For example, Francisco Rodríguez, the chief economist for the Venezuelan National Assembly from 2000 to 2004, asserts that economic "inequality has actually increased during the Chávez administration," and that "official figures show no significant change in the priority given to social spending during his administration."[23] It *is* ironic, in light of Cold War conflicts in the region, and the apparent demise of leftist alternatives there when the Cold War ended, that Daniel

Ortega with his long-standing Sandinista ties rules in Nicaragua, and that Mauricio Funes of the FMNLN is the president of El Salvador. But shortly after he was elected, Funes declared that "strengthening relations with the United States will be the priority of our foreign policy,"[24] and Ortega has expressed support for the Central American Free Trade Area, an organization which includes the United States, and one that strengthens trading ties among all of its members. And President Luiz Inacio Lula da Silva rose to power out of the Workers Party, whose colorful name is indicative of its formally socialist character. But Lula has "continued the market-friendly economic policies begun by previous governments that tamed inflation and stimulated private investment."[25]

Indeed, ideological and political differences among Latin American states seem in the current era to bring periodic threats of serious conflict among them. In 2009, Colombia agreed to allow US troops to use seven military bases in Colombia. Hugo Chávez complained that these bases amounted to a declaration of war, and the presidents of Bolivia and Ecuador agreed with him. At a meeting of the Union of South American Nations in Argentina in September 2009, Chávez and his allies called for a condemnation of the cooperation between Colombia and the United States, but "instead, the South American leaders simply signed a document reiterating that their continent was a 'zone of peace.'"[26] Also in 2009, the leftist leader of Honduras, Manuel Zelaya, was ousted in military coup. Hugo Chávez threatened military action against the coup, putting his troops on alert. In a reaction distinctly different from that by President Bush when Chávez was the victim of a coup in 2002, President Obama said that "existing tensions and disputes must be resolved peacefully," and the State Department issued a statement to the effect that Zelaya was the "only elected and constitutional leader of Honduras."[27] Despite the recent "pink tide" in Latin America, it is a long way from being uniformly committed to socialist solutions, or relentlessly and universally antagonistic to the United States.

NOTES

1. Mention of the last acquisition might seem out of place in an otherwise somber and proper discussion, but Elisa Lynch reputedly had a significant impact on the policies of Solano López. Pelham H. Box, for example, asserts that "the nature of the influence that for sixteen years the 'lorette parisienne' expressed over the mind of Francisco Solano López has not been adequately investigated. That it was considerable admits of no doubt." Box, *The Origins of the Paraguayan War* (Urbana: University of Illinois Press, 1927), pp. 181–182.

2. Vera Blinn Reber, "The Demographics of Paraguay: A Reinterpretation of the Great War, 1864–1870," *Hispanic American Historical Review*, May 1988, p. 290. For a standard source making the higher estimate of the Paraguayan casualties of the kind referred to by Reber, see Charles J. Kolinski, *Independence or Death: The Story of the Paraguayan War* (Gainesville: University of Florida Press, 1965), p. 198.

3. Robert N. Burr, "The Balance of Power in Nineteenth-Century South America: An Exploratory Essay," *Hispanic American Historical Review*, February 1955, pp. 40–41.

4. Hubert Herring, *A History of Latin America*, 3d ed. (New York: Knopf, 1972), p. 655.

5. Walter Russell Mead, *Special Providence* (New York: Knopf, 2001), p. 19.

6. G. Pope Atkins, *Latin America in the International Political System* (New York: Free Press, 1977), p. 323.

7. J. David Singer and Melvin Small, *The Wages of War 1816–1965: A Statistical Handbook* (New York: Wiley & Jones, 1972), p. 67.

8. Minerva M. Etzioni, *The Majority of One: Towards a Theory of Regional Compatibility* (Beverly Hills, CA: Sage, 1970), pp. 118–119.

9. This section relies heavily on my earlier discussion of integration in Latin America in James Lee Ray, *Global Politics,* 4th ed. (Boston: Houghton Mifflin, 1990), pp. 429–440, as well as on an updated analysis in James Lee Ray, *Global Politics,* 6th ed. (Boston: Houghton Mifflin, 1995), pp. 392–397.

10. David Mitrany, *A Working Peace System* (London: Royal Institute of International Affairs, 1943); and Ernst Haas, *The Uniting of Europe* (Stanford: Stanford University Press, 1958).

11. Joseph Grunwald, Miguel S. Wionczek, and Martin Carnoy, *Latin American Economic Integration and US Policy* (Washington, D.C.: Brookings Institution, 1972), p. 51.

12. Roger W. Fontaine, *The Andean Pact: A Political Analysis* (Beverly Hills, CA: Sage, 1977), p. 19.

13. Thomas J. Biersteker, "The Illusion of State Power: Transnational Corporations and the Neutralization of Host-Country Legislation," *Journal of Peace Research* 17 (1980): 207–221.

14. Ricardo French-Davis, "The Andean Pact: A Model of Economic Integration for Developing Countries," in *Latin America and the World Economy,* ed. Joseph Grunwald (Beverly Hills, CA: Sage, 1978), pp. 165–194. Venezuela withdrew from the organization in 2006. Although the remaining four members have a cooperation agreement with MERCOSUR (see below), Bolivia, Ecuador, and Peru share domestic and foreign policy outlooks far different from that of Colombia.

15. James Brooke, "The New South Americans: Friends and Partners," *New York Times,* April 8, 1994, p. A3.

16. "Free Trade on Trial," *Economist,* January 3, 2004, p. 14.

17. Ibid., p. 13.

18. Sam Quinones, "State of War," *Foreign Policy* 171 (2009): 76.

19. Peter Hakim, "Is Washington Losing Latin America?" *Foreign Affairs* 85 (2006): 48.

20. Francis Fukuyama, "Poverty, Inequality, and Democracy: The Latin American Experience," *Journal of Democracy* 19 (2008): 70.

21. "Most Latin Americans were dumbfounded by US actions at Abu Ghraib and Guantanamo Bay." Hakim, "Is Washington Losing," p. 48.

22. Will and Ariel Durant, *The Lessons of History* (New York: MJF Books, 1968), p. 62.

23. "An Empty Revolution: The Unfulfilled Promises of Hugo Chávez," *Foreign Affairs* 87 (2008): 53. Rodríguez also points out that "the Gini coefficient (a measure of economic inequality . . .) increas[ed] from 0.44 to 0.48 between 2000 and 2005" (p. 53).

24. "Journalist Mauricio Funes Wins El Salvador Presidency," *Guardian,* March 16, 2009, www.guardian.co.uk/world/2009/mar/16/el-salvador-presidential-election-funes/print.

25. Juan de Onis, "Brazil's Big Moment: A South American Giant Wakes Up," *Foreign Affairs* 87 (2008): 110.

26. "US Troops to Use Colombian Bases," *Economist,* September 11, 2009, p. 16.

27. Hannah Strange, "Honduras President Manuel Zelaya Ousted in Military Coup," *TimesOnLine,* June 29, 2009, www.timesonline.co.uk/tol/news/world/us_and_americas/article6596689.ece.

SUGGESTED READINGS

"A 'Left Turn' in Latin America." *Journal of Democracy* 17, no. 4 (2006): 19–109. Several writers analyze recent domestic political developments in Latin America generally, and in Chile, Colombia, and Peru.

Atkins, G. Pope. *Latin America in the International Political System.* 2d ed. New York: Free Press, 1989. A good broad and basic introduction to inter-American relations, as well as to the relationship of the Latin American region with the rest of the world.

Burr, Robert N. "The Balance of Power in Nineteenth-Century South America: An Exploratory Essay." *Hispanic American Historical Review*, February 1955, pp. 37–60. An informative discussion of relations among the South American states in the nineteenth century, with a focus on the impact of the interstate wars in that time period.

Casteñeda, Jorge. "The Forgotten Relationship." *Foreign Affairs* 82 (2003): 67–81. A former Mexican minister of foreign affairs pleads for a US recommitment to Latin America in the wake of September 11, 2001, and in the midst of its war on terrorism.

Connell-Smith, Gordon. *The United States and Latin America.* New York: Wiley, 1974. One of the liveliest historical accounts on US foreign policy toward Latin America.

De Soto, Hernando. *The Other Path.* New York: Harper & Row, 1989. An English translation of this Peruvian work, which has apparently become a kind of bible among advocates of neoclassical reforms in Latin America. There is a rather lengthy introduction by Mario Vargas Llosa.

Herring, Hubert. *A History of Latin America.* 3d ed. New York: Knopf, 1972. A comprehensive, authoritative history of the region that discusses each country in some detail.

Levinson, Jerome, and Juan de Onis. *The Alliance That Lost Its Way.* Chicago: Quadrangle, 1970. A penetrating analysis of the Alliance for Progress. Especially good on the problems faced by the United States in its attempts to mold the internal political systems of Latin American states.

Malloy, James M., and Mitchell A. Seligson, eds. *Authoritarians and Democrats: Regime Transition in Latin America.* Pittsburgh: University of Pittsburgh Press, 1987. An analysis of the transition to democracy in several Latin American countries with a general theoretical discussion of the phenomenon in both the introduction and a concluding chapter.

Mora, Frank O., and Jeanne A.K. Hey, eds. *Latin American and Caribbean Foreign Policy.* Lanham, MD: Rowman & Littlefield, 2003. A state-by-state analysis of the foreign policies of most of the countries of Latin America.

Oelsner, Andrea. *International Relations in Latin America.* New York: Routledge, 2009. A constructivist analysis of relations between Argentina and Brazil, and Argentina and Chile.

Smith, Peter H. *Talons of the Eagle: Dynamics of US–Latin American Relations.* New York: Oxford University Press, 1996. An analysis of US–Latin American relations broken down into three periods, from the 1790s to the 1920s, the Cold War era, and the contemporary era.

Szulc, Tad. *Fidel: A Critical Portrait.* New York: Avon, 1986. A very readable biography with lots of interesting tidbits about, for example, how the CIA helped Fidel financially in the 1950s, and how Fidel contacted and developed a close relationship with the traditional Communist Party in Havana almost from the moment he came to town in 1959.

Chapter 14

THE UNITED STATES
AND LATIN AMERICA

Into a New Era

WAYNE S. SMITH

US–LATIN AMERICAN relations are at a historic turning point. It is not simply that the Cold War is over: that, after all, was a phenomenon of only the past half century. Rather, it is that the basic strategic calculations that shaped US policy over the past 200 years or more—or virtually since the birth of the republic—are now obsolete.

The most central of these was the concept of strategic denial.[1] Simply put, this was the response of US leaders to the calculation that while no state or potential state to the south was powerful enough to threaten the security of the United States, the very weakness of these states rendered them vulnerable to the control of outside powers. The United States had first the Atlantic and later the Pacific, the two great oceans, between it and those who might intend it harm. The latter, however, might overcome those natural barriers by positioning themselves south of the United States. Thus an early and enduring US objective was to keep other powers out of the Western Hemisphere.

At first, of course, two European powers were already positioned to the south: Spain and Portugal. But Portugal was never viewed as a threat, and by the beginning of the nineteenth century Spain had come to be seen as the weakling of Europe. So long as the colonies were in their hands, there was little cause for concern. Transfer to a more powerful state, however, was unacceptable, and thus the No-Transfer Resolution passed by the US Congress in 1811 with respect to the Floridas. This concern also informed secretary of state Henry Clay's assertion in 1825 that "we could not consent to the occupation of those islands [Cuba and Puerto Rico] by any European power other than Spain under any contingency whatever."[2] That warning was repeated several times over the next few decades.

With the Louisiana Purchase, Cuba had come to be seen as the most strategically vital piece of territory outside the continental limits of the United States. From 1803 onward, the Port of New Orleans was the window onto the rest of the world for the vast interior of the United States. All trade and communications funneled through that window and out through the Gulf of Mexico. And what sat in the entrance to the gulf, like a cork in a bottle? The island of Cuba. Not allowing Cuba to fall into the hands of a powerful enemy that might block vital US trade routes became a maxim for US leaders.

The second basic calculation was that the United States must assert hegemony over the lands to its south. The second in effect flowed from the first, for keeping other powers out obviously required some degree of control by the United States. As Gaddis Smith has put it, the Monroe Doctrine was an assertion of a US sphere of influence.[3] Ideas as to the form that might take changed over time. Early leaders tended to assume the US flag was destined eventually to fly over the entire continent, that is, the United States would exercise outright sovereignty. By the end of the nineteenth century, however, control was seen as more important—and cheaper—than sovereignty. Thus secretary of state Richard Olney could say with satisfaction in 1895 that the United States "is practically sovereign on this continent, and its fiat is law upon the subjects to which it confines its interposition."[4]

One may smile at Olney's statement and others like it (though at the time few Latin Americans found them amusing), for they certainly exaggerated the degree of control actually enjoyed by the United States. It was in fact never "practically sovereign" in the hemisphere (though it came close to it for a time in Central America and the Caribbean). The point, however, is that Americans tended to believe it was and, more importantly, to believe that their security required that degree of control.

Obviously that is no longer the case. With the collapse of the Soviet Union, there is now no power in the world capable of positioning itself in Latin America so as to threaten US security. In today's world, a far more realistic danger lies in the clandestine introduction of a nuclear device by terrorists—or some other terrorist act on the magnitude of the attacks on September 11, 2001. But no Latin American base would be required for that. There are various terrorist organizations against which the United States must be alert, and there are still a few adversary nations that perhaps wish us harm—countries such as North Korea. But none has the capability—or the need—to mount a threat from the south; nor do the terrorist organizations.

The nature of warfare has so changed that the old concepts are now obsolete. One thinks today in terms of terrorist bombs or of intercontinental missiles that reach their targets from the other side of the world in less than forty minutes. The great oceans are no longer much protection and have not been for decades. Having nearby naval bases so as to position a fleet off American shores is a tactic of the past.

Thus the entire concept of strategic denial has become invalid. So too has the rationale for the Monroe Doctrine, and with it any need for the United States to assert hegemony over the rest of the hemisphere. The problems that face the United States today require efforts at cooperation, not the exercise of hegemony. The United States needs to rethink its entire position and base its policies on today's realities, not yesterday's. But old habits die hard. Whether US policymakers can make the necessary mental adjustment and fashion an effective policy for today remains to be seen. Certainly the administration of George W. Bush did not make that adjustment. On the contrary, it took a unilateralist, do-it-our-way-or-else approach that alienated other countries around the world—and in Latin America. This is not the place to comment on Bush's march to war in Iraq in virtual defiance of the UN Security Council, because, he said, Iraq had weapons of mass destruction ready to fire and we could not wait. But then no weapons of mass destruction were found. This *is* the place to note that US standing in Latin America reached its lowest point in memory—perhaps ever. This is little short of tragic. Why did it turn out that way? Mexico is a perfect example. President Bush and President Vicente Fox of Mexico had been expected to forge a warm personal relationship and bring relations between the two countries into a period of unprecedented friendship and cooperation. President Bush had promised to negotiate a comprehensive agreement on immigration matters that was of key importance to Fox. But then Mexico opposed the United States in the UN Security Council on the matter of the war in Iraq. That was the end of the special relationship—and of a comprehensive agreement on immigration. Fox was left holding the bag.

Before we turn to an analysis of the post–Cold War and post-9/11 situation, however, a historical review would seem to be in order. Since the future of US–Latin American relations is uncertain, we need to be clear as to how we got here.

Manifest Destiny, 1823–1898

Since the Monroe Doctrine has been described as the "great American shibboleth" for over a century, one would imagine that it was issued with great fanfare and comment. But it was not. Europeans were momentarily irritated by its brashness but paid it little heed, realizing that the United States had no means of enforcing it. For over two decades there was little further reference to Monroe's statement in the United States itself. If European powers were dissuaded from adventures in the Caribbean basin, it was largely because of the presence of a powerful British naval squadron, not because of anything the United States said or did. For the United States had to grow into the role of protector; it first had to become strong. US leaders expected the Stars and Stripes to fly over the rest of the hemisphere, yes, but that was for the future. For the moment, they focused on consolidating their hold over the vast territory already within US borders.

By 1845, however, the United States was looking beyond those borders. It not only had decided to bring Texas into the Union but was also casting covetous eyes at California and Oregon, areas on which Great Britain and perhaps other European powers had designs as well. President James Polk therefore saw fit to revive the Monroe Doctrine, restating it twenty-two years to the day, December 2, 1845, after President Monroe's famous message to the Congress. The Western Hemisphere, he emphasized again, was not open to colonization by outside powers. Because the United States was focusing on Texas, California, and Oregon at that point, he added that this was especially true of North America.

In early 1846, war broke out with Mexico, a short-lived conflict that ended with US troops occupying Mexico City and the United States seizing half of Mexico's territory, including California. It thus became a continental power, with shores on both the Atlantic and Pacific oceans. Manifest Destiny was on the march. As cargo and passengers bound from one coast to the other now more often than not moved across the Central American isthmus, control of that area took on new importance.

It was no coincidence that the United States encouraged William Walker's filibustering expeditions to Central America and his successful efforts to establish himself (briefly) as the ruler of Nicaragua.

As early as 1823, John Quincy Adams had described Cuba as a ripening fruit destined to fall into the lap of the Union. Guarding one of the approaches to the isthmus, the island took on even greater strategic importance after 1848, and US administrations began a series of efforts to acquire it, beginning with President Polk's attempted purchase that very year. Over the next half century, four other US presidents tried to buy Cuba outright. There were also a number of abortive and certainly less straightforward schemes to transfer the island to US ownership.[5] In addition, there were three major filibustering expeditions against the island. One of these, led by a Venezuelan-born former Spanish army officer named Narciso López, came in 1850 and in many ways was a preview of the Bay of Pigs disaster more than a century later. Just as did the CIA in 1961, López assured his little band of invaders that as soon as they landed, the Cuban people would rise in arms against their government. That turned out to be as wild a dream in 1850 as it was in 1961.

The acquisitive tendencies that were so much a part of Manifest Destiny were interrupted by the Civil War, that great and bloody conflict that tested the very survival of the nation. Further, while the United States was locked in its own mortal combat, the Monroe Doctrine was challenged more clearly than ever before. Louis Napoleon of France occupied Mexico and imposed an emperor, Maximilian of Hapsburg, to rule it—on the points of French bayonets. Maximilian's reign came to a tragic end, however, as the Civil War concluded and the United States warned Louis Napoleon to withdraw his troops. He did, leaving Maximilian defenseless. An honorable man, the latter would not abandon his few Mexican supporters. He fought on and was captured and shot by Mexican patriots led by Benito Juárez. The Monroe Doctrine and Mexican sovereignty (not always easy traveling companions) had been preserved.

At midcentury, it had seemed that more and more territory in Latin America was destined to come under the US flag, but by the end of the century US perceptions of its security needs were changing. Washington wished to assert hegemony and turn a profit, especially in the areas nearest to it, that is, in Central America and the Caribbean, but it had growing reservations about the need, or even the desirability, of bringing these areas into the Union or incorporating them into the US system in some other way. That would be expensive and would require permanent occupying forces. That was one objection. Probably a more important one was chauvinistic. As E. L. Godkin, editor of the *Nation* magazine put it, "semicivilized Catholic states" had no place in the American system.[6]

As the other states were to remain independent, something might be gained by developing a hemispheric grouping of nations, with the United States as primus inter pares. Thus in 1889 the first Pan-American Conference was held in Washington under the stewardship of Secretary of State James G. Blaine. All independent states attended except for the Dominican Republic. With the Argentine delegation taking the lead, the majority of Latin Americans present made it clear that they were not to be dictated to by the United States, and a number of US proposals were rejected. Even so, a permanent secretariat was established in Washington that eventually became the Pan-American Union, and a system of arbitration was set up for handling disputes between nations—a system, however, that was all too rarely used. The governments apparently were not prepared to go as far as the delegates to the congress.

Even long-standing US designs on Cuba were altered by this new reluctance to incorporate territories into the US system. Despite all its past efforts to acquire the island, in 1898, just as Cuba's war of independence against Spain was reaching its climax and the United States was on the verge of entering the conflict on Cuba's side, that is, just as conditions seemed most favorable for annexation, the United States stepped back. Under the famous Teller Amendment attached to the declaration of hostilities, the United States vowed not to acquire Cuba as the result of those hostilities. Nothing was said about the Philippines or Guam or Puerto Rico. As a result of the war with Spain, the United States took them all, and in the process became a global power. But Cuba was left with its independence—not fully independent to be sure; rather, under the Platt Amendment, which the United States forced Cuba to attach to its constitution, Cuba became virtually a US protectorate.

The United States in effect supervised Cuba's foreign affairs, including foreign loans, and had the right to intervene whenever it saw fit to preserve peace and stability. "It is not the absolute independence we had dreamed about," mused the embittered old Cuban military leader Máximo Gómez.[7] He nonetheless urged his fellow countrymen to accept the amendment as the price of US withdrawal. It was better to accept limited sovereignty and be rid of the occupying forces, he reasoned. Perhaps in the future, the dream of the republic might be realized. (In 1959 it was.)

Gunboat Diplomacy, 1898–1929

This was the pattern followed over the next thirty-four years. The United States considered everything to the south to be its sphere of influence, and it often exercised outright control in Central America and the Caribbean basin. US capital flooded into those same nearby regions. Banks, utility enterprises, and companies such as United Fruit soon virtually controlled the economies of several states. By 1929, for example, over 65 percent of the Cuban economy was in the hands of US owners. It was an age of dollar diplomacy backed up by US gunboats.

The United States continued to meet periodically with the other governments at Pan-American conferences. The fiction of juridical equality was maintained, and the United States did not seize any more territory, not even to build a canal in Panama, one of President Theodore Roosevelt's overriding priorities. The United States first negotiated with Colombia, of which state Panama was a province. When those negotiations did not prosper, Washington engineered a rebellion in the province, immediately recognized the breakaway rebels as the government of a new Panamanian state, and in 1903 signed an agreement with them to build a canal. US forces made certain Colombia did not intervene. But the new state remained independent (though, like Cuba, with a circumscribed form of independence) and almost eight decades later would assume control of the canal.

Elsewhere, US insistence that extra-hemispheric states not meddle in its sphere of influence raised difficulties. It was all well and good for the United States to say that other powers could not intervene, but what, then, if the states of the hemisphere defaulted on their debts or, in the parlance of the times in the United States, "behaved irresponsibly"? Who was to police them? In his annual message to Congress in 1904, President Theodore Roosevelt gave the answer: the United States would become the policeman of the Western Hemisphere. "Chronic wrongdoing," he said, "or an impotence which results in a general loosening of the ties of civilized society, may in America, as elsewhere, ultimately require intervention by some civilized nation, and in the Western Hemisphere the adherence of the United States to the Monroe Doctrine may force the United States, however reluctantly, in flagrant cases of such wrongdoing or impotence, to the exercise of an international police power."[8]

This became known as the Roosevelt Corollary to the Monroe Doctrine. The United States wasted no time in implementing it. In 1905 it intervened in the Dominican Republic to set up a customs collection operation to pay off that country's debt to several European creditors. It did the same thing in Nicaragua in 1912 and in Haiti in 1915, with marines remaining in those countries off and on for many years. On various other grounds, it intervened no less than twenty-six times in other states of Central America and the Caribbean. Even President Woodrow Wilson landed marines in Veracruz and sent US troops under General John Pershing into northern Mexico. By 1927, US hegemony over Central America was so complete that undersecretary of state Robert Olds could say, "Central America has always understood that governments we recognize and support stay in power, while those we do not recognize and support fail."[9]

Olds's statement was a direct assertion of hegemony. Perhaps in part it was the very brazenness of the attitudes behind such statements—a brazenness that clashed painfully with US idealism—that caused opinion in the United States to begin to swing toward a more cooperative relationship. Shifting opinions were pushed also by growing resistance in Latin America. Offended by the condescending paternalism of the Roosevelt Corollary, Latin Americans increasingly protested US interventions and high-handed actions. By the Pan-American Conference held in Havana in 1928, the other states were demanding a rectification of US policy. Perhaps to their surprise, the United States listened. There was a greater spirit of equality and cooperation than ever before, and issues such as intervention in the internal affairs of the member states were discussed frankly. In the past, they had not even been on the agenda. As the conference broke up, participants understood that an anti-intervention resolution would be on the agenda at the next meeting. The stage was set for the Good Neighbor Policy.

THE GOOD NEIGHBOR POLICY, 1929–1953

Many chronologies mark the beginning of the Good Neighbor Policy in 1933, with the inauguration of President Franklin Delano Roosevelt. In fact, however, it was begun under President Herbert Hoover. He deplored US interventionism, and during his presidency, 1929–1933, US Marines were pulled out of every country in Latin America except Haiti. Hoover also ordered a review of the historical rationale for interventionism. In response, a memorandum prepared by undersecretary of state J. Reuben Clark and published in 1930 held that nothing in the

Monroe Doctrine had ever given the United States the right to intervene in the internal affairs of its neighbors. This removed the underpinning from the Roosevelt Corollary, and it was never again cited as the basis for US policy.[10]

The trend away from interventionism was given new impetus during the presidency of Franklin Roosevelt. He stressed strong economic ties with Latin America, not political domination, and favored collective security over unilateral actions by the United States. He abrogated the Platt Amendment, thus removing the protectorate infringement of Cuban sovereignty. And, as promised at Havana in 1928, at the 1933 Pan-American Conference in Montevideo, Uruguay, the United States pledged itself to the principle of nonintervention. The following year, Roosevelt pulled the last marines out of Haiti and, true to his word, did not send them into any Latin American country during his long presidency (1933–1945).

Good relations were further spurred by World War II. With the exception of Argentina, which tended to sympathize with the Axis powers (until a last-minute change of sides in 1945), all the Latin American states were allies of the United States and made no small contribution to the war effort, assuring natural resources and other needed commodities, providing air and naval bases, and, in the case of Mexico and Brazil, even sending troops. A Brazilian army division fought in Italy, a squadron of Mexican fighter aircraft in the Pacific. As the war ended, US–Latin American relations were more harmonious than they had ever been.

Even warmer, more cooperative relations seemed to lie ahead. Roosevelt's successor, President Harry S. Truman, continued Roosevelt's noninterventionist policy and in 1947 also helped bring into being the so-called Rio Pact, a collective security treaty that made defense of the Western Hemisphere the responsibility of all member states. This was followed in 1948 by the creation of the Organization of American States (OAS), which provided for the adjudication of disputes among members and for collective peacekeeping measures. The OAS, in effect, took the old Pan-American Union to a new level of cooperation and organizational cohesion.

If the hemisphere still had to be defended from outside powers, those who had framed the OAS charter and the Rio Pact clearly did not think that was any longer the responsibility of the United States alone. Rather, it now became the duty of all member states. As US political leaders and scholars commented at the time, the Monroe Doctrine was thus to become a multilateral instrument.[11] And so it might have. Unfortunately, as the OAS was being formed, the Cold War between the United States and the Soviet Union was heating up. Soon it was to become an all-consuming struggle to which all other considerations and objectives were sacrificed.

THE COLD WAR, 1953–1992

In the same year that the Rio Pact was signed, 1949, China fell to the communists and the Soviet Union exploded its own atomic bomb. The next year, 1950, saw the outbreak of the Korean War. The Cold War was on in earnest. That had little immediate effect on US–Latin American relations, however. Latin America was perceived to be far removed from the Soviet Union and safely within the US sphere of influence. Indeed, Latin American states were perceived as important allies on whose votes in the UN General Assembly the United States could always count. The Truman administration continued its noninterventionist policies. Thus, despite the growing Cold War hysteria in the United States as reflected by McCarthyism, and despite some rumblings in the Policy Planning Bureau of the State Department that a harder line might be in order, the Good Neighbor Policy toward Latin America continued until 1953.

In that year, however, with the inauguration of Dwight Eisenhower as president and the appointment of John Foster Dulles as secretary of state, the Cold War came to Latin America full force. The concept of strategic denial now had but one focus: the Soviet Union. Thus Dulles, on the basis of no hard evidence, immediately warned of increasing communist influence in the hemisphere that the Soviet Union was determined to exploit. He pointed to Guatemala as a case in point. At the meeting of OAS foreign ministers in Caracas that year, he presented a resolution stipulating that any hemispheric government under communist influence represented a threat to peace and security against which the other states would take multilateral action. Dulles made it clear that the other states could either accept the resolution and cooperate with the United States or risk a return to unilateral interventions. The resolution was accepted, but only after it had been changed to provide for "consultations" rather than immediate multilateral action.

Undaunted, the Eisenhower administration moved ahead with plans to oust the "communist-controlled" government of Jacobo Arbenz with a coup clandestinely organized by the CIA. In June 1954, Colonel Castillo Armas, a disaffected Guatemalan officer, led a group of several hundred armed men in an uprising against Arbenz.[12] The United States could maintain that it was not intervening, that this was a Guatemalan reaction. Few believed it, but all that was needed was a fig leaf. As the Guatemalan army would not fight for the government, the coup quickly succeeded. The Guatemalan revolution, which might best be described as a liberal reform movement begun in 1944, ended. What followed, thanks to US intervention, was a long series of bloody military dictatorships occasionally interrupted by elected governments—that served at the sufferance of the military and were rarely allowed even to serve out their terms. Repression was massive. Tens of thousands of Guatemalans were slaughtered by the army in the next fifty years. Only recently has there been encouraging movement toward democracy and an end to the bloody guerrilla warfare that plagued the country since the early 1960s.

In retrospect, it is clear that there was no communist—let alone Soviet—threat in Guatemala. Arbenz himself was not a communist. On the contrary, though elected by the people, he was a colonel in the Guatemalan army. There were no communist cabinet ministers in his government and only four Communist Party members in the National Assembly. The Soviet Union had not even bothered to establish diplomatic relations with Guatemala and was providing no assistance of any kind. The government was progressive, however, and was carrying out an agrarian reform. In the process, it nationalized some land belonging to United Fruit, which may have been what actually triggered Arbenz's overthrow. John Foster Dulles's law firm had handled the United Fruit account and his brother, CIA director Allen Dulles, UN ambassador Henry Cabot Lodge, and several other senior government officials had all been members of the United Fruit board.

The Eisenhower administration adopted a policy of supporting any right-wing dictatorship, no matter how repressive, so long as it professed itself to be anticommunist. For eight years, from 1953 until 1961, the United States forgot about the pursuit of democracy and seemed to see dictators as more reliable allies. At one point Secretary Dulles even described Venezuela under Pérez Jiménez, that country's comic opera military dictator, as pursuing the kind of political and economic policies the United States would wish to see emulated by every Latin American country.[13]

In the Guatemalan case and in most other US interventions in Latin America during the Cold War, the perceived communist takeover threats were more figments of the imaginations of US leaders, fed by Cold War hysteria, than real. Only in the Cuban case was there legitimate cause for concern. Not that Fidel Castro was a communist when he took power in 1959. But his objectives of sharply reducing US influence in the hemisphere and encouraging the emergence of a whole series of other revolutionary regimes seemed likely to carry him toward an alliance with the Soviet Union. They were objectives, after all, that he could not achieve on his own. By early 1960, the United States concluded that such an alliance was in formation and began preparing to overthrow the Castro government. That effort was made at the Bay of Pigs in April 1961, with disastrous results. The idea that the 1,200 men of the Cuban exile brigade could defeat Castro's 60,000 army troops, who had tanks and artillery, was preposterous. They could have succeeded only with the support of US troops. President John F. Kennedy, who had taken office in January 1961 and inherited the invasion plan from the Eisenhower administration, had stated flatly that no US forces would be used, but the CIA counted on a change of orders once it became clear that the brigade could not hold the beach. They were wrong. Kennedy stuck by his determination not to commit US forces, and the invasion failed, resulting in the destruction of any internal opposition and the consolidation of a Cuban-Soviet alliance.

The latter led, in October 1962, to the Cuban missile crisis. Suddenly the worst nightmare US policymakers could imagine in Latin America was upon them. For almost 150 years, the Monroe Doctrine had been intended to keep other powers out of the hemisphere and thus prevent any threat to US security from the nation's southern frontier. Now the principal US global adversary, the Soviet Union, was doing just that, threatening with nuclear missiles. The crisis was eventually resolved through the Kennedy-Khrushchev Understanding: the Soviet Union agreed to withdraw its missiles in return for a US pledge not to invade Cuba. Even so, US policymakers were badly traumatized by the missile crisis and from 1962 onward were absolutely determined that there would be no more Cubas.

The Kennedy administration followed a two-track policy toward that objective. (1) It moved to contain Castroism by trying to isolate him in the hemisphere and by giving military assistance to other governments to defend themselves against Castro-backed guerrillas. (2) It launched the Alliance for Progress, a program of economic and technical assistance. This recognized that revolutionary conditions resulted from economic and social distress and that addressing these problems was as important as military aid. For the same reason, the Kennedy administration also gave greater emphasis to supporting democratic regimes rather than dictatorships.

With Kennedy's death, however, the Alliance for Progress was for all practical purposes abandoned by the harder-line administration of Lyndon Johnson. In 1964 the latter also made it clear to the Brazilian generals that the United States would endorse their overthrow of the democratically elected government of Jango Goulart, who was regarded by the United States as too far to the left. The generals proceeded to do just that, thus aborting the democratic process in Brazil and ushering in two decades of military rule.

Johnson also sent troops into the Dominican Republic in 1965 when political instability threatened to open the way to "a Castroite take-over." Johnson was able to get OAS cover for the intervention (the grateful Brazilian generals providing many of the troops). What he was unable to do was to come up with any evidence of a communist conspiracy.[14]

Eight years later, Richard Nixon and Henry Kissinger played a role in Chile similar to that of the Johnson administration in Brazil. Regarding the Popular Front government of Salvador Allende as communist influenced, they at the very least indicated to the Chilean military that they would welcome his overthrow, if indeed they did not actively encourage it. True, Allende was a socialist and the Communist Party was part of the ruling Popular Front. On the other hand, Allende had been democratically elected (in 1970), and all Chilean national institutions were intact and functioning. Allende either had to play within the constitutional parameters or face impeachment. There was no need to overthrow him, since he could be voted out of office in the next election. But neither the Chilean military nor the Nixon administration wanted to wait. On September 11, 1973, the coup was launched—and not in the cause of democracy. The seventeen years that followed witnessed the bloodiest military dictatorship in Chile's history, a period during which tens of thousands of Chilean citizens were tortured and murdered, often because they simply looked like leftists. Not until 1990 did democracy return to Chile. To its credit, the United States, which must bear some responsibility for those seventeen years of horror in Chile, encouraged Chile's return to democracy.

The last significant Cold War chapter in the hemisphere was played out in Central America, with one small sideshow in Grenada. In Nicaragua, where the Somozas had ruled since 1936, the administration of Jimmy Carter found itself in an uncomfortable position. It was glad to see the Somoza dictatorship end in 1979 but was concerned that the Sandinista guerrillas who had ousted him were avowedly Marxist and friendly to Fidel Castro, although they quickly vowed to move toward elections and to address US security concerns. The Carter administration, albeit nervously, was prepared to meet them halfway, to handle differences through negotiations and even to provide limited economic assistance as an incentive. Not so the administration of Ronald Reagan, which took office in January 1981. It regarded the Sandinistas as nothing less than instruments of Soviet aggression and was determined to get rid of them one way or another.

Meanwhile, encouraged perhaps by the Sandinista victory in Nicaragua, left-wing guerrillas in El Salvador had launched an all-out effort to topple the government, and with it the traditional control of the landowning elite. The Carter administration focused as much on the need for economic and social reforms as on the need to contain the guerrillas, and the US ambassador, Robert E. White, insisted that the government curb the right-wing death squads (which had been responsible for the murder of Archbishop Romero) as a condition for US assistance.

The Reagan administration had no such qualms. As it came into office in 1981, it in effect told the government and the military to do whatever they deemed necessary to defeat the guerrillas. Atrocities on the government's side shot up at an appalling rate, often carried out by troops or death squads trained by the United States. Equally determined to win in Nicaragua, the Reagan administration eschewed negotiations and other efforts at peaceful solutions. Instead, it armed former Somoza national guardsmen and other anti-Sandinista elements, organized them into a force called the Contras, and launched them as a guerrilla force against the government in Managua. The ensuing conflict raged from 1982 until 1989. During that time, the United States pulled Honduras into the conflict by having the Contras operate from its territory and by training Honduran death squads to go after suspected leftists. In 1984 it also mined Nicaraguan harbors, an act that resulted in a 14–3 decision by the International Court of Justice (ICJ) declaring the United States to be in violation of international law. The United States, having already taken the position that the ICJ did not have jurisdiction in the matter, simply ignored the decision.

In their frantic efforts to do away with the Sandinistas, officials of the Reagan administration also lied to the Congress and then, in their efforts to circumvent congressional restrictions on aid to the Contras, initiated what became known as Iran-Contra-gate, a bizarre operation that began with efforts to divert to the Contras "profits" made by overcharging for arms the United States illegally sold Iran as part of a deal to bring about the release of Americans held hostage by Islamic groups in Lebanon. Eventually the operation involved secret donations made by a whole series of governments and shady individuals, and all in direct violation of congressional directives.[15] The US Army even trained Central American officers in methods of torture and assassination and wrote manuals advocating methods that were used in the infamous School of the Americas.[16]

In short, during the last chapter of the Cold War the United States seemed to lose its way and forget the values on which the country had been founded. As Gaddis Smith has so well put it:

> James Monroe in 1823 had contrasted American principles of candor, self-government, and respect for national independence with the devious, autocratic, imperial ways of Europe. The [Monroe] doctrine was proclaimed as protection of the first against the second. The abandonment after 1945 of its original ideals made the last years of the Monroe Doctrine a history of moral degradation. Sometimes the words and principles of the Monroe Doctrine were embraced openly, enthusiastically, and with complete candor. More often they were muffled in secrecy, tainted by lies, and in conflict with the public creed of democracy and human rights.[17]

In the end, the Central Americans ended the conflict through their own peace process, with little encouragement or support from the United States. Indeed, the United States opposed the negotiations until late in the day. US opposition frustrated the so-called Contadora process, an effort on the part of the Central American and Mexican presidents begun in 1983 to work out solutions to the region's conflicts. As this stood near the verge of collapse, however, it was followed by a new effort begun in 1987 at a meeting of presidents in Esquipulas, Guatemala. The prime mover of this new negotiating effort was Oscar Arias, the new president of Costa Rica and a man of great determination. Over the next two years, agreements were hammered out that eventually led to an end to the civil war in El Salvador, phased out fighting between the Contras and the Sandinistas in Nicaragua, and held elections in that country in 1990. When the Sandinistas lost, they peacefully turned power over to the opposition.

And so the conflict ended in Central America—no thanks to the United States. Oscar Arias won the Nobel Peace Prize, much to the disgust of some in the Reagan administration who had dismissed his plan for negotiations as a means of appeasing the communists. Meanwhile, back in 1983, in something of a sideshow performance, the Reagan administration had used US forces to invade the island of Grenada. Relations with Grenada had deteriorated steadily after the New Jewel movement took power there in 1979. It was led by Maurice Bishop, a friend of Castro's, whom both the Carter and Reagan administrations considered too far to the left. On the other hand, Grenada was a tiny island that threatened no one. Even so, in October 1983 the Reagan administration took advantage of internecine political strife on the island to send in US forces and remove the New Jewel movement from power. The specific pretexts for the invasion were (1) to assure the safety of US students at a medical school on the island and (2) to prevent the completion of an airfield that President Reagan warned was probably intended for use by the Soviets.

In fact, subsequent investigations made clear that the students were in no danger and in any event could have been peacefully evacuated had it not been for the invasion. It also turned out that the United Nations Development Program had recommended construction of the airfield as part of an effort to expand tourism on the island. And once the invasion was over, the US taxpayers forked over $19 million to help the new Grenadian government complete that same airfield—to expand tourism! In other words, the pretexts were phony.

The United States did at least have a legal fig leaf for its invasion, however. The other governments of the eastern Caribbean said they had urged the United States to step in. They said it only after the fact, however, and that was the case also of the alleged invitation from the British governor-general, which no one remembered to mention until the invasion was over. No one was fooled by these after-the-fact invitations. Certainly the British government was not. Prime Minister Margaret Thatcher, friend though she was of President Reagan's, roundly condemned the invasion. Still, by holding to its fig leaf, the United States was at least suggesting that it cared about the diplomatic and legal niceties, and it was sticking to the pattern that had existed since the withdrawal of the last marines from Haiti in 1934 of not intervening unilaterally with its own forces—without, that is, at least some shred of multilateral endorsement.

Strangely, with the Cold War virtually over, President George H.W. Bush broke that pattern, sending US forces to invade Panama in December 1989 without any invitation from the OAS, the Central American countries, or anyone else. And unlike all other US-organized interventions since 1954, the invasion of Panama was not aimed at thwarting some thrust on the part of the Soviet Union or Cuba. Indeed, it had nothing to do with the dwindling Cold War. Rather, Panama was invaded in order to arrest its president, Manuel Noriega, who was said to be involved in major drug trafficking. Noriega, once a paid asset of the CIA, had made the mistake of courting Cuba's Castro and of thumbing his nose at the United States. He paid the price. In blatant violation of international norms, US forces stormed into Panama, arrested Noriega, and brought him back to the United States to stand trial, much as conquering Roman legions once brought their prisoners back to Rome in chains.

Few shed any tears for Noriega, who had indeed won election by fraud and was something of a thug. The US invasion was nonetheless illegal and was so condemned by a nearly unanimous vote in the OAS. For the first time since 1934, US troops had intervened in Latin America without trying to win multilateral approval. Some wondered if the end of the Cold War meant a return to US gunboat diplomacy.

Meanwhile, the Soviet Union was in the throes of cataclysmic change. Mikhail Gorbachev had taken power there in 1985 and tried to revive the sputtering Soviet economy by introducing liberalizing reforms. In effect, he tried to fashion a socialist system with a more democratic face. Some said he went too far too fast. Others held that the system depended on coercion and ground to a halt when Gorbachev removed it. Whatever the case, the Soviet system began to collapse.

Gorbachev also changed the thrust of Soviet foreign policy. In the past, it had been geared to the Marxist tenet that worldwide revolution was a historical inevitability. In other words, it had been geared to expanding the socialist system to the extent possible. Quite understandably, the West had perceived this to be aggressive and threatening. But Gorbachev abandoned the whole concept. No more would the Soviet Union try to extend the reach of socialism; rather, it was now strictly up to each country to determine its internal arrangements without outside interference. With that, the Cold War began to wind down.

When an abortive coup by hard-liners in late 1991 failed, the almost seventy-five years of Communist Party rule was swept aside in reaction. The other republics then pulled out of the Soviet Union, and by 1992 the latter had disappeared, replaced by the Russian Republic and a loose grouping of the former union republics. The Cold War was over.

POST–COLD WAR, 1992 TO THE OBAMA PRESIDENCY

As already noted, with the end of the Cold War, the imperatives that had driven US policy for almost 200 years became obsolete. If the United States had treated the Caribbean as an American lake in order to protect the approaches to the Panama Canal, there was now no other power that wished to hinder those approaches; the canal passed into the hands of Panama and in any event was no longer of vital importance to the United States. The factors that had once riveted US attention to the Caribbean had gone the way of the three-mile limit to territorial waters (because that had once been the range of a cannon shot). There was no need to treat the Caribbean as an American lake. There was no need either to assert US hegemony in the Caribbean or Central America and certainly not in the rest of the hemisphere. US interests and objectives in the hemisphere today need the cooperation of other governments, not their subservience. This requires a new approach geared to vastly changed circumstances. This was true under the first post–Cold War presidency of William Clinton (1993–2001), and certainly so under the administration of George W. Bush (2001–2009), given the terrorist attacks on the World Trade Center and the Pentagon on September 11, 2001. The latter, in effect, opened a whole new chapter in US foreign policy, in which US efforts and attention will be focused on the struggle against terrorist forces in the world (Al Qaeda, the Taliban, and several others) intent on destroying US—and Western— influence and values in the world at large.

Under these circumstances, what are US interests and objectives in the hemisphere? The most pressing ones, not necessarily in order of priority, are as follows: (1) to contribute to our struggle against terrorism in a balanced way, so as not to lose sight of our other objectives in the hemisphere; (2) to halt or at least sharply reduce the flow of drugs into the United States; (3) to encourage the economic development of the countries to our south, both so as to (a) keep the populations in place (the United States does not want to receive vast flows of illegal immigrants or refugees from the south), and (b) increase trade, especially US exports; and (4) to help protect the environment on which we all depend.

Is the United States developing a more cooperative approach to address these interests? Let us examine them case by case.

THE STRUGGLE AGAINST TERRORISM

Following the September 11 attacks against the United States, virtually all the countries of the Western Hemisphere, including Cuba, condemned the acts themselves and terrorism in general, indicating at the same time their solidarity and willingness to cooperate with the people of the United States. That remained the case for some time. Indeed, on October 28, 2003, the Organization of American States approved a new multifaceted security agreement to "fight terrorism in all its forms" and to expand the hemisphere's "traditional concept and approach . . . to encompass new and nontraditional threats, which include political, economic, social, health, and environmental aspects."[18]

Other countries were willing to cooperate in the struggle against terrorism. The "with-us-or-against-us" attitude of the Bush administration did cause problems, however. Countries that opposed the US war in Iraq, such as Mexico, for example, were, in effect, sent to stand in a corner. But most of the OAS countries disagreed with the war in Iraq, and certainly their populations did. They took a dim view of the fact that the United States went in virtual defiance of the UN Security Council, thus weakening the United Nations. And when no weapons of mass destruction were found, the foray was seen as unjustified, irresponsible, and a blatant violation of the UN Charter. As a result of all this and other factors, US prestige in Latin America fell to its lowest point in many years, perhaps ever. At a meeting of the OAS in Santiago, Chile, in June 2003, the other countries for the first time ever voted to exclude the United States from membership on the Inter-American Human Rights Commission.

As always, Cuba was a special problem (see below), not so much because of Cuban attitudes but because of the almost fanatical determination of the Bush administration not to see or say anything positive about the Castro government. Immediately after the September 11 attacks, Cuba expressed its solidarity with the American people and opened Cuban airspace to any American planes caught in the air when US space was closed. Subsequently it offered to cooperate with the United Nations and with all governments, including the United States, in the fight against terrorism. It signed all twelve UN antiterrorist resolutions and offered to sign an agreement with the United States on cooperation in fighting international terrorism, an offer that the State Department almost insultingly rejected.

And the State Department continued to include Cuba on the list of "terrorist nations." The evidence for its inclusion, however, ranged from totally false to irrelevant. The department maintained, for example, that Cuba had harbored Chilean terrorists wanted for murder in Chile. It pointedly neglected to report the findings of the Chilean government itself, which had thoroughly investigated the case, even sending a delegation to Cuba, and concluded that Cuba had in fact not harbored or assisted the Chileans at all.[19]

DRUG INTERDICTION

The United States cannot reduce the flow of drugs over its borders by sending battleships and marines to the Caribbean and Central American states, and certainly not by landing troops in South America. Further, the drug problem is two-sided: consumption and production, with the former centered in the United States. It is up to the United States to address the matter of demand, for so long as there is a market for any product, it will be produced, no matter how energetic the efforts to turn it off. So far, the United States has done almost nothing to reduce consumption. That would require a major effort and outlay of funds, for which US political leaders have simply not had the stomach. Unless they do make such a commitment, however, their seriousness of purpose is in question, their vows to come to grips with the drug problem not really credible.

As to the second side, neither the United States nor the Latin American governments can eradicate production through legislation and police action, though those are of course necessary components. The result of those efforts over past years has been to contain production to a 10 percent per year increase![20] The cartels are only part of the problem. By and large, coca and other narcotics are grown by poor peasants in Bolivia, Peru, Colombia, and other countries. They depend on their crops of coca leaves, poppies, and marijuana to eke out a meager existence. They have raised these plants for centuries and have little concept of the havoc they cause elsewhere. They are not likely to give up their major source of income just because the United States and their own governments demand it. (This was a factor in the October 2003 overthrow of Bolivian president Gonzalo Sánchez de Lozada; see Chapter 25) They must find alternative crops and sources of income, and this will require a major cooperative effort among the United States, individual Latin American governments, and international organizations. Such an effort would involve a large-scale input of resources, most of which would have to come from the United States. It would be a small price to pay, however, if, as President

George H.W. Bush told Americans some years back, drugs are the principal threat to national security.[21] So far, the United States has shown not the slightest interest.

The system of certification imposed by the United States in 1987 was, as many Latin American governments saw it, simply a matter of shifting the blame to Latin America. Many took it as confirmation that the United States saw itself as judge and jury of whether the efforts of Latin American governments to interdict drugs were adequate. If it deemed them inadequate, then that government was no longer eligible for certain economic benefits. Never mind what the Latin American governments might think of the inadequacy of US efforts and its failure to commit resources. Clearly this was not a cooperative effort among equal partners.

The major US effort in the drug war has been in Colombia. With Plan Colombia, President George W. Bush promised to reduce coca production in Colombia by 50 percent by the year 2005. This proved wishful thinking, however. State Department reports indicated that coca production in Colombia from 2003 onward actually increased."[22]

PROTECTION OF THE ENVIRONMENT

The United States also needs the cooperation of the Latin American governments in protecting the environment, or the habitat in which we all live, but has yet to provide the necessary leadership and resources. The so-called Earth Summit in Rio in June 1992 (or more formally, the United Nations Conference on the Environment and Development) offered a perfect opportunity at least to provide leadership. However, the administration of President George H.W. Bush raised objections to the two major treaties to be signed at the conference even before it opened. In the event, it refused to sign the treaty to preserve the world's plants, animals, and natural resources, much to the disgust of the other delegates and even of many in the US delegation. It signed the other major treaty, dealing with the problem of global warming, but only on the condition that the strict timetable for curbing harmful emissions be deleted. Rather than leading and encouraging cooperation, the Bush administration played an obstructionist role and was almost completely isolated in its position.[23]

The intentions at least of the administration of Bill Clinton were an improvement over those of the first Bush administration. In 1993 Clinton called for "a new covenant for environmental progress." His administration then negotiated a multilateral agreement aimed at halting the depletion of the ozone layer in the upper atmosphere, and in 1996 it began massive negotiations for a worldwide effort to address the critical problem of global climate change. These were steps in the right direction, but Congress refused to come up with the money to fund them. The United States did not even supply seed money for the project to reduce CFCs worldwide and thus reduce the depletion of the ozone layer. Even under Clinton, the United States was the biggest debtor in the Global Environmental Facility, the principal international funding mechanism for the effort called for by the Climate Change Convention.[24]

The heart of the matter in the Western Hemisphere is the need to halt the destruction of the Amazon rain forest, often described as the lungs of the world. But halting deforestation is linked to responsible economic development. Alternatives must be offered so that destruction of the forest is no longer profitable, but that requires a carefully coordinated developmental effort and, again, the outlay of resources. As one Brazilian official put it, "We of course want to protect the environment. In the best of all possible worlds, we'd like to preserve the rain forest. On the other hand, we must develop, must offer our people a better way of life. We can't afford to be the lungs of the world if we are also to pay off our foreign debt and finance our development plans."[25]

Worse, with the inauguration of George W. Bush in 2001, any pretense that the United States was interested in the Amazon or even took seriously the protection of the environment as a whole went out the window. From undercutting the Clean Air Act to proposals promoting wholesale clear-cutting of our own national forest in the guise of "fire prevention," the administration moved almost across the board to weaken measures to protect the environment. In March 2003 it announced that the United States would not cooperate with the Kyoto treaty aimed at reducing greenhouse gas emissions to slow global warming. Under George W. Bush, any interest in cooperating with the other nations of the hemisphere to protect the environment was put on hold.

ECONOMIC DEVELOPMENT

During the Cold War, US representatives often answered Latin American requests for economic assistance by pointing to the huge US defense expenditures. Were it not for the need to defend the rest of the world against the aggressive intentions of the Soviet Union, politicians said, the United States would have ample resources to assist the economic development efforts of its neighbors. As it was, those resources had to be diverted to defense. But in the decade between the end of the Cold War and the September 11 attacks, there was virtually no change of attitude on the part of the United States, no appreciable decrease in military spending, and no increased willingness to consider economic development programs of a magnitude required to get the other nations on the road to prosperity. And with its attention on the struggle against terrorism since the September 11 attacks, it is even less willing. (More on that below.)

This US cold shoulder is difficult to understand, given that such developmental efforts would advance US interests. It is not simply that an economically imbalanced hemisphere is unhealthy and morally unsustainable; rather, such a situation fuels one of Washington's major headaches: the influx of illegal immigrants from the south. There is only one way to encourage these unstable populations to remain in place (i.e., not to head for the United States), and that is by giving them some hope of a better future in their own countries. But rather than developmental programs involving even small-scale transfer of public resources, the United States urged the countries to its south to privatize and to depend on private investment, both local and foreign. In short, it urged a neoliberal approach. This was accompanied during the administration of George H.W. Bush by rhetoric centering around the Enterprise for the Americas, a vague program of trade preferences, incentives for private investment, calls for limited debt reduction, and promises of movement toward a hemispheric free trade zone. While praiseworthy in its concept, little came of it. Few of the necessary legislative packages were ever even presented. The George

H.W. Bush administration did succeed in negotiating and winning congressional approval for a free trade agreement with Canada, the first step in putting in place a North American Free Trade Agreement (NAFTA). It initiated the process with Mexico, which the Clinton administration completed. In 1994, at the urging of the Clinton administration, NAFTA was extended to Mexico as well.

Much hoopla attended the so-called Summit of the Americas held in Miami in December 1994. The heads of thirty-four governments met and signed a Declaration of Principles and Plan of Action involving twenty-three separate initiatives on everything from efforts to end corruption to the extension of the free trade zone to virtually all states of the hemisphere by the year 2005. The Clinton administration did little to push the initiative. As we shall see below, another meeting was held in Miami in November 2003, supposedly to follow on the work of the Miami Summit and form the Free Trade Association for the Americas, with disappointing results.

Meanwhile, the results of the new economic policies advocated by Washington were decidedly mixed. Over the first five years of the 1990s, most countries succeeded, with their new neoliberal economic measures, in controlling inflation, reducing budget deficits, attracting foreign investment, and getting growth rates up around a respectable 3 percent (after a nearly stagnant decade during the 1980s). The downside, however, was that the reforms produced higher unemployment, more people living in poverty, a greater disparity between rich and poor, and declining standards of living for the majority. According to the World Bank, income distribution in Latin America "approaches the most unequal in the developing world."[26]

This was exacerbated by the neoliberal policy of reducing social welfare programs. The poor not only got poorer but found only a frayed safety net to arrest their descent into need. Even in Argentina, once one of the bread baskets of the world, the poor simply went hungry.

Mexico went through a dramatic economic crisis during the Clinton presidency. Shortly after becoming part of NAFTA and as a direct result of mistakes in adjusting to the agreement, in December 1994 its economy virtually collapsed. Only a massive bailout led by the US Treasury kept Mexico from going under. By late 1996, it had begun to recover. Growth rates were back in the black and foreign investment was again beginning to flow into the country. But the disparities were worse than ever. Mexico could boast of fifteen billionaires (only four other countries had more), but 50 percent of the Mexican population was living in abject misery, and more were falling beneath the poverty line every day.[27] Social and political tensions rose, as evidenced by the peasant uprisings in Mexico's southern states. These were muted by the election of Vicente Fox of the opposition PAN party in July 2000 and, as indicated above, an era of warm relations with the United States was supposed to ensue. The problem of illegal aliens coming in from Mexico was to have been addressed in a comprehensive way. But the warm relationship broke down quickly and the migration problems were not addressed. The flow of illegal aliens from Mexico continued to increase.

Meanwhile, whether belonging to NAFTA has benefited or harmed Mexico is increasingly debated. A study by the Carnegie Endowment for International Peace in November 2003, for example, concluded that real wages in Mexico were lower than when the agreement was adopted, and that income disparity (as suggested above) had increased. A World Bank Study also issued in 2003, on the other hand, contended that Mexico would have been worse off without the agreement as it struggled to recover from its financial crisis of the mid-1990s (see above). That, however, left aside the argument of many that the crisis was caused precisely by Mexico's entry into NAFTA. [28]

The George W. Bush administration did even less than its predecessor to address economic problems in Latin America. The Argentine economy collapsed on its watch, and the Bush administration stood aside and did nothing to rescue it. The Argentine problem was, by and large, caused by the mismanagement and corruption of Argentina's political leaders. Some part, however, was the result of the neoliberal economic model urged by the United States, and which the Bush administration continued to favor until the end.

With the election of Nestor Kirchner in 2003, Argentina began to recover, both economically and politically. It remained deeply resentful of US neglect, however, and suspicious of US intentions. Those suspicions continued under Cristina Kirchner, who followed her husband in the presidency in 2007.

Rather than supporting economic development programs, the Bush administration tended to offer the Latin American nations free trade agreements—on decidedly unequal terms. The United States did not want agriculture or nontariff barriers to be on the table. At the same time, it wanted the Latin American states to compromise their national sovereignties by agreeing to investor "protections." It signed such agreements with Chile (in June 2003) and with the Central American states, except for Costa Rica, in December 2003. Costa Rica finally signed in January 2004.

As part of that same tendency, the Bush administration pressed for all countries to support an agreement for a Free Trade Area for the Americas (FTAA), and it hosted a hemispheric meeting in Miami in November 2003 to sign agreements that would lead to the formation of the FTAA by 2005. There was strong opposition, however, led by Brazil but seconded by Argentina, Venezuela, Bolivia, and a number of other states, in part over US agricultural subsidies and other trade barriers, which the other countries said were unfair and would neutralize any positive effects of the agreement. Sentiment against free trade agreements has also come to be linked to growing rejection of neoliberal economic policies. The Miami meeting of 2003 could be called a standoff. The United States refused to give up its agricultural subsidies, and Brazil refused to agree to rules on intellectual property rights, or investment and government procurement. The meeting adjourned early with a call for continued discussions, but clearly the Latin American states had deep reservations. And public opinion in Latin America was turning massively against the United States. In November 2005, for example, at the Summit of the Americas in Mar del Plata, Argentina, not only did representatives of virtually all countries flatly reject the only thing President Bush had to offer—the Free Trade Agreement for the Americas—but there were massive demonstrations against him. From that point forward the Free Trade Agreement was seen as a dead letter, except possibly in Colombia.

In sum, US efforts to stimulate economic development in Latin America failed to convince and were rejected. The flow of illegal aliens meanwhile continued unabated. And economic underdevelopment continued to affect US interests in another area: trade. Countries with growing numbers of impoverished masses are not good markets. Thus, rather than booming trade, with balances in favor of the United States, trade increased little at all, and the balances against the United States continued to escalate. In 1992 the balance against the United States was only $991 million. By 1995 it was almost $9 billion, and by 2003 over $10 billion.[29]

FAILURE OF US POLICY

Clearly the United States failed to formulate a policy that worked in the post–Cold War world. It needed the cooperation of the other governments, but it provided little leadership and few resources under the first Bush and Clinton administrations, and even less under that of George W. Bush. At least until 2009, US leaders seemed to have become so wholly consumed by the war on terrorism that Latin America had largely disappeared from their radar screens.

Worse, the United States gave evidence of moving back toward a kind of unilateralism more appropriate to the days of gunboat diplomacy than to the post–Cold War world. During the Cold War, the United States often spoke of committing itself to abide strictly by the United Nations Charter and international law if the Soviet Union would but do so also.[30] With the Soviet Union having collapsed and its successor state, the Russian Republic, having committed itself to adhere to the charter, hopes rose that the United States would return to the spirit of multilateralism that had briefly prevailed with the formation of the Rio Pact in 1947 and the Organization of American States in 1948. That spirit had been undermined by the anticommunist hysteria of the Cold War. Might it now be possible to resuscitate it and to construct a hemispheric system based on rule of law?

At least until 2009, the answer seemed to be no. For one thing, the United States continued to behave as though the Cold War was not over, at least with respect to Cuba. During the 1980s, the US position was that relations with Cuba could improve if the latter would (1) remove its troops from Africa, (2) stop fueling revolutionary situations in Central America and elsewhere, and (3) reduce its military ties with the Soviet Union. As of 1992, all those conditions had been met. Yet rather than moving to relax tensions and improve relations with the island, the United States did exactly the opposite. With passage of the Cuban Democracy Act of that year, it actually tightened the embargo against the island. Congressman Robert Torricelli (D–New Jersey), the act's principal proponent, assured one and all in a television debate in December 1992 that as the result of his legislation Castro would be gone within months.[31]

That proved to be a farcically rosy prediction. Even so, ultraconservative forces in the US Congress came up with even more draconian legislation aimed at forcing other countries to reduce trade with and investments in Cuba. The Helms-Burton Act, signed into law in March 1996, was extraterritorial in nature and violated international law and various international agreements to which the United States is a party, including NAFTA. It represents nothing less than a unilateral US effort to dictate to the rest of the world without regard to the rules of the international system.

Not surprisingly, Helms-Burton was roundly condemned by the international community and had almost no effect in bringing down the Cuban economy, much less the Castro government. In November 1996, the United Nations General Assembly condemned the US embargo, including Helms-Burton, by a vote of 138–3. Only Israel and Uzbekistan voted with the United States that year, and they both trade with Cuba! The vote has followed a similar pattern every year since.

What this points up is that Helms-Burton is an irrational act on the part of the United States. With the Cold War over, Cuba no longer represents even a potential threat to US security and certainly not to US economic interests. In fact, in terms of US interests, Cuba is of little importance at all. US commercial ties with Canada, Europe, and Mexico, on the other hand, are vital. That the United States is willing to place at risk that which is important over that which is not is simply illogical.

Unfortunately, Helms-Burton seemed to be part of a pattern. If some saw the end of the Cold War as an opportunity to construct a more stable international system based on international law and adherence to rules of conduct agreed to by all in such international forums as the UN and the WTO, others, such as Senator Jesse Helms (R–North Carolina) (let us call them the unilateralists) saw it in quite another light. To them it meant that the United States, as the only remaining superpower, could and should order things to suit its own purposes, paying little attention to such abstractions as international law and international organizations. The United States wanted to bring down the Castro government and so insisted that other governments cooperate with it or face the consequences.

It also wanted to be rid of Venezuelan president Hugo Chávez. The evidence that George W. Bush supported the abortive coup against Chávez in April 2002 was not conclusive, but was enough to convince Chávez and turn him into a foe of US policy so long as George W. Bush was in the White House.

Almost immediately after taking office, Bush announced that the United States would withdraw from the Anti-Ballistic Missile Treaty of 1972, one of the foundation stones of the international arms control system that had functioned well for many years. He then issued a thirty-three-page report, *The National Security Strategy of the United States,* which discarded the policy of détente and containment and, rather, endorsed preemptive or preventive military actions against states with which we are at peace, with or without the approval of the United Nations Security Council.[32]

In March 2003, in defiance of the Security Council, which did not vote to approve the US action, the Bush administration launched its war against Iraq, claiming the latter had weapons of mass destruction virtually ready to fire and that it had to take immediate and preemptive measures. No weapons of mass destruction were found, but the Bush administration was not in the least apologetic. The fact that its actions had seriously undermined the United Nations system founded by earlier American presidents and supported by all until George W. Bush seemed not to concern it in the least.

The Bush administration also became even more threatening toward Cuba, claiming that it was somehow a "potential threat" to US security, thus raising the possibility of some preemptive strike against it as well as Iraq. And indeed, in October 2003, the Bush administration confirmed that the objective of US policy toward Cuba was to get rid of the Castro government. As assistant secretary of state Roger Noriega put it to the Senate Foreign Relations Committee on October 2,

2003: "The president is determined to see the end of the Castro regime and the dismantling of the apparatus that has kept him in office for so long."

Cuba took this threatening attitude seriously. The day that the United States invaded Iraq, it launched a massive crackdown against dissidents on the island, fearing, apparently, that it might be next on the list for a preemptive attack and that it had to batten down the hatches. This was almost certainly an overreaction. The United States had its hands full in Iraq and appeared to have no intention of attacking Cuba—no matter what its threats of the moment. What the episode illustrates yet again, however, is that US threats and bellicose posturing toward Cuba are almost always counterproductive. Indeed, they produce exactly the opposite of the desired results. If we want solutions to our disagreements, this is not the way to achieve them.

REACTION TO BUSH POLICIES

As noted above, under George W. Bush, US standing in Latin America reached its lowest point in memory—perhaps ever. Virtually to a nation, the Latin American states rejected the various components of Bush's so-called Washington Consensus (e.g., unfettered capitalism, free trade, and hostility toward Cuba). And given that Cuba was seen as the principal and longest-standing victim of US policy, the other Latin American states indicated rapprochement with Cuba as a prerequisite to a new US relationship with Latin America as a whole. Gone were the days when the United States could dictate policies to the other nations of the hemisphere.

Bush's Latin American policy was of course not his only failure. There was also the war in Iraq, his failure to respond adequately to the tragedy that was Hurricane Katrina, and by the end of his presidency, the United States was in the throes of a deep economic recession. Not surprisingly, the American people urgently wanted change. In November 2008, they elected Barack Obama, who was inaugurated as the forty-fourth president of the United States on January 20, 2009.

THE OBAMA PRESIDENCY—SO FAR

Obama was greeted enthusiastically by the American people and by most of the international community. He brought in sweeping new economic reforms and stimulus packages in an effort to get the economy working properly again. He moved ahead with his plan to remove most American troops from Iraq, though many would simply be transferred to Afghanistan. He announced that the infamous prison at Guantanamo would be closed within a year. He closed secret CIA prisons and outlawed torture. And he vowed that from now on, the United States would respect international treaties and be a law-abiding member of the international community.

All this met with the applause of the international community and the great majority of American citizens. As of this writing, several months into the Obama presidency, it is too early to predict with any certainty the results of the economic programs, the outcome of the war in the Middle East, or of various other of the new administration's initiatives. Since this chapter focuses on Latin America, let us turn to the Obama administration's approach there.

Given pressing economic problems and critical challenges in other areas, Latin America was not a priority issue during the presidential electoral campaign. Obama did on a number of occasions, however, indicate that as president he intended to have a more cooperative relationship with the Latin American states.

His first major opportunity to articulate a new policy came at the Summit of the Americas Conference held April 17–19, 2009, in Trinidad and Tobago, where he pledged to the other members of the hemispheric body to "seek an equal partnership," with no "senior partner or junior partner in our relations, [but] simply engagement based on mutual respect and common interests and shared values."[33]

His statement of the new US position and his generally more forthcoming attitude were well received by the Latin American representatives, with a reservation. They wanted the United States to support Cuba's reintegration into the hemispheric system. As Lula da Silva, president of Brazil, had already indicated to Obama, a US shift on Cuba was a necessary first step if the United States wished to rekindle Latin America's faith in Washington's ability to lead.[34]

And in his speech on April 19, Patrick Manning, the prime minister of Trinidad and Tobago and the chairman of the Summit Conference, insisted on change with respect to Cuba's exclusion from the inter-American system: "There was a clear consensus," said Manning, "that the reintegration of Cuba in the inter-American relations is an essential step toward the building of a more cohesive and integrated Americas."[35]

In the same speech, Manning complimented Obama's more "open and conciliatory stance," but the marker had nonetheless been put down. The other governments wanted to see more than a conciliatory stance; they wanted to see Cuba's reintegration into the hemispheric community.

And what of Obama's initiatives on Cuba? On April 13, knowing that Cuba would be an issue at the approaching summit, he in effect removed restrictions on Cuban-American travel and remittances. Henceforth, he said, rather than every three years, they could travel when they wanted, stay as long as they wished, and send as much money to family members as they wished.[36]

This was something of a disappointment, since the unofficial word out of the Obama camp up until April 13 had been that restrictions on academic travel and people-to-people travel would be removed as well as those on Cuban Americans. All these restrictions had been imposed by the Bush administration in 2004, and so it had seemed appropriate, if we were to return to the status quo ante Bush, that all be removed. But it was not to be. Obama only restored the rights of Cuban Americans, and in his speech at the summit tended to exaggerate the importance of that step. The United States sought a new beginning with Cuba, he said. "There are critical steps we can take toward a new day. I've already changed a Cuba policy that I believed failed to advance liberty or opportunity for the Cuban people. We will now allow Cuban-Americans to visit the islands whenever they choose and provide resources to their families."[37]

Clearly restrictions on academic and people-to-people travel had not advanced liberty or opportunity for the Cuban people anymore than had restrictions on the travel of Cuban Americans. President Obama did not explain why, then, he had left the first two in place.

Lifting travel restrictions on Cuban Americans did not, of course, go nearly as far as the Latin American governments had hoped. They wanted the United States to help reintegrate Cuba into the inter-American system, not simply lift a few travel controls. Doubtless to keep everyone happy by suggesting that there might be more, President Obama indicated that he was prepared to talk, prepared to have his administration engage with the Cuban government on a wide range of issues. "I do believe," he said," that we can move US-Cuban relations in a new direction."[38]

Perhaps, but there was no evidence the United States was really moving in that direction following the summit. US-Cuban relations were at center court again at the OAS meeting in San Pedro Sula in early June. The Latin American states were determined to cancel the 1962 resolution that had expelled Cuba from the OAS and bring Cuba back into the organization. The Obama administration, on the other hand, was opposed, with Secretary of State Hillary Clinton insisting that Cuba would have to adopt democratic reforms before it could possibly again become a member.[39]

The disagreement may have been seen as somewhat unrealistic in that whatever the Latin Americans and the United States wanted, Cuba had already said it had no interest whatever in rejoining the OAS, which it regarded as nothing more than a creature of the United States!

Even so, the debates at the San Pedro Sula meeting were animated and there was speculation that the OAS might split, with the Latin American states in one organization and the United States in another. In fact, however, diplomacy won out and a compromise was reached, embodied in a June 3 resolution declaring (1) that the resolution of 1962, which had excluded Cuba from participation in the inter-American system, now ceased to have effect, and (2) that Cuba's participation would be the result of a dialog initiated by Cuba and in accordance "with the practices, purposes, and principles of the OAS."

In other words, the Latin Americans had done away with the hated resolution of 1962 and left it up to Cuba as to whether she wished again to become part of the OAS, knowing in fact that she did not. It was a compromise, but more a Latin American victory than one for the United States. What all this points up is that the United States can no longer simply call the shots in Latin America—and Cuba has been a factor in bringing about that change. In 1962 the United States could force through a resolution ousting Cuba from the OAS. Today—when all hemispheric states save the United States have full diplomatic relations with Cuba and when all, again save the United States, are pushing for her reintegration into the inter-American system—it could not do so.

US standing among the other nations was briefly bolstered when it joined the other nations in opposing the removal of Honduran President Zelaya by a conservative-backed military coup on June 28. Claiming that Zelaya was committing treason by advocating a change to the constitution to permit presidents to serve more than one term, he was removed by force from his residence and put on a plane to Costa Rica. The conservative majority in the congress then voted him out of office and declared Roberto Michelli to be the new president.

Every government in the hemisphere, plus the Organization of American States, denounced the coup and demanded that Zelaya be returned to power. The

Michelli government refused and was therefore expelled from the Organization of American States.

At first the Obama administration condemned the coup and cooperated with the other governments in efforts against it. Over time, however, its position became more ambiguous. In November 2009, it seemed to have worked out a deal whereby Zelaya would briefly return to the presidency prior to elections. But it then abandoned that position entirely and supported elections for a new president under the ruling dictatorship, a position rejected by virtually all other OAS governments and by the OAS itself. The US action provoked deep resentment and distrust throughout the hemisphere. It was one of the issues that caused the other governments in February 2010 to come up with a new hemispheric organization, one that excluded the United States and Canada.

In sum, the Obama administration's relations with Latin America are not off to a good start. One of the issues between them is what the rest of the hemisphere sees as an outdated and irrational US policy toward Cuba—a policy that the Obama administration begins to appear incapable of changing.

NOTES

1. Lars Schultz, "Inter-American Security: The Changing Perceptions of U.S. Policy-makers" (paper, 1990). See also Wayne S. Smith, "The United States and South America: Beyond the Monroe Doctrine," *Current History,* February 1991.

2. Quoted in Julius W. Pratt, *A History of U.S. Foreign Policy* (Englewood Cliffs, N.J.: Prentice-Hall, 1955), p. 165.

3. Gaddis Smith, *Last Years of the Monroe Doctrine* (New York: Hill & Wang, 1994), p. 8.

4. Pratt, *History of U.S. Foreign Policy,* p. 348.

5. Wayne S. Smith, *Portrait of Cuba* (Atlanta: Turner Publishing, 1991); p. 41 n.

6. George Black, *The Good Neighbor* (New York: Pantheon, 1988), p. 16.

7. Louis A. Perez Jr., *Cuba Between Empires* (Pittsburgh: University of Pittsburgh Press, 1983), p. 327.

8. Quoted in Black, *Good Neighbor,* p. 23.

9. Quoted in Wayne S. Smith, "Will the U.S. Again Send in the Marines?" *World Paper,* November 1983.

10. J. Reuben Clark, *Memorandum on the Monroe Doctrine* (Washington, D.C.: U.S. Government Printing Office, 1930).

11. Ann Van Wynen Thomas and A. J. Thomas Jr., *The Organization of American States* (Dallas: Southern Methodist University Press, 1963), p. 356, conclude that "the Rio Treaty is the final step to date in the multilateralization of the Monroe Doctrine." See also Samuel Guy Inman's account of Republican senator Arthur Vandenberg's conclusion that this would be the effect of the OAS, in *Inter-American Conferences, 1826–1954: History and Problems* (Washington, D.C.: University Press of Washington, 1965), pp. 221–222.

12. See Smith, *Last Years,* pp. 78–84. For perhaps the most penetrating study of US intervention in Guatemala, see Piero Gleijeses, *Shattered Hope* (Princeton, N.J.: Princeton University Press, 1991).

13. See Stephen G. Rabe, *Eisenhower and Latin America* (Chapel Hill: University of North Carolina Press, 1988), p. 94.

14. Smith, *Last Years,* pp. 122–129.

15. Ibid., pp. 196–199.

16. Dana Priest, "U.S. Instructed Latins on Executions, Torture," *Washington Post,* September 21, 1996.

17. Smith, *Last Years,* p. 7.

18. Associated Press, Mexico City, October 28, 2003.

19. Cuba on the terrorist list, International Policy Report of the Center for International Policy, November 2000.

20. James Brooke, "Peru Suggests U.S. Rethink Eradication in Land Where Coca Is Still King," *New York Times,* November 18, 1990, p. 3.

21. Ibid., p. 3.

22. See the State Department's 2008 report on international narcotics production.

23. See discussion in the following articles in the *New York Times:* Sanjoy Hazarika, "India Is Facing Ecological Quandary in Plans to Dam River," April 11, 1992, p. 8; Gwen Ifill, "Clinton Links Ecology with Jobs," April 23, 1992, p. 22; Keith Schneider, "U.S. to Reject Pact on Protection of Wildlife and Global Resources," May 30, 1992, p. 1; James Brooke, "U.S. Has a Starring Role at Rio Summit as Villain," June 2, 1992, p. A10.

24. See article by deputy secretary of state Strobe Talbott, "Our Mission and the Global Environment," *State Magazine,* December 31, 1996, pp. 15–32.

25. Interview with a senior Brazilian diplomat who requested anonymity, Washington, D.C., May 1990.

26. Molly Moore, "Three Years After Mexico Embraced Free Trade, Rural Poor Still Flock to the Capital," *Washington Post,* December 31, 1996, pp. A12–13.

27. Ibid., pp. A12–13.

28. See "Report Finds Few Benefits for Mexico in NAFTA," *New York Times,* November 19, 2003.

29. Figures are taken from Tables 6 and 8 of *U.S. Foreign Trade Highlights, 1995* (U.S. Department of Commerce, International Trade Administration, Office of Trade and Economic Analysis, 1996); and from Table 8 of *Trade and Economy: Data and Analysis,* a report issued by the Department of Commerce's International Trade Administration on August 25, 2003.

30. See the interesting debate in Council on Foreign Relations, *Might vs. Right* (New York: Council on Foreign Relations, 1989). See especially the presentation by Jeane Kirkpatrick and Allan Gerson, "The Reagan Doctrine, Human Rights, and International Law," pp. 37–71, in which they make the point that respect for international law is based on reciprocity, that is, if I respect it, so must you.

31. See the transcript of *Crossfire* on CNN, December 30, 1992.

32. See Office of the President, *National Security Strategy of the United States* (Washington, D.C., 2002). See also comments under *Bush League Diplomacy* (New York: Prometheus, 2003), chap. 6.

33. See the text of the president's speech issued by the White House on April 17, 2009.

34. Quoted in Robert White, "Temperate Zone: Obama and Latin America," *Commonweal,* May 22, 2009.

35. See the text of Manning's speech issued by the Fifth Summit of the Americas on April 17, 2009.

36. See memo issued by the White House on April 17, 2009.

37. See the text of the president's speech issued by the White House on April 17, 2009. Note, however, that instructions have not been brought in line with the president's

words. As of July 2009, Cuban-Americans could travel only once a year, rather than whenever they wanted, as the president had promised.

38. Barack Obama, speech issued by the White House on April 17, 2009.

39. See *New York Times,* May 22, 2009.

Suggested Readings

Langley, Lester. *America and the Americans.* Athens: University of Georgia Press, 1989.

Munro, Dana. *Intervention and Dollar Diplomacy.* Princeton, N.J.: Princeton University Press, 1964.

Morley, Morris, and Chris McGillion, eds. *Cuba, the United States, and the Post-Cold War World.* Gainesville: University of Florida Press, 2005.

Prins, Gwyn, ed. *Understanding Unilateralism in American Foreign Relations,* London: Royal Institute of International Affairs, 2000.

Schoultz, Lars. *Beneath the United States: A History of U.S. Policy Toward Latin America.* Cambridge: Harvard University Press, 1998.

Smith, Gaddis. *Last Years of the Monroe Doctrine.* New York: Hill & Wang, 1994.

Smith, Peter. *Talons of the Eagle: Dynamics of U.S.–Latin American Relations.* New York: Oxford University Press, 1996.

Smith, Wayne S. *The Closest of Enemies, A Personal and Diplomatic Account of U.S.-Cuban Relations Since 1957.* New York: Norton, 1987.

Whitaker, Arthur. *The Western Hemisphere Idea.* Ithaca, N.Y.: Cornell University Press, 1954.

Wood, Bryce. *The Dismantling of the Good Neighbor Policy.* Austin: University of Texas Press, 1985.

———. *The Making of the Good Neighbor Policy.* Austin: University of Texas Press, 1961.

Part VI

MEXICO AND
CENTRAL AMERICA

Chapter 15

MEXICO

A Revolution Laid to Rest?

FRED R. HARRIS AND
MARTIN C. NEEDLER

ALL NATIONS AND peoples are, more or less, products of their own history.[1] Mexico and Mexicans are more so than most. Mexican sociologist Raúl Béjar Navarro has shown that studies seeking to prove that there is a unique Mexican "character" are largely impressionistic and unscientific.[2] But there certainly is, in Mexico, such a thing as national experience, a shared history.

History is not only a chronological recording of past events but also an attempt to explain those events. In order to understand a country and a people, then, we must know not only what has happened to them but also what they choose to remember and what they choose to make of what they remember—what they teach.

HISTORICAL FOUNDATIONS

"To say Benito Juárez is to say Mexico. To say Mexico is to say sovereign nation." Those were the beginning words of a patriotic speaker at the annual Mexico City ceremony on Benito Juárez Day, March 21, 1982—the 176th anniversary of the birth of the Zapotecan Indian who rose to be president of Mexico. Virtually every Mexican town and city has a monument to Juárez or a principal street named for him—this stern "man of law" who stripped the Catholic Church of its property and privileges; reformed Mexican politics; instituted public education; ended the rule of the Mexican dictator Santa Anna; and later, drove the French from Mexico.

Reform. Respect for law. Nationalism and resistance to foreign aggression. Civilian control of the government. The importance of "great leaders." Public morality. Separation of church and state. Pride in Indian history. These are some of the concepts that the memory of Benito Juárez evokes for Mexicans—and is used to evoke. To Mexicans, Juárez was an Indian who became a Mexican, as Mexico was an Indian nation that became a Mexican nation. But it was Indian first.

THE PRE-CORTÉS PERIOD

Within the great sweep of Middle America lies the Valley of Mexico (in which present-day Mexico City is situated). It is 7,000 feet (2,134 meters) above sea level and encompasses some 5,000 square miles (12,950 square kilometers). The valley is bounded on all sides by snowy volcanic mountains. In prehistoric times, much of the valley floor was covered by large, shallow lakes. By around 8000 BC, people had begun farming in the valley. After 1500 BC, population centers began to develop. Stratifications of power and wealth evolved. Trade flourished over wide areas. Agriculture became highly advanced.

Civilization was already ancient—great cities, like Teotihuacán and Tula, had already risen and then fallen—by the time the Aztecs came into the Valley of Mexico in the thirteenth century. They were an especially industrious, vigorous, and expansionist people. By 1425, they had subjugated, or made alliances with, all the other peoples of the valley. Eventually, their influence reached from the Mexican highlands to the coasts on either side and as far south as present Guatemala. Only the Tlaxcalans to the east, the Tarascans to the west, and some of the Mixtecs to the south remained apart.

By the time Moctezuma II became its principal lord in 1502, the capital city of the Aztecs, Tenochtitlán, was a clean, healthy, bustling metropolis, one of the largest cities of the world, with a population as high as 200,000 people. (By contrast, Seville, the Spanish city from which the conquistadores were later to sail, had a population of around 40,000, and only four European cities—Paris, Venice, Milan, and Naples—had populations of 100,000 or more.) There were some fifty other cities in the Valley of Mexico. Millions and millions of people lived in an area of one of the greatest population concentrations in the world.

THE SPANISH CONQUEST

When Hernán Cortés and the conquistadores came over the snowy pass to the east and first saw Tenochtitlán and the other cities in and around the lake, they could hardly believe their eyes. Bernal Díaz del Castillo, who was in the party, later wrote that "we were amazed and said that it was like the enchantment they tell of in the legend of Amadis, on account of the great towers and cues and buildings rising from the water, and all built of masonry." Within three years thereafter, Cortés was the ruler of all he had at first surveyed—except that, by then, the great city was in ruins.

Why did Moctezuma II, the Aztec ruler, let the Spaniards come freely into Tenochtitlán? Cortés's monstrous use of terrorism as a tactic must have been puzzlingly and terrifyingly different from any kind of war that Moctezuma II had known. Why destroy a huge tribute city like Cholula and the income one could derive from it, as Cortés did? Why kill such great numbers of people for no useful purpose? Moctezuma II must also have let the Spaniards come because he was certain that at any later moment when he wanted to, he could easily defeat and capture Cortés and his army. Moctezuma must have been influenced, too, by Cortés's continued and effusive expressions of friendly intention. And, philosopher and thinker that he was, intellectually curious, Moctezuma must have been intrigued by these strange white men and anxious to know more about their identity and their place of origin.

In any event, Cortés did indeed come in. Once inside Tenochtitlán, he seized Moctezuma and held him prisoner. But Cortés soon had to leave for the gulf coast to defeat a rival Spanish army sent by the governor of Cuba. While he was away, the Aztecs at last rose up and attacked the Spaniards. Moctezuma was killed in the bloody fighting. Cortés, with his Tlaxcalan allies, marched back to Tenochtitlán to relieve the embattled Spanish garrison there. But the Aztecs had had enough, and they drove Cortés and the Spaniards from the city.

Then came into play one of the most terrible factors in the success of the conquest—European disease, in this case, smallpox. The European plagues—smallpox, influenza, typhus, typhoid, diphtheria, measles, whooping cough, and others—were unknown in the New World. The native peoples of the Western Hemisphere had built up no immunities to them. Time after time, then, with first contact, one or another of the European diseases decimated whole populations in the Americas. Such was now the fate of Tenochtitlán. Smallpox swept through the city with devastating effect, throwing social and political organization into disarray and shaking religious beliefs. Thousands upon thousands died within the span of a week. Bodies piled up and could not be disposed of rapidly enough. Cuitlahuac, the nephew of Moctezuma who succeeded him, was one of those who died. Cuauhtémoc assumed the leadership. As one historian has written, "Clearly, if smallpox had not come when it did, the Spanish victory could not have been achieved in Mexico."[3] Another historian concurs, writing that "the glorious victories attributed to Spanish arms would not have been possible without the devastation wrought by Spanish disease."[4] Cortés had time to regroup. When he attacked, he fought a weakened enemy. Still, Cuauhtémoc and the Aztecs resisted fiercely until, at last, they were defeated—and Cuauhtémoc captured—in the suburb of Tlatelolco on August 21, 1521. By that time, Tenochtitlán had been destroyed.

As Robert E. Quirk and others have written, one can tell a great deal about a country by the monuments it chooses to erect—and by the monuments it chooses *not* to erect. There are no monuments in Mexico to Cortés. Neither are there monuments to Malinche, the collaborating Indian woman who became mistress of and interpreter for Cortés (indeed, in Mexico today, *malinchismo* is the act of selling out one's country to foreigners). There are no monuments to Moctezuma. Cuauhtémoc is the Indian hero of Mexico history.

SPANISH COLONIALISM

Cortés had cut off the head of the Aztec empire. In the next years, the body followed. The Spanish captain rewarded his men—and himself—as richly as he had promised. There were great quantities of gold. Cortés took for himself vast estates of rich land and huge *encomiendas* (entrustments or grants of Indians) to work them. He gave land and *encomiendas* to his followers, also.

The first year, Cortés began growing sugarcane. With this and other crops, the plow was also introduced. Soon, great herds of sheep and cattle were imported and set to graze. Slave labor built *ingenios*, or sugar mills. Forests were felled to provide fuel, lumber for building, and charcoal for cooking. Thus began, from the first year of Spanish colonialism, the overplowing, overgrazing, deforestation, and desertification that have continued to plague Mexico to this day.

Gold and silver mines were established, expanded, and worked, under incredibly brutal conditions, by Indian slave labor. *Obrajes*, or sweatshops, were everywhere set up to produce the coarse cloth and other products needed for domestic consumption. When the *encomienda* system and slavery were later made illegal, these monarchical edicts were often ignored, or were replaced by debt peonage, which was just as bad. Brutal treatment and European diseases wiped out more than two-thirds of the native population in the Valley of Mexico between 1519 and 1650!

Spanish colonialism, then, was characterized by exploitation of people and natural resources. It was also characterized by mercantilism—the crown's practice of keeping Mexico a producer of raw materials only and a purchaser of Spain's manufactured goods. Education was a privilege in colonial Mexico, not a right. The Roman Catholic Church was the established church. After a first period of missionary zeal, the Church fell, in many instances, into dissolution. The Church, itself, became a great landholder and exploiter of Indian labor. There were wholesale conversions to Catholicism, but the Indian converts still held on to much of their old religion. The Spaniards built churches on sacred Indian sites. The Virgin of Guadalupe appeared to an Indian convert, Juan Diego, at a site where there had previously been a shrine to an Aztec goddess.

After 1700, the Mexican and Spanish economies, both of which had been depressed, began to revive. The population in Mexico began to grow—mostly among the mestizos. The numbers of the *criollos* (Spaniards born in the New World) also grew, and they began to develop a pride in Mexicanness, which paralleled their increasing resentment of the privileged position of the *peninsulares*, who had been born in Spain.

Spain's wars in Europe meant more taxes in Mexico, more "forced loans" to the crown, and confiscation of Church charitable funds. Then, Napoleon Bonaparte imposed his brother on Spain as its ruler. At this, some *criollos* in Mexico attempted a revolt against the *peninsulares*, but this revolt was put down. Political dissatisfaction was soon joined by economic troubles.

INDEPENDENCE AND EMPIRE

Throughout Mexico, groups of dissidents began to meet in 1809, some to plot. One such group met regularly in Querétaro. Among its members were a young cavalry captain, Ignacio Allende, thirty-five, and a fifty-seven-year-old priest, Miguel Hidalgo y Costilla, whose parish was in the small nearby village of Dolores. Hidalgo, a *criollo*, had been investigated twice by the Inquisition for his political views. When word leaked out about the conspiracy in Querétaro, its members were warned by the wife of the local *corregidor*, or governor (she is celebrated in Mexican history as *la corregidora*). In Dolores, with Allende by his side, Father Hidalgo rang his church bell to summon his parishioners and issued what came to be called the *grito de Dolores*, a call to rebellion, on September 16, 1810. Many *criollos* were alarmed by the excesses of the mestizos and Indians who fought for Hidalgo and independence. Government forces rallied. Hidalgo and Allende were defeated, captured, and killed.

A mestizo priest, José María Morelos y Pavón, took up the sword of leadership, and in the congress that he called in 1813, he made clear by his stirring speech to the delegates that the sword he carried was meant to cut the *criollo,* as well as the *peninsular,* bonds that had for so long held down the mestizos and Indians of Mexico. The constitution adopted by this congress was a liberal document. Principles could not stand up to guns, however. *Criollos* and *peninsulares* joined together in opposition to this rebellion, and by 1815, Morelos, too, had been captured and killed. Still, the war—or wars—for independence sputtered on for another five years.

In Spain, Ferdinand VII had been restored to the throne in 1814, but the *criollos* of Mexico felt increasingly separate from Spain. In 1823, led by a conservative military man, Agustín de Iturbide, the *criollos,* backed by the Church, declared Mexican independence—a conservative independence, much different from that for which Morelos and Hidalgo had fought and died. Spain, after years of war, had no alternative but to agree to Mexican independence. The Mexican economy was in shambles. And after all the fighting, the lives of the great mass of the Mexican people had not changed. The identity of their oppressors had changed, but the nature of the oppression remained the same. Iturbide had himself declared emperor of Mexico—the first of its *caudillo,* or strongman, rulers. But the imperial grandeur in which Iturbide lived and ruled lasted only ten months.

Now, there rode onto the Mexican scene one of the most flamboyant and most enduring *caudillos* of Mexican history, the Veracruz military commander, a twenty-nine-year-old *criollo,* Antonio López de Santa Anna. Santa Anna had switched from the Spanish army to support Iturbide. After Iturbide dissolved the Mexican congress, Santa Anna switched and led the forces that unseated Iturbide. He could be a monarchist or an antimonarchist. He could be a liberal or a conservative. He could be a defender of his country, or he could sell it out. For him, expediency and self-interest were the first principles. In February of 1823, Iturbide was driven into European exile, and his rule was replaced by that of a provisional government, run by a three-man military junta.

Needless to say, there are no statues in Mexico honoring Iturbide. By contrast, both Hidalgo and Morelos had states named after them, and there are many monuments to them. On each anniversary of the *grito de Dolores,* the president of the Mexican republic rings the old bell, now at the National Palace, in commemoration of that important event.

THE MEXICAN REPUBLIC

A new Mexican constitution was promulgated in 1824. It established the Estados Unidos Mexicanos, which consisted of nineteen states and four territories. Patterned after the constitution of the United States and influenced by the writings of the French philosopher Montesquieu, the Mexican constitution established a national government of three branches—executive, legislative, and judicial—a bicameral legislature, and a president to be elected by nationwide popular vote. Roman Catholicism was continued as the established religion. Military men and priests were guaranteed their special privilege of the *fuero*—that is, the right to be tried for any offense not by the civil courts but by military or Church courts.

After Manuel Félix Fernández Guadalupe Victoria was elected as the first president, poor Iturbide mistakenly thought he heard a call of the Mexican people—all the way over in Italy. He unwisely returned home, where he was arrested and executed. In 1827, Santa Anna put down another attempted revolt. In 1830, he was called on to defend the country and the government once more. When the second republican president had pushed through legislation expelling all Spaniards from Mexico, Spain had invaded Mexico at Tampico. Santa Anna laid siege to the Spanish forces and eventually forced their surrender. By then, he was easily the most popular figure in Mexico. The president of Mexico was then thrown out of office and executed by his vice president. Santa Anna rose up and threw this usurper out of office. He was then elected president of Mexico in 1833.

It turned out that Santa Anna was not very much interested in governing. His vice-president, though, began to push through liberal reforms. So the army, the Church, and other conservatives banded together to overthrow the constitutional government and rescind the reforms. And who should lead this revolt but the president of the republic himself, Antonio López de Santa Anna. Now the foremost conservative, Santa Anna abolished the constitution of 1824 and made the states into military districts. He required that he be addressed as Your Serene Highness. He was to occupy the presidency again and again, off and on, until 1855. During those years, the army became larger and larger, the bureaucracy became ever more bloated, taxes became higher and higher, the economy stagnated, bribery and corruption of officials became outrageous, and there were conflicts with foreign governments—first with the Republic of Texas, then with France, and finally, and disastrously, with the United States.

For years, Mexico had encouraged emigration from the United States to the sparsely settled, vast lands of Texas—provided only that the new emigrants were Catholics, would be loyal to the Mexican government, and would use Spanish as their official language. As the years passed, little was done to enforce these requirements. The flood of emigration swelled. Eventually, people from the United States greatly outnumbered Mexicans in Texas, and they became increasingly critical of the central government, until, at last, they rebelled and declared the establishment of the Lone Star republic in 1836. Santa Anna took personal command of the Mexican army and marched to San Antonio, where, at the Alamo on March 6, 1836, he defeated the Texas defenders there and killed them all. Another part of the Mexican army captured the small town of Goliad, taking 365 prisoners, all of whom Santa Anna had executed. Then, on April 21 of that same year, Santa Anna was himself defeated at the San Jacinto River and was taken captive.

To save himself, Santa Anna promised the Texans that Mexico would not again fight against Texas and that the Mexican cabinet would receive a formal mission from the Lone Star republic. When the cabinet heard of these agreements, they immediately repudiated them and sent Santa Anna back to his estate near Veracruz. Soon, however, the trumpets sounded again for Santa Anna. Provoked by Mexico's refusal—actually an inability—to pay its French debts, France ordered a shelling and invasion of Veracruz. Santa Anna led the Mexican forces that eventually drove the French away.

WAR WITH THE UNITED STATES

Then came the war between the United States and Mexico (1846–1848). US attitudes toward Mexico and Mexicans were highly derogatory, even racist—especially after the war with Texas. Furthermore, the people and government of the United States felt that it was their Manifest Destiny to stretch their country's boundaries westward, all the way to the Pacific. The United States annexed Texas as a state of the Union in 1845. Mexican officials seethed, but were largely powerless to do anything else. Then, without any discoverable basis in law or fact, Texas claimed that its border went, not just to the Nueces River, but much past it to the Rio Grande (which the Mexicans call the Rio Bravo). Not only had Mexico suffered the loss of Texas, but it was now expected to accept the doubling of Texas territory— to include additionally, for example, San Antonio, Nacogdoches, and Galveston in Texas as well as Albuquerque, Santa Fe, and Taos in present New Mexico.

It is known from President James K. Polk's diary that he had made up his mind early to engage in a war with Mexico and was only waiting for a provocation. He sent US troops into the area between the Nueces and the Rio Grande. When they skirmished with Mexican cavalry, Polk went before Congress, declared that he had made every effort at reconciliation, that the Mexicans had invaded US territory and "shed American blood on American soil," and asked for a declaration of war. Congress complied.

The US Army of the West was divided into three attack groups, which rapidly took New Mexico, California, and Chihuahua. The Army of the Center attacked Monterrey, where it was stopped by none other than Santa Anna. The main US attack came from the Army of Occupation at Veracruz, which eventually marched all the way to Mexico City. The last battle there was on September 13 at Chapultepec Castle, the site of a military academy. Young Mexican cadets fought alongside the Mexican regulars, many preferring death to surrender. Mexico was defeated.

Peace was even more humiliating for Mexico than the war had been. According to the Treaty of Guadalupe Hidalgo, Mexico lost half of its territory in return for a payment of a little over $18 million—all of California, some of present-day Colorado, and most of the present states of New Mexico and Arizona. More humiliation was to come. When Santa Anna again came to power in 1853, needing money, he sold the rest of present New Mexico and Arizona (in the so-called Gadsden Purchase) to the United States for $10 million.

Today, one of Mexico's principal national monuments is located in Chapultepec Park. It is dedicated to the *niños héroes* ("boy heroes") of the war with the United States. Similar national monuments commemorating the patriotism and courage of the young cadets have been erected in villages and towns throughout Mexico. There are no monuments to Santa Anna.

THE REFORM

By 1854, the liberals of Mexico had had enough of dictatorial government. Among them was Benito Juárez, the lawyer of Zapotec Indian origin who had been governor of his home state, Oaxaca. They rose up in arms behind the liberal Plan of

Ayutla. Santa Anna was driven into exile in 1855. Thus began what is called La Reforma (the Reform). Benito Juárez, as secretary of justice in the new government, was instrumental in having promulgated three important new reform laws: *ley Juárez, ley Lerdo,* and *ley Iglesias.* The first law abolished the *fuero,* the right of priests and military men to be tried in their own courts. The second law prohibited the Church and public units (including *ejidos,* the communal landholdings of Indian villages) from owning more property than was necessary for Church or governmental functions. The extra lands were not divided among the people. They were put up for sale. The unfortunate result was that large landholdings went to those who had the money. The third law struck again at the Church—making registration of births, deaths, marriages, and adoptions a civil, not a Church, responsibility; giving control of cemeteries to civil authorities; and prohibiting priests from charging high fees for administering the sacraments.

The constitution of 1857 incorporated these and other reforms. Pope Pius IX declared any who followed the constitution heretics. The lines were sharply and bitterly drawn between the liberals on one side and the conservatives and supporters of the Church on the other. The War of the Reform broke out in 1858. Conservative forces overran the capital. Benito Juárez, who had earlier been elected chief justice and was, therefore, next in line for succession to the presidency, took over that office when its occupant resigned. Juárez eventually made his capital in Veracruz.

The conservative government in Mexico City renounced the Reform laws and swore allegiance to the pope. The Juárez government, on the other hand, issued even stronger decrees against the Church. The Church and the state were formally separated. Monastic orders were outlawed. All Church properties and assets were nationalized. Taking advantage of dissension within conservative circles, the liberal forces began to win some battles. Finally, on January 1, 1861, Mexico City fell to them.

FRENCH INTERVENTION

Juárez entered Mexico triumphantly in March and was officially elected president. But before 1861 was over, foreign troops invaded. Mexico owed debts to France, Spain, and Great Britain, which it had not been able to pay. Napoleon III of France persuaded the other powers to join with him in an invasion of Mexico. The Spanish and British withdrew after they learned that Napoleon III was bent on conquest. The French troops were then reinforced, and they began to march toward Mexico City. On the *cinco de mayo* ("the fifth of May"), the French troops were defeated near Puebla by the Mexican army. After this victory, Juárez, incensed by the fact that many priests had urged their parishioners to support the French, issued a decree prohibiting priests and nuns from wearing distinguishing garments and from speaking against the government.

The *cinco de mayo* victory was short-lived. Juárez retreated northward, eventually all the way to El Paso del Norte (later to be renamed Ciudad Juárez). Now began one of the most bizarre and tragic episodes in Mexico's political history—the imposition in 1864 by Napoleon III of the Hapsburg prince from Austria, Ferdinand Maximilian, as emperor of Mexico. Poor Maximilian and his wife, Carlota, believed the Mexican conservative, monarchist, and pro-Church emissaries who came to urge Maximilian to accept the Mexican throne. They were told that the people would welcome them with warm enthusiasm. They also believed Napoleon III when he said he would finance Maximilian's rule and sustain him on the Mexican throne with French troops as long as necessary. They also believed their Mexican advisers who told them that Juárez was defeated and had fled to the United States. These things were not true.

When the US Civil War ended, the United States again turned its attention to Mexico and began to pressure France to withdraw. At the same time, the US government began to furnish munitions and other supplies to Juárez. In late 1865 and early 1866, the French troops were called home, and Napoleon III announced that he could no longer pay the costs of Maximilian's government. Carlota went to Rome to secure the pope's help; when this effort was unsuccessful, she lost her mind. Maximilian began a final and hopeless resistance to the republican army—being soundly defeated and captured in Querétaro on May 15, 1867. Despite a great number of petitions by numerous heads of state, Juárez denied clemency for Maximilian and had him executed. Juárez entered Mexico City once more, reinstituted the constitution of 1857, and in December of 1867, was elected to a third term as president. During this "restored republic," Juárez reduced the size of the army, instituted economic and educational reforms, and began construction of a railroad system to pull Mexico together as one nation.

Mexico had developed a strong sense of nationalism—and significantly, this nationalism had flowered in struggles against foreign powers. There are, of course, no monuments in Mexico to Maximilian. There are many monuments dedicated to Juárez, and Mexico City's principal boulevard is named the Paseo de la Reforma.

THE PORFIRIATO

Perhaps Juárez stayed in office too long. There were complaints that he centralized too much authority in the presidency, manipulated and dominated the congress, caused the alienation of *ejido* land, and increased the power of the national government, to the detriment of state and local governments. Nevertheless, Juárez announced for election to a fourth term in 1871. There was a three-way contest, and no candidate received a majority of the vote. The election was thrown into the congress, which chose Juárez. One of the other candidates, a military hero of the battles with the French, Porfirio Díaz, attempted a revolt under the slogan of No Reelection. The attempt failed. The revolt was quashed. But, in July of 1872, before he could take office, Juárez died.

The chief justice, one of the other candidates, Sebastián Lerdo de Tejada, succeeded to the office and in special elections in October of that year, was elected president. Lerdo continued the basic policies of Juárez and then announced for reelection to a second term. Porfirio Díaz took to the field with his military supporters again. This time, his No Reelection slogan caught fire. By force of arms and general support among those who counted, Díaz took over the presidency in 1876. This Mexican *caudillo* was to rule Mexico for over a third of a century. True to his No Reelection theme, Díaz did not seek reelection in 1880. After the undistinguished administration of his successor, Díaz became president again in the election of 1884. Thereafter, he remained in office until he was forced out in 1911.

The Porfiriato, as the Díaz reign is called, was a time of stability, law and order, and overall economic growth. It was dominated by men whom detractors later came to call *científicos*—followers of French positivism (a belief in progress through scientific knowledge and the scientific method), pragmatism, and Social Darwinism. Chief among the *científicos* was the son of a French emigrant, José Yves Limantour, who became secretary of the treasury. Porfirio Díaz and his backers believed, among other things, that Mexico needed a period of "administrative power"—a nice way to say dictatorship—if the country was to be transformed from a backward nation into a modern one.

Díaz created a powerful political machine, run from the top. He practiced a shrewd politics of conciliation and coalition. There were great political and economic benefits for those who joined up—jobs and positions, land, subsidies, concessions. Constitutional local government continued in theory, but real local power was vested in some 300 *jefes políticos* ("political chiefs"), named by Díaz. The military was also a part of the Díaz coalition. Key generals were allowed to dominate their states. Government policies encouraged bigness in agriculture, as in everything else. New laws allowed surveying companies to keep a portion of any idle, unclaimed, or public lands they surveyed. Great land grabs resulted. Four surveying companies, for example, were able to obtain two-thirds of all the land in the northern state of Sonora, territory equal to the size of England and Wales combined!

The *científicos* believed that Mexico's economic development depended upon attracting foreign capital through special subsidies and concessions. By 1910, US interests controlled 75 percent of Mexican mines, 72 percent of the metal industry, 68 percent of the rubber business, and 58 percent of oil production. Other foreigners—mostly British, French, German, and Dutch—controlled 80 percent of the rest of Mexico's industry.

The theme of the Porfiriato was "peace, order, and progress." A modern railroad network was built. This helped to double cotton production. Mining flourished; so did industrialization. Some ports were modernized and others opened. Exports mushroomed—and Mexico became dependent upon them. Mexico's population doubled.

But the costs were exorbitant. The great majority of Mexicans lived in misery or in otherwise intolerable conditions. The Indians, who Limantour believed were biologically inferior, were considerably worse off by 1910 than they had been a hundred years earlier, prior to independence. The rural *peones,* or laborers, were also worse off. The *peones,* as well as the miners, were paid, not in money, but in scrip or special coins, which could be spent only at the *tienda de raya,* the company store, and they were perpetually behind in what they owed. *Rurales* ("rural police") hunted down and brought back anyone who tried to escape. Debts were passed on from one generation to another. Because Mexico's agriculture had increasingly been converted to cash crops and to the cattle and sheep business, especially for export, Mexico was producing less corn and beans in 1910 than it had produced in 1867—and was a large importer of food.

Railroad, mining, and industrial workers became increasingly hostile to the owners, to foreigners, and to their own government. Labor agitation and attempts at organization began in the 1880s—some of it encouraged by the Catholic Church following the issuance of a papal encyclical in 1891 that called for greater recognition of the rights of labor. Between 1881 and 1911, there were 250 strikes. In the worst of these, against French- and US-owned companies, federal troops were used to break the strikes.

A growing Mexican middle class was also increasingly unhappy with the government. The economic policies and the educational programs of the Díaz regime had helped to create this middle class. But, as Porfirio Díaz and his administration aged, they turned more and more to a politics of exclusion. Liberal intellectuals began to speak out against the undemocratic practices of the government and the exploitation of Mexican labor. Two Flores Magón brothers, Jesús and Ricardo, started a liberal publication, *Regeneración,* to call for change. The publication was closed down by the government, and the Flores Magón brothers fled to the United States, where their writings and calls for action became increasingly radical.

On top of all this came bad economic times. The year 1907 was one of both severe drought in Mexico and severe economic problems in the world. A financial panic in the United States cut off credit to Mexico. The worldwide economic problems deprived Mexico of its export market, upon which it had come to depend so heavily. Mines were shut down. The economy stagnated. The prices of food and clothing rose rapidly—the costs of flour, beans, wheat, corn, and chili nearly doubling.

Then, in an interview with a US magazine in 1908, Porfirio Díaz announced— and this was widely publicized in Mexico—that he felt the time had come for Mexico to choose its own president in the elections of 1910. Nevertheless Díaz himself eventually became a candidate for reelection. In the meantime, Francisco Ignacio Madero, the son of a Coahuila *hacendado* who had studied for five years in France and eight months at the University of California in Berkeley, wrote a very important book, *The Presidential Succession of 1910,* in which he called for political reform (although he said virtually nothing in regard to land, labor, or other economic or social reforms). Madero formed an Anti-Reelection Party and began to expound his views in well-attended meetings around the country. Actually doubtful that Díaz would really allow a free election, Madero nevertheless announced as a candidate for president. Madero's doubts were well founded. He was arrested and jailed. Díaz was declared the winner in the 1910 elections; Madero went into exile in San Antonio, Texas.

THE REVOLUTION

With this latest usurpation of power by Porfirio Díaz, Madero's frustrations at last rose to a level that matched Mexico's. In October of 1910, he issued his Plan of San Luís Potosí, reiterating his call for political reform and asking Mexicans to rise up in arms against the Díaz regime on November 20. Rise up they did! This moderate man, with his moderate plan, became the lightning rod that attracted all of the dissident elements of the country. Some who joined him were more conservative than Madero; many were more radical. Some joined him to secure a share of the power and wealth, others to fight for social and economic, as well as political, reforms.

There was an uprising in Yucatán. The Flores Magón brothers led an uprising in Baja California. In Chihuahua, Pascual Orozco Jr., a muleteer disgruntled by the political and economic stranglehold of the *hacendados,* raised an army and began to achieve significant victories over the federal forces. Among his lieutenants was a man who called himself Francisco "Pancho" Villa. Born Doroteo Arango into a poor family living on a hacienda, Villa had spent most of his life as a bandit and a cattle rustler.

In February of 1911, Madero returned to Mexico and took command of the revolutionary army. In the state of Morelos, Emiliano Zapata, a charismatic and dedicated leader for land reform, announced his support for the Madero revolution. It turned out that the federal army had become as debilitated by power and corruption as the government itself. It could not stop Zapata in the state of Morelos nor Orozco and Villa in the northern states. Zapata took Cuautla; Orozco and Villa captured Ciudad Juárez. It became clear to Díaz and those around him that after a third of a century, his government had lost its legitimacy and, with it, control of the country. Limantour went to Ciudad Juárez and negotiated a transfer of power. Díaz abdicated on May 25 and left for Europe, never to return. The Porfiriato had ended. Madero thought that the revolution had also ended, but it had only begun.

The war was to continue for another decade. Countless Mexicans, including Madero himself, were to be killed by other Mexicans. The country was to be ravished, the economy devastated. The population of Mexico, which had been rapidly growing, was to suffer a decline of nearly 1 million people between 1910 and 1920. But all that was somewhere in the future when a triumphant Madero boarded the train for Mexico City. The troubles to come were presaged, though, by a harsh confrontation Madero had with Orozco and Villa just before he left Ciudad Juárez. In Mexico City, Madero made a strategic mistake. A stickler for legality, he allowed an interim president to serve until Madero could be formally elected in October of 1911. By then, perhaps, his moment had passed. Madero was to govern for only thirteen months. His meager and timid reforms did nothing to satisfy labor and land-reform demands. He continued the fiscal policies of Díaz and retained many of the Porfiriato's high officials.

Orozco took to the battlefield again. Zapata issued his Plan of Ayala, which demanded immediate land reform; denounced Madero; and recognized Orozco as the true leader of the revolution. Now, Madero made another mistake, this one literally a fatal mistake. He called upon a Porfiriato general, Victoriano Huerta, a mestizo from the state of Jalisco, to head the federal army against Orozco and Zapata. Huerta was successful against Orozco (who later, opportunistically, joined forces with him), and he began to put pressure upon Zapata. Then came another challenge—from the right. Felix Díaz, a nephew of the former president, rose in arms in Veracruz against the Madero government. Again, Huerta was successful. This rebellion too was quashed, and Felix Díaz was brought to Mexico City and jailed. Soon, however, other conservative forces freed Díaz and threatened the government again. There then ensued what is called in Mexican history the decena trágica ("the ten tragic days"). The killing and destruction wrought by the Díaz and the Huerta forces, fighting against each other, were horrible. It appears now that Huerta might have been going through a sham in order, purposely, to cause the decimation of his own government army, because he was, at the same time, opening secret negotiations with Díaz. These negotiations culminated in an agreement, which was reached under the direction and guidance of the US ambassador, Henry Lane Wilson. Huerta switched sides and the US ambassador supported him. Herta immediately took over the government, arrested Madero, and had the president's brother killed. Madero was imprisoned. Despite the pleas for help by Madero's wife to Wilson, the ambassador did nothing, and Madero and his vice-president were taken out and cruelly murdered.

In the United States, President Woodrow Wilson refused to recognize the Huerta regime. But, in Mexico, most state governors did. Zapata, of course, did not recognize Huerta. Neither did Villa, and he was joined in arms by Alvaro Obregón, a former schoolteacher and *cacique* ("political boss") in Sonora, and a former revolutionary commander. The leadership of these constitutionalist forces was assumed by Venustiano Carranza, nearly sixty years old, the governor of Coahuila, and the patriarch of a distinguished *criollo* family there. Carranza took as his title First Chief. He issued his Plan of Guadalupe, a moderate plan, promising, again, only political reforms. As the fighting worsened and widened, as villages were taken first by one side and then another, many people began to wonder what it was all about. Even the soldiers—in both the federal and constitutionalist armies—were not agreed among themselves on what they were fighting for.

Although, interestingly, Huerta probably achieved more in the way of reforms and in support of education than did Madero, he also severely suppressed the press, jailed opponents, countenanced the use of assassination as a political tool, and practiced harsh repression generally. Huerta also initiated forced conscription to supply his army with soldiers—producing an inferior army and depleting the Mexican work force, adding injury to the Mexican economy. President Wilson possessed a moralistic zeal for democracy. He replaced Henry Lane Wilson and, using the pretext of a Mexican affront to some US sailors, sent an armed force to capture the port of Veracruz in 1914. This caused a new wave of severely anti-US feeling in Mexico. The vigor and successes of the constitutionalist army, augmented by the facts that Huerta had to divert troops to Veracruz and that his outside sources of supply had been cut off by the US occupation of that port, brought down the Huerta government in July of that same year. Huerta resigned, blaming the United States for his fall (he later died in a Texas jail in 1916, still plotting to return to Mexico).

The First Chief, Venustiano Carranza, took control of the Mexican government. Partisans of social and economic reform soon found out that he was not one of them. To consolidate his position, Carranza called a military convention in Aguascalientes in 1914. *Carrancistas, Villistas,* and *Zapatistas* met to pull the country together and to decide upon a provisional president until elections could be held. But the convention soon got out of hand. Led by the *Zapatistas,* a majority of the delegates, in a burst of revolutionary fervor, elected a provisional president who was opposed by Carranza. The First Chief disowned the convention and called for his representatives to withdraw from it. Fatefully, as time would show, one of those who decided to obey this order was Alvaro Obregón.

The troops of Villa and Zapata marched on Mexico City. Carranza withdrew his headquarters to Veracruz (from which, incidentally, the US occupation forces were eventually evacuated). The provisional president chosen by the Aguascalientes Convention was installed in office. But Obregón was a student of the new tactics of war being used at the time in Europe. At Celaya, in April of 1915, he met an old-style massed cavalry charge with a deadly stationary defense. Thousands of Villa's men were killed and wounded, and Villa himself withdrew northward. Zapata thereafter confined himself and his forces to the state of Morelos.

Carranza returned to power in Mexico City. His government was recognized by President Woodrow Wilson. The First Chief then called another convention, this one a constitutional convention in Querétaro. To avoid his earlier mistake, he decreed that none of the delegates to be elected could include anyone who had fought with Huerta, Villa, or Zapata. But when the convention met, these restrictions proved unavailing. A majority of the delegates quickly rejected the moderate model constitution that Carranza had sent them. Instead, they wrote an organic law—still in effect in Mexico—which was a radical document for its day. It limited the president to one four-year term. Its Article 3 was vigorously anti-Church, incorporating all such earlier restrictions and prohibitions and, further, taking primary education away from the Church (making education purely secular as well as mandatory and free). Article 27 incorporated the basic philosophy and provisions of the Plan of Ayala in regard to land reform, made private ownership a privilege subject to the public interest as the government might define it, and restricted the right to exploit Mexico's water and mineral resources to Mexican nationals. Article 123 mandated extensive labor reforms—an eight-hour day, a six-day week, equal pay regardless of sex or nationality, and a minimum wage. The right of labor to organize and to strike was guaranteed.

Shocked as he was by the product of this second runaway convention, Carranza nevertheless accepted the constitution, although he made it clear that he had no intention of following it. He was elected president in March of 1917. Carranza distributed very little land. His labor reforms were also minor, although he did permit the organization of Mexico's first nationwide union, the Regional Confederation of Mexican Labor (CROM). In the north, Villa was relatively quiet—and wealthy—on his hacienda. But from Morelos, Zapata wrote a defiant open letter to Carranza, calling on him to resign and charging that Carranza and his friends had fought in the revolution only for "riches, honors, businesses, banquets, sumptuous feasts, bacchanals, orgies." Carranza had tried direct military action against Zapata, to no avail. Now he decided upon treachery. On Carranza's orders, an officer of the federal army in Morelos, indicating that he wanted to defect to Zapata, led Zapata into a trap and killed him in 1919. Carranza rewarded the assassin with an army promotion and a generous cash prize.

But things were far from settled in Mexico, and the battered country had not seen the last of political violence—nor of political assassinations. General Obregón, the one-armed hero of the constitutionalist forces, had gone back to his native Sonora after Carranza's government had been firmly put in place. As a *hacendado,* a grower and "merchant of garbanzos," a cattleman and an exporter of beef and hides, and an all-around entrepreneur, Obregón had grown very wealthy. But power interested him as much as wealth. So, when he thought Carranza had passed over him in choosing the "approved" presidential candidate for 1920, Obregón led a military revolt against Carranza—a successful one. Sadly, Carranza was killed while retreating toward Veracruz. Obregón's subsequent election as president in 1920 was not the last time a presidential election would ratify a result earlier achieved by military means. But Obregón's revolt was the last successful revolt against the government.

The Mexican revolution was over, and it was soon enshrined forever—with a capital *R*—in Mexican history. With time, the Mexican constitution came to be regarded as a nearly sacred document—though it was a long way from actually being implemented. Time did not improve the image of Huerta, whom Mexican history remembers as "the bloody usurper." No Mexican monuments were erected in memory of Porfirio Díaz (although, ironically, a street in El Paso, Texas, still bears his name). But plenty of Mexican monuments and street names, today, pay homage to Madero, Carranza, and Zapata. Mexican history makes Madero "the apostle" of the revolution and of Mexican democracy, Carranza "the father of the constitution," and Zapata the heroic fighter for the Mexican masses.

THE NORTHERN DYNASTY

Alvaro Obregón and his fellow Sonoran, Plutarco Elías Calles, who had fought with Obregón, apparently soon worked out an arrangement by which they agreed to pass the presidency back and forth between them in the years that were to follow. Obregón was elected president in 1920. He was a charismatic leader and a dynamic orator, and he gathered power into the presidency. Obregón was also a conciliator. He made a kind of peace with the Church and with his former foes. He had another rich hacienda bought for Pancho Villa, and the mellowing revolutionary of the North settled down (and was later assassinated in 1923). The economy recovered. Mexico became the world's third largest producer of oil. The first national system of education was established, and rural schools were built. Obregón allowed some cautious labor advances to be made and endorsed some cautious land reform. A sense of what came to be called revolutionary nationalism began to develop in the country—in its writings, in its music, and in its art. In the United States, Warren G. Harding, a friend of big oil, became president in 1921. He pressured Mexico to recognize the US oil holdings there, and Obregón yielded.

Calles became president in 1924—after an attempted rightist rebellion was put down by military force. Taking office, Calles became the strongest—and, as it turned out, the longest-lived—president and *caudillo* since Díaz. He put down his enemies without mercy. He built up Mexico's economy, pushed health programs, expanded education, helped make labor more powerful, and established a cooperative relationship with CROM. He also vigorously enforced, as Obregón had not, the anti-Church provisions of the constitution. Militant Catholics rose up in a bloody rebellion, their cry being "Viva Cristo Rey!" ("Long live Christ, the King!"). Calles dealt very harshly with this *cristero* rebellion and, after much shedding of blood on both sides, eventually suppressed it.

Calles also confronted the United States in regard to oil. It was decreed that all interests that predated the constitution of 1917 would have to be renegotiated with the government—and these new concessions were to be limited in duration. The United States sent a Wall Street investment banker, Dwight Morrow, to Mexico as its ambassador. His quiet negotiations eventually worked out a compromise. The oil interests were allowed to continue their concessions without the duration lid.

Calles caused the presidential term to be changed from four years to six years. He then prepared to turn the government back over to Obregón in the 1928 presidential election. There was a rebellion, again, and it was again put down. The election ratified the earlier military victory. But before Obregón could take office, he was killed by a religious mystic. Calles assumed power again—ruling through puppets as the *jefe máximo* ("maximum chief") until 1934. During this period, called in Mexican history the *maximato*, Calles established Mexico's ruling party in order to institutionalize his political control, since he was not charismatic or dynamic enough to rule by power of personality. Calles shifted the revolution to the right. Powerful leaders of labor, business, and government became immensely wealthy during the Calles *maximato*. Calles, himself, seemed to own property almost everywhere.

The Cárdenas *Sexenio*

With the end of the 1928–1934 *sexenio*, the *maximato* had run its course. Calles was the last survivor of the great revolutionary *caudillos*—Madero, Zapata, Villa, Carranza, and Obregón had all been assassinated—and he was now to lose control. But Calles did not know that that was about to happen when he chose the populist and popular governor of Michoacán and his former minister of war, Lázaro Cárdenas, as the National Revolutionary Party (PNR) presidential candidate in the elections of 1934. Elected, Cárdenas turned out to have a mind of his own. Once he had cut down the strength and influence of the military and had bolstered his own political position with labor, the peasants, and other elements in the country, he confronted Calles and exiled him from the country.

Cárdenas undertook more land reform—mostly by delivering land to *ejidos*—than all of his predecessors put together. He instituted socialist education in the schools and expanded education generally. He reorganized the national labor union into the Confederation of Mexican Workers (CTM) and made this organization a much more aggressive and representative body. The minimum wage was raised. The old hacienda system was broken. A limited peace was achieved with the Church. The railroads were nearly all nationalized. Nationalistic artists were encouraged. A cultural nationalism blossomed. The ruling party, PNR, was reorganized to make it much more broad based and more truly representative of the people to the government, rather than, as it had been, from the government to the people. The name of the party was changed to Mexican Revolutionary Party (PRM).

Then, in 1938, came the major decision of the Cárdenas *sexenio*, the confrontation with big oil. Oil workers had gone on strike. By modern standards, their demands in regard to wages, hours, and working conditions were modest. But the oil interests, chiefly based in the United States and Great Britain, were adamant in their rejection of the demands and in their intention to crush the strike. When the companies showed their arrogance toward the president himself and, thus, toward Mexican sovereignty, Cárdenas invoked Article 27 of the constitution and nationalized the oil industry. He did not turn the industry over to the workers as they wanted, but he did create a public corporation, Petróleos Mexicanos (PEMEX), to run it. He saw to it that this public company dealt generously with the *petroleros*, or oil workers, as it has done ever since.

In the United States, the powerful oil industry called upon the United States to take action—from economic sanctions to outright invasion—to protect their oil holdings and businesses. The US government, and the government of Great Britain, were only too happy to back the companies. They boycotted Mexican oil and sought to isolate PEMEX from oil-production and exploration technology and technical assistance (thus, it turned out, forcing Mexico to build what is today a first-rate oil industry of its own).

Cárdenas had spent a great part of his term walking among the ordinary people of Mexico. Unannounced, he would visit small villages and, on the spot, sign orders for irrigation projects, for distribution of land, for clinics, and for other responses to local petitions that were humbly presented to him. The people of the country saw Cárdenas as one of their own. Now, with the expropriation of oil, the people—including even leaders of the Church and many conservatives—stood up with Cárdenas and with their country against the "greedy" oil companies and against foreign powers—particularly *el coloso del norte* ("the colossus of the North"), the United States. Never had there been such an outpouring of popular support for a president and his government.

Today, Cárdenas remains the greatest hero of Mexico's modern history. The anniversary of his birth and the anniversary of his expropriation of Mexico's oil are national holidays (by contrast, Calles is not considered to have been one of the "revolutionary family"). Under Cárdenas, Mexico's political system became more firmly institutionalized—in the presidency and in the official party (later renamed Institutional Revolutionary Party, PRI).

MEXICO SINCE 1940

Mexico's history since 1940 can best be capsulized by considering a series of "lasts" and "firsts" among its presidents during that period and earlier. Calles was the last presidential exemplar of *continuismo,* continued control past one term. Cárdenas (1934–1940) was the last of the openly and consistently leftist and populist presidents. After his *sexenio,* the Mexican government increasingly focused its attention and efforts on rapid economic growth—the *milagro mexicano* ("Mexican miracle")—to the detriment of economic equity.

Avila Camacho (1940–1946), chosen by Cárdenas to succeed him, was the last military man to serve as president. Interestingly, it was he who disbanded the military arm of the official party (though this action by no means eliminated the influence of the military on government and policy). Miguel Alemán Valdés (1946–1952) was the first civilian president popularly elected for a full term. He allowed new parties to form (some had formed earlier, too). But the PRI's monopoly was not seriously challenged. Alemán was the first Mexican president to exchange visits with a US president. Trade with the United States flourished, as did US private investment in Mexico. Alemán was the last president to devote a really substantial portion of Mexican public investment to agriculture. After his term, the trends toward rapid industrialization and urbanization were accelerated, and Mexico eventually became an urban nation and a net importer of food.

Gustavo Díaz Ordáz (1964–1970) was the last Mexican president to come from outside the metropolis of Mexico City, and he was the last president to have held prior elective office. His political experience did not protect his popularity, though, when economic conditions worsened. The legitimacy of the Mexican political system was seriously strained when students at the national university and other protesters mounted huge demonstrations against government policies and were brutally attacked, with many killed and imprisoned, at Tlatelolco. Still, Díaz Ordaz was the last president under whom Mexico's foreign debt was below double-digit billions of dollars. He was the last president, too, during whose administration the rate of inflation remained at tolerable levels and the value of the peso continued to be stable.

Luís Echeverría Alvarez (1970–1976) was the first of four "insider" presidents—Echeverría, José López Portillo, Miguel de la Madrid Hurtado, and Carlos Salinas de Gortari; each came from the Federal District, had built his career in federal-government positions, and had served in the cabinet of his predecessor. Echeverría was also the first president since 1954 to devalue the peso. He was the first president to lead Mexico into an activist role in foreign affairs, particularly in regard to its own region and Third World countries, and this role increasingly diverged from US policy. Echeverría was the first Mexican president to institute government-backed family planning—none too soon, since Mexico's population had gone from 16.5 million in the 1930s to around 51 million by 1970 (and over 80 million and growing by 1987).

José López Portillo (1976–1982) was the first Mexican president to expropriate Mexican private banks. He did so after hopes had soared at the beginning of his term, when new oil was discovered, only to plummet with a drop in world oil prices. This drop in prices, coupled with skyrocketing federal deficits, inflation, foreign borrowing, and two devaluations, as well as reports of widespread corruption, produced a crisis of confidence for his government.

Miguel de la Madrid Hurtado (1982–1988) was the first president to institute a *sexenio*-long austerity program, causing increased Mexican unemployment and poverty. Pressured to follow this course by the International Monetary Fund and the foreign banks that held Mexico's mammoth $100 billion foreign debt, he was the object of increasing public criticism and opposition during his term.

Carlos Salinas de Gortari (1988–1994) was the first modern president to take office with questioned legitimacy, his victory having been clouded by serious charges of widespread election fraud, as were previous PRI-claimed victories in certain northern state elections. He was the first president to face heavy parliamentary opposition and the first president whose inaugural ceremony in the great hall of the Chamber of Deputies was marred by a raucous demonstration and a protest walkout. Improvement in economic conditions and restoration of the legitimacy of the Mexican system—these were the fundamental challenges Salinas de Gortari had to confront. The economy was at first restored, and Salinas de Gortari signed the North American Free Trade Agreement. But it was suspected that after the nationalized banks and other enterprises were re-privatized, Salinas himself benefited personally, and after a *Zapatista* rebellion in Chiapas exploded and the handpicked PRI presidential candidate, Luís Donaldo Colosio, was assassinated, a severe financial crisis and economic depression ensued.

The succeeding PRI nominee and president, Ernesto Zedillo (1994–2000), was truly elected but took office when the legitimacy of the system and the hegemony of PRI were being challenged as never before. The brother of Carlos Salinas de Gortari was imprisoned for complicity in political assassination and for unlawful enrichment, and at the end of his term Carlos Salinas himself fled into exile. President Zedillo struggled to restore political and economic stability, and had at least the satisfaction of acquitting himself with honor, presiding over scrupulously fair elections in which for the first time ever in Mexican history an opposition candidate for the presidency won.

THE LEGACY OF REVOLUTION

Mexican politics and government are of course products of Mexican history. Authority is still concentrated in the national government and, within it, in the president. Mexicans have a justified cynicism about government and a skepticism about the rhetoric of candidates and officials. Yet at the beginning of each *sexenio,* there is hope anew (tinged, of course, with some skepticism). Each new president becomes the symbolic leader of the country as well as its official leader, the repository of national authority and national honor, and the focus of Mexican aspirations. For more than fifty years, the Mexican system was stable, and the country's governmental system generally was seen as legitimate by Mexicans—despite gross inequities that existed, and a good deal of misery. The "institutionalization" of the revolution and the legitimacy of the "official" PRI government faced serious questioning and challenge, however, after the early 1980s and in the 2000 elections the long hegemony of the PRI, the party of the Mexican revolution, was finally brought to an end.

MEXICO IN THE TWENTY-FIRST CENTURY

The present is a particularly difficult time for those who try to understand Mexican politics and economics. The system's parameters are undergoing a fundamental shift, and it is not clear, even to the major participants themselves, what directions change will take. To try to understand that change, we must understand its starting point.

The system might have been difficult to characterize, but it was not hard to understand. It was established after the Mexican revolution had stabilized. Behind the façade of a constitutional democratic system similar to that of the United States, it was dominated by a hegemonic political party growing out of the coalition of those who had fought successfully for the revolution. In this respect it was similar to other dominant parties that claimed origins in a national revolution, such as those in the developing countries of Africa and Asia, and even those in the Communist countries of Eastern Europe. Like them, its social and economic policies reflected at least in part its revolutionary and nationalist rhetoric. But after a period of experimentation the ruling elite had come to terms with the facts of the world capitalist system and Mexico's position as a neighbor of the dominant country in that system. Although the economy was mixed, with some government ownership of basic utilities and major industries and with central government guidance and planning, the bulk of the economy was in private hands, and foreign investment was encouraged.

The rules that were supposed to protect Mexico's independence from foreign control by carefully stipulating the areas in which foreign investment was allowed, and the circumstances in which only state investment or investment by private Mexican nationals was to be tolerated, could often be evaded. Indeed, evasion of the law was widespread, Political figures became wealthy by one means or another, and the various police forces of the republic were notorious more as a cause of crime than as a deterrent to it. But Mexico was not simply a kleptocracy, a government that existed only so that its rulers could steal; the ideals of the revolution lived on and were frequently embodied in policy, and many government officials were capable and progressive servants of the public interest.

The Political System

The formal political system resembles that of the United States in its major structural features, but it was modified to meet objections raised by opposition parties to the fact that the same party, the Institutional Revolutionary Party (PRI), occupied the presidency and dominated the legislature and the state governments from its founding in 1929 until 2000. Before the administration of President Zedillo, however, the changes in the system that made it easier for opposition parties to win lesser offices never threatened PRI control of the presidency or its majority in the federal legislature.

There is a constitutional separation between the president and the two houses of the legislature; they are elected independently of each other and each has powers specified in the constitution. The president is directly elected by the voters for a single six-year term and can never be reelected. Members of the senate, now four from each state (the number increased from two to make it easier for the opposition parties to elect senators), are not elected for staggered terms, as they were formerly, but all at the same time as the president. Members of the chamber of deputies are elected for three-year terms by a method similar to that pioneered by the German Federal Republic but increasingly adopted elsewhere; under it 300 members represent individual districts, but another 200 are chosen by proportional representation on party lists—again, so that opposition parties would have a better chance of electing representatives.

It is a federal system, with each state having its own constitutional structure and elections for governor and a single-chamber legislature. When the PRI dominated the system, gubernatorial autonomy was often overridden by high-handed presidential acts. President Carlos Salinas (1988–1994), especially, used to treat governors as though they were his political appointees, moving them into cabinet or party positions or ordering them to resign if he thought the local political situation required it.

President Ernesto Zedillo (1994–2000) found himself in a much weaker political position than Salinas, however. Not the most popular or politically skilled of possible successors, Salinas picked him (behind the formal procedures, the outgoing PRI president in effect designated his successor) after the popular nominee, Luís Donaldo Colosio, was assassinated under circumstances that have never been satisfactorily explained. Zedillo was never able to impose his authority on a disciplined PRI, and local party machines resisted his attempts to comply with promises to fully democratize and constitutionalize Mexican political life by guaranteeing honest elections, impartial media, and an uncorrupt police and judiciary.

Nevertheless, a 1996 reform diminished the possibility of political manipulation of election results by establishing an electoral tribunal independent of the executive branch (along with providing for the direct election of the governor of the Federal District, which includes Mexico City) and paved the way for an opposition victory in the 2000 presidential election.

The second oldest party, founded in 1940, is the PAN, the Party of National Action. Its leadership core has traditionally consisted of those educated in Catholic secondary schools and active in Catholic lay organizations, working in the professions and small business. But as its access to local and state-level political power grew, it attracted some big business support and the votes of opponents of the PRI regime from across the class and income structure. Its national organization is uneven, being stronger in the northern border states and some other specific regions, such as Yucatán, but its presidential candidate Vicente Fox, governor of Guanajuato, finally won the presidency in 2000, and it retained the presidency in the 2006 elections.

This meant fewer policy changes than might have been expected, since PRI policy positions had shifted to the center-right of the political spectrum, with acceptance of neoliberal economic theory. Thus the PRI and the PAN had already formed an implicit alliance on some policy issues in the legislature, especially when two-thirds of the votes were required to pass a constitutional amendment, more than the PRI could muster on its own.

Such cooperation was made necessary by the growth of the third major party, the PRD, or Democratic Revolutionary Party. The PRD developed out of a secessionist movement from the left of the PRI, a movement loyal to the nationalism, agrarianism (support of land reform), and semisocialism that had characterized the PRI's rhetoric, and to some extent its policy, before the shift to the right that began under President Miguel de la Madrid (1982–1988) and was carried further by Carlos Salinas (1988–1994). That secessionist movement managed to attract substantial support for its 1988 presidential candidate, Cuauhtémoc Cárdenas, the decidedly uncharismatic son of the leftist revolutionary general who served from 1934 to 1940 as probably the most popular president of Mexico ever.

While Salinas may perhaps have received more votes than Cárdenas, the official results were universally regarded with skepticism. Cárdenas's incompetent campaigning and indecision on policy questions, however, together with the apparent success of Salinas's economic policies and a strong showing by a dynamic PAN candidate, put the PRD in a weak third place in the 1994 presidential elections. The disgrace into which Salinas fell after the end of his term, however, led to an upswing in support for the PRD and the election of Cárdenas, then vindicated, as governor of the Federal District in 1997.

The PRD has held the governorship of the Federal District—essentially the mayoralty of Mexico City—since then, and the mayor who took office in 2000, Manuel López Obrador, proved able, popular, and a strong candidate for the presidency in 2006. By then, however, the PAN administration had managed to repoliticize the independent electoral commission set up by President Zedillo, and the 2006 election was characterized by a suspiciously narrow victory for the PAN candidate after López Obrador's lead disappeared during a computer malfunction.

With electoral reforms making for a multiparty system—essentially of three major parties and a few much smaller ones—with weak party discipline, President Vicente Fox (2000–2006) was unable to register any significant departures in policy, especially since control of the bureaucracy also eluded him. In historical retrospect, his achievement will simply be to have been elected and breaking the political monopoly of the PRI. The second president from the PAN, Felipe Calderón (2006–2012), more low-key and less dramatic than his predecessor, had to confront the indignant PRD street demonstrations against the election result; the failure of the United States to honor some provisions of NAFTA, such as the right of Mexican trucks to travel on US roads; a harsh campaign in the US against immigration from Mexico; then the consequences of the financial and economic downturn in the United States during 2008 and 2009, which meant declining revenue from trade, lower oil prices, and declining remittances from Mexicans working in the United States, further complicated by an epidemic of swine flu severe enough to cause hundreds of deaths and a lot of panic.

However, the major long-term policy problem the country faces is the deterioration of law and order as the burgeoning drug trade, primarily to supply US demand, means gang wars and assassinations, the corruption of the police and the judiciary, and increasing lawlessness and violence generally. Responding to pressure from US authorities, keen to seem to be doing something about drugs but afraid for political reasons to crack down on the availability of weapons or the replacement of the punitive approach to the problem by a medicalized "harm reduction" approach, Calderón assigned the Mexican army to antidrug operations in place of hopelessly corrupt police forces, only to see the same corruption and breakdown of discipline begin to affect the military too.

EXTRA-SYSTEM OPPOSITION

As the PRI moved to the right, it abandoned the principles of land reform under which land expropriated from large owners was owned in common (but usually farmed individually) by *ejido* collectivities. This provided the occasion for a revolt of rural workers who had been mobilized through Catholic liberation theology grassroots organizations by activists left over from the student movements of the late 1960s. Taking the name of the great agrarian reformer of revolutionary days, Emiliano Zapata, the movement was catalyzed in the southern border state of Chiapas by the collapse in coffee prices and competition from immigrant Guatemalan agricultural workers. As notoriously mistreated people espousing noble goals, the Chiapas Indians who made up the Zapatista forces that took up arms on January 1, 1995, and especially their ironic and quotable leader, Subcomandante Marcos, aroused sympathy among the Mexican public. Although the Zapatista forces were too weak to win any military victories, the government correctly perceived that a straightforward military attempt to wipe them out would create an endless Vietnam War in southern Mexico, with all the political costs that would entail, and instead settled down to an indefinite process of negotiating, making agreements that were never fully implemented and continuing tactics of local repression that fell below the radar of the major international media.

The mountainous state of Guerrero, which lies west and south of Mexico City, has always been home to bandit and even guerrilla forces. From time to time, guerrilla movements appear there and sometimes in other mountainous states, but it is out of the question that guerrilla movements of this kind could come to power by force. The country is too big, too complicated, and too sophisticated; as weak as the government may be, it is stronger by many orders of magnitude than any conceivable guerrilla army.

ECONOMIC STRUCTURE AND PERFORMANCE UNTIL 1980

The economic performance of the country was very impressive until the early 1980s. The long-term rate of growth in the gross national product between 1940 and 1980 was 7 or 8 percent annually. Industry grew, producing both for the domestic market and, under special tariff arrangements, for export; but today about 8 million Mexicans still work on the land. Commercial farmers in the north of Mexico grow many specialty crops, such as winter vegetables, that are exported to the United States and constitute a valuable source of foreign exchange.

Since the middle of the 1970s, Mexico's major industry and major export has been petroleum. Early in the century, before the coming of the automobile era, when demand for the product was limited, Mexico was the world's leading petroleum producer. The international oil companies were active in Mexico until 1938. They played the obstreperous role they have often played elsewhere, mixing in the country's politics to try to minimize their tax payments and labor costs and making themselves generally disliked. The 1938 expropriation of the oil companies by Lázaro Cárdenas was thus very popular in Mexico and was looked on as a kind of economic declaration of independence. After the expropriation, the international corporations got their crude elsewhere, however, and Mexican production declined to the level necessary simply to supply the domestic market. The state oil corporation, now called Petróleos Mexicanos (PEMEX), contented itself with producing mostly from established wells, lacking the incentive or the funds for serious exploration.

However, over the years, PEMEX built up the technical capabilities necessary for all phases of the industry—exploration, production, refining, and marketing—except for offshore drilling. With the development of an adverse balance of payments and the sharp rise in world petroleum prices that took place in the early 1970s, PEMEX undertook explorations that established Mexico's possession of huge reserves; in mid-1997 proven and potential reserves exceeded 300 billion barrels. Yet this figure represents the exploration of only a fraction of the sedimentary basins that could contain hydrocarbon deposits. Mexico advanced to fourth place among the world's petroleum producers and became the third largest exporter after Saudi Arabia and Venezuela.

The ambiguity of the economic system, which combined capitalism with a strong dose of nationalism and socialism, paralleled the ambiguity of the political system, whose democratic institutions were belied by its underlying authoritarian character. In foreign policy, similarly, Mexico combined a wariness of its giant neighbor that reflected a long history of intervention, insult, and loss of territory, with a lively appreciation of the relative political and economic power of the two countries, which meant that defiant confrontation was not a viable option. Thus, equally well-informed observers believed that Mexico had a nationalist foreign policy behind a façade of cooperation with the United States or that it had a policy of subservience to the United States behind a nationalist façade.

Despite its revolutionary rhetoric and the many social welfare and economic projects undertaken by the government, twentieth-century Mexico fell a long way short of meeting the goals of the revolution. Although Mexico's economic growth was undeniable, the benefits of that growth were concentrated in the upper and middle ranges of the income distribution. Moreover, privilege and corruption were widespread, and the country never came close to achieving full employment. Nevertheless, by the relative standards appropriate to an imperfect world, on the whole most observers accounted the Mexican experiment a success until late in the century.

Political stability was underwritten by economic growth. For most of the period, the economy grew steadily; indeed, Mexico had more years of continuous uninterrupted economic growth than any other country. The political system remained stable, and since 1920 the constitutional succession has been unbroken, although perhaps bent a few times. The possibility of a military seizure of power, a daily worry in many of the Latin American countries, has long been a thing of the past in Mexico.

There was room for steady expansion of the domestic market as remote rural areas and indigenous populations that had been self-sufficient were progressively incorporated into the national market. In a country that lacked so much, government expenditure on infrastructure—communications, social investment, or the provision of basic utilities—was bound to generate a substantial return. Mexico's geographic position next to the United States guaranteed a constant inflow of capital and income from tourism and border transactions, plus assembly plants (*maquiladoras*) in special duty-free zones importing components from and re-exporting the finished product to the United States. The steady stream of convertible currency that these activities provided normally made unnecessary the fiscal austerity to avoid inflation that put brakes on economic growth elsewhere. After the oil boom unbalanced the economy, however, poor handling of public finances led to a major crisis in each decade of the end of the century and the beginning of the next one.

THE INEVITABILITY OF CHANGE

When democracy triumphed with the collapse of the Soviet Union, so did the world capitalist system, which flexed its muscles and decided it no longer needed to tolerate socialist- or nationalist-inspired restrictions on its ability to seek maximum profits across state boundaries. So the classic Mexican mixed economy would have been under pressure to change in any case. However, the change in the Mexican economic model, like most major events in history, was overdetermined; that is, several factors were working in the same direction to make it happen.

It had been clear to students of development that the political and economic model that characterized the middle years of the century could not last indefinitely. For one thing, the social changes that were occurring would clearly put intolerable strains, sooner or later, on the single-party system. As the country developed so-cially, more students went to the university, more illiterates learned to read, more peasants moved to the city. A nation of illiterate peasants may believe that their government always does everything right and public officials are invariably com-petent and public-spirited. A nation of sophisticated urban dwellers led by a large university-trained elite is likely to be more skeptical. A growing managerial class is likely to chafe at government controls, and it is not possible to provide comfortable, well-paying positions for all members of a rapidly growing educated elite.

Mexico's steady economic growth was based on the gradual incorporation into the market of hitherto marginalized Indian peasants, gradually growing foreign earnings, and a stable exchange rate of the peso to the dollar. In the late 1970s, however, a volatile new factor was introduced into this equation when the rise in international petroleum prices made it worthwhile for PEMEX, the national oil monopoly, to incur the costs involved in exploring for new sources of petroleum. The tremendous reserves that were found made it possible for Mexico to earn huge amounts of money on the international oil market. But the sudden affluence brought by oil exports, like the touch of King Midas, proved in the long run a curse rather than a blessing. Corruption grew to new levels; the ready availability of foreign exchange made it easier to import everything than to produce it in Mex-ico, and Mexico's own factories closed down. Government employment mush-roomed, and growing inflation hurt the standard of living of everyone not in a position to benefit from oil revenues.

When the inevitable downturn in oil prices came, the government of President José López Portillo (1976–1982) refused to adjust and instead borrowed abroad to cover the government's inflated expenses, hoping that prices would quickly re-bound. When that didn't happen, Mexico's international creditors forced a drastic retrenchment in expenditures, so that all available resources could be devoted to paying down the debt. The result was that it was precisely those who had benefited least from the oil boom who were forced to bear the brunt of the policies of aus-terity that became necessary in its wake.

The abandonment by the governments of de la Madrid and Salinas of the dis-tinctive Mexican mixed economic model, as they moved to align Mexico with the norms of the world capitalist economy, was thus presented as a painful but neces-sary process of adjustment that would get the economy on a sound footing and make renewed growth possible. During Salinas's presidential term, it appeared that the formula was successful. The value of the currency stabilized, economic growth resumed, and for a while the ruling PRI seemed to have regained the legitimacy it had lost with the economic crisis.

The shift in the economic model was drastic, involving not only changes in the laws governing the freedom of action of foreign capital but also a colossal sell-off of industries that had been in the public sector and the introduction of private en-terprise norms into the reformed sector of agriculture, whose collectivist principles had until then been viewed as sacred cows of revolutionary ideology. Out of the profits of the privatization program (which would have been greater if state prop-erty had not been sold to the president's friends and family at bargain prices), Sali-nas managed to mount a significant poverty reduction program, called Solidarity, which softened the blow that structural reform dealt to Mexicans of lower income.

It also contributed to the president's popularity and looked for a time as though it could provide a new generation of political activists Salinas would use to replace the "dinosaurs" of the PRI party organization.

However, the economic stabilization successes of the Salinas administration were based in part on a sort of confidence trick. Long-term monetary stability and economic growth were financed by short-term and potentially volatile investment funds, many of them attracted into high-interest government bonds. Not wanting to damage his image as a financial wizard, which he thought would help him win the post of secretary-general of the new World Trade Organization, Salinas did not devalue the peso when it would have been appropriate to do so. His successor, Ernesto Zedillo, then mishandled the overdue devaluation, when it finally came, with the result that capital fled the country, the value of the peso dropped, and a new wave of foreign borrowing, "structural reform," and declining living standards ensued.

Much was hoped for from the North American Free Trade Area (NAFTA), which went into effect in 1995 and purported to integrate the economies of Mexico and Canada with that of the United States. Mexico already had a partially integrated zone along its US border, where *maquiladoras,* or assembly plants, could import raw materials and components from the United States and export finished products, without being subject to tariffs and other restrictions. As is the case with such arrangements, some interests benefited and some were disadvantaged, though the overall balance was supposed to be advantageous on both sides of the frontier. But a stronger power can be expected to bias the arrangement in its own favor (e.g., NAFTA allowed the free movement of capital but not of labor) and although provisions were added to the agreement embodying antipollution rules and fair labor practices, enforcement mechanisms were weakened by political pressures from US industry so as to make them ineffective. Meanwhile, capitalism's relentless pursuit of lower costs and higher profits meant that the jobs which had left the United States often did not stay long in Mexico before moving on to China.

SOCIAL STRUCTURE AND PROBLEMS

During the years of steady economic growth, before the borrowing, inflation, and austerity of the 1980s and 1990s, things gradually got better for most Mexicans. Life expectancy at birth, a good general measure of well-being, increased from forty-eight years in 1950 to sixty-eight years in 1986. Literacy climbed during the same period from about 66 percent to about 90 percent of the population. The high rate of annual population increase—which made social problems more difficult to resolve—dropped from 3.2 percent in the 1960s to 2.9 percent in the 1970s and 2.4 percent in the 1980s.

Thereafter, however, social indicators stopped improving and indicators of economic well-being deteriorated as gains in income were nullified and the average standard of living in the mid-1990s dropped back to about where it was in the 1960s. Income inequality increased. By 1995 the top 10 percent of Mexicans received 41 percent of national income, while 3.2 percent went to the 20 percent at the bottom of the scale. As much as half of the urban population lacks regular paid employment and makes do with occasional temporary work, street vending, marginal and dubiously legal activity. In the rural areas, about half of those engaged in agriculture are landless laborers, while most of the rest have small plots that provide hardly more than a subsistence living.

Problems of Mexico City

Even if the rate of population increase should decline further, however, it will come too late to avoid the onset of some major problems. The combination of population growth and migration to the cities has made Mexico City the largest urban agglomeration in the world. This has meant an avalanche of problems in the areas of housing, employment, transportation, sanitation, and so on. Government performance has fallen short of a satisfactory resolution of these problems, which were worsened by the effects of the 1985 earthquake. Unemployment and underemployment are acute; housing standards are uneven, ranging down to very poor in the satellite city of Netzahualcoyotl; and pollution sometimes reaches health-threatening proportions. Surface transportation can be an ordeal; a worker may have to travel as much as two hours each way to get to work and back each day. Construction of a subway system has alleviated the problems somewhat, however; the energetic mayor, Manuel López Obrador, and his successors from the PRD have generally been credited with making sincere efforts to attack the city's other problems, and even managed, at least for a while, to reduce corruption among the District's bureaucrats and police.

Change in the Political System

The political effects of these economic developments reinforced tendencies in the political arena that grew out of other causes. The general strategy adopted by the ruling PRI for dealing with the political pressures arising from the changes going forward in Mexican society was to negotiate a long drawn out strategic retreat that kept opposition political forces engaged in the political game and willing to channel their opposition into constitutional means within the system, by delivering a phased series of concessions. These, it was thought, were enough to enable the opposition parties to feel they were gaining ground but not enough to affect the substance of power at the national level. From time to time, electoral laws were reformed so as to enable opposition parties to win a few more legislative seats; some opposition victories in municipal elections were recognized. Over time, the concessions became greater: opposition victories were recognized for governorships, and senators from opposition parties were seated. Finally, all of the little changes coalesced into one big change, and political life in Mexico began to approximate the façade it had always had, that of a constitutional democracy.

After so many years of distinctiveness, Mexico faces the future of a "normal" country. Today, however, that means a country in which money strongly influences the media and the political process, and the PAN has given signs of wanting to make itself the permanent governing party by hook or by crook. Mexico is still next door to a hegemonic country dominated by powerful economic interests and is embedded in an unforgiving international financial system. Will it make any difference, in years to come, that Mexico was the locus of one of the great social revolutions of the twentieth century?

NOTES

1. The "Historical Foundations" section of this chapter was written by Fred R. Harris; "Mexico in the Twenty-First Century" by Martin C. Needler.

2. Raúl Béjar Navarro, *El Mexicano: Aspectos culturales y psicosociales* (Mexico City: Univérsidad Nacional Autónoma de México, 1979).

3. William C. McNeill, *Plagues and People* (Garden City, N.Y.: Doubleday Anchor, 1976), p. 207.

4. John Duffy, "Smallpox and the Indians in the American Colonies," in Roger L. Nichols, ed., *The American Indian: Past and Present,* 2d ed. (New York: Wiley, 1981), p. 64.

SUGGESTED READINGS

Barry, Tom, ed. *Mexico: A Country Guide.* Albuquerque, N.M.: Inter-Hemispheric Education Resource Center, 1992. A detailed report and analysis of Mexico's politics, government, and economy.

Basáñez, Miguel. *El Pulso de los Sexenios: 20 años de crisis en México.* 2d ed. Mexico City: Siglo XXI, 1991. An account of the shifts in popular attitudes as revealed in opinion polls.

Collier, Ruth Berins. *The Contradictory Alliance: State-Labor Relations and Regime Change in Mexico.* Berkeley, Calif.: International and Area Studies, 1992.

Grayson, George W. *The United States and Mexico: Patterns of Influence.* New York: Praeger, 1984. This is an excellent history and assessment of relations between Mexico and the United States, with particular emphasis on key issues, including marketing of oil and gas, policy toward Central America and Cuba, and illegal immigration of Mexicans to the United States.

Hellman, Judith Adler. *Mexico in Crisis.* 2d ed. New York: Holmes & Meier, 1983. A good critique of Mexican political practice from the left.

Informe. This annual report by Mexico's president is one of the most valuable sources on Mexican politics and policies. It consists of a compendium of figures, a review of the previous year's performance (hardly an impartial one, of course), and a prognosis of what is to come. The report is reproduced in the major newspapers, and it is usually made available as a separate document by the office of the president (and sometimes in translation by the US embassy).

Levy, Daniel, and Gabriel Székely. *Mexico: Paradoxes of Stability and Change.* 2d ed. Boulder: Westview, 1987. A brief text of outstanding quality, this book discusses Mexican politics and government from precolonial days to the time of President de la Madrid.

Lustig, Nora. *Mexico: The Remaking of an Economy.* Washington, D.C.: Brookings Institution, 1992.

Meyer, Michael C., and William L. Sherman. *The Course of Mexican History.* New York: Oxford University Press, 1979. This is a highly readable and well-researched history of Mexico from pre-Cortés times to the election of President José López Portillo.

Needler, Martin C. *Mexican Politics: The Containment of Conflict.* 3d ed. New York: Praeger, 1995. This general book covers the country's history, geography, economy, and social structure—as well as its politics—from the same point of view as this chapter.

———. *Politics and Society in Mexico.* Albuquerque: University of New Mexico Press, 1971. Interpretive essays, generally optimistic and favorable in tone.

Pastor, Robert A., and Jorge Castañeda. *Limits to Friendship: The United States and Mexico.* New York: Knopf, 1988. Two scholars who have also held high government positions have written alternating chapters in this illuminating book about US-Mexican relations and the misperceptions that have hampered greater cooperation.

Paz, Octavio. *The Labyrinth of Solitude.* Translated by Lysander Kemp. New York: Grove, 1961. A brilliant discussion of the national character of Mexico by one of the country's leading men of letters.

Philip, George. *The Presidency in Mexico.* New York: St. Martin's, 1992. Examines the terms of some recent presidents and takes into account psychological as well as political and economic factors.

Raat, W. Dirk, and William H. Beezley. *Twentieth-Century Mexico.* Lincoln: University of Nebraska Press, 1986. This highly worthwhile anthology contains chapters that usefully explain Mexico "from Porfirio Díaz to petrodollars."

Ruíz, Ramón Eduardo. *The Great Rebellion: Mexico, 1905–1924.* New York: Norton, 1980. This is a well-researched and fully footnoted study of the events, conditions, and leaders that made the Mexican revolution. It characterizes the revolution as a bourgeois revolt led by middle-class dissidents that did not produce the social and economic justice some of its rhetoric promised.

Selee, Andrew D., ed. *Mexico in Transition*, Washington, D.C.: Woodrow Wilson Center, 2003. Summary reports on various aspects of Mexico's society, economics, and politics by leading commentators.

Wilkie, James W., and Albert L. Michaels. *Revolution in Mexico: Years of Upheaval, 1910–1940.* New York: Knopf, 1969. This excellent sourcebook reprints works by various authors, as well as some original documents, and contains several useful chronologies.

Wolf, Eric. *Sons of the Shaking Earth.* Chicago: University of Chicago Press, 1959. Written by an anthropologist, this history of Mexico is particularly useful in regard to the pre-Cortés and colonial periods.

Womack, John, Jr. *Zapata and the Mexican Revolution.* New York: Random House, 1970. This is a detailed, step-by-step account of the Mexican revolution and the role of the heroic fighter for agrarian reform.

Chapter 16

CENTRAL AMERICA

From Revolution to "Low-Intensity Democracies"

THOMAS W. WALKER
AND CHRISTINE J. WADE

THE 1970S AND 1980s were a tumultuous time in Central America. Decades of economic and political marginalization resulted in violent struggles between the status quo and those challenging the system. The victory of the Sandinista Front for National Liberation (FSLN) in Nicaragua in 1979 gave way to revolutionary rule and a bloody and costly US-orchestrated counterrevolution for almost eleven years before its people elected a conservative government more compatible with the whims of Washington. Prolonged armed struggles between revolutionary insurgents and elite-dominated regimes led eventually to comprehensive peace settlements and democratization in El Salvador (1992) and Guatemala (1996). Although they avoided armed struggle, Honduras and Costa Rica were strongly buffeted by events taking place in neighboring countries.

The region's transitions to democracy were accompanied by changes in economic policy as well. The dominant economic model of the time, the so-called Washington Consensus, demanded strict adherence to neoliberal economic policies. The resulting structural reforms resulted in cuts in government bureaucracy and social services, the privatization of former government enterprises, the redirection of credit away from the peasantry into large private export activities, and a variety of other socially regressive policies designed to stimulate export. They were implemented to earn foreign exchange and ultimately service the region's enormous foreign debt. Many of these "neoliberal" policies were reminiscent of the laissez-faire, agro-export measures promoted by the region's liberal politicians of the late nineteenth and early twentieth centuries. The consequences of these policies had serious implications for the new democracies.

Although the violent conflicts ended, new threats to the civilian population and democratic governance emerged. Soaring crime, increasing marginalization and inequality, and corruption and impunity resulted in widespread loss of confidence and support for democratic governance in the region's most fragile countries. Less than two decades after the historic transitions, prospects for meaningful change had given way to "low-intensity democracies." After two decades of neoliberal policies, an increasingly dissatisfied populace brought the left to power in each of the Central American countries. Effectively resuscitating support for democratic governance would be the greatest challenge for these countries.

Contemporary Differences and Their Historical Determinants

Within this matrix of sweeping change, however, there were significant differences among the countries that deserve examination and explanation. Why, for instance, did Nicaragua, El Salvador, and Guatemala experience violent upheaval while Costa Rica and Honduras remained relatively peaceful? The answer, as John Booth, Christine Wade, and Thomas Walker have suggested, probably lies in five centuries of historical formation.[1] Put in very simple terms, the large native populations of what would become Guatemala, Nicaragua, and El Salvador were quickly conquered by invading Spaniards at the beginning of the sixteenth century, thus forming a vast, racially distinct underclass that could be exploited for the enrichment of a small European ruling class. In those countries the foundations of very inegalitarian societies were already firmly set within decades of the arrival of the conquistadors. In Costa Rica, in contrast, the native population resisted fiercely and, for their troubles, were largely exterminated or driven out of the fertile highlands where the Spanish eventually settled. With no racially distinct underclass to exploit, the society created by the Spanish settlers in Costa Rica was relatively more egalitarian. For its part, Honduras until the twentieth century was so underpopulated and such an economic backwater that a self-confident and exploitative ruling class was slow in developing.

By the 1970s, as a result of these distinct social histories, Costa Rica had developed a functioning democracy and welfare state; Honduran governments, though not always democratic, were normally willing at least to pay lip service to grassroots demands; and the dictatorships in the other three countries had become accustomed to responding with violence to growing demands for social justice from the impoverished majority. While social problems existed throughout the region, they had been allowed to build to explosive levels only in Nicaragua, Guatemala, and El Salvador. It was primarily this built-up pressure rather than some sort of sinister "communist" conspiracy—as the US government would claim—that led to the armed revolts of the 1970s and 1980s.[2]

The Revolutionary Three

Though Nicaragua, El Salvador, and Guatemala share the experience of prolonged armed revolt, only in Nicaragua did the insurgents actually seize power. It is interesting to ask why insurgents succeeded there and not in the other two countries. Perhaps the best explanation is given by Timothy Wickham-Crowley.[3] Rejecting single-factor theories, he argues that four conditions were met in Nicaragua that were not fully met elsewhere in Latin America, except in Cuba two decades earlier. (1) Nicaragua (and Cuba) had the right social conditions (an impoverished and exploited rural population living in very precarious circumstances). (2) There was an intelligent and flexible guerrilla movement. (3) The target regime was so despicable that it had alienated most of its political base. (4) The right international environment existed (i.e., a temporary lapse in US support for the local dictator).

Guatemala and El Salvador met only the first two conditions. In both countries, military and civilian presidents succeeded each other at relatively short intervals. Though brutal and undemocratic, these governments were hardly caudillo-dominated "mafiacracies" of the type run by Fulgencio Batista in Cuba or Anastasio Somoza in Nicaragua. As a result, much of the Salvadoran and Guatemalan upper and middle classes remained loyal to their respective regimes. In addition, alarmed by the Sandinista victory in Nicaragua, the United States—which had been immobilized by the contradictions inherent in trying to promote human rights in Somoza's Nicaragua—now focused on preventing leftist victories in the other two countries, often with little regard for human rights. Even though they did not come to power, the rebels in both countries eventually forced their foes to accept major changes in historically repressive systems as their price for peace.

Nicaragua

The Sandinista Period. From July 19, 1979, to April 25, 1990, Nicaragua had an avowedly revolutionary government. However, sobered by an awareness of the weakness of the socialist model of the Soviet Union and the Eastern European countries and some obvious excesses of the Cuban experiment (the cult of personality, overnationalization of the economy, etc.), the Sandinistas developed policies that were moderate and pragmatic.[4]

The Sandinista revolution can be divided into two periods: transition and reconstruction (1979–1984) and the constitutional period (1985–1990). The first was a time of innovation, experimentation, some excess, and a number of successes. In the second, the US-orchestrated Contra war, though never a military threat, inflicted such heavy economic and human damage that the revolution began to unravel and was eventually voted out of office.

The Period of Transition. The economic policy adopted during the period of transition and maintained thereafter favored a mixed economy. Confiscation of property was confined mainly to land and enterprises owned by ousted dictator Anastasio Somoza and his henchmen. Though these were turned into public enterprises or cooperatives or parceled out to the poor, around 60 percent of the productive capacity of the country remained in private hands throughout the revolution. Indeed, though very nervous about the intent of the Sandinistas, the private sector was actually encouraged, through favorable exchange rates and other measures, to remain productive.

Complementing these domestic economic policies, the Sandinistas pursued international policies—renegotiating and servicing the national debt and writing liberal foreign investment laws—designed to maintain Nicaragua's credit in Western circles. These policies paid off. From 1979 through 1983, Nicaragua's gross domestic product per capita grew a total of 7 percent, while Central America as a whole suffered a decline of 14.7 percent.[5] It was only in the wake of the full impact of the Contra war and a US-orchestrated international credit boycott that the Nicaraguan economy began to decline (1984) and then plummet (1985 onward).

The new government also oversaw innovative and highly successful social projects during this period. Inexpensive, grassroots-based programs for literacy (1980) and health (beginning in 1981) brought such positive change that by 1984 even President Reagan's Kissinger Commission had to admit that "Nicaragua's government has made significant gains against illiteracy and disease."[6]

There was also much innovation and some success in the area of politics and government. First, the government encouraged the creation or strengthening of massive grassroots organizations representing neighborhoods, women, youth, urban and rural workers, and peasants. These groupings in turn were given the responsibility of articulating the interests of their constituencies and delegated the task of implementing programs designed to help the people (the literacy crusade, health work days, neighborhood watch, etc.). By 1984, an in-house US embassy report placed membership in these organizations at 700,000 to 800,000, the equivalent of about half of the population aged sixteen or over.[7]

During this time the revolution moved from transitional to elected constitutional government. The first institutions of government were a multiperson executive, or junta; a corporative legislature (Council of State); and a judiciary composed of the usual lower and higher courts plus People's Anti-Somoza Tribunals set up to process Somoza-era war criminals but later used to deal with Contras. By 1983, however, the Council of State was writing election and party laws (designed with the advice of the Swedish Electoral Commission and modeled after Western European practices) that would produce a clean, competitive, internationally monitored[8] election in November 1984 and the swearing-in of a constituent assembly and an elected president, Daniel Ortega, in 1985.

Finally, in the area of human rights, Sandinista performance, though not perfect, was better than that of most other contemporary Latin American governments—and strikingly good compared with that of US client regimes in northern Central America. There were restrictions of civil liberties, as take place almost anywhere when a country is under siege, but freedom of religion was generally respected, there were no death squads, and extralegal deprivation of life was relatively infrequent.[9]

The worst problems Nicaragua encountered during the early 1980s were in foreign affairs, particularly with the United States. Though the Sandinistas (FSLN) repeatedly expressed their interest in having good relations with the superpower to the north, the victory of revolutionaries in Nicaragua—and the specter of a "second Cuba"—had alarmed Washington from the very beginning.[10] While the Carter administration was frigid but correct in its relations with the new government in Nicaragua, the Reagan administration, inaugurated in January 1981, immediately set out to destroy what it portrayed as a dangerous extension of Soviet and Cuban influence into Central America. It began training, equipping, and directing a Nicaraguan exile counterrevolutionary (Contra) army to fight against its own government, used its influence to block normal World Bank and Inter-American Development Bank loans to the upstart state, and orchestrated a massive propaganda campaign and program of dirty tricks to discredit the Sandinistas.[11]

The Constitutional Period. The second half of the Sandinista period was marked by both significant achievements and serious economic, social, and political setbacks. Respect for human rights continued at a relatively high level. New governmental institutions were created by the constituent assembly elected in 1984. After much open public debate, a new constitution was promulgated in 1987. That same year, an innovative autonomy law for the peoples of the Atlantic coast was formalized. Later, new parties and electoral laws were passed (1988) and amended (1989) laying the groundwork for a second clean, internationally supervised election in February 1990. Two months later, the losing FSLN turned over the reins of power to the victorious opposition.

But this was also a time of hardship that ultimately led to the defeat of the FSLN at the polls. The cost of the Contra war, US-orchestrated international economic strangulation, and some Sandinista mismanagement combined to produce such a collapse of the economy that by 1988 hyperinflation had reached over 33,000 percent annually. Though the Sandinistas implemented structural reforms that year and the next that would cut inflation to 1,690 percent by 1989,[12] the unemployment and social pain these early neoliberal policies caused were enormous. Added to this, cutbacks in government social programs and the tremendous human cost of the war (almost 31,000 dead and many more wounded and maimed)[13] created an environment in which the National Opposition Union (UNO)—organized, managed, and funded by the United States—was able to defeat the Sandinistas handily in the 1990 election.[14]

The Post-Sandinista Period.[15] Violeta Barrios de Chamorro, elected president with 55 percent of the vote, was inaugurated in April 1990. A political novice with a high school education, Chamorro eventually scored some important successes. Her economic policies cut inflation to relatively low levels and by the mid-1990s actually led to modest overall growth for the first time in over a decade.

Her greatest achievements, however, lay in the area of peacemaking and reconciliation. After months of negotiation, the Contra war was brought to an end in mid-1990. By cleverly allowing Sandinista general Humberto Ortega to oversee that otherwise difficult task, Chamorro was able to bring the size of the Sandinista People's Army down from over 80,000 to under 15,000. Finally, Chamorro steadfastly eschewed pressure from the United States (until 1993) and right-wing members of UNO to engage in a vengeful "desandinization" program for the country. As a result, a new political "normalcy" gradually developed. Negotiations in the National Assembly led to the promulgation of a new military code (1994) and some revisions in the 1987 constitution (1995). Elections on the Atlantic coast (1994) and nationwide (1996) were carried out without a major hitch. In January 1997, Chamorro passed the reins of office to Arnoldo Alemán of the National Liberal Alliance (ALN).

There were also notable failures in this period, many in the social area. The neoliberal economic policies urged on Nicaragua by Washington and the international financial community and enthusiastically implemented by the Chamorro administration pummeled the poor majority. The downsizing of government, cutbacks in social services, privatization of state enterprises, the credit emphasis on agro-export rather than peasant production of domestic foodstuffs, and so on, combined to exacerbate the misery of ordinary people. Unemployment, underemployment, crime rates, drug addiction, domestic violence, and homelessness (especially among children) soared.

This was accompanied by a growing cynicism about politicians and government institutions. In ethically dubious, self-serving legislation, some top Sandinista leaders had appropriated large amounts of property in the last months of their administration. Also it soon appeared that both Arnoldo Alemán and Antonio Lacayo (Chamorro's son-in-law) had increased their fortunes through corruption while serving, respectively, as mayor of Managua and minister of the presidency before launching their presidential campaigns in 1996. Thus, ironically, while Nicaraguans retained faith in elections and the electoral process, many by the mid-1990s were bitterly skeptical about politicians, parties, and most institutions of government.

The unprecedented corruption of the Alemán administration further depleted funds that might have been available to help impoverished Nicaraguans. This corruption, combined with the further destruction of the social service infrastructure, defined Alemán's presidency. It was dramatically illustrated in the wake of Hurricane Mitch in October 1998, which left 2,400 Nicaraguans dead and another 700,000 displaced. Spending cuts in social services and the armed forces left the Nicaraguan government incapable of responding to the crisis in any meaningful way, and it relied heavily on international aid. When Alemán tried to channel relief funds through departments where the Liberal Party (PLC) was in control or through Liberal Party headquarters where it was not, international donors resorted to the unusual practice of channeling assistance through nongovernmental organizations rather than the government.

Negotiations between Alemán and Daniel Ortega hurt Nicaragua's democracy in late 1999 with the Ortega-Alemán Pact, which sought to consolidate the emerging two-party system. The electoral laws passed in early 2000 by the FSLN/PLC legislative majority represented an effort to eliminate third parties.[16] Additionally, the Supreme Court, the Office of the Comptroller General, and the Supreme Electoral Council were all packed with FSLN/PLC partisans. Finally, former presidents were made legislators for life and hence received immunity from prosecution.

The 2001 elections were relatively clean procedurally despite being designed to favor the two major parties. Enrique Bolaños, Alemán's vice president, defeated the FSLN's Ortega by pledging to battle corruption and impunity in Nicaraguan politics. Ortega argued, with justification, that the United States had actively worked to prevent his reelection. As in 1990 and 1996, US pressure shaped the outcome of the 2001 elections. Playing on the events of September 11, 2001, the United States alleged connections between Ortega and "terrorists," while actively supporting the Bolaños candidacy. When Bolaños entered office in 2002, he appealed to the National Assembly to repeal Alemán's legislative immunity and used the legal system to pursue him and other individuals in his corrupt administration. While Alemán was convicted and sentenced for his crimes, the Supreme Court overturned his conviction in January 2009. The battle over Alemán's prosecution provoked a constitutional crisis that paralyzed the Nicaraguan government.

The FSLN's Daniel Ortega returned to power following the 2006 elections. Ortega, who traded in his revolutionary image in favor of peace, love, and reconciliation, narrowly won the presidency with 38 percent of the vote. The FSLN also won the most seats in the National Assembly (38), followed by the PLC with 25, the ALN with 24 and the MRS with 5. Ortega implemented numerous policies, including health, education, and literacy programs, to address Nicaragua's persistent poverty. He also established citizens' power councils (CPCs) to administer antipoverty programs at the local level. These achievements, however, were undermined by accusations of fraud in the 2008 municipal elections, the most contentious in nearly two decades. Preelection violence, a ruling by the Supreme Electoral Council (CSE) that prohibited two of the smaller parties from participating, and the denial of accreditation to international and independent election observers led even regime supporters to question the validity of the results. The FSLN reportedly won 105 of the 146 municipalities where voting occurred. Protests and allegations of fraud followed, which led to the suspension of aid from the European Union and United States. In 2009 a Supreme Court packed by Ortega issued a ruling that allowed him to run for office again in 2011, potentially further consolidating his power.

El Salvador

Insurgency and Counterinsurgency: 1979–1992. The 1970s had been a time of tremendous mobilization in Salvadoran society. Social democratic and Christian democratic parties as well as segments of the Catholic Church and even USAID and the US Peace Corps had promoted development projects and grassroots participation. Salvadoran elites and the military regimes they supported, however, responded to it with repression. Apparent opposition victories in both the 1972 and 1977 elections were overturned as increasingly brutal military regimes used security forces and associated death squads to kill party, interest group, and religious leaders working with the masses. Responding to this repression, groups of various political affiliations fielded small guerrilla armies that united in 1980 to form the Farabundo Martí National Liberation Front (FMLN).

The Sandinista victory in Nicaragua alarmed the status quo and heartened popular organizations in El Salvador. Convinced that it was now possible to topple the dictatorship, the FMLN began preparing for its (unsuccessful) "final offensive" of 1981. At the same time, sobered by events in Nicaragua, the Salvadoran elite and the US government took measures to prevent a repetition. Within days of the Nicaraguan victory, planners in Washington had decided that in order to justify beefing up the Salvadoran military, the existing regime would have to be replaced with a cosmetically more acceptable government run by a junta combining both progressive military and civilian members.[17] On October 15, 1979, a military coup by "moderates" essentially implemented this objective.

For the following twelve years, the forces of the status quo pursued a two-pronged strategy for containing revolution. On the one hand, until the end of the Cold War, Washington insisted on military victory over the insurgents. The United States spent over $6 billion in aid—much of it military aid to security forces that were responsible for killing most of the 75,000 people (mainly civilians) who died during the conflict—in its war against "communism." Though Salvadoran regimes would occasionally go through the motions of negotiating, no serious effort to arrive at a peace accord was made.

On the other hand, in order to get a reluctant US Congress to provide the arms necessary to implement the overall military strategy, it was also necessary for Salvadoran governments to appear both democratic and progressive. Accordingly, after several years of civilian-military juntas in which civilians had no real power, elections for a constituent assembly (1982) and then president (1984) were held. Staged against a background of state-sponsored terror and in the absence of a free press, these elections—in which voting was obligatory and the sequentially numbered, translucent ballots were deposited in clear plastic ballot boxes—produced the presidencies of conservative Christian Democrat José Napoleón Duarte in 1984 and right-wing Nationalist Republican Alliance (ARENA) Party member Alfredo Cristiani in 1989.

At the same time, government social policy took an apparently more humane turn. Immediately after the Sandinista victory in Nicaragua, Salvadoran regimes (under tremendous US pressure) actually seemed to be competing in the social realm with the Nicaraguan revolution.[18] The first junta, like the Sandinista government, implemented sweeping agrarian reform programs and nationalized the banking industry. Though some of this reform was stillborn and much of the rest was reversed after a right-wing victory in the 1982 constituent assembly elections, heavy aid from the United States allowed various civic action and other programs to continue throughout the period.

Meanwhile, responding to international reality, the FMLN modified its objectives in the early 1980s. By 1982 the guerrillas had come to realize that an all-out victory would, in the words of their civilian ally Rubén Zamora, "be ashes in our mouths."[19] They had seen what the United States was already doing to the Nicaraguan revolution. Although they still had confidence that they could win militarily, they had decided instead to fight only until the regime agreed to a peace treaty instituting major changes in the military, political, and social character of the system.

The war dragged on, with Washington and the Salvadoran military pushing for all-out victory and the guerrillas fighting to achieve a negotiated settlement. By the end of 1989, the stalemate was beginning to break. Early that year the government refused an opposition request to delay the national election in order to institute democratic safeguards so that FMLN candidates might participate. That November, in response, the FMLN staged a massive assault on San Salvador, taking over and holding whole neighborhoods for weeks at a time. In addition, under the cover of the turmoil, the US-trained Atlacatl Battalion entered the grounds of the Central American University and executed six prominent Jesuit intellectuals, their maid, and her daughter.

As a result of all this, it was clear that (1) the FMLN was still alive and effective and (2) the regime was still badly in need of reform. Thus when the Soviet Union collapsed a little over a year later, the Bush administration decided to cut its losses in El Salvador by reversing its position on negotiations. As a major report on El Salvador prepared for the US Defense Department put it, with the end of the Cold War, "'Winning' in El Salvador no longer matters much. A negotiated solution, or even 'losing,' would no longer carry the same ominous significance."[20] Now, with the full backing of Washington and even such right-wing Salvadorans as Roberto D'Aubuisson, the United Nations could move ahead and broker a formal peace.

The Imperfect Peace: 1992 Onward. The peace accords of January 1992 encompassed most of the reforms and changes the FMLN had proposed almost a decade earlier. Under UN supervision, the government was to depoliticize and drastically reduce the size of its army. It was obliged to abolish "rapid deployment" forces (such as the Atlacatl Battalion), the treasury police, and the National Guard. The hated national police would be replaced by a civil police as veterans of the conflict would be drawn equally from both sides and, together, would constitute less than half of the force. An ad hoc commission was to be named to provide a list of war criminals to be purged from the armed forces. After that, a truth commission was to make a report on war crimes committed by both sides and by civilians. On another plane, there were to be significant reforms of electoral mechanisms and the judiciary. And land and resources were to be set aside to resettle former combatants from both sides. In return, the FMLN was to demobilize.

The peace accords were in fact implemented, if imperfectly and slowly. The FMLN demobilized, if a bit behind schedule, and turned over most—but apparently not all—of its weapons.[21] The ad hoc and truth commissions performed their duties bravely. The armed forces were reduced, reorganized, and purged, though at a slow pace and not as originally stipulated. Sweeping changes were made in the police forces, though not to the extent envisioned in the accords. Limited changes were made in the corrupt judicial system. In 1994 a closely observed national election took place in which the FMLN was allowed to participate—but not on a "level playing field."[22] As a result of the 1994 election, the candidate of the ruling ARENA Party, Armando Calderón Sol, was inaugurated president on June 1. Though ARENA won the largest bloc of seats in the Legislative Assembly, the FMLN came in second ahead of the Christian Democrats, who had been discredited by corruption and ineffective rule.

Calderón Sol deepened Cristiani's neoliberal program by reducing tariffs, increasing the already regressive value-added tax from 10 to 13 percent, privatizing the Salvadoran telecommunications and electrical industries, and establishing a convertibility plan that pegged the Salvadoran colón to the US dollar. This uncompromising pursuit of neoliberal policies was the source of great tension within ARENA, pitting the industrialists against the traditional agricultural elites. From 1990 to 1995, economic growth averaged 6 percent annually but dropped to only 3 percent from 1996 to 2000.[23] Despite overall economic growth, poverty remained rampant with nearly half of Salvadorans living below the poverty line.[24]

The FMLN capitalized on ARENA's internal troubles and increasing public dissatisfaction with neoliberal policies in the 1997 legislative and municipal elections, winning twenty-seven legislative seats and forty-eight mayoral contests, including the capital. While ARENA maintained a majority of the seats in the Legislative Assembly and mayoralities, the FMLN clearly demonstrated its fortitude as a political party. The FMLN's electoral success at the legislative and municipal levels failed to translate into a presidential win in the 1999 presidential elections. FMLN candidate Facundo Guardado was easily defeated by ARENA's Francisco Flores.

The Flores administration continued the neoliberal thrust of his predecessors, overseeing conversion to the US dollar in 2001. The plan to privatize segments of the health care sector resulted in two bitter and prolonged strikes, which occurred against the backdrop of the 2000 and 2003 elections. Like his predecessors, Flores resolutely applied the neoliberal model. However, El Salvador managed to avoid significant popular opposition to the neoliberal model due to the influx of remittances from Salvadorans living abroad, which were $2 billion in 2002.[25]

In the 2000 elections the FMLN became the largest political party and secured some of the largest municipalities, gaining four seats in the Legislative Assembly and winning seventy-seven (ten in coalition races) mayoralties. While the FMLN did not make significant gains in the 2003 legislative and municipal elections, the party kept its thirty-one seats in the Legislative Assembly while ARENA lost two seats. Additionally, the FMLN retained its mayoral post in San Salvador despite losing popular two-time mayor Héctor Silva as a candidate. Little more than a decade after the signing of the peace accords, the FMLN had clearly demonstrated its potency as a political party. Such potency caught US attention, prompting the former US ambassador and other officials to express their "concern" over the prospect of a FMLN presidential victory in 2004.

The FMLN, however, did not win the election. Former guerrilla commander Shafik Handal was easily defeated in the first round of voting by ARENA's Antonio Elías Saca. Saca continued ARENA's neoliberal policies, using populist rhetoric to appeal to voters in the *campo*. Saca's method of dealing with crime and social unrest was to replace failed *mano dura* (iron fist) policies with super *mano dura* and an antiterrorist law that criminalized most forms of protest.

In 2009, for the first time since 1994, elections for all offices were held at once.[26] Twenty years of ARENA's neoliberal policies had yielded little socioeconomic progress in a country increasingly dependent on remittances, which totaled $3.8 billion in 2008. Moreover, the failure of *mano dura* policies to reduce crime made El Salvador the most violent country in the hemisphere and one of the most violent in the world. In 2007 the homicide rate was 67 per 100,000. The FMLN nominated popular television journalist Mauricio Funes as its presidential candidate. Funes, who had not been a guerrilla, offered a more centrist option than prior candidates. ARENA, which had been in power since 1989, selected former national police director Rodrigo Avila. Throughout the campaign, ARENA revived its Cold War rhetoric, frequently referring to the "socialist threat" posed by an FMLN victory. The message lacked the potency of 2004 thanks, in part, to the moderate Funes, who defeated Avila in the first round of voting. His inauguration in June 2009 represented the first transfer of power from one party to another in competitive elections.

Guatemala

The Guatemalan experience in the same period bore both striking similarities to and important differences from that of El Salvador. As in El Salvador, bloody civil war raged throughout the late 1970s and 1980s, and the possibility for real peace emerged only after the Cold War ended and Washington changed its policies. And as in El Salvador, the guerrilla strategy of fighting to reform a brutal system seemed to pay off by 1996. However, unlike the case in El Salvador, the US role in the conflict—though very real—was somewhat less visible, and the Guatemalan military appeared to be a bit more autonomous. In addition, the peace settlement would be negotiated (and implemented) in a step-by-step fashion over a period of more than half a decade rather than all at once as in El Salvador.

By the late 1970s, Guatemala had already experienced almost two decades of bloody civil war. Frustrated by the destruction of the democratic revolution in 1954 and by a US-approved military coup that blocked the return to elected civilian rule in 1963, some Guatemalans turned to armed insurrection. In response, the United States trained the Guatemalan army and security forces in the methods of counterinsurgency and "counterterror." By 1966, death squads had begun to operate and the term "disappeared" was first used as a noun to refer to victims of these tactics. By 1979, thousands of people—mainly civilians—had already been killed and a long series of military dictatorships had ruled the country.

As in El Salvador, US policy toward Guatemala was often two-tracked.[27] On the one hand, there was the primordial need to "stop communism." On the other, it was always important to appear concerned with human rights and democracy. Early in his administration, Jimmy Carter's criticism of Guatemalan human rights violations led to a rupture in the flow of open military aid to that country. Though Washington obviously hoped for a Salvador-type coup that would justify a resumption of such aid, the military clung to power until the mid-1980s, thus making it impossible to get such assistance approved by Congress. To some extent, the Reagan administration got around the problem by relabeling as "civilian" such obviously military items as helicopters; by successfully pressuring Israel—the world's leading recipient of US assistance—to increase arms assistance to Guatemala; and by continuing both covert CIA assistance and the US military's counterinsurgency advisory role.[28]

But by the early 1980s things seemed to be getting out of hand. President/General Lucas García (1978–1982) sharply increased already high levels of repression. As a result, the divided guerrilla opposition came together in one organization, the Guatemalan National Revolutionary Unity (URNG), in 1982. Replacing Lucas in a coup d'état that same year, President/General Efraín Ríos Montt increased the repression even more. Altogether, in a scorched-earth war that lasted from 1981 through 1983, between 100,000 and 150,000 civilians were killed, hundreds of villages were destroyed, and over 1 million persons were displaced.[29]

Though the United States had approved of Guatemala's dirty war, it eventually pushed for the emergence of a more cosmetically acceptable system. The vehicle for this policy was General Oscar Humberto Mejía Victores, who overthrew Ríos Montt in 1983. Though the brutality did not cease, a new constitution was written, an election was held, and a civilian president, Christian Democrat Vinicio Cerezo, was inaugurated in 1986.

It would be hard to argue that democracy in Guatemala was born again in 1986. Though the constitution was a reasonably good one and the elections were fairly clean from a procedural standpoint, the fact that the former was frequently violated, that the latter had been held against a background of state-sponsored terror, and that the military, rather than the new president, continued to hold real power obviated such claims. Nevertheless, an atmosphere of possibility began to emerge. For its part, the URNG—by now convinced that outright military victory was neither possible nor desirable for the guerrillas—began calling for a negotiated settlement. In August of the following year, President Cerezo and the other four presidents of Central America signed the Esquipulas Peace Accord, which, after the end of the Cold War four years later, would serve as a rough framework for peacemaking in Guatemala.

With its ally's surface "democratization" in the mid-1980s, the Reagan administration was able to get Congress to approve military aid for Guatemala. The war dragged on, and not much was done to promote a general settlement throughout the rest of the Cerezo administration.

However, as the Cold War was winding down, the Catholic Church and then important civilian groups began to establish a dialog with the URNG. Finally, in 1991, newly inaugurated, conservative president Jorge Serrano began negotiating directly with the guerrillas. In 1992 an agreement on democratization and some discussion of human rights took place. The following year, after Serrano tried (and failed) to seize dictatorial powers, he was removed from office by the military and replaced with former human rights ombudsman Ramiro de León Carpio. Though negotiations stalled for a while, they picked up again in January 1994 and resulted in a framework accord for the negotiation of a settlement to be brokered by the United Nations. This was followed in rapid succession by a global human rights accord in March and two accords in June, one dealing with the resettlement of displaced populations and the other with the creation of a truth commission. In March 1995 a landmark identity and rights of indigenous peoples accord was signed—very important for a country in which over 60 percent of the population is indigenous.

In November 1995, the possibilities of a comprehensive peace moved forward as Alvaro Arzú, a conservative who understood that civil war is bad for business, was elected president. Negotiations were accelerated. In March 1996, the URNG declared an open-ended cessation of hostilities, and the army soon followed suit. This was followed in September by the landmark Accord on the Strengthening of Civilian Power and the Function of the Army. Finally, in December, the two sides signed a "definitive cease-fire," an "Accord on Constitutional and Electoral Reforms," "Bases for the Incorporation of the URNG into Legality," and, at the end of the month, the final comprehensive peace settlement. All said, these appeared to constitute a truly revolutionary end to the war.

The revelry of the Guatemalan peace process was short-lived. In April 1998 Bishop Juan Gerardi was assassinated shortly after his report *Recovery of Historical Memory* (REMHI) revealed atrocities committed during the war, most of which were attributed to the armed forces. This tragedy was a sober reminder that the road to peace would not be smooth.[30] This atmosphere was reinforced when the truth commission report was unveiled in 1999. President Arzú downplayed the report and openly rejected the commission's recommendations. The peace accords received another blow in May 1999, when a referendum on constitutional reforms (including judicial and military reform) required to implement some provisions of the accords was defeated at the polls.

Arzú's failure to address the socioeconomic concerns of the Guatemalan people was a far greater factor in the 1999 elections than issues surrounding the peace accords. Alfonso Portillo, candidate of a rival conservative party, the Guatemalan Republican Front (FRG), easily defeated the PAN candidate in the second round. The FRG, whose membership included numerous former army officers, dominated the congress—with former dictator Ríos Montt presiding.[31] Portillo fared no better than his predecessors in battling corruption, improving social conditions, or furthering the peace accords. His administration was plagued by corruption and stagnation.

Guatemala's peace process had not been as successful as El Salvador's. The lack of political will was the most persistent problem in ensuring their successful implementation. Additionally, the URNG did not hold the political clout or support that the FMLN continued to enjoy in El Salvador. As such, many important terms of the peace accords were ignored or delayed. Additionally, human rights abuses and intimidation of human rights workers persisted in Guatemala. Maneuvers by Rios Montt, whose candidacy was outwardly shunned by the United States, to insert himself into the 2003 presidential race further demonstrated that Guatemala's peace was imperfect.

Although he came in a distant third, Ríos Montt won nearly 20 percent of the vote.[32] His presence was enough to force a second round of voting between National Unity of Hope (UNE) candidate Alvaro Colom and Great Alliance (GANA) candidate Oscar Berger. Former Guatemala City mayor Berger defeated Colom in the second round, promising jobs and a renewed focus on peace accords. As in other Central American countries, Guatemala experienced a surge in social violence after the end of the civil war. Unlike other Central American countries, much of the crime was conducted by organized crime syndicates and clandestine security organizations that had never been fully dismantled following the war.[33] Femicides were a particularly troubling aspect of the crime wave. More than 2,000 young women were murdered between 2002 and 2007. Few of these crimes were ever prosecuted, demonstrating both institutional ineffectiveness and high levels of corruption. To deal with the growing problem, the Berger administration and the United Nations created the International Commission Against Impunity in Guatemala (Comisión Internacional Contra la Impunidad en Guatemala—CICIG) to "investigate and dismantle violent criminal networks," assist in prosecutions, and recommend policies, including the 2007 murders of three Salvadoran representatives to the Central American Parliament (PARLACEN) and their driver.

The 2007 election season was particularly violent, with more than fifty congressman, candidates, and activists killed in preelection violence.[34] UNE candidate Alvaro Colom narrowly won the first round of voting and faced retired general Otto Pérez Molina of the Patriot Party (Partido Patriota–PP) in a runoff. Colom defeated Pérez Molina in the second round, 53 percent to 47 percent. Increasing crime and violence threatened Colom's government and distracted from the country's glaring social problems. More than half of the population lived below the poverty line in the most unequal country in the region. The situation was even more dire for the country's indigenous population, whose poverty rate was 12 percent higher than the rate for ladinos.[35]

The "Tranquil Two"

Honduras

Having experienced decades of military rule, Honduras was certainly no democracy as it entered the period examined in this chapter. However, its military differed from that of the three neighboring republics in that it responded to grassroots mobilization with reform and cooptation rather than repression.[36] As a result, tiny guerrilla groups that appeared in the 1960s and 1970s never gained legitimacy or support.

In the late 1970s, as part of its policy of promoting human rights, the Carter administration began pressuring Honduras to return to democratic forms. The regime of President/General Policarpio Paz García responded by holding constituent assembly elections in 1980 and full national elections in 1981. The winner of the presidential race, Liberal candidate Roberto Suazo Córdova, was inaugurated early in 1982.

As it turned out, Suazo Córdova was president in name only. By the time he donned the sash of office, the United States was deeply involved in containing "communism" in El Salvador and programming the Contra war in Nicaragua. Nestled between the two, Honduras was seen as an ideal base of operation for many aspects of these two projects. Salvadoran military personnel would be trained in Honduras to circumvent a ceiling the US Congress had placed on the number of US military advisers to be sent to El Salvador. Honduran and Salvadoran forces would perform pincer operations on the border to annihilate Salvadoran civilian populations thought loyal to the guerrillas. Nearly continuous joint US-Honduran military "training" exercises—designed to intimidate the Sandinistas—would be conducted on Honduran territory close to the Nicaraguan border. Several US military bases would be built. And Honduran troops and civilians would be moved out of some territory bordering Nicaragua to allow the Nicaraguan Contras sanctuaries out of which to operate against their own government.

To do all of these things, the United States worked closely with the Honduran military while essentially ignoring the weak civilian government. In the early 1980s, Honduras received hundreds of millions of dollars in US aid, much of it military. CIA asset General Gustavo Alvarez became the head of the military and virtual dictator of the country in 1982. For the first time in Honduran history, "death squads" became active, as opponents to the military were murdered or disappeared by the hundreds. Meanwhile, Alvarez and his clique reportedly "embezzled over $30 million of public funds."[37]

By 1984, Alvarez, who had gone beyond bounds acceptable even to the military, was replaced in an internal military coup by another general with CIA connections, Wálter López Reyes. From then until the end of the Cold War, a growing segment in Honduran society would call for a return to real civilian rule, an end to human rights abuses, and greater US respect for their country's sovereignty. Nominal civilian presidents came and went as Suazo Córdova was succeeded in 1986 by fellow Liberal José Azcona Hoyos, who in turn passed the presidential sash to Nationalist Leonardo Callejas in 1990.

In August 1987, Honduras agreed to the Esquipulas peace framework for Central America. However, under pressure from the United States (which was still pursuing the dream of military victory over the "communists" in Nicaragua and El Salvador), it failed to fulfill its obligation to prevent its territory from being used by irregular troops (the Contras) attacking the government of a neighboring country (Nicaragua). Widespread dissatisfaction with US and Contra troops in Honduras simmered throughout the 1980s. On April 7, 1988, after the United States engineered the illegal extradition of an accused drug trafficker from Honduras, thousands of enraged students set fire to the US consulate building in Tegucigalpa. It is probably significant that the Honduran police took over two hours to respond to calls for assistance from the embassy.

In the long run, the Honduran people would have to wait until the end of the Cold War and the demobilization of the Contras for their country to return to some form of normalcy. Even then, Rafael Leonardo Callejas in the early 1990s would refuse to reform the military, and human rights abuses, a legacy of the early 1980s, would continue at high levels. To make matters worse, as part of an overall package of neoliberal reforms, the Agricultural Modernization Act was passed in 1992 that partially dismantled Honduras's earlier agrarian reform laws, thus threatening the interests of members of agricultural cooperatives.

Understandably, the 1994 inauguration of human rights lawyer Carlos Roberto Reina of the Liberal Party as president inspired hope in many Hondurans. The new president, while pursuing generally neoliberal economic policies, was at least willing to negotiate with those sectors of society (peasants, workers, etc.) on which these policies had the biggest negative impact. In addition, he moved decisively to curb the inordinate power of the military. The secret police was abolished. Obligatory military service was ended in 1994. In 1997 police control was transferred from the military to civilian authority, and a civilian police force was created. Military officers charged with atrocities during the early 1980s were tried and their convictions were upheld by the Supreme Court—despite three amnesty laws passed during previous, more subservient administrations. The administration also ended military control of various nonmilitary entities such as the telecommunications industry and immigration services.

In 1997 Carlos Flores Facussé of the Partido Liberal (PLH) defeated former Tegucigalpa mayor Nora Gunera de Melgar of the Partido Nacional (PN).[38] Flores's economic plan proposed to strengthen the neoliberal model through expanding the maquila industry, increasing tourism, and strengthening the agro-export sector. The neoliberal reforms of the 1990s exacerbated decades of environmental devastation, including deforestation, soil erosion, and urban migration.[39] Many peasants displaced by agribusiness settled on the unstable hillsides of Tegucigalpa and Choluteca. The results would be horrific.

In October 1998, Hurricane Mitch devastated Honduras. Official records indicate 5,657 dead, 8,058 missing, 12,272 injured, and 1.5 million displaced. Many of those affected were migrants who had settled on the crowded hillsides surrounding Tegucigalpa. Some 35,000 homes were destroyed and another 50,000 damaged. The hurricane caused nearly $4 billion in economic losses. The costs of Hurricane Mitch forced Honduras to seek relief under the World Bank's Heavily Indebted Poor Countries (HIPC) initiative, permitting the suspension of payments on its $4.4 billion debt until 2007 and cancellation of $768 million of its debt balance.[40] The military's incompetent response to Hurricane Mitch prompted congress to further demilitarize the country. In 1999 the military was placed under civilian rule, the president was given direct command of the armed forces, and the first civilian defense minister with real power was appointed.

Like other Central American countries, Honduras experienced a prolonged crime wave. Gang activity, extrajudicial killings, and common street crime became all too frequent in Honduras. Much of the crime wave was blamed on youth gang activity, despite the fact that only a small portion of the murders committed in Honduras were attributed to gangs. One of the most disturbing trends of the crime wave was the extrajudicial killings of Honduran youth. Between 1998 and 2002 more than 1,500 youths were murdered, over 40 percent of them under the age of 18. Human rights organizations, such as Casa Alianza and Amnesty International, attributed some of these deaths to "social cleansing" by state police and private security forces. Equally disturbing is the impunity with which these murders were committed.[41]

Crime was a major theme of the 2001 presidential elections. Ricardo Maduro (National Party), former central bank president and successful businessman, promised to crack down on crime, corruption, and inequality. Maduro, whose own son was killed in a bungled kidnapping, defeated Liberal Party candidate Rafael Pineda. Maduro enlisted 10,000 officers to wage his war against crime and appointed a military official as the head of security, which led to concerns of a regression toward the militarization of the police force.[42] Maduro's *mano dura* policies were imitated throughout the region, although they failed to decrease crime.

As in 2001, crime, the economy, and corruption took center stage in the 2005 elections. Liberal Party candidate Mel Zelaya won the presidency by the narrowest margin in Honduran history, defeating National Party candidate Porfirio Lobo by 4 percent. Zelaya continued Maduro's *mano dura* policies despite their ineffectiveness. In 2006 the homicide rate was 46.2 per 100,000. His tenure was also plagued by organized crime activity and drug trafficking. The socioeconomic realities of Honduras complicated efforts to reverse the crime wave. More than half of the Honduran population lived in poverty. Unemployment and income inequality persisted at high levels. All of these conditions were exacerbated by Hurricane Mitch and the subsequent drought. Additionally, Honduras' ability to address such vital issues was hindered by its debt burden and implementation of neoliberal reforms. While Zelaya supported a number of neoliberal policies such as CAFTA, he also built alliances with other leftist governments. Zelaya secured Honduras's membership in Petrocaribe and ALBA, which angered many within his own party. In March 2009 Zelaya announced a nonbinding referendum for a constituent assembly to rewrite the Honduran constitution. If approved, the measure would be submitted to voters at the polls during the 2009 elections. His opponents questioned the constitutionality of the referendum and attributed it to an attempt by Zelaya to remain in power.[43] Zelaya defied a Supreme Court ruling on the referendum and vowed to hold the election anyway. In June Zelaya was removed from his residence by the army and flown to Costa Rica. It was the first post–Cold War coup in the region. National Congress president and Zelaya rival Roberto Micheletti was sworn in as president. The international community condemned the coup and called for Zelaya's return. Despite widespread international statements of concern, the Micheletti government held the previously scheduled 2009 elections against a background of violent repression. National Party presidential candidate, conservative Porfirio Lobo, was proclaimed the victor. The United States stood practically alone in quickly recognizing the results. Zelaya, who was not restored to office, was exiled to the Dominican Republic hours after Lobo's inauguration.. Clearly Honduras experienced a rockier transition to democracy than did its revolutionary neighbors.

Costa Rica

Costa Rica has the strongest democratic traditions and most egalitarian society in Central America. Its formal democratic system has continued to function without a major hitch, although increasing voter abstention is cause for concern. Conservative Unity (Unidad) president Rodrigo Carazo (1978–1982) was followed in office by Party of National Liberation (PLN) presidents Luís Alberto Monge (1982–1986) and Oscar Arias (1986–1990), Social Christian Unity Party (PUSC) president Rafael Angel Calderón (1990–1994), PLN president José María Figueres (1994–1998), PUSC president Miguel Angel Rodríguez (1998–2002), and PUSC president Abel Pacheco (2002–).

Similarly, Costa Rica's relatively more egalitarian social structures appear to be holding their own. Between 1980 and 1990, even though population grew from slightly less than 2.3 to over 3 million and gross domestic product per capita declined slightly from $2,032 to $1,829, the portion of households in poverty stayed constant at 19 percent, infant mortality actually dropped from 19 to 15 per 1,000, and life expectancy increased from 72.6 to 75.6 years.[44] Costa Rica's economy was strong throughout the 1990s, averaging 5 percent growth throughout the decade. Economic growth slowed significantly in 2000, dropping from 8.4 in 1998 to 1.7 in 1000 and 1.1 in 2001. Despite this, life expectancy increased to 77.6 and the infant mortality rate dropped to 9 per 1,000 in 2001.[45]

But even for Costa Rica, all was not well in this period. First, the Cold War struggles to the north during the 1980s inevitably had their impact on the region's most democratic republic. Attempts by the Reagan administration to involve Costa Rica in the US crusade against Sandinista Nicaragua caused serious problems. During the presidencies of Rodrigo Carazo and Luís Alberto Monge, the United States operated a Contra "southern front" out of Costa Rica.[46] At the same time, it built a military airstrip and subverted Costa Rica's tradition of not having a military by pouring tens of millions of dollars into that country's "civil guard." Meanwhile, the CIA carried out dirty tricks and disseminated anti-Sandinista propaganda via segments of the Costa Rican media that it came to influence. There were even credible charges that CIA planes carrying weapons for the Contras were off-loading in Costa Rica and returning to the United States with drugs to help pay for the Contra war.[47]

All of this offended the national sensibilities of many Costa Ricans and led to the February 1986 electoral victory of Oscar Arias, who had promised to bring such affronts to his country's sovereignty to an end. Almost immediately the airstrip was shut down for fear that "it was being used by counterrevolutionaries or by drug traffickers."[48] Arias also defied the will of the United States—at the time still bent on outright military victory over its chosen enemies—by working on a comprehensive peace plan for Central America. The Esquipulas Peace Accord of August 1987 won that year's Nobel Peace Prize for Arias. Apparently annoyed by Arias's disloyalty, the United States subsequently channeled large sums of money through the National Endowment for Democracy into the conservative Costa Rican Association for the Defense of Democracy and Liberty, whose executive director, Rafael Calderón Fournier, would win the 1990 presidential election.

Though Costa Rica's Contra war–related problems would fade by the late 1980s, economic difficulties would quickly take their place. A growing government deficit and foreign debt combined with intensified pressures from international lenders would cause the country's leaders to implement neoliberal economic reforms in the late 1980s and 1990s that would threaten the relatively egalitarian nature of the country's social system. Social spending would drop in 1989 to 1992 from slightly under 22 percent to slightly under 19 percent of gross domestic product.[49] By the mid-1990s, neoliberal policies were in play as José María Figueres was downsizing the government payroll and reducing social services, selling state enterprises, lowering tariffs, raising taxes, and "reforming" Costa Rica's unique state pension system.

The PUSC and PLN continued to dominate Costa Rican politics throughout the 1990s. In 1998 PUSC candidate Miguel Angel Rodríguez defeated PLN candidate José Miguel Corrales. Voter abstention, typically 20 percent, was 30 percent in the 1998 elections. While Costa Rica had been more successful than its neighbors in offsetting the costs of adjustment, opposition to neoliberal policies and public displeasure at corruption scandals began to emerge. In fact, increasing evidence suggested that Costa Ricans' confidence in political parties and government was only marginally better (and sometimes worse) than in other Central America countries.[50]

Costa Rica's traditional two-party dominant system was challenged in the 2002 elections when a coalition dedicated to transparency, accountability, and citizen participation entered the race. The Citizen's Action Party (PAC) was founded in 2001 by Ottón Solís Fallas, formerly of the PLN and the minister of planning under Oscar Arias. The anti-neoliberal PAC platform opposed privatization of the remaining state enterprises—telecommunications, electricity, oil processing, and social security among others. Its campaign against corruption and neoliberal policies was particularly appealing to the urban middle class, which had been become poorer as a result of neoliberal policies.[51]

The PAC's presence forced a runoff in the presidential election, a first in Costa Rican history.[52] In it Abel Pacheco (PUSC) defeated Rolando Araya (PLN), 58 percent to 42 percent. The election was the first time that the PUSC held the presidency for two successive terms. As evidence of increasing public displeasure with politics as usual, the abstention rate for the second round was 39 percent. The PAC also prevented the PUSC and PLN from holding a majority in the Legislative Assembly.[53] It was the beginning of a significant shift in Central America's most stable democracy. By 2006 the dynamics of Costa Rican politics had shifted. Former president and PLN candidate Oscar Arias narrowly defeated the PAC's Solís. The PLN also won twenty-five seats in the legislature, followed by the PAC with seventeen seats. The PUSC continued its decline, displaced by the PAC. Voter turnout also continued to decline as Costa Ricans tired of politics as usual. CAFTA, which Arias supported, was at the heart of the 2006 campaign. Costa Rica was the only country to put the contentious issue to a popular vote. There was widespread concern that the agreement would increase inequality and poverty, which had increased under neoliberal policies. The agreement was so unpopular that the government feared losing the referendum. An internal government memorandum advising a "campaign of fear" to generate support for CAFTA surfaced shortly before the election. The treaty was approved 51.6 percent to 48.4 percent. Costa Rica became the last country in the region to implement the agreement in 2009. Thus even Costa Rica did not emerge from the neoliberal onslaught unscathed. While its social structures were measurably better than those of its neighbors, implementation of the neoliberal model had significant consequences for Costa Rica's political structures. Unlike other countries in the region, this dissatisfaction did not translate into an electoral victory for the left. In 2010 PLN candidate and Arias ally Laura Chinchilla won the presidential election with 45 percent of the vote, becoming the country's first woman president.

Central America in the Twenty-First Century

Clearly the previous quarter century under review brought advances as well as tragedy and problems to Central America. The insurrectionary wars, and especially the US-coordinated reaction to them, cost the lives of well over 300,000 people, mainly innocent civilians. Yet the political landscape of Central America was radically transformed. The political systems in Nicaragua, El Salvador, and Guatemala, though not perfect, were far more democratic than they were in the 1970s. Costa Rica remained resilient despite declining voter turnout and the demise of one of its dominant parties.

However, all was not well. Neoliberalism had a significant impact on the region. Increasing disparities in wealth led to rising disenchantment among the new democracies in the region and in Costa Rica as well. The social violence of peace replaced the political violence of war, contributing to increased levels of insecurity and disillusionment with the democratic process. Despite economic growth throughout the 1990s, poverty continued to plague the region and threatened the fragile peace. The 2009 coup in Honduras that removed President Zelaya from office served as a stark reminder about the serious challenges that lay ahead for the region.

Notes

1. John A. Booth, Christine J. Wade, and Thomas W. Walker, *Understanding Central America* (Boulder: Westview, 2009).

2. Washington's point of view was articulated in the Kissinger Commission report of 1984. *Report of the National Bipartisan Commission on Central America* (Washington, D.C.: Government Printing Office, 1984). While mentioning social injustice, the report stresses the communist conspiracy explanation.

3. Timothy P. Wickham-Crowley, *Guerrillas and Revolution in Latin America: A Comparative Study of Insurgents and Regimes Since 1956* (Princeton, N.J.: Princeton University Press, 1992).

4. Daniel Ortega once argued, if immodestly, that "it is the Sandinista Revolution which invented perestroika." In his first meeting with Mikhail Gorbachev in April 1985, he claims to have informed the new Soviet leader—who had not yet gone public with his reformist ideas—that Nicaragua was following a path very different from that of the Soviet Union with its command economy. To his surprise, Gorbachev responded with ap-

proval. From an Ortega interview with Pierre Hurel, "Ortega ne rend pas les armes," *Paris Match*, March 22, 1990, pp. 78–81.

5. Michael E. Conroy, "Economic Legacy and Policies: Performance and Critique," in Thomas W. Walker, ed., *Nicaragua: The First Five Years* (New York: Praeger, 1985), pp. 219–244.

6. National Bipartisan Commission on Central America, *Report of the National Bipartisan Commission*, p. 30.

7. This information was revealed by an official of the US embassy to a group of which Thomas Walker was part on June 25, 1985.

8. For a discussion of that election and citation of the pertinent British Parliament and House of Lords, Irish Parliament, Dutch government, and other observer reports, see Thomas W. Walker, *Nicaragua: Living in the Shadow of the Eagle* (Boulder: Westview, 1991), pp. 52–53; 71–72 nn. 23, 25.

9. Michael Linfield, "Human Rights," in Thomas W. Walker, ed., *Revolution and Counterrevolution in Nicaragua* (Boulder: Westview, 1996), pp. 275–294.

10. On August 2, 1979, less than two weeks after the Sandinista victory, coauthor Walker had the unusual experience of being one of three academics to deliver short presentations at a dinner seminar on Central America hosted by CIA director Admiral Stansfield Turner in his executive dining room. (By prior agreement, his presentation consisted of a sharp criticism of US policy in Central America.) Turner, who had just left a long meeting with President Carter, set the tone of the evening with his first six words: "There can be no more Nicaraguas."

11. See Thomas W. Walker, ed., *Reagan Versus the Sandinistas: The Undeclared War on Nicaragua* (Boulder: Westview, 1987).

12. Both inflation figures are from United Nations ECLAC, "Balance Preliminar de la Economía de la América Latina y el Caribe, 1990," *Notas Sobre la Economía y el Desarrollo* 500/501 (December 1990): 27.

13. This figure is from eight pages of charts on the human cost of the war provided Walker by the ministry of the presidency in January 1990.

14. William I. Robinson, *A Faustian Bargain: The US Involvement in the Nicaraguan Elections and American Foreign Policy in the Post–Cold War Era* (Boulder: Westview, 1992).

15. For coverage of this period, see Thomas W. Walker, ed., *Nicaragua Without Illusions: Regime Transition and Structural Adjustment in the 1990s* (Wilmington, Del.: Scholarly Resources, 1997).

16. Sandinista Front for National Liberation (FSLN); Liberal Constitutionalist Party (PLC)

17. In fact, that solution was openly discussed at the August 2, 1979, CIA dinner seminar mentioned in note 11.

18. Indeed, State Department official James Cheek, addressing a plenary session of the Latin American Studies Association congress in Washington on October 18, 1980, argued passionately—if unconvincingly—that Salvador's was the "real" revolution.

19. As part of the Presbyterian Task Force on Central America, coauthor Walker had the opportunity to interview both Rubén Zamora (once) and several official spokespersons of the FMLN (twice) in Managua in November 1982.

20. Benjamin C. Schwarz, *American Counterinsurgency Doctrine and El Salvador: The Frustration of Reform and the Illusion of Nation Building* (Santa Monica, Calif.: Rand Corporation, 1991), p. xii.

21. A large cache of FMLN weapons exploded in Managua in March 1993.

22. For good coverage of the implementation of the Salvadoran peace accords, see Hemisphere Initiatives, *Justice Impugned: The Salvadoran Peace Accords and the Problem of Impunity* (Cambridge, Mass.: Hemisphere Initiatives, 1993); Jack Spence and George Vickers, with Margaret Popkin, Philip Williams, and Kevin Murray, *A Negotiated Revolution: A Two Year Progress Report on the Salvadoran Peace Accords* (Cambridge, Mass.: Hemisphere Initiatives, 1994); and Jack Spence, David R. Dye, and George Vickers, with Garth David Cheff, Carol Lynne D'Arcangelis, Pablo Galarce, and Ken Ward, *El Salvador: Elections of the Century: Results, Recommendations, Analysis* (Cambridge, Mass.: Hemisphere Initiatives, 1994).

23. El Salvador Central Bank (BCR).

24. CEPAL (2001). Total poverty in 1997 was 48 percent, while rural poverty was 62 percent and urban poverty was 26 percent.

25. In 2002 remittances accounted for 10 percent of El Salvador's GDP, and were largely responsible for bolstering consumerism and managing inflation.

26. The elections for municipal and legislative seats, however, were held more than a month earlier than the presidential elections.

27. See Susanne Jonas, "Dangerous Liaisons: The US in Guatemala," *Foreign Policy* 103 (Summer 1996): 144–160.

28. For lengthy documentation, see Booth and Walker, *Understanding Central America*, pp. 224–225 n. 27.

29. Jonas, "Dangerous Liaisons," p. 147.

30. In June 2001 three members of the military were convicted in his death. The convictions, however, are on appeal.

31. On a positive note, the URNG coalition had a better than expected showing, winning 13 percent of the vote.

32. URNG candidate Rodrigo Asturias garnered less than 3 percent of the vote.

33. Washington Office on Latin America (WOLA), *The Captive State: Organized Crime and Human Rights in Latin America*, pp. 7–8.

34. Marc Lacey, "Drug Gangs use Violence to Sway Guatemala Vote," *New York Times*, August 4, 2007; Luis Solano, "Political Violence Takes a New Twist,"*Central America Report*, October 19, 2007.

35. Latin American Database, "Hardly a Dent in Guatemalan Poverty," *NotiCen*, October 4, 2007.

36. Rachel Sieder, "Honduras: The Politics of Exception and Military Reformism (1912–1978)," *Journal of Latin American Studies* 27, pt. 1 (February 1995): 99–127.

37. James D. Cockcroft, *Latin America: History, Politics, and US Policy* (Chicago: Nelson Hall, 1996), p. 191.

38. The Liberals continued to hold a majority in congress as well as mayoral posts.

39. Jeff Boyer and Aaron Pell, "Mitch in Honduras: A Disaster Waiting to Happen," *NACLA Report on the Americas*, September-October 1999, pp. 36–43.

40. Debt servicing consumed 46 percent of the annual budget, or nearly 23 percent of GDP.

41. United Nations Report of the Special Rapporteur, *Civil and Political Rights, Including the Question of Disappearances and Summary Executions* (United Nations Economic and Social Council Commission on Human Rights, 2003).

42. Ismael Moreno, "A New President and Cracks in the Two-Party Structure," *Envio*, January-February 2002, pp. 37–43.

43. "Sin condiciones para romper Constitución," *La Prensa*, March 14, 2009, www.laprensahn.com/Pa%C3%ADs/Ediciones/2009/03/15/Noticias/Sin-condiciones-para

-romper-Constitucion; "Artículos pétreos no pueden reformarse ni con plebiscito ni refe-rendo," *La Prensa*, May 26, 2009, www.laprensahn.com/Ediciones/2009/05/26/Noticias/Articulos-petreos-no-pueden-reformarse-ni-con-plebiscito-ni-referendo.

44. Proyecto Estado de la Nación, *Estado de la nacion en desarrollo humano sostenible* (San Jose, Costa Rica: Estado de la Nación, 1996), p. 4.

45. World Bank Development Report 2001.

46. Former US ambassador Lewis Tambs as quoted in Cockcroft, *Latin America,* p. 240.

47. Martha Honey, *Hostile Acts: US Policy in Costa Rica in the 1980s* (Gainesville: University of Florida Press, 1993).

48. Costa Rican minister of public safety Hernán Garrón Salazar, as quoted in Cockcroft, *Latin America,* p. 240.

49. Proyecto Estado de la Nación, *Estado de la Nación,* p. 68.

50. Amaru Barahona, "Costa Rican Democracy on the Edge," *Envio*, May 2002, pp. 22–29.

51. Ibid.

52. The PAC won 26 percent of the vote. The PUSC and PLN won 38.5 percent and 31 percent respectively.

53. The PUSC won 19 of the 57 seats, while the PLN won 17 and the PAC won 14. Two smaller parties, the PML and PRC, won 6 and 1 respectively.

Chapter 17

PANAMA AND THE CANAL

STEVE C. ROPP

PANAMA IS A COUNTRY that should be well known to every citizen of the United States because the United States was literally present at the creation. Panama gained its independence from Colombia in 1903 largely because the United States, under President Theodore Roosevelt, was interested in constructing a canal across the isthmus. After independence, US citizens in large numbers journeyed to Panama to dig "the big ditch." Upon completion of the canal in 1914, many chose to stay, becoming permanent residents of the US-controlled Canal Zone. In subsequent decades, the US political and economic presence on the isthmus was massive. On December 31, 1999, the canal was formally transferred to Panama and US control officially ended.[1]

During the 1980s, Panama caught the public eye because of the confrontation between the US government and General Manuel Antonio Noriega. The administration of President Ronald Reagan at first supported Noriega and the Panamanian Defense Forces (PDF) in exchange for the help Noriega provided in dealing with the crisis in Central America. But a policy shift began to occur in 1986 for a number of reasons, including increasing national concern about the drug problem. Beginning in 1987, both the Reagan and first Bush administrations used economic sanctions and other means in an attempt to unseat Noriega.[2] When these measures failed to remove him, President George H.W. Bush launched a military invasion in December 1989 that resulted in Noriega's capture and transport to the United States to face drug trafficking charges.

Despite the deep US involvement in isthmian affairs, there is little understanding today of Panama and its people in the United States. Although many US leaders and citizens once had an interest in the strategic importance of the Panama Canal and the associated large civilian and military presence in the Canal Zone, such interest evaporated when the last US military troops left the isthmus in 2000.

With these thoughts in mind, we turn to a closer examination of the country called Panama. This chapter consists of four parts. In the first, we examine the historical setting. In the second, we look more closely at some of the ways in which Panama's socioeconomic structures have been shaped by the country's unique development as a transit area. The third section focuses on the changes in government structure and policy substance that have taken place during the past two decades of civilian rule that followed two decades of military rule. Finally, we take note of Panama's relationship with the United States and its changing place in the world.

Historical Setting

Although geography is not always destiny, Panama has been influenced more than most countries by its location. Panama is an isthmus, a narrow strip of land 420 miles (676 kilometers) long, that joins Central and South America. As the narrowest and the lowest point in the Southern Hemisphere, the isthmus historically served as a transit route from the Atlantic Ocean to the Pacific. The first Europeans to take advantage of Panama's location were the Spaniards, who occupied the isthmus soon after Vasco Núñez de Balboa discovered in 1513 that it linked the Atlantic to the great "south sea." With the Spanish discovery and conquest of the Incan empire after 1532, Panama became a major transit route for treasure shipped back to Spain and for slaves and foodstuffs flowing to Peru.

The social and economic system that emerged on the isthmus during colonial times reflected Panama's importance as a strategic "bridge." A small urban elite developed that derived its influence from the ability to control isthmian trade. The political and economic position of this urban elite was strong until the middle of the eighteenth century because the Spanish crown had made Panama City one of only three ports in all of Latin America through which trade with the home country could be conducted. However, Panama City (and hence the urban elite) lost its favored position in the Spanish empire during the seventeenth and eighteenth centuries when the Spanish trade monopoly in Latin America began to erode. By 1655, the British had established a military and trading base in Jamaica from which they began rapidly to expand their reach. The final blow to Panama's favored economic position came in 1739, when the British destroyed the forts protecting the isthmian trade route.

Termination of Panama's port monopoly undermined the economic base of the urban commercial and administrative elite. Some members of this elite managed to maintain their power positions, but on greatly reduced sources of income. Although they no longer controlled the port, they were able to turn to contraband trade with the British or to provisioning military garrisons that continued to occupy the isthmus under Spanish, and later Colombian, rule. Most importantly, termination of Panama's port monopoly led to diversification within the social and economic system. Although many of the high-ranking Spanish-born administrators returned to the metropole or found bureaucratic posts elsewhere in Latin America, the locally born Creoles were forced to find other local sources of income, particularly in the countryside, where they could invest in cheap rural land. Because there was no large indigenous labor force like that found in the Andes, cattle raising became the major rural activity. Termination of the port monopoly and the attendant decline in trade thus led to the creation of a new economic class of small property owners in the interior.[3]

During the nineteenth century, those who remained on the isthmus had to adjust to a new set of relationships with outside powers. On November 28, 1821, Panama declared its independence from Spain. After considerable debate, a decision

was made to affiliate with the former viceroyalty of New Granada. This led in turn
to Panama's becoming a province of Colombia when Colombia went its separate
way.

As a small but strategically important province of a weak Latin American country, Panama was tugged in a number of directions. Lacking any strong historical
allegiance to Colombia, Panamanians made numerous attempts to achieve either
outright independence or increased autonomy within the Colombian political
system. Both Great Britain and the United States were interested in the isthmus
because of its central importance to the existing and potential hemispheric transportation network. As the United States expanded across the North American continent, it came to view the isthmus as a major component of the "domestic"
transportation system, linking the industrialized cities of the East Coast to the
rapidly expanding settlements in the West.[4] In 1851, US financiers underwrote the
construction of a railroad across the isthmus. To forestall any possible conflict over
future canal rights, the United States and Great Britain had signed the Clayton-
Bulwer Treaty in 1850. This treaty guaranteed that any canal constructed by either country anywhere in Central America would not be exclusively fortified or
controlled.

The social and economic consequences of Panama's new relationship with these
outside powers during the nineteenth century cannot be overestimated. Renewed
attention to the transit function restored the economic vitality of the urban transit
area and even led to the creation of an entirely new city, Colón, on the Atlantic
side of the isthmus. Panama City once again became an economic magnet, drawing workers from the interior to construct the railroad and later to work on the
canal project undertaken by the French in 1878. A second major effect of these
new external relationships was to change the composition of Panama's urban lower
class. Until the middle of the nineteenth century, the urban lower class consisted
largely of Hispanicized blacks who had come to Panama as slaves during the colonial period to work in the transit area. Beginning with construction of the railroad,
English-speaking black workers were imported in great numbers from the
Caribbean islands. At the height of the US canal-building efforts in 1910, the
Panama Canal Company employed over 35,000 such workers. Many remained in
urban Panama after the canal was completed in 1914. Their English language and
Protestant religion set them apart from the Panamanian culture and society.

Growing US interest in constructing a canal across the isthmus led to Panama's
independence from Colombia in 1903. President Theodore Roosevelt gave tacit
encouragement to Panamanian nationalists intent on liberating the isthmus from
Colombian rule. The result was an uprising on November 3, 1903, that led to the
creation of the Republic of Panama.

It is not surprising that US influence in early Panamanian politics was extensive.
Article 136 of the new constitution granted the United States the right to "intervene in any part of Panama, to reestablish peace and constitutional order if it has
been disturbed."[5] Panamanian politicians frequently called on US officials in the
Canal Zone for help in restoring order when it suited their purposes. Additionally,
many high-level positions in the Panamanian bureaucracy were held by US citizens. The United States also exercised overwhelming economic influence in the
new republic. The primary source of such influence was the Canal Zone, the ten-

mile-wide (16 kilometer) strip of US-controlled land that cut the isthmus in half. Employing a large number of US and Panamanian workers, it was both an employer and a market for Panamanian products. Furthermore, large banana plantations established by the US-owned United Fruit Company in the interior employed many Panamanians and served as a primary source of export income for the new nation.

As in several other Latin American nations, the highly visible US political and economic presence eventually caused a strong national reaction, particularly in the 1920s and 1930s. During this period, a number of factors worked to seriously undermine the economy. There was a massive reduction of the canal workforce after the locks were completed in 1914, and the national government incurred heavy debts, leading to a cutback in public sector employment after 1916.

On August 19, 1923, a semisecret nationalist group was formed that embodied much of the resentment Panamanians felt toward the United States as well as toward the Antillean blacks who held many of the jobs in the Canal Zone. Called Community Action, it espoused Hispanic nationalism. Arnulfo Arias soon emerged as its leader. Born on a small cattle ranch in the interior in 1901, Arias graduated from Harvard Medical School and returned to Panama, where he practiced medicine and began to dabble in politics. Although elected president on three separate occasions (1940, 1949, and 1968), he was never allowed to complete a full term.

The populist political movement led by Arias (henceforward called the Panameñistas) was partially displaced by another emerging political force beginning in the 1950s. After Panama achieved independence in 1903, the army was disbanded because of the threat it posed to the political elite and to the United States. Only a small police force was retained. However, during the 1930s the national police gradually began to gain political influence under the guidance of José Antonio Remón. By the late 1940s, Colonel Remón and his police organization had become important arbiters in the feuds among leaders of the traditional political parties. Using the police as a springboard, Remón won the presidential election in 1952. Several years later, the national police was converted into the national guard and given a new, expanded military role.

With the rise in the power and influence of the national guard in the 1950s, the base was laid for several subsequent decades of military government. Although the government returned to civilian hands after Remón's assassination in 1955, the national guard retained much of its political influence. During this period, the guard became increasingly professionalized as more officers with academy training entered it. Because of the Cold War, the United States greatly expanded its military assistance programs during the 1950s, and many Panamanian soldiers were trained at US installations.

On October 11, 1968, the civilian Panameñista government of President Arnulfo Arias was overthrown by a military coup. The young lieutenant colonel who emerged as the central figure in the national guard was Omar Torrijos. He quickly moved Panamanian policy in a symbolically anti-US direction and restored diplomatic relations with Castro's Cuba. Although Torrijos and the national guard never displayed the same degree of anti-US sentiment that existed in the early days of Community Action, the restoration of the armed forces to a central position in

Panamanian politics created an important new institutional base from which nationalist sentiments could be voiced.

TRANSIT AREA GROWTH AND SOCIOECONOMIC STRUCTURES

Panama's social and economic structures are largely the product of its unique development as a transit area. The perceived need in the United States for hegemonic control of this transit area led to the 1903 creation of an enclave (the Canal Zone) in the heart of urban Panama. Although foreign-controlled enclaves were common elsewhere in Latin America, the economic importance and geographic centrality of the Canal Zone were such that they largely determined not only the rate and direction of national economic growth but also the nature of the domestic class structure. Urban commercial groups and rural cattlemen depended heavily on the Canal Zone as a market for their products. Perhaps most important, the existence of the zone played a determining role in the evolution of Panama's urban working class.

In many Latin American countries, the urban working class has served as an important base of support for political leaders intent on restructuring relations between elites and masses or between the nation and outside powers. However, in Panama the working class has remained quite dormant except for a brief period while the military governed during the 1970s and 1980s. Workers traditionally operated within the context of an alliance between Canal Zone and Panamanian elites that limited their opportunities for protest and political mobilization. During the early years of the republic, repression of working-class interests was often brutal and exercised through the direct use of military force. For example, when canal workers living in Panama City went on strike in 1925 to stop rent increases, Panamanian slumlords called on US troops from the zone to quell the rioting.

Historically, the ease with which working-class demands have been repressed was also rooted in two features of the transit area that negatively affected labor's bargaining power. First, Canal Zone workers were organized into unions that had primary ties to the United States rather than to Panama. Second, the Canal Zone workforce was largely composed of English-speaking blacks who enjoyed little sympathy among the Spanish-speaking Panamanian population. Because Canal Zone workers received higher wages by national standards, a perception arose that they were a "labor elite," privileged and culturally distinct from Panamanians elsewhere in the republic.

Rapid growth of economic activities in the transit area during the 1960s and 1970s led to the mass migration of people from the interior provinces. As in many other Latin American countries, Panama's urban population grew very rapidly, increasing from 36 percent of the national total in 1950 to 48 percent by 1970.[6] The result of this massive internal migration was the creation of a large, culturally and economically heterogeneous class of urban poor living in numerous squatter settlements around Panama City.

The magnetic attraction of the transit area during the 1960s and 1970s served in turn to reinforce the historic marginality of the countryside. The interior provinces continued to be neglected by urban civilian politicians representing the interests of commercial elites, so that neither the rural cattlemen nor the peasants really prospered. However, the structure of the rural economy was significantly altered during these two decades. Traditionally, the Panamanian peasant engaged in subsistence farming on small plots of land owned by the government. The expansion of commercial cattle raising greatly reduced the amount of land available to peasants. In addition to forcing many of them off the land and into the cities, this development increased the tension between cattlemen and peasants.

The military regime that controlled politics from 1968 until 1989 came to power partly because of the marginality of those living in the countryside and related changes in the structure of the rural economy. Power was taken away from the urban economic elite who had held sway since 1903. In contrast to members of this elite, General Torrijos was born and raised in the interior. And although his antiurban biases were not as strong as the smoldering antagonism of the marginalized cattlemen who had supported Arnulfo Arias, his concern for the culture and economy of rural Panama was just as real.

Industrial growth after World War II created an economy that by the 1960s consisted of three major parts. Supplementing the traditional service and agricultural activities was an expanded industrial light manufacturing sector, which led to growth of the industrial working class. The most important economic development in the 1970s and 1980s was the dramatic change in the overall importance of these three sectors. Although the service economy continued to expand at a rapid rate, industrial manufacturing activities began to level off. The same was true for the agricultural sector, which experienced a number of problems related to international competition, marketing, and farm technology.

Panama's transit area and related service sector continued to play a central role in the domestic economy following the transition to civilian rule in the 1990s and the US departure from Panama in the year 2000. During the previous two decades of military rule (the 1970s and 1980s), global multinational corporations had begun to use Panama as a location for servicing their financial transactions with a minimum of red tape, as well as for a variety of transportation, communication, and warehousing activities. These practices continued during the following two decades, but the pace of service sector growth accelerated following the end of the Cold War and rapid expansion of the world economy.

This rapid economic expansion (a process often referred to as globalization) was largely driven by the symbiotic relationship that developed between Asia's export-oriented economies and more consumer-driven ones in North America and Europe. During this phase of globalization, Panama's role was to move raw materials to Asia and then move the finished product (clothes, electronics, and the like) back to the consumers. Increasingly, the world demand for Asian manufactured goods led to an explosion of demand for containerized shipping and associated port facilities. As a result, Panama today is home to a number of large container ports run by North American, European, and Asian corporations.

By 2008, Panama had one of the fastest growing economies in the world, the country benefited from not only the rapid growth of world trade but also the large number of North American and European baby boomers who moved there to retire. However, when global credit began to dry up and the scale of the financial meltdown became apparent, the Panamanian economy quickly went into reverse. Whereas unemployment had dropped steadily from 2004 to 2008, it began to move higher in 2009. Worse yet, the economy's informal sector (made up of marginal, self-employed people), which already accounted for over 40 percent of all workers, began to grow again.

In sum, the same global forces that drove transit area activity to new heights during the past decade are now slowing it dramatically. Container traffic through the canal has been reduced, and this in turn has led to a decrease in associated activities involving the transshipment and processing of goods. Complicating things even further, the Panamanian government has committed itself to a major expansion of the canal which involves the construction of a third set of locks. Time will tell whether this grand project will lead to renewed growth in the transit area or to another phase of national economic stagnation.

GOVERNMENT AND POLITICAL DYNAMICS

For some two decades (1968–1989), Panama was dominated by the military.[7] During these years, government structures were altered in order to give the military a greater role in policy formulation and implementation. The substance of policy also changed because military officers viewed themselves as representing previously marginalized rural and urban working-class groups. Military leaders used heavy state intervention in the economy and enlarged governmental structures to pursue economic development strategies aimed at improving the lot of their class allies.

In the two decades since the US military invasion, there have also been major changes in government structure and policy associated with Panama's return to civilian rule, although the constitution adopted by the former military government remains in place. These changes in structure and policy have been associated with four different civilian presidents who completed their five-year terms and a fifth (Ricardo Martinelli) who has yet to complete his. What is interesting from a political standpoint is that the two large populist political parties that historically had served as the major source of civilian/military instability in the political system appear to have become the primary source of its strength. Alternating in power from 1989 until 2009, the Panameñistas (the legacy of Arnulfo Arias) and the PRD (the legacy of Omar Torrijos) have governed within the context of what has apparently become a more stable political system. Consequently there has been no break in the continuity of civilian governance in more than two decades.

Although there have been many changes in government structure over the past forty years of military and civilian rule, it is important to note that *both* military and civilian leaders have been heavily influenced by the nation's Iberian political heritage. When Panama declared its independence from Colombia in 1903, a new constitution was drafted that was based on Colombian law. A centralized unitary government would be composed of three branches: executive, legislative, and judicial. The president was to be elected for a four-year term and would not be ineligible for immediate reelection.

The legislative branch historically centered around a unicameral National Assembly whose members were elected for four-year terms at the same time as the president. Assembly representatives were elected from circuits corresponding to the nine provinces into which the country was divided. This traditional political system was eminently "presidential," since the chief executive normally dominated both the legislative and judicial branches. The president's power to appoint provincial governors extended his authority into the countryside and influenced administration on the local level. Although the municipalities theoretically possessed more autonomy than the provinces, it was seldom manifest in practice.

After the military coup in 1968, the dominance of the executive branch became even more pronounced, but power was concentrated in military rather than civilian hands. A new constitution promulgated in 1972 made General Omar Torrijos "maximum leader of the Panamanian Revolution." As for the legislative branch, the new constitution substituted a system of representation based on the nation's 505 municipal subdistricts for the National Assembly. Members of this reconfigured legislature were elected for longer terms in a process that was tightly controlled by the executive branch. Traditional parties played no role.

The military's domination of these civilian political institutions was contingent on its ability to circumvent legal mechanisms designed to curb military power and maintain strict discipline within the ranks. Prior to the 1968 coup, the president of the republic was commander in chief of the armed forces as specified by the 1946 constitution. As such, the president had the right—if not always the power—to appoint and remove military personnel. Under provisions of the 1972 constitution, the president (appointed, in fact, by the military) had no such powers. Furthermore, Article 2 stated that government agencies were to act in "harmonic collaboration" with the armed forces.

General Torrijos and his successor, General Noriega, maintained control of the military through a highly centralized administrative apparatus. Lines of authority ran directly from the commander in chief to all military units without being channeled through the General Staff. Torrijos maintained direct control over all seven of Panama's infantry companies, and no officer assignments were made, even at the lieutenant level, without his express approval.

An important change following the 1968 coup was that the traditional political parties were banned, largely because they were perceived as representing the interests of the traditional elites. In 1978 the Democratic Revolutionary Party (PRD) was formed to incorporate and guide the various groups that supported the military regime. According to its declaration of principles, the PRD was to be democratic, multiclass, unitary, nationalistic, revolutionary, popular, and independent.[8] In many respects, it resembled other Latin American political parties historically established by military leaders to give civilian institutional form to their ideas. Like Mexico's Institutional Revolutionary Party (PRI), the PRD exercised close collaboration among military, government, and party leaders to carefully channel the participation of opposition groups.

In sum, a form of "guided democracy" existed in Panama for two decades. Military leaders adopted economic policies that were tailored to improving the lot of their multiclass popular constituency and relied on heavy state intervention to implement them. During this period, the government bureaucracy experienced considerable growth, organized labor gained more influence, and the social safety net was expanded to include a large number of new and previously marginalized social groups.

When civilians returned to power in Panama following the US invasion in 1989, most of the country's democratic institutions were reestablished, including the unicameral National Assembly. At the same time, problems of democratic governability soon emerged that related to three major factors. First, many Panamanians were unconvinced that the coalition of political and economic groups that had been returned to power on the backs of US tanks was fully legitimate and would govern in the best interests of the Panamanian people. Second, there were serious political divisions within the coalition. And finally, changes in the global economy forced the first and second of these civilian presidents to undertake harsh economic reforms that were perceived as negatively affecting the most vulnerable groups and classes.

Guillermo Endara (1989–1994) became Panama's first civilian president after the invasion and was sworn into office on a US military base. A longtime supporter of Arnulfo Arias and the Panameñistas, he headed an alliance of political parties that General Noriega had prevented from assuming power following fraudulent elections held in 1989. With regard to the economy, Endara's administration initially focused its attention on efforts to restore the government's credibility in international financial circles. As a consequence, it made some rather halfhearted and unsuccessful attempts to reduce the size of the public sector in order to allow for larger payments on the country's national debt. At the same time, his administration had to react to the sea change that had taken place during the late 1980s in thinking about development. The new neoliberal economic model that gained ascendancy following the collapse of Soviet communism emphasized lowering national tariff barriers, reducing the size of the public sector through the privatization of state-owned companies, and shifting from the traditional import substitution model to export-oriented industrialization.

While Endara was president, the government did start restructuring the economy along neoliberal lines. However, it was only during the subsequent presidency of Ernesto Pérez Balladares (1994–1999) that the government began to make serious and sustained efforts to implement economic reforms. The curious aspect of this situation was that Pérez Balladares represented the old military governing party (the PRD) that had been responsible for doubling the size of the government bureaucracy and increasing state economic intervention during two decades of prior military rule.

Panama's third postinvasion president rode to victory on a wave of popular revulsion against President Pérez Balladares's harsh neoliberal reforms. Mireya Moscoso (1999–2004) was the first woman president in the country's history and the daughter of a schoolteacher who lived in an impoverished rural part of the interior. After joining the Panameñista Party, she married its founder, Arnulfo Arias, and accompanied him into exile following the military coup of 1968. President Moscoso's years in office were dominated by attempts to soften the impact of the two previous administrations' economic reforms on Panama's poorest citizens. However, her ambitious populist agenda fell prey to a combination of economic difficulties, personal ineptitude, and corruption.

The fourth and final Panamanian president to complete a full term since 1989 was Martín Torrijos (2004–2009). The son of General Omar Torrijos, who ruled Panama from 1968 until his death in 1981, Martín Torrijos received his business education in the United States and continued former President Pérez Balladares's practice of using a "reinvented" PRD to push through reform measures related to fiscal policy and social security. Although he was partially successful in this regard, President Torrijos may be best remembered for shepherding through a 2006 national referendum on future expansion of the canal. On the negative side, he was widely perceived as failing to stabilize the price of basic necessities, failing to control drug-related violence, and opening the door for renewed military participation in national affairs.

With Panama's two traditionally dominant political parties alternating in power since 1989, a pattern of relative stability and continuity has been established that was largely unforeseen by most academic observers (including this author) twenty years ago. While there are still some disturbing questions related to the quality of Panama's current democracy and the potential for renewed military influence in politics, a preference for democratic governance seems to be well established. Panama's new president, Ricardo Martinelli (2009–), has held high office during the recent presidential administrations of both the PRD and the Panameñistas. As such, his administration has the potential to serve as a "bridge" to the future of an even broader and more inclusive national party system.[9]

Panama's Changing Place in the World

Because of its small size and unique geographical position, Panama's foreign relations have been heavily influenced by outside powers.[10] By 1903, the United States had emerged as the dominant outside power with multiple sources of influence over Panama's foreign initiatives. The large US troop presence in the Canal Zone and the strategic importance of the isthmus to the United States limited the contacts the Panamanian government was allowed to develop with global US adversaries, such as Hitler's Germany and the former Soviet Union. In addition to this military presence, US economic dominance meant that independent foreign policy initiatives had to be cautiously pursued. During the Cold War, Panama's economic reliance on the US government and private companies was probably greater than that of any other country in the world.[11]

Owing to US domination throughout most of the twentieth century, Panama pursued a largely bilateral foreign policy. The commercial elites who controlled the foreign ministry were primarily interested in extracting the maximum economic benefits from their relationship with the United States. A secondary concern was to modify the worst colonial aspects of the US-Panamanian relationship, particularly as it related to the Canal Zone. According to terms of the original 1903 treaty, the United States could act "in perpetuity" in the Canal Zone "as if it were the sovereign of the territory . . . to the entire exclusion of the exercise by the Republic of Panama of any such sovereign rights, power, and authority."[12] Over the years leaders of various political persuasions tried repeatedly to negotiate treaties that did not so egregiously violate the country's sense of sovereignty.

In spite of these attempts, the major provisions of the 1903 treaty remained unchanged until 1978. In that year, the US Congress ratified two completely new treaties, the Panama Canal Treaty and the Treaty of Neutrality. The former recognized Panamanian sovereignty over the Canal Zone and specified that US troops would be withdrawn completely from this area by the year 2000; the latter guaranteed that the waterway would remain permanently neutral in time of peace or war.

It would be hard to overstate the degree of change that occurred in US-Panamanian relations when Panama assumed control of the canal in 2000 as a result of the 1978 treaties. Before the year 2000, Panama had been a major seat of US diplomatic and military power in the Western Hemisphere—a place from which the United States could project power, whether to deal with a threatened guerrilla insurgency or a looming humanitarian crisis. Following the transfer of the canal, however, Panama became more of a problem than a solution in the eyes of the US diplomatic and military planners, requiring special attention because of its logistical importance to regional drug and arms smugglers and its potential vulnerability to the continuing crisis in the northern part of South America.[13]

Over the past decade Panama has become deeply entangled in the civil and drug wars that have engulfed large parts of neighboring Colombia. For many years, this war has spilled over the border and created numerous problems for Panama, including increased drug trafficking, floods of refugees, and increased crime. As if all of this were not enough, Panama has also been affected by the continuing political and economic crisis in Venezuela. A former army colonel named Hugo Chávez became president as head of a populist movement that challenged the traditional oligarchy. Because of the ongoing turmoil, more and more Venezuelans are seeking refuge in Panama.

As a result of changes in Panama's traditional bilateral relationship with the United States and its place in the world, Panamanians have had to think long and hard about their future. This has resulted in the emergence (or perhaps reemergence) of two different views concerning Panama's fundamental nature as a global entity, views that predominate among different segments of the population. The first is the belief that Panama is more of a transnational global city than a true nation-state. This view is deeply rooted in the historical memory of the white ruling classes. It stresses Panama's unique place in the world as a result of its geographical location and its attendant role as a strategic bridge within the global transportation network.

The second view, long dominant among the followers of Arnulfo Arias as well as among followers of the old military regime, suggests that Panama is just another nation-state, a rather small one that must learn to survive on its own in a harsh global political and economic environment. From this perspective, Panamanians need to stop looking back nostalgically to the "good old days" of its close relationship with the United States or looking forward to a new role as a transglobal city. Rather, Panamanians need to focus on strengthening domestic institutions and building interstate alliances in a way that will protect vital national interests.

Regardless of how this domestic debate about Panama's fundamental nature and place in the world is resolved, its relationship with its global environment will be much more complex in the future. The simple and straightforwardly hegemonic relationship between Panama and the United States that existed until 2000 has been replaced by one that includes many other states and global entities. Most pronounced in this regard are the strong ties that the Panamanian government has developed with both the Republic of China on Taiwan (ROC) and the People's Republic of China (PRC). It remains to be seen whether President Ricardo Martinelli will change foreign policy from one that has historically favored the ROC to one that fully recognizes the PRC's growing role in the global economic system.

Conclusion

Panama's geographical location has played a critical role in determining the country's global function as a transit area, in shaping domestic socioeconomic structures, and in defining and redefining its place in the world. Because Panama has long served as a strategic "bridge," it has historically attracted the attention of Great Powers (such as Spain, Great Britain, France, and the United States) intent on enhancing their geostrategic position. This continues to be the case today as Panama struggles to define a role for itself in the world following the US withdrawal from the isthmus.

With the return to democratic government in the 1990s, Panama's civilian presidents and their administrations have struggled with the question of how best to balance the need for economic reforms in order to remain competitive within the global economy with the need to protect Panamanians from the threat of growing unemployment, increasing class inequality, and the like. This is no easy task, and is surely one that future Panamanian presidents will continue to struggle with.

As noted at the beginning of this chapter, the people of the United States have a short memory when it comes to thinking about our deep historical relationship with Panama. However, since we were involved in the creation of the country, we have a moral obligation to help ensure the continuing welfare of the people of Panama in the future. Panama played a critical role as a trusted regional ally during most of "the American century"—a role that we should never forget.

Notes

1. This transfer was the end result of the so-called Carter-Torrijos Treaties signed by US president Jimmy Carter and Panamanian general Omar Torrijos in 1978.

2. President George H.W. Bush outlined his administration's reasons for opposing Noriega and launching the subsequent invasion in an address to the nation on December 19, 1989. These reasons included the obligation to protect American lives, to uphold terms of the Carter-Torrijos Treaties, to defend democracy, and to suppress drug trafficking. Some observers, including General Noriega himself, also suggested that officials in both the Reagan and Bush administrations had become increasingly frustrated with what they perceived as Noriega's unwillingness to allow Panama to be used as a launching pad for US operations against Nicaragua's Sandinista government. See President George H.W. Bush, Panama Invasion Address (retrieved March 8, 2010, from www.youtube.com/watch?v=GlaewpvuEAY); and Steve C. Ropp, "The Bush Administration and the Invasion of Panama: Explaining the Choice and Timing of the Military Option," in John D. Martz, ed., *United States Policy in Latin America: A Decade of Crisis and Challenge* (Lincoln: University of Nebraska Press, 1995), p. 83.

3. Omar Jaén Suárez, *La Población del Istmo de Panamá del siglo XVI al siglo XX* (Panama City: Impresora de la Nación, 1978), pp. 187–190, 301.

4. Walter LaFeber, *The Panama Canal: The Crisis in Historical Perspective* (New York: Oxford University Press, 1979), p. 8.

5. Juan Materno Vásquez, *Teoría del estado Panameño* (Panama City: Ediciones Olga Elena, 1980), p. 122.

6. Panamá, Dirección de Estadística y Censo, Contraloría General, *Panamá en cifras: 1973–1977* (Panama City, n.d.), p. 38.

7. For an attempt to explain this long period of military rule, see Steve C. Ropp, "Explaining the Long-Term Maintenance of a Military Regime: Panama Before the US Invasion," *World Politics*, January 1992, pp. 210–234.

8. Partido Revolucionario Democrático, *Documentos fundamentales* (Panama City, 1979), pp. 16–17.

9. Martinelli breaks the mold of his predecessors in office while at the same time providing elements of continuity. Unlike the mostly career politicians who had previously occupied the presidential palace, he is a wealthy businessman who founded his own political party (Democratic Change) in 1998. At the same time, he began his career serving in the two largest traditional political parties. His style is in most respects that of a typical Panamanian populist politician.

10. Jan Black, "The Canal and the Caribbean," in Richard Millett and W. Marvin Will, eds., *The Restless Caribbean: Changing Patterns of International Relations* (New York: Praeger, 1979), pp. 90–91.

11. Neil R. Richardson, *Foreign Policy and Economic Dependence* (Austin: University of Texas Press, 1978), pp. 103–106.

12. US Congress, Senate, Committee on Foreign Relations, *Hearings on the Panama Canal Treaties*, 95th Cong., 1st sess., September 1977, pt. 1, p. 588.

13. One major symbol of this changing US presence is the transfer of the US embassy from downtown Panama City to a remote hilltop near the canal.

Suggested Readings

Greene, Julie. *The Canal Builders: Making America's Empire at the Panama Canal*. New York: Penguin, 2009. The story, told from the bottom up, of the diverse workforce that the US government brought to Panama to construct the canal.

McCullough, David. *The Path Between the Seas: The Creation of the Panama Canal, 1870–1914*. New York: Simon & Schuster, 1977. An epic book dealing with French and US efforts to build the Panama Canal.

Pearcy, Thomas L. *We Answer Only to God: Politics and the Military in Panama, 1903–1947*. Albuquerque: University of New Mexico Press, 1998. A well researched study of the historical role of the military in Panamanian politics.

Perez, Orlando J., ed. *Post-Invasion Panama: The Challenges of Democratization in the New World Order*. Lanham, Md.: Lexington, 2000. An excellent collection of essays concerning political developments following the US military invasion of 1989.

Sanchez, Peter M. *Panama Lost? US Hegemony, Democracy, and the Canal*. Gainesville: University Press of Florida, 2007. A theoretically sophisticated account of the historical interplay between US hegemony and the development of Panamanian democracy.

Ward, Christopher. *Imperial Panama: Commerce and Conflict in Isthmian America, 1550–1800*. Albuquerque: University of New Mexico Press, 1993. Solid account of developments in Panama during the colonial period.

PART VII

CUBA AND THE CARIBBEAN

Chapter 18

THE CUBAN REVOLUTION

NELSON P. VALDÉS

A SOCIAL REVOLUTION is a radical, abrupt, thorough, and systematic alteration of the social relations, the patterns of behavior, and the institutional structures that exist in the economic, political, cultural, and social life of a country. By definition, a social revolution touches every facet of interaction in society. It often attempts a total break with tradition. But even revolutionaries cannot escape their material and historical context.

The agendas of social revolutions have changed through time. From the seventeenth century on, Western Europe dealt with a series of critical problems, ranging from nation building (the creation of national institutions, a central system of authority, and a national economy) to the creation of representative political institutions and industrialization. The development of the modern capitalist nation-state took centuries to unfold and was often plagued with social conflict at home and war abroad. During this century, the countries of the Third World (including most of those in Latin America) have confronted some of the same difficulties (nation building, economic development, the problems of citizenship) as well as new ones (national self-determination and ending foreign control and neocolonial institutions and practices).

In general, revolutionaries have defined their tasks in such a manner that their aims are, to say the least, awesome. Social revolutions are supposed to bring about the full blossoming of national sovereignty, fight foreign influence, develop national resources, distribute the economic benefits of growth, centralize political power while increasing the sense of citizenship and the degree of political participation, and totally transform the country's major institutions. And all of these tasks are to be done in a short period of time with the few resources the country may have at its command.

The Cuban revolution is worthy of study because it presents us with an example of what a revolutionary state tried to do, how it went about it, and what resulted from the effort. Multifaceted and complex, this revolution is a unique phenomenon that other countries have attempted to emulate. Finally, the revolution catapulted this small island into the center of the struggle between the superpowers. The impact of the Cuban revolution, in other words, has been felt not only within its own borders but beyond its shores as well.

The Historical Context

Social revolutions occur in particular places and times. They cannot escape either of the two. The fact that Cuba is an island in a strategic location has made it a crossroads of trade and cultures. And the fact that it lies only 90 miles (145 kilometers) from the US mainland has preoccupied US as well as Cuban authorities, particularly since 1959.

Yet the islanders have been somewhat isolated from the rest of Latin America by a certain attitude of self-containment and self-sufficiency. Cubans are not sufficiently aware of the dramatic differences between a country that developed a plantation economy early in its history and the agrarian, peasant, and other traditional forms of social interaction that exist elsewhere in the hemisphere. This has led some Cubans to consider their experience a model that can be emulated elsewhere—a vanguard rather than an exception.

Social revolutions are shaped and bound by history—a dynamic, ever changing process. How that process unfolds and how it is interpreted do not have to coincide. Yet the interpretation that a society or a segment of a population gives to that process may have a power all its own. Historical interpretation may also function as a tool for understanding as well as a call to action. Revolutionaries know this well.

Spanish Colonial Period

The basic pattern of Cuba's history has differed from that of most of Latin America. From the onset of the Spanish conquest, the island became a springboard for the conquest of Mexico, Central America, and even portions of South America. Lacking mineral wealth and a large native labor force, Cuba offered little incentive for settlement. The population was fairly small, and the economy was geared toward servicing the fleet that visited the port of Havana once or twice a year. Most of the population tended to concentrate in the small towns. Colonial institutions were not as strong as in Peru or Mexico, and the Catholic Church held sway only in the urban milieu.

From the 1760s on, Cuba experienced dramatic changes in its economic, social, and political organization. These changes were initiated by the development of the sugar plantation economy and, with it, of a cohesive class of sugar planters (referred to in Cuba as the *sucarocracia*). As sugar production rose, the demand for labor also increased. Since this shift in production occurred just as the British began their industrial revolution, the steam engine was soon introduced into the refining of sugar. This generated a greater demand for sugarcane and the labor force that cut it. Hence, with the sugar plantation and the modernization of production, black slaves arrived in ever larger numbers. Sugar production was essentially for profit, although dependent on slave-master relations. The sugar economy dominated the western part of the island, particularly around Havana. In the eastern region, however, a small farming class, mainly white, produced coffee, tobacco, and cattle—a significant portion for barter or direct use.

The sugar areas were held by people born in Spain (*peninsulares*), and the rest of the land was essentially in the hands of poor farmers who had little contact with the Spanish colonial system. The latter were, in a sense, the early *criollos;* the first indications of a Cuban national identity developed in the eastern part of the island. The differences between the two economic regions, with their distinct modes of production, gave rise to tensions between the Spaniards and the Cubans. The latter, of course, were barred from political power.

The early nineteenth century witnessed independence struggles throughout most of Latin America. Cuba, however, remained under Spanish control, due to three factors. First, the economic prosperity achieved through sugar cultivation kept much of the population contented. Second, the defeats suffered by Spanish military forces throughout the hemisphere meant that a large proportion of the defeated personnel ended up in Cuba—thus fortifying colonial rule there. Finally the sugar planters, as well as many other whites who were not directly connected to the sugar economy, feared that a war of independence would be transformed into a slave revolt, as had happened in Haiti after 1791.

In 1868 Cuba began a war of independence led by the small, independent white farming class of eastern Cuba. The war went on for ten years but ended in defeat for the rebels as well as the total destruction of the nonsugar economy. The plantation became increasingly powerful and began to expand to the east. The class system, at the same time, was simplified, and a basic tension surfaced between the slave owners and the slaves. In this confrontation, the Catholic Church sided with the plantation and the colonial system. Thus sugar plantation slaves and colonial rule became one side of the equation, while emancipating the slaves, limiting the dominance exerted by the plantations, and Cuban independence became united themes. During this period the antisugar mentality arose that has dominated the thinking of Cuban revolutionists ever since.

In 1895 the war of independence broke out again, this time led by the Cuban Revolutionary Party (PRC) under the guidance of Cuba's leading poet, national hero, and thinker: José Martí. The PRC was a unique development. No other Latin American war of independence was organized by a political party. The PRC maintained political and military control of the entire struggle. This was new as well. But the PRC went even further. José Martí had studied conditions in Latin America and concluded that even though many countries had attained political independence, the laws, traditions, practices, and institutions of colonialism had survived. The PRC therefore had a decolonization program. In that respect, the party foretold a process that would take root throughout the Third World in the second half of the twentieth century.

THE AMERICAN PROTECTORATE

But the war of independence did not achieve its goal. The international situation was far different from what it had been when the rest of Latin America became free of Spain. Late in the nineteenth century, the United States was emerging as a major power in the hemisphere. Manifest Destiny had numerous adherents in Washington, DC, and the Caribbean was considered an American lake. The Cuban war of independence was lost when the United States and Spain went to war in 1898. US military intervention in the island brought to an end Spanish colonial rule, only to initiate a new period of US hegemony.

The island became an integral part of the US economy, and the culture and education of the Cubans became increasingly Americanized. The United States imposed a new economic arrangement, new trade partners, and a new political system. The US dollar became the main currency. From 1899 to 1902, the US military ruled over Cuba, restructuring its socioeconomic system to meet US needs. US investors began to control the strategic sectors of the Cuban economy (sugar, transportation, utilities, trade). All communal lands were lost, passing into US ownership.

An amendment to the Cuban constitution, dictated by US military authorities, allowed the US government to pass judgment on the acceptability of Cuban public policy through the Platt Amendment, reserving the right to intervene militarily to ensure that its dictates were honored.

A new regime in Cuba, ushered in by the so-called Sergeants' Revolt, unilaterally repudiated the Platt Amendment in 1933. However, other progressive and nationalistic reforms that followed the Sergeants' Revolt were soon undermined as the leader of that revolt, Fulgencio Batista, assumed dictatorial powers and curried favor with the United States.

The Cuban Revolutionary Party, which had spearheaded the struggle for independence from Spain, disintegrated after the death of its leader, Martí. But in 1944, a new populist party, using the same name and drawing on the same inspiration, won election and ruled until 1952, when Batista displaced it and reestablished a dictatorship.

From 1953 to 1958, the opposition to Batista was led by the 26th of July Movement formed by ex-members of the Cuban People's Party (PPC), a splinter of the PRC, many of whom remained committed to populism, nationalism, and general concepts of social justice. Led by a young lawyer, Fidel Castro, they waged a guerrilla war that managed to overthrow a military regime for the first time in Latin American history. The United States apparently misunderstood the degree to which these revolutionaries were committed to thorough and rapid social change. But their dedication soon became obvious.

FROM NATIONALISM TO SOCIALISM

The young revolutionaries sought to gain control of the major economic decisions affecting their country in order to redistribute wealth and promote development. There is no evidence that they envisioned either a complete break with the United States or a thorough socialization of the economy. But the US government and business community equated the revolutionaries' policies in regard to foreign investments and land reform with communism. US countermeasures, which included slashing Cuba's sugar quota and later imposing an economic embargo, pushed the Cubans to further expropriations.

By late 1960, the state owned a significant portion of the means of production in Cuba. No one had planned this. Cuba's capitalist economy became socialized through a process of confrontation, actions, and reactions, even though the Cuban state did not have the personnel to run all the enterprises. At issue was Cuba's right to make decisions within its own borders, and failure to reply to the

US challenge to its independent decision-making power would have amounted to forfeiting sovereignty.

It was nationalism that led the Cuban revolutionaries to socialism. The United States represented capitalism and imperial power; in reaction, Cuban nationalism and socialism became integrated into a new revolutionary ideology.

The Bay of Pigs invasion, organized and financed by the CIA, captured the capitalist–socialist dichotomy well. On April 15, 1961, airplanes piloted by Cubans working for the CIA bombarded the airports at Santiago de Cuba and Havana prior to a planned invasion by Cuban exiles. Seven persons died. Speaking at the burial ceremony the next day, Fidel Castro said that a counterrevolutionary invasion, seeking to restore capitalism, was imminent. On that day, he characterized the Cuban revolution as socialist. The invasion began on April 17 and was defeated within two days. Again, just as cutting the sugar quota led to socialization of the basic means of production, the Bay of Pigs invasion made Cuba's identification with socialism the only possible reaction that a radical nationalist movement could take.

This turn in the revolution surprised the United States as well as the Soviet Union. In fact, the Cuban experience defied some basic tenets of orthodox Marxist theory. Communists, following the views of Lenin, had believed that without a revolutionary theory (i.e., Marxism-Leninism), there could be no revolutionary party or movement. And without the party, there could be no revolutionary practice—seizing political power and socializing the means of production. In Cuba, the formula was reversed. Power was seized without a revolutionary theory or party. The state took over a significant part of the economy and months later called the outcome socialism. Only much later, on December 2, 1961, was Marxism-Leninism formally adopted. It was only in early 1962 that a revolutionary party began to form, and it held its first party congress thirteen years later. Thus the Cuban experience with revolution is unique in many ways.

The Political System

During the first sixteen years of revolutionary rule, Cuba's leaders successfully merged charisma with patrimonialism and a high degree of mass mobilization. The Communist Party did not play an important role during that first phase of the revolution, since the very nature of a political party runs counter to charismatic authority. Until 1970, political and organizational work was concentrated on the growth and development of mass organizations. (Cuba has six mass organizations: Cuban Confederation of Labor, Federation of Cuban Women, National Association of Small Farmers, Federation of Secondary School Students, the Union of Young Pioneers, and the Committees for the Defense of the Revolution.)

The institutionalization of the revolution after 1975 redefined the role of the Communist Party. It was to coordinate, control, lead, and supervise the tasks of the state and the mass organizations, without administering. But to assume such roles, the party had to grow, train its cadres, develop efficient methods of leadership, establish internal discipline, and improve its political training as well as the educational level of its members.

In 1965 the Communist Party had just 45,000 members; ten years later, the number had increased to 211,642, and in 1980, the membership numbered 434,143. The educational level has changed as well. In 1970, 33.6 percent of the members did not have a sixth grade education; nine years later, that proportion had declined to 11.4 percent. The proportion of members with higher education has also been rapidly increasing, from 2.8 percent in 1970 to 6.2 percent in 1979. Party cadres have shown even greater improvement, with 16 percent having had a high school education in 1975 and 75.5 percent five years later. Meanwhile, membership in the mass organizations has ceased to grow. Since the 1970s, the revolutionary leadership has been preparing the party to play the "leading role" that Marxist-Leninist theory had claimed for it. However, since 1991 there has been very little mention of Marxism or Leninism in the Cuban mass media or in the speeches of government figures.

COMMUNIST PARTY ORGANS

The present system of government is characterized by a complex web of interlocking power relations. The Communist Party, the state, and the government are functionally differentiated, although some individuals occupy more than one post in each of these three centers of power. The Communist Party, at present the locus of political power, is highly structured. At the base, the party membership is organized in cells, or *núcleos,* 26,500 of them in 1980. The party is organized on a territorial basis (local, municipal, provincial, and national).

On the national level, the party congress is formally the highest authority, but it meets only once every five years. Delegates to the party congress, elected from subordinate territorial levels, elect (actually, ratify) from their ranks the members of the Central Committee (CC). Because of its size, and the fact that its members have other responsibilities, the CC has only about two one-day plenums annually. At these meetings, the CC selects the members of the Political Bureau (PB) and the Secretariat.

The PB makes policy between congresses and plenums on behalf of the CC and the party. Its task consists of translating general principles and aims into more precise policy, and its decisions are binding.

The Secretariat is also a powerful institution. The PB may appear to be more powerful than the Secretariat because the latter answers to the former (just as the PB answers to the CC, and it in turn responds to the party congress). However, it is more useful to see the PB and the Secretariat as functioning in different arenas.

The Secretariat is responsible to maintain the party apparatus. It decides who joins and who is expelled. It oversees internal political education and promotion within party ranks. The Secretariat also transmits the PB guidelines to the institutions of the state, government, and mass organizations. In 1992, as the Soviet bloc disappeared, the Secretariat was abolished but was reestablished in 2005.

The internal organization of the Communist Party parallels that of the administrative and political divisions of the island, with 14 committees representing the provinces and 169 representing municipalities. Below the municipal committees are the party cells, organized at work centers, schools, and military barracks. At the base, then, the party is organized by function rather than by territory (which discriminates against people who are not employed, do not study, or are not in the military).

The functions and hierarchical lines of the CC, the PB, and the Secretariat are clearly demarcated, but in practice the demarcations seem to be insignificant. Many of the same individuals serve in all three bodies. The Secretariat has nine members—five are full members of the PB, and two are alternates. Political power is interlocked for the simple reason that the same person can have two entirely different statuses and roles. In 1982 thirty men and one woman comprised the core of revolutionary power in Cuba (what in Mexico is known as "the revolutionary family").

The Communist Party makes decisions but does not execute them, guides but does not administer. The implementation of policy—practical day-to-day decision making and policy formulation—is carried out by a different set of institutions. From 1959 to 1975, the people who had political power and those who held key government posts were the same. In 1976, however, a constitution was issued proclaiming the socialist nature of the Cuban state and establishing the rules of government. Executive, legislative, and judicial powers were separated. Granted, the executive still had some legislative prerogatives, but nothing similar to those that existed between 1959 and 1975.

In the 1980s a number of changes took place within the Communist Party. Some of these were due to the internal dynamics of the revolution. The party grew from just 50,000 persons in 1965 to 523,639 members in 1986. There was some fluctuations, but party recruitment increased faster than the population grew. Between 1975 and 1980, it grew almost 21 percent; between 1980 and 1986 it dropped to 4.1 percent. After 1986 there was a renewed effort to recruit members, particularly young ones. Tied to the reduction in membership age was an improvement in educational level. In 1975, 19.6 percent of the members had a ninth grade education or more; in 1986 the figure was 72.4 percent. This shift reflects the overall improvement in the educational level of the population at large.

There have been some changes in party organization over the years. The Central Committee membership can be divided into full members (who actually participate in decision making) and alternates (who may take the place of full members due to death, promotion, etc.). There were 100 full members in the CC in 1965. As the PCC membership grew, new members were incorporated into leadership positions. The PCC avoided demoting CC full members, however, by inventing the concept of alternates. By 1986 the Central Committee had 146 members and 79 alternates.

The Political Bureau also expanded. Whereas it had eight members when the party was organized in 1965, it had thirteen full members and fourteen alternates in early 1990. Eleven of the fourteen alternates had assumed their positions since 1986.

At the 1986 party congress, Fidel Castro noted that "we had to renew or die." Thus, he went on, "we must trust our youth." Indeed a policy of affirmative action that targeted women, the young, and blacks began from the 1986 congress on. At previous congresses the party stressed the recruitment of workers and peasants. In other words, class had priority. By 1980 special attention was being given to increasing the number of women in the PCC. The same theme was repeated at the third congress, but the PCC went further this time, enunciating a policy of affirmative action for women, blacks, and the young. The main report read by Fidel Castro stated, "The mechanisms that ensure the correct selection, permanence and promotion of cadre must be improved constantly on the basis of thorough, critical, objective and systematic evaluations and with appropriate attention to development and training. Women's representation in keeping with their participation and their important contribution to the building of socialism in our country must be ensured, along with the existence of a growing reserve of promising young people born and tempered in the forge of the Revolution."

In 1986 women accounted for 21.5 percent of party membership. (The number of women in the CC had increased to 18.8 percent of the combined CC membership.) Ethnicity has become an important issue in the party, perhaps related to the growing influence, education, and expectations of the black population. A Communist Party document stated that "in order for the Party's leadership to duly reflect the ethnic composition of our people, it must include those compatriots of proven revolutionary merit and talents who in the past had been discriminated against because of their skin color."

Fidel Castro has noted that the "rectification of historical injustices" such as racial discrimination "cannot be left to spontaneity." By 1986, only 28.4 percent of the CC membership was black or mulatto. But the affirmative action policies adopted by the revolutionary leadership suggested that the failures in this area were acknowledged and steps were to be taken to address them.

The Communist Party's internal organization was also confronted by the changes begun in 1985 in the Soviet Union, and then taken up by Eastern Europe in the late 1980s, as well as by Communist parties throughout the rest of the world. Thus, in mid-February 1990, the Communist Party leadership announced plans to transform itself. The promised changes, however, did not imply the abolition of the one-party state. A party document stated, "What we are talking about is the perfecting of a single, Leninist party based on the principles of democratic centralism." (This happened precisely as the Soviets abandoned a constitutional monopoly on power.)

In 1990 the ten-member Secretariat was reduced, without explanation, to six persons. As a consequence of the changes, the labor movement no longer had a representative (the peasant/farmer sector had no direct voice either). The representative of the labor movement (former head of the Cuban Confederation of Labor) was also dropped from the Political Bureau at that time.

In summary, while the permanent full-time membership of the Political Bureau remained fairly constant throughout the 1980s, the alternate membership experienced drastic change. However, the alternates have little power as long as they remain in that position. In a sense, the increasing number of alternates suggests that rising stars within the revolutionary ranks have been promised power and authority but are not permitted to shape decisions within the Political Bureau and the Secretariat. True, the alternates have power vis-à-vis the society at large. They participate in controlling key social, economic, and governmental institutions; but since the core of power resides within the party, they merely implement decisions made elsewhere.

At the 1991 Communist Party congress, the congress announced that religious persons could become members of the Communist Party and outlined the major policy changes that would follow, for example, opening major areas of the economy to foreign investment, developing a mixed economy under the guidance of the state, allowing a greater role to private enterprise, and establishing party cells at the neighborhood level (until that time, party cells were found only at the workplace). At the fourth PCC congress in 1992, the Secretariat was abolished. The position of candidates to the Political Bureau was also abolished, but its membership was increased to twenty-five.

The Communist Party was supposed to have a congress in 1996, but it was postponed until the following year. The 1997 fifth congress of the Communist Party allowed the membership to reassess the results of the economic policies adopted since the collapse of the Soviet bloc (post 1991), when the country decriminalized the use of the dollar, fostered foreign investment, stressed the importance of tourism, and legalized family remittances to the island, as well as small private entrepreneurship in some areas of the urban economy, the privatization of most state farms, and the widespread use of market relations among state enterprises. From 1991 to 1996 some party members dropped out or "lost their perspective" during those difficult and critical years. In August 1994, urban unrest led to serious concerns about the country's political stability. A 1996 party document noted that during the early years of the "special period" the PCC had to deal with objective material shortages as well as with "selfishness, a mercantile outlook, the desire of some to just make money, consumerism and the loss of revolutionary ethical norms." During the same period pressure from the US government had increased, as manifested in the Torricelli Act (1992) and the Helms-Burton Bill (1996) (Chapter 14).

From 1994 to 1997, the PCC leadership—led by Raúl Castro—traveled around the country striving to revitalize its methods and membership. The national leaders demanded a more critical attitude from the lower political levels of the party, stressing that local political and economic resources were needed to solve pressing problems. The key message was "it can be done" if the party ranks took the initiative without expecting assistance from above. By 1994, despite the social problems, the Cuban economy began to improve. Over the next two years economic growth became significant, and the political leadership was in a stronger position to have its Communist Party congress.

Prior to the fifth party congress of October 1997, the mass organizations held their own respective congresses, with the themes of political unity and grassroots initiative. In the face of such difficulties, membership was opened to a greater number of workers. The fifth congress recognized the need to extend to all state enterprises the *nuevo sistema empresarial,* a managerial experiment initiated within the armed forces that provided incentives to workers, including the option of being paid partly in dollars or having access to dollar-based goods. Fidel Castro did not speak at the fifth congress, leading many analysts to assume that he was ill. However, having Raúl Castro play such a central role showed that Fidel was indeed replaceable. In the 1980s, on a yearly average, about 27,000 persons joined the PCC. From 1992 to 1996, about 233,000 workers joined, an average of 46,000 annually. That meant that the political organization had about 30 percent new members during the most difficult period of the revolutionary period.

By May 2003 the PCC had 856,262 members organized in 62,800 grassroots cells, which are organized at workplaces, schools, military units, and by place of residence, the latter a uniquely Cuban feature. Since 1992 there has been significant leadership change at the municipal, provincial, and national levels of the Communist Party. Even some of the historical figures have been replaced, although control remains in the hands of older members. Nonetheless, a growing number of cabinet members and state legislative and administrative leaders are now under the age of fifty. The majority of the new party leaders are professionals with technical training. The youthfulness of the PCC at the provincial and municipal levels is even more extraordinary; the typical party leader is thirty-four years old.

At the fifth congress, the Central Committee membership was reduced from 225 to 150 members while the Political Bureau declined from 26 to 24. This was a mechanism to reduce the influence of the so-called *históricos*, or "old guard," within the revolutionary ranks. The Political Bureau had taken over functions previously undertaken by the Secretariat, such as dealing with the party's internal matters. A PCC congress was due in 2003, but it has not yet been held. In 2005 the Secretariat was restored. It is expected that in 2010 a party congress will finally be held to decide the economic and political arrangements of the country. As of 2010 the PCC had approximately 800,000 members.

THE NATIONAL ASSEMBLY

In 1977, a National Assembly (NA) with formal legislative powers was established for the first time. The NA is a representative institution whose members are elected for five-year periods. Election is indirect, delegates being chosen by provincial assemblies. (Provincial elections are popular and direct.) The NA has 481 delegates and meets twice a year, usually for less than a week. It can generate legislation as well as approve it, but laws must be consonant with the general guidelines of the Communist Party. How much real power the NA possesses is debatable. Sessions are so short that there is little time to study, analyze, and debate. Recently some delegates have tried to represent their respective local constituencies, but the NA is not receptive to that idea. In general, the NA serves to legitimize decisions made elsewhere.

The real work of the NA is done by standing work committees and the Council of State (CS). Committee members are appointed. Chosen for their specialized knowledge rather than for their political credentials, they need not be delegates to any legislative body. The NA has fifteen committees, fourteen commissions, and nine departments. It should be noted that the persons elected to the assemblies, whether on the national, provincial, or municipal level, do not run on a particular political platform. They have no individual set of policy proposals; instead, they are chosen for their personal characteristics. It is a given that a candidate's political platform will be that of the Communist Party.

The National Assembly has come under criticism from the general population, its members, and members of the Communist Party. The people, at meetings with their elected representatives, have expressed dismay at the institution's lack of power and its incapacity to deal with substantive issues. The members of the municipal and provincial assemblies, on the other hand, have begun to lobby their own constituencies as well as the National Assembly, in order to acquire a greater role in making policy decisions, particularly in the area of economic and social policy. Finally, National Assembly members have complained that they ought to be able to work for a longer period of time, taking for themselves the powers enjoyed by the executive committees. They also have demanded a say in determining budgetary priorities, the size of the budget, and real control over matters of foreign policy.

At the Communist Party congress in 1991, these matters were addressed, and in 1992 the Cuban constitution was drastically changed in order to provide more power and influence to the National Assembly. The 1993 elections of the National Assembly produced a major overhaul of the elected members; new people entered the scene, most of them in their thirties. Direct elections were established at each legislative level: municipal, provincial and national.

When the NA is not meeting, its functions and prerogatives are assumed by its executive committee, the Council of State, which is selected by the NA from its own ranks. The CS carries out the decisions of the NA as well as tasks outlined in the 1976 constitution. In 1982 the CS had forty members. Since the CS issues laws when the NA is not functioning, the CS, in a sense, is the country's real legislature. The CS also interprets the law, exercises legislative initiative, declares war or makes peace, removes or appoints members of the Council of Ministers, gives instructions of a general nature to the office of the attorney general and to the judiciary, supervises the diplomatic corps, vetoes ministerial decisions as well as those made at any other level, and exercises any other power that the NA may give it.

The president of the CS is expected to control and supervise the activities of all government ministries and administrative agencies. He could take over any ministry or government post and nominate CM members to the NA. He is also commander in chief of the armed forces. The president, first vice president, and five vice presidents of the CS are all in the Political Bureau. The president and the first vice president also head the Secretariat. The other thirty-three members of the CS have been in the PB, the CC, or, until recently, the Secretariat.

Since 1992, the National Assembly has had elections in 1993, 1998, 2003. The most recent legislature has 390 (64.04 percent) males and 219 females (35.96 percent). The average age is 47 years; 67 percent of the deputies are white and 378 of them (62 percent) are new to the office. Since 2005 the National Assembly has played a more active role, particularly through its specialized commissions, which meet throughout the year and also monitor how the executive branch operates.

THE COUNCIL OF MINISTERS

The government proper is the Council of Ministers (CM), whose members are appointed by the president of the Council of State and ratified by the NA. The CM has one president, one first vice president, twelve vice presidents, thirty ministers, forty-eight commission members, eight advisers, one deputy secretary, and one minister secretary. The CM administers the state apparatus, executes the laws, issues decrees in accordance with existing laws, develops and administers the national budget, carries out foreign policy, and organizes and directs social, economic, cultural, scientific, and military matters. The CM's Executive Committee (comprising the president, first vice president, and the twelve vice presidents) is the real power in government. In 1982, of the fourteen persons on the Executive Committee, nine were in the PB, two were in the Secretariat, five were full members of the CS, and six others were alternates.

Before 1976, the same individuals performed numerous functions although they had one role. They were revolutionaries with power—revolutionary leaders assumed both political and administrative functions. Political leadership and administration are now separate. Charismatic authority is being transformed into a legal-rational system of authority, but during that transition, which may take years, the rules and regulations of the new political structure are elaborated, defined, and given content as well as life by the charismatic authority.

Fidel and Raúl Castro have a tremendous amount of power over the key institutions of Cuban society. But this is to be expected. A charismatic system of authority transfers legitimacy to a legal-rational type of authority by placing the representatives of the previous system in key positions. As time goes on and the charismatic leaders play by the new rules, the institutions themselves gain legitimacy. Of course, it remains to be seen whether such a process will continue to unfold in the future. In 1982 Fidel Castro held the following posts: first secretary of the Political Bureau and the Secretariat; member of the Central Committee; deputy to the National Assembly; president of the Council of State, the Council of Ministers, and the Executive Committee of the Council of Ministers; and commander in chief of the armed forces. Raúl Castro was the second secretary of the Political Bureau and the Secretariat; member of the Central Committee; deputy to the National Assembly; first vice president of the Council of State, the Council of Ministers, and the Executive Committee of the Council of Ministers; and minister of the armed forces. Thus the answer to the perennial question, What will happen when Fidel Castro dies? has to be—on the basis of the institutionalization of authority and the resources that Raúl Castro commands—that Raúl would succeed his brother. And that is what occurred after Fidel Castro became seriously ill in late July 2006.

The succession question, a problem confronted by any political system based on charismatic authority, seemingly has been handled very well without any traumatic consequences. Moreover, the issue that many scholars mentioned—the concern that a gerontocracy was ruling the island—has been handled as well. The new team members that Raúl Castro put in place beginning in 2008 were, on the average in their forties and fifties, including high-ranking military positions (although there they are a little older). Of course, there is not much of a Communist movement. There is no longer a Soviet bloc. The East-West conflict has been replaced by the US government war against "terrorism." Cuba, in a sense, no longer commands much attention in Washington.

The European Parliament, as well as traditional leftist friends of the Cuban revolution, is demanding the establishment of a more open political system in the island. By its very success, the revolution has created a more sophisticated political culture, a more educated population, and a more generalized belief that the people can rule themselves. The period of charismatic rule is gone. The transfer of authority from charismatic leader to representative institutions has taken place since 2008.

How this will be accomplished has not yet been resolved. Nor is there a consensus within Cuba that this should be done. Many people still identify solely with Fidel Castro, the charismatic leader (*el original,* the man who conceived, organized, made, consolidated, and maintained the revolution for over thirty-eight years). In fact, those who wish to preserve the charismatic type of political regime note that "in the face of the crisis of socialism and the aggressive euphoria of North American imperialism" it is impossible to play with Western political models. Their reasoning suggests that the United States is now ready to attack Cuba, as the revolution becomes one of the few surviving socialist/revolutionary regimes in the world. In their view the only possibility for survival is to be in a permanent state of readiness, which only the mass mobilization qualities of charismatic authority can ensure. Perhaps this reasoning would be easily dismissed if the revolutionaries thought that the United States had no intention of attacking the revolution, but US policymakers, in a sense, have contributed to the fear of attack. (See "US-Cuban Relations" below.)

From 1989 to 1992, the Cuban revolutionaries returned to the methods of earlier years. Mass mobilization and calls to nationalism have become a daily occurrence. The revolutionary leadership asserts that Cuba's independence and the very future of socialism depend on the survival and durability of the revolution. Thus political reforms have been defined as concessions that could lead to revolutionary defeat. According to Fidel Castro, in a number of speeches given in late 1989 and early 1990, Cuba's independence, national sovereignty, and the defense of "socialism" are inexorably linked. The battle cry "Fatherland or Death" of earlier years has been transformed into "Socialism or Death."

After the 1991 Communist Party congress and the 1992 constitutional reform, the political picture changed again. The nationalist theme was replaced by stress on economic efficiency and reorganization. One heard less talk of socialism as seminars on management, quality circles, and profitability became the order of the day. The regime had begun building a state capitalist economy without private capitalists.

Calls to emulate the experience of Eastern Europe are dismissed by Cuban revolutionaries as another form of "intellectual and political colonialism." Cuba's realities, they say, are different from those of Europe. Cuba and the other countries of Latin America must find their own answers on the basis of their own material and cultural conditions. Moreover, the recent return to power by electoral means of socialists and even Communists in Eastern Europe had given cause for hope to those in power in Havana. The dismal economic problems in Russia and elsewhere in Eastern Europe further strengthen the point held by the Cuban revolutionaries that the state has to play a central role in economic policy. Moreover, the recent tilt to the left in the political landscape in Latin America (Lula in Brazil, Kirchner in Argentina, Chávez in Venezuela, Correa in Ecuador) means that Havana has new allies in this hemisphere. The right-wing, interventionist foreign and military policies of the George W. Bush Administration have made new friends for Cuba throughout the world as well.

Cuba, by 2010, is seriously discussing at every level of the society what is to be done. National sovereignty will continue to be defended, but it is clear that the political institutions will be revised, changed somewhat, and that a new model of what a socialist Cuba would look like. The role of state enterprises will not be dismissed or abolished, but how they operate will certainly change. The same is true as to the increasing role that cooperatives will have in the urban economy, just as it has been the case in agriculture. Private farming has made a significant return, becoming the most productive sector of in agriculture.

REDISTRIBUTION AND ECONOMIC EXPERIMENTATION

Cuba is a poor and underdeveloped country. When the Cuban revolutionaries attained power, the country confronted serious economic problems. Foremost among these was dependence on one crop—sugar—and one buyer—the United States. How much sugar the United States bought was determined by the US Congress and the Agriculture Department. The sugar harvest lasted, at best, four months; thus Cuba also faced serious unemployment and underemployment.

Prior to the revolution, the unemployment rate averaged 16.4 percent of the available workforce. However, when the sugar harvest ended, it could climb to 20–21 percent. In 1957, only 37.2 percent of the labor force worked the entire year. Social inequality was also a problem. According to a Labor Ministry report issued in 1957, 62.2 percent of the employed received an average monthly salary of less than 75 pesos (peso value was then equal to the dollar). Only 38 percent of the male workers earned more than $75 per month. In 1956, 34 percent of the total population of Cuba received 10 percent of the national income, and only 7.2 percent of the employees earned more than $1,000 a year. A family of six, on the average, had a yearly income of $548.75 and could spend about $0.17 per person for food on a daily basis. In the first year of the revolution, 73 percent of all families had an average income of $715 per year. Poverty was widespread, particularly in the rural areas.

Land was unequally distributed. A small portion of the landowners owned most of it. In 1959, 8.5 percent of all farms comprised 71.6 percent of the land area in farms; on the other hand, 80 percent of all farms comprised 13.8 percent of the farmland. At the time, 94.6 percent of the land was privately owned; the state controlled just 5.4 percent. Only 32.2 percent of the landowners worked their own land; 25.5 percent of the farmland was administered on behalf of the landowners, and 42.3 percent was rented out or sharecropped. One-quarter of the best agricultural land was owned by US companies, while 63.7 percent of the agricultural workforce had no land of its own. Most of those who owned their land were usually engaged in production for family use since their parcels were very small. Altogether, US corporate interests controlled 2 million acres (810,000 hectares) of land in the island, out of a total surface of 23 million acres (9.3 million hectares)—8.7 percent of the national territory. In Camagüey province, six companies controlled 20.7 percent of the land.

US interests could be found elsewhere as well. Total US investments had reached a little over $1 billion when the revolutionaries took power; this was the equivalent of 40 percent of the GNP. US capital dominated 90 percent of the utilities, 50 percent of the railways, 40 percent of the production of raw sugar, 25 percent of all bank deposits. US interests controlled more than 80 percent of mining, oil production, hotels, pharmaceuticals, detergents, fertilizers, auto dealerships, tires, imports, and exports. Of 161 sugar mills, US companies owned 36. US capital was shifting away from traditional investments (sugar, utilities, mining) and moving toward new areas (loans, imports, exports, light industry). The reported rate of return on US investments was 9 percent, but Cuban revolutionary authorities have estimated that the real rate was about 23 percent. From 1952 to 1958, US companies repatriated an average of $50 million yearly (new investment during the period was $40 million yearly).

In 1958, the United States supplied 72 percent of Cuban imports and bought 69 percent of Cuban exports. Cuba's balance of trade from 1948 to 1958 was positive with most of the world, except the United States. It has been estimated that the rate of economic growth from 1945 to 1958 averaged 4.3 percent per year while the per capita income growth was 1.8 percent.

When the revolutionaries seized power, they found an economy that relied on sugar production, primarily controlled in its numerous facets by US capital, as well as an economy that was unable to generate sufficient jobs in the primary or secondary sector to absorb the surplus labor. The Cuban economy was essentially capitalist, with a large proletarian labor force in the countryside (over 64 percent of the rural laborers were wage earners).

In the first two years of the revolution two major trends developed. On the one hand, a progressive redistribution of income took place.

- February 2, 1959: All debts owed to the Cuban state were suspended
- March 10, 1959: House rents lowered 50 percent
- May 17, 1959: Agrarian Reform Law began redistribution of land
- December 23, 1959: Social security made available to all workers
- October 14, 1960: Urban Reform Law established procedure by which renter would use rent payments as amortization in order to purchase home
- June 7, 1961: Free universal education established
- August 1, 1961: Transportation costs lowered
- September 21, 1961: Child care centers subsidized by the state
- March 12, 1962: Rationing introduced, price of all food items frozen (remained frozen until the early 1980s)

The second trend was a radical change in prevailing property relations. By the end of 1960, the critical areas of the Cuban economy had been taken over by the state. All banking, export-import operations, energy, and utilities were owned by the state. More than three-quarters of industry, construction, and transportation was also in the hands of the government. Only the bulk of agriculture was in the hands of the private sector, and that was primarily the result of the redistribution of land.

Between 1959 and 1960, there was no talk of socialism among the authorities. Economic thinking revolved around the ideas of rapid industrialization, import substitution, and reducing the role of sugar while diversifying agriculture. There were no real controls of an economic nature. The capitalist market was not replaced; it disappeared, and nothing took its place. No one seemed to pay attention to capital accumulation. The central idea was simply to establish greater equality by increasing the income and resources of the lower classes. This was the distributionist phase of the revolution. As the state moved into the private economy, it found that it lacked the personnel to run the new enterprises; often those who were considered loyal were put in command. They had to learn their jobs while performing them. Consumption improved across the board, but it led to shortages because no effort was made to increase stocks.

In 1961, after the revolutionaries discovered that they had socialism, they began looking for a model to emulate. The Czechoslovakian model was copied and industrialization was stressed; sugar was set aside. From 1961 to 1963, some problems developed with the emerging rural middle class. Since the revolutionary regime had little use for sugar and industry seemed more appealing, a second agrarian reform was issued that abolished the remaining medium-size landholdings. During this period, the state further socialized the means of production so that it controlled 70 percent of the agricultural sector and more than 95 percent of industry, transportation, and construction. The private sector could sell only to the state. The Cuban economy had the highest index of state control in the world. A generalized process of centralization of economic decision making took root, led by Ché Guevara from the Ministry of Industries.

During this period Cuba and the United States had reached the equivalent of a state of war (in 1961, the Bay of Pigs; in 1962, the October missile crisis). Within Cuba, the revolutionaries continued their distributionist policies. Health care, for example, became free. Unemployment disappeared, primarily because the productivity of labor declined and several people were hired to do a job that in the past had been performed by one person. Also, many of the previously unemployed were absorbed by the service sector. From 1961 to 1962, sugar output dropped from 6.8 million tons to 3.8 million. Yet few sectors were growing or generating the necessary foreign exchange. This led to a rectification of the economic policy.

In 1963 the revolutionary authorities abandoned their stress on industrialization; sugar was to be the pivot of Cuba's economic development. The new economic strategy was to be based on modernizing Cuban agriculture, introducing up-to-date forces of production, while improving the skills of the workers. The effort would be centered on the state farms. At the time, two entirely different economic models for constructing the future socialist society were being discussed.

Meanwhile, the United States had imposed an economic blockade on the island in 1962, and Mexico was the only country in the hemisphere that traded with the Cubans. Moreover, Cuba's terms of trade deteriorated from 1964 to 1966 due primarily to the drop in the price of sugar (in 1963, the price was 8.3 cents per pound; by 1966, it had dropped to 1.8 cents). So the cost of imports increased greatly.

Cuba's most original phase began in 1966 and lasted until 1970. The goal was to produce increasing amounts of sugar, regardless of the world market for sugar. Moreover, since the country did not have the material resources to reward effort, moral (i.e., political) incentives were to be used to motivate the workers. The highly centralized economic plans of the previous period were replaced by sectoral, independent, decentralized plans. The plans (and enterprises) received money allocated through a central budget. Enterprises did not engage in mercantile relations with one another, and they did not have to show a profit. Cost accounting was disregarded altogether. Efficiency depended on meeting output goals, regardless of cost. During this period, a concentrated effort was made to avoid bureaucratic rigidity and to discourage criticism of the approach. Revolutionary consciousness and commitment, it was believed, would do the trick.

At the same time, the state controlled industry, construction, 98 percent of transportation, and every single retail business. The labor force involved in harvesting sugar was militarized in 1969. Sugar output went through cycles. From 1966 to 1967, it went up from 4.5 million tons to 6.2 million; then it dropped to 5.1 million in 1968 and to 4.4 million in 1969. The 1970 harvest was the largest in the history of the country, but it had a tremendous negative impact on the larger economy since most of the national resources were concentrated on meeting the goal of producing 10 million tons of sugar.

Economic efficiency dropped abruptly during this period. Economic growth averaged just 0.4 percent. The revolutionary authorities had ended the connection between output and salaries; that is, workers got paid regardless of production. Moreover, during this period, the state distributed, free of charge, water, public phone service, and child care, among other things. Gratuities were on the increase, and labor productivity declined. As excess money circulated, purchasing power exceeded goods available, contributing to labor absenteeism. During the period, the country invested up to 30 percent of its material product on economic growth, which forced it to rely more than ever on imports. The economy did not fare as poorly as might have expected because the price of sugar consistently climbed during these years (in 1966, the price was 1.8 cents per pound; 1967, 1.9; 1968, 1.9; 1969, 3.2; 1970, 3.68).

In 1970 the revolutionary authorities reconsidered their strategy and revised it, shifting from the budgetary system of finance to what is called *cálculo económico,* or self-finance system. The new system stressed centralized economic planning, cost accounting and enterprise profitability, material rewards, mercantile relations among enterprises, and contracts between enterprises and labor unions. Productivity and efficiency came to be measured on the basis of the rate of return (connected to the cost of production). Managerial expertise on the administrative level began to take precedence over revolutionary zeal. The role of sugar was deemphasized as more attention was paid to the diversification of agriculture and the development of mineral resources. The *cálculo económico* had become nationwide in its application by 1977. Thus 1971 to 1976 were years of transition as the shift away from the budgetary system coincided with the move toward institutionalization. This was not coincidental. Cuba's economic and political organizations are highly interrelated. Charismatic authority went hand in hand with moral incentives and mass mobilization to achieve economic goals; rational-legal authority now permeates the political as well as the economic spheres.

The new economic and political organization seemed to pay off very well. The gross material product (GMP)—the gross value of production from agriculture, industry, and construction—has shown some remarkable developments; for example, the GMP growth rates for the 1970s were as follows.

1971: 4.2 percent
1972: 9.7 percent

1973:   13.1 percent
1974:   7.8 percent
1975:   12.3 percent
1976:   3.5 percent
1977:   3.1 percent
1978:   8.2 percent
1979:   2.4 percent

The improvement and subsequent deterioration of the economy in the 1970s, however, were not due to internal conditions. Rather, the price of sugar in the world market affects the general performance of the Cuban economy. Sugar prices rose from 4.5 cents per pound in 1970 to 29.6 in 1974 and 20.3 in 1975 before they began to drop, reaching 7.4 cents in 1982. The cycle was reflected in the Cuban economy because, more than twenty years after the revolution, the export of sugar has remained crucial to the overall functioning of the economy. Sugar accounts for 80 percent of foreign earnings.

That the revolutionary government worked out an arrangement with the Soviet Union which allowed the island to escape, to some extent, the cycles of the capitalist economy as far as sugar is concerned. Since the 1960s, the Soviets paid Cuba a much higher price for sugar than the price in the open world market. Only on three occasions (1963, 1972, 1974) were world market prices higher than those paid by the Soviets. By 1979, when the world price had reached a low point of 9.6 cents, the Soviets were paying 44 cents. The treatment that the revolutionary government received from the Soviet Union was positive and extraordinary. In 1972 the USSR agreed to postpone the payment of Cuba's debt until 1986. The debt covered a period of twenty-five years during which Cuba paid no interest.

Approximately 20 percent of Cuba's trade in the early 1980s was with the capitalist market economies. The terms of trade were such, however, that while the price of sugar declined, the prices of the products Cuba had to buy to process the sugarcane and produce sugar went up. (A metric ton of urea in 1972 sold for $76, but by 1980 the price was $303. Similarly, the price of ammonia nitrate rose from $206 to $506.) In constant 1970 prices, a pound of sugar in 1982 sold for 2.8 cents. In order to import the same amount of goods, then, Cuba had to export much more.

Cuba's economic performance in the first five years of the 1980s was significantly better than that of the rest of Latin America. But the Cuban situation started to change in 1986, the year that Fidel Castro announced the initiation of the "rectification" campaign in the economy. The campaign denounced and took steps against private enterprise (the free peasants market created in 1980, private urban businesses, and the reliance on profitability as an indicator for the allocation of resources). The rectification campaign, in other words, put political decisions rather than economic logic in command. The overall performance of the economy suffered as a result.

Moreover, events in Eastern Europe and the Soviet Union damaged external trade. The Eastern European countries shifted toward convertible currency transactions, and the democratization of the Soviet political system led to a greater demand for consumer goods just as the situation produced tremendous uncertainty

| TABLE 18.1 | Imports | |
Year	Growth Rate	Total (millions USD)
1989:	3.4%	8,608
1990:	–5.7	8,017
1991:	–37.0	4,702
1992:	–45.3	2,737
1993:	–5.4	2,339
1994:	–19.2	2,849
1995:	11.5	3,565
1996:	24.3	4,125
1997:	11.0	4,628
1998:	8.0	4,800

| TABLE 18.2 | Gross Internal Investments, Growth Rate |
Year	Growth Rate
1989:	10.1
1990:	- 2.9
1991:	-45.9
1992:	-58.3
1993:	-39.7
1994:	1.9
1995:	35.2
1996:	22.8
1997:	13.7
1998:	7.3

in the supply of goods from abroad. Cuban economic planning and performance hence suffered. The revolutionary government, with little foreign exchange in hand, adopted a policy of more import substitution. The strategy was accompanied by greater stress on export diversification.

In early 1990 Fidel Castro told the Cuban people that very difficult years could be expected and that rationing might be extended to new products. At the same time, the Cuban authorities contacted Mexican, Brazilian, and Japanese investors and made new offers to transnational corporations in hopes of overcoming the shortage of capital. Cuban foreign reserves in 1988 and 1989 were less than $100 million.

Between 1991 and 1992, Cuba's traditional economic allies disappeared, and so did all aid, credit, suppliers, and buyers. The Cuban economy suffered an almost overwhelming blow. From 1992 to 1993, imports collapsed, as did exports. Table 18.1 shows the pattern of imports from 1989, just prior to the collapse of the Soviet bloc, its impact on Cuba, and then the island's improvement, without any real assistance.

The absence of supplies and raw materials meant that economic output declined between 30 and 35 percent in just two years. Decline and renewed growth in internal investment in the 1990s is indicated in Table 18.2.

By 1994 the economy touched bottom. The following year it grew by about 3 percent, and in 1996 it achieved a growth of 7.8 percent (Table 18.3). Bouncing back, however, has not meant that the overall standard of living has improved significantly. In the late 1990s, Cuba still produced at a level below that of 1985. Yet the positive turn in the economy has been quite extraordinary. Foreign investments, tourism, and nickel exports were the three major contributors to the recovery. However, more recently, the export of human capital as to obtain foreign exchange has increased. Cuba provides doctors, nurses, and technical personnel worldwide. Cuban biotechnology products and medicines have been remarkable and successful.

TABLE 18.3   Gross National Product

Year	Growth Rate	Per Inhabitant
1989:	1.5%	1.0
1990:	-2.9%	-3.9
1991:	-9.5%	-10.4
1992:	-9.9	-10.6
1993:	-13.6	-14.2
1994:	0.6	0.2
1995:	2.5	2.2
1996:	7.8	7.2
1997:	2.5	2.1
1998:	1.3	0.9

TABLE 18.4   Population Growth and Growth Rate

Year	Total	Growth Rate
1989:	10.5 million	0.5%
1990:	10.6	1.1
1991:	10.7	1.0
1992:	10.8	0.8
1993:	10.9	0.7
1994:	10.9	0.4
1995:	10.9	0.3
1996:	11	0.4
1997:	11	0.4
1998:	11	0.5

The population of Cuba is about 11 million. Table 18.4 shows absolute population growth and rate of growth over the course of a decade.

The country is highly urban (in 1958, 58.7 percent of the people lived in cities; by 1983 the figure was 64.5 percent). The mortality rate is 7.1 per 1,000 inhabitants, and life expectancy increased from 58 years in 1959 to 74.8 years in 2001. The infant mortality rate, a major index of how much poverty and inequality a society has, has changed radically, dropping from a high of 33 to 6.5 in 2002. The age distribution of the population has changed as well. Before the revolution, 36.2 percent of the population was younger than fifteen; in 2000 the figure was 21.3 percent. At the same time, the percentage of people over sixty increased from 4.2 percent in 1958 to 14.5 percent in 2000. By 2002, 1.4 million Cubans lived on income from pensions. While the population is getting older and living longer, the birth rate has declined. In 1955 the population growth rate (per thousand) was 16, but in the year 2000 the rate stood at 2.3. As the population gets older, there is further decline in the population growth rate. Opportunities offered to women further contribute to a drop in the natality of the female population. The dependency ratio continues to increase (it stood at 55.0 in the year 2000). The city of Havana contains 17 percent of the population over the age of 60. The Cuban family tends to be small. In 1995 the typical household had 3.4 members, with little variation between urban and rural areas; 53.7 percent of the families are nuclear, that is, two generations living under the same roof; however, 42 percent have three generations under the same roof or in close proximity. The population in 2002 was 76 percent urban. From 1990 to the present the urban population has grown by 0.7 percent per year (the growth rate was 2.1 percent from 1970 to 1991).

Illiteracy has been reduced to less than 4 percent, and almost the entire population has received a primary education. At present, 96–97 percent of all the children of primary school age go to school. More than a million people have received a secondary education since 1959. One out of every 2.83 Cubans studies today. Full employment was achieved, although in the last few years unemployment has begun to grow (an estimated 2–4 percent of the male labor force in 1982). The social benefits that the population receives in the form of old-age pensions; workers' compensation; and maternity, illness, and social security allowances place Cuba at the forefront of all Latin American countries. It is by this means that the popularity and legitimacy of the revolution have been maintained. The distributionist policies of Cuba's revolutionary government have been far more successful than its economic policies, although numerous external political constraints have been imposed on the country.

Since 1993, however, the economic policies that have been introduced for the sake of survival have increased the degree of social inequality in the society. Despite government policies to counter the trend, social stratification and inequality have gained ground. This phenomenon has been exacerbated by the remittances sent by Cubans living abroad, the increasing role of the market as a mechanism to distribute goods, and the emergence of tourism. As Cuba has become a more complex socioeconomic system, poverty has become a real problem. Since the mid-1990s the Cuban government began to address the issue of a "population at risk." This was a serious matter in the eastern part of the island (Oriente), where by 1996 about 30 percent of the people were not earning enough to meet their basic needs; the estimated figure for the urban areas was 20 percent. Yet according to the Economic Commission for Latin America, Cuba remains the society with the greatest degree of social equality in all of Latin America (CEPAL, Equidad, Desarrollo y Ciudadanía, Santiago de Chile, 2001). Between 1996 and 1998, Cuba's Gini coefficient was 0.38 in urban areas (CEPAL, *Política Social y Reformas Estructurales: Cuba A Principios del Siglo XXI*, Mexico, 2004).

Lately, climate changes have impacted Cuba too. Hurricanes batter the island almost yearly. In 2008 three major hurricanes and two smaller ones reduced the island to rubble. The island lost over $15 billion, or 10 percent of its gross domestic product, half a million dwellings were damaged or destroyed, adding to a housing deficit of approximately 2 million. In the same year the world financial crisis also hit Cuba and affected it in numerous ways, producing a decline in exports, a drop in foreign remittances, and a reduction in tourist income. In fact, the Cuban people faced an economic crisis that was even more serious than the one that ensued soon after the fall of the Soviet Union. The next few years promise to be difficult for Cuba economically, in the absence of Fidel Castro and his style of governing. Whether Cuba's tremendous investment in human capital will pay off in the foreseeable future remains to be seen.

US–CUBAN RELATIONS

From 1959 to 1961, relations between the United States and Cuba progressively deteriorated. From 1961 to 1965, the two countries were in a state of semiwar. After 1965 the situation relaxed somewhat, but the two had no contact with each other. This situation continued until the last years of the Nixon administration, when unofficial talks began. Relations finally began to thaw during the Carter administration. Diplomatic relations were renewed on the section level (as opposed to the embassy level), but no steps were taken toward restoring trade relations. The US economic embargo was relaxed somewhat, as were travel restrictions between the two countries. When Ronald Reagan arrived in the White House, however, every major social upheaval in Latin America was interpreted as the work of Cuban subversion. Consequently the United States returned to policies reminiscent of the Eisenhower administration. Some Cubans even claimed that the Reagan administration attempted to assassinate the leaders of the revolution.

After eight years of the Reagan administration, the Cuban government assumed that President George Bush would improve bilateral relations, but they deteriorated. Dramatic changes in world Communism led the White House to conclude that Cuba would be one more "domino" and that there was no need to take any initiatives that would change the island's isolation. Rather, the White House began to broadcast television programs to the island and tightened the economic embargo, while attempting to link improvement in the relations between the United States and Eastern Europe with the severance of their ties with the revolution.

In 1992, an election year, both Democratic and Republican parties ended up supporting the Torricelli Bill, which imposed stricter US government policies on Cuba and shifted policymaking away from the executive branch and into the hands of the US Congress. Presidential candidate Bill Clinton campaigned in support of a harder line against the Cuban government. Once Clinton was elected president, the government in Havana adopted a wait-and-see policy but soon discovered that the new administration addressed Cuban policy on the basis of domestic political needs. The Clinton administration took a fairly aggressive approach of supporting human rights activists and political opposition, and the Cuban government reacted by imposing even harsher restrictions on anyone considered a political enemy. During the summer of 1994, as the standard of living deteriorated and political repression tightened in Cuba, the number of boat people leaving the island climbed. As the US government continued to welcome the so-called *balseros,* the Cuban government opted to allow anyone to leave the island by sea in order to reach the United States. The initiative forced the White House to begin negotiations with Havana. The end result was a break with past migration policy on Cuba. The United States no longer allowed Cubans to enter the country unless they followed proper procedures, including obtaining a visa.

Throughout 1995 there were hints and indications that perhaps relations between the two longtime adversaries would improve. Tension between the White House and the conservative exile organizations was manifested on many occasions. The conservative victory in congressional elections in 1994 meant that new forces pushed for a tougher stance on Cuba in US politics. Exile organizations believed that the time was right to manufacture a crisis. In the fall of 1995 and early 1996, conservative exiles initiated a series of ventures against the Cuban government, the best known led by Brothers to the Rescue, a Miami group that began to fly over Cuban territory to drop political leaflets. In early 1995, two of the planes were shot down by the Cuban air force. This incited the Congress to pass the Helms-Burton Bill, which President Clinton quickly signed. The legislation signified a return to the worst days of US interference in Cuba's domestic affairs, at the same time creating a mechanism to impose a policy of economic isolation by third countries on Cuba. Thus the policy of extraterritoriality was made into law and applied against Cuba and other countries as well.

With the George W. Bush administration, right-wing Cuban exiles got into strategic positions in Latin American policymaking in general, and Cuba in particular. Relations between the two countries have deteriorated in a number of areas, with the White House even announcing policies that further limit the travels of Americans and Cuban Americans to Cuba. The numerous people-to-people and cultural as well as educational contacts established during the Clinton administration have, for all practical purposes, come to an end. Family remittances by Cuban Americans have been reduced since the Bush Treasury Department restricted the very definition of what constitutes a Cuban family. Moreover, the administration has announced its commitment to produce "regime change" by providing more financial and other resources to the political opposition on the island (as long as it answers to the right-wing exiles). In early May 2004, the US government released a 500-page document indicating what it intends to do once the revolution has been overthrown. It outlined how Cuba's economy, politics, society, and culture should be organized, all under the direct supervision of the executive branch. The announced policy went beyond the Platt Amendment.

The political opposition in Cuba doesn't have much of a future. Moderate and liberal opponents on the island will be more isolated now than ever, since the United States does not recognize them. Seeking assistance from social democrats in Western Europe does not seem promising either (the European Union has toyed with developing an alternative approach to Cuba, but Washington has torpedoed the initiative). The opposition on the island is disorganized and thoroughly penetrated by the Cuban police.

In the United States, both the House of Representatives and the Senate have gone on record favoring closer relations with Cuba. Their position corresponds to what a growing sector of the business community wants. Moderate Cuban Americans also support such a change. Moreover, the demographics of the Cubans who live in the United States have changed; a greater number left the island in the 1990s, and they did so—primarily—for economic reasons. Eventually those trends will assert themselves. Cuban society has become more complex, and the same can be said of Cubans abroad.

Cuba has a policy of opening to anyone who is willing to engage in respectful communication, as long as Cuba's right of self-determination is acknowledged. Havana has improved relations with a large segment of the Cuban American community, even dropping the requirement that an exile needed a visa to enter the island. Normalization among Cubans on both sides of the Straits of Florida is paving the way for such action by the politicians in Washington.

The policy of confrontation reinforces the fortress mentality in Havana. Thus the revolutionary authorities reply by establishing worldwide ties of all types with every country that is willing to engage them. Tourism has become a sort of self-defense, since the more people get to know about Cuba and its revolution, the less they will consider using military means against it. Relations between the United States and Cuba did not improve during the George W. Bush administration. (See also Chapter 14.) However, US export of agricultural products to the island increased significantly after 2001. But so did US intervention into Cuban domestic affairs.

Cubans welcomed the election of Barack Obama. Expectations were high that relations would improve under his administration. Certainly the limitations that Bush II imposed on the travel of Cuban Americans and Americans hurt the island economy as well as cultural and professional exchanges. Obama abolished the limitations on Cuban American travel and did away with the regulations on remittances that people of Cuban ancestry could send to relatives and friends. Yet as of early 2010, the Obama team has not returned US policy to what it was under the Clinton or the first Bush administrations. In fact, commercial transactions between US corporations abroad and Cuba were freer under Richard Nixon and Gerald Ford. The US government has moved so far to the right on Cuba that those days are no longer remembered.

The Cuban revolution is there to stay. It has radically affected every facet of Cuban life as well as of the country's international relations. What will happen as the population becomes better educated and the political system further institutionalized, no one knows. It is clear, nonetheless, that internal developments—as is the case with other social revolutions—will be affected by the international context.

SUGGESTED READINGS

Periodical Literature

There are many useful periodical sources that can help students of Cuba keep up with events.

Bohemia. This major Havana weekly covers social, economic, cultural, and political events.

Cuba internacional. A glossy monthly portraying achievements of the revolution.

Cuba Resource Center Newsletter. The main English-language publication presenting a friendly view of revolutionary Cuba. Published in New York City.

Cuban Studies. The best scholarly journal on Cuba. It concentrates on the post-1959 period. Each issue contains the best bibliography available on publications dealing with Cuba.

Foreign Broadcast Information Service. Daily translations of Cuban radio and television broadcasts monitored by US intelligence agencies. Available on microfiche.

Temas. This is the leading cultural and social sciences journal in Cuba, required reading for anyone who wishes to understand the country.

Translations on Latin America. Translations of the documents and articles that are considered most important by the US intelligence community. Deals with all of Latin America and has a section on Cuba. Published at least twice a week.

There are numerous Internet resources that offer information on Cuba. The best one is http://sitioscubanos.cuba.cu.

Books

Chomsky, Aviva, Barry Carr, and Pamela Maria Smorkaloff, eds. *The Cuba Reader: History, Culture, Politics.* Duke University Press, 2004.

Domínguez, Jorge I. *Cuba: Order and Revolution.* Harvard University Press, 1978.

Gott, Richard. *Cuba: A New History.* Yale University Press, 2004.

Hernandez, Rafael. *Looking at Cuba: Essays on Culture and Civil Society.* University Press of Florida, 2003.

MacEwan, Arthur. *Revolution and Economic Development in Cuba.* St. Martin's Press, 1981.

Mesa-Lago, Carmelo. *The Economy of Socialist Cuba: A Two-Decade Appraisal.* University of New Mexico Press, 1981.

Perez, Louis A. *Cuba: In the American Imagination.* University of North Carolina Press, 2008.

Perez Sarduy, Pedro, et al. *Afro-Cuban Voices: On Race and Identity in Contemporary Cuba.* University Press of Florida, 2000.

Perez-Stable, Marifeli. *The Cuban Revolution: Origins, Course, and Legacy.* Oxford University Press, 1998.

Rosset, Peter, and Medea Benjamin. *The Greening of the Revolution: Cuba's Experiment with Organic Agriculture.* Ocean Press, 1995.

Scarpaci, Joseph L., Roberto Segre, Mario Coyula, Andres Duany. *Havana: Two Faces of the Antillean Metropolis.* University of North Carolina Press, 2002.

Schoultz, Lars. *That Infernal Little Cuban Republic.* University of North Carolina Press, 2009.

United Nations, Economic Commission for Latin America. *Cuba: Estilo de desarrollo y políticas sociales.* Mexico City, 1980.

Chapter 19

THE CARIBBEAN

The Structure of Modern-Conservative Societies

A N T H O N Y   P.   M A I N G O T

In a geopolitical sense, the Caribbean is best defined in terms of all the countries that border on that sea. This includes the islands as well as the countries of the mainland whose eastern coasts form the western perimeter of the Caribbean. Together, they make up a "basin" of which the sea is the crucial geopolitical feature.

Geographical definitions, however, are ultimately arbitrary. Their validity depends on the purpose or ends pursued, that is, on their utility. So El Salvador, which has no border on the Caribbean Sea, is regarded by some as a Caribbean basin country, whereas Mexico, Colombia, and most Central American countries are two-ocean countries that look more toward the Caribbean than toward the Pacific. A simple explanation lies in the fact that colonization and subsequent trade and cultural contacts developed as part of the Atlantic expansion, first of Spain and later the rest of Europe.

In this chapter, "the Caribbean" is considered to be the islands plus mainland territories that until recently were part of the British, Dutch, and French colonial empires. Generalizing on any level about countries as varied as these is difficult. Haiti has almost six times more land and five times the population of Trinidad and Tobago but only 20 percent of the gross domestic product (GDP). Haitians speak Creole, and a liberal estimate is that 50 percent of them are illiterate; Trinidadians speak English, and 96 percent are literate (see Table 19.1). Haiti has been governed by dictators throughout most of its 180 years of independence; Trinidad had a functioning parliamentary system even before it became independent in 1962.

As with any other geographical region or expression ("Africa," "Latin America," "Asia"), each unit in the region deserves to be studied individually. And yet there is value in an understanding of the broader continuities and similarities that make any region a culture area. Keep in mind, as Melville Herskovits reminds us, that the concept of culture area does not denote a self-conscious grouping. Rather than focusing on the details, it points to the broad lines of similarities and differences between cultures. In the Caribbean, these continuities and similarities result from a blending of modern and conservative features in the composition of major

TABLE 19.1   The Insular Caribbean: Basic Statistics

Independent States[1]	Population (1000)	Area (Km.²)	GDP (2005) per cap.	Language
Cuba	11,000	114,500	——	Spanish
Dominican Republic	9,000	49,000	2,130	Spanish
Haiti	9,000	28,000	400	French/C
Jamaica	3,000	11,000	2,980	English
Trinidad & Tobago	1,290	5,000	7,790	English
Bahamas	272	13,900	12,944	English
Barbados	261	430	7,894	English
St. Lucia	153	620	3,907	English/C
St. Vincent/Grenadines	127	390	2,635	English
Grenada	108	340	3,347	English
Antigua/Barbuda	92	440	8,559	English
Dominica	96	750	3,310	English
St. Kitts/Nevis	48	270	6,716	English

On Mainland

Guyana	760	215,000	825	English
Suriname	457	163,000	710	Dutch/C
Belize	211	23,000	2,725	English

Dependent Territories[2]

Guadeloupe (F)	413	1,710	12,287	French/C
Martinique (F)	371	1,100	14,524	French/C
French Guiana (F)	135	90,000	13,044	French/C
Netherland Antilles (Neth.)	197	800	11,698	Dutch/C
Aruba (Neth.)	77	90	16,186	Dutch/C
Cayman Islands (UK)	33	264	23,966	English
British Virgin Islands (UK)	17	150	14,010	English
Turks & Caicos (UK)	14	417	7,061	English
Montserrat (UK)	11	102	3,846	English
Anguilla (UK)	10	90	6,937	English
Puerto Rico (USA)	4,000	9,000	17,000	Spanish
U.S. Virgin Islands (USA)	104	347	12.038	English

Sources: (C= Local creole language)
(1) Norman Girvan, "Societies at Risk? The Caribbean and Global Change," Paris: UNESCO Discussion Paper No.17 (Aug. 1997), Table No.1. (2) Victor Bulmer-Thomas, "The Wider Caribbean in the 20th C.," *Integration and Trade* Vol. 15 (2001), Table 10, note 1.

institutions as well as in social and behavioral dynamics. It is useful to call Caribbean societies modern-conservative systems.

THE CONCEPT OF MODERN-CONSERVATIVE SOCIETIES

Like all concepts or heuristic devices in the social sciences, the concept of modern-conservative societies is used to explain complex social structures and social processes. This is especially important in a region as varied as the Caribbean. The concept appears to describe Caribbean social structure well, and we conclude therefore that it will also help explain the political manifestations of that social structure.

Note that we are not talking about traditional societies: relatively static, passive, and acquiescent societies that resist change. They approximate what Michael Oakeshott calls societies underpinned by "skeptical conservatism," a peculiar mixture of political conservatism and radical individualism and skepticism. In addition, the modern-conservative society is often prone to dramatic calls or movements for change. Several cases from the English-speaking Caribbean illustrate the latent explosive character of the modern-conservative society.

In 1970 the island state of Trinidad and Tobago was suffering from both declining oil production and falling world prices for oil. OPEC had not yet managed to control the market; it would do this in 1972. The economy had been radically changed by oil. The production of sugar, cacao, and other agricultural commodities was now subsidized; the state became the largest employer. By 1970 there was 22 percent open unemployment and 23 percent hidden unemployment, while the unemployment among moderately educated youth (more than eight years of schooling) was 40 percent higher than the average. Additionally, since 80 percent of the women indicated no desire to work outside the home, the problem was squarely centered on young males. These youth were integrated into the modern sector: urban, educated, organized, and in close contact with the outside world.

With the black power movement in full bloom in the United States and Canada, two events outside Trinidad lit the spark of Trinidad's own black power uprising. One occurred in Jamaica, where authorities prohibited a Guyanese university lecturer, Walter Rodney, from reentering Jamaica from Canada. The so-called Rodney affair stirred university students in Trinidad, as did a "riot" staged by a dozen Trinidadian students in Canada claiming racial discrimination. Racial grievances, unemployment, unrest among professional military men, and accusations of graft and corruption against certain government ministers all came to a head in a massive movement against "the system." And yet the motor, the driving force, was not class conflict but a deep sense of righteous indignation. The target of the movement, Prime Minister Eric Williams, was repeatedly invited to join the moral crusade for black identity and ownership. Clearly he had lost his moral authority but not his political legitimacy.

In 1970 in Trinidad, righteous indignation took on psychological and cultural dimensions: a return to history, to a purer and more integral past as a means of collective and individual cleansing and redemption. African names and apparel were adopted and modern European ways rejected to such an extent that the movement's leadership began to alienate large sectors of the Indian and colored populations as well as the black middle class. A reorganized police force put an end to the armed phase of the movement. Ten years later, when the same leaders competed in a free election, they were soundly defeated. Had the massive influx of oil revenues since 1973 solved Trinidad's problems? Not at all. In 1983 fully 83 percent of those who felt that life was getting worse on the island blamed corruption. Although the incumbent party won a sizable electoral victory in 1981, race again showed its strength: the victorious People's National Movement (PNM) won the safe black seats; the opposition United Labour Force (ULF), the safe Indian seats. The case of St. Lucia in early 1982 illustrates this aspect of political behavior in a modern-conservative society. On January 16, 1982, the prime minister of St. Lucia resigned under pressure. This forced the dismissal of parliament and mandated the calling of elections within a few months. The caretaker government was led by a member of a radical party, the smallest of St. Lucia's three main parties. It was not this party, however, that had led the antigovernment movement, nor were the issues in the movement ideological ones in the political sense. That movement was headed by the chamber of commerce and other middle sectors, protesting what they regarded as official corruption and abuse of government authority.

The upheaval in St. Lucia was similar to that in Grenada three years earlier. Incompetence, corruption, and abuse of authority had engendered a massive sense of indignation among a multiplicity of sectors. In Grenada, the opposition movement was called the Committee of 21, indicating the number of groups involved in the opposition to Prime Minister Eric Gairy. The difference between Grenada in 1979 and St. Lucia in 1982 was that in Grenada a small clique managed to wrest power by force of arms, teaching a lesson to the middle classes in St. Lucia. Although all groups participated in the 1982 elections in St. Lucia, the moderates won every seat in the House of Assembly. Radical parties had suffered similar defeats in Dominica, St. Vincent, St. Kitts, Jamaica, Barbados, and Trinidad. Elections in the Dominican Republic in mid-1982 also indicated a tendency toward the center in political-ideological terms; it appeared to be a Caribbean-wide phenomenon.

A decade later, similar moderate tendencies were evident in Trinidadians' response to an armed insurrectionary attempt. In 1991 a Black Muslim group, the Jamaat al Muslimeen, played on the deep sense of malaise among the urban masses. After assaulting police headquarters, taking the prime minister and most of his cabinet hostage and taking control of the television station, the rebels called on the populace to rebel. They did no such thing, and the terrorists had to surrender to the authorities. Although 60 percent of those who responded to a national poll expressed sympathy with the Muslimeen's grievances, fully 75 percent rejected the use of force to achieve redress. Equal numbers rejected the religious intolerance evident in the Muslimeen's early proclamations.

These illustrations allow us to identify some of the characteristics of the modern-conservative society. Speaking of "structures" does not imply anything static but means that certain underlying factors or interrelationships are more durable, tenacious, and retentive than many of the immediate and observable manifestations of those relationships suggest. Such ideas or concepts as history, life, being, and essence are central to this conservative view of life and are logical products of ex-colonial, multiethnic, and deeply religious societies, as we shall see. As Karl Mannheim has noted, these patterns of thought, far from becoming superfluous through modernization, tend to survive and adapt themselves to each new stage of social development.[1] Because it has a real social basis, conservative thought is functional and useful as a guide to action.

The modern-conservative society, then, tends to mobilize politically around issues that strike chords of a conservative type, issues that engender a collective sense of moral indignation. Mobilization occurs, however, through modern mechanisms and institutional arrangements. The most conservative of values, if widely shared and if the spokespeople have access to modern institutions and mechanisms, can have impacts that have revolutionary manifestations though something less than revolutionary goals—if "revolutionary" implies a complete overthrow of the existing sociopolitical structure, not merely the regime.

The myth of the modern, revolutionary nature of Caribbean societies stems from a misunderstanding of the nature of many of the movements that brought revolutionary elites to power. Even in modern-conservative societies (as Lenin theorized and demonstrated), a determined elite can bring about a designed outcome. This is so because after the initial mobilization, the movement tends to enter into a qualitatively new phase. The dynamics of this phase tend to represent a combination of the unpredictability and complexity of all mass actions and the more predictable—or at least understandable—actions of revolutionary cadres and elites. The latter can turn a movement in a revolutionary direction even in modern-conservative societies; they are less capable, however, of initially generating a revolutionary mobilization in such societies.

This explains why the Suriname revolution (1980) and the Grenadian revolution (1979), like the Nicaraguan revolution, coexisted with a strong private sector, established churches, and other aroused but hardly revolutionary sectors. These regimes were confronted with the complexity of the modern-conservative society, which explains as much about the failure of revolution as does the implacable opposition of Washington (which certainly played its part).

Understanding the nature of political change in these societies, then, requires an analysis of not only the immediate political happenings in the area—the political landscape—but also what might be called the structural or enduring aspects of Caribbean political dynamics: the political substructure. What is required, thus, is a political economy approach to the area in which culture, demographics, and economics are central, though not exclusive, topics of analysis.

The central questions, however, remain. Who reacts, why, and over what? What do the answers tell us about the ongoing and therefore relatively predictable aspects of Caribbean political culture and dynamics? Some answers might be forthcoming from an analysis of the ideology and behavior of a few of the major political leaders in recent Caribbean history.

POLITICAL-IDEOLOGICAL LEADERSHIP

The career of Trinidad's Eric Williams, who was prime minister from 1956 until his death in 1981, illustrates the complexity of style and orientation of the region's leadership. Much has changed in the Caribbean since 1956, when Williams first came to power as a celebrated scholar-administrator. His PhD thesis at Oxford University, "Capitalism and Slavery," had become the standard radical interpretation of European industrialization (made possible by the triangular slave trade) and emancipation (made necessary by the very success of that industrialization). He was living proof that a man of color was capable of great achievements in a mother country's highest centers of learning.

This success and his courage in "telling off" of the English, Americans, French, and Dutch in the Caribbean Commission—an agency set up by the colonial powers to assist in Caribbean development—made him the man to lead the island's decolonization movement. "Massa day done" became Williams's battle cry, a welcome prospect to the black and colored middle and working classes who followed his charismatic leadership. The psychic scars of colonialism had found their soothing balm. But where to turn for models?

Asia and Africa were also going through the pains and pleasures of decolonization, and those continents—more than neighboring Latin America—provided some, but not all, of the models. Nehru, Nkrumah, Sukarno, and Kenyatta, for Williams, represented the post–World War II, nonwhite decolonization process. Like those leaders, Williams understood very early that decolonization had both racial and political connotations. The very concept of empire had been based on ideas of racial superiority and inferiority. These men had to give living rebuttals to the imperial myths that people of color could not govern themselves and that non-Western societies could never be viable nations. Not only did they have to prove their people's capacity by leading the political struggle, they also had to prove their personal worth through exceptional achievement. In colonial situations, the burden of proof is always with the colonized.

It is no surprise, therefore, that the decolonizers began to perceive themselves as the very—if not the sole—embodiment of their countries. This perhaps was the genesis of their eventual sense of indispensability. Williams acted for twenty-five years on that belief. Repeated victories at the polls did little to dispel the illusion.

But Trinidad, like the rest of the English-speaking West Indies, was in the Western Hemisphere, where the majority of the independent countries were Spanish speaking and most were far from being democratic models. Surrounded by dictators who enjoyed warm relations with Washington and London, Williams understood that the decolonization of the English-speaking Caribbean was to be a lonely process in the Latin American setting. The parliamentary system adopted by the West Indies differed from the executive system of Latin America, and Williams always felt that the former suited the West Indies better.

This belief was shared by an array of truly exceptional West Indian leaders: Alexander Bustamante and Norman Manley in Jamaica, Grantly Adams and Errol Barrow in Barbados, and Cheddi Jagan in Guyana (a true constitutionalist despite his Marxist rhetoric). By the mid-1960s, these leaders had laid the foundations of West Indian constitutional democracy, thereby giving the lie to colonial racists and modern ideologists who argued that only authoritarian one-party states fit the Caribbean reality.

Williams governed long enough to deal with two elected Manleys (father and son) and two elected Adamses (father and son), to see the OPEC-created explosion in revenues from gas and oil, to see the collapse of the West Indian Federation and the rise of the Caribbean Common Market, and to see the decline of Britain and the rise of Cuba and Venezuela as regional powers. He lived long enough to see the rise and fall of Michael Manley's "democratic socialism" in Jamaica (1972–1980), and he appeared ready to deal with Jamaica's new leader, Edward Seaga, who emphasized the role of the private sector.

By the time of Williams's death in 1981, the Caribbean had witnessed many a social and economic experiment and was quite a different area. Although there were some governments "for life" (Cuba, Haiti, and probably also Guyana), there were now democratic governments in virtually all the other Caribbean island states, making the Caribbean the largest area governed by democratically elected regimes in the hemisphere. The parliamentary system was working in the West Indies.

The first generation of postindependence leaders in the English-speaking Caribbean had sown well and, in so doing, left their marks on the immediate postcolonial era. By the mid-1980s, there were indications that the passing of that era meant not only generational change but also the passing of the charismatic, "indispensable" leader as a part of the political culture. This change was demonstrated by a trend in the region's politics: the emergence in the 1980s of the less than charismatic "manager" political type. Edward Seaga of Jamaica, Mary Eugenia Charles of Dominica, Tom Adams of Barbados, George Chambers in Trinidad, and Antonio Guzmán and Jorge Blanco in the Dominican Republic all fit this mold.

What explains this shift in leadership? Certainly there is some truth to the view that the trend is partly reactive: a response to the dismal administrative performance of some of the area's most celebrated charismatic leaders of the 1960s and 1970s—Fidel Castro of Cuba, Michael Manley of Jamaica, and Forbes Burnham of Guyana, for example. But a fuller explanation would bring us closer to the issue of complexity that was posited earlier—a dual process involving enduring, underlying relationships, values, and interests (substrata) and the changing political landscape. The careers of Caribbean leaders of Marxist or non-Marxist socialist persuasion—the secular modernizers—are illustrative.

One such case is Aimé Césaire, mayor of Fort-de-France, Martinique, and Communist *député* to the National Assembly in Paris for over thirty-five years. When Césaire resigned from the French Communist Party in 1956, it was a sensational event. "Thinking of Martinique," he wrote, "I see that communism has managed to encyst us, isolate us in the Caribbean Basin." To Césaire, there was an alternative path: "Black Africa, the dam of our civilization and source of our culture." Only through race, culture, and the richness of ethnic particulars, he continued, could Caribbean people avoid the alienation wrought by what he called the "fleshless universalism" of European communism.[2]

This return to history, to culture, and ultimately to race has been a fairly consistent response to many Caribbean socialist modernizers—who never stop referring to themselves as socialists—faced with the difficulties of attempting secular revolutionary change in large, nonrevolutionary and conservative societies. The counterpoint between a rational secular universalism and a particularism of "being" has resulted in some original and dynamic West Indian ideological modifications to Marxism and non-Marxist socialist thought. In Césaire's case, it led to his fundamental contributions to négritude, a literary-political movement highlighting African contributions to contemporary society, as well as to an accommodation with continued French-Caribbean integration (though not assimilation) into the French system. None of this is new.

Trinidad's first major socialist activist in the 1920s, Andrew Cipriani, yearly paid homage to Fabian thought and the British Labour Party. But after decades of militancy he withdrew in the face of two challenges to his basic conservative view of the world: the divorce bill, which he saw as a threat to the family, and the use of violence in strike actions. Those who used violence (such as Uriah Butler, the "spontaneous" leader in Trinidad's 1937 labor movement and uprising) ended up turning to religion (quoting biblical passages) and to English history (studying the rule of Henry VIII). The "pull" on the leadership of the conservative values and norms of the masses has been powerful. Even Eric Williams, whose early historical writings were gems of Marxist thought and careful documentation, would eventually abandon what one admirer called "the infinite, barren track of documents, dates and texts" to write "gossip . . . which experience had established as the truth."

A review of Trinidadian C.L.R. James's five decades of thought on Trotskyite socialism and revolution indicates that he never resolved the universalism-particularism counterpoint. In his classical study of the Haitian war of independence, *The Black Jacobins* (1938), perhaps the most influential West Indian work of the twentieth century, James vacillates and hedges but ends up on the side of the Dessalinean black revolution as distinct from the universalist experiment of Toussaint L'Ouverture.

It is not at all evident that there can be in practice a working and productive relationship between racial or ethnic populism and a program based on premises of secular modernism, whether socialist or not. Even in theory, the reconciliation appears improbable. A case in point is the work of the Martinican Frantz Fanon. Like Césaire—whom he knew and greatly admired—Fanon wished to be liberated from the "fleshless shackles" of European thought; thus he searched for a key to what he called the "psycho-affective equilibrium" of the angry Third World intellectual. This search is central to an understanding of the dynamics of modern-conservative societies with their emphasis on culture. Fanon felt compelled to describe and explain what he perceived as the relentless determination of revolutionary elites to return to history: to "renew contact once more with the oldest and most pre-colonial springs of life of their people." Fanon understood the enduring consequences of the racial hurts and angst inflicted during colonialism. "This state belief in national culture," he wrote, "is in fact an ardent despairing turning toward anything that will afford him anchorage."[3] Even such a lifelong and dedicated Marxist as Guyana's Cheddi Jagan found a practical and perhaps psychological need to blend his Marxism with an ongoing devotion to Hinduism. Clearly, then, race and a desire for a return to history have been powerful forces blocking a universalist and secular approach to politics.

The rational and secular view of the world that is necessary for modern (especially socialist) revolution is not easily sustained in these societies. For Césaire, Williams, Norman Manley, Forbes Burnham, and others, Marxist or socialist thought was mediated by pressures from the multiethnic, religious, and conservative societies they led—and which eventually forced them to succumb to the particularistic note in the particularism-universalism counterpoint. It is a fundamental characteristic of a conservative society that views of the world and of social change resist any notions of dealing with problems in any way other than in terms of their historically perceived cultural uniqueness. This characteristic has been, more often than not, part of the Caribbean experience.[4]

The experience explains how Dr. François Duvalier ("Papa Doc") could come into power in Haiti in 1957 advocating a radical black power revolution but revert to a traditional form of political barbarism. He played retrograde chords of a deeply conservative society to entrench himself—and then his son, Jean-Claude—in power.

CARIBBEAN POLITICAL ECONOMY

In part because it involves modern societies with relatively skilled labor and a high degree of unionization, and thus high wages, the development process in the Caribbean has tended to be industrial and capital intensive. The overflow of available labor (because of reduced migration) has tended to be absorbed by the public sector. The financial and economic retrenchments made necessary by the energy crisis (and consequent balance-of-payments difficulties) have forced a slowing down of this public employment. The result is not merely unemployment but rather a process that is creating a whole generation of "never employed." The vast majority of this group has attained at least some high school education and has aspirations and some skills—but not the skills that are in demand or the aspirations that would encourage needed activities such as agricultural enterprises. Only the latter, with its labor intensity, could in fact absorb the large numbers of people who annually enter the labor market.

Such an agricultural orientation and direction is to be found nowhere in the Caribbean except Haiti, which is still 50 percent rural. The decline of the agricultural sector is a fundamental fact of Caribbean political economy. The movement is toward the urban areas and, critically, migration abroad. In the English-speaking Caribbean, migration accounted for a 46,000-person decrease in the labor force during the 1960s. Because of a slowdown in migration, this labor force is calculated to have increased by about 400,000 during the 1970s, nearly 70 percent of the increase being among young adults.

On every Caribbean island except Cuba, youthful adults make up an ever-increasing percentage of the total population, and everywhere they share the restlessness of youth the world over. But the "complexity" approach cautions that it would be a terrible mistake to associate a priori all this modern political ferment and activity with a state of social revolution. Such an association might preempt a close look at the substratum—the political economy—of Caribbean society. Although the configurations and expressions of this conservatism vary, the following aspects of Caribbean society show great similarities from one country to another.

Throughout the area, there is a deep and dynamic religiosity, even though the intensity and pervasiveness of religion—as doctrine and as institutions—do vary and are in a rapid process of change. It is startling, for instance, to discover that in Jamaica traditional religions such as Anglicanism and Roman Catholicism are now professed by only 5.5 percent and 4.1 percent respectively, while new US-based faiths, such as the Church of God, claim 21.2 percent of the faithful.[5] The traditional picture of the dominant church in the central plaza, attended by women and children once a week, is giving way to the storefront churches attended by the whole family. This is true of the whole Caribbean, Hispanic and non-Hispanic alike. Cuba and Puerto Rico were perhaps the least structurally conservative of the Caribbean societies, in large measure because of the considerable influence of secular North American values and interests. The rebirth of the Catholic faith and the widespread belief in the syncretistic Santería religion in Cuba reflect the fact that not even five decades of secular state control of virtually all means of socialization have dimmed religious fervor.

In the English-speaking West Indies, one finds multiple denominations and neighborhoods, urban and rural. This case illustrates a living presence of religion greater than a ceremonial one and is typical of countries such as Haiti where Christianity combined with West African religions to create a syncretism called voodoo (called Santería in Cuba and Shango in Trinidad). This religiosity impinges on other spheres of life.

One attitudinal spin-off from the doctrines of the major religions in the area is the belief in private property, especially land. There is an intense love and respect for the land and a desire to own a piece of it. The popular Haitian saying *Se vagabon qui loue kay* ("Only vagabonds rent their homes") expresses the desire for ownership, for full possession. On Nevis, 80 percent of the homeowners own their house lot; on St. Vincent, the figure is 75 percent. Although the figure is only 46.8 percent on Barbados, even the smallest house has a name, which represents the emotional dimension of property ownership. The little picket fence around the house is the physical expression of the emotional dimension. That picket fence (or cactus fence in the Netherlands Antilles) also expresses another characteristic of Caribbean peoples. In the midst of their gregariousness, they like their privacy, an expression of their intrinsic independence. This characteristic, usually identified as a rural phenomenon, is pervasive even in urban areas. This explains the living presence in West Indian language of old English sayings such as "A man's home is his castle" or, as used with an additional meaning in Creole, "Two man rats can't live in same hole."

This latter saying expresses the idea that in any house only one of the partners can wear the pants. In these patriarchal societies, it is taken for granted that the male partner does. And yet these societies are fundamentally matrifocal and matrilocal. Because of the high illegitimacy rate in the working class, it is the mother who raises the child, and the child lives where the mother and often where the maternal grandmother lives. As the 1981 study by Gary and Rosemary Brana-Shute demonstrates, there is a deep underlying conservatism in the socialization processes and aspirations of even the hard-core—and angry—unemployed youth in the area.

And yet, as Caribbean history has repeatedly shown, these generally moderate and family-oriented societies, and especially the youth, are capable of sudden, unpredictable political and social outbursts. This was evident in Curaçao, in the Netherlands Antilles, in 1969 when a minor industrial strike exploded into a class and race attack on the system. Half of the buildings in the main commercial sector of the island were burned to the ground.

The basically conservative substrata of Caribbean societies also sustain modern, highly mobilized societies and their corresponding agencies. Note the following dimensions and configurations of that modernity—with certain exceptions, such as Haiti, the populations are literate and schooled. On island after island, from 90 to 100 percent of the children of primary school age are in school, and literacy rates everywhere are above 85 percent. Although there is some evidence that conservative attitudes are positively correlated with greater degrees of education,[6] the fact is that a population that participates in the articulation of grievances and wishes and can utilize the modern techniques of communication is one that has an increased capability for mobilization. Throughout the Caribbean, people are politically mobilized. There are everywhere political parties and interest groups with capacities for extensive articulation of interests and aggregation of these into policy options. No government today, of the left, middle, or right, can ignore the demands of the groups. Literacy and education also make the labor union system more effective in the West Indies, since 30 to 50 percent of the workforce is unionized, and historic ties with political parties give unions additional leverage in the bargaining processes.

Another of the modern agencies that a literate and schooled population makes possible is the state bureaucracy, which, according to Max Weber, is the most "rational" of all forms of organization. Such state bureaucracies are found throughout the Caribbean in the form of a relatively skilled public or civil service. In Trinidad, there are three and a half times more people with diplomas or degrees in the public service than in the private sector, and in Jamaica the institutionalization and legitimacy of the public service are evident in its capacity to survive dramatic shifts in political party fortunes. The top echelons of these bureaucracies are now being educated in the area. The University of the West Indies (UWI), with campuses in Jamaica, Trinidad, and Barbados, now makes university education accessible to a much broader sector, as do the universities in Guyana, Martinique, Suriname, Curaçao, Aruba, and elsewhere. Whereas in 1957 there were 2,632 West Indians studying at universities abroad compared to only 566 at UWI, by 1982 the number abroad had doubled, but the number of students at UWI had increased twelvefold.

Caribbean modernity is reflected also in other areas. Caribbean working people have developed both the habits and the skills required of labor in modern societies, making them very desirable as immigrant workers. This explains the long tradition of migration, and return, of Caribbean workers; they are and always have been a mobile population. Whether building the Panama Canal and Central America's railroads and ports or running the London public transportation system, Caribbean workers have had the attitudes and skills of urban workers. They return with new skills, but also with the hope of buying that house or piece of land for which they have saved. In Haiti, the "Bahamas" house was built with remittances from Haitians working in the Bahamas, whereas the newer "Miami" house points to the new destination of Haitian migrants and the source of their remittances.

While abroad, Caribbean workers are able to communicate with their compatriots. Mailboxes stand along every road; there is widespread use of radio and newspapers and direct-dialing telephones from the United States to many islands, and in the French West Indies, Netherlands Antilles, Jamaica, Trinidad, and Barbados, television is popular. Modern communications assist both in modernizing the Caribbean and in preserving ethnic attachments. Literacy in one or more of the major languages of the world (English, Spanish, and French) gives Caribbeans access to the main currents of ideas and technology, while their native variations on those languages (Creole in Haiti, Papiamento in Curaçao, Sranang—also known as Taki-Taki—in Suriname) strengthen the sense of *Volk*, or nation, of *Gemeinschaft*, or community.

If one adds the fact that any particular sector of the islands is within, at most, a two-hour bus ride of some urban center, one understands something of the modernity of the society as well as its continued proximity to rural village life. Ties to the land and to tradition are not broken by a move to the city; rather, those links provide something of the underpinnings of the conservative values and orientations of the urban residents even as the diversification of memberships and involvements (churches, sport clubs, unions, political parties, service clubs) contributes to and expresses the society's modern dimensions. The glue that holds all together is the Caribbean family, both the nuclear and the extended family with its *compadres* (godfathers), *comadres* (godmothers), "cousins," and "aunties."

These, then, are some of the native aspects of these modern-conservative societies. Yet an analysis of the substrata also has to take into account the external factors affecting change. Although on balance internal factors tend to carry more weight in any causal analysis of social change, the small size of the Caribbean states makes external factors somewhat more important than they would be for most states.

Smallness makes them vulnerable to a host of problems. One of these is national insecurity, as was illustrated by the extraordinary 1981 attempted invasion and subversion of the government of Dominica by US mercenaries in league with local politicians. Furthermore, securing a degree of national representation abroad is costly. But such representation is important not only to facilitate contact with foreign nations through traditional diplomatic ties but also to attract attention from international and multilateral banking or lending agencies.[7]

Also contributing to the vulnerability are the cleavages created by the race and ethnic divisions that characterize the politics of nations such as Trinidad and Tobago, Guyana, and Suriname. In each of these countries, Indians (originally from British India) compose half or more of the population. Predominantly Hindu in religion (some 20 percent are Muslim), these sectors are prototypical modern-conservative groups. Reconciling Hinduism with secular ideologies such as Marxism is a difficult task; to do so in a context in which major elements of that Indian population are capitalists, landowners, and merchants (as in the case of Guyana and Surinam) is an even more complex proposition. Whether the cleavage is black versus white, Indian versus black, or black versus mulatto, race and race conflict contribute to social division and to the vulnerability of Caribbean societies.

An awareness of the vulnerabilities resulting from smallness have led to many attempts at regional or subregional integration. Dreams of a united Caribbean are not new. They were expressed in José Martí's theme that Cuba and Puerto Rico were wings of the same dove; in Haitian president Jean Pierre Boyer's dream of liberating all the slaves, first of neighboring Santo Domingo (which his armies occupied from 1822 to 1844), then of other islands; and in the West Indies Federation, which lasted from 1958 to 1961. The repeated failures of such attempts, however, created skepticism about the viability and indeed the desirability of such union.

Despite constant talk about integration, such as the mid-1990s creation of the thirty-five-member Association of Caribbean States, the mini nation-state is now a reality of the Caribbean scene, and we probably have not seen the last of the newly independent entities. By the 1990s, the area was limiting itself to attempts at economic integration through such instruments as the Caribbean Common Market (CARICOM) and the Caribbean Development Bank. Even the Organization of Eastern Caribbean States[8] emphasizes the economic aspects of association, leaving politics, including foreign policy, to each individual member.

Unfortunately, while insularity gathers strength on each island, globalization, impelled by international politics and transnational forces (including multinational corporations), presses for a reduction in state sovereignty. And today, as in the past, size and isolation make these territories targets for international expansion. During the Cold War (the 1950s through the 1980s), escalating ideological competition among international forces made the Caribbean a cockpit, the modern-day equivalent of the European battlegrounds of the seventeenth and eighteenth centuries. Marxism-Leninism, the Socialist International, the Christian Democrats, and international labor organizations as well as new regional actors such as Cuba, Venezuela, and Mexico all joined the battle for the minds of Caribbean peoples. The United States has long been engaged in the competition. To these may be added many proselytizing religious and semireligious groups, from Islam to the Seventh-Day Adventists and Mormons, to the Rastafarian movement (now of pan-Caribbean character). Since the foreign offices and intelligence services of the major states never left the area, the ideational scene in the Caribbean was a bewildering panorama of competing radio broadcasts; roaming sports, cultural, and scientific missions; state visits; and sojourning consultants from international aid agencies—and these activities were only the overt ones. By the 1990s, with the end of the Cold War, the "taming" of Cuban internationalism, and the shocks of the denouements of the Grenadian and Surinamese revolutions, all that changed. The new Caribbean geopolitics have more to do with economics. In the search for markets and foreign investment capital, import substitution economies have been opened up (i.e., "liberalized") and forced to become export-driven. The private sectors, not the state, have been given the responsibility for economic development. Whether this will prove to be a more productive development strategy is not yet clear. It certainly is global in application and strongly pushed by the single power whose influence still predominates in the region—the United States. There are new challenges to that American predominance but it is doubtful that they will change the region's political culture in any fundamental way. Not even the formidable efforts of President Hugo Chávez of Venezuela with its Petro-Caribe program, a generous provision of oil on concessionary terms, and its financing of Cuban medical staff (who are now serving admirably in virtually every country in the region), has shaken the islands' basic system of democratic governance and economic relations. Every island now has diplomatic relations with Cuba, conducted with the utmost respect on traditional state-to-state reciprocal relations. The structural elements revealed in this bare-bones sketch of the internal nature and dynamics of Caribbean societies dispute the generalized idea that these societies were invariably or structurally revolutionary in nature. To be sure, these societies were never static; they often reacted violently when the sense of moral indignation and the collective democratic sensibilities were challenged. These were the deep-rooted cultural responses of modern-conservative societies.

By the late 1990s and early 2000s, a new and arguably greater threat faced these vulnerable states: the threat of organized international crime, pushing every form of illegal activity from drugs to guns to money laundering to financial scams of every conceivable type. Accompanying these structural changes are new sources of threat: the fear that the greatest menace to these small states comes from the internationalization of crime, corruption, and violence. International criminal cartels are capable of corrupting whole states, subverting their electoral, legal, and police systems. Formal sovereignty does not mean much under such circumstances. The question is whether the moral conservatism that was so instrumental in withstanding the totalitarian temptation will also serve as a bulwark against the onslaught of organized crime. I conclude by addressing this question, the central challenge at the end of the twentieth century.

CONCLUSION

The first thing to keep in mind in analyzing the "new" Caribbean is the degree of social change, both in speed and in kind. Such rapid social change never occurs without consequences, and this region is no exception. Two distinct processes can be identified. First, these recently decolonized societies are increasing their contacts with their former metropolitan masters. There are benefits to be derived from membership in the European Union, including assistance in many social and economic areas. The association clearly brings some relief from the sense of economic vulnerability in the context of globalization and, perhaps more immediately, from the challenges represented by the demand for economic "openness" and liberalization coming from the North American Free Trade Area (NAFTA). With an increased European military presence, it also means a greater sense of security in the increasingly important area of law and order operations.

The second set of processes derive from the fact that race and ethnicity continue to be bridges that contribute to better understanding and relations with the United States. And yet, since nothing ever stands still, the erstwhile special relationship with the predominantly Afro-Caribbean islands is in relative decline as the US racial and ethnic composition changes. Specifically, the rise of Hispanic political mobilization and the comparative decline of black political power in the United States has meant the relative decline of Afro-Caribbean influence. It is vital that politically important US cities such as Los Angeles and Miami, the former a gateway to Mexico and the latter a veritable gateway to the Caribbean, are essentially Latin cities. The growing Puerto Rican and Dominican populations in New York have come out of the shadow of the much older West Indian enclaves to assert an influence of their own. Competition for the attention of Washington has, and continues to be, a fundamental task of the foreign policies of Caribbean states, and it is becoming more difficult.

Both these processes challenge the region's sense of national identity and perception of sovereignty and highlight the vulnerability of small states in a globalized world. Yet there is no reason to despair. The stalwart people of these islands have faced many threats and challenges before. As they say in the islands, "We have seen the best of times and the worst of times." Certainly this is an uplifting message. Hard facts, however, indicate that the new transnational challenges will surely test their mettle as never before. Be that as it may, the interpretation of Caribbean societies presented here does provide some grounds for cautious optimism. The wide acceptance of democratic forms is but one expression of political cultures that are at once conservative about basic social and political issues and yet modern and adaptable in their capacity to adjust and even innovate. Such predispositions to incorporate the new without discarding what has worked historically will surely come in handy in the new era. Thus it is useful to characterize Caribbean societies as modern-conservative societies, an ideal construct that helps us understand what otherwise might appear to be contradictory or even unintelligible in the behavior of this multilingual, multiracial, and multistate area.

NOTES

1. Karl Mannheim, "Conservative Thought," in Paul Keckskemeti, ed., *Essays on Sociology and Social Psychology* (New York: Oxford University Press, 1953), pp. 77–164.

2. Aimé Césaire, "Lettre à Maurice Thorez," *Présence Africaine* (Paris), 1956, p. 15.

3. Frantz Fanon, *The Wretched of the Earth* (New York: Grove, 1968), p. 217.

4. One interesting exception wa the New Jewel movement, which came to power in Grenada in 1979, attempting to portray that experience as an extension of a Caribbean decolonization process begun in Cuba. It was ended by internecine conflict and US military intervention.

5. Martin Mordecai and Pamela Mordecai, *Culture and Customs of Jamaica* (Westport, Conn.: Greenwood, 2001), 41.

6. See Selwyn Ryan, Eddie Greene, and Jack Harewood, *The Confused Electorate* (St. Augustine and Trinidad, 1979); and Anthony P. Maingot, "The Difficult Path to Socialism in the English-Speaking Caribbean," in Richard R. Fagen, ed., *Capitalism and the State in US–Latin American Relations* (Stanford: Stanford University Press, 1979).

7. This is a question not only of asymmetical power but also of commanding respect and dignity.

8. Antigua/Barbuda, St. Vincent/Grenadines, Dominica, St. Lucia, and Grenada.

SUGGESTED READINGS

A good general treatment of the Caribbean as a whole is Franklin W. Knight, *The Caribbean: The Genesis of a Fragmented Nationalism*, 2d ed. (New York: Oxford University Press, 1980). Knight also edited, with Margaret E. Crahan, *Africa and the Caribbean: The Legacies of a Link* (Baltimore, Md.: Johns Hopkins University Press, 1979). On the English-speaking Caribbean, several of Gordon K. Lewis's books are being republished. *The Growth of the Modern West Indies* (1968) was republished in 2004 by Ian Randle Publishers of Jamaica with a new introduction by Franklin W. Knight. Gordon Lewis's *Puerto Rico: Freedom and Power in the Caribbean* (1963) also reappeared under the Ian Randle imprint with a new introduction by Anthony P. Maingot. Maingot also wrote the new introduction to Lewis's classic, *Main Currents of Caribbean Thought* (1983), republished by the University of Nebraska Press in 2004. He edited and supplied the introduction to Gordon K. Lewis, *Race, Class, and Ideology in the Caribbean* (Kingston: Ian Randle, 2010). David Lowenthal's *West Indian Societies* (New York: Oxford University Press, 1972) is especially strong on race relations and the analysis of the "plural society." On the development of socialist politics and the region's conservative responses, see Anthony P. Maingot, *The United States and the Caribbean* (Boulder: Westview, 1994).

Contemporary affairs are best followed through the London newsletter *Caribbean Insight* and the magazine *Hemisphere* (Florida International University).

PART VIII

THE ANDES

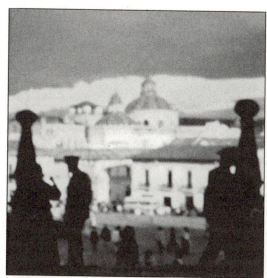

Chapter 20

COLOMBIA'S SPLIT-LEVEL REALITIES

JAN KNIPPERS BLACK WITH WILLIAM H. GODNICK

For most of the past century, Colombia has been formally identified as a democracy, often in fact as South America's oldest democracy. And by some standards it has been an extraordinarily stable one, underpinned by a growing and modernizing economy. For those who enjoyed *abolengo*—notable names—and lived in gated and guarded neighborhoods, the landed gentry and captains of industry whose family histories were threaded through the highest offices of Church and state, this formal identity may have seemed real enough. Even for the less well endowed middle-class families who lived within a hundred mile radius of the capital, Bogota, or one of the other major cities, the social strife that has ravaged the countryside almost continuously may have intruded only episodically.

Those episodes of intrusion have called forth a variety of explanations or rationales and a continuous process of labeling and relabeling, from the wars of conquest and of independence to partisan wars, to banditry and ideological wars overlain by the Cold War, and more recently to the ongoing drug war and the war on terrorism. All such wars are power struggles, of course, from local to global arenas, and all to some degree are about resources, particularly land.

Changes over the years in slogans and flags and in the resources at issue have served to obscure what is unchanging in this equation of anarchy: the hand played by Mother Nature herself–the divisions imposed by the steep and rugged ridges and isolated valleys of a three-pronged mountain range. In Colombia, as in Afghanistan and Appalachia, Papua New Guinea and the Caucasus, the ultimate saboteur of national or regional unity and the effective sovereignty of a central government is topography. But there is no glory, no partisan advantage, no budgetary windfall, and no victory to claim in fighting a mountain range.

The anarchy and generalized insecurity that constitute the ground floor of the Colombian reality—at least in rural areas and the urban shantytowns where peasants driven off their land seek shelter—may be almost as old as the mountains that sustain it. But a couple of circumstances have caused it to intrude on the national consciousness more persistently and insistently in the past two decades. In the first

381

place, while the spread of cash cropping and agro-export in general implies concentration of land ownership—turf wars—and thus a degree of violence, the cultivation and trafficking of cocaine is particularly conducive to violence. Addiction and criminalization ensure an inelastic market and high market value. The monetary stakes attract thieves from all classes and sectors, and criminalization enhances the budget, power, and autonomy of security forces, especially as they continue to be heavily supported by military aid from the United States.

Finally, over past centuries the Colombian government, like many governments elsewhere, had generally been willing to settle for the illusion of centralized control over the rugged mountainous territory claimed by the state. But in the twenty-first century, with seemingly unqualified US support, the Colombian government has become increasingly ambitious, and at times delusional, about what it is able or should be able to control. Given the changing structure of the global economy and the emergence in neighboring countries of governments less subject to US influence such ambition threatens to turn a condominium of split-level realities into a conflated reality of free-fire-zoned wasteland, spreading across national borders.

A PENTHOUSE PERSPECTIVE ON COLOMBIAN REALITY

The Origins of Oligarchy

Virtually all analysts of the Colombian political system use modifiers when speaking of the country's democracy. John D. Martz Jr. characterized the system as a "qualified" democracy. Others have spoken of limited or elitist democracy. Robert E. Scott went so far as to label its leadership a "ruling caste." While the frontier area between the upper and middle classes lacks the structure that might be provided, for example, by titles of nobility, and while there are varying interpretations by students of Colombian society of degrees of upward and downward mobility, there is considerable objective and subjective evidence that a self-perpetuating minority controls the key power resources of the society.

Robert H. Dix's study of the Colombian elite, among the first to involve survey and interview techniques as well as correlations among leadership positions in the major political parties, the professions, private enterprise, and economic pressure groups found that most of those in the upper class had their roots in the hacienda. Prestigious family names (*abolengo*) have been historically associated with land ownership, although they have served to some extent as autonomous sources of elite status. Light complexion, higher education in the arts or traditional professions, and cosmopolitanism are generally concomitants of *abolengo*. Wealth acquired from industrial or commercial pursuits or professional expertise may confer elite status but by no means assure it. Some interlocking of landowning and industrial families has occurred through marriage, however, and many landowning families have invested in industrial and commercial enterprises, while some industrial entrepreneurs have invested in land. Dix noted that the Colombian equivalent of *Who's Who* confirmed a high degree of fusion among the elites of property, social standing, education, and political power. Members of both Liberal and Conservative Party hierarchies, for example, have been officers of the powerful National Federation of Coffee Growers.

The two-party system, which in the early development of most Latin American countries involved only the upper classes and in most cases gave way in the twentieth century to a multiparty system, was so pervasive in Colombia that as late as 1969 a leader of the National Popular Alliance (ANAPO), the only political movement that posed a credible threat to the dominance of the two traditional parties, described ANAPO as a bipartisan movement rather than a third party. Colombia's two-party system has reflected and reinforced, rather than mitigated, a system of rigid socioeconomic stratification and a traditional political culture that favors control by a relatively closed societal elite over the expansion of political participation. More recent developments with parties and pseudoparties, such as the Alternative Democratic Pole (Polo Democrático) and the Party of the U, emerging from both the left and right of the political spectrum, have had more to do with political personalities than challenging the structural underpinnings characteristic of the Conservative versus Liberal divide.

Partisanship Takes Root

Although partisanship began to develop in Colombia in the 1830s, the Liberal and Conservative parties did not appear as such until 1848, when they took positions, respectively, against and for the government of Tomás Cipriano de Mosquera. Since that time the two parties, through armed conflict, electoral competition, or collaboration, have largely maintained control of the country's political system. In the nineteenth century that competition was manifested more often in armed conflict than in elections.

The constitution drawn up by the Conservatives in 1886 established a unitary system and provided for separation of church and state, although a concordat with the Holy See established a close working relationship between the government and the Catholic hierarchy. Coffee production and export provided a financial base for centralizing state power and promoting investment also in industry. Coffee accounted for 70 percent of the country's export earnings by the 1930s. The Conservative Party ruled, largely in authoritarian fashion, from 1886 to 1930, successfully thwarting two attempts by the Liberals to gain control by force. The essentially partisan so-called Thousand Day War (1899–1902) devastated the country and left some 100,000 dead.

The constitution of 1886 lasted more than a century, until it was superseded in 1991. It was amended, however, by the Liberals to give the government power to deal with economic affairs, which were in turmoil when Enrique Olaya Herrera came to power in 1930. The country was ruled by four Liberal presidents between 1930 and 1946. The first term of Alfonso López Pumarejo, 1934–1938, saw numerous reform measures enacted. As a result, the more centrist elements of the Liberal Party withdrew their support from López, who was then succeeded by Eduardo Santos, leader of the centrist faction. López was reelected in 1942 but resigned in 1945, his term being completed by Alberto Lleras Camargo.

Conservative Mariano Ospina Pérez was elected president in 1946 on a platform of quasi-bipartisanship, but partisan rivalry erupted into civil war after the Bogotazo—the 1948 uprising in Bogota that followed the assassination of Jorge Eliécer Gaitán. A Liberal, Gaitán had achieved national recognition as a dynamic spokesman for peasant and working-class interests. Laureano Gómez assumed the presidency in an uncontested election in 1948 and completed the trend toward authoritarianism that had been initiated by his predecessor, including the use of the armed forces and police to fight Liberals. Some 200,000 people were killed, mostly between 1949 and 1953, in an awful bloodletting that came to be known as *la violencia*.

In 1953 Lieutenant General Gustavo Rojas Pinilla, after uncovering a plot apparently inspired by Gómez for his assassination, engineered a coup d'état and assumed control of the government. Although this move was initially greeted with broad popular support, the military government became increasingly arbitrary and repressive. Following a display of public discontent in 1957, the armed forces, backed by political party leaders, removed Rojas Pinilla from office.

City-States, the Vertical Two-Party System, and Social Structure

By the mid-twentieth century the major issues that distinguished Liberals and Conservatives in the nineteenth century—a unitary versus a federal governmental system and the extent of the special prerogatives of the Church—were no longer seriously contended. Even so, almost all Colombians consider themselves either Liberals or Conservatives, though this has begun to change in recent times with the emergence of stronger alternatives. This affiliation is a part of one's family heritage and, especially among the rural middle and lower classes, strongly influences marriage, business ties, and social contacts, although the majority of the adult population does not vote and actual participation in party affairs is extremely limited. The parties are similar in composition and organization, incorporating persons of all social classes but deriving their leadership from the oligarchy. While on paper the parties have much of the framework of modern parties, in the functioning of their internal machinery, in methods of financing, in the role of the press, and in the approach to mass organization they reveal the patron client orientation of their societal environment. In the rural areas, for example, landowners are expected to "deliver" the votes of the peasants in their domains.

The isolation of the various population centers, resulting from settlement patterns and topographic extremes, has fostered a type of political rivalry reminiscent of city-states or fiefdoms. In many towns and villages almost the entire population consider themselves either Liberals or Conservatives. Thus the structures of the two parties merely reflect the pyramidal structure of the larger society, and the pervasiveness of the traditional parties has left little room for the emergence of modern parties organized along horizontal lines of common socioeconomic interests. Furthermore, armed clashes in the nineteenth century, resulting from political and economic rivalry in which peasants were called upon to defend their landlords, consolidated the political uniformity of some regions and communities to such an extent that to change one's party affiliation was to be considered a traitor. The more recent versions of right wing–paramilitary forces have been particularly brutal in obliging entire towns to support "their" candidate to the point that in many rural towns there is often only one candidate in the running.

Despite the general blurring of ideological differences between Conservatives and Liberals, positions traceable to the inception of the two parties—order, hierarchy, and strong central control by Church and state versus secularization of society, decentralization of government, and laissez-faire economic policy—regain significance from time to time. And new differences have emerged on occasion as one party or the other sought to expand its base. The Liberal Party was responsible for a considerable body of welfare legislation, for example, enacted in the twentieth century. Political expediency, however, has generally been more apparent than ideological considerations in the voting patterns of both parties and their factions, and the leadership of both parties remains firmly in the hands of the elites. While the leaders have been able to compromise on occasion when upper-class interests appeared to be threatened, members of the lower classes, with less comprehension of the ideological and practical issues dividing the parties, have been less able to overcome traditional party enmity in order to identify and articulate their common interests.

Until the mid-twentieth century only the elite evidenced a politically significant degree of class consciousness. A potential source of conflict that might have diluted the power of the upper class was avoided as the large landowners recognized that through accommodating the new industrialists they could prevent a major challenge to traditional political patterns. By the 1930s a middle class had begun to develop sufficient numerical strength to challenge elite dominance, but individuals of this group recognized few common interests or values distinct from those of the elites. Thus the ruling families were generally able to coopt individuals who exhibited potential for leadership of a middle-class movement into the service of the existing two-party system.

Commercial associations with members from both upper and middle classes began to replace social clubs as arenas for the discussion of policy interests, but the elites maintained a veto over middle-class aspirations. By 1936 there were a few persons of middle-class background in congress, but they joined the traditional parties rather than seeking a power base among the middle and lower classes. The failure of the lower class to develop class consciousness and structures for articulating and aggregating class interests may be attributed in part to the paternalistic attitude of the elites, the vertical organization of virtually all social institutions, the lack of leaders from the middle class (with the notable exception of Jorge Eliécer Gaitán) and the paucity of large concentrations of the disadvantaged in a given social environment.

Where wage-earning rural laborers have been concentrated in plantation "factories," such as in the sugar industry in the Cauca Valley, unionization and political radicalization have been common, but throughout most rural areas *minifundio* owners, squatters, tenants, and sharecroppers, who have little contact among themselves, predominate. The fact that industrial labor forces have been dispersed among several urban centers rather than concentrated in a few large cities has inhibited the development of the labor movement. In fact, each of the two major labor confederations developed under the tutelage of one of the two major parties, and until the 1970s suspicion and rivalry prevented effective aggregation of interests even on the most basic issues affecting labor.

The clientelistic orientation of both parties, the hegemony of the party in power, and the pervasiveness of the spoils system has made the position of one's party appear to be a matter of more vital concern than the welfare of a particular occupational or income group. The party is seen as a source of potential benefit for the individual rather than as an arena for the articulation of group interests. There is a general disinclination to exercise local initiative through collective action, and in rural areas the patron-client relationship in the party structure is reinforced by a tendency among peasants to look to their landlords for the fulfillment of their needs and the redress of grievances.

Among elites, on the other hand, interest articulation often circumvents the party structures entirely. Informal ties based on kinship, friendship, or interlocking business interests allow individuals to take their appeals directly to the executive branch regardless of which party is in power. Periodic consultations between the president and representatives of the country's major pressure groups, such as the National Coffee Growers Federation and the National Association of Industrialists, designed to reach mutual accommodation on matters of economic and social policy, have become virtually institutionalized.

A Brush with Ground Floor Reality: La Violencia

Ironically, the protracted civil war known as *la violencia,* or the violence, initially fought on behalf of clashing loyalties in the traditional regional partisan pattern, uprooted masses of people and planted the seeds of class consciousness. By the late 1950s, evidence of change in the political culture, fostered largely by the *violencia* and by urbanization, raised the specter of a modification in the two-party system and a challenge to elite control.

The partisan war (or perhaps class war disguised as partisan conflict) largely dissipated during the period of military rule but revived to a degree in the late 1950s and early 1960s, as some who had led Liberal Party guerrilla operations established occupied enclaves in rural areas and supported themselves through banditry. Some, including the Revolutionary Armed Forces of Colombia (FARC) and the Army of National Liberation (ELN), also declared independence for their carved out domains and learned the language of Marxism.

Widespread mistrust in the institutions of authority was to some extent both cause and effect of the *violencia.* Gaitan's denunciation of the elites, or *oligarquia,* and the sacking of buildings identified with the government or the Church after his assassination were indicative of the depth of alienation. The direct involvement of the police and the armed forces in the partisan conflict that followed further undermined authority and the power structure on which it was based. Skepticism toward governmental institutions and mistrust of the oligarchy grew out of the *violencia* and corresponded with a growing awareness among spokesmen of the lower class of their potential political strength and their right to be heard on policies affecting them. What began as a partisan conflict evolved into a diffuse manifestation of an incipient class struggle.

Urbanization, spurred by rapid industrialization since the 1930s and accelerated in the 1950s by the *violencia,* has had a measurable impact on political attitudes. Rivalries based on kinship and community ties have been less relevant in the more anonymous context of urban life, and changing of hereditary affiliations in the city, while requiring some corresponding changes in personal relationships, has not assured social ostracism.

Furthermore, urban dwellers have been exposed more intensively to the communications media and to organizations such as unions where class interests are articulated. More or less spontaneous protest demonstrations have taken place with increasing frequency in response to the implementation of unpopular measures, such as increases in the costs of public services. Urbanization has been seen as a major factor in the general midcentury shift from a Conservative to a Liberal nationwide majority of voters. In the elections of March 1962 every city with a vote amounting to 25,000 or more returned a Liberal majority.[1]

Elite Consensus and Stabilization: The National Front

The temporary coalescence of Liberal and Conservative Party leadership to effect a political truce or a gradual transfer of power that had taken place prior to 1958 had been short-lived, and had given way to the hegemony of one party and the virtual exclusion of the other from representation in government. In the late 1950s, however, the undercurrent of class consciousness that had revealed itself in the latter stages of the *violencia*, the assumption of power by the military (1953–1957) for the first time in the twentieth century, and the complex demands that a rapidly developing economy made on government apparently served notice on the elites of both parties that only through genuine sustained cooperation could they avoid losing control of the direction and pace of change. Thus a bipartisan agreement drawn up before the overthrow of Rojas Pinilla established a coalition system to be known as the National Front.

The arrangement embodied in the Sitges Agreement in 1957 and incorporated by plebiscite into the constitution institutionalized monopolistic control of the Liberal and Conservative parties over the machinery of government that was to remain in effect until 1974. The three basic pillars of this arrangement—parity in all elective and appointive offices, alternation of the presidency, and the requirement of a two-thirds vote on all legislation—contributed further to a system favoring accommodation over resolute action. Such accommodation did indeed pave the way for substantial economic growth, as a number of new products were added to the agro-export list.

In pitting faction against faction within each party, however, the arrangement magnified existing tendencies toward factionalism and personalism and often obscured from the public the issues of national policy involved in elections and in the legislative process. The low priority allocated to legislation by the legislators themselves was indicated by the high rate of absenteeism and the frequency with which congressmen yielded their seats to alternates.[2]

The system of proportional representation among the factions of the two major parties and the tolerance of the coalition government for the participation of other groups willing to run candidates under the traditional party labels operated as an escape valve for mounting pressures of opposition to the bipartisan arrangement and gauged the extent of that opposition. As dissident factions of the major parties and incipient third party movements generally based their platforms on opposition to the system, elections between 1958 and 1974 were viewed, in effect, as plebiscites on the continuation of the National Front arrangement.

Between 1958 and 1969 the combined votes cast for opponents of the National Front rarely exceeded a third of the total vote. The alienation and apathy, however, evidenced by abstention rates of some two-thirds of the eligible voters in the elections of 1964, 1966, and 1968 weakened the credibility of the government's claim to a popular base. Voter turnout decreased from a high of about 70 percent in the 1957 plebiscite to approximately 30 percent in the 1968 congressional elections.

The abrupt dissolution of the National Front in 1974, called for in the original agreement, had been viewed by elites with anxiety as an invitation to recourse to violence. A major constitutional revision, however, adopted in 1968, alleviating many of the adverse aspects of the bipartisan arrangement and paving the way for a gradual transition over an eight-year period, raised hopes that the return to a more competitive system could be achieved peacefully.[3]

Another major subject of speculation and concern was whether the transition would result in a reversion to two-party dominance or the emergence, for the first time in the country's history, of an authentic multiparty system. The major parties appeared geared up for the former eventuality. The Liberal Party was strengthened in 1967 by a merger, the first since the late 1930s, of its two largest factions, and the major Conservative factions were vociferous about the need for unity. It was assumed, however, that in the event that the Conservatives failed to unite and the Liberal merger came unglued, the right wing of the Liberals and the left wing of the Conservatives might unite to form a center party. As it turned out, partisan elites were to be blindsided by new power contenders who shunned electoral arenas or hijacked electoral processes.

REALITY FROM THE BOTTOM UP: CHRONIC WARFARE, DISPLACEMENT, AND DESPERATION

Frustrated Reform and Ill-Gotten Gain

Formally, the National Front arrangement was laid to rest on schedule in 1974 with the inauguration of President Alfonso López Michelsen of the Liberal Party. Nevertheless, in accordance with the constitutional amendment of 1968, the pattern of partisan parity in executive and legislative positions was followed by López and by his Liberal Party successor, Julio Cesar Turbay Ayala. Some aspects of the pattern were also revisited in the 1990s.

Over the course of the extended National Front period, the issues and interests that had previously divided Conservatives and Liberals and had even driven them twice to civil war—Church versus state, urban versus rural, agriculture and commerce versus industry—had almost become moot, and on both sides of the partisan divide, competition had moved inside the parties.

The public in general was not expected to weigh in on this kind of competition and in fact did not. Voter turnout, less than half of those eligible during the official period of the National Front, did not rebound thereafter.

Until the advent of the National Front, minor parties offered little challenge to the two-party system. Most of them were short-lived and were personalist- or Marxist-oriented or both. Few had sufficient membership to operate in all parts of the country. The Communist Party was the oldest and most durable of the minor parties, having functioned continuously since the 1920s, but it rarely received more than 1 percent of the vote, and it was often sharply divided between pro-Moscow and pro-Beijing factions.

The National Popular Alliance (ANAPO), initially a personalist party, was organized in the 1960s under the leadership of former dictator Gustavo Rojas Pinilla.

It made steady gains, electing candidates on primarily Conservative but also Liberal lists. Despite the strange bedfellow nature of its membership, the vagueness of its platform, and the confusion as to whether it was a party or a bipartisan movement, it aroused considerable uneasiness among the elite. Such uneasiness proved well founded in 1970, when ANAPO came very close, at least, to winning the presidential election. In fact, it was widely believed to have been deprived of victory by electoral fraud.

Frustration with a seemingly impregnable system gave rise in the 1970s to a new underground organization drawing participants, especially from ANAPO and from the FARC. Formally calling itself the April 19th Movement after the date of the alleged electoral fraud, it came to be known simply as M-19. Unlike earlier guerrilla movements, it was urban based from the start. Meanwhile other organizations representing lower-class interests began to break with their Liberal Party roots—as in the case of a peasant organization nurtured initially by the government of Carlos Lleras Restrepo (1966–1970)—or to rise independently of partisan support, like the union movement that culminated in 1986 in the formation of the United Workers Central (CUT).

Meanwhile rural violence, exacerbated by the spread of a new cash crop—cocaine—drove peasants from their land and into unsecured and unserviced shantytowns on the fringes of the cities. Thus the violence and vulnerability that had long plagued many rural areas moved into town and became a fact of city life as well.

Already in the 1970s, Colombia's homicide rate was among the world's highest, and it continued to climb sharply. By the late 1980s, 20,000 people were being murdered each year, a roster that included party and union leaders, mayors and city councilors, journalists and newspaper editors, judges and prosecutors, a minister of justice, an attorney general, and in 1989 and 1990 three presidential candidates.[4] Responsibility for the atrocities lay in part with the FARC and, to a lesser degree, with the ELN. Human rights monitors have found them to be responsible for most of the kidnappings, early on a fund-raising strategy and more recently leverage as well for prisoner exchange. Monitors found, however, that the great majority of the murders were carried out by official security forces or the rapidly growing paramilitary death squads. Massacres have generally been the work of paramilitaries. Americas Watch, the Western Hemisphere branch of Human Rights Watch, reported in December 1992 that 40 percent of Colombia's political assassinations were attributable to government agents, 30 percent to paramilitary groups, 27.5 percent to the guerrillas, and 2.5 percent to the drug mafia.[5]

Paramilitaries, supported financially by landowning drug barons and strategically by the military, were operating with impunity in urban as well as rural areas. Whole villages were massacred with the open collusion of the army, which, incidentally, was also growing—from 80,000 members in 1978 to 135,000 in 1988—and operating with increasing autonomy from civilian authorities. On one occasion, in 1985, when M-19 guerrillas had occupied the Palace of Justice, the army stormed the palace, killing ninety-five people, including many staff members and visitors as well as twelve of the twenty-five Supreme Court justices.[6] Parts of the palace were torched, including those where narco-trafficking case files were being processed.

The storming of the Palace of Justice appeared to be an affront to President Belisario Betancur (1982–1986) of the left wing of the Conservative Party, who had made a serious effort to de-escalate insurrection and to rein in the repression practiced by security forces. Human rights concerns received official attention under his government, and the activities of right-wing death squads were investigated. Amnesty was offered to guerrillas who would lay down their arms. Many accepted the offer, and former FARC affiliates went on to form a legitimate political party, the Patriotic Union (UP). The UP had considerable success initially in fielding and electing candidates, especially to local offices, but its leadership ranks were decimated between the mid-1980s and the early 1990s by more than 2,000 assassinations. Drug mafias shared responsibility for these murders with police, military, and paramilitary forces.

Violence continued to escalate under the presidency of Liberal Virgilio Barco, who succeeded Betancur in 1986 and who also attempted, to little avail, to make the political system more inclusive. The assassination in 1989 of the Liberal Party's popular presidential candidate, Luís Carlos Galán, by drug lords precipitated an all-out campaign against the leaders of the major Medellin- and Cali-based narco-trafficking organizations. That campaign had the effect of splintering and dispersing mafia operations. That plus the balloon effect of earlier US-sponsored drug wars in pushing major operations out of Peru and Bolivia and into Colombia greatly expanded the territory under coca cultivation and the geographic distribution of cocaine-processing laboratories. Meanwhile, laundered drug money was burrowing more deeply into legitimate business and mainstream politics and competing more forcefully with government for the loyalty of security forces.

The Making of a Humanitarian Catastrophe

Peasants driven from the countryside by the *violencia* between the late 1940s and the mid-1960s doubled the urban population; and those driven out from the mid-1960s to the mid-1980s by the commercialization of agriculture doubled it again. The urban population reached about 20 million, 70 percent of the overall population, in the mid-1980s. Urban life, particularly in the largest cities—Bogotá, Cali, and Medellin—benefited in the 1960s and 1970s from a flourishing of diversified domestic industry. By the 1980s, however, deregulation and foreign competition, inflation, and debt had taken their toll. Government intervention in the late 1980s stopped the slide, but local industry did not recover to 1970s levels.

Narco dollars helped finance the external trade balance, saving Colombia from the depths of recession experienced elsewhere in Latin America during that decade, but the off-budget windfall fueled inflation and, of course, corruption. Moreover, new economic growth was not matched by growth in jobs, much less in wages. Most employment was in the so-called informal sector, unprotected by labor organization or legislation.

The 1990 elections saw the withdrawal of the Patriotic Union, following the assassination of its leader and presidential candidate, Bernardo Jaramillo; the emergence of another party on the left—the Democratic Alliance, a vehicle primarily of former members of M-19—with 12.5 percent of the vote; a schism within the Conservative Party; and a victory for the centrist Liberal Party candidate César Gaviria Trujillo. Only slightly more than 25 percent of the eligible electorate turned out to vote. Twice as many as voted for Gaviria, however, voted in favor of a Constituent Assembly to draw up a new constitution. That constitution, optimistically opening up more avenues for popular political participation, was adopted in 1991.[7]

Assuming office in 1990, Gaviria embraced neoliberal economic policies, stressing trade liberalization, privatization, competitiveness, elimination of price subsidies, and sharp reductions in public expenditures. Foreign investment rose sharply but wage levels dropped, prices and unemployment figures rose, and public services declined. As popular opposition mounted, Gaviria's successor, Ernesto Samper (1994–1998), proposed social pacts with labor. But he resumed implementation of neoliberal measures as the US Congress, citing allegations that narco dollars had corrupted Samper's election campaign, found the Colombian government insufficiently committed to derailing the drug trade. Colombia was thus "decertified" in 1996 as a drug war collaborator, triggering disruptions in trade with and aid from the United States. Disruptions in legitimate trade and slippage in the legitimate economy set in relief the importance of the country's most lucrative cash crop.

Andres Pastrana of the Conservative Party (son of an earlier president) came to the presidency in 1998 with an ambitious plan. Along with strengthening security forces, *Plan Colombia* envisioned the strengthening of investigatory, judicial and other capabilities of the civilian government as well as the promotion of rural development; but most of all the plan originated as a peace initiative. Under that plan, Pastrana recognized a zone (under the de facto control of FARC), about the size of Switzerland, in the southern part of the country, as an autonomous—or demilitarized—zone, in which negotiations for a peaceful settlement might take place. Latin American and European countries offered their good offices, and for a time optimism prevailed.

Negotiations between the Pastrana government and the FARC leadership got under way at the beginning of 1999 and continued off and on for three years without producing so much as a cease-fire agreement. On the one hand, prospects for negotiation were stymied, particularly after 2000, by the insistence of the US government—the major funding source for operations of the semiautonomous Colombian security forces—on the militarization of Plan Colombia. On the other hand, prospects were hampered by the FARC's distrust of the government. Such distrust was born in part of the betrayal of FARC political and diplomatic leaders who had set themselves up for assassination by accepting amnesty and integrating the legitimate political system. That betrayal set in relief the underlying weakness of the traditional civilian partisan elite—especially its inability to control security forces—weakness heavily underscored by the fate of the Patriotic Union Party.

At the beginning of 2002, a new plan for the peace process and a timetable for a cease-fire were produced through a Colombian government ultimatum, aided by the intercession of United Nations envoy James LeMoyne, accompanied by Church officials and representatives of ten countries. Sadly, this seeming breakthrough was to be short-lived. In the weeks that followed, FARC provocations continued, culminating in the hijacking of a domestic airliner and the kidnapping of a senator who was on board. Thereupon, President Pastrana declared the peace process dead; on February 20, aerial bombardment signaled the beginning of a military campaign to retake the recently demilitarized zone.[8]

If Pastrana's election in 1998 had been seen as a mandate to pursue peace, the election in 2002 of Alvaro Uribe Vélez, a dissident Liberal, was seen as a mandate for security, or closure by reconquest. President Uribe, who assumed office in August 2002, had a reputation as a hardliner, and he promised to do all-out battle against the FARC. After two years of staunch refusal to negotiate, Uribe surprised the country on August 18, 2004, by offering the FARC conditions for a prisoner exchange. The conditions, however, were such that both the FARC and relatives of some of its hostages dismissed the offer as unserious. Since polls indicated that most Colombians support a prisoner exchange, some commentators linked the government's apparent about-face on the issue to the then pending congressional approval of a constitutional change that eventually opened the way for Uribe to serve a second term.[9]

The Demographics of Desperation

In May 2004, Jan Egeland, UN undersecretary for humanitarian affairs, called a press conference in New York to draw attention to the situation in Colombia, which he called "by far the biggest humanitarian catastrophe in the Western Hemisphere." Intractable warfare over political and military advantage, old and new grudges, the bounty of the illicit drug trade, and straightforwardly now over control of territory, had generated 2 million refugees. Colombia had become, after the Congo and the Sudan, the country with the third greatest number of displaced persons in its midst and the largest number of land mine victims worldwide.[10]

The two major guerrilla groups, the FARC and the ELN, were engaged in armed combat with official military forces and right-wing paramilitary groups. The contemporary cash crop of choice sustained combatants on all sides. Left-wing guerrillas and right-wing paramilitaries alike financed themselves directly through drug trafficking as well as through collecting protection "taxes" from coca growers. Taxation notwithstanding, small-scale growers, who produce most of the national crop, can earn far more on cocaine than on any other traditional or non-traditional crop.

Revolutionaries: The FARC and the ELN

Taxes paid in exchange for security are more important to the guerrillas and the territories they control than to the paramilitaries, who gain much of their territory by killing off or driving off the previous inhabitants and taking possession of the land. Though the FARC has become more involved in trafficking in recent years, most of its cocaine windfall, estimated at $500 million a year, derives from the 10 percent tax it collects from growers. With that treasury, the FARC has been able to field an army of more than 20,000—swelled at times by peasants driven off their land by the paramilitaries—and to control, or at least to move freely in, 40 to 60 percent of the national territory.[11] The ELN is much smaller, having about 4000 troops, and has been less intransigent with respect to negotiation for peaceful settlement. It has been noted particularly for continual sabotage of operations and pipelines of the petroleum multinationals.

Now the hemisphere's oldest and most powerful revolutionary body, the FARC originated as a Maoist-inspired peasant co-op under the leadership of Liberal Party combatants "retired" after *la violencia* subsided. The isolated community in south-ern Tolima department known as the Independent Republic of Marquetalia was transformed into a guerrilla organization after a US-supported attack on the com-munity in May 1964. Survivors reported that the raid pitted 16,000 military per-sonnel against 1,000 villagers, of whom only 48 were armed.[12]

A peasant-based and peasant-led movement from the start, there can be little doubt that the FARC is serious about social change. The movement, however, hardly lends itself to the self-sacrificial, romantic revolutionary image of the Zap-atistas, for example, of Mexico's southern province of Chiapas. As has so often been the case in Colombia and elsewhere, a war without foreseeable end has gen-erated its own sustainable economy; and the FARC would be highly unlikely to place it on a bargaining table, even if it could place full faith and credit in the gov-ernment's bargaining position.

A factor contributing further to the intractability of this war is the nature and experience of the FARC leadership. Until early 2008 it remained in the hands of its septuagenarian founder, Manuel Marulanda (better known as Tirofijo, or Sure-shot) who had been a warrior for half a century, since the onset of *la violencia*. In early 2008 he died of age-related illness. The FARC's then number two, Raúl Reyes, was killed subsequently while in hiding in Ecuadorean territory in March 2008 by a Colombian military strike supported by US counternarcotics surveil-lance. This latter incident was a violation of Ecuadorean sovereignty that has had lasting consequences in bilateral relations. In 2009 the FARC under the leadership of Alfonso Cano, an intellectual with a background in anthropology, continued to be mired in conflict, weakened by the Uribe government's Democratic Security campaign, a military surge sustained by US Plan Colombia.

Counterrevolutionaries: The Paramilitaries and the AUC

It is hardly surprising that where threadbare peasants organize to defend their in-terests, armed bodies acting on behalf of estate or plantation owners will also ap-pear. And when the cash crop cultivated on many such estates comes to be cocaine, those armed bodies will become increasingly robust. Compensation for such secu-rity services usually comes largely in the form of impunity—the right to rape and pillage. The longer such forces enjoy impunity and the greater the available loot, the more likely it is that they will soon cease simply to serve private or public pow-ers and rather become wielders of those powers.

The trajectory of Colombia's paramilitaries is not so different from those of vig-ilante groups or death squads elsewhere (e.g., Central America), where rigid class structure and increasing inequity were challenged from below. That trajectory has led from private and locally contained activity to cooptation, disguised or open, by official military and intelligence operatives, and finally to major or commanding roles in government itself.

Paramilitaries, in order to coordinate their operations at the national level, in 1997 formed a loose confederation, the United Self-Defense Forces of Colombia (AUC); it tripled in size from 1998 to 2002, when its members numbered about 15,000. As generalized insecurity has moved into town, along with displaced peas-ants and dismissed workers, Support for the paramilitaries has spread also within the urban middle class. This expanded base was manifested in the congressional and presidential elections of 2002. For reasons, reportedly, of affinity on the one hand and intimidation on the other, the AUC gained control of about 35 percent of the congressional seats as well as several governorships.

President Uribe's support base included both Liberals and Conservatives, but it was expanded by nontraditional participants like the paramilitaries. Uribe, a former governor of the drug mafia–infested department of Antioquia, had been linked to the paramilitaries, reportedly, in myriad ways and to their collaborators in official military positions, and he was clearly their undeclared candidate. The United States had also weighed in, signaling its support for Uribe both privately and publicly. Though only 38 percent of the eligible voters turned out, Uribe's margin of 53 percent in a field of four was impressive. The official Liberal candidate, Horacio Serpa, came in second, trailing at 31.7 percent.

Paramilitaries were also found to have sent their members of congress to horse trade with close advisers to President Uribe in order pass the legislation in congress to allow Uribe to run and win a second term in 2006.[13] In this election, Uribe won with more than 60 percent of the vote and with total voter turnout of 45.1 percent.[14] Despite increasing evidence of paramilitary influence in the Uribe government, referred to as *parapolítica*, a majority of Colombians responding to recent opinion polls continue to support Uribe and even a possible referendum to allow him to run for a third time either in 2010 or nonconsecutively in 2014. Interestingly, the cult of personality around Uribe has weakened the relative power of the Conservative and Liberal parties and made way for the left-wing Alternative Democratic Pole to take second place in the 2006 presidential election and gain its second consecutive mayorship in Bogotá as well as the governorship of the southern department of Nariño.

Deepening US Involvement

In the aftermath of the September 11, 2001, terrorist attacks on New York City and Washington, DC, the Bush administration began to speak of its left-wing antagonists around Latin America, including Colombia, as terrorists. An emergency supplemental appropriations bill to expand counterterror capabilities worldwide, rushed through the US Congress in March 2000, included money for Colombia and language that allowed the mission there to expand from fighting drugs to fighting terrorists as well. The Democratic Party opposition, unable to prevent passage of the legislation, managed nevertheless to designate the AUC, along with the FARC and the ELN, as terrorist organizations.

In the name of Plan Colombia, the US government by 2004 had spent some $3 billion, more than 75 percent of it on military assistance. Until the US invasion of Iraq, Colombia was the third-largest recipient of US assistance, after Israel and Egypt. About 400 military personnel were serving in Colombia, along with another 400 so-called civilian contractors, and the administration had proposed nearly doubling those numbers. The United States had used hundreds of thousands of gallons of highly toxic herbicides in aerial spraying of coca fields—and also, incidentally, of food crops and villages. Such spraying is most likely in the long term to increase the acreage planted in coca; the coca plant is more resilient than most and will grow in soil too damaged for replanting in food crops. In the short term, peasants whose food crops have been eradicated will be driven onto less fertile land that is fit for little else than the extraordinarily robust coca. There is no indication, in any case, that the almost $40 billion a year cocaine traffic into the United States—some 80 percent of it from Colombia—has abated.[15]

When the Democratic administration of Barack Obama took office in 2009, it sent mixed signals, despite earlier rhetoric indicating a potential shift in approach to Colombia and the wars on drugs and terrorism. On the one hand, the Obama administration took a more diplomatic line toward Colombia's neighbors. On the other, it accelerated military collaboration through a series of counternarcotics/counterterrorism basing arrangements designed to replace the US base in Manta, Ecuador, since its lease was not renewed by the Ecuadorean government. Nonetheless, total US government security assistance reached $420 million for 2009 in contrast to $243 million for economic and social aid, with much of the latter still overly influenced by the logic of the military support package and its objectives.[16]

No Winners; Only Losers and Unsung Heroes

While paramilitary organizations have literally gained ground under the Uribe government, it has been less clear who might emerge in the longer term as winners of the seemingly endless Colombian free for all. But there has been no doubt at all about the losers. Civilians who were not targeted by the guerrillas were thereby under suspicion of being guerrilla sympathizers and thus were targeted by the paramilitaries. Some were targeted by both and others were simply crushed in passing when their ancestral homes got in the way of bullets and bombs and herbicides, or in the case of some indigenous groups, in the way of the ambitions of multinational petroleum interests.

By 2009, some 40,000 combatants, mostly from the AUC, had been demobilized through the Justice and Peace law passed by the Uribe government and the Colombian congress in 2003. High-level military leaders have either been jailed under VIP conditions or extradited to the United States to face drug trafficking charges rather than being held accountable for massacres and widespread displacement of poor peasants, Afro-Colombians, and indigenous groups. While overall rates of violence, as measured in homicides, have dropped considerably in Colombia over the past ten years, particularly in large cities, evidence is mounting that this reflects a transition rather than the end of violence.[17]

The Uribe administration claims its democratic security policy and the AUC demobilization process are responsible for declining homicide rates, particularly in Bogotá and other large urban centers. However, other analysts attribute these improvements to a combination of two important factors.[18] First, to those who had wondered whether the "decommissioning," or laundering, of the AUC was to be a cold shower or a warm bath, it is now clear that the paramilitary organizations dominate key economic sectors so completely that they no longer need to engage in the same levels of violence to maintain control. Second, Bogotá, Medellín, and other large cities have been governed in recent years by left of center governments that focused on improving policing at the local level and a range of important social programs designed to reduce violence and improve civic cohesion.

Despite the façade of economic modernity observed in major cities, Colombia was the second most unequal country in Latin America, after Brazil in terms of income distribution; more than 60 percent of families live below the poverty threshold.[19] Health care has been generally unavailable for those in the herbicide spray zones who suffer from rashes, respiratory problems, and temporary blindness. Education has not been readily available either. Though at least 75 percent of the population is now urban, one-third of the children of primary school age have never attended school. In the mushrooming shantytowns, children lacking schools or jobs had often been impressed into one or another category of armed band or lured into prostitution.

Ninety percent of the land is owned by 10 percent of the population, and the trend is toward ever greater concentration. It is hardly surprising that land seized by terror from the poor finds its way into the grasp of the already wealthy. Paramilitaries began in 2001 to sell off great chunks of land under their control to drug traffickers willing to pay fees based on cocaine production.[20] The growth of agroindustry for export has only exacerbated these dynamics.

The process of peace and justice for the displaced and the families of those killed by paramilitary forces moves forward at a snail's pace, with no law mandating reparations for those killed by military forces. Meanwhile, there was no escape from nagging insecurity for the rural poor. Wealthy businessmen can build higher walls around their property and hire more security guards; but even they cannot avoid becoming prisoners in their own homes. Some Colombians hunker down and assume a low profile. But those who by profession or avocation have chosen to deal in truth and justice put themselves at risk, and the poor, of course, are always vulnerable. Colombia continues to be a very dangerous place for human rights activists, environmentalists, union workers, and indigenous leaders. [21]

All wars have their heroes. But the heroes of the most inglorious of wars, especially wars of the rich against the poor—of conquest and endless reconquest—are certain to be unsung. Among the unsung heroes and heroines of Colombia's chronic conflict are the citizens of rural communities—particularly in the province of Cauca—who have organized and declared themselves "peace communities" despite continuing threats from marauding bands. At great personal and collective risk, they stand firm in unarmed resistance to guerrillas or, more often, paramilitaries who would drive them off their land and out of their villages. The best known and presumed oldest of these is San Jose de Apartado, which has maintained its integrity against all odds over some three decades of resistance. Victories are partial and always reversible, but the network of communities is spreading rapidly, capturing imagination and drawing support from many religious and nongovernmental organizations in Europe and the United States.

Even so, if there is to be a breakthrough to sustainable peace and human security at ground level—as opposed to the penthouse suites where "peace process" can so easily become the new designation of an ongoing war—its outline is yet to emerge. For now, the famous lament of the Liberator of South America, Simón Bolívar, remains sadly applicable to Colombia: "America is ungovernable; those who have fought the revolution have plowed the sea."

NOTES

1. Robert H. Dix, *Colombia: The Political Dimensions of Change* (New Haven: Yale University Press, 1967), p. 242.

2. James L. Payne, *Patterns of Conflict in Colombia* (New Haven: Yale University Press, 1968), pp. 238–267.

3. Ninety-first Congress, 1st sess., Senate Committee on Foreign Relations, *Colombia: A Case History of US Aid.* (Washington: GPO, 1969), pp. 57–59.

4. Jenny Pearce, "Colombia," in Peter Calvert, ed., *Political and Economic Encyclopedia of South America and the Caribbean* (London: Longman, 1991), pp. 123–133.

5. Charles Bergquist, Ricardo Penaranda, and Gonzalo Sánchez, *Violence in Colombia, 1990–2000: Waging War and Negotiating Peace* (Wilmington, DE: Scholarly Resources, 2004), p. xiv.

6. Pearce, "Colombia." see also Marc Cooper, "Plan Colombia: Wrong Issue, Wrong Enemy, Wrong Country," *The Nation,* March 19, 2001, pp. 11–18.

7. A sampling of the reforms embodied in that new constitution is found in Charles Bergquist et al., *Violence,* p. 213.

8. William Monning and Jeffrey Fields, "A Multilateral Negotiation/Mediation Simulation: The Civil Conflict in Colombia," Monterey Institute of International Studies, 2004.

9. Latin America Database, NotiSur–South American Political and Economic Affairs, ISSN 1060–4189, vol. 14, no. 33, September 3, 2004.

10. Peter Canby, "Latin America's Longest War," *The Nation,* August 16/23, 2004, pp. 31–38; Radio broadcast on United Nations Radio, "Colombia es el país con más víctimas de minas" ["Colombia is the country with most landmine victims"], December 4, 2008.

11. Monning and Fields, "Multilateral Negotiation."

12. Ibid.

13. Santiago Martinez Castilla. 'Justicia y gobernabilidad en Colombia: De la 'Ley de Justicia y Paz' a la "Yidispolítica," *Delaware Review of Latin American Studies,* July 30, 2008.

14. Daniel Zovatto, *Balance Electoral Latinoamericano Noviembre 2005–Diciembre 2006* (Stockholm, International IDEA, 2007).

15. Canby, "Latin America's Longest War."

16. See *Just the Facts: A Civilian's Guide to US Defense and Security Assistance to Latin America and the Caribbean,* http://justf.org/Country?country=Colombia.

17. Douglas Porch and María José Rasmussen, 'Demobilization of Paramilitaries in Colombia: Transformation or Transition?" *Studies in Conflict and Terrorism* 31, no. 6 (2008).

18. Adam Issacson, *Plan Colombia: Six Years Later* (Washington, D.C.: Center for International Policy, 2006).

19. United Nations Development Program, *Human Development Report* (New York: UN, 2007); United Nations Economic Commission for Latin America and the Caribbean, *Anuario Estadístico 2007* (Santiago: ECLAC, 2007).

20. Robin Kirk, *More Terrible Than Death: Violence, Drugs, and America's War in Colombia* (New York: Public Affairs, 2004).

21. Virginia Bouvier, *Civil Society Under Siege: Special Report.* Washington, D.C.: US Institute for Peace, 2004.

SUGGESTED READINGS

Bergquist, Charles, Ricardo Penaranda, and Gonzalo Sánchez, eds. *Violence in Colombia, 1990–2000: Waging War and Negotiating Peace.* Wilmington, DE: Scholarly Resources, 2001.

Dix, Robert H. *Colombia: The Political Dimensions of Change*. New Haven: Yale University Press, 1967.

———. *The Politics of Colombia*. New York: Praeger, 1987.

Dudley, Steven. *Walking Ghosts: Murder and Guerrilla Politics in Colombia*. London: Routledge, 2004.

Fluharty, Vernon J. *The Dance of the Millions: Military Rule and Social Revolution in Colombia, 1930–1956*. Pittsburg: University of Pittsburg Press, 1957.

Galbraith, W.O. *Colombia: A General Survey*, 2nd ed. London: Oxford University Press, 1966.

Hartlyn, Jonathan. *The Politics of Coalition Rule in Colombia*. Cambridge: Cambridge University Press, 1988.

Holmes, Jennifer S., Sheila Amin Gutiérrez de Piñeres, and Kevin M. Curtin. *Guns, Drugs, and Development in Colombia*. Austin: University of Texas Press, 2009.

Holt, Pat M. *Colombia Today and Tomorrow*. New York: Praeger, 1964.

Hunter, John A. *Emerging Colombia*. Washington, D.C.: Public Affairs, 1962.

Kirk, Robin. *More Terrible Than Death: Massacres, Drugs, and America's War in Colombia*. New York: Public Affairs, 2004.

Kline, Harvey F. *Colombia: Democracy Under Assault*. Boulder: Westview, 1995.

Livingstone, Grace. *Inside Colombia: Drugs, Democracy, and War*. New Brunswick, NJ: Rutgers University Press, 2004.

Martz, John D., Jr. "Colombia: Qualified Democracy." in Martin C. Needler, ed., *Political Systems of Latin America*. Princeton: Van Nostrand, 1964.

———. *The Politics of Clientelism in Colombia: Democracy and the State*. New Brunswick, NJ: Transaction, 1996.

Molano, Alfred. *Loyal Soldiers in the Cocaine Kingdom: Tales of Drugs, Mules, and Gunmen*. Trans. James Graham. New York: Colombia University Press, 2004.

Payne, James L. *Patterns of Conflict in Colombia*. New Haven: Yale University Press, 1968.

Smith, T. Lynn. *Colombia: Social Structure and the Process of Development*. Gainesville: University of Florida Press, 1967.

Stokes, Doug. *America's Other War: Terrorizing Colombia*. London: Zed, 2005.

Tate, Winfred. *Counting the Dead: The Culture and Politics of Human Rights Activism in Colombia*. Berkeley: University of California Press, 2007.

Taussig, Michael. *Law in a Lawless Land: Diary of a Limpieza in Colombia*. New York: New Press, 2004.

Chapter 21

VENEZUELA

The Challenge to a "Model Democracy"

STEVE ELLNER

VENEZUELA WAS AN unlikely nation for the type of social and political turbulence that began during the 1990s and peaked following the election of Hugo Chávez in 1998. For years political scientists had labeled Venezuela a "showcase" or "model" democracy in large part because of its mass-based political parties, which provided organized labor and other institutions with input into decision making, thus assuring political stability. Leaders of the struggle against the dictatorship of Juan Vicente Gómez (1908–1935) founded Venezuela's largest party, Democratic Action (AD), and subsequently came to power during a short-lived democracy from 1945 to 1948. AD and the nation's second largest party, the Social Christian Party (COPEI), alternated in power several times during the modern period of democracy beginning in 1958, at a time when military coups interrupted democratic rule in the rest of Latin America. Cold War imperatives contributed to the international renown of AD and COPEI leaders, who played a leading role in Washington's efforts to banish Cuba from the community of Latin American nations shortly after Fidel Castro's rise to power.

A week of mass disturbances in February 1989 known as the Caracazo signaled the end of AD and COPEI hegemony and coincided with other abrupt and difficult changes. Controversial formulas, which included the privatization of the telecommunications and steel industries and the national airline, replaced the strategy of state intervention in the economy (known as "sowing the oil"), which had enjoyed a near consensus among major political actors after 1958. In addition, erratic international oil prices since the mid-1980s contrasted with the relative stability of the previous half century and underlined Venezuela's dependence on the export of that commodity, leading Venezuelans to question the notion that they were a privileged Third World nation.

Another rupture occurred with Chávez's presidential election. The constitution of 1999 drafted by Chávez supporters established the model of direct popular participation known as participatory democracy, in the process undermining the all-encompassing influence and privilege of political parties. In addition, Chávez's foreign policy, which was designed to promote a multipolar world, distanced

Venezuela from the US orbit more than at any moment until then. In other respects, however, Chávez's appeal to the marginalized poor who worked outside the formal economy was not completely new for Venezuela and Latin America. To a certain extent it represented a throwback to the 1930s and 1940s when radical Latin American leaders known as populists (such as Juan Domingo Perón in Argentina) promoted the incorporation of excluded sectors into their nation's social and political life.

VENEZUELA PRIOR TO THE OUTSET OF THE MODERN DEMOCRATIC PERIOD IN 1958

Colonial Venezuela's backwater setting and delayed institutional growth molded future developments, including resistance to Spanish rule in the early nineteenth century. Thus, due to Venezuela's backwardness and poverty, few Spanish women arrived to marry into the native elite. As a result the colony was characterized by high rates of miscegenation both in rural areas and towns, and soon virtually all colonists were of mixed blood. Furthermore, the weak presence of Spanish authorities gave rise to widespread contraband, which in turn cemented ties with Spain's traditional adversary England and eventually generated interest in free trade. At the same time it facilitated contact with republican ideas, which also contributed to the wars for independence. Spain's neglect of Venezuela in the sixteenth and seventeenth centuries helped convert town councils (known as *cabildos*), controlled by the local elite but responsive to all citizens, into centers of decision making. Attempts by eighteenth-century Spanish Bourbon kings to centralize power enhanced Caracas's position at the expense of the *cabildos* and created discontent. The relative weakness of Spanish authority in the colony goes a long way in explaining why an army led by Venezuela's Simón Bolívar not only liberated his nation from Spanish rule but went on to win independence in Colombia, Ecuador, Peru, and Bolivia.

Traditional historiography portrayed the period between the death of Bolívar in 1830 and that of Gómez in 1935 as a lost century devoid of meaningful change, characterized by ongoing clashes among caudillos (strongmen) lacking in scruples and programs. Such a simplistic thesis, which is still accepted by many Venezuelans, belies the popular and democratic banners of the struggles and certain changes that occurred during those hundred years. A dynamic view of history would recognize the long-term importance of mobilization around radical social and political slogans, and their influence on popular consciousness, even though most of those demands were neither well defined nor achieved at the time.

As a result of the Federal War between 1859 and 1863, the Liberal Party, which appealed to nonprivileged sectors, gained power from the Conservatives, who had previously dominated politics. When the Liberal leaders landed at the port city of Coro marking the beginning of the war, they proclaimed the abolition of both the death penalty and imprisonment for debt, as well as religious liberty, direct elections, and equality before law. Their arrival at Coro sparked uprisings in several places, including the San Carlos prison in Maracaibo. The Liberal rallying cry "Federation" lacked a precise definition, but for the lower classes it signified a call for liberty, equality, and distribution of land. To raise money for the war effort, the most radical Liberal, General Ezequiel Zamora, decreed a 5 percent tax on the possessions of wealthy Venezuelans. Zamora, however, was killed in battle, possibly on orders from fellow Liberals.

Eventually the rival Liberal leader Antonio Guzmán Blanco gained control and ruled Venezuela between 1870 and 1888. Guzmán Blanco was notoriously corrupt and abandoned the Liberals' democratic commitments. Nevertheless, in his first year in power he decreed obligatory primary education, and subsequently the number of public schools increased nearly tenfold. At the same time, he curtailed the prerogatives of the Catholic Church, a bulwark of the oligarchy, by establishing a civil registry and giving the state a monopoly on legally recognized marriages. Guzmán Blanco also established a mechanism known as the *situado* for distributing a fixed percentage of the federal budget to the states. The *situado* placated the regional caudillos by compensating for the central government's jurisdiction over customs and mineral wealth and the elimination of internal tariffs. Venezuelan historian Germán Carrera Damas has argued that the Liberals in power embraced a "national project" consisting of incipient state centralization and policies that favored the "advanced" enterprising sectors of the elite over the traditional oligarchy.

The next important political change occurred in 1899 when a makeshift army from the state of Táchira led by Cipriano Castro (who governed from 1899 to 1908) and Juan Vicente Gómez (1908–1935) took control of Caracas. Their war cry, "New Men, New Ideals, New Methods," proved deceptive as Castro ruled as a dictator and Gómez as a ruthless one. Nevertheless, Castro, who even before the invasion had embraced a nationalist rhetoric in opposition to British territorial claims, displayed courage in facing up to powerful national and foreign interests that were themselves linked. He put down an uprising known as the Revolución Libertadora in 1902–1903 supported by US and European investors who were irked by Castro's stiff requirements toward foreign capital. During the conflict the rebels hailed the blockade of British, Italian, and German ships sent to force the Venezuelan government to meet its debt obligations. Castro reacted by appealing to national unity and even had a leading political adversary, José Manuel Hernández, released from jail. Hernández called on Venezuelans to put aside differences to face the foreign invaders. Although Castro requested US help in settling the dispute, Washington ended up aiding his ex-comrade in arms, Gómez, in staging a successful coup in 1908.[1]

In promoting centralism and building national institutions, Castro and Gómez continued where Guzmán Blanco left off. Most importantly, Castro created a standing national army while Gómez promoted its professionalization and centralized its command. As a result, the Venezuelan government was able to rein in regional caudillos and avoid a repetition of the Revolución Libertadora uprising.

Oil revenue under Gómez facilitated state building and the formation of a well-equipped standing army. In the early 1920s, Venezuela began to export significant quantities of oil and by the end of the decade had become the largest international supplier. Venezuela's status as a single-product exporter was maintained as the production of coffee and cacao, the nation's main cash crop during the previous century, declined precipitously in the 1920s. The state bureaucracy and programs fed by oil revenue produced opportunities for a burgeoning middle class and working class, which went on to form the social base of democratic political movements that challenged the Gómez dictatorship.

The year 1936 began the modern period of Venezuelan history. Even though President Eleazar López Contreras (1936–1941) and Isaías Medina Angarita (1941–1945) were former Gómez military officers and were called *gomecistas* by their adversaries, they promoted gradual democratization, including legalization of political parties and labor unions, freedom of expression, and electoral reforms. Equally important, both presidents contributed to the institution building and centralism that began with Guzmán Blanco. Thus, for instance, López passed the Social Security Law in 1940 while Medina implemented it by creating the Venezuelan Social Security Institute (IVSS) in 1944.

The October 1945 coup that initiated the *trienio* period of AD rule between 1945 and 1948 deepened the steps toward reform, modernization, and democracy of the previous ten years. An example of gradual change was the *trienio* government's policy of 50-50—for every dollar of oil company profits, the state received at least one dollar in revenue. Although AD called the policy "revolutionary," President Medina had established the 50-50 arrangement as a guiding principle in his Law of Hydrocarbons of 1943 (but in practice the calculation of taxes on oil profits during the next two years fell short of that goal). In some aspects, the *trienio* represented a qualitative change in favor of democracy and modernization. Most importantly, politics was characterized by popular mobilization and participation, including the proliferation of labor organizations, in contrast to the more elitist, restrictive political system operating up until then. Another novelty was the government's strategy of assigning a significant portion of the national budget to the Venezuelan Development Corporation (CVF) in order to grant credit and subsidies to national enterprises.

The military rule under General Marcos Pérez Jiménez between 1948 and 1958 also combined elements of rupture with continuity. By outlawing AD, the Communist Party, and hundreds of labor unions and holding a notoriously rigged election (for a constituent assembly) in 1952 and plebiscite in 1957, the dictatorship broke the "constitutional thread" dating back to 1936. It also halted the *trienio* government's policy of subsidizing national enterprises to promote economic development. Nevertheless, in carrying out ambitious development plans in the industrial Guayana region, including the creation of the state-owned steel company SIDOR, the government rejected laissez-faire (or state nonintervention) economics, thus adhering to general policy dating back to 1936.

THE MODERN DEMOCRATIC PERIOD:
THE STABLE YEARS, 1958–1988

Following the overthrow of Pérez Jiménez as a result of popular mobilization and a broad alliance including political parties, dissident officers, and representatives of the Catholic Church hierarchy, Venezuelan politics evolved into a two-party system based on AD and COPEI. For the first three presidential elections, AD's Rómulo Betancourt (in 1958), AD's Raúl Leoni (in 1963), and COPEI's Rafael

Caldera (in 1968) ran in an open field of candidates and were elected with less than 50 percent of the vote. In 1961 the diverse parties converged to draft a national constitution, which remained in effect for nearly forty years.

Pro-establishment AD and COPEI emerged as the dominant parties due in part to a fatal decision by the Venezuelan left, inspired by the Cuban revolution, to participate in guerrilla warfare. The political tensions that led the left to take up arms were partly the product of economic difficulties stemming from the international competition posed by emerging Middle Eastern oil producers. During Leoni's presidency, the pro-guerrilla Communist Party put forward the slogan "Democratic Peace" in order to negotiate its way back into legal life. Upon taking office, President Caldera granted amnesty to the Communists and subsequently to the insurgent Movement of the Revolutionary Left (MIR).

The guerrilla defeat was testimony to the attractiveness of the model of state intervention in the economy embraced by AD and COPEI as an alternative to the socialist system of exclusive state ownership defended by the left. Thus AD and COPEI governments actively promoted economic development and attempted to fulfill social objectives. While Venezuela was basically capitalist, the constitution of 1961 reserved "basic industry" for the state, although it failed to formulate a precise definition of the term. Along these lines, the Betancourt administration expanded the plans for Guayana formulated under the Pérez Jiménez dictatorship by creating the Venezuelan Corporation of Guayana (CVG) in order to run the steel and hydroelectric power industries of the region. In addition, Betancourt created the Venezuelan Petroleum Corporation (CVP), although he stressed its more limited objective of gauging private oil company profits for tax purposes over the more ambitious objective of competing on the international market. Throughout the period, the nation's main labor confederation, the AD-controlled Confederation of Venezuelan Workers (CTV), put forward specific proposals to enhance the central government's role in the economy and in doing so championed the interventionist model even more than the governing parties did. Nevertheless, the limitation of the reformist thrust of these governments was demonstrated by the Agrarian Reform Law passed in 1960, which distributed publicly owned land and property confiscated from Pérez Jiménez's closest followers, but not from large landholders.

The 1974 election of Carlos Andrés Pérez as president initiated a new period in which the combined presidential vote of AD and COPEI approximated 90 percent of the voting population. Pérez's full-fledged application of the interventionist model in the form of ambitious social and economic programs was made possible by a windfall in oil revenue beginning in his first year in office. Pérez nationalized the iron and oil industries (in 1975 and 1976), increased state ownership of the aluminum industry, and invested vast sums of money in the expansion of the state steel company SIDOR.[2] Shortly after he left office, Pérez claimed that the state takeover of private companies under his administration formed part of a strategy of "evolutionary socialism."

Sharply rising international oil prices provided President Pérez and his successor, COPEI's Luís Herrera Campins (1979–1984), with a golden opportunity to promote national development. The subsequent economic contraction and deteriorating social conditions throughout the 1980s served as a reminder that the development strategy of previous decades had failed to produce the expected results. Neoliberal thinking, which minimizes the role of the state, attributed the stagnation to the inherent shortcomings of the interventionist strategy.

Other explanations for the economic shortcomings of the democratic period focus on certain priorities and practices. In the first place, the interventionist policies of the Venezuelan government were biased in favor of social as opposed to developmental objectives (a tendency that has led some political scientists to call Pérez and other presidents of the period "populists"). Thus, for example, the need to create job opportunities overshadowed the goal of increasing productivity and consequently generated artificial employment. In the second place, in spite of Venezuela's image as a showcase democracy, the widespread corruption and patronage practiced by the dominant parties were responsible for the state's low levels of productivity, particularly in telecommunications, steel, aluminum, and airlines companies that were subsequently slated for private takeover. Indeed, there is evidence that the deteriorating conditions in state-run industries in the 1980s were partially induced in order to pave the way for privatization. In the third place, the post-1958 governments generally failed to prioritize the goal of severing dependence on foreign capital and promoting technology and sophisticated products such as capital goods. Finally, even though the nation was awash in hard currency as a result of oil price hikes, the Pérez and Herrera Campins administrations greatly increased the foreign debt, thus limiting budgetary options for many years to come. Political scientist Terry Lynn Karl points out that the magnitude of such indebtedness in a time of prosperity had parallels only with Spain in the sixteenth century.

The Deepening Political Crisis, 1989–1998

Critics of Venezuelan democracy have pointed to two distinct dates signaling the changes that inflicted the most damage on the nation and its political system. President Chávez and his supporters claim that the democratic system was flawed from the outset in 1958 due to the central role assigned to political parties and the key decisions that were reached by a political elite far removed from the general population. Such a view ignores the popular will in favor of the electoral democracy that replaced the Pérez Jiménez dictatorship. In addition, the politics of state intervention in the economy that was a hallmark of the post-1958 regime, for all its shortcomings, promoted economic development and diversification.

A second view pinpoints 1989 as the date when the economic policies implemented under the second presidency of President Carlos Andrés Pérez (1989–1993), coupled with an extended period of relatively low oil prices, aggravated social inequality and sparked social unrest. Over the next ten years, the number of marginalized poor lacking steady work in the formal economy grew steadily, reaching nearly 60 percent of the population. As a result, leading actors such as Carlos Andrés Pérez and other politicians and AD, COPEI, and pro-establishment political parties lost credibility. Pérez's shock treatment—sudden application of neoliberal reforms—included deregulation of exchange rates (which led to the devaluation of the local currency), retail prices, and interest rates. Like Pérez in 1988,

Rafael Caldera in 1993 won the presidential elections on a platform that defended the interventionist model, only to implement neoliberal formulas in his third year in office on terms negotiated with the International Monetary Fund (IMF). In his last two years as president, Caldera signed legislation modifying the system of worker severance payments and privatizing social security along the lines that President Pérez had proposed in 1989 but then had dropped due to lack of sufficient support. Both measures were widely perceived as tinkering with long-standing worker benefits that protected them in difficult circumstances. The CTV (along with business and state representatives) formed part of a presidentially created tripartite commission that drafted the legislation, and in doing so abandoned its traditional insistence on leaving both systems intact. Electoral abstention, which had increased moderately in the 1980s, rose dramatically in the 1990s as a result of widespread disillusionment with the nation's major political parties.

Undoubtedly the most important neoliberal policy promoted by the Pérez and Caldera administrations was the Oil Opening, which deepened the policy of insulating the oil industry from government interference and popular pressure. The new approach allowed private capital to become majority shareholders in joint ventures with the state oil company PDVSA. Much, but not all, of the Oil Opening took in nonconventional, heavy oil and oil wells with reduced productive capacity, which required considerable capital and advanced technology. Nearly all the companies that associated with PDVSA under the terms of the Oil Opening were multinationals. Critics of oil policy feared that the Oil Opening formed part of a PDVSA strategy to bring about the total privatization of the oil industry, thus undoing the nationalization of 1976. They also warned that the sharp increase in Venezuela's productive capacity as a result of the Oil Opening weakened OPEC in that it disregarded the organization's policy of limiting supply in order to increase prices. Indeed, some PDVSA executives considered OPEC's system of production quotas contrary to Venezuelan interests in exploiting its immense reserves, and virtually favored Venezuela's withdrawal from the organization.

The reaction against Pérez's neoliberal reforms was immediate and at times violent. A week of nationwide disturbances known as the Caracazo broke out on February 27, 1989, just minutes after transportation price hikes went into effect. A wave of organized protests and spontaneous street actions encompassed Pérez's four years in office. On February 4, 1992, an abortive coup was staged by middle-level army officers led by Hugo Chávez, and ten months later a second and bloodier revolt was spearheaded by senior officers, including air force and navy ones. The following year Pérez was impeached, ostensibly on accusations of misuse of public funds, but undoubtedly his removal was related to the widespread discontent generated by his economic policies. Subsequently the series of protests subsided, in large part because of President Caldera's more sagacious approach. Not only did Caldera follow a policy of protracted implementation of neoliberal formulas, but he created the tripartite commission and forged a tacit alliance with AD that brought key actors into the decision-making process.

The presidential election of 1998 confirmed the popular repudiation of the political establishment. Chávez with 56 percent of the vote and Henrique Salas Römer with 40 percent both blamed the major parties, and the coterie that ran them, for the nation's woes. In his antiparty rhetoric, Chávez, as an ex-rebel who had tried to overthrow an AD government, outdid Salas Römer, who formerly belonged to COPEI and received an eleventh-hour endorsement from AD and COPEI. Chávez's popularity rose during the nearly two-year presidential campaign at the same time that he subordinated or modified radical positions such as nonpayment of the foreign debt and emphasized political objectives. His main campaign banner was the convocation of a constituent assembly in order to replace "representative democracy," which was underpinned by political parties, with "participatory democracy" consisting of direct popular input.

The Chavez Presidency

In elections held in July 1999, voters gave Chávez's party, the Fifth Republic Movement (MRV), absolute control of the National Constitutional Assembly. A national referendum in December of the same year approved the document by 71 percent of the votes. The framers of the new constitution rejected the model embodied by those who drafted the constitution of 1961 that privileged political parties. Instead, the new constitution established mechanisms for the direct participation of civil society and citizens as a whole in decision making. For instance, while a majority of the members of the national electoral commission in the decades following 1958 had belonged to political parties, the 1999 constitution stipulated that they all had to be independents, and assigned civil organizations a major role in selecting them. The 1999 constitution also allowed for recall elections of elected officials and referendums on policy and legislation.

In his bid for the presidency in 1998, Chávez received campaign contributions from various powerful economic groups as well as political moderates such as the Movement toward Socialism (MAS) party. Chávez, however, did not hide his intentions of going beyond an initial political stage to a more radical one highlighted by socioeconomic changes at a future date, although the moderates and business representatives who backed him may have underestimated his resolve. In 2001 Chávez radicalized his discourse and simultaneously passed forty-nine controversial laws. This legislation included an agrarian reform that forced owners of unproductive land to accept a state plan for cultivation or face expropriation, the Organic Law of Hydrocarbons, which assigned the state majority control of mixed oil ventures, and another law that undid the privatization of the social security system enacted under Caldera. According to an executive decree of February 4, 2002, committees established in slum areas that undertook surveys could distribute deeds to longtime residents who had settled the land illegally.

The opposition—AD, COPEI, MAS, the CTV, the business organization FEDECAMARAS, and the communications media in general—accused Chávez of moving in an authoritarian direction. The opposition pointed out that the new constitution strengthened the executive at the expense of the congress, which, for example, lost the right to veto proposed promotions of military officers to higher ranks. Opposition leaders added that President Chávez's domination over the various branches of government violated the system of checks and balances.

The opposition-sponsored indefinite general strike in April 2002 led to a coup that in turn set off mass mobilizations of slum dwellers in defense of Chávez, paving the way for his return within forty-eight hours. During those two days, FEDECAMARAS president Pedro Carmona assumed the presidency and proceeded to abolish congress and other elected institutions. The US and Spanish ambassadors met with Carmona while the governments of both nations issued statements in support for the new regime, unlike the official positions pronounced in the rest of the hemisphere; the International Monetary Fund also offered to assist Venezuela. The Carmona government announced its intention to revoke the commercial agreement supplying Cuba with oil.[3] A second effort to oust Chávez occurred in December of the same year with a ten-week general strike. Given FEDECAMARAS's leading role in the strike, it was difficult to determine whether the shutdown was supported by the workers or was (as the Chavistas claimed) a management-decreed lockout.

Until 2004, the Chavista government was on the defensive. Two attempts to topple Chávez in 2002 almost succeeded and the recall election two years later threatened to vote him out of office. These opposition offensives limited Chávez's options. Nevertheless, the government's economic program during these years refrained from implementing plans inherited from the previous administration of Rafael Caldera to privatize such sectors as aluminum, petroleum, and the social security system, and thus can be characterized as anti-neoliberal.

Further radicalization had to await the consolidation of the Chávez government and the weakening and demoralization of the opposition. Electoral triumphs opened a window of opportunities for Chávez, specifically his victory in the recall election in August 2004 with 58 percent of the vote and the municipal-gubernatorial contests two months later, when the Chavistas took all the governorships except Zulia and Nueva Esparta. Chávez went on to win the presidential elections in December 2006 with 63 percent of the vote and seventeen of twenty-two governorships and 80 percent of the mayoral positions in the elections of 2008.

In 2005 the government redefined the rights of private property by insisting that the private sector was responsible to fulfill certain basic national objectives. The government broke up various agricultural estates in accordance with the Lands Law of 2001, which required agricultural producers to maintain production levels at 80 percent of capacity or more. At the same time, the government, in keeping with its policy on company closings, nationalized a paper factory that had shut down several years before, and in the following months did the same with several other medium-size firms.

On the social front, the government allocated large sums of money to provide free educational and health services and job opportunities and to undertake public works projects mainly to the benefit of underprivileged sectors. The government promoted the creation of tens of thousands of cooperatives by providing them with generous amounts of credit, lenient terms of payment, contracts from state companies, and tax-exempt status. The majority of cooperatives consist of not many more than five members (the minimum number required by law), taking in mostly members of the same extended family. A law passed in 2006 encouraged the creation of 20,000 community councils representing 200 to 400 families, which approve priority projects in assemblies. The councils plan, administer, and finance public works and housing construction in the community and represent a radical break with the past, when these activities were undertaken by local government. In addition, school "missions" consist of literacy and educational programs in the barrios that, in the case of the pre-university levels, use video cassettes, many of them made in Cuba. Another mission program involves about 20,000 Cuban doctors in poor areas who provide health service and medicine free of charge. Both missions have met resistance from the political opposition, even though the anti-Chavista parties recognize their relative success. In the case of the health mission, for example, physicians in regular hospitals often oblige patients remitted by Cuban doctors to start from scratch by repeating exams and medical consultations.

On the economic front, the government embraced state control of strategic industries, a banner that was first raised in the 1930s and then abandoned in the 1990s. Shortly after being reelected in December 2006, Chávez announced the state takeover of companies that had been privatized during the previous decade. The Venezuelan government bought the controlling shares of the telephone company CANTV (from Verizon) and the electrical utility Electricidad de Caracas (from AES Corporation). In addition, the government assumed greater control over the oil industry. Foreign interests were forced to accept the Venezuelan state's 60 percent ownership of the mixed companies established in the petroleum industry during the neoliberal period of the 1990s, and their employees were transferred to the payroll of the state oil company PDVSA. In 2007 the government took control of the steel company SIDOR (which had been privatized in 1997) and three foreign-owned cement companies, followed by one of the nation's largest banks, the Spanish-owned Banco de Venezuela.

The nationalization of strategic sectors of the economy was designed to promote national development and social objectives, including a more humane treatment of the workforce, goals that overshadowed profit making. Indeed, the newly nationalized companies boasted of accomplishments along these lines. In the first place, the companies took steps to incorporate workers employed by contractor firms into their own workforce, thus fulfilling a long-standing labor union demand. The oil company PDVSA took over several scores of contractor companies, particularly in the area of transportation and gas injection, and committed itself to absorbing all continuous operations in the industry. By 2009 its workforce reached 80,000, double that of 2002. In the second place, both SIDOR and the state-owned cement company began to emphasize satisfying national demand as opposed to export sales.

Prior to 2007, the opposition parties suffered a series of electoral defeats. Refusing to recognize the legitimacy of the Chávez government, they boycotted the National Assembly elections in 2006, thus forfeiting representation at the congressional level. In addition, their unsuccessful efforts to topple the government led to the erosion of confidence in the opposition-led Venezuelan Workers Confederation (CTV), which was replaced by the pro-Chávez National Workers Union (UNT) as the nation's largest worker organization. In response to this development, in 2005 the International Labour Organization (ILO) removed the CTV from its governing council. The opposition modified its tactics by participating in the 2006 presidential elections with the candidacy of the ex-AD leader Manuel Rosales, who went on to recognize Chávez's triumph. In 2007 the opposition managed to defeat Chávez's constitutional reform proposal that was submitted to a national referendum, though by only 1 percent of the vote. In early 2009 Rosales, who was mayor of Maracaibo, sought asylum in Peru, claiming that he was a victim of political persecution. At the same time Antonio Ledezma, the principal mayor of Caracas, who was also a former AD leader, objected to the government's encroachment on his authority in the areas of health, education, and security and appealed to world public opinion to help block Chávez's alleged dictatorial plans. One of the main challenges facing the opposition was the definition of programs and ideology. Over a ten-year period, opposition leaders had sacrificed programmatic clarity in favor of maintaining unity in their effort to oust Chávez, which eclipsed all other objectives and activities.

US-VENEZUELAN RELATIONS UNDER CHÁVEZ

The radicalization of Chávez's government during his first five years in office was accompanied by deteriorating relations with Washington. During the 1998 presidential campaign, Chávez avoided criticizing the United States, even though the Clinton administration denied his request for a visa to address the international business community in New York. John Maisto, the US ambassador in Caracas under Clinton, set the tone for the strained tolerance that characterized relations during Chávez's first two years in office. Maisto argued that in spite of Chávez's leftist discourse, the United States should avoid open confrontations with his government. The ambassador pointed out that Chávez was elected by a large majority of votes, and that Venezuela continued to supply oil and make payments on its foreign debt. The most important source of friction at the outset was Chávez's refusal to allow US surveillance planes to pursue drug smugglers from neighboring Colombia into Venezuelan space.

Diverse positions assumed by Chávez aggravated relations between the two nations, particularly after George W. Bush assumed the US presidency in 2001. Most importantly, Chávez played a leadership role in OPEC, a position facilitated by the fact that Venezuela was the only non-Muslim member of the organization and thus exempt from internal feuds with religious implications. Chávez's efforts to promote OPEC unity led him to travel to each member nation and personally invite heads of states to OPEC's second summit meeting held in Caracas in September 2000. Subsequently Washington rebuked Chávez for meeting with Iraq's Saddam Hussein and Libya's Muammar Qaddafi.

Chávez's rhetoric favoring a multipolar world with various centers of power, such as the European Union, the Latin American bloc of nations, and OPEC, implicitly (and eventually explicitly) questioned the legitimacy of US hegemony. Other stands and actions that annoyed Washington included Chávez's close ties with Cuba, as reflected by the sale of oil at discounts and the presence of a large mission of Cuban doctors in Venezuela; his vocal opposition to the Free Trade Area of the Americas (FTAA) promoted by Bush; Venezuelan criticism of Plan Colombia to combat the drug trade and guerrilla movement in that nation; and Chávez's decision to order a US military delegation to vacate the Venezuelan army's Caracas headquarters on grounds that such an arrangement was no longer necessary in the aftermath of the Cold War.

Relations with the United States worsened after the September 11, 2001, attacks, when the Bush administration explicitly ruled out a middle ground between Washington's allies and enemies. Although Chávez condemned the attacks, he also criticized the US bombing of Afghanistan. Shortly thereafter, secretary of state Colin Powell accused Chávez of failing to be fully supportive in the war against terrorism. The National Endowment of Democracy (NED) funneled money through conduits to opposition organizations, including political parties, NGOs, and the staunchly antigovernment Confederation of Workers of Venezuela. The NGO Venezuelan Solidarity Network claimed that the NED had allocated $800,000 to Venezuelan organizations in 2002 and 2003. The NED web page included the names of over a dozen Venezuelan recipients of the foundation's grants, some of which were in the anti-Chávez camp.

The White House at first attributed the April 11, 2002, coup to Chávez's errors. On April 12, the Bush administration's Otto Reich, who had met with opposition leaders including coup head Pedro Carmona numerous times in the months prior to April 11, summoned Latin American ambassadors to his office. Reich assured them that the coup would not endanger democracy throughout the region. Nevertheless, as soon as the OAS condemned the coup and internal resistance to it began to mount, the United States adopted a more neutral stand. In the aftermath of the coup relations assumed a lower profile until the general strike in December of that year, which set off an escalation of hostile rhetoric between the two nations. President Chávez for the first time used the term "imperialism" and denounced Washington for its close ties to the opposition. Washington, for its part, distinguished the nationalistic governments in Argentina and Brazil from the more leftist Venezuelan government, and questioned Chávez's democratic credentials.

In subsequent years, President Chávez pursued an activist foreign policy on diverse fronts. Within OPEC, Venezuela abandoned the moderate conciliatory position it had defended since the organization's founding in 1960 and assumed a hard line in favor of oil production reductions and price hikes. At OPEC meetings, minister of energy and petroleum Rafael Ramírez urged member nations to follow Venezuela's example by asserting greater state control over the oil industry as a step to shore up prices. At the continental level President Chávez played a decisive role in defeating the US-sponsored Free Trade Area of the Americas (FTAA) at the Fourth Summit of the Americas held in Mar del Plata, Argentina, in 2005. As an alternative, Venezuela and Cuba founded in 2004 the Bolivarian Alliance for the People of our America (ALBA), which committed itself to priority treatment for national companies and worker cooperatives and the retention of workers' historical gains and respect for existing legislation.

Chávez's scathing denunciations of the foreign policy of the Bush administration were at first replaced with a more friendly tone toward President Obama that led to a warm, well-publicized encounter between the two heads of state at the Fifth Summit of the Americas in Trinidad in April 2009. Nevertheless, the clash between Chávez's hard-line and anti-imperialist rhetoric, on the one hand, and Washington's objectives in the region, on the other, was predictable. Chávez was instrumental in persuading the OAS to condemn the coup staged in Honduras in June 2009 that overthrew his ally Manuel Zelaya; at the same time he criticized Washington for not cutting off economic ties with the de facto regime, a position which the deposed Honduran leader subsequently began to express. Shortly thereafter, Venezuela characterized the US decision to establish several military bases in neighboring Colombia as an act of hostility.

Conclusion

The founding and preservation of democracy in Venezuela after 1958 represented a major achievement for the nation, but the system also had serious defects and limitations. Modern democratic rule contrasted favorably with the previous century and a half of caudillos and military dictatorships following independence. Venezuelan democracy also stood in contrast to the rest of Latin America in the 1960s through the 1980s, which was largely subject to military governments. Furthermore, Venezuelan democracy after 1958 established a model of active state intervention in the economy, which promoted industrial diversification for the internal market, thus substituting many consumer products that were previously imported. On the downside, corruption, the patronage system, and electoral manipulation at all levels became a standard feature of life. In addition, the governments of the period took but timid steps to break dependence on foreign technology and capital.

The difficulties that Venezuela faced in the 1990s clearly demonstrated that it was not a "privileged" Third World nation, as many had thought. Thus Venezuela's two dominant political parties lost considerable prestige as a multiparty system replaced the prevailing two-party system. In addition, two military coup attempts occurred against the backdrop of intense social unrest. Finally, government economic policy failed to relieve the stagnation that characterized the nation's economy since the early 1980s. Developments along these lines forced many Venezuelans, including political analysts, to reconsider their view that Venezuela was a showcase for democracy due to its social and political stability. Most importantly, Venezuela's dependence on petroleum pegged the performance of the nation's economy to fluctuating world oil prices, thus accounting for the economic instability that translated into political instability. These concerns and criticisms provide the backdrop for understanding Hugo Chávez's rise to power and his impressive electoral successes over a ten-year period.

Notes

1. Gómez's more lenient policy toward foreign investors became evident at the outset of his rule when he eliminated the fines imposed on the New York and Bermudez Company for supporting the 1902–1903 rebellion.
2. The terms of nationalization generated controversy. Shortly after nationalization in 1976, a pro-leftist magazine published secret technological and commercialization contracts signed between the state oil company (PDVSA) and Exxon, Shell, and Gulf, which had dominated the Venezuelan petroleum industry for half a century. PDVSA executives defended the contracts as ensuring a smooth transition to state control. At the same time they rejected public debate on grounds that the issues involved were technical matters that nonspecialists could not easily grasp. They also feared that excessive government interference would undermine long-term planning based on technical criteria.
3. The documentary *The Revolution Will Not Be Televised*, produced by two Irish filmmakers sympathetic to Chávez, captures the events of the day of the coup. See, Rod Stoneman, *Chávez: The Revolution Will Not Be Televised: A Case Study of Politics and the Media* (London: Wallflower).

Suggested Readings

Buxton, Julia. *The Failure of Political Reform in Venezuela*. Aldershot, UK: Ashgate, 2001.

Coppedge, Michael. *Strong Parties and Lame Ducks: Presidential Patriarchy and Factionalism in Venezuela*. Stanford: Stanford University Press, 1994.

Coronil, Fernando. *The Magical State: Nature, Money, and Modernity in Venezuela*. Chicago: University of Chicago Press, 1997.

Ellner, Steve. *Organized Labor in Venezuela: Behavior and Concerns in a Democratic Setting*. Wilmington, DE: Scholarly Resources, 1993.

———. *Rethinking Venezuelan Politics: Class, Conflict, and the Chávez Phenomenon*. Boulder: Lynne Rienner, 2008.

———. "The Perennial Debate over Socialist Goals Played Out in Venezuela." *Science and Society*, January 2010, 63–84.

Ellner, Steve, and Miguel Tinker Salas, eds. *Venezuela: Hugo Chávez and the Decline of an "Exceptional Democracy."* Lanham, MD: Rowman & Littlefield, 2007.

Ewell, Judith. *Venezuela: A Century of Change*. Stanford: Stanford University Press, 1984.

———. *Venezuela and the United States: From Monroe's Hemisphere to Petroleum's Empire*. Athens: University of Georgia Press, 1996.

Friedman, Elisabeth J. *Unfinished Transitions: Women and the Gendered Development of Democracy in Venezuela, 1936–1996*. University Park: Pennsylvania State University Press, 2000.

Jones, Bart. *Hugo! The Hugo Chávez Story: From Mud Hut to Perpetual Revolution*. Hanover, NH: Steerforth, 2007.

Karl, Terry Lynn. *The Paradox of Plenty: Oil Booms and Petro-States*. Berkeley: University of California Press, 1977.

Kozloff, Nikolas. *Hugo Chávez: Oil, Politics, and the Challenge to the United States*. New York: Palgrave Macmillan, 2006.

Lombardi, John. *Venezuela: The Search for Order, the Dream of Progress*. New York: Oxford University Press, 1982.

McCaughan, Michael. *The Battle of Venezuela*. London: Latin American Bureau, 2004.

McCoy, Jennifer L., and David J. Myers, eds. *The Unraveling of Representative Democracy in Venezuela*. Baltimore: Johns Hopkins University Press, 2004.

McCoy, Jennifer, Andrés Serbin, William C. Smith, and Andrés Stambouli, eds. *Venezuelan Democracy Under Stress*. New Brunswick, NJ: Transaction, 1995.

Tinker Salas, Miguel. *The Enduring Legacy: Oil Culture and Society in Venezuela*. Durham, NC: Duke University Press, 2009.

Wilpert, Gregory. *Changing Venezuela by Taking Power: The History and Policies of the Chávez Government*. London: Verso, 2007.

Wright, Winthrop R. *Café Con Leche: Race, Class, and National Image in Venezuela*. Austin: University of Texas Press, 1990.

Yarrington, Doug. *A Coffee Frontier: Land, Society, and Politics in Duaca, Venezuela, 1830–1936*. Pittsburgh: University of Pittsburgh Press, 1997.

Chapter 22

ECUADOR

Political Turmoil, Social Mobilization, and a Turn Toward the Left

PABLO ANDRADE A. AND LIISA L. NORTH

IN NOVEMBER 2006, Ecuadoreans chose a president, Rafael Correa, who embodied the regional turn toward a new left politics aimed at reversing the market friendly neoliberalism that had prevailed since the early 1980s. In the following two years, Correa won four more elections by resounding majorities. In April 2007, 82 percent of the electorate voted for his proposal to rewrite the constitution; five months later, in September, the president's political vehicle, Alianza País, won 80 of the 130 seats in the new Constitutional Assembly; in September 2008, the new constitution was approved by 64 percent of all votes cast; and in April 2009, he won an absolute majority in the first round of the presidential elections held under the terms of the new constitution. But the margin of victory was narrower than before and his alliance failed to garner a majority in the legislature. Correa's victories reflected both voter disgust and hope: disgust with the existing party system that was blamed for the social decay, political instability, corruption, and economic crises of the neoliberal years, and hope in the realization of Correa's promised *revolución ciudadana* (citizen revolution) and the payment of what the president called the "social debt" by a revitalized state.

The two decades prior to Correa's first election were marked by increasing social inequality and poverty, rising debt service costs, the dismantling of state capacity, and economic decline and instability that fed migration out of the country, estimated to have reached 1 million people, or 8 percent of the population during the 1990s.[1] Remittances from the migrants rather than income earned at home provided for the needs of increasing numbers of Ecuadoreans. Real GDP per capita at the time of Correa's first election in 2006 remained below its 1980 level (International Crisis Group 2007, 28). These dismal social and economic conditions were cause and consequence of political turmoil. The first four presidents during the period of transition from military rule (see Table 22.1) finished their constitutionally mandated terms in office, but the party system, which appeared to be consolidating during the early

413

1980s, was in shambles by the mid-1990s. Between 1996 and 2006, six presidents rotated through the executive office. A combination of elite opposition and massive popular protest brought down the populist coalition of Abdalá Bucaram in February 1997, after only six months in office; the centrist government headed by Jamil Mahuad lasted eighteen months, toppled by an indigenous-military rebellion in early 2000; and yet another populist coalition, led by retired Colonel Lucio Gutiérrez, the military head of the movement that overthrew Mahuad, disintegrated amid massive urban middle-class protests in April 2005.

While the political party system was discredited and fragmented, social movements gained importance, the indigenous movement most prominently among them. Led by the Confederación de Nacionalidades Indígenas del Ecuador (Confederation of Indigenous Nationalities of Ecuador, CONAIE), the indigenous peoples of the highland and Amazonian regions united in nearly nationwide but peaceful *levantamientos*, or uprisings, against government social and economic policies in 1990, 1994, 1997, 2000, and then again in 2001. Although neither the indigenous movement nor other social movements—the new and vital women's and environmental activism or the old labor unions that dated to the early 1920s—were able to secure policies that might have counteracted deteriorating social trends, Correa rode into the presidency on the protest ground prepared by these social movements.

What explains Ecuador's dismal socioeconomic performance and political instability? A good part of the explanation lies in the historical evolution of the country's highly dependent primary export-oriented economy, its profound social class and ethnic divisions, and its weak and exclusionary political institutions that led repeatedly to destabilizing street politics and military interventions. Following a brief review of this historical legacy, we turn to Ecuador's incomplete democratization since 1979, drawing attention to the fragmentation of the political party system, the rise of vibrant indigenous and other social movements, and the adoption of two new constitutions (in 1989 and 2008), the latter strongly nationalist, socially progressive, and centered on a renewed state role in the economy and society. The final sections look at Ecuador's debilitating dependency and the limits it places on government policies and at its foreign relations, with particular reference to the United States and Colombia's civil war.

THE HISTORICAL LEGACY

The prevailing patterns of Ecuador's twentieth-century development, which excluded the majority of the population from political participation and the benefits of economic growth, can be traced back to the colonial period. However, it was during the first two great waves of modern export growth—the cacao (roughly 1860–1920) and banana (1948–1972) eras—that the basic contours of contemporary patterns of exclusionary economic development and social inequality hardened into place. The efforts of reformist military governments to generate a more inclusive model of economic growth and social transformation, first in the late 1930s and then in the mid-1960s and once again at the beginning of the decade-long petroleum boom (1972–1982), remained truncated (Larrea and North 1997).

The Constitution of an Exclusionary Primary Export Economy

During Ecuador's first modern export era, a powerful oligarchy of cacao producers, who also controlled banking and the export-import trade, was formed in the coastal city of Guayaquil. Employing cheap semi-servile (or semi-waged) labor on their great estates, these landlord-financial-commercial families concentrated political power and the profits of export growth in their few hands. Idealizing their European roots and inclined toward ostentatious consumption, at the beginning of the twentieth century these elite families transferred an estimated 20 percent of cacao export profits to relatives who lived abroad, especially in Paris (Guerrero 1980).

The second great export era of banana production expanded the network of intermarrying oligarchic families in Guayaquil and was associated with important investment in infrastructure (roads and ports), the acceleration of migration from highland to coastal regions, steady urbanization, the beginnings of import substitution industrialization, the growth of the middle class, and the foundation of state economic and social planning institutions. The banana boom thus distributed its profits more broadly than cacao had done, but the basic patterns of social inequality remained intact and the political system highly exclusionary. Indeed, in the highlands, indigenous peoples, who then formed the majority of the rural population, remained disenfranchised and subject to servile labor relations. The triad of the prefect, the priest, and the landlord continued to control the lives of rural Andean peoples.

In the 1960s and 1970s ten Guayaquil-based business empires, linked through elite family ties, controlled most commercial, financial, industrial, communications, and agricultural enterprises along the coast.[2] A parallel, although somewhat less concentrated set of Quito-based elite families reigned over the highlands. The political power of these two sets of oligarchies was sufficient to block any thoroughgoing social and economic reform aimed toward redistribution of services, incomes, and assets (most importantly agricultural land).

The divergent economic interests of the coastal and highland elites (and a third elite cluster in the city of Cuenca in the southern highlands) led to regional tension and conflict. The coastal elites were outwardly oriented while the highland elites were more dependent on production for internal markets. Also, to the extent that the productive apparatus and social relations of production varied from region to region, regional political cultures emerged. These regional divisions/cultures divided both subordinate and dominant classes. But whereas regional elites, when faced with threats from below, united to defend their common interests, subordinate classes—divided by ethnicity, class, and region—found political unity difficult to achieve.

Civilian Authoritarians and Military Reformers

As Ecuador's civilian elites equated their narrow private interests with national interests, military governments pursued social reforms in response to pressures from below, and turned the state into a sponsor of economic development. Military governments recognized indigenous communities in the Ley de Comunas of 1937, carried out the first agrarian reform that abolished the highland *huasipungo* in 1964 (a response to peasant demand, the threats posed by the Cuban Revolution, and a then reform-supportive US foreign policy, as expressed in the Alliance for

Progress), decreed a second agrarian reform in 1973, and during the remainder of that decade, promoted industrial diversification and economic planning, and invested in physical and social infrastructure—education in particular (North 2004). The last of those military governments (1972–1979) coincided with the petroleum boom (1972–1982) that provided unparalleled resources to the state to pursue reformist and developmental policies. However, the reformist initiatives of the government headed by General Rodríguez Lara (1972–1976) were blocked by the country's dominant elites, who engineered his overthrow and replacement by a military Triumvirate (1976–1979). In effect, elites managed to access petroleum income to diversify their portfolios into industrial activities in collaboration with foreign capital. Redistributive reforms remained truncated, although the petroleum boom's resources were spread widely enough to generate the rapid growth of an urban middle class. The institutional and social transformations of the decade also set the context for the social mobilizations of the past quarter century, to which we turn below.

The Democratic Transition and the Ups and Downs of New Social Forces

In the course of the various export booms and their attendant social transformations, Ecuador failed to develop a strong party system, and the existing system—weak, clientelistic, and fragmented—was regionally based. Moreover, since political organization had been throttled under the military regime of the 1970s, the transition to civilian rule did not begin under favorable circumstances. Nevertheless, an incipient party system appeared to be forming in the 1980s, with major parties spanning the ideological spectrum from left to right. However, populism and political instability reemerged in the mid-1990s, along with new social movements.

The Political Party Spectrum of the Transition to Democracy

The transition to civilian rule in 1979 added a new element to Ecuador's politics: the electoral participation of illiterates (provided for in the constitution of 1978), which meant the enfranchisement of the rural poor, who in the highlands were largely indigenous peasants. This liberating political reform took place in a countryside where the agrarian reform initiatives of 1964 and 1973, although they had not distributed much land, had transformed the traditional structures of political power that were based on domination by large estate owners. However, neither the traditional regionally based right-wing parties that had been linked to the landlord classes of the coast and the highlands nor the left that had spurred the creation of a peasant movement managed to establish strong, stable linkages with the new rural voters who enjoyed citizenship rights for the first time in the country's history. (On the political right, since the nineteenth century, these parties were the Conservatives in the highlands and the Liberals on the coast and, in recent times, the Social Christians also on the coast; on the left, they were the Communist and Socialist parties since the 1930s and the Maoist Popular Democratic Movement since the 1970s.) Nor did the center and center-left parties (the Christian Democratic Popular Democracy Party and Democratic Left respectively) fare any better.

Thus until 1996, when indigenous organizations and social movements coalesced to form the Pachakutik United Pluricultural Movement (MUPP), the indigenous and peasant populations, for all practical purposes, did not enjoy political representation in the national congress or in provincial and municipal governments.

The rapid urbanization and growth of peri-urban settlements that began in the 1950s turned the attention of all parties toward conquering the votes of recently arrived migrants from the rural areas. The population residing in towns and cities climbed steadily from 28.6 percent in 1950 to 55.4 percent in 1990 and 65 percent in 2000. Following patterns of behavior whose origins can be traced back to Ecuador's first period of twentieth-century democracy (1946–1963), political parties focused on creating clientelistic networks to capture the votes of urban middle classes and the more or less recently arrived migrants who made up the urban popular sectors. On the one hand, political clientelism involved the direct exchange of goods and services provided by national and municipal governments for the votes of the popular sectors. On the other hand, the transformation of clientelistic networks into electoral machines depended on attracting and promoting the leaders of popular sector neighborhood organizations, as well as the leaders of middle-class professional and business associations. These leaders were then transformed into the political figures who occupied positions in congress, the executive branch, and local governments (Menéndez Carrión 1986; Conaghan 1995).

The alliances among the political leaders and the various parties remained fluid, however, and the parties were not able to transform their capacity to win votes into a capacity to create stable groups of cadres. Perhaps even more importantly, the first four presidents of the contemporary democratic period—in order to implement the neoliberal structural adjustment policies (SAPs) demanded after the debt crisis of 1982 by the International Monetary Fund (IMF), the World Bank, and the US Treasury—effectively abandoned their electoral machines and governed with ad hoc technocratic teams (Conaghan and Malloy 1994). Consequently they dug a trench between their governments and the political parties that were supposed to support their policies. The highly unpopular SAPs, pursued by all governments until the inauguration of Correa in January 2007, undercut both popular and elite support for the representatives the parties elected. And all this was reflected in the turbulent relations between governments and their representatives in congress and in local governments, contributing to the further fragmentation of the parliamentary alliances and the political parties.

In this political milieu, the parties that were most successful in attracting votes were not necessarily the same ones that best expressed the interests of the dominant groups—the networks of Quito- and Guayaquil-based bankers, industrialists, large merchants, and landowners. Thus the quintessential *bête noir* of Ecuadorean politics, the erratic and flamboyantly populist leader of the Ecuadorean Roldosist Party, Abdalá Bucaram, was elected president in 1996, and the leader of the turn of the century military indigenous revolt, Colonel Lucio Gutiérrez, won in 2002 with the support of Pachakutik (Beck and Mijeski 2006). The party that was supported by the indigenous movement was subsequently discredited by its participation in Gutiérrez's government. Yet another populist movement, Alianza País, carried Rafael Correa into the presidency in the November 2006 elections.

TABLE 22.1   Ecuadorian Heads of State and Their Political Affiliations, 1972–2009

1972–79: Military Rule
Reformist (1972–76); Conservative Right (1976–79)

1979–81: Jaime Roldós
Populist, Concentration of Popular Forces

1981–84: Osvaldo Hurtado
Centrist, Popular Democracy (Christian Democratic)

1984–88: León Febres Cordero
Rightist, Social Christian Party

1988–92: Rodrigo Borja
Center-Left, Democratic Left Party

1992–96: Sixto Durán-Ballén
Rightist, Conservative Party

1996–97: Abdalá Bucaram
Populist, Ecuadorian Roldosist Party

1997–98: Fabián Alarcón (Interim)
Center-Right, Liberal

1998–2000: Jamil Mahuad
Center-Right, Popular Democracy

2000–02: Gustavo Noboa (Interim)
Center-Right, Popular Democracy

2002–05: Lucio Gutiérrez
Populist, alliance including Pachakutik

2005–07: Alfredo Palacio (Interim)
Centrist, based on ad hoc political arrangements

2007-2009 & 2009-: Rafael Correa
Left Populist, *Alianza País* movement

Emerging Social Movements

The period beginning in the mid-1990s is one of the most dramatic in Ecuador's recent political history. It included the massive popular mobilizations surrounding the deposition of President Bucaram in 1997, President Jamil Mahuad in 2000, and President Lucio Gutiérrez in 2005, and the rise and at least momentary decline of Ecuador's indigenous political movement. During the 1990s, that movement converted itself into a leading and legitimate force in Ecuadorean politics, both through its principal organization, the Confederation of Indigenous Nationalities of Ecuador (CONAIE) and the entry of the associated Pachakutik/MUPP into increasingly successful electoral competition. Pachakutik, however, suffered serious setbacks as a consequence of its participation in the Gutiérrez administration. Its share of the vote dropped dramatically from over 20 percent in the first round of the 2002 presidential elections to just over 2 percent in the 2006 first round. It received little support in the 2009 elections. Nevertheless, indigenous organizations remained significant forces in the local politics of some highland provinces and Amazonian areas.

The historical origins of Ecuador's indigenous movement can be traced to the peasant movements of the 1930s (Becker 2000; Striffler 2002). Its recent origins, as noted above, can be located in the transformation of the social relations of rural power that originated from the agrarian reforms of the 1960s and 1970s and the modernization of agriculture, which liberated the mostly indigenous highland peasant populations from the ties of political domination that had prevailed in the countryside (Zamosc 1994; Clark 1998). This liberation was accompanied by the presence of two religious transformations that favored the reconstruction of the indigenous community: the embrace of liberation theology by the Catholic Church and the growth of evangelicalism.

Inspired by liberation theology, the Catholic Church abandoned its traditional orientation in favor of the country's landlord elites and moved toward support for the indigenous peasantry. The new orientation sought to address the conditions of extreme poverty among indigenous and peasant populations through land transfers, agricultural cooperatives, and literacy training in native languages. The best known of these experiences took place in the province of Chimborazo. There, a prominent bishop of the Latin American liberation theology movement established Quichua-language community radios, literacy programs, and leadership schools for indigenous people. These programs not only propelled linguistic identity reconstruction among the indigenous but also fed into the creation of a new center of power in the political vacuum left by the retreat of the old landlord structure. That center was the indigenous community, and it became the foundation on which the indigenous movement established itself and grew in the 1980s and 1990s (Korovkin 2001). Meanwhile, the leadership education initiatives undertaken by the Church in the early 1980s formed the people who became the political leaders of CONAIE and Pachakutik.

A similar although less well-known role was played by evangelical missions in the highlands (Muratorio 1980). Contrary to the stereotyped image of US-based evangelical missions as "agents of imperialism" that encourage political passivity among peasants, the Protestant churches in the two most indigenous provinces of highland Ecuador—Chimborazo and Cotopaxi—played a broadly emancipating role by favoring peasant organization and literacy in Quichua. These processes, which evolved over the last quarter of the twentieth century, culminated in the creation of the Ecuadorian Federation of Indigenous Evangelicals (FEINE), one of the most politically active indigenous organizations of recent times.

The new indigenous leaders began their political careers as intermediaries between indigenous communities, the national state, and international development aid agencies. The links with development agencies made it possible for some well-known figures of the late 1990s, both CONAIE and Pachakutik founders, to connect with the international indigenous rights movement (Maiguashca 1992). Thus, unlike the fragmenting middle- and upper-class-led and urban-based political parties and the declining labor movement, a rural indigenous leadership emerged in the early 1980s which, step by step, became capable of controlling, and disputing vis-à-vis the parties of the left, the representation of the peasant and indigenous sectors of the highland and Amazonian regions. The process culminated in the establishment of CONAIE, which burst dramatically on the political stage with the national indigenous uprising of 1990 (Guerrero 1993).

During the 1990s, the demand for cultural rights and an anti-neoliberal political-economic platform gained importance within the indigenous movement, whereas the traditional peasant movement had demanded land. The indigenous peoples insisted on running their own affairs—taking charge of their own development and governing themselves according to their own laws and customs. These were rights that they claimed on the basis of international accords and treaties signed by Ecuador. The solidarity that these demands awakened among intellectuals and public and private sector union activists culminated, in 1996, in the establishment of a coalition between CONAIE and various popular organizations that formed part of the Coordinator of Social Movements (CMS). This was the coalition that ultimately founded the Pachakutik/MUPP, which participated successfully in national and local elections from 1996 to 2002. As already noted, Pachakutik/MUPP's support for and participation in the Gutiérrez government cost it dearly. It won only two (out of 130) seats in the National Constitutional Assembly elections of September 2007. However, five Alianza País assembly representatives came from various indigenous organizations, and indigenous claims were incorporated into the 2008 constitution, as they had been in 1998. Moreover, activists and leaders from a broad range of social movement organizations who were sympathetic to the indigenous case won seats on the Alianza País slate.

The Adoption of New Constitutions: 1998 and 2008

Contrary to the expectations of its proponents and authors, who included members of the entire political spectrum from the parties of the right to the indigenous and other social movements, the 1998 constitution did not produce political stability or deepen social democracy by improving the mechanisms of political representation. By facilitating the creation of political electoral movements and establishing mechanisms to transfer control of public resources from the central government to local governments (municipal and provincial), the 1998 constitution actually fed into the chronic factionalism within political parties and among the indigenous and social movements. These negative effects became particularly noticeable among the larger political parties that had dominated national politics since 1984—the centrist Popular Democracy (Christian Democratic), the rightwing Social Christian Party, the center-left Democratic Left, and the populist Ecuadorean Roldosist Party (Pachano 2004; Andrade 2006). All these parties, in addition to suffering from intense internal factionalism, had to confront a more competitive political scene with the rise of the new social movements that reduced their capacity to win national elections.

On the other hand, the collective rights and increased representation that the 1998 constitution accorded to indigenous and women's organizations and various popular sectors, which should have ensured their greater influence on decision-making processes in congress, local governments, and various state agencies, proved useless in correcting the destructive impacts of neoliberal policies. The poverty and inequality that the 1998 constitution was supposed to help reverse, by giving greater voice to the sectors most prejudiced by the neoliberal economic model, were actually accelerated by the financial crisis of 1998–2000, making it clear that reforms in the system of political representation could not change the direction and impacts of the prevailing economic policies. This was also demonstrated by the rightward turn of the economic policies pursed by the Gutiérrez administration and Pachakutik's exit from its alliance with the colonel who had led the military-indigenous movement against Mahuad.

Taking all of this into account, perhaps it was not surprising that one result of Gutiérrez's demise in 2005 was an increasingly vociferous demand on the part of just about all social and popular organizations, as well as sectors of the middle class, for yet another constitution in order to enshrine a socially progressive legal order. President Palacio's weak interim government could not satisfy these demands or fundamentally change the direction of economic policy, but it did introduce a new charismatic leader to the country: Rafael Correa, who served briefly as its minister of economy. As the traditional parties and the indigenous movement weakened, the new dynamism gained by social movements and middle-class organizations during the protests against Gutiérrez, in the cities of Quito and Cuenca in particular, was converted into a broad coalition, the Alianza País, that won the presidential elections of 2006. After inauguration, Correa immediately proposed convening elections for a National Assembly that would write a new constitution.

The proposal faced a hostile congress in which the president did not have majority support. A complex political and juridical confrontation followed in which the Tribunal Supremo Electoral (the Electoral Court) eventually dismissed two-thirds of the elected deputies and replaced them with their *suplentes* (substitutes), who voted for the president's proposal. As noted above, in April 2007 the electorate overwhelmingly approved the creation of a National Assembly that would not only write a new constitution but would exercise "full" legislative powers, assuming the functions of congress. With the clear victory of Alianza País in those elections, congress was definitively suspended, legislation proposed by the Executive was passed by the newly elected assembly, and a socially progressive (albeit rather contradictory) constitution was drafted. It was largely written by leaders of the many nongovernmental organizations (NGOs) and social movements who formed the core of Alianza's representation in the assembly.

The opposition campaign against a new constitution failed for two reasons. First, in contrast to Alianza País, which managed to keep itself united during both the assembly elections and the drafting stage of the constitution, the opposition was unable to bridge differences among its member parties. Second, the opposition's public campaigns focused on the wrong targets. In April 2007 it defended the 1998 constitution and a clearly corrupt congress that were highly unpopular. As the assembly deliberated, the opposition tried unsuccessfully to create outside pressure, for example, by raising the phantom of Guayaquil's possible secession. Later, during the plebiscite campaign, it appealed to religious sentiment, attempting to falsely raise fears of the legalization of gay marriage and abortion (Ospina 2008).

In sum, the 2008 constitution was the result of two factors. One is historical and has to do with the rise and consolidation of opposition to neoliberalism; the other is conjunctural and lies in the weaknesses of the opposition and the capacity of the president and his party to rally popular support. The constitution is arguably the result of deliberations and decisions within the Alianza País and negotiations with (on some occasions, impositions by) the executive. However, given the broad spectrum of progressive opinion incorporated within Alianza País and the vagueness of its anti-neoliberal program, the document does not move in a single direction. Rather, it combines at least three clearly different elements that have been, and will most likely continue to be, supported by different political actors.

The first of those elements involves concentrating power in the hands of the executive and converting it into the sovereign representative of the people and seriously devaluing the role of parliament. A second tendency involves creating new rights or expanding existing rights for social groups that opposed neoliberal policies and saw themselves as especially harmed by them. For example, the concept of *Sumak Kawsay—Buen Vivir* or the "Good Life"—grants universal access to water sources and proscribes their privatization. Finally, a third source for the constitutional text comes from neodevelopmentalist thought, expressed in numerous articles that refer not only to the state's·role in the economy but to the relationships between state, society, and nature.

Overall, the new constitution has a clear anti-neoliberal bias with regard to the economy: it places limits on private property; includes clauses with great potential redistributive impacts (especially with reference to land and incomes); grants great powers to the state for planning the economy, regulating international trade and finance, and promoting savings and investment in domestic productive spheres; and it visualizes a more centralized provision of basic services as well as universal social security. Opposition groups have also identified an anti-liberal political bias in the constitution, given the strengthening of the executive vis-à-vis the legislative and judicial branches. Nevertheless, the constitution also creates other potentially powerful balances that can make all political representatives and state administrators more responsible to the citizenry (for example, the new constitutional court). Finally, the document refers to nature's rights, a concept that environmentalists are using to struggle against government plans to encourage mining as a new leading export sector for Ecuador.

Exacerbated Dependency and Government Policies

Ecuador is a small, dependent country with little capacity to buck international trends and pressures. Its dependency has been both economic (on foreign investment and fickle export markets) and ideological (an incapacity to formulate policies distinct from those imposed from the outside). If change took place in the 1980s and 1990s, it was essentially in the direction of intensifying these historical trends, specifically through the adoption of neoliberal SAPs imposed by the IMF, the World Bank, and the US Treasury, which reconfigured the relations between the state, economy, and society.

The most notable results of those neoliberal policies were a renewed reliance on primary export commodities (petroleum and bananas as in the past, with cut flowers and maritime products added to the mix recently); dependency on foreign private capital in export production, commercialization, and finance; the lowering of labor standards, along with a weakening of the labor movement to attract domestic and foreign investment; the invasion of domestic markets by cheap imports, especially after the adoption of the US dollar as the official currency; the general abandonment of redistributive reforms, with a resulting growth in inequality and poverty; and weak and erratic, when not negative, growth. The social violence generated by these policies and their consequences led to the rapid growth of private security forces, in the urban as well as the rural areas, that cooperated with public forces to control the increased number of crimes against property and new waves of protest in the countryside. And all this meant contraction of the domestic market—indeed, the abandonment of the policies that favored the domestic market growth and diversification that were pursued, albeit in erratic ways, by developmentalist governments in the 1960s and 1970s.

The negative impacts of neoliberal adjustment policies were aggravated during the financial crisis of 1997–2000, when almost 60 percent of the financial system went bankrupt. The financial crisis intensified the vulnerability of Ecuador's government to external pressures to adopt policies favorable to domestic and international financial sectors at the same that it made government more susceptible to the demands of domestic export and financial groups for measures that would protect their interests. Eventually President Mahuad adopted the US dollar as Ecuador's official currency in an effort to buy the support of the great commercial and banking groups of the city of Guayaquil. Dollarization, however, did not save Mahuad's government or the country's economy. Even though inflation slowed, economic growth was restricted, since the costs of production in Ecuador were increased in comparison to its neighbors whose currencies continued to devalue. Consequently exports were punished and imports were favored, even food imports. Indeed, according to the Guayaquil chamber of commerce, nearly half of the country's export companies went bankrupt between 2000 and 2003. It was the legacy of the neoliberal era, which had reinforced the country's historically exclusionary dependent development path that Correa inherited (see summary table below).

Upon assuming the presidency, Correa tackled all these issues quickly and forcefully, thus raising and maintaining his popularity with the electorate. First, with regard to dependency, Correa distanced himself from the World Bank and the IMF. He also appointed a commission to study Ecuador's foreign debt and used its findings regarding what Correa called the "illegitimate, corrupt, and illegal" character of the debt to negotiate better terms for Ecuador (Serrano Narváez 2008). At the same time, Correa announced that he would support the creation of an international tribunal for arbitration of foreign debt at the United Nations. Second, with regard to poverty and inequality, the government increased social spending substantially. It doubled the so-called human development bonus received by the poorest sectors of the population to $30 per month and also increased the housing bonus subsidy (doubling it for urban residents and raising it even more for rural dwellers) (International Crisis Group 2007, 20). Third, with regard to relations with Ecuador's leading oligarchic families, his government investigated how the Mahuad presidency handled the financial crisis and took steps to confiscate property from one great banking family. At the same time, action was taken to reduce tax fraud and improve revenue collection. And fourth, with regard to development promotion, the president took steps to protect local industries (and therefore employment) against cheap imports from Asia and elsewhere.

While Correa's actions were remarkable on many fronts, his hands were tied in other areas. Although he had argued against adopting the dollar as Ecuador's currency, he did not consider the economic conditions propitious for reversing that policy. Correa also ran into deep conflict with environmental and indigenous groups over mining issues. As the country's petroleum reserves declined, the government sought to identify new sources of export revenue, and mining became its choice as the new dynamic export sector. By late 2008, dependency on the global

TABLE 22.2   Ecuador: The Historical Legacy of Dependent Development

Late 19th Century	Late 20th Century
Reliance on primary exports with strong, albeit boom-bust, growth under increasing US dominance.	Reliance on primary exports with weak and erratic growth under IFI/US dominance.
Reliance on foreign private capital for export commerce and finance.	Reliance on foreign private capital for export production, commerce, and finance.
Expropriation of church and indigenous community lands to favor "export oligarchies," with increases in inequality and the maintenance of forced labor regimes.	Reduction of labor standards, weakening of unions, and abandonment of redistributive reforms to favor foreign and local investors, with increases in inequality and poverty.
Organization of professional military and police forces, alongside the private security forces of estate owners, to control rural rebelliousness and banditry.	Booming growth of private security forces in both urban and rural areas, often in cooperation with state forces, to control increasing waves of crime against property and new waves of protest or rebellion in the countryside in the context of increased US police and military assistance.
Political opening toward urban middle and working classes, but with continued concentration of economic policy making power in the hands of "export oligarchies" and allied foreign interests.	Political opening toward some social sectors, women and indigenous people in particular, but with increasing concentration of economic policy making power among local and foreign financial elites, including the IFIs.

economy, now in crisis, was taking its toll once more: declining petroleum prices (35 percent of the state budget), a sharp reduction in remittances sent by the hundreds of thousands of Ecuadoreans who had left the country during the crises of the late 1990s and early 2000s, and the appreciation of the dollar, which made Ecuador increasingly uncompetitive vis-à-vis its neighbors and other Third World exporters were all threatening economic and social stability along with the government's policy maneuvering room. Despite mounting and looming problems, Correa won a new presidential term in April 2009, although the vote for both him and his party dropped vis-à-vis the previous elections.

FOREIGN POLICY

Three periods can be identified in Ecuador's relations with the United States during the twentieth century. A formative period from 1900 to 1942 was characterized by the predominance of trade issues as the United States became Ecuador's principal market for its exports and industrial imports. This relationship was strengthened by the opening of the Panama Canal and reached a high point during the Kemmerer Mission's reorganization of the Ecuadorean economy in the 1920s; the US mediation of the 1942 war with Peru and the negotiation of the Treaty of Rio de Janeiro;

and Ecuadorean cooperation with the United States during World War II, as reflected in the establishment of a US air base in the Galapagos Islands.

The second period, from the end of World War II to the turn of the century, was characterized by Ecuador's search for a "special relationship" with the United States. It acquired its definitive form during the 1950s, in the context of US international development aid policies (Montúfar 2003). During the 1950s and 1960s, Ecuador's attempts to establish close ties to the United States were facilitated by modernizing governments, both civilian led (1948–1963) and military (1963–1966). The relationships established in the 1950s and 1960s endured through the 1970s, with only slight variation during the radical phase of the military government headed by General Rodríguez Lara (1972–1976), which, in addition to redistributive reforms, tried to pursue moderately nationalist policies. Although that government sought to maintain a multilateral Third World orientation (e.g., by working to consolidate the Andean Pact, joining the movement of nonaligned nations, and becoming an OPEC member), economic ties to the United States became more important than ever before. Two factors accounted for this. On the one hand, to exploit and export petroleum, the Ecuadorean state established an alliance with an American multinational corporation, Texaco, and that relationship endured until 1986. On the other hand, the economic development strategies of the military governments favored alliances between Ecuador's private sector (the most important national business groups of the oligarchy described earlier) and US multinational corporations and financial institutions.

A third distinct period in US-Ecuadorean relations began in the early 1980s, with the transition to democracy. Three themes characterized those years. The first involves the adoption of neoliberal economic policies, accompanied by cooperation with the United States regarding hemispheric trade liberalization. Second came the concern for democratic stability in Ecuador and the hemisphere, as promoted by Washington and the multilateral organizations—the OAS, the United Nations, and the Andean Community of Nations most importantly. Finally, after 1998, the "war against drugs" became more and more important in relations with the United States.

The adoption of Washington's diagnosis and the Ecuadorean government's own interest in drug control favored practical (but not always rhetorical) support for the US war on drugs (Bonilla 2002). That support manifested itself in the creation of a forward observation base (FOB) at the air force base in Manta on the north coast of Ecuador. It also involved increased cooperation between Ecuador's armed forces and police and US government agencies. In 1999 Ecuador adopted an antidrug strategy that included a combination of police and military initiatives against drug trafficking, and the national police established the National Antinarcotics Division (DNA). Then in 2000 mixed police-army task forces were created that operated in the three provinces that border on Colombia. In sum, the channels for achieving a special relationship with the United States became the country's alignment in the drug wars, and, after September 11, in the war on terrorism, and all this was accompanied by a step-by-step institutionalization of the ties between Ecuadorean security forces and US agencies.

From the first days of his government, Rafael Correa announced that he would pursue a different kind of foreign policy vis-à-vis that of his predecessors. Three distinctive characteristics can be identified. First, although the government has maintained its collaboration in the drug wars, its initiatives in this realm were nationalized as the past unconditional alignment with Washington was abandoned. Second, Ecuador's policies toward Colombia changed, with (1) an emphasis on humanitarian assistance for the victims of the Colombian conflict who have been displaced to Ecuadorean territory and (2) a distancing from the policies of Alvaro Uribe's government in Colombia. Third, the Ecuadorean government renewed efforts to maintain close relations with like-minded Latin American governments (Venezuela, Bolivia, and Cuba in particular) and to diversify its diplomatic initiatives with the European Union, Iran in the Middle East, Libya in North Africa, and China. Even though this new foreign policy was oriented toward achieving greater autonomy, it was not exclusively based on ideological or principled considerations. In fact, with the exception of the stance toward the Uribe government, Correa's foreign policy could be considered pragmatic.

Establishing distance from the United States, although marked by nationalist and anti-imperialist rhetoric, has been rather moderately pursued and refers for the most part to three issues. Similar to the governments of Argentina, Chile, and Bolivia, Ecuador, as noted above, has attempted to limit and even suppress the influence of the World Bank and the IMF in the management of the domestic economy. Second, cooperation in the war on drugs has been reformulated to ensure national control over it. To accomplish this, the government has not renewed the treaty with the United States for the continued operation of the Manta base (a treaty that expired in 2009), and it has created two new domestic organizations to replace the former direct relations between the Ecuadorean and North American security agencies: the Ministry of Domestic and International Security and Plan Ecuador. These changes have affected the Ecuadorean armed forces and the national police more than they have affected relations with the United States. A third change in policy toward the United States, initiated under President Palacio, was rejection of free trade agreements, not only with the United States but also with the European Union. This last change in policy must be examined with reference to Ecuador's limited commercial importance. The United States actually decided to exclude both Ecuador and Bolivia from any free trade deal with the Andean countries already in August 2006, and Europe made a similar decision in October of that year.

The policy turn toward Colombia, as pointed out above, is derived from ideological considerations. At the end of 2007, the creation of the Ministry of National and International Security and Plan Ecuador was accompanied by a failed Ecuadorean attempt to intervene diplomatically in the domestic conflict in Colombia. Then in April 2008, an incursion by the Colombian army into Ecuadorean territory destroyed a clandestine base of the Revolutionary Armed Forces of Colombia (FARC) and killed an important FARC leader, Raúl Reyes. Ecuador responded by breaking diplomatic relations with Bogotá and requesting the intervention of the Organization of American States (OAS). Diplomatic relations were not reestablished until early 2010. Throughout the suspension of relations, Ecuador, nevertheless, continued to maintain its policy of denying FARC access to Ecuadorean territory, and through Plan Ecuador it provided humanitarian assistance to displaced Colombians who sought refuge in Ecuador (Ramírez and Montúfar 2008).

Although the Ecuadorean government is using the notion of multipolarity to refer to the general orientation of its foreign policy, its search for a new diversity in its foreign relations is based on pragmatic rather than ideological considerations (Bonilla 2008). Correa has oriented Ecuador's efforts in the realm of Latin American integration toward the Union of the South (UNASUR), the emerging scheme for economic integration between the Andean Community and the Southern Cone, and the creation of a new organization of Latin American and Caribbean states without the United States and Canada. Ecuador's renewed membership in the Organization of Petroleum Exporting Countries (OPEC), from which the country withdrew in 1994, arises also from pragmatic considerations: the need to maintain high petroleum prices. Similarly, efforts to increase the density of relations with the Middle East and China are justified by commercial considerations.

Conclusion

President Correa's policies mark the most important Ecuadorean initiatives since the transition to democracy to break out of the cycle of exclusionary dependent development that has characterized the country's history. His government has attempted to chart an independent nationalistic path in terms of international relations while it has taken important steps domestically to reduce poverty and inequality and to make elites accountable. But the challenges are formidable for a small country with a legacy of dependency and limited resources, not only natural but also human, given the neglect of investment in health, public education, and social security of the past quarter century. Those challenges are all the more formidable in the current global economic crisis, which has reduced significantly the resources available to the government.

Notes

1. For the statistical data on levels of poverty and inequality in the 1990s, see Larrea and Sánchez 2002.

2. On the constitution of the elites, see Navarro 1976; Fierro 1991; Conaghan 1988; Handelman 2002.

Recommended Readings

Andrade, Pablo. 2002. "Fuerzas sociales y políticas en la Constitución ecuatoriana de 1988." Paper delivered at the I Encuentro de Ecuatorianistas, Latin American Studies Association (LASA), Quito.

Beck, Scott H., and Kenneth J. Mijeski. 2006. "The Indigenous Vote in Ecuador's 2002 Presidential Election." *Latin American and Caribbean Ethnic Studies* 1, no. 2 (September).

Becker, Marc. 2002. "Ecuador." In *The South American Handbook*. Edited by Patrick Heenan and Monique Lamontagne. London: Fitzroy Dearborn.

Bonilla, Adrián. 2002. "Alcances de la autonomía y hegemonía en la política exterior ecuatoriana." In *Orfeo en el infierno: Una agenda de política exterior ecuatoriana*. Edited by Adrián Bonilla. Quito: FLACSO-CAF-Academia Diplomática.

Clark, Kim. 1998. "Racial Ideologies and the Quest for National Development: Debating the Agrarian Problem in Ecuador (1930–1950)." *Journal of Latin American Studies* 30.

Conaghan, Catherine M. 1988. *Restructuring Domination: Industrialists and the State in Ecuador*. Pittsburgh: University of Pittsburgh Press.

Conaghan, Catherine M. 1995. "Politicians Against Parties, Discord, and Disconnection in Ecuador's Party System." In *Building Democratic Institutions in Latin America.* Edited by Scott Mainwaring and Timothy Scully. Stanford: Stanford University Press.

Conaghan, Catherine M., and James M. Malloy. 1994. *Unsettling Statecraft: Democracy and Neoliberalism in the Central Andes.* Pittsburgh: University of Pittsburgh Press.

Fierro, Luís. 1991. *Los grupos financieros en el Ecuador.* Quito: CEDEP.

Guerrero, Andrés. 1980. *Los oligarcas del cacao.* Quito: Editorial El Conejo.

———. 1993. "La desintegración de la administración étnica en el Ecuador." In *Sismo étnico en el Ecuador. Varias perspectivas.* Edited by José Almeida et al. Quito: CEDIME & Abya-Yala.

Handelman, Howard. 2002. "The Origins of the Ecuadorian Bourgeoisie: Its Implications for Democracy, Challenges, and Limits to Latin American's Democratic Revolution." *Canadian Journal of Latin American and Caribbean Studies* 27, no. 53.

International Crisis Group. 2007. *Ecuador: Overcoming Instability.* Latin America Report no. 22. August 7.

Larrea, Carlos, and Liisa North. 1997. "Ecuador: Adjustment Policy Impacts on Truncated Development and Democratization." *Third World Quarterly* 18, no. 5.

Larrea, Carlos, and Jeannette Sánchez. 2002. *Pobreza, empleo y equidad en el Ecuador: Perspectivas para el desarrollo humano sostenible.* Quito: Programa de las Naciones Unidas para el Desarrollo.

Maiguashca, Bice. 1992. "The Role of Ideas in a Changing World Order: The International Indigenous Movement." In *Occasional Papers in Latin American and Caribbean Studies,* no. 4. Toronto: CERLAC/York University.

Menéndez-Carrión, Amparo. 1986. *La conquista del voto: De Velasco a Roldós.* Quito: FLACSO-Corporación Editora Nacional.

Montúfar, César. 2003. *Hacia una teoría de la asistencia internacional para el desarrollo: Un análisis desde su retórica.* Quito: Corporación Editora Nacional-Centro Andino de Estudios Internacionales, Universidad Andina Simón Bolívar.

Muratorio, Blanca. 1980. "Protestantism and Capitalism Revisited in the Rural Highlands of Ecuador." *Journal of Peasant Studies* 8, no. 1.

Navarro, Guillermo. 1976. *La concentración de capitales en el Ecuador.* Quito: Ediciones Solitierra.

North, Liisa. 2004. "State Building, State Dismantling, and Financial Crisis in Ecuador." In *Politics in the Andes: Identity, Conflict, Reform.* Edited by Jo-Marie Burt and Philip Mauceri. Pittsburgh: University of Pittsburgh Press.

Ospina Peralta, Pablo. 2008. *El refrendum y después: Un camino despejado?* Quito: Comité Ecuménico de Proyectos (CEP).

Pachano, Simón. 2004. "El territorio de los partidos: Ecuador 1979–2002." In *Partidos políticos en la región Andina: Entre la crisis y el cambio.* Edited by Simón Pachano. Stockholm: IDEA.

Ramírez, Socorro, and César Montúfar, eds. 2007. *Colombia y Ecuador: Cercanos y distantes.* Bogota: Universidad Nacional de Colombia, Instituto de Estudios Políticos y Relaciones Internacionales/Universidad Andina Simón Bolívar.

Serrano Narváez, Helga. 2008. *Ecuador Seeks Non-payment of Illegitimate Foreign Debt.* Americas Policy Program, Center for International Policy. November 24. http://americas.irc-online.org.

Striffler, Steve. 2002. *In the Shadows of State and Capital: The United Fruit Company, Popular Struggle, and Agrarian Restructuring in Ecuador, 1900–1995.* Durham, NC: Duke University Press.

Zamosc, León. 1994. "Agrarian Protest and the Indian Movement in the Ecuadorian Highlands." *Latin American Perspectives* 29, no. 3.

Chapter 23

PERU

Precarious Democracy amid Dependent Development in a Divided Nation

CYNTHIA MCCLINTOCK

ALTHOUGH DEMOCRACY HAS regularly been undertaken in Peru, to date no constitutional regime has been uninterrupted for more than twelve years. Since the restoration of democracy in 2000, for the first time in history Peru simultaneously enjoyed economic growth, political peace, and one-person, one-vote elections. Nonetheless, the governments were unpopular and many Peruvians considered leftist or populist alternatives.

As Jan Knippers Black highlights in the introduction to this volume, blame for the tenuousness of democracy in Peru can be placed in part on the Iberians, who provoked the nation's deep divides. Peru's renowned novelist Mario Vargas Llosa wrote that the country was "an artificial gathering of men from different languages, customs, and traditions whose only common denominator was having been condemned by history to live together without knowing or loving one another."[1] The Spaniards' abuse and betrayal of the Incas have not been forgotten and constitute one reason for today's pervasive social mistrust.[2] The divides were deepened by geography. In contrast to other Andean nations, Peru's capital is on the coast, separated from the country's indigenous peoples by some of the highest mountains of the Andes.

And as Black points out too, blame can be placed also on elites in Peru, Europe, and the United States, who were tied to patterns of dependent development that did not do enough to bridge the country's historic divides. Currently and for most of its history, Peru has had "liberal" or "free market" economic policies; economic growth has been based primarily on raw-material exports, and the country has been vulnerable to cycles of boom and bust. The priority for the US government has usually been its immediate economic objectives rather than democracy.

In the context of dependent development, Peru, like most Latin American nations, has a disappointing record on growth and poverty alleviation. Between 1900 and 1987 Peru's real GDP growth averaged approximately 3.6 percent, versus 3.8 percent for the region.[3] Despite robust growth since the mid-1990s, per capita income in Peru for 2007 was $7,240, more than 20 percent below the average of

$9,321 for Latin America and the Caribbean.[4] As late as the 1960s, two poles en-dured in Peru: at one pole were "the oligarchy" and perhaps another 10 percent of the population who were Caucasian, Catholic, Spanish-speaking, wealthy, and based in Lima; at the other pole were some 40 percent of the population, called "In-dians," who were dark-skinned, only nominally Catholic, Quechua-speaking, im-poverished, and based in the Andean highlands, in particular the southern highlands. These poles are less stark today, but regional disparities remain severe.

The precariousness of Peru's democracy cannot be blamed, however, on Peru-vians' disinterest. For example, in the 2006 election, more than 80 percent of the voting-age population cast ballots, the highest turnout rate in Latin America save Uruguay.[5] Although Peru's elected governments have been the victims of coups, authoritarian governments have also been brought down by popular demand for elections and democracy. As of 2005, Peru's population was more than 70 percent urban; also, more than 90 percent of the relevant age-group was enrolled in sec-ondary school and more than 30 percent in postsecondary education.[6]

THE SPANISH CONQUEST AND COLONIZATION

Given that Peru was the home of one of the Western Hemisphere's largest and most sophisticated indigenous civilizations and subsequently one of Spain's two viceroyalties, the Spanish conquest and colonial rule were especially traumatic.

The Spanish conquest was devastating for Peru's indigenous peoples. The Inca Empire extended from present-day Chile to Ecuador and embraced more than 7 million people; with vast irrigation networks and excellent food storage and distri-bution facilities, it was prosperous. Yet in 1532, fewer than 200 Spaniards led by Francisco Pizarro brutally overwhelmed an Incan army that might have numbered as many as 80,000 warriors. Despite their small numbers, the Spaniards won be-cause of their horses, gunpowder, swords, and successful ambush strategy—and also because of Incan internal conflicts. After capturing the Incan emperor, Atahualpa, the Spaniards betrayed him. They promised him freedom in exchange for a huge ransom, but murdered him after he paid. About forty years later, Túpac Amarú, the last Incan ruler, was seized and asked to convert to Christianity; he complied but was nonetheless beheaded.

Peru became one of Spain's two viceroyalties in the hemisphere. Peru's gold, sil-ver, and mercury mines were extremely rich. The Spanish forced the indigenous peoples to work in these mines under brutal conditions. By 1600, these labor con-ditions and new European diseases decimated the indigenous population. The Spanish also seized much of the best agricultural land in Andean mountain valleys. Angry, the native peoples rebelled sporadically, often proclaiming that their goal was the restoration of Incan rule. In 1780, a descendant of the Inca royal family, Túpac Amaru II, led the largest rebellion against the Spanish during the colonial era. Lasting almost two years, the rebellion gained substantial peasant support but was brutally crushed by the Spanish crown.

When the movement for independence grew in the early nineteenth century, Lima was Spain's administrative center in South America and it became the center of the Spanish counterattack. Peru's *criollos* (descendants of the Spanish born in the colonies) were wary of independence, worried that they would not be able to control the large indigenous population. Accordingly, predominantly foreign forces, led by the Argentine José de San Martín and the Venezuelan Simón Bolívar, brought independence to Peru in 1824.

INDEPENDENCE TO 1930: THE RISE OF PERU'S OLIGARCHY

The hundred-odd years between Peru's independence and 1930 were turbulent. There were periods of robust economic growth, but it was export-led and marked by the emergence and consolidation of "the oligarchy"—forty-odd families who controlled large landholdings that produced Peru's key exports, in particular sugar and cotton on the coast. Although these elites tended to favor elected civilian regimes, they severely restricted suffrage and pursued export-led growth without a great deal of concern for its impact on poverty.

For the first twenty years after independence, military officers from different regional bases (caudillos) competed for power and fought over national boundaries. Then guano (bird droppings), abundant on small islands off Peru's coast, was discovered to be an excellent fertilizer; during the guano boom (1840–1879), millions of tons of guano were sold to Europe and North America. The Peruvian state owned a monopoly on the guano and sold licenses for its extraction and export. With enormous new revenues, the country established political order and built state bureaucracies and railroads. However, graft and mismanagement were rampant. By the time Peru's guano was exhausted, the country was deeply in debt. Peru had failed to "sow its oil"—channel the revenues from its export bonanza for the benefit of the country as a whole.

The guano boom enriched a number of merchants and businesspeople who became the social base for Peru's first political party, the Civilista Party. They were angry at what they saw as the incompetence and corruption of the "men on horseback" who had been governing. Also, many had used their new wealth to establish coastal haciendas and, with an eye to their own future economic prosperity, they sought low tariffs and other free market policies. In 1872, in Peru's first "elections" (there were 3,778 voters), the Civilista candidate triumphed.[7]

This liberal experiment ended amid the 1879–1883 War of the Pacific, which pitted Peru and Bolivia against Chile. Nitrates (also a valuable fertilizer) had been discovered in the Atacama desert, where hundreds of miles of territory were disputed by the three countries. The Civilistas did not want to fight an all-out war; they feared that if the indigenous peasants were mobilized against the Chileans, the peasants would subsequently turn against large landowners. (This did happen in some parts of the highlands.) Ostensibly to secure foreign loans and new ships, the Civilista president sailed for Europe. After a series of victories, the Chilean military occupied Lima in January 1881. In 1883, Peru ceded a southern nitrate-rich province to Chile (among other concessions) and peace was achieved. But there was a widespread belief that Peru's elites had betrayed the country in favor of their own interests.

In the aftermath of the war, Peruvians were demoralized and the country's economy ravaged. After several years of negotiations, a military government reached an agreement with Great Britain that restored Peru's international credit; export-led growth finally resumed.

In 1895 military rule ended with the establishment of the "Aristocratic Republic." Suffrage was severely restricted and electoral manipulation was common, but (with the exception of a coup in 1914) the constitutional order was maintained until 1919. Amid robust export-led growth, Peru's oligarchy was consolidated and its Civilista Party was dominant. Economic growth increased the demand for labor, and a working class emerged; education expanded. However, large haciendas were extending at the peasants' expense, and mining operations devastated the ecology of contiguous communities. Working conditions were dismal.

At the end of World War I, commodity prices fell and export production declined. Strikes erupted. The 1919 presidential elections were won by Augusto Leguía, a former Civilista president who campaigned as a populist reformer. Backed by the military, Leguía terminated the constitution of the Aristocratic Republic. Leguía enjoyed close ties with the United States, and US capital flowed into Peru. At first, the Leguía government funded road, school, and irrigation projects and implemented some reforms (the eight-hour day, the minimum wage, and legal standing for peasant communities), and was not unpopular. However, Leguía became corrupt and repressive, and he was overthrown amid the global depression in 1930.

1930–1968: OLIGARCHIC POWER UNDER STRESS

From 1930 to 1968, Peru's oligarchy and its free market economic model confronted serious challenges, in particular from a new political party, the American Popular Revolutionary Alliance (APRA). The prevailing perception was that Peru was trailing other Latin American nations in the effort for social justice and national integration and that dramatic redistributive reform was necessary. However, virtually throughout this period, Peru's oligarchy and military on the one hand and APRA on the other remained intransigent opponents, and reform initiatives failed. Whereas many Latin American nations adopted import substitution industrialization policies, Peru retained an open, export-led model without a significant redistributive component.

Indeed, by most measures Peru was behind other Latin American nations. Peru's income distribution was one of the most unequal in the region; in 1961 the wealthiest 1 percent of the economically active population received a staggering 30 percent of the national income.[8] Also, the Gini index of land distribution was the most skewed among fifty-four nations for which data were reported; a mere 280 families—less than 0.1 percent of all farm families—owned approximately 30 percent of the land and more than 50 percent of the best land.[9] Moreover, the disparity in living standards between the capital and the hinterlands—in Peru's case between Lima and its southern highlands—was unusually severe.[10] On numerous measures of political participation Peru was also behind its neighbors.

Founded in 1924 by Haya de la Torre and based on Peru's sugar-growing north coast, APRA became Peru's only institutionalized political party. Haya de la Torre was not only a charismatic speaker and brilliant intellectual but also the architect of a cohesive, disciplined political organization. While various leftist leaders of the 1920s, in particular José Carlos Mariátegui, embraced Marxism, Haya did not. He did, however, denounce US imperialism and advocated dramatic economic and political reforms. Proclaiming that "Only APRA will save Peru," he also called for moral renewal.

In bitterly fought elections in 1931, Haya was defeated by Luís Sánchez Cerro, a military commander who had toppled Leguía. Although Sánchez Cerro enjoyed the support of the oligarchy, his modest, provincial background and mestizo appearance appealed to popular groups as well. Sánchez Cerro denounced APRA as anti-Catholic, antimilitary, and closet-communist. Without evidence, APRA repudiated the 1931 electoral result as fraudulent and quickly became obstructionist in the legislature. In retaliation, Sánchez Cerro deported APRA's entire congressional representation. In 1932 APRA members rebelled in Trujillo, executing sixty-odd members of the army. In reprisal, the military killed 1,000 to 2,000 Apristas. In 1933 Sánchez Cerro was assassinated by an Aprista. Sánchez Cerro's successor intensified the repression of APRA, and Aprista militants continued to resort to violence. Also, APRA sought out allies in the military and plotted with them against the government—tactics that deeply antagonized officers.

Between 1931 and 1968, elections were held, but APRA was proscribed to one degree or another. The only civilian president to complete his term during this period was Manuel Prado (1939–1945). During World War II, the United States and the Prado government were strong partners; rejecting fascism, APRA collaborated with Prado.

At the end of the war, hopes for democracy and reform were high. In the 1945 elections, distinguished legal scholar José Luís Bustamante triumphed; he led a new political alliance that incorporated the APRA party. The Bustamante government implemented import substitution industrialization policies; the government raised tariffs, introduced import and exchange controls, and increased workers' wages and benefits. However, while these policies did not go far enough for APRA, they outraged Peru's oligarchy. Politically inexperienced, Bustamante was unable to negotiate effectively with either APRA or the oligarchy. Also, the Bustamante government was unable to secure support from the US government; the Truman administration did not sustain the pro-democratic policies of Franklin D. Roosevelt. In 1948, amid political polarization and economic deterioration, Bustamante was ousted in a military coup.

The coup was led by General Manuel Odría, who immediately banned APRA, reestablished free market policies, and reinvigorated cooperation with the United States. With the onset of the Korean War, mining boomed and the economy grew. But in 1953 with the end of the war and export bust, support for Odría plummeted.

Elections held in 1956 were won by former president Manuel Prado. Although Prado did not launch reforms, he ameliorated tensions by reaching out to APRA, which was allowed to run in the 1962 presidential elections. The election results were inconclusive, however; in part to prevent an APRA presidency, the military staged a coup. New elections were organized in 1963 and won by Fernando Belaúnde, leader of the new party Popular Action.

At this time, in the wake of the Cuban revolution and the Kennedy administration's Alliance for Progress, reformist tides were sweeping Latin America. Peruvians' hopes for reform were high. However, although public expenditures for education and for infrastructure increased dramatically, overall these hopes were not realized. Constrained in part by his own aristocratic proclivities and in part by APRA obstructionism, Belaúnde did not deliver on key promises. Agrarian reform was minimal. Belaúnde failed to resolve quickly a dispute with the International Petroleum Company (IPC), a US company that had provoked intense nationalistic sentiments among Peruvians. Although Peruvians considered Belaúnde too accommodating toward IPC, the Johnson administration considered him too harsh. The United States did not provide the support that Belaúnde, as a democratic reformer, expected during the Alliance for Progress.

THE 1968–1980 MILITARY GOVERNMENT

In 1968, reflecting Peruvians' perception that the last chance for reform by a democratic government had been lost, General Juan Velasco Alvarado led a military coup. Proclaiming a "revolutionary government of the armed forces" that would build a "fully participatory social democracy," the Velasco government finally curtailed the power of Peru's oligarchy. Subsequently Peru's elites were more likely to have earned their position through work rather than to have inherited it. Peru's income distribution improved, and the middle class expanded. Also, the Velasco government distanced Peru from the United States.

The Velasco government's reforms were dramatic. Not only did the government implement one of the most sweeping agrarian reforms in Latin America, but it expropriated a broad spectrum of other enterprises—from fishing, mining, and banking companies to daily newspapers—most of which had been owned by oligarchic families. Further, the government expropriated numerous US companies, including IPC. The state came to own more than 20 percent of the economy, and peasants' and workers' cooperatives owned another 10 percent. Tariffs were raised, and manufacturing grew rapidly within the closed economy.

Ultimately, however, the military government's reforms did little to alleviate the lot of Peru's poorest—the highland peasants. Per capita, there was not enough quality land to redistribute in these areas to make a major improvement in living standards. Further, public expenditure was not shifted toward highland agriculture. The government did, however, continue to expand educational opportunities, and it recognized Quechua as the second national language of Peru.

The Velasco government's political agenda was incoherent. Although the government was not repressive by the Latin American standards of the time, it severely restricted political parties, and the expropriated newspapers gradually became mouthpieces for the regime. The government created a political agency, the National System for the Support of Social Mobilization (SINAMOS, an acronym that meant "Without Masters"), but its role was muddled. Still, worker and peasant organizations expanded dramatically, to a considerable degree under the banner of the Marxist left. Political attitudes became more democratic, more participatory, and also more radical and confrontational.

In 1975 Velasco was ousted in a palace coup by General Francisco Morales Bermúdez. Velasco had fallen ill, factionalism within the military had intensified, and Peru's economy had weakened. As the International Monetary Fund (IMF) demanded austerity, popular protest mounted. In 1977, less than two weeks after a massive nationwide strike, Morales Bermúdez announced a transition to democracy.

The 1980–1992 "Electoral Democracy"[11]

In 1980 the prospects for democracy in Peru appeared more favorable than ever before. No longer was an oligarchy looking out first and foremost for its own interests, and no longer was APRA politically excluded. A new political left was expected to push for greater social justice; for the first time in the 1979 constitution, illiterates were enfranchised. Peru's democratic transition was coinciding with a return to democracy in much of the region and a rhetorical US commitment to democracy and human rights. However, these democratic prospects were dashed amid economic crisis and the concomitant rise of the Shining Path insurgency.

In 1980, seventy-year-old Belaúnde was reelected president. Unfortunately, the aging leader seemed unable to focus on the country's increasingly formidable problems. Like most countries in the region, Peru faced a debt crisis: an increase in external interest rates, a decrease in prices for its exports, and payments on its foreign debt that exceeded 35 percent of its export earnings. As per capita GDP declined, the subsistence of southern highlands peasants was threatened.

Mounting the most serious guerrilla challenge in Peru's history, the Shining Path was savage, sectarian, and virulently Maoist; among its victims were political leaders from other Marxist groups, development engineers, church people, and peasants. Based in the impoverished southern highlands, the Shining Path appealed to some peasants and to provincial teachers and young people whose professional aspirations had been frustrated. For almost two years, the Belaúnde government did nothing but then endorsed repressive military action. Subsequently many victims of human rights violations turned against the government.

In 1985 Alan García, a young, charismatic APRA leader, won the elections in a landslide. On the debt crisis, García staked out a leftist position. In his inaugural address, blaming the crisis on imperialism and the United States, García said that Peru would pay no more than 10 percent of its export earnings to service its debt. García's position pleased Peruvians (almost 80 percent of whom had voted for either García or the leftist party's candidate), but deeply alienated the international financial community and the Reagan administration. García introduced expansionary fiscal policies that appeared to work—until the end of 1987, when Peru's international reserves ran out. The ultimate result was economic debacle.

At the same time, the Shining Path expanded—seemingly inexorably. García understood *Sendero* as a serious problem that was the result of the destitution of the southern highlands and rejected an exclusively military approach to the problem; he sought to provide economic aid to the area and to raise the military's respect for human rights. However, these efforts failed. One reason was a perception that García was hypocritical. In June 1986, when the military was ordered to quell riots staged by Shining Path prison inmates, more than 200 inmates were killed and García was considered complicit. By 1989, the Shining Path guerrillas numbered approximately 10,000 combatants, had the support of roughly 15 percent of Peru's citizens, and controlled about 28 percent of the country's municipalities.[12]

As the 1990 elections loomed, APRA was seriously discredited. The odds-on presidential favorite was Mario Vargas Llosa, the renowned novelist, but during the campaign he appeared aloof and arrogant. Ultimately Alberto Fujimori, a former mathematics professor and university head, was the surprise runner-up in the first round and the easy winner of the runoff. Whereas Vargas Llosa called for a free market "shock," Fujimori promised to restore prosperity through gradual changes. The son of humble Japanese immigrants, Fujimori appeared, in the words of his slogan, "A president like you." Another campaign motto, "Work, Honesty, and Technology," highlighted the qualities that Peruvians respected in persons of Asian origin. With no prior political experience, Fujimori was a political outsider; a vote for him was a vote against what many Peruvians considered a failed, corrupt political class.

Fujimori was a bold, confrontational leader who sought to aggrandize his power; within months, Peru's media satirized him as a would-be Japanese emperor. Fujimori soon lurched to the right, reversing his campaign promise and implementing a drastic shock policy. State expenditures were slashed, foreign investment laws eased, tariffs reduced, and privatization initiated. Although Fujimori's party held only about a quarter of the seats in the legislature, his initiatives were backed by Vargas Llosa's political coalition. Also, with the support of Vladimiro Montesinos (a former army captain and lawyer for drug traffickers), Fujimori gained control over appointments and promotions in the military. The government repeatedly expressed disdain for human rights and government-authorized death squads emerged.

As 1991 ended, however, Fujimori faced some resistance from Peru's legislature. Disagreement about draconian new counterinsurgency measures was particularly intense. In part as a result, on April 5, 1992, Fujimori launched an *autogolpe* (coup by the president himself): he suspended the 1979 constitution, arrested several opposition leaders, padlocked the congress, and moved to dismantle the judiciary. The *autogolpe* was supported by almost 80 percent of Peruvians; if these Peruvians had not considered most of Peru's politicians and judges corrupt prior to Fujimori's drumbeat to this effect, they did by April 1992.

THE FUJIMORI GOVERNMENT AFTER THE 1992 *Autogolpe*

After the *autogolpe*, the Fujimori government became what scholars have called an "electoral authoritarian" regime.[13] In such a regime, elections are held and democratic institutions persist, but at the same time any real threat to presidential power is blocked by whatever means necessary. From 1992 until September 2000, Fujimori and Montesinos, de facto head of the National Intelligence Service (SIN) and Fujimori's "Rasputin," rode roughshod over Peru's democratic institutions.

The first six months after the *autogolpe* were rocky. The Organization of American States (OAS) and the US government were seeking to establish hemispheric democratic norms, and they opposed the *autogolpe*. Negotiations ensued. Ultimately, in November 1992, the Fujimori government held elections for a new legislature that would also write a new constitution. Although the government's electoral machinations were manifold, the international community decided that it would tolerate the new regime.

The international community's tolerance in part reflected the Fujimori government's successes. In September 1992, a small, elite squad within Peru's antiterrorist police (established under García) captured the Shining Path leader, Abimael

Guzmán. Within the next few weeks, using information found in Guzmán's hide-out, police arrested more than 1,000 suspected guerrillas. During the next few years, the Shining Path was decimated. Also, as in much of Latin America, the economy recovered. Peru's foreign debt was renegotiated and Peru returned to the good graces of the international financial community.

In the 1995 elections, Fujimori won a landslide victory. His popularity was due to his counterinsurgency and economic successes and also to an increasingly pop-ulist strategy; funds from the privatization program were spent in part on social pro-grams and infrastructure for poor communities. Dressed in a poncho and Andean-style hat, Fujimori frequently helicoptered to highland communities to in-augurate new schools and roads.

Gradually, however, support for Fujimori eroded. Again as in much of Latin America, the economy slowed. Also, the government's authoritarian proclivities were increasingly obvious. Although the new constitution limited a president to two consecutive terms, Fujimori's congressional majority passed a law affirming his eligibility for a third consecutive term. The government derailed efforts by the Na-tional Elections Board, the Constitutional Tribunal, and a coalition of opposition leaders to deny, in one way or another, Fujimori's eligibility.

As the 2000 elections neared, Fujimori and Montesinos steeply tilted the elec-toral playing field. Television news was blatantly biased; it was subsequently proven that Montesinos paid millions of dollars in bribes to media magnates. Opposition candidates were slandered and their campaigns obstructed. Large sums were spent on food programs and their continuation conditioned on residents' votes. The gov-ernment sought to ensure that election officials were, at a minimum, spineless.

However, most Peruvians were fed up, and one of the opposition candidates, Alejandro Toledo, began to rise in the polls. Born in the mountains of Peru, the dark-skinned Toledo boasted an impressive résumé that included a PhD from Stanford University and employment with the World Bank. The founder of his po-litical party (Perú Posible), Toledo was effective on the stump, emphasizing his commitment to job creation. In the first round of the elections, Toledo finished with more than 40 percent of the vote, and a runoff was scheduled for May 28. However, in mid-May, Peru's electoral authorities announced the introduction of a new computer program, and OAS election monitors worried that the government was plotting fraud. When the government refused to postpone the runoff to give the OAS monitors time to verify the new program, they declined to monitor the exercise and declared Peru's electoral process "far from one that could be consid-ered free and fair." Toledo boycotted the runoff. Undeterred, Fujimori claimed that he won with 51 percent of the vote.

While the rigged election angered international monitors, it did not appear to dismay the most powerful sectors of the US government. Rather than call for new elections or threaten to suspend aid, the US ambassador maintained a cordial rela-tionship with Fujimori. Despite the Fujimori government's abuse of democratic principles, it was succeeding on other Clinton administration priorities for Latin America: it was opening Peru's economy and achieving victories in the war on drugs. Also, after Ecuador had provoked a border war with Peru in 1995, the Fu-jimori government had negotiated effectively and a peace accord had been achieved. The Central Intelligence Agency and Montesinos enjoyed a close relationship and cooperated for such initiatives as the 1997 raid that rescued almost all the hostages who had been seized by rebels at the Japanese Ambassador's residence.

Almost immediately, however, the regime collapsed. In August, the US Department of State was upset by revelations that Montesinos had masterminded the smuggling of arms to guerrillas in Colombia. In September, a video that showed Montesinos bribing an opposition congressman was leaked to Peru's media. The video was the smoking gun that definitively proved the regime's corruption; Peruvians exploded in disgust. Montesinos fled the country, and Fujimori faxed his resignation from Tokyo in November.

PERU'S POST-2000 DEMOCRACY

After Fujimori's flight, the head of Peru's congress, Valentín Paniagua, became the president of a transition government and Peru returned to democracy. On the one hand, as this chapter was being written in 2009, the achievements of Peru's post-2000 democracy were unprecedented. Peru has enjoyed legitimate governments, political peace, and outstanding economic growth. Peru became the first Latin American country to convict one of its own former elected presidents on human rights grounds. Yet most Peruvians are dissatisfied and there is a distinct possibility that a populist (from the left or the right) will be elected in 2011. This section will explore this apparent contradiction between this successful record and Peruvians' dissatisfaction.

The primary responsibility of Paniagua's government was to clean up Peru's political, judicial, and other institutions so that free and fair elections could be held in April 2001—which it did, to considerable acclaim. As the key victim of the 2000 fraud, Toledo was well positioned for the 2001 contest and he won the first round with 37 percent of the vote and the runoff with 53 percent.

The Toledo government had important accomplishments. As elaborated below, export-led economic growth began in 2002 and continued. The government was not, however, unresponsive to opposition to its free market policies. In 2002, after three days of violent protest in the southern highlands city of Arequipa over the privatization of electricity companies, the government backed down rather than risk a high death toll.

The government's human rights record was excellent. It remained vigilant toward the Shining Path and, to better understand the political violence of the 1980s and 1990s, it appointed the Commission for Truth and Reconciliation, which produced a detailed and rigorous, albeit controversial, report. An important decentralization law was passed; for the first time, elections were held for regional governments. The government also sought to hold ex-officials accountable for corruption and human rights violations. Montesinos, who had been captured in Venezuela, was imprisoned and convicted. Prosecutors sought to extradite Fujimori from Japan and then from Chile, where the ex-president flew in 2005. In all, approximately 1,500 individuals were investigated on corruption charges; two finance ministers, a president of congress, and several generals were convicted.[14]

Yet for most of Toledo's term, the president's approval rating was below 20 percent and at times he seemed in danger of impeachment. In his first year, he lost moral authority when he refused to acknowledge paternity of a daughter born out of wedlock. As Peru's first president of indigenous descent since Sánchez Cerro in 1931, Toledo faced particular cultural challenges. Although his lifestyle was not extravagant by the standards of Latin American presidents—he enjoyed fine scotch and liked to vacation at a beach resort on Peru's north coast—it was perceived as frivolous. Peruvians were measuring Toledo by standards they considered appropriate for indigenous persons (and also by the standards of Fujimori, who on Montesinos's orders had been portrayed in the media as an austere workaholic).

The Toledo government faced other challenges as well. His party, Perú Posible, did not enjoy a majority in the legislature; neither of the two major opposition parties, the APRA and the center-right National Unity party, was particularly constructive and the government had to reach out to a small fourth party for the approval of numerous initiatives. Further, Perú Posible was a hodgepodge of politicians who often wrangled over government jobs. Probably the most formidable challenge, however, was the onslaught from elites who were threatened by the Toledo government's judicial investigations. These elites, dubbed the Montesinos Mafia, still had money and friends in important positions and schemed for Toledo's downfall in the hope that a new government would provide amnesty.

Peru's 2006 election was a cliffhanger that showed the continuing alienation of Peru's hinterlands. Ollanta Humala, a fiery former lieutenant colonel allied with Hugo Chávez, won the first round and came within five points of winning the runoff. Of Peru's twenty-five departments, Humala won fifteen, including all but two in the country's interior, and averaged 75 percent of the vote in Peru's southern highlands. Humala had no previous elected experience and no coherent political party. Humala's family proclaimed an ultra-nationalistic ideology, *etnocacerismo,* named after a Peruvian general who had heroically rallied Peruvian highlanders against the Chilean invaders during the War of the Pacific.

Ultimately, however, former president Alan García, who had just squeaked into the runoff, prevailed. Despite García's calamitous 1985–1990 government, he was a brilliant politician. For several years, he had been introducing economic proposals that integrated the left's concern for the poor and the right's respect for the global free market; in the first round of the election, García deftly staked out the political center. For example, while the center-right candidate Lourdes Flores applauded the US-Peruvian free trade agreement and Humala excoriated it, García promised to review it line by line. In the runoff, García played Chávez's support for Humala to his own advantage.

For a congressional majority, García turned to the rightist parties, in particular the Fujimorista Party, which was now led by Fujimori's daughter Keiko. At times, García even adopted confrontational Fujimori-style tactics and threatened civil society groups. Overall, however, democratic principles were maintained and, despite the APRA-Fujimorista alliance in the legislature, the government did not appear to interfere in the trial of Alberto Fujimori. Extradited from Chile in 2007, Fujimori was convicted of human rights crimes in May 2009 and sentenced to twenty-five years in prison; the trial was widely considered the precedent of accountability for a former president, a historical landmark.

Despite García's campaign promises, his economic policies were to the right; the reasons for García's ideological conversion were hotly debated. García's leitmotiv was Aesop's fable of the "Dog and the Manger," in which a dog lying in a manger of hay prevents the oxen from eating. García's analogy was to indigenous peoples who are unable to exploit Peru's resources but prevent others from doing so; the message was that investment should be welcomed. García fervently backed the US-Peruvian free trade agreement as it was, and it went into effect in February 2009. Free trade agreements were also concluded with numerous other countries, including China.

As a result of the Toledo and García governments' policies and strong global demand for Peru's raw materials—in particular its gold, silver, copper, zinc, and tin—trade and investment boomed. As of 2008, Peru's exports were approximately quadruple the annual average of 1998–2002; as of 2007, foreign direct investment in Peru was more than triple the annual average of 1998–2002.[15] From 2002 through 2008, annual GDP growth averaged 7.4 percent versus a 4.6 percent regional average, and Peru vied with Panama for the accolade of the highest growth rate in Latin America.[16]

But was Peru's economic growth benefiting most Peruvians and helping to bridge Peru's divides? Some indicators were positive. Nationwide in 2007, unemployment was less than 5 percent.[17] According to official estimates, poverty fell from 55 percent of the population in 2001 to 44 percent in 2006, 40 percent in 2007, and 35 percent in 2008.[18] The infant mortality rate, which in 1990 had been about 25 percent higher than in various poorer Latin American countries, was slashed and as of 2006 was at the rates in these countries.[19]

Yet there was cause for concern. Wages were stagnant.[20] The official poverty figures were questioned on various grounds.[21] Regional disparities remained severe; for example, in 2005 chronic malnutrition was suffered by 7 percent of children under five in Lima, but 43 percent in the highlands, which was the same rate as in Burkina Faso and Mali.[22] Despite Peru's growth rate, in Latinobarómetro polls Peruvians were more skeptical than most other Latin Americans about their country's economic situation.

Also, conflict over the extraction of natural resources was mounting, and in June 2009 it exploded in the northern jungle town of Bagua. As already noted, for most of Peru's history its resources have been extracted primarily for the benefit of elites. In recent years, as the operations of international mining, energy, and logging companies have expanded, concerns about their impact have intensified. As in the past, the key concerns are the takeover of untitled and communal land by unscrupulous investors and damage to the ecology of the area. With these worries, for two months the natives of Bagua were protesting several government decrees; they were blocking roads and waterways. Rather than negotiate concessions, in June 2009 the García government sent the police to retake the area by force. In the ensuing clashes, twenty-three police officers and at least ten protesters were killed and more than one hundred hospitalized. Finally the decrees were repealed, but García continued to denigrate the native groups and blame the unrest on political allies of Hugo Chávez.

In the wake of the deaths in Bagua, García's approval rating sank nine points to 21 percent.[23] At the same time, amid the global recession, Peru's economy was slowing down. Numerous cities were paralyzed by protests. It appeared that the final two years of García's term would be difficult.

PROSPECTS FOR THE FUTURE

Since 2001, elections in Peru have been free and fair, and Peruvians have turned out at the polls in large numbers. Yet in Latinobarómetro polls, satisfaction with the way democracy is working is very low in Peru relative to other Latin American nations. Until majorities of Peruvians are at least somewhat satisfied with their democracy, it will remain at risk. In this context, although it appears very likely that the upcoming 2011 elections will be free and fair, the outcome is very uncertain. Among the front-runners in the crowded field are the successful Lima mayor, Luis Castañeda Lossio, and a populist from the right, Fujimori's daughter Keiko. Humala remains strong in Peru's highlands; Toledo is also likely to compete. However, amid Peruvians' discontent, an outsider candidate may once again emerge. At the same time, the achievements of the first decade of the 2000s have been considerable, and it is also possible that the 2011 elections will be an important step toward democratic consolidation in Peru.

NOTES

1. Mario Vargas Llosa, "Questions of Conquest: What Columbus Wrought, and What He Did Not," *Harper's*, December 1990, p. 52.

2. On mistrust in Peru and Latin America, see the annual polls at www.latino barometro.org.

3. Shane Hunt, "Peru: The Current Economic Situation in Long-Term Perspective," in *The Peruvian Economy and Structural Adjustment*, ed. Efraín Gonzales de Olarte (University of Miami: North-South Center Press, 1996), p. 15.

4. World Bank, *World Development Report 2009: Reshaping Economic Geography* (Washington DC: World Bank, 2009), p. 353. The figures are for purchasing power parity dollars.

5. J. Mark Payne, Daniel Zovatto, G. Fernando Carrillo Flórez, and Andrés Allamand Zavala, *Democracies in Development: Politics and Reform in Latin America* (Washington, DC: Inter-American Development Bank, 2007), appendix 2. The comparison is for the most recent election in the countries.

6. World Bank, *World Development Indicators 2007* (Washington, DC: World Bank, 2007), pp. 79, 163.

7. Julio Cótler, *Clases, estado, y nación en el Perú* (Lima: Instituto de Estudios Peruanos, 1978), p. 109.

8. Richard Webb, *Government Policy and the Distribution of Income in Peru, 1963–1973* (Cambridge; Harvard University Press, 1977), pp. 6–7.

9. Charles L. Taylor and Michael C. Hudson, *World Handbook of Political and Social Indicators*, 2nd ed. (New Haven: Yale University Press, 1972), p. 267; and Daniel Martínez and Armando Tealdo, *El Agro Peruano, 1970–1980* (Lima: CEDEP, 1982), pp. 15–16.

10. Comparisons for inequality between regions are available for Peru, El Salvador, and Ecuador in Cynthia McClintock, *Revolutionary Movements in Latin America: El Salvador's FMLN and Peru's Shining Path* (Washington, DC: U.S. Institute of Peace Press, 1998), pp. 167–173.

11. "Electoral democracy" is a concept for political regimes that hold free and fair elections while lacking most other key features of democracy; see Larry Diamond, "Is the Third Wave Over?" *Journal of Democracy*, July 1996, pp. 21–25.

12. McClintock, *Revolutionary Movements,* p. 73.

13. Steven Levitsky and Lucan A. Way, "The Rise of Competitive Authoritarianism," *Journal of Democracy,* April 2002, pp. 51–65.

14. *El Comercio,* June 25, 2003.

15. Figures are from the Economic Commission for Latin America and the Caribbean and the Economist Intelligence Unit; see Cynthia McClintock and Fabián Vallas, "The United States and Peru in the New Millennium," in Jorge I. Domínguez and Rafael Fernández de Castro, eds., *Contemporary Inter-American Relations* (New York: Routledge, forthcoming).

16. Figures are from annual editions of *Perú en Números* and from the International Monetary Fund; see McClintock and Vallas, "United States and Peru."

17. Richard Webb and Graciela Fernández Baca, *Perú en Números 2008* (Lima: Cuánto, 2008), p. 653.

18. Webb and Fernández Baca, *Perú,* p. 599; and "La Pobreza Hizo Click," *Caretas,* May 21, 2009, p. 34.

19. World Bank, *World Development Indicators 2008* (Washington, D.C.: World Bank, 2008), pp. 118–119.

20. Webb and Fernández Baca, *Perú,* pp. 676–677, 691.

21. Richard Webb, "Quizás, Quizás, Quizás," *El Comercio,* June 2, 2008.

22. Webb and Fernández Baca, *Perú,* p. 345; World Bank, *World Development Indicators 2008,* pp. 106–107.

23. *El Comercio,* June 21, 2009, p. A8.

Chapter 24

BOLIVIA

An Indigenous Movement Consolidates Power

JOSÉ Z. GARCIA

ON DECEMBER 6, 2009, voters in Bolivia reelected President Evo Morales to another five-year term as president, with a margin of 64 percent, nearly two out of every three votes. His political party, the Movimiento al Socialismo (MAS) won more than two-thirds of the seats in each chamber of the bicameral legislature, giving him an enviable ability to control legislation. For the past few years, under Morales's leadership, power in Bolivia has shifted away from a wealthy, outward-looking white minority that dominated Bolivian politics under the banner of neoliberalism, toward a much poorer, inward-looking indigenous majority excluded in recent decades from exercising power on a national scale.

Bolivian indigenous majorities empowered themselves in the early 1950s with the revolution of 1952, but the white leadership was soon coopted by more conservative forces, including the armed forces, which came to dominate politics in the 1960s and 1970s. After a period of institution building through trade unions and peasant organizations, which redistributed income downward, the movement slowly disintegrated. By the late 1980s power had shifted back to a white, wealthy elite allied to foreign interests that dominated economic and social policy under the ideology of neoliberalism. The elites' growing power was challenged by the charismatic leader of coca producers in the Chapare region, Evo Morales, who forged a coalition with indigenous leaders in the highlands near La Paz, trade unions, urban masses in Cochabamba, and other groups, to win presidential elections in 2005. A nationalistic, redistributive regime has consolidated power since then. Like the leaders of the revolution of 1952, MAS understands the importance of institution building to consolidate gains. Unlike the revolution of 1952, the top leader is an Aymara-speaking Indian, with roots in labor unions and peasant organizations.

HISTORICAL BACKGROUND

Colonial authorities distinguished between Upper Peru, or Charcas—roughly the area now comprising Bolivia—and Lower Peru, site of contemporary Peru. Charcas was subordinated to Lower Peru throughout most of the colonial period, although

443

geographic isolation in practice permitted a good deal of local autonomy. In 1545 a phenomenal silver deposit was discovered at Potosí, which made Chuquisaca (today Sucre) and Potosí two of the richest cities in the world. While these cities nurtured an outstanding tradition of religious painting and developed superb universities during the sixteenth and seventeenth centuries, the wealth that made this possible derived from the forced labor of indigenous populations on behalf of foreign-born white elites. Gradually silver production declined due to rising costs of imports essential to mining operations (especially mercury), periodic weaknesses in the international silver market, and exhaustion of silver supplies. The area now encompassing Bolivia has been extremely poor by Latin American standards for well over 200 years.

During the drive for independence Upper Peru was torn between royal authorities representing Rio de la Plata (Argentina) and Lower Peru, defending the crown, and rebels fighting for independence. Power was seized by a native-born conservative, Pedro Antonio de Olañeta, who refused to acknowledge the legitimacy of either Spanish authorities after the Liberal Revolution in Spain in 1820 or the rebel army under Venezuelan Simón Bolívar. Antonio José de Sucre, an officer under Bolívar, defeated Olañeta's army in 1825. Bolivia became independent and Simón Bolívar became its first president (hence the name Bolivia) for five months before leaving Sucre in charge. Independence, however, brought on a period of instability caused in part by disagreement over the relationship between Peru and Bolivia. President Andrés de Santa Cruz, who had been president of Peru in 1826, tried to resolve the issue by creating a federation between the two countries, but this elicited opposition from Argentina and Chile, and the federation broke up after Chilean forces defeated Santa Cruz in 1839.

Traditional trade routes were severed by the independence movement in the early part of the nineteenth century, nearly causing the mining industry to collapse. Power shifted away from mining elites, dominant in political life for centuries, toward a landed aristocracy. As land became more valuable, the government confiscated Church-owned lands, selling or renting them on behalf of the state. Then the government began to confiscate communal lands—some cultivated by Indian communities since before the conquest—forcing Indian residents to purchase individual plots and destroying part of the foundation of Indian society. Mariano Melgarejo, a caudillo who ruled from 1864 to 1871, abrogated land titles of more than 100,000 peasants, about 10 percent of the population of Bolivia. Grievances resulting from these policies would reawaken during the revolution of 1952.

Within a few decades after independence Bolivia had lost half of its territory to more powerful neighbors: Brazil, Argentina, Chile, Peru, and, later, Paraguay. In 1867 Melgarejo ceded territory to Brazil for questionable commercial advantages. A war with Brazil in 1903 resulted in further losses. In 1879 Chile occupied Bolivia's small coastal strip on the Pacific Ocean between Peru and Chile. With support from Peru, Bolivia declared war. In 1884 a truce was declared, and in 1904 Bolivia formally ceded the territory to Chile. Bolivia has been landlocked ever since.

Bolivia's economy revived during the 1870s with the discovery of huge tin deposits near the old silver mines. Tin prices remained high on world markets for several decades, generating revenues that helped modernize the country. Three railroad lines were built, connecting Bolivia with the rest of the world for the first time. Foreign investors were invited. New highways integrated large areas of the country, and a new era of prosperity set in.

With the economy finally generating surpluses, Bolivians began to debate alternative roles for government. Traditional silver mining interests and large landowners, geographically centered in Potosí and Sucre, formed the base of the Conservative Party, which advocated development of transportation networks and encroachment of large haciendas onto traditionally Indian communities. These latter policies resulted in Indian uprisings and the migration of Indians to mining and urban areas, where they encountered ethnic discrimination. Tin mining entrepreneurs were centered near La Paz, and formed the base of the Liberal Party, advocating a stronger military and better international ties. As revenues in the tin industry soared, the balance of power shifted to the Liberal Party. Liberal governments moved the capital city from Sucre to La Paz, although they left the national judiciary in Sucre. The Republican Party was formed in 1914, representing the growing middle classes in urban areas. In the 1920s socialist parties began to appear. In short, economic growth produced competing interests, upsetting the traditional balance of political power held by the tiny elite representing landowners and mine owners.

Although the tin mining industry dominated much of the economy, its structure left the tin barons vulnerable to these new social forces. By the early 1920s three families—Patiño, Hochschild, and Aramayo—had driven out smaller enterprises and owned the vast proportion of the tin industry. However, the complexities inherent in the organization of the tin industry required that the three families hire hundreds of middle-class overseers and create strong relationships with government officials and foreigners. When Simón Patiño, who owned more than half of the tin mines of Bolivia, and his family left Bolivia in the early 1920s to live in Europe, his estate was left in the hands of managers who did not always share his interests. One of Patiño's accountants, Víctor Paz Estenssoro, would later nationalize the tin mines and lead one of the few social revolutions in Latin American history.

The Chaco War

A dispute between Bolivia and Paraguay led to a protracted war between the two countries. The Chaco, a deserted area the size of Colorado, was believed to contain important oil deposits, and the boundary lines within the Chaco between Paraguay and Bolivia were contested. Bolivian president Daniel Salamanca, representing a conservative coalition of the Liberal and Republican parties, began building a powerful army, paying for it by cutting government services. During a border dispute in 1932 Salamanca ordered troops to invade Paraguay. The Paraguayan armed forces put up a spirited defense, inflicted many casualties, and eventually entered Bolivian territory in a rout of the Bolivian army. A peace treaty was signed in 1935, in which Bolivian territory in the Chaco was ceded to Paraguay.

Several groups in Bolivia were embittered by this experience. Military officers were outraged that a civilian president had instigated an unwinnable war with an unprepared military. For the next two decades military officers ruled the country. Moreover, the war had mobilized 10 percent of the population of Bolivia, including Indian peasants and tin miners. The segregation of the army into castes—white officers, mestizo noncommissioned officers, and Indian frontline soldiers—led to obvious inequalities in casualty rates, raising ethnic consciousness among Indians. Finally intellectuals, labor union activists, and disaffected urban groups, frustrated by their inability to help set the national agenda, saw in the defeat an opportunity to play a stronger role in the political life of the country. The loss of the Chaco War helped unify middle and lower class groups and served to discredit the traditional political parties responsible for the war.

From the end of the Chaco War in 1935 until 1939, young military officers undermined the conservative political system that had ruled Bolivia since the 1880s. Standard Oil Company was nationalized without compensation, the first such confiscation in Latin American history. A constitutional convention in 1938 created an activist state for the first time, approving a far-reaching labor code favorable to the laboring classes. Large mining concerns were required to turn over their foreign exchange to the national bank, enabling the government to tax them more effectively. During this period various middle-sector groups, including the armed forces, strengthened the power of the state at the expense of conservative upper classes. But they were unable to consolidate reform or establish a ruling coalition.

THE RISE OF THE MNR AND THE BOLIVIAN REVOLUTION OF 1952

With the weakening of the traditional parties after the Chaco War, several new political parties appeared. The most talented leadership came from the National Revolutionary Movement (MNR), led by Víctor Paz Estenssoro. The MNR openly advocated nationalizing the tin mines and granting stronger rights to workers. When conservative parties tried to regroup in the early 1940s behind the government of General Enrique Peñaranda, the MNR conspired with sympathetic officers in the armed forces, overthrew the government, and backed a military government headed by Major Gualberto Villarroel. Villarroel, however, was unable to control conservative opposition, demands from the left, and conspiracies against him from the armed forces and sectors of the MNR. In 1946 he was attacked by a mob of students, teachers, and workers who marched on the palace of government, killed him, and hanged his body from a lamppost. Traditional conservative parties regained power and exiled MNR leaders, while struggling to manage an ailing economy hurt by deteriorating tin prices, high inflation, labor unrest, and stagnant agricultural production. Presidential elections were held in 1951, and Paz Estenssoro received the highest number of votes. But the armed forces prevented the MNR from taking power; a year later the MNR received assistance from a faction within the armed forces. The MNR seized arsenals and distributed arms to supporters. Miners marched on La Paz, blocking loyalist troops from reaching the city. The army finally surrendered and Paz Estenssoro became president of Bolivia.

Once he was in power, Paz acted quickly. During the revolt Indians had overtaken many haciendas and distributed the land among themselves, and tin miners had occupied the tin mines. Now the MNR formalized the takeovers and granted Indians full citizenship rights for the first time since the conquest. Peasants were allowed to keep their arms, and an agrarian reform law expropriated large, unproductive estates for distribution to peasants. Tin miners organized themselves into a powerful new labor federation (COB), and the armed forces were purged of officers associated with previous conservative governments. Finally, the MNR nation-alized the tin mines of the three major families, creating a state-owned monopoly to administer the sale of all minerals.

At the head of a successful, extremely popular social movement—composed of miners, peasants, government workers and other urban middle class groups—that had endowed the government with extraordinary power, Paz Estenssoro began preparing for long-term rule. A pact was forged among the top four leaders to ro-tate their candidacies for president under the MNR party for sixteen years until 1968. Paz would serve a term from 1952 to 1956. He would be followed by Hernán Siles Suazo (who ran for vice president with Paz in 1951) from 1956 to 1960. Siles would be followed by Wálter Guevara Arce, another leader of the MNR, until 1964, when mineworker organizer Juan Lechín would become the candidate. Dissolution of the pact would drive a wedge within the MNR, permit-ting conservative forces to rise again.

Siles Suazo indeed followed Paz as the presidential candidate in 1956. He was elected and served out his term, consolidating the reform program of the MNR. But in 1960 Paz intervened to block the agreed-upon candidacy of Wálter Guevara in favor of his own. Paz became president again, splitting the MNR. In office, Paz acted swiftly to strengthen the armed forces, badly weakened under President Siles and increasingly allied with conservatives. Then, as the 1964 presidential elections approached, Paz used his influence to amend the constitution to permit him to run for yet another term in office. In this effort he was assisted by elements of the US government as well as the armed forces, both concerned that Juan Lechín, a Trot-skyite, might come to power. In return for their support, however, the armed forces insisted that the vice presidential candidate would be a member of the military.

Paz was duly elected under these circumstances. But a few months later the armed forces overthrew him, allowing Vice President (General) René Barrientos to become president. Barrientos, a truly popular leader who tried to create a multiclass power base of his own, was killed three years later in a helicopter incident. A suc-cession of military governments followed. The most unusual was the regime of General Juan José Torres, who allowed students and labor union activists to form a Popular Assembly, which elected Juan Lechín as its president and began passing leg-islation. Another general, Hugo Banzer, ousted Torres from office in less than a year. Banzer forged a power base that included a conservative newly emerging elite from Santa Cruz in the east, as well as conservative sectors throughout the country.

Under pressure from the US Carter administration to hold elections after years of dictatorship, Bolivia had some difficulty reestablishing constitutional rule. In elec-tions scheduled for 1978, former president Siles Suazo ran in a contest that also in-cluded General Juan Pereda Asbún, favored by President Banzer. The tally eventually found that neither had received a majority of votes, throwing the election to the legislature. Siles apparently counted on enough votes, but before congress could meet, Pereda staged a coup and assumed dictatorial powers. He was ousted a few months later by General David Padilla. New elections were scheduled in 1979.

The major candidates this time were former presidents Siles and Paz. Again nei-ther candidate received enough votes to win outright, throwing the election to the legislature, which then wrestled over the issue for days. It finally selected Wálter Guevara Arce, who had been betrayed by Paz in 1960 and was now president of

the Senate. Guevara had not been a candidate in the 1979 elections and the constitutionality of his selection is still disputed. His election, however, was widely
viewed as an effort to correct an injustice committed two decades earlier. Guevara
was overthrown a few months later by General Alberto Natusch Busch, who had
known connections to international cocaine traffickers. Facing strong opposition,
Natusch stepped down. The legislature was reconvened to select a new president.
Lydia Gueiler, the first woman president of Bolivia, was chosen interim president
until new elections could be held.

In 1980 Paz and Siles ran against each other again. Siles won a plurality of votes,
but once again not enough. Before the legislature could convene to settle the issue,
General Luís García Meza toppled the government. Connected to drug trafficking,
he was ousted after a year and later convicted of corruption and sentenced to jail.
In 1982 the legislature reconvened and selected Siles president. Of the four MNR
leaders who in 1952 agreed to alternate their candidacies, three eventually became
president; all were deposed at one time or another, and all remained active through
the 1980s. The fourth, Juan Lechín, remained an outsider; but as undisputed
leader of the labor movement, he was a force to be reckoned with until he retired
in the late 1980s.

Bolivia from 1982 to 2005

After the armed forces were removed from power in 1982, constitutionally
elected governments struggled to balance the conflicting demands of the nation's
organized interest groups in a reasonably equitable manner—the normal task of
government—while on the other hand struggling to satisfy the doctrinal demands
for neoliberal reform from agents of the international system. The two projects
were not compatible, and the neoliberal faction was predominant until 2005. During this period Bolivian governments, encouraged by US support, opted to accept
neoliberal reforms, altering the domestic balance of power among the various actors (e.g., trade unions, peasant groups, teachers, business groups, etc.) that
emerged from the revolution of 1952, often in favor of small, well-connected
groups of Bolivians allied with wealthy international partners. Since the electoral
constituency for neoliberalism was small, politicians often adopted anti-neoliberal
slogans at election time. After elections the honest broker, conflict-resolving function of government was deeply compromised, with widespread corruption at the
highest levels of the political class. These patterns surfaced under the governing
watch of the same party, the MNR, that spearheaded the revolution of 1952,
heightening the people's sense of betrayal.

President Siles Suazo tried governing in the traditional post-1952 style, from
1982 to 1985. His government secured loans from the International Monetary
Fund (IMF) to service heavy foreign debts incurred during the military regimes
of the 1970s. Since the debt repayment schedule amounted to 70 percent of export earnings, Siles faced painful decisions about which government programs to
cut to pay for the debt service. Relying on a well-established fiscal pattern in Bolivia under such circumstances, he tried to temporize by granting concessions to
many groups, setting off an inflationary spiral—nothing new in Bolivian history—
escalating to well over 10,000 percent in early 1985. This angered IMF officials

and provoked a political crisis that led to Siles's resignation later that year. Subsequent presidents were more careful to adhere to the discipline advocated by the IMF, but they did so at the cost of popular support.

In one of the great ironies of Bolivian history, Víctor Paz Estenssoro took the first major steps toward undermining the social compact that he, more than any single figure, had galvanized during the revolution of 1952. Immediately after being elected president for the fourth time in 1985, he introduced the neoliberal model to Bolivia: rapid privatization of government corporations, reduction in state subsidies, a diminished role for government in social investments such as education, health care, and welfare. He resolved the immediate economic crisis with a mixture of economic austerity, severe repression of labor, and martial law. At one point, when debt service payments equaled 84 percent of the value of exports, his government virtually stopped spending on social programs altogether. During his tenure in office expenditures on education dropped from nearly 20 percent of the national budget to less than 10 percent. Illiteracy and infant mortality rose significantly as social spending dropped. These policies stabilized the economy, satisfying potential foreign investors, but alienated the major protagonists of the 1952 revolution: peasant organizations, tin miners, labor unions, and the poor in general. Paz Estenssoro's stature as founder of the MNR and leader of the 1952 revolution enabled him to enact these reforms without serious civil strife. Subsequent governments were not so fortunate.

Paz Estenssoro's nephew, Jaime Paz Zamora, was elected president in 1989 after promising to reverse the direction of his uncle's policies. Once in office, however, his party formed an alliance with General Banzer's Acción Democrática Nacionalista (ADN), a right-wing, pro-business party, agreeing to share cabinet positions and to continue neoliberal policies. In 1993 the MNR selected Gonzalo Sánchez de Lozada, one of the primary architects of Bolivian neoliberal reform, as its candidate for president. Sánchez had grown up in the United States, had a degree from the University of Chicago, and spoke Spanish with a strong American accent. Within weeks after being elected president Sánchez announced he would sell 49 percent of the government-owned oil company to private interests and transfer the tin mining industry to the private sector. Foreign investors would be given access to 49 percent ownership in state-owned airline, railroad, and electric power facilities, allowing foreign firms to assume managerial control over these firms. These measures passed through the legislature with little opposition. Severe employment cutbacks within these industries weakened the trade union movement, formerly the core of the MNR, and raised the unemployment rate. Pressures within the political system began to build.

COCA PLANTATIONS AND THE RISE OF MAS

In Bolivia 12,000 hectares of coca is planted legally in the Yungas region north of La Paz, to satisfy the local demand generated by indigenous groups who have consumed coca leaves for centuries. However, as demand for cocaine escalated in the United States during the 1980s, illegal cultivation of coca rose dramatically in the Chapare region, where up to 35,000 hectares of coca were harvested for conversion to cocaine. Illegal coca plantations in the 1990s provided a livelihood for over

70,000 peasant families, some of whom had migrated to the Chapare after the collapse of the tin industry in the 1980s. Up to 10 percent of the gross domestic income of Bolivia derived from coca production, and as many as 300,000 peasants—8 to 10 percent of the national workforce—depended on coca production in the Chapare. Facing extraordinary pressure from the US embassy, which insisted on eradication of illegal coca plantations as a condition of further assistance, Bolivian governments agreed to initiate a program of crop substitution combined with coca crop destruction. From 1995 to 2001 Bolivian antinarcotics operations, assisted by the US government, destroyed about 70 percent of the country's illegal coca plantations, by far the most effective antidrug effort in the Western Hemisphere. But as in the case of neoliberal reform, cooperation with the United States damaged relations between the Bolivian government and large sectors of the population.

In the early 1990s coca producers began to organize. A talented young coca producer, Evo Morales, organized a confederation of six growers' associations representing over 35,000 producers. He also organized the Movement Toward Socialism (MAS), a political party, and ran for congress. Morales led strikes and demonstrations against US drug policy. He was jailed repeatedly. He was elected to congress and then expelled from congress. But MAS, allied with other groups opposing neoliberal policies and advocating a return to national control over natural resources, kept gaining popularity. In 2003 he ran for president, coming in a close second, in spite of (or perhaps because of) public warnings from the US ambassador to Bolivia that his election would seriously jeopardize continued US assistance.

In 1995 teachers, health workers, and public utilities employees organized dozens of work stoppages demanding higher salaries, protesting privatization policies, and protesting the coca eradication program. President Sánchez suspended constitutional rights, imposed a nighttime curfew, and allowed the government to hold people without trial. In 1996 protests broke out against an agrarian reform bill approved by congress, apparently reneging on promises made to various agrarian constituent groups. Opposition to the bill included peasants, coca growers, labor unions, tenant farmers, and agribusiness leaders.

In 1997 former dictator Hugo Banzer was elected president, promising to "humanize" the face of neoliberalism on behalf of a conservative party, and Evo Morales was elected to the national congress. Under pressure from the US government, Banzer made coca eradication a centerpiece of his administration. Three thousand troops were sent into the Chapare to conduct military operations. They destroyed the livelihoods of thousands of peasants in a failed effort to reduce the availability of cocaine in US markets 3,000 miles away. Meanwhile, several scandals broke out implicating high-level government officials in large-scale drug trafficking activities. In one case a cargo plane loaded with four tons of cocaine was seized in Peru, part of a drug enterprise run in Bolivia and protected by officials at all levels. Former presidents Jaime Paz Zamora and Víctor Paz Estenssoro were accused of accepting large quantities of campaign contributions from Bolivian drug dealers. By 2003 the US State Department was reporting that coca cultivation in Bolivia had increased 23 percent, despite destruction of 12,000 hectares in 2002.

The Cochabamba Water War, the Bolivian Gas War, and the Election of Evo Morales

In the late 1990s, World Bank officials pressured Bolivian government officials to privatize the water utility of Cochabamba, Bolivia's third largest city, with a population then of 600,000. In 1999 Bolivian officials, in secrecy and with no bidding process, leased the Cochabamba water utility company to Aguas de Tunari, a subsidiary of Bechtel Corporation, a large multinational engineering company. The contract guaranteed Bechtel a profit of 16 percent each year for forty years. Shortly after Aguas de Tunari took over the utility in January 2000, it announced water rate hikes of up to 200 percent, raising the effective rate to about $10–$20 per month per household, in a city where the minimum wage was $60 per month. Almost immediately large-scale demonstrations formed in protest and the city was paralyzed from January to April. Violent confrontations with authorities led to the declaration of a state of siege, as government officials negotiated with organizers of the revolt.

In one of his first nationally covered moves, Evo Morales, now a congressman, joined the demonstrations, showing solidarity with the protesters and demanding an end to the US-sponsored coca plantation eradication program. Government officials argued his presence meant that the protesters were part of a conspiracy financed by cocaine traffickers carrying out subversive activities. The government finally announced that the contract had been rescinded and that Bechtel had left Bolivia. Water rates were rolled back to where they had been before the contract, and the water system was not improved. But most residents of Cochabamba were grateful for the congressman from the Chapare who had joined their cause.

A few months later the country was paralyzed by demonstrations, strikes, and roadblocks—the worst social unrest in two decades—when students, teachers, peasant organizations, and coca growers, again led by Morales, began protesting low teachers' wages, government agrarian policies, and the military campaign to eradicate coca plants in the Chapare. The month-long protests ended in October when the government negotiated an end to the strikes, which caused widespread food shortages in several cities. In 2002 Gonzalo Sánchez de Lozada, of the MNR, was again elected president, forming a coalition government with the MIR, headed by former president Jaime Paz Zamora. But by this time the MAS, headed by Evo Morales, was the second largest political organization in the country. Morales immediately challenged Sanchez's policies, including Bolivia's participation in the Free Trade Area of the Americas, financial deals made to export Bolivian natural gas, the continued eradication of coca fields, and the neoliberal project that had come to be identified with Sánchez. For the next three years groups that had been left out of the neoliberal project of the previous two decades—peasant organizations, trade unions, small-scale farmers, and the unaffiliated poor—took to the streets to demonstrate their displeasure with the neoliberal project and its partners.

In January 2003, more than twenty persons died in clashes between the government and coca growers, joined by Bolivia's largest labor confederation, headed by Aymara leader Felipe Quispe. In February more than thirty persons died in protests during a police strike for higher wages. Police were supported by many groups, including the Confederation of Private Business, upset by a government plan, under IMF pressure, to impose an income tax for the first time. In June opposition legislators went on a hunger strike to force the government to debate key bills dealing with land rights and agricultural subsidies, and miners blocked major highways demanding government support to reactivate the mining industry. In July, landless peasants began seizing haciendas in various parts of the country and demanding land. Soldiers evicted peasants from occupied estates.

In September protests broke out against plans to export natural gas to Chile. Bolivia has the second largest natural gas reserve in Latin America and the government had reached an agreement with Pacific LNG, an international consortium, to invest $6 billion in a pipeline to the Pacific coast for export to Mexico and the United States. Opposition groups demanded that 250,000 Bolivian homes be supplied with gas before permitting any exports, and strongly objected when Pacific LNG insisted on building the pipeline to Chile, instead of Peru. Many Bolivians still resent Chile for taking away Bolivia's access to the sea in 1884. Evo Morales and MAS organized an umbrella coordinating committee, incorporating dozens of peasant and trade unions, and insisted that the government receive 50 percent of gas royalties rather than the 18 percent paid by foreign companies. After clashes in October had killed another thirty persons, Sánchez resigned and fled to the United States.

His successor, Vice President Carlos Mesa, tried to defuse the violence by decreeing a referendum on the gas deal, but by this time many were calling for the complete nationalization of hydrocarbons. The referendum, held in July 2004, only presented the option of the state recovering ownership *after* gas arrived from underground to the wellhead, an option that received 92 percent support. Protests continued and Mesa tendered his resignation to Congress in March 2005. This move was seen as cynical, since the line of succession would have elevated the president of the senate to the presidency, a man widely believed to have been corrupted repeatedly by foreign interests seeking government support. The legislature refused to accept the resignation. Protests continued, taking on increasingly racial overtones, as indigenous leaders in El Alto, above La Paz, blocked access from the airport to La Paz at a strategic choke point called *la ceja del Alto* (the eyebrow of El Alto). Legislative leaders agreed to step down as potential replacements for Mesa, the armed forces threatened action, and Mesa resigned in June, leaving Supreme Court Judge Eduardo Rodríguez as a caretaker president. Elections were held in December, two years early, and Evo Morales became the first president in many decades elected on the first ballot, receiving 54 percent of the vote.

EVO MORALES AS PRESIDENT

MAS is a socialist political party, firmly nationalist, with strong indigenous roots, uniting many disparate factions that had been left out of the neoliberal project of the previous quarter century. One of the most talented politicians in Latin America, Evo Morales, came to embody the massive public rejection of a political class which, under the banner of neoliberalism, had captured power only to sell off, often for private gain, the country's patrimony to foreign interests at discount prices. He also represents a rejection of the heavy-handed US counternarcotics policy and global institutions like the IMF and the World Bank, which in recent decades have imposed neoliberal doctrines as a condition for assistance.

Once in office Morales quickly acted to decapitate the armed forces, choosing top leaders from the ranks of persons loyal to him. He nationalized all reserves of natural gas on May 1, 2006, giving foreign companies six months to renegotiate contracts for exploitation or lose them altogether. This measure was hugely popular throughout the country.

Elections for a Constitutional Assembly were held in July 2006 and delegates began deliberating in August. In December 2007 the national assembly ratified the constitution with the required two thirds majority vote. The new document strengthened indigenous rights and provided greater autonomy for the nine departments and all municipalities. Areas governed by indigenous people were allowed to incorporate traditional, community-based forms of local justice.

The Morales government was exceptionally fortunate during its first term in office to benefit from a rapidly expanding economy, driven by rising prices for silver, natural gas, zinc, and tin. Exports rose from about 30 percent of GDP to over 40 percent of GDP from 2005 to 2008. After the government nationalized hydrocarbon industries in 2006, government revenues increased dramatically, up to nearly 50 percent of GDP, enabling the government to increase spending; the government, however, was fiscally conservative, accumulating surpluses. Bolivia's economic growth during Morales's first term averaged over 5 percent per year, including 2009, the latter year in spite of declining remittances from abroad, the revocation of favored trade status by the United States, declining export prices, and a worldwide recession.

In part because of a strong economy, the government was able to increase spending on social programs for the poor. One program provides a small stipend to children as an incentive to continue education through sixth grade, another provides grants to impoverished elderly citizens, and another provides funds to mothers for prenatal care. The government has also considered strengthening traditional communities, called *ayllus*, by extending them neighborhood governance privileges. In urban indigenous areas like El Alto, indigenous families coming from rural areas frequently live in closely-knit neighborhoods composed largely of *ayllu* members from the original community. Government services will flow to these communities through local, *ayllu*-organized governance structures, reinforcing ethnic bonds and ethnic-government relations.

In his foreign policy Morales distanced himself during his first term from the US government, at first curtailing and then expelling the large DEA mission in Bolivia, and improving relations with Venezuela, whose president, Hugo Chávez, had led a Latin American movement to challenge US foreign policy. Venezuela offered to buy textiles from Bolivia equivalent to twice the exports of Bolivia to the United States when the latter retaliated against the DEA expulsion by dropping preferential tariff treatment for Bolivia. Bolivia also strengthened relations with Libya, Iran, and Russia, countries not always friendly with the United States. In 2008 Morales declared Ambassador Philip Goldberg persona non grata, expelling him from Bolivia after finding out Goldberg had attended a secret meeting with an opposition leader.

Opposition to the Morales government is organized geographically in the Amazon areas of Bolivia. As demographic and political changes have isolated relatively wealthy, white minority groups in these regions, especially Santa Cruz, Tarija, and

Beni, leaders have called for greater autonomy in a region called the Media Luna (half moon). Much of the nation's gas reserves are found in these provinces, and local populations would like more of the tax revenues to remain in the region. A separatist movement led by right-wing groups such as the Nación Camba and the Unión Juvenil Crucenista have at times seemed racially motivated and resorted to violence. In the elections of 2009, however, MAS mobilized significant support in these departments, reducing its losses, and Morales has been willing to reach out to political leaders, listening to their grievances.

It is not surprising that Morales was extremely popular in his first term, given the pent-up frustration of millions of Bolivians with neoliberal politics, the exceptionally strong economic performance of the economy, and his own talented, charismatic, and pragmatic leadership. Whether the government can consolidate the coalition of forces supporting it into a more permanent social contract will depend on the country's economic fortunes in the next few years, the quality of government management, and the willingness of the outside world to allow Bolivia, one of the poorest countries in the hemisphere, to go its own way.

SUGGESTED READINGS

García Linera, Alvaro. *Sociología de los movimientos sociales en Bolivia: Estructuras de movilización, repertorios culturales, y acción política*. Oxfam, 2004. The author is currently vice president of Bolivia.

Good, Peter. *Bolivia: Between a Rock and a Hard Place*. Plural Editores, 2006.

Hylton, Forest, and Sinclair Thomson, *Revolutionary Horizons: Past and Present in Bolivian Politics*. Verso, 2007.

Klein, Herbert S. *Bolivia: A Concise History.* Cambridge University Press, 2003.

Lazarte Rojas, Jorge. *Entre los espectros del pasado y las incertidumbres del futuro: Política y democracia en Bolivia a principios del siglo XXI*. Friedrich Ebert Stiftung, 2005.

Marcy, William L. *The Politics of Cocaine: How U.S. Foreign Policy Has Created a Thriving Drug Industry in Central and South America*. Lawrence Hill, 2010.

Munoz-Pogossian, Betilde. *Electoral Rules and the Transformation of Bolivian Politics: The Rise of Evo Morales*. Palgrave Macmillan, 2008.

Olivera, Oscar, and Tom Lewis. *Cochabamba: Water Rebellion in Bolivia*. South End Press, 2008.

Weisbrot, Mark, Rebecca Ray, and Jake Johnston. "Bolivia: The Economy During the Morales Administration," December 2009. www.cepr.net/documents/publications/bolivia-2009–12.pdf.

PART IX

BRAZIL AND THE SOUTHERN CONE

Chapter 25

BRAZIL

From Military Regime to Workers' Party Government

DAVID FLEISCHER

"I WAS DREAMING THE wrong dream!" With these words, on October 14, 2003, Rio de Janeiro deputy Fernando Gabeira highlighted his disengagement from the Workers' Party (PT).[1] Considered an icon of the Brazilian left, Gabeira participated in the kidnapping of US ambassador Charles Elbrick in August 1969 that permitted the ransom of fifteen political prisoners, including José Dirceu, who became President Lula's all-powerful chief of staff in January 2003. Calling the new PT government "Fernando Henrique Cardoso's third term," Gabeira voiced the disappointment of many Brazilians with the conservative, neoliberal policies pursued by the new PT government elected in October 2002, after twenty-two years of political and electoral struggles against the last military government and its four successors.

What happened to Brazil in this forty-year period from 1964 to 2003? After twenty-one years of military rule, a civilian president was "elected" indirectly by the Electoral College in January 1985. On the eve of his inauguration on March 15, president-elect Tancredo Neves was stricken with an intestinal disorder, hospitalized, operated on five times in Brasília and São Paulo, and finally died on April 21. His vice president, José Sarney, who had been until June 1984 the president of the Social Democratic Party (PDS), which supported the military government, became president for the five-year term until March 1990. In essence, this was the first "dream gone wrong." Brazil's final transition from the military regime was in the hands of a former governor and senator who had been allied with the military government and governed under close tutelage by the military.

TWO BRAZILS: "BELINDIA"

Brazil has often been portrayed and characterized as a nation existing on two levels—the "two Brazils"—where an incredibly rich, developed, educated, and very small minority managed to dominate the poor majority, many living on a subsistence level, passive, semieducated, unorganized, leaderless. This duality was first described by two French sociologists in the late 1950s—Roger Bastide's "contrasts" and Jacques Lambert's "archaic" and "modern" Brazil.[2] Economist Edmar Bacha characterized this dualism as a "Belindia" (Belgium versus India).[3] Two Brazils sharply cut into various dichotomies: rural and urban, social and cultural environments, industrial and agrarian economies, coast and hinterland, plains and rain forests. The growing gap between the rich and the poor (less than 10 percent of the population currently owns 50 percent of the national wealth) and conflicting demands for material modernization and social change that weak formal political institutions were unable to mediate led to an impasse in the early 1960s. The consequent demand for "order" against the "chaos" deriving from incipient social mobilization paved the way for the civilian-military coup of 1964.

Considerable change has occurred in Brazil's regional contrasts in recent years. In terms of the so-called rich families (monthly income over BRL22,487, approximately US$7,500) in 2000, 1,162,164 such families were encountered. They constituted 2.4 percent of all families (58 percent of them in São Paulo), concentrating 33 percent of national income, and wealth equivalent to 45.85 percent of Brazil's GDP. In 1980 rich families were only 1.8 percent of the total.[4] The differences indicate that Brazil's wealth is no longer generated by production and labor, but by a "financialization" of the economy. In 2000 the average income of rich families was fourteen times the national average compared to ten times in 1980. In this twenty-year period, the proportion of rich families in São Paulo increased by 102.9 percent, by 78.4 percent in Piauí and 17.9 percent in Ceará; the proportion declined by 14.2 percent in Pará and by 28.8 percent in Bahia.

In terms of quality of life, Brazil scored 0.775 on the Human Development Index (HDI) elaborated by UNDP in 2004 and was ranked 72nd out of 177 nations: 62nd rank on education (0.88), 111th rank on life expectancy (0.72), and 63rd rank on income (0.73). In 1990, Brazil was in 71st rank (0.712) and in 1975 in 81st rank (0.643) on the HDI scale. In terms of income distribution, however, Brazil was ranked "the 4th worst" worldwide—only better than Namibia, Lesotho, and Sierra Leone. In Brazil, the 10 percent richest segment had 46.7 percent of national income while the 10 percent poorest had only 0.5 percent (a differential of 85 times). This was worse than in the 2003 HDI, where the differential for Brazil was 65.8 with the 9th worst income distribution. In Namibia, the difference was 128.8 times. Brazil's Gini index for income distribution was 0.591 and that of Namibia was 0.707. In contrast, Brazil is the 5th largest nation (slightly larger than the continental United States) and 5th in population with the 15th largest GDP, but is ranked 63rd in terms of per capita income.

THE 1964 COUP AND THE TWENTY-ONE-YEAR MILITARY REGIME

After achieving independence from Portugal in 1822, Brazil evolved into a constitutional monarchy with the son of the Portuguese king (Dom João VI), Dom Pedro I, as emperor. After a brief regency, Dom Pedro II ruled Brazil from 1840 until he was toppled in 1889 when a republic was installed, with two successive general presidents until 1894 when a civilian president was elected. This first republic, based on coffee exports and dominated politically by the two largest states (São Paulo and Minas Gerais), which alternated the presidency during much of this thirty-five-year period, continued until the 1930 revolution. After the period of centralized empire, the new political system was more decentralized, with considerable autonomy for the states.

The 1920s produced great social and economic turmoil with growth of the main urban centers, large volumes of immigrants (especially from Italy and Spain), incipient industrialization, two military rebellions in 1922 and 1924, a long march led by army captain Luís Carlos Prestes that crisscrossed the nation in an attempt to stir resistance to the regime. Finally in the 1930 election São Paulo broke the "alternation" agreement (with Minas Gerais) and proceeded to elect a second consecutive president from that state.

In October 1930, discontent with this situation and fearing that "we must make the revolution [from above] before the people do," the governors of Minas Gerais and Rio Grande do Sul organized a revolt that ended the decadent oligarchic system and installed Getúlio Vargas as "provisional" president. Except for a brief democratic interim (1934–1937), Vargas ruled as a dictator until the military removed him from power in November 1945, one month prior to general elections. This fifteen-year Vargas period was marked by modernization, political centralization, industrialization, and Brazilian participation in World War II in support of the Allies in the Italian campaign (1943–1945).

The 1946 constitution instituted a liberal, multiparty democracy with moderate autonomy for the states. Vargas returned to the presidency by direct election in 1950, but was again removed by the military in August 1954. Vargas then committed suicide, becoming a martyr and symbol for his Brazilian Labor Party (PTB) of the struggle of Brazilian workers against economic oppression.

In November 1955, the PSD governor of Minas Gerais, Juscelino Kubitschek, was elected by a simple majority, threatened by a military coup, and took office in January 1956 following a three-month state of siege. Most thought that he would not complete his five-year term. However, Kubitschek proceeded to mobilize Brazilians for "fifty years of progress in five," built the new interior capital city of Brasília, spurred industrial growth, expanded the country's highway and electric power infrastructure, and pushed Brazil into the twentieth century.

Kubitschek's successor, Jânio Quadros, took office in January 1961, stressing austerity. He condemned the irresponsible spending of his predecessor, visited Cuba, decorated Ernesto Ché Guevara, and instituted a new independent foreign policy. Seven months later, constrained by a minority in congress, Quadros abruptly resigned. Part of the military then attempted to impede Vice President João Goulart (PTB), considered a Vargas protégé, from acceding to the presidency. The military was divided, and with the threat of a civil war, congress devised a solution by installing a parliamentary regime. Goulart was allowed to become president, with reduced powers, in September 1961.

The first parliamentary cabinet, with Tancredo Neves (PSD) as prime minister, was quite successful until it had to step down four months before the October 1962 elections. Goulart then appointed a series of weak prime ministers, and in late 1962 congress authorized a national plebiscite for January 1963 that voted to end the short-lived parliamentary system and restore Goulart's presidential powers. The nation was undergoing considerable unrest caused by increased inflation, massive rural-urban migration, slowed economic growth, farm invasions by landless peasants, and successive labor and student strikes that frequently outpaced

Goulart's feeble attempts at achieving basic reforms—changes in land tenure, the banking system, university reform, and the political system. Regarding political reforms, progressives (especially in southern, more developed Brazil) proposed a one-man, one-vote system for Brazil to reduce the political weight of the underdeveloped, smaller, and more conservative states in the northeastern and northern regions. They also called for the enfranchisement of illiterates, state military police, and noncommissioned army officers.

While Brazil had undergone considerable political, social, and economic changes since 1930, it was still not a modern nation by twentieth-century standards. Although women had been enfranchised in 1932, illiterates were still prohibited from voting. In the 1962 elections, only about 25 percent of Brazil's population was registered to vote and some 70 percent of the population still lived in rural areas.

The 1962 elections had produced some renovation in congress, and the PTB and PSD each controlled about 28 percent of the 409 seats in the lower house. In 1961 and 1962, Goulart's brother-in-law, Governor Leonel Brizola, expropriated the foreign-owned electric power and telephone companies in their home state of Rio Grande do Sul. Brizola was elected federal deputy from the new state of Guanabara with the then largest vote total on record. The conservatives controlled a majority that blocked approval of Goulart's basic reforms, which required a two-thirds constitutional quorum.[5] As a result, in early 1964, President Goulart initiated some reforms by decree. When he appeared to be stimulating the unionization of army sergeants and other noncommissioned officers articulated with the CGT labor union central, in late March the armed forces led a coup that ousted Goulart and instituted the twenty-one-year military regime.[6]

The Brazilian military regime can be divided into four distinct periods: (1) the pseudo-constitutional interval from April 1964 to December 1968, when President Castelo Branco and President Costa e Silva governed under the aegis of the 1946 and 1966 constitutions but with some exceptional changes; (2) the descent into dictatorship with the AI-5 (Fifth Institutional Act) signed on December 13, 1968, that abolished all constitutional guarantees for ten years, covering the second part of the Costa e Silva presidency and the Médici period; (3) the presidency of Ernesto Geisel (1974–1979) that promoted controlled liberalization and reduced the powers of the military; and (4) the last military president, João Figueiredo (1979–1985), who processed the final political opening without the exceptional powers of the AI-5.

Differing from the military regimes of its South American neighbors (Argentina, Peru, Uruguay, and Chile), where the generals prohibited all political activities with short exceptional periods, the Brazilian armed forces maintained what President Geisel called "relative democracy"—regular elections for legislative office and local mayors (but with constant changes in the rules, and indirect elections for president and state governors). Political parties continued to function (but with two total realignments forced by the military), and the national congress remained open (but with reduced powers and prerogatives, and was closed three times).

After President João Goulart was removed by the military coup in late March 1964, the military high command issued the First Institutional Act (AI-1) that legitimated the intervention and imposed certain limits on civil liberties. This AI-1 also allowed the military to cancel elected mandates, remove civilians and military from the public service, and decree the loss of political rights for ten years. Congress was convened on April 11 to ratify the choice of General Humberto Castelo Branco and Deputy José Maria Alkmin as president and vice president. Many political leaders were purged and lost their political rights, including former presidents João Goulart, Jânio Quadros, and Juscelino Kubitschek. By the end of the AI-2 in 1966, sixty-seven deputies and two senators were stripped of their mandates and five governors were removed, in addition to hundreds of labor union leaders, professors, intellectuals, civil servants, and military officers.

The Castelo Branco presidency was marked by tension between hard-line and soft-line factions in the military. The former pressured for major surgery on Brazil's political system requiring a long period of military rule, while the latter envisioned a short intervention, minor plastic surgery, and a quick return to a civilian president after the October 1965 presidential elections. However, the prospects for such a quick transition became quite difficult, and eventually President Castelo decreed indirect elections for the next president and extended his own mandate until March 1967. However, he maintained the direct elections for governor in eleven states for October 1965 and promised that those elected would take office. Although conservative candidates performed well in these elections, two Kubitschek protégés were elected in the important states of Minas Gerais and Guanabara (city-state of Rio de Janeiro) and two days later JK returned from exile in Paris to savor this "victory." The negative reaction of the hard-line military officers was intense and the mobilization of army officers in Rio de Janeiro threatened to depose President Castelo Branco. The minister of war, General Arthur Costa e Silva, stepped in to calm the situation, extracted concessions from the president, avoided a coup, and consolidated his political position to be Castelo's successor in 1967. Those elected were allowed to take office, but the president decreed the end of the post-1945 multiparty system and established criteria for a new two-party system to be enacted for the 1966 elections.

In 1966 two new political parties were organized, the National Renovating Alliance (ARENA, pro-government) and Brazilian Democratic Movement (MDB, opposition). The rules required a minimum of 120 deputies and 20 senators to form a new party. Initially, the MDB could muster only eighteen senators, but President Castelo Branco convinced two ARENA-leaning senators to temporarily join the opposition party. Deputies from three major parties during the 1945–1964 period joined ARENA and MDB in distinct patterns. Those from the largely anti-Goulart UDN joined ARENA (84 out of 94), whereas those from Goulart's PTB mainly joined the MDB (75 out of 109). In a more even split, a majority from the conservative PSD joined ARENA (80 out of 124).[7] Castelo Branco had read the works of Maurice Duverger[8] and understood the connection between two-party systems and majority (district) election systems. The president instructed the TSE (National Election Court) to divide Brazil into 409 election districts for the 1966 elections, but later abandoned the idea after the ex-UDN politicians complained that this system would favor their arch rivals (ex-PSD deputies) in Brazil's vast interior regions.

By mid-1966, ARENA counted 260 deputies and MDB 148. On October 3, 1966, the state legislatures in the twelve states that had not held direct elections for governor in 1965 convened to select their respective "bionic" governors.[9] Direct elections were held for senator, state and federal deputies, mayors, and city councils on November 15. In view of the restrictions imposed by the regime, ARENA fared quite well at the polls and elected 276 deputies (67.5 percent) versus 133 for the MDB. ARENA achieved 47 members (71.2 percent) of the upper house. Thus the second military president, Arthur Costa e Silva, took office on March 15, 1967, with comfortable majorities in congress and a new constitution. The latter had been hastily elaborated by the lame duck congress in December 1966 and January 1967 under heavy tutelage from the outgoing Castelo Branco government.[10]

The Economic Miracle and Repression

The 1967 constitution left the new president without the most oppressive powers available to the regime in the 1964–1966 period. However, repression of public assembly, labor union strikes and articulations, student demonstrations, and so on, was frequent. Although the government support party (ARENA) enjoyed strong majorities, congress was now immune to summary removal of its members by the military government. As discontent increased, ARENA found it increasingly more difficult to approve government bills, especially in 1968.

Following a period of economic stagnation (1960–1964), the Castelo Branco government enacted public policies to curb inflation, reduce public deficits, and control labor's economic demands. That provoked a recession, with declining GDP and rising unemployment. In 1967 Costa e Silva's economic czar, finance minister Delfim Netto, enacted policies to stimulate consumer demand, new domestic and foreign investments, and incentives for Brazilian exports. These initiatives, together with a favorable international economic environment, produced the so-called economic miracle (1967–1973). During this "miracle" phase, average annual GDP growth was 11.1 percent, led by the industrial sector at 13.1 percent. Imports grew faster than exports to feed this economic expansion, but the resulting trade deficits were offset by large inflows of capital resulting in balance of payments surpluses.[11] The military government expropriated all electric power and telephone concessions, and quickly consolidated the latter into modern state enterprises—Eletrobrás and Telebrás.[12]

Labor and student unrest and protests against the authoritarian system swept Brazil in 1968, with the "March of 100,000 [students]" in Rio de Janeiro, and numerous strikes in São Paulo that were repressed by police. Similar student and labor protest movements erupted in Western Europe and the United States in the spring and summer of 1968. In August, police closed the state university in Belo Horizonte and invaded the University of Brasília, and censorship and repression increased dramatically. Urban guerrilla actions and bank robberies became very frequent and produced even more repression.

Just prior to Brazil's national Independence Day (September 7), an outspoken MDB deputy, Márcio Moreira Alves, delivered a fiery speech at the chamber of deputies on September 2. Alves exhorted Brazilians to "boycott militarism" and not attend the military parades on Independence Day. Furthermore, he urged young Brazilian women not to date military officers. The armed forces were outraged, claiming that their dignity had been offended. In reprisal, the Costa e Silva government demanded that the chamber suspend Deputy Moreira Alves's parliamentary immunity, so that he could be stripped of his mandate and prosecuted for this offense.

In early December, this political challenge to the military regime reached its climax. On December 11, the chamber of deputies Justice Committee (following the substitution of 9 ARENA deputies) reported in favor of Alves's removal. However, the following day, the full chamber rejected the request by a 216 to 141 vote (with some 90 nay votes from ARENA deputies). On December 13, the military government issued the AI-5 that closed congress until October 1969 and instituted ten years of full dictatorial discretionary powers. In the following months, ninety-four deputies (28 from ARENA) and four MDB senators were expelled from congress.

In 1969 the military government perpetrated new waves of purges, including many university professors, such as sociologist Fernando Henrique Cardoso from the University of São Paulo. Reportedly, President Costa e Silva had constituted a group of scholars and jurists to prepare a new constitution that would embody many of the regime's "exceptional rules" but restore a state of law to Brazil. Before this task could be completed, the president suffered a crippling stroke on August 27 and the three military ministers formed a junta to impede civilian vice president Pedro Aleixo from assuming the presidency. During this confusing interval, guerrillas kidnapped US Ambassador Charles Burke Elbrick in Rio de Janeiro on September 4 and demanded the release of fifteen political prisoners. The ransomed prisoners were flown to Mexico two days later.[13]

Finally, the army high command selected General Emílio Garrastazú Médici to succeed Costa e Silva, and on October 25 congress was reconvened to ratify this decision. The Médici government maintained harsh political repression while the economy boomed, and in 1970 imposed considerable changes on the election system. The chamber of deputies was reduced from 409 to 310 members, and state delegations became proportional to their respective electorates, rather than population. Proportionately, this measure increased the representation of the more developed states with large electorates (Minas Gerais and São Paulo), and reduced that of less developed states with smaller electorates. Pernambuco, for example, had its delegation reduced from twenty-four to fifteen deputies.[14]

The 1970 elections were held with harsh restrictions on the opposition MDB. Many candidates were not permitted to run; radio, TV, and press advertising was censored; many politicians had been purged; freedom of expression and assembly were reduced; and a general economic euphoria helped promote ARENA candidates. Brazil's victory in the World Soccer Cup in mid-1970 enhanced government support even more. The result was a near landslide victory for ARENA, and the MDB was reduced to eighty-six deputies (27.7 percent) and seven senators (10.6 percent). In 1971, some discouraged members of the opposition proposed the dissolution of the MDB.[15] The mayors and city councils elected in 1970 were given two-year mandates. This change was adopted to set municipal elections two years out of phase from the elections for congress and state legislatures. Two such elections were held in 1972 and 1976.

1974: Economic Downturn and Political Opening

By 1973, the economic miracle was waning, and the first petroleum shock imposed by OPEC after the Yom Kippur Arab-Israel conflict impacted heavily on Brazil because of its heavy dependence on imported oil. As a result, capital flows to Brazil declined and its balance of payments became negative. This situation caused the country to borrow heavily from international financial markets to maintain minimal economic growth. The economic legitimacy that had sustained the military regime since 1967 was eroding and needed a quick political fix.

Enter General Ernesto Geisel, a nationalist officer of German descent who began his career just prior to the 1930 revolution and participated in anti-Vargas military revolts in 1945 and 1954, as well as the movements against his successors in 1961 and 1964. He had been a close adviser to President Jânio Quadros and President Castelo Branco and had directed Petrobrás after 1967. His older brother, Orlando, was the outgoing army minister under President Médici.

Aided by the chief of staff, General Golbery do Couto e Silva, the Geisel presidency pursued three policy objectives: (1) maintaining economic growth with a deepening of industrialization; (2) managing a political opening or liberalization, paving the way for a return to civilian rule; and (3) reducing the power and influence of the military by reasserting the command powers of the presidency.[16] President Geisel still had the all-powerful AI-5 at his disposal to enforce his policy decisions.

In late 1973, Geisel had been challenged by an "anticandidate," Deputy Ulysses Guimarães (MDB-SP), who crisscrossed the country with his quixotic crusade and garnered 76 (15 percent) out of a total of 505 votes in the January 15, 1974, Electoral College. Two months later, Geisel was sworn as the fourth military president for a five-year term, through March 1979. Thus he became the only military president to oversee two general elections—in 1974 and 1978.

The first petroleum shock, of late 1973, was impacting strongly on Brazil in early 1974. Although exports remained strong, Brazil's terms of trade were drastically reduced. Capital flows declined, forcing an increase in foreign borrowing and consequently exploding current-account deficits. GDP growth remained relatively strong—6.9 percent on average from 1974 to 1980—but the current-account deficit rose from US$1.7 billion in 1973 to US$12.8 billion in 1980, and the foreign debt soared to US$54 billion by 1980. The rising foreign debt was sustained by an international financial market awash in petrodollars. This situation was further aggravated by the second oil shock and the interest rate shock in the late 1970s. Inflation also increased considerably—from 16.2 percent in 1973 to 110.2 percent in 1980—with salaries adjusted by monetary correction once a year, and biannually as of 1979. The economic miracle phase had ended, and the military regime was in need of an alternate source of legitimacy.

Geisel and Golbery sought to enhance legitimacy through a decompression, or political opening, with more or less unfettered elections in 1974. The MDB opposition party was allowed to select its candidates with little official coercion, and the campaign suffered few restrictions. Embratel (Brazil's long-lines telecommunications state enterprise) had completed the system of microwave TV transmissions that unified coverage in all states and nationwide, after the initial hookup was put in place just in time to cover Brazil's victory in the 1970 World Soccer Cup. Thus the "free" TV time made available to the parties by the TSE covered all states in the evening prime time period. Unlike the 1970 campaign, in 1974 the MDB (and ARENA) candidates had live access to TV campaigning, and in many states debates were organized between the senate candidates.

In most states, the MDB did not foresee a favorable election outcome and its traditional leaders avoided the "sacrifice" of running for the senate. For example, in São Paulo, deputies Franco Montoro and Ulysses Guimarães ran for reelection, while a young city council member, Orestes Quércia, became the party's senate candidate. In 1970 the opposition party had polled 28.6 percent of the national vote and elected only three senators, and thus MDB leaders were justifiably apprehensive.

However, Brazilian voters reacted quite differently in 1974 than in 1970. Although ARENA out-polled the MDB in votes for federal deputy (42.0 percent vs. 36.6 percent with 21.3 percent blank and null votes), the opposition achieved 50.1 percent of the vote for the twenty-two senate seats up for election and, more importantly, elected sixteen senators. From 19.5 percent of the total vote for federal deputy in 1970, the MDB amassed 36.6 percent in 1974 and advanced from 87 (28.1 percent) to 165 (45.3 percent) deputies, thus impeding the government from amending the constitution (at that point a two-thirds majority was required) in the 1975–1979 period.[17] The MDB also elected majorities to six state legislatures that in principle would allow the opposition party to indirectly elect the next governors in 1978.

Many of the new MDB senators were excellent orators so that in 1975 the senate galleries were packed with spectators (including many deputies) to observe the eloquent and fiery debates between ARENA and MDB senators. In 1975, the fanatical hard-liners in the armed forces began an insidious campaign against Geisel and Golbery, accusing them of favoring the left in the 1974 elections. In October, Geisel countered with what appeared to be a pendulum strategy and struck hard against the clandestine Brazilian Communist Party (PCB) in São Paulo. That month, journalist Vladimir Herzog was found dead in his cell at the infamous Sao Paulo Division of Intelligence (DOI) detention/torture center. Massive student demonstrations ensued with violent protest speeches in congress. In January 1976, labor union leader Manoel Fiel Filho was found dead in the same São Paulo DOI. With the death of Herzog, Geisel had extracted a promise from the army generals that such an incident would not be repeated, or else. The Fiel Filho repetition caused the president to immediately sack the commander of the II Army in São Paulo, General Ednardo D'Avila Mello, and many hard-line officers were retired or transferred to remote garrisons. Many of Geisel's advisers counseled the sacking of the minister of the army.

In an effort to stem what was perceived as a possible MDB tidal wave approaching with the 1976 municipal elections, the Geisel government enacted restrictions on TV propaganda that year as well as campaign activities. This resulted in modest gains for the MDB. In 1977 Geisel adjourned congress for two weeks and decreed the April Package, which modified the rules for the 1978 elections, in which two senate seats were up for election in each state. The base for calculating the number of deputies per state was changed back to population (in 1970 and

1974, the base was the electorate), thus increasing the representation of states in the north and northeast, where ARENA was stronger. One of the two senate seats became "bionic" (indirectly elected by an electoral college in each state). These same state electoral colleges (with ARENA majorities in all states but the state of Rio de Janeiro) would also elect the new state governors in 1978. The constitutional quorum was reduced from a two-thirds to an absolute majority, thus allowing ARENA to amend the constitution. These changes were expected to stem the opposition tide in 1978 and guarantee continued ARENA majorities in both houses of congress. During his term, Geisel used the AI-5 powers to sack six MDB deputies and one ARENA senator. The latter had been accused of corruption.

Also in 1977, army minister Sylvio Frota began frequent visits to congress and initiated an active political dialogue with ARENA politicians, clearly demonstrating his presidential ambitions for the 1979–1985 period. When Frota's activities began to challenge and erode Geisel's authority, the president reacted decisively. On the Columbus Day holiday, Geisel summarily dismissed Frota from the cabinet. The general attempted a reaction by convoking a meeting of the army high command but to no avail. General Fernando Bethlem was swiftly sworn in as the new army minister and proceeded to impose order in the military sector. Geisel then had a free hand to conclude his term and install his handpicked successor.[18]

Ernesto Geisel enacted a foreign policy—responsible pragmatism—that distanced Brazil from the United States. His predecessors (Castelo Branco, Costa e Silva, and Médici) had maintained closely articulated relations with the United States.[19] In 1975 Brazil signed a nuclear cooperation agreement with West Germany to build seven nuclear power plants to generate electric power in Brazil's southeast industrial region. However, some US officials suspected that this agreement could permit Brazil to gain access to technology that would allow the nation to master the complete nuclear cycle and construct a nuclear weapon. At the same time, President Geisel was attempting to reduce human rights violations and torture in Brazil. In early 1977, the new US president, Jimmy Carter, began to pressure Brazil and West Germany to end their nuclear agreement. At the same time, the White House released a report prepared for Congress describing the negative human rights situation in Brazil. Geisel reacted strongly, and in March 1977 renounced the military agreement that had been signed with the United States in the 1950s. The military aid involved was insignificant but Geisel's gesture had symbolic resonance. In June, Geisel received Rosalynn Carter coolly in Brasília after she had visited an American lay Roman Catholic volunteer who had been imprisoned and tortured in Recife. In 1978 President Carter made a state visit to Brazil. However, Germany and Brazil maintained their nuclear agreement. Geisel visited Japan, Germany, France, and the United Kingdom but was the only military president not to visit the United States. In 1975 Brazil became the first Western power to recognize the MPLA regime in newly independent Angola (the United States favored UNITA). On the other hand, Brazil followed the US lead and established diplomatic relations with the People's Republic of China. In 1977 Brazil forced Uruguay to cancel the political asylum it had granted to Leonel Brizola in 1964, and immediately President Carter offered asylum in the United States.

Geisel completed his last year in office (1978) with the election of his successor, General João Batista Figueiredo, and ARENA majorities in the congress that took office in February 1979. Neither victory was easy. In 1974 Geisel had named Figueiredo, then a two-star general, to head the SNI (National Information Service). He had served as chief of military household under President Médici (1969–1974), and together with Geisel on the senior staff of President Castelo Branco. To ready Figueiredo as candidate for the fifth and last military presidency, Geisel had to bend army promotion rules and pass over several more senior generals to promote his *in pectore* candidate to the fourth star by early 1978. This accomplished, the docile ARENA majority in the Electoral College duly elected Figueiredo to the presidency and the civilian governor of Minas Gerais, Aureliano Chaves, as vice president.

The April Package of alterations of the electoral system for 1978 helped produce the ARENA majorities, especially in the senate. These changes had little effect on the election of federal deputies, accruing perhaps four additional seats for ARENA. In the case of the senate, however, without these modifications (appointed— bionic—senators and the creation of 3 new seats from the new state of Mato Grosso do Sul), in the best of hypotheses, the MDB would have eked out a 33 to 31 senate majority. The package delivered a 42 to 25 majority to ARENA, in spite of a 46 percent versus 35 percent plurality vote favoring the MDB. The national vote for the chamber was evenly split, ARENA with 39.9 percent and MDB with 39.4 percent. However, the regional inequalities of state delegations produced a 231 to 189 majority for the military government support party. The MDB counted 45 percent of the deputies, quite similar to the 45.3 percent in 1974.[20]

General Figueiredo was sworn in to a six-year term in March 1979 but without the AI-5 exceptional powers that had been abolished by Geisel two months earlier. Golbery continued as chief of staff. The hard-line radicals who had been muffled by Geisel in 1977 again began to agitate military opinion and bombed newspaper stands, the Brazilian Bar Association (OAB) headquarters in Rio de Janeiro, and the Riocentro convention center. In the latter attempt, an army captain was badly injured and a sergeant was killed. However, some significant positive changes were made in 1979: the social security system was modified; a two-way amnesty was voted by congress; the end of the two-party system was approved by congress in late 1979; direct elections for governor were set for 1982; new legislation was approved that benefited renters; a two-year extension of the mandates of mayors and city councils elected in 1976 was enacted; amnesty was granted to purged labor union leaders; and biannual salary readjustments were made. As a result, most exiles began to return to Brazil after September 1979, including Leonel Brizola.

The two-party system had been useful to the military government, but after the economic downturn and the results of the 1974 and 1978 elections this mechanism became a straitjacket. All discontent (even among business leaders) was channeled into support for the single opposition party (MDB). Government strategists thought that, with the creation of a "moderately" plural party system having five or six parties, the government would have more room to negotiate its proposals and build party coalitions in congress. ARENA was more or less transformed into the Social Democratic Party (PDS) but with a slight reduction from 231 to 225 deputies. The MDB became the PMDB, but was split in half (reduced from 189 to 94 deputies). A new swing party, the Popular Party (PP), was organized with sixty-eight deputies that on occasion could ally with the PDS. Finally, the old PTB was resurrected with twenty-three deputies and the Workers Party (PT) was organized with five deputies. However, in May 1980 the TSE allocated the PTB label to Ivette Vargas (niece of Getúlio Vargas), and Leonel Brizola was forced to form his own Democratic Labor Party (PDT).

The extra two years for local officials' mandates synchronized local and general elections for November 1982. This change was necessitated because in 1980 the new political parties were still being organized, and it was thought that concurrent elections would benefit the new military government party—PDS. This move reversed the 1969 decision by the military government that set municipal elections two years out of phase in 1972 and 1976.

In September 1981, President Figueiredo suffered a heart attack in Rio de Janeiro. His doctors recommended total rest with no political activity and cardiac bypass surgery. Some of his advisers wanted a "Reagan solution": the vice president would not assume the presidency and Figueiredo would govern from his hospital room. When the doctors countered that this alternative would quickly kill him, chief of staff Leitão de Abreu reminded the president's staff that the "Costa e Silva solution" did not work in 1969, and counseled that they must allow vice president Aureliano Chaves to occupy the presidency; otherwise some general would take over. "They" (the Figueiredo advisers) would be out, and even though Figueiredo might recover, he would not return to the presidency. Chaves was duly sworn in as acting president for two months. Figueiredo had successful bypass surgery in Cleveland, Ohio, and reassumed the presidency in mid-November—in time to sign the creation of the new state of Rondônia to further reinforce the PDS majority in the senate after the 1982 elections.

However, SNI research discovered that the PDS would have great difficulty in the November 1982 elections, in spite of the inclusion of municipal elections, because of coalition building already under way. Thus in December 1981 the Figueiredo government again altered the election rules, as Figueiredo's four predecessors had done so many times. Voters were to use a tied, straight ticket ballot (obliged to vote for candidates of the same party for all offices), coalitions were prohibited, and the parties had to run full tickets and not leave the top of the ticket (governor and/or senator) vacant. In October, congress had already defeated an attempt to adopt sublists for senator and governor that could have helped unify the diverse PDS factions. As a result, leaders of the PP felt that these rule changes had severely limited their party's electoral chances. Consequently, in early 1982 they abruptly abolished the party and merged with the PMDB.[21] In June 1982, congress approved a government-sponsored amendment that altered the date and composition of the next Electoral College, permitted a short period of party switching, and returned the quorum for constitutional amendment to a two-thirds majority. The latter change anticipated that the PDS would lose its absolute majority in the chamber.

1984–1985: POLITICAL TRANSITION AND TRANSACTION

This election strategy (bottom-up "coattails" effect) functioned well with the "tied ballot" in the northeastern region, where all 9 nine states elected PDS governors and senators. However, in the other regions, where voters had more freedom from oligarchic tutelage, the coattails effect was top-down; the PMDB elected nine governors and the PDT elected Leonel Brizola governor of the state of Rio de Janeiro. As a result of the tied effect, the PMDB elected a large number of mayors in these states. The PDS maintained a 46 to 23 majority in the senate, but lost its absolute majority in the lower house, 235 out of 479 deputies (49.1 percent). Through an unstable coalition with the thirteen PTB deputies, the government eked out a 51.8 percent majority.

As the nomination phase (for the Electoral College) approached in mid-1984, the PDS suffered preelection tension with several precandidates, the most important being Vice-President Aureliano Chaves, interior minister (retired army colonel Mário Andreazza), and former São Paulo governor Paulo Salim Maluf. In April, an absolute majority of the chamber of deputies approved a constitutional amendment calling for direct presidential elections in November 1984, but was short by 21 votes of the necessary 2/3 majority. When President Figueiredo abruptly vetoed the idea of a PDS presidential primary (that Chaves probably would have won), a dissident PDS faction (the Liberal Front) declared its independence by supporting the PMDB candidate, Minas Gerais governor Tancredo Neves, and supplying his running mate—former PDS national president, Senator José Sarney from Maranhão—forming the Democratic Alliance ticket. To become a candidate, Sarney was obliged to join the PMDB. Paulo Maluf eventually was nominated in the PDS national convention for the January 15, 1985, Electoral College. The June 1982 amendment had changed this body's composition to give each state six delegates (in addition to its deputies and senators), and the 1982 elections had produced a 359 out of 680 (52.3 percent) majority. With the party loyalty law, it was thought that Maluf would be easily elected; but that was not to be. The Tancredo-Sarney ticket campaigned vigorously and attracted many PDS governors, senators, deputies, and delegates, especially from states in the northeast. The army high command communicated an informal nihil obstat (no objection) vis-à-vis the Democratic Alliance. Finally, in November 1984, the Supreme Court ruled that the party loyalty law did not apply to the Electoral College, thus facilitating an avalanche in favor of the opposition candidates; the PMDB ticket was elected by a 480 to 180 margin over the PDS candidate.[22]

Tancredo assumed several commitments on his route to the presidency and in the constitution of his new government. First, he established pacts with Aureliano Chaves and Ulysses Guimarães in early 1984. With the latter (PMDB pact), it was agreed that if the direct elections amendment passed, Guimarães would be the ideal PMDB candidate; if not, Neves would be the better candidate in the indirect election. With Chaves (Minas Gerais pact), it was agreed that whichever politician achieved the nomination of his respective party, the other mineiro would close ranks at the state level in support of the successful candidate. Neves also established hundreds of commitments with politicians from the PMDB and other parties regarding public policies, appointments, and pork barrel politics after his inauguration on March 15, 1985. Most of the latter were oral agreements made during one-on-one conversations. His cabinet, announced in late January, was an eclectic patchwork of leaders from nearly all parties and factions and included his nephew, Francisco Dornelles, as finance minister.

Unfortunately Tancredo was never sworn in. After falling ill on March 14, the eve of his inauguration, he was admitted to the central hospital in Brasília with severe diverticulitis (intestinal inflammation). The surgery resulted in blood poisoning, and he was subjected to three additional operations. He was transferred to a São Paulo hospital and finally died on April 21. But the question remained on the night of March 14: who should be sworn in as president? Some interpreted the constitution to read that the president of the lower house, Deputy Ulysses Guimarães (PMDB), should become acting president for sixty days, and if Tancredo became incapacitated (or died) new elections should be convoked by the Electoral College. Most thought that this solution would be unacceptable to the military. Supreme Court judges suggested that José Sarney be sworn in as vice president and occupy the presidency until Tancredo recovered. This alternative was accepted, but outgoing President Figueiredo refused to pass the presidential sash to Sarney and left the Alvorada palace by the back door.

Thus José Sarney assumed the presidency for what was to be a six-year term and came under considerable military tutelage by the two key generals who had articulated the nihil obstat in the army high command in late 1984. Leonidas Pires Gonçalves and Ivan de Sousa Mendes had been named army minister and chief of the SNI, respectively, by Tancredo Neves. Sarney was also under tutelage by many PMDB leaders who never really accepted him in the party, much less as Tancredo's successor. Sarney was soon besieged by politicians asking him to honor commitments that Neves had supposedly made with them. The Liberal Front faction that had split off from the PDS organized the Liberal Front Party (PFL) in early 1985 and absorbed many party switchers. By mid-1985, the Democratic Alliance counted 199 PMDB and 100 PFL deputies. In mid-1986, the count was 222 and 127, respectively. On the other hand, this party migration in the lower house reduced the former military support party (PDS) considerably—from 235 elected in 1983, to 135 in mid-1985, 68 in mid-1986, and only 35 seated in the National Constituent Assembly (ANC) in February 1987.

In May 1985, congress approved several measures to advance the process of redemocratization: direct elections for president were adopted; illiterates were allowed to vote; the party system was "unchained," allowing the formation of new parties, including the PCB and PCdoB; a National Constituent Assembly (ANC) was to be elected in 1986 and convened in 1987; and direct elections were set for November 15, 1985, in towns and cities that still had "bionic" mayors held over from the military regime. Inflation was becoming a serious problem, and in August 1985 Sarney replaced Dornelles at finance with business leader Dilson Funaro. The new minister recruited a group of young economists to prepare a novel stabilization plan for 1986.

Constituent Assembly and Direct Elections

The initial strategy of this task force was altered in February 1986, following Sarney's cabinet reshuffle, which PMDB leaders considered conservative. Sarney ordered economists to devise a crash stabilization plan to reinforce his legitimacy, and thus the Cruzado Plan was born on February 28, 1986. This plan consisted of a wage-price freeze that corrected salaries from their last readjustment and greatly stimulated consumer buying power and demand. Sarney's popularity soared, and the PMDB joined this new bandwagon. GDP experienced strong growth during the first two years of the Sarney period—8.3 percent in 1985 and 8.0 percent in 1986. The stabilization plan became a powerful election tool and enabled the PMDB to elect every governor but one in the November 1986 elections, giving the party an absolute majority—302 (257 deputies and 45 senators) out of a total of 559—54 percent in the 1987 National Constituent Assembly. Not since the PSD elected 54.1 percent of the 1946 ANC members had one party held an absolute majority in congress.

The ANC labored diligently until September 1988 and produced a new constitution from scratch. Final log rolling left some 300 points for posterior regulation, which has hampered policymakers ever since. While the new Charta Magna was considered liberal in the areas of political and social rights, it was considered conservative or status quo in the section dealing with the economic order and reinforced the role of the state in the economy, the role of state enterprises, and central planning. The ANC rejected a parliamentary system, reduced Sarney's mandate to five years, and introduced the *medida provisória* (provisional measure, MP), a modification of the decree-law concept that went into effect immediately. The progressive group that had produced the first draft of the new constitution was superseded by a new conservative Big Center (Centrão) majority and was able to reverse the content of some of the articles on the second round item-by-item votes.[23] To placate the supporters of the parliamentary system, the ANC determined that a plebiscite would be held five years (1993) after the promulgation of the new constitution to decide Brazil's system of government—presidential or parliamentary republic, or a constitutional monarchy. Unfortunately (some remembered retrospectively), the ANC had finished its work prior to the fall of the Berlin Wall (1989), German reunification (1990), and the subsequent demise of the socialist systems in Eastern Europe, followed by major changes in the world economic order.[24]

In anticipation of the November 1988 municipal elections, a progressive faction in the PMDB splintered in June 1988 to form the PSDB (Brazilian Social Democratic Party) along the lines of the Western European social democratic parties—with forty deputies and eight senators. By 1989 the party counted fifty deputies, and by 1990, sixty. However, after the 1990 elections, the PSDB was reduced to thirty-eight deputies and ten senators, with one governor—Tasso Jereissati (Ceará).[25] The PMDB also lost deputies to other parties in the 1988–1990 period, and was reduced from 257 elected in 1986 to 108 in 1990, similar to the fate of the PSD after the 1946 Constituent Assembly. In these elections, the PT more than doubled its representation from sixteen elected in 1986 to thirty-five in 1990.

Brazil's first direct elections for president since 1960 were scheduled for November 15, 1989, and twenty-two parties fielded candidates. The PMDB chose the president of the ANC, Deputy Ulysses Guimarães. The PFL ran former vice president Aureliano Chaves and the PDT chose former governor Leonel Brizola, while the PT selected charismatic metalworkers labor union leader Luiz Inácio "Lula" da Silva.[26] A little known governor from Alagoas, Fernando Collor de Mello, organized the PRN (Party of National Renovation) in early 1989, mounted a flashy media campaign, and took the lead as an antiparty candidate, in a style reminiscent of Jânio Quadros in 1960. Collor received 30.48 percent of the valid vote on the first round, followed by Lula with 17.19 percent and Brizola with 16.51 percent. The PT candidate had edged Brizola out of the second round by some 455,000 votes. The ANC had imposed the absolute majority concept on Brazilian elections for executive office, so Collor and Lula disputed the second round runoff on December 17. Collor was victorious over Lula by a 49.9 percent to 44.2 percent margin.[27]

THE COLLOR DISASTER AND IMPEACHMENT

President Collor was sworn in on March 15, 1990, and immediately issued a series of MPs that imposed a heterodox stabilization plan whereby all financial liquidity (over a certain minimum) was confiscated, held by the government for eighteen months, and then dribbled out to the owners in twelve monthly payments with a below par monetary correction. This desperate operation was an effort to stem Brazil's inflation that was running at about 90 percent per month. GDP growth in the final part of the Sarney presidency declined considerably: 2.9 percent in 1987, 0.0 percent in 1988, and 3.6 percent in 1989. The Collor Plan stabilized prices quickly, and inflation dropped below zero (deflation). The US dollar exchange rate dropped from Cr$84 to Cr$40 in two days. However, this stabilization plan lacked the staying power of the 1986 Cruzado Plan, so that before the November 15, 1990, elections the initial effects had dissipated into economic stagnation. Collor attempted a disorganized modernization of Brazil by consolidating and reducing the number of cabinet ministries, extinguishing twenty-four state enterprises, sacking many public servants, raising taxes on industrial and agricultural production, beginning a privatization program for state firms, deregulating markets, and liberalizing trade with successive reductions in import levies and quotas—in harmony with the main lines of the so-called Washington Consensus. However, Collor's popular approval rating declined from 71 percent in February 1990 to 34 percent seven months later (September). Inflation had returned and in December 1990 reached 20 percent per month. The Collor Plan caused a strong recession in 1990, as GDP declined by 4.2 percent and then stagnated in 1991 and 1992.[28]

The November 1990 elections did not produce a majority in congress for Collor's support coalition. Collor's group counted 170 deputies (34 percent) as follows: PRN, 40; PFL, 82; PTB, 38; PTR, 4; and PSC, 6. The opposition was led by the PMDB, 108; PSDB, 37; PDT, 47; and PT, 35. In 1990 Collor tried to induce the PSDB to join his coalition and offered several cabinet positions, including foreign minister (Senator Fernando Henrique Cardoso). The PSDB refused this overture, as did several other parties.

In early 1992, an avalanche of corruption accusations culminated in a long denunciation in a *Veja* magazine interview in late May by his younger brother, Pedro Collor, who revealed extensive "bag man" bribe operations. A congressional investigating committee (CPI) was installed in June. Finally, the lower house approved the suspension of President Collor's mandate in late September (on an open televised roll call vote), just four days before the municipal elections; the senate then deliberated his impeachment. Finally, on December 30, 1992, Fernando Collor was duly impeached (the first such case in a democratic presidential system) by another open roll call vote in the senate and his political rights were suspended for eight years.[29]

The Itamar Franco Interim

Collor's vice president, former PMDB senator Itamar Franco (Minas Gerais), became interim president in late September and president de jure in late December 1992 to complete the remainder of Collor's term through December 1994. He assembled his first cabinet based on many of his former senate colleagues, including Senator Fernando Henrique Cardoso (São Paulo), who became foreign minister. The problem of how to reactivate the economy that had stagnated in the Collor period plagued Franco during the first seven months of his government. After four finance ministers and strengthened by the April 21 national plebiscite that reaffirmed Brazil as a presidential republic, on May 21 Franco named F. H. Cardoso to the Finance Ministry. Cardoso proceeded to recruit a team of top economists who elaborated new policies to stimulate GDP growth (4.9 percent in 1993) and develop a strategy for a different type of stabilization plan.

Nearly a year after the chamber of deputies had voted Collor's impeachment, in October 1993 the so-called Budgetgate crisis erupted in Brasília. Testimony by the former chief of staff of the Joint Budget Committee in congress revealed a complex conspiracy to rig the budget for construction projects. A CPI was installed and discovered that (1) the committee leaders made sure that these items remained in the budget; (2) key executive branch staff arranged the inclusion of these items in the budget proposal and assured the intended result of each procurement bid; and (3) the cartel of these firms designated the winner and loser for each contract.

The CPI filed its report in January 1994 and recommended sacking several of the deputies and senators involved. The senate declined to take action against its members, but the chamber expelled eight deputies and absolved twelve; another four opted to resign. New procedures for budget elaboration by congress were suggested.[30]

The Real Plan Elects Cardoso

In March 1994, finance minister Cardoso and his economic team launched the new stabilization plan, based on the reference value unit (URV), which became the price and wage reference unit. Every day the currency value of the URV was adjusted. Congress approved the Emergency Social Fund (FSE), which allowed the government to impound (and/or transfer) up to 20 percent of constitutional bloc grants in order to reduce the fiscal deficit. After four months of price-wage alignments by the URV, this unit was converted into the new *real* currency unit on July 1, 1994, at the final rate of Cr$2.75 to each URV/*real*. A totally new currency (bills and coins) had been created with the assistance of government mints in the United States and Europe. Brazil's GDP expanded by 5.9 percent in 1994, and annual inflation declined from 916.5 percent in 1994 to 22.4 percent in 1995.[31]

However, Cardoso was no longer finance minister when the Real Plan was launched, for in April he had stepped down to become a PSDB presidential candidate in the October 1994 elections. At that point, the Real Plan had not been launched and inflation was still rampant. For this reason, the PT candidate (Lula) was leading public opinion and had reached 42 percent in the Datafolha poll conducted in early May, versus only 16 percent for Cardoso. However, by mid-July (two weeks after the Real Plan was launched), popular preferences were 34 percent versus 25 percent, and in early August Cardoso was leading 36 percent to 29 percent, and by the end of September Cardoso led by 47 percent to Lula's 23 percent. In the October 3 election, Cardoso achieved a first round victory with 54.3 percent of the valid vote and Lula trailed with 27 percent. The Real Plan had propelled Cardoso into the presidency.

The 1994 elections confirmed the PMDB as the largest party in congress—107 deputies and 22 senators, followed by the PFL (89 deputies and 19 senators). President Cardoso's party (PSDB) enhanced its chamber delegation vis-à-vis the 1990 elections, from thirty-eight to sixty-two deputies, but remained at ten senators. The PT increased from thirty-five to forty-nine deputies. Cardoso's election alliance (PSDB-PFL-PTB) counted 182 deputies (35.5 percent). To achieve an absolute majority, Cardoso's support coalition in the chamber needed to be expanded. Moving to the left was numerically impossible, and so Cardoso moved his support locus to the right to include the PMDB (107), the PDS (53), and the PP (36) and composed a comfortable 378 (73.7 percent) majority.

Although the Real Plan had stabilized inflation and elected Cardoso in 1994 in spite of the FSE control of revenue transfers to state and municipal governments, the federal deficit continued to expand due to state enterprises and the social security system. For this reason, Cardoso's top priority in 1995 was reform of the economic order section in the 1988 constitution to permit further privatizations and restructuring of the economy. In rapid sequence, congress approved constitutional amendments to permit privatization of the telecommunications and electric sectors, gas distribution, plus coastal and river shipping. The main jewels of Brazil's state enterprises were privatized—CSN (steel) (1994), CVRD (mining) (1997), and Telebrás (1998)—plus most of the state-owned electric generation and distribution systems and banks. The revenues from these privatizations helped reduce federal deficits somewhat in lieu of further reforms (fiscal/tax, social security, and administration).[32]

Cardoso made some advances in administrative reform and attempted social security reforms. In 1998 and 1999, congress passed a social security reform package that would have reduced the deficit caused by benefits paid out to retired public servants—had not the Supreme Court declared this unconstitutional. Several attempts by congress to approve tax/fiscal reform packages were derailed by Cardoso's finance minister, Pedro Malan. Finally, after much debate, congress approved the Fiscal Responsibility Law in April 2000, which imposed severe penalties (including jail terms) on governors and mayors who overspent their budgeted revenues. In 1997 and 1998, Minister Malan negotiated debt consolidation packages with each Brazilian state government. The federal government assumed the public debts of each state to be paid off in thirty years at 6 percent adjusted annually, with monthly installments of up to 13 percent of the state's revenues.

Former president Itamar Franco was conveniently removed from Brazilian politics when President Cardoso appointed him ambassador to Portugal and then to the OAS in Washington, DC. However, in 1998 he returned to Brazil to run for president. In 1997, after considerable arm twisting, congress approved the reelection amendment allowing presidents, governors, and mayors to be elected to a second consecutive term. Thus Cardoso could stand for reelection in the October 1998 elections. At that time, Itamar Franco was a member of the PMDB, and in two national conventions (March and June 1998) the party decided not to field a presidential candidate, nor to support any other party's candidate that year. Itamar was offered the PMDB candidacy for governor of Minas Gerais as a "consolation prize" that he grudgingly accepted, and he was duly elected. However, in early January 1999, Itamar's comeuppance was devastating. In his first week in office, Governor Itamar Franco suspended payments of some his state's foreign loans that produced a run on Brazil's currency and forced Cardoso to intervene in the Central Bank to float the real with a devaluation of some 60 percent. The new governor of Rio Grande do Sul, Olívio Dutra (PT), followed Itamar's lead. Finance Minister Malan wrote letters to the World Bank and Interamerican Development Bank withdrawing federal cover of loan operations with these states and immediately both institutions suspended all loan disbursements. Dutra quickly capitulated, but Itamar stubbornly held out for a few months.[33]

Enhanced by the Real Plan, Cardoso's PSDB made big gains in the 1996 municipal elections. Having elected 317 mayors in 1992, the party's so-called *tucanos,* nearly tripled this number to 917 in 1996. From this expanded municipal base, the PSDB was able to increase its chamber delegation from sixty-two to ninety-nine deputies in the 1998 elections.[34] Cardoso's reelection was relatively tranquil in 1998, with 53 percent of the valid vote. This time, the PT and PDT formed a coalition, with Leonel Brizola as Lula's running mate, and they polled 31.7 percent of the valid vote. This team more or less repeated the sum of the vote totals each had received in 1994 (PT 27 percent plus PDT 3.2 percent = 30.2 percent). Former Ceará PSDB governor, Ciro Gomes, who became Itamar Franco's last finance minister in 1994, ran on the PPS-Popular Socialist Party (former PCB) ticket in 1997 and received 11 percent of the valid vote.

The PSDB elected seven governors and the PFL and PMDB three each. The opposition elected six governors—PT, 3; PSB, 2; and PDT, 1. The PMDB increased its senate delegation to twenty-seven, the PSDB expanded to sixteen, and the PFL remained at nineteen, while the PT-PDT-PSB-PPS bloc to the left totaled fifteen. In the lower house, the PMDB declined to eighty-three while the PFL (105) and PSDB (99) gained deputies. The left bloc elected 112, led by the PT with fifty-nine deputies. Of the twenty-seven governors, twenty-two ran for reelection, but only fifteen (68 percent) were victorious, and the elections in thirteen states went to a second round. For the first time, a 25 percent quota for women candidates for deputy was used. In spite of this "advantage," only twenty-nine women (5.7 percent) were elected to the chamber versus thirty-four (6.6 percent) in 1994 (without the quotas).

Cardoso's legislative initiatives in his second term were less successful than in his first. In part this was due to a burgeoning list of scandals that threatened to affect some governors, senators, and deputies. Finally, in 2000, for the first time in Brazilian history, a senator was sanctioned by his peers, and later in 2001 three others decided to resign rather than be sacked. All three of the latter were reelected in 2002 (one to the senate, and two as federal deputies). In late 2001, the Election Court removed the governor of Piauí for election law violations but in 1998, but he was elected to the senate in 2002. Also, the impact of the Real Plan on the economy had declined as GDP growth slowed in 2001 and 2002, following the electric sector crisis and blackouts in May 2001.[35]

The left made further gains in the 2000 municipal elections. The PMDB (1,257), PFL (1,028), and PSDB (990) made modest gains over their performance in 1996. The PT elected 187 mayors, including that of Brazil's largest city, São Paulo. The left advanced in urban Brazil and captured 49 of the 100 largest cities (vs. 32 in 1996), as well as of the twenty-six state capitals where its candidates won twelve races (8 in 1996). To a certain extent, these results were cues for what would happen in the 2002 general elections.[36]

2002: LULA WINS THE PRESIDENCY

In late 2001 and early 2002, the PT's perennial candidate, Lula, was again leading in the polls, as he had in 1994, before the Real Plan was introduced. However, 2002 would not have another such stabilization plan and the earlier Cardoso coalition was disorganized. The PFL had left the Cardoso support bloc and his cabinet in 2001, and in March 2002 severed all links with the PSDB because of the "implosion" of the precandidacy of the PFL governor of Maranhão—Roseana Sarney—the daughter of former president José Sarney. This time the PFL decided not to run a presidential candidate or support any other candidate in coalition. The PSDB chose Senator José Serra (SP) and then began organizing a coalition with the PMDB. With great difficulty, PMDB leaders were able to force approval of this linkage in late June at the party's national convention and selected Deputy Rita Camata (ES) as Serra's running mate. However, many state sections of the PMDB rejected this alliance and threw their informal support to Lula.

The PT, on the other hand, understood that it needed a different strategy for the 2002 race, and proceeded to move to the center. First, Lula's party concluded a coalition with the more conservative PL (Liberal Party) that chose a self-made businessman, Senator José Alencar from Minas Gerais, as Lula's running mate. Second, the PT reached out to progressive business leaders for financial and political support. Third, the party drafted a letter to Brazilians explaining its policy objectives for the 2003–2006 period in a realistic and moderate proposal, quite different from past PT platforms.

The PPS again ran Ciro Gomes, but this time in coalition with the PTB (which had supported Cardoso in 1994 and 1998) and the PDT (which had supported Lula in 1998). Finally, the PSB (Brazilian Socialist Party) governor of Rio de Janeiro, Anthony Garotinho, stepped down to become a candidate, with considerable support from evangelical Protestants.

Coalition building in 2002 was more complicated than in 1994 and 1998 because in February 2002 the TSE imposed the verticalization of coalitions concept that obliged parties to maintain the same coalitions for governor that they had joined for president. That meant, for example, that the PSDB-PMDB presidential coalition would be replicated in all twenty-seven elections for state governor. Of the major parties, only the PFL and the PPB (which did not participate in any presidential election coalition) were free to join any state coalition. Initially it was thought that this TSE decision would favor the PSDB candidate, but the election results proved otherwise.

In the October 6 first round, Lula came close to an outright victory with 46.4 percent of the valid vote versus 23.2 percent for Serra, 17.9 percent for Garotinho, and 12 percent for Ciro Gomes (equal to his 1998 result). Three weeks later, Lula obtained a resounding victory in the runoff election—62.5 percent of the valid vote. Like Salvador Allende in Chile and François Mitterrand in France, Lula was finally elected on his fourth attempt.

The parties that had been allied with Cardoso fared well in the races for governor, but their base declined in congress. The PSDB elected seven governors, the PMDB five, and the PFL four. On the left, the PT gained three governorships, the PSB four, the PDT one, and the PSB two. In the senate, the PMDB was reduced from twenty-seven to nineteen, the PFL was steady at nineteen, and the PSDB declined from sixteen to eleven, while the PT doubled its delegation from seven to fourteen. In the lower house, the Cardoso support group declined considerably, the PFL from 105 to 84, the PMDB from eighty-three to seventy-five, and the PSDB from ninety-nine to seventy-one. Capitalizing on its gains in the 2000 municipal elections and on Lula's 2002 coattails, the PT delegation jumped from fifty-nine to ninety-one deputies to become the largest delegation, allowing Lula's party to elect the president of the lower house in February 2003. Many thought that these results augured profound reforms and changes for economic and social policies in Brazil, but they were mistaken.[37]

2003–2004: DREAMING THE WRONG DREAM

Twenty-two years after it had been organized, the Workers Party finally achieved national political power with Lula as president. The pent-up election anxieties and vocations for political power climaxed with the inauguration of Lula and Alencar on January 1, 2003. However, during the transition in November and December 2002, president-elect Lula initiated a series of "heresies" that surprised many PT militants. Most expected Lula to abandon his 2002 campaign rhetoric and revert to the PT's original policy objectives—reverse privatization measures, adopt developmentalist economic policy, enhance state participation in the economy, and so on.

The first heresy involved Lula's choice for Central Bank president, a key appointment aimed at restoring the confidence of the international financial community. The choice fell to the former Bank of Boston CEO Henrique Meirelles, who had just been elected federal deputy by the PSDB in Goiás. He promptly resigned his seat and his membership in the PSDB, and Lula requested President Cardoso to send the nomination to the senate so that it could be approved before the Christmas recess.

The second disappointment for the PT militants was the appointment of former PT mayor of Ribeirão Preto, SP, Antônio Palocci Filho, to be finance minister. A medical doctor by training, Palocci had been Lula's campaign manager in 2002. He quipped to the press, "You say Brazil's economy is in the intensive care unit, so Lula chose a doctor to cure the patient." Although the PT has a number of militants who are trained economists, Palocci set finance off-limits and none were recruited for the economic team.

The third heresy that went against all past PT demands was the continuation of the fifteen-month emergency agreement that Cardoso and Malan had signed with the IMF in August 2002. For twenty years the PT had ranted against the IMF and its policies as highly detrimental to Brazil.

The fourth heresy was announced at the new government's first cabinet meeting in January 2003—continuation of the Cardoso fiscal austerity modus operandi with a BRL14 billion cut in the 2003 budget. Stricter fiscal targets were adopted (the primary surplus goal was upped from Cardoso's 3.75 percent to 4.35 percent of GDP), and the Central Bank monetary policy committee quickly increased the basic interest rate to 26.5 percent adjusted annually.

The fifth heresy was announced in February—a major social security reform that aimed at reducing the massive deficits in the public sector where employees were allowed to retire at full salary. Traditionally, public servants had been staunch PT supporters and now they felt "their" PT had betrayed them. This reform was approved by congress in December; it placed caps on public salaries and retirement benefits, and imposed a new model on all new entrants to the public service as of 2004 (limited benefits and a parallel private pension fund arrangement).

The final 2003 heresies involved the construction of Lula's support base in congress in 2003. The coalition that had supported Lula in the second-round runoff against Serra (PT, PL, PCdoB, PPS, PTB, PDT, and PSB) had elected 218 deputies (42.5 percent) and 31 senators (38.3 percent) in October 2002. Thus comfortable absolute majorities had to be constructed. Lula's chief of staff, Deputy José Dirceu (SP), and his operatives began this task, and before the newly elected deputies were sworn in on February 1, 2003, the Lula bloc could count 252 deputies (49.1 percent). These party migrants were attracted away from the PFL (8), PSDB (7), PMDB (5), and PPB (5). The PT did not accept any of these joiners, who were channeled to the PTB (+15), PL (+7), PSB (+6), and PPS (+6). By the time Lula submitted the social security and tax reforms to congress on April 30, the PMDB and the PPB had joined the Lula bloc, which swelled to 370 deputies (72.1 percent) and 53 senators (65.4 percent). The PPB is the party of PT anathema Paulo Maluf. In four months, the Lula team had achieved nearly the same size congressional coalition that Cardoso had assembled in 1995. This and other comparisons led some critics to call the Lula government "Cardoso's third term." Newspaper cartoons depicted Lula and Cardoso fighting over the agenda.

Lula chose his cabinet ministers from the coalition allies with a predominance of the PT, concentrated in São Paulo and Rio Grande do Sul. Several defeated PT candidates (for governor and senator) were rewarded with cabinet appointments. Lula's first round adversary, Ciro Gomes, became minister of national integration. In late January 2004, Lula processed his first cabinet reshuffle. The PMDB had supported all the reform and legislative packages in 2003 and finally received two cabinet posts. Three social promotion posts were consolidated into a new Social Development Ministry; other ministers were switched or sacked. However, in mid-February the first of a series of scandals erupted and the Lula government was thrown into turmoil. The chief of congressional relations was accused of taking bribes from numbers racket operators and attempting to "intermediate" certain contract renewals. In the process the Lula bloc lost its majority in the senate, as five PDT senators and three PL senators left the coalition. The government lost key votes—the new minimum wage, outlawing bingo games, and an amendment to allow the reelection of the presidents of the senate and chamber of deputies. In early May, the *New York Times* published an article questioning the impact of Lula's excessive "tippling."[38] The president reacted angrily and ordered the correspondent's visa revoked. Cooler heads prevailed subsequently and the order was rescinded. Later, at the end of June, the *New York Times Magazine* published a long cover story about Lula, his origins, political ascent, and presidency.[39]

However, in May 2005 a much worse scandal—known as the Mensalão, or big monthly allowance—irrupted in the chamber of deputies. It was revealed that some PT leaders had engineered a massive kickback scheme funded by skimming off funds from federal service contracts—mostly for advertising—operated by two ad agencies in Belo Horizonte that channeled these funds to certain political parties to ensure cohesion in voting for government measures—the PMDB, PTB, PL, and PPB.[40]

Several deputies were *cassados* (expelled from the chamber) by their peers, including Lula's all-powerful chief of staff Deputy José Dirceu as well as PTB floor leader Deputy Roberto Jefferson. President Lula, claiming that he had no prior knowledge of this scheme, was spared. However, the president's approval rating in the polls tumbled by the end of the year, from 62 percent in December 2004 to 42 percent in December 2005, and was surpassed by possible PSDB presidential candidate José Serra in a simulation of the October 2006 election, in a survey conducted by *Ibope*.[41] The PSDB-PFL opposition thought that Lula, who had been weakened by the Mensalão scandal, would be easily defeated in the upcoming elections. In June 2005, President Lula replaced Dirceu with Dilma Rousseff, who had been minister of mines and energy since 2003.

However, in 2006 Lula recovered in the polls and went on to defeat the PSDB candidate, Geraldo Alkmim, by 60.8 percent to 39.2 percent in the October 29 second-round runoff election. Lula's support in Brazil's poorer municipalities largely came from the 10 million families who were receiving the *bolsa famíliar* (monthly family cash transfer).[42] José Serra, who had been defeated by Lula in 2002, was elected mayor of São Paulo in 2004, and governor of São Paulo in 2006.

In 2007 another scandal paralyzed congress, this time in the senate, where the president of the upper house, Renan Calheiros (PMDB), was accused of fathering a child out of wedlock with a TV *Globo* journalist and a major lobby group was making the support payments. In his subsequent efforts to document his income to justify these payments (which were larger than his senate salary), Calheiros became involved in corruption accusations and was forced to resign the senate presidency in December 2007 to avoid being *cassado*. In the process, that same month, the government lost a crucial senate vote to continue the CPMF (tax on financial transactions to fund national health programs).

Because Brazil uses the open list variant of proportional representation, its political parties are considered weak, with little party loyalty and little accountability among those elected. After each election, the president is forced to construct a support coalition in congress that involves considerable party switching by deputies and senators in order to join the government bandwagon. In both the 2002 and

2006 elections, the PFL elected the largest number of senators and thus would have had the prerogative of electing the new senate president. However, between the October election and the new legislative session that opened on February 1 (in 2003 and 2007), the PMDB regained the status of largest party via party switching. For this reason, the DEM (ex-PFL) sought redress at the TSE, arguing that the mandate belonged to the party and not to the individual politician, and that those who switched parties should lose their mandate and be replaced by the next alternate on the party list.

In March 2007, the TSE declared that the mandate belongs to the party rather than the politician and the switchers should lose their mandate in favor of the next alternate. Six months later, the Supreme Court confirmed the TSE decision, but not retroactively. Over the next two years, congress was unable to resolve this party loyalty question, and a series of other political reform measures were defeated in the chamber of deputies in June 2009.

The October 2008 municipal elections saw the PT and its allied parties increase their share of municipal governments. The PT gained an additional 146 mayors, the PMDB added 149, and the PSB gained 116. The opposition parties suffered losses—the PSDB lost 83 mayors, the PFL-DEM lost 288, and the PPS lost 172.[43]

Yet another scandal irrupted in congress in 2009 in the wake of José Sarney being elected senate president for a third time. A scheme that involved manipulating appointments and contracts and nepotism, run by the chief staff officer of the senate since 1995, was revealed, with the involvement (or connivance) of Sarney and other PMDB senators. Sarney was pressured to resign his post after several influence schemes pertaining to large areas of Brazil electric and other sectors were reported by the press. In July 2009 Sarney's son, Fernando Sarney, was indicted by the federal police and on July 31 the Sarney family pressured a local court in Brasilia to order prior censorship of the *O Estado de São Paulo* newspaper not to report on Fernando's indictment. This created a very negative international image of Brazil regarding freedom of the press.[44]

As the 2010 presidential election campaign began heating up in late 2009, Lula chose his chief of staff, Dilma Rousseff, as the PT precandidate. The PSDB precandidate, Governor José Serra, had a strong lead in the polls. PSB deputy Ciro Gomes posted a strong third position and Lula's former environment minister, Senator Marina Silva (who left the PT for the PV-Green Party in August 2009), was trailing in fourth.

CONCLUSION

Rhetorically, the *New York Times Magazine* story asked whether Lula was "Latin America's last leftist leader." More likely, Brazil's PT president is neither the first nor last national leader from a left-socialist political party to assume power only to enact neoliberal policies and reforms that his more conservative predecessors were unable to accomplish. This was the case with French socialist François Mitterrand (1981), Spanish socialist Felipe Gonzales (1983), and Polish labor leader Lech Walesa (1990). These three leaders were followed in office by more conservative parties. However, two leftists aligned with Venezuelan president Hugo Chávez were elected president—Evo Morales in Bolivia and Rafael Correa in Ecuador, while President Michelle Bachelet was faring well in Chile, with 80 percent approval ratings in late 2009. In late 2009, the Frente Amplio president Tabaré Vásquéz was able to elect his successor, former Tupamaro guerrilla fighter, José "Pepe" Mújica.

Lula has declared several times, "I am not, nor have I ever been, a socialist or a leftist." Fernando Henrique Cardoso followed a similar sequence. He began his academic career at the University of São Paulo in the late 1950s as a Marxist, evolved into a progressive social democrat in the senate after 1983, and finally enacted neoliberal reforms as president (1995–2002).

The policies, programs, and reforms introduced by President Lula in 2003 and 2004 led PT deputy Fernando Gabeira (RJ) to abandon the party in October 2003 and declare, "I was dreaming the wrong dream."[45] During the crucial rounds of voting on social security reform in 2003, a small group of PT deputies agreed with Gabeira and either voted against parts of the reform, abstained, or was absent. As a result, in mid-December 2003, three PT deputies and one senator were expelled from the party by its national executive committee. In mid-2004, twelve senators from parties in the Lula coalition declared themselves independent of government directives.

Once in power, the PT quickly discovered the hard and difficult political and economic restraints on governing. Its leaders complained about the negative inheritance received from the Cardoso presidency. The ensuing austerity policies enacted by the PT in 2003 constricted the economy, unemployment increased, average wages declined, and Brazil's GDP shrank by 0.2 percent. On the other hand, the former government parties (PFL and PSDB) had difficulty adjusting to their new opposition role, especially vis-à-vis Lula's social security reform proposal, which was very similar to what Cardoso had proposed and seen rejected by the Supreme Court.

Since the end of the military regime in 1985, Brazilian representative democracy has suffered considerable trials and tribulations. Tancredo Neves died on the eve of his inauguration; the first popularly elected president since 1960 was constitutionally impeached in 1992; several major congressional investigations shook the foundations of Brazil's political and economic institutions. Thirteen elections, one plebiscite and one referendum have been held since 1985; illiterates have been enfranchised; the voting age was reduced to sixteen; and some 65 percent of Brazilians are now eligible to vote. In mid-2009, the nation appeared united and economically and politically stable; but Lula's presidency was seeing declining approval ratings after eighteen months in office. But Lula and his political allies consolidated their position in the 2004 local elections and Lula was reelected president in 2006. Further consolidation occurred in the 2008 municipal elections due to the *bolsa famíliar*.

When the world financial crisis hit Brazil in late 2008, the impact was quite negative—falling industrial production, declining exports, rising unemployment, and contractions in Brazil's GDP in the fourth quarter of 2008 and first quarter of 2009. However, the Lula government quickly enacted selective tax reductions and other incentives to spur consumer demand, and the Central Bank provided foreign exchange cover for exports so that Brazil returned to positive GDP results in the second and third quarters of 2009.

The question remains, Have the PT and its allies further expanded their political base enough to repeat the 2006–2008 algorithms in the next general election in 2010? Will Lula's charisma and high approval ratings (near 80 percent) be sufficient to boost the election of his handpicked successor, Dilma Rousseff?

NOTES

1. *Folha de São Paulo,* October 15, 2003, p. A-5.

2. The two Brazils concept was first used by Jacques Lambert, *Os dois Brasis* (Rio de Janeiro: INEP/CBPE, 1959). The concept of contrasts was applied by Roger Bastide, *Brésil: Terre des contrastes* (Paris: L'Harmattan, 1957). For an extensive discussion of the basic dualism of Brazilian society, see Hélio Jaguaribe, *Alternativas do Brasil* (Rio de Janeiro: José Olympia Editora, 1989), chap. 2.

3. Edmar Bacha and Herbert S. Klein, eds., *Social Change in Brazil, 1945–1985: The Incomplete Transition* (Albuquerque: University of New Mexico Press, 1989). For a treatment of Brazil's regional socioeconomic differences and their impact on the unequal distribution of political power before 1964, see Glaucio Soares, *A democracia interrompida* (Rio de Janeiro: Fundação Getúlio Vargas, 2001), chap. 11.

4. Márcio Pochmann, ed., *Atlas da riqueza no Brasil* (São Paulo: Editora Cortez, 2004). In 2000, the average monthly income of Brazilian families was BRL1,608 (US$563).

5. For an analysis of this deadlock in the early 1960s, see Glaucio Soares, *A Democracia Interrompida,* chaps. 12–14; and Barry Ames, *Political Survival: Politicians and Public Policy in Latin America* (Berkeley: University of California Press, 1987).

6. See Élio Gaspari, *A ditadura envergonhada* (São Paulo: Companhia Das Letras, 2002), pt. 1; and René A. Dreifuss, *1964: A conquista do estado: Ação política, poder e golpe* (Petrópolis: Editora Vozes, 1981).

7. Robert Wesson and David Fleischer, *Brazil in Transition* (New York: Praeger, 1983), pp. 103–105.

8. Maurice Duverger, *Les partis politiques* (Paris: Armand Colin, 1951).

9. Because the TV series *Bionic Woman* was popular in Brazil, persons indirectly elected to office were nicknamed "bionics."

10. For an analysis of this period, see Élio Gaspari, *A ditadura envergonhada* (São Paulo: Companhia Das Letras, 2002), pp. 129–266.

11. For a description of this economic expansion phase, see Werner Baer, *The Brazilian Economy: Growth and Development* (New York: Praeger, 1989).

12. Ironically, the progressive left had called for the expropriation of foreign-owned public utilities in the early 1960s.

13. This episode is described in Fernando Gabeira, *O que é isso, companheiro?* (Rio de Janeiro: Codecri, 1980); and the movie *Four Days in September,* released by Miramax films in 1997.

14. For an analysis of the never ending sequence of election law changes in Brazil, see David Fleischer, "Political Reforms: Cardoso's Missing Link," in Font, ed., *Reforming Brazil* (Lanham, MD: Lexington, 2004), pp. 121–139. For an analysis of the regional inequalities in the chamber of deputies produced by the election system prior to 1964, see Glaucio Soares, *A democracia interrompida,* chap. 12.

15. For a description of the tribulations of the MDB in the early 1970s, see Maria D'Alva Kinzo, *Legal Opposition Politics Under Authoritarian Rule in Brazil: The Case of the MDB, 1966–1979* (London: Macmillan, 1988).

16. Geisel's taped recollections of his presidency are found in Maria Celina D'Araujo and Celso Castro, eds., *Ernesto Geisel* (Rio de Janeiro: Fundação Getúlio Vargas, 1997), pp. 255–415. For a broader analysis of this period, see Élio Gaspari, *A ditatura encurralada* (São Paulo: Companhia Das Letras, 2004).

17. For details regarding this MDB victory, see Maria D'Alva Kinzo, *Legal Opposition Politics*; and Sebastião Nery, *As 16 derrotas que abalaram o Brasil* (Rio de Janeiro: Francisco Alves, 1975).

18. Élio Gaspari. *A ditatura encurralada*, pp. 407–481.

19. Jan Knippers Black. *United States Penetration of Brazil* (Philadelphia: University of Pennsylvania Press, 1977).

20. Maria D'Alva Kinzo, *Legal Opposition Politics*.

21. Wesson and Fleischer. *Brazil in Transition*, pp. 110–116.

22. The 1985 Electoral College sequence is described in David Fleischer, "Manipulações casuísticas do sistema eleitoral durante o período militar, ou como usualmente o feitiço se voltava contra o feiticeiro," in Soares and D'Araujo, eds., *21 anos de regime militar* (Rio de Janeiro: Fundação Getúlio Vargas, 1994), pp. 188–194.

23. Maria D'Alva Kinzo, "O Quadro Partidário na Constituinte," *Revista Brasileira de Ciência Política* 1, no. 1 (1989): 91–123.

24. For analysis of the ANC, see Xavier Martinez-Lara, *Building Democracy in Brazil: The Politics of Constitutional Change, 1985–1995* (London: Macmillan, 1996); Celina Maria de Souza, *Constitutional Engineering in Brazil: The Politics of Federalism and Decentralization* (London: Macmillan, 1997); and Luiz Werneck Vianna, *A transição: Da constituinte à sucessão presidencial* (Rio de Janeiro: Ed. Revan, 1989).

25. For the chronicle of the *tucano* party, see Jales Ramos Marques and David Fleischer, *PSDB: De Facção a partido* (Brasília: Instituto Teotonio Vilela, 1998). For an analysis of the *tucanos'* performance in the state of Ceará, see Judith Tendler, *Good Government in the Tropics* (Baltimore: Johns Hopkins University Press, 1996).

26. Margaret E. Keck, *The Workers Party and Democratization in Brazil* (New Haven: Yale University Press, 1992).

27. Emir Sader and Ken Silverstein, *Without Fear of Being Happy: Lula, the Workers Party, and the 1989 Elections in Brazil* (New York: Verso, 1991).

28. For a review of economic policy in this period, see Edmund Amann, "Economic Policy and Performance in Brazil since 1985," in Maria D'Alva Kinzo and James Dunkerley, eds., *Brazil Since 1985* (London: ILAS/University of London, 2003), pp. 107–137.

29. A detailed analysis of the Collor impeachment is found in Keith S. Rosenn and Richard Downes, eds., *Corruption and Political Reform in Brazil: The Impact of Collor's Impeachment* (Coral Gables: University of Miami Press, 1999).

30. For an analysis of Budgetgate, see David Fleischer, "Beyond Collorgate: Prospects for Consolidating Democracy in Brazil through Political Reform," in Rosenn and Downes, eds., *Corruption and Political Reform in Brazil*, pp. 49–71.

31. For a review of the Real Plan and its consequences, see Edmund Amann, "Economic Policy and Performance in Brazil Since 1985," in Kinzo and Dunkerley, eds., *Brazil Since 1985*, pp. 116–126.

32. Brazil's reform program is evaluated in Kurt Weyland, *Democracy Without Equity: Failures of Reform in Brazil* (Pittsburgh: Pittsburgh University Press, 1996).

33. David Fleischer, "Political Reforms: Cardoso's 'Missing Link,'" in Mauricio Font et al., eds., *Reforming Brazil* (Lanham, MD: Lexington, 2004), pp. 112–139.

34. For a review of the *tucanos'* performance in the 1996 and 1998 elections, see Marques and Fleischer, *De facção a partido*, pp. 109–123, 133–155.

35. Analysis of the Cardoso presidency is found in "Brazil: The Challenge of Constitutional Reform," a special issue of the *Journal of Interamerican Studies and World Affairs*, Winter 1998; Bolivar Lamounier and Ruben Figueiredo, eds., *A era FHC: Um balanço* (São Paulo: Cultura Editores, 2002); and Mauricio Font et al., eds., *Reforming Brazil*. Studies of Cardoso, intellectual and politician, are found in, respectively, Carlos Michiles, *Ciência e política sobre a perspectiva do realismo utópico* (Brasília: University of Brasília Press, 2003); and Mauricio Font, *Transforming Brazil*.

36. For an analysis of the 2000 municipal elections, see David Fleischer, "As eleições municipais no Brasil: Uma análise comparativa (1982–2000)," *Opinião Pública* 8, no. 1 (2002): 80–105.

37. For a review of these expectations, see Sue Brandford et al., *Lula and the Workers Party in Brazil* (New York: New Press, 2004).

38. Larry Rohter, "Brazilian Leader's Tippling Becomes National Concern," *New York Times*, May 9, 2004.

39. Barry Bearak, "Poor Man's Burden: The Hard Times and Letdowns of Lula," *New York Times Magazine*, June 27, 2004.

40. Peter Flynn, "Brazil and Lula, 2005: Crisis, Corruption, and Change in Political Perspective," *Third World Quarterly* 26, no. 8 (2005): 1221–1267.

41. "José Serra já ultrapassa Lula no 1º turno e lidera com vantagem de 13 pontos no 2º," *Veja*, December 14, 2005.

42. Wendy Hunter and Timothy J. Power, "Rewarding Lula: Executive Power, Social Policy, and the Brazilian Elections of 2006," *Latin American Politics and Society* 49, no. 1 (2007): 1–30.

43. David Fleischer, "Political Outlook in Brazil in the Wake of Municipal Elections: 2009–2010" (paper presented at the Brazil Institute of the Woodrow Wilson International Center for Scholars, Washington, DC, November 10, 2008).

44. Juliana Lima, "Brazilian Daily Marks 90 Days of Court-Ordered Censorship," *Jornalism in the Americas*, Knight Center for Journalism in the Americas, November 2, 2009. www.knightcenter.utexas.edu/blog/?q=pt-br/node/5661.

45. Cited in the *Folha de São Paulo*, October 15, 2003.

SUGGESTED READINGS

In English

Abers, Rebecca Neaera. *Inventing Local Democracy: Grassroots Politics in Brazil*. Boulder: Lynne Rienner, 2000.

Amann, Edmund. "Economic Policy and Performance in Brazil Since 1985." In Maria D'Alva Kinzo and James Dunkerley, eds., *Brazil Since 1985: Economy, Polity, and Society*, pp. 107–137. London: ILAS/University of London, 2003.

Ames, Barry. *Political Survival: Politicians and Public Policy in Latin America*. Berkeley: University of California Press, 1987.

———. *The Deadlock of Democracy in Brazil*. Ann Arbor: University of Michigan Press, 2001.

Bacha, Edmar, and Herbert S. Klein, eds. *Social Change in Brazil, 1945–1985: The Incomplete Transition*. Albuquerque: University of New Mexico Press, 1989.

Baer, Werner. *The Brazilian Economy: Growth and Development*. New York: Praeger, 1989.

Bearak, Barry. "Poor Man's Burden: The Hard Times and Letdowns of Lula." *New York Times Magazine*, June 27, 2004.

Bethell, Leslie. "Politics in Brazil: From Elections Without Democracy to Democracy Without Citizenship." In Maria D'Alva Kinzo and James Dunkerley, eds., *Brazil Since 1985: Economy, Polity, and Society*, pp. 21–41. London: ILAS/University of London, 2003.

Black, Jan Knippers. *United States Penetration of Brazil*. Philadelphia: University of Pennsylvania Press, 1977.

Branford, Sue, and Bernardo Kucinski. *Carnival of the Oppressed: Lula and the Brazilian Workers Party*. London: Latin American Bureau, 1995.

Branford, Sue, and Bernardo Kucinski et al. *Lula and the Workers Party in Brazil*. New York: New Press, 2004.

Branford, Sue, and Jan Rocha. *Cutting the Wire: the Story of the Landless Movement in Brazil*. London: Latin American Bureau, 2002.

Figueiredo, Angelina C., and Fernando Limongi. "Congress and Decision-Making in Democratic Brazil." In Maria D'Alva Kinzo and James Dunkerley, eds., *Brazil Since 1985: Economy, Polity, and Society*, pp. 62–83. London: ILAS/University of London, 2003.

Fleischer, David. "Government and Politics." In Rex A. Hudson, ed., *Brazil: A Country Study*, pp. 253–332. Washington, DC: Library of Congress, 1997.

———. "Beyond Collorgate: Prospects for Consolidating Democracy in Brazil through Political Reform," In Keith S. Rosenn and Richard Downes, eds., *Corruption and Political Reform in Brazil: The Impact of Collor's Impeachment*. pp. 49–71. Coral Gables: University of Miami Press, 1999.

———. "Political Reforms: Cardoso's 'Missing Link.'" In Maurício A. Font et al., eds., *Reforming Brazil*, pp. 112–139. Lanham, MD: Rowman & Littlefield, 2004.

Flynn, Peter. "Brazil and Lula, 2005: Crisis, Corruption, and Change in Political Perspective." *Third World Quarterly* 26, no. 8 (2005): 1221–1267.

Font, Maurício A. *Transforming Brazil: A Reform Era in Perspective*. Lanham, MD: Rowman & Littlefield, 2003.

Font, Maurício A., et al., eds. *Reforming Brazil*. Lanham, MD: Rowman & Littlefield, 2004.

Hudson, Rex A., ed. *Brazil: A Country Study*. Washington, DC: Library of Congress, 1997.

Hunter, Wendy. *Eroding Military Influence in Brazil: Politicians Against Soldiers*. Chapel Hill: University of North Carolina Press, 1997.

Hunter, Wendy, and Timothy J. Power. "Rewarding Lula: Executive Power, Social Policy, and the Brazilian Election of 2006." *Latin American Politics and Society* 49, no. 1 (2007):1–30.

Keck, Margaret E. *The Workers Party and Democratization in Brazil*. New Haven: Yale University Press, 1992.

Kingstone, Peter R., and Timothy J. Power, eds. *Democratic Brazil*. Pittsburgh: Pittsburgh University Press, 1999.

———. *Democratic Brazil Revisited*. Pittsburgh: University of Pittsburgh Press, 2008.

Kinzo, Maria D'Alva. *Legal Opposition Politics Under Authoritarian Rule in Brazil: The case of the MDB, 1966–79*. London: Macmillan, 1988.

———. "Parties and Elections: Brazil's Democratic Experience Since 1985." In Maria D'Alva Kinzo and James Dunkerley, eds., *Brazil Since 1985: Economy, Polity, and Society*, pp. 42–61. London: ILAS/University of London, 2003.

Kinzo, Maria D'Alva, and James Dunkerley, eds. *Brazil Since 1985: Economy, Polity, and Society*. London: ILAS/University of London, 2003.

Macaulay, Fiona. "Democratization and the Judiciary: Competing Reform Agendas." In Maria D'Alva Kinzo and James Dunkerley, eds., *Brazil Since 1985: Economy, Polity, and Society*, pp. 84–104. London: ILAS/University of London, 2003.

Mainwaring, Scott. *The Catholic Church and Politics in Brazil, 1916–1985.* Stanford: Stanford University Press, 1986.

―――. *Rethinking Party Systems in the Third Wave of Democratization: The Case of Brazil.* Stanford: Stanford University Press, 1999.

Martinez-Lara, Xavier. *Building Democracy in Brazil: The Politics of Constitutional Change, 1985–1995.* London: Macmillan, 1996

Mueller, Charles C., and Werner Baer. "The Economy." In Rex A. Hudson, ed., *Brazil: A Country Study,* pp. 137–252. Washington, DC: Library of Congress, 1997.

O'Donnell, Guillermo. "Challenges to Democratization in Brazil: The Threat of a Slow Death." *World Policy Journal,* Spring 1988, pp. 281–300.

Porto, Mauro P. "Mass Media and Politics in Democratic Brazil." In Maria D'Alva Kinzo and James Dunkerley, eds., *Brazil Since 1985: Economy, Polity, and Society,* pp. 288–313. London: ILAS/University of London, 2003.

Power, Timothy J. *The Political Right in Brazil: Elites, Institutions, and Democratization.* University Park: Pennsylvania State University Press, 2000.

Rosenn, Keith S., and Richard Downes, eds. *Corruption and Political Reform in Brazil: The Impact of Collor's Impeachment.* Coral Gables: University of Miami Press, 1999.

Sader, Emir, and Ken Silverstein. *Without Fear of Being Happy: Lula, the Workers Party, and the 1989 Election in Brazil.* New York: Verso, 1991.

Sallum, Brasilio, Jr. "The Changing Role of the State: New Patterns of State-Society Relations in Brazil at the End of the Twentieth Century." In Maria D'Alva Kinzo and James Dunkerley, eds., *Brazil Since 1985: Economy, Polity, and Society,* pp. 179–199. London: ILAS/University of London, 2003.

Sawyer, Donald R. "The Society and Its Environment." In Rex A. Hudson, ed., *Brazil: A Country Study,* pp. 90–156. Washington, DC: Library of Congress, 1997.

Skidmore, Thomas. *Politics in Brazil.* New York: Oxford University Press, 1966.

―――. *The Politics of Military Rule in Brazil, 1964–85.* New York: Oxford University Press, 1988.

Souza, Celina Maria de. *Constitutional Engineering in Brazil: The Politics of Federalism and Decentralization.* London: Macmillan, 1997.

Stepan, Alfred. *Rethinking Military Politics: Brazil and the Southern Cone.* Princeton: Princeton University Press, 1988.

Stepan, Alfred, ed. *Democratizing Brazil: Problems of Transition and Consolidation.* New York: Oxford University Press, 1989.

Taylor, Matthew M. *Judging Policy Courts and Policy Reform in Democratic Brazil.* Stanford: Stanford University Press, 2008.

Tendler, Judith. *Good Government in the Tropics.* Baltimore: Johns Hopkins University Press, 1996.

Tolefson, Scott D. "National Security." In Rex A. Hudson, ed., *Brazil: A Country Study,* pp. 333–412. Washington, DC: Library of Congress, 1997.

Wesson, Robert, and David Fleischer. *Brazil in Transition.* New York: Praeger, 1983.

Weyland, Kurt. *Democracy Without Equity: Failures of Reform in Brazil.* Pittsburgh: Pittsburgh University Press, 1996.

In Portuguese

Avelar, Lúcia M., and Antônio O. Cintra. eds. *O sistema político brasileiro: Uma introdução.* São Paulo: UNESP, 2007.

Avritzer, Leonardo, and Fátima Anastasia, eds. *Reforma política no Brasil.* Belo Horizonte: Editora da UFMG, 2006.

Bastide, Roger. *Brasil: Terra de contrastes.* São Paulo: DIFEL, 1959.

Benevides, Maria Victória et al., eds. *Reforma política e cidadania*. São Paulo: Editora Fundação Perseu Abramo, 2003.

Bresser Pereira, Luiz. *Pactos políticos: Do populismo à redemocratização*. São Paulo: Editora Brasiliense, 1985.

Carreirão, Yan de Souza. *Decisão do voto nas eleições presidenciais brasileiras*. Rio de Janeiro: Fundação Getúlio Vargas, 2002.

D'Araujo, Maria Celina, and Celso Castro orgs. *Ernesto Geisel*. Rio de Janeiro: Fundação Getúlio Vargas, 1997.

D'Alva Gil Kinzo, Maria. "O quadro partidário e a constituinte." *Revista Brasileira de Ciência Política*, March 1989, pp. 91–124.

DaMatta, Roberto. *O que faz O Brasil, Brasil?* São Paulo: Rocco, 1986.

Dreifuss, René A. *1964: A conquista do estado: Ação política, poder e golpe do estado*. Petrópolis: Editora Vozes, 1981.

———. *O jogo da direita*. Petrópolis: Editora Vozes, 1989.

Faoro, Raymundo. *Os donos do poder: Formação do patronato político brasiliero*. Editora Globo, 1958.

Fleischer, David. "Manipulações casuísticas do sistema eleitoral durante o período militar, ou como usualmente o feitiço se voltava contra o feiticeiro." In Glaúcio Soares and Maria Celina D'Araujo, eds., *21 Anos de Regime Militar*, pp. 154–197. Rio de Janeiro: Fundação Getúlio Vargas, 1994.

———. "As eleições municipais no Brasil: Uma análise comparativa (1982–2000)." *Opinião Pública* 8, no 1(2002): 80–105.

Gabeira, Fernando. *O que é isso, companheiro?*. Rio de Janeiro: Codecri, 1980.

Gaspari, Élio. *A ditatura envergonhada*. São Paulo: Companhia Das Letras, 2002.

———. *A ditadura escancarada*. São Paulo: Companhia Das Letras, 2002.

———. *A ditadura derrotada*. São Paulo: Companhia Das Letras, 2003.

———. *A ditatura envergonhada*. São Paulo: Companhia Das Letras, 2004.

Jaguaribe, Hélio. *Alternativas do Brasil*. Rio de Janeiro: José Olympio Editora, 1989.

Kinzo, Maria D'Alva. "O quadro partidário e a constituinte." *Revista Brasileira de Ciência Política* 1, no. 1 (1989): 91–123.

Krause, Silvana, and Rógerio Schmitt. eds. *Partidos e coligações no Brasil*. Rio de Janeiro: Konrad Adenauer Stiftung, 2005.

Lambert, Jacques. *Os dois Brasis*. Rio de Janeiro: INEP/CBPE, 1959.

Lamounier, Bolivar, ed. *De Geisel a Collor: O balanço da transição*. São Paulo: Ed. Sumaré.

Lamounier, Bolivar, and Rubens Figueiredo, eds. *A Era FHC: Um balanço*. São Paulo: Cultura Editores, 2002

Marques, Jales Ramos, and David Fleischer. *PSDB: De facção a partido*. Brasília: Inst. Teotonio Vilela, 1998.

Nery, Sebastião. *As 16 derrotas que abalaram o Brasil*. Rio de Janeiro: Francisco Alves, 1975.

Pochmann, Márcio, ed. *Atlas da riqueza no Brasil*. São Paulo: Editora Cortez, 2004.

Soares, Glaucio A.D. *A democracia interrompida*. Rio de Janeiro: Fundação Getúlio Vargas, 2001.

Soares, Glaucio A.D., and Maria Celina D'Araujo, eds. *21 Anos de regime militar: Balanços e perspectivas*. Rio de Janeiro: Fundação Getúlio Vargas, 1994.

Soares, Glaucio A.D., and Lúcio R. Rennó. eds. *Reforma política: Lições da história recente*. Rio de Janeiro: Fundação Getúlio Vargas, 2006.

Vianna, Luiz Werneck. *A transição: Da constituinte à sucessão presidencial*. Rio de Janeiro: Ed. Revan, 1989.

Chapter 26

CHILE

The Development, Breakdown, and Recovery of Democracy

J. SAMUEL VALENZUELA AND
ARTURO VALENZUELA

CHILE, A COUNTRY ON an elongated strip of land running 2,650 miles into the farthest southern reaches of the earth, was among the world's pioneers in experimenting with democratic constitutional principles. After gaining independence from Spain, the nation unfailingly renewed national and municipal authorities through electoral contests from the late 1820s until well into the twentieth century, creating a pattern of political stability that was unusual in Latin America. Given the frequency and importance of elections, Chile also developed, from the mid-nineteenth century on, strong political parties that, while changing over time, have dominated its political life. Running the full range of the ideological spectrum from a communist and socialist left to conservative parties on the right, the Chilean party system has paralleled those of Latin Europe rather than those of its neighbors in the Americas.

This unusual party system permitted the election in 1970 of President Salvador Allende, whose leftist government tried to lead the nation to socialism while respecting its democratic institutions. Allende's program of change attracted worldwide attention, but could not withstand the tensions generated by the Cold War. On September 11, 1973, General Augusto Pinochet, with the support of the Nixon administration, staged a military coup that destroyed Chile's democracy. Prior to Pinochet's regime, Chile had been governed by a military junta only once before, for less than five months in 1924–1925. The crisis years of 1891 as well as 1932 produced juntas with military and civilian figures that lasted a few weeks. With the exception of a president who ran unopposed in 1927, all Chilean presidential elections since the first one in 1829 had more than one candidate in them, and all presidents had been replaced by their successors following constitutional procedures. The national congress, a key institution in Chilean history, was also closed by Pinochet's dictatorship for the first time since independence.

With the inauguration of President Patricio Aylwin on March 11, 1990, Chile finally recovered its hundred-year-plus democratic tradition. Since then Chile has reconsolidated its democracy, perfected its welfare state, and grown economically. It has the highest score of any Latin American nation on the United Nations human development index, and is the first South American country to join, at the beginning of 2010, the Organization of Economic Cooperation and Development (OECD).

This chapter examines the origins, evolution, characteristics, and breakdown of Chile's democratic system. It also reviews the main features of Pinochet's dictatorship and discusses the reestablishment of its democracy.

An Overview of Chilean Political History, 1818–1970

Founding a Proto-Democracy (1818–1850)

Chile's first experience in self-government began in September 1810, but the last of the Spanish king's forces were only defeated finally in 1826, a full eight years after Chile declared independence in 1818. The break with Spain brought important changes: Chile was declared a republic, all titles of nobility were abrogated, and slavery was abolished.

The nation's mostly rural population, located mainly between Copiapó in the North and Concepción in the South, continued to live off the fruits of the land while a merchant, mining, and landed elite drew its income from exporting copper, animal products, and grain. The break disrupted the monarchic colonial political system, but its judicial institutions, civil servants, and most of the colonial army continued to form the backbone of the incipient independent state. The very first constitutional strictures stipulated that the nation's authorities had to be divided into an executive power in the hands of a president, a legislature with a bicameral configuration, and an independent judiciary. By the mid-1820s, Chilean electoral laws had established a secret paper ballot, an electoral registry, territorial representation through districts that elected a variable number of congressmen on the basis of their population, indirect elections for the presidency, and direct elections for the lower house of congress. Access to suffrage was given to all males who had a fixed domicile and income, regardless of literacy. These laws were the most advanced of any nation in the world that experimented with democratic constitutionalism.

Several constitutions were enacted in the 1820s before an elected Constituent Assembly approved the constitution of 1828. By that time the electoral contests had generated a sharp division in Chilean politics between two parties, one conservative and the other liberal. The tragically ambiguous constitutional rules for the selection of the vice president by the congress—once the contest could not be decided by the Electoral College—ended in a brief civil war between the two forces which the conservative sector won. A drastically reduced electorate chose a new president and congress in 1831, and it approved the constitution of 1833, which proved to be long lasting. It called for a strong central government but preserved judicial independence and limited the powers of the president by giving congress the right to approve the annual budget law as well as a law authorizing the stationing of regular army troops in Santiago, the capital city.

If by the consolidation of a political order we mean the acceptance of its legitimacy by a nation's elites and by a broader informed public, then it is clear that the consolidation of the new nation's republican order, with its regular elections of all executive, legislative, and municipal authorities, took place under the constitution of 1833. The most important reason Chile's democratic constitutional order was consolidated comes back to the fact that the conservative forces (*pelucones*) that won the civil war of late 1829 to early 1830 continued to be committed to enacting a republican constitution that included periodic elections according to a legally defined electoral calendar. They kept the same electoral laws that had been enacted in the 1820s. This is hardly surprising, because they had been written by Mariano Egaña, a prominent conservative jurist who was also one of the main redactors of the constitution of 1833.

In practice, however, the elections became less democratic because the *pelucón* governments of the time began to mobilize national guard forces and public employees in an effort to gain majorities for an official list of candidates that they began to sponsor. While this was a reversal when compared to the lively and much more participatory elections of the 1820s, it nonetheless sustained the commitment of the Chilean upper class to the ritual of renewing authorities through electoral contests because the results were a foregone conclusion.

The consolidation of Chilean institutions was also aided by the triumph of Chilean forces over those of a Peru-Bolivia Confederation. Its leader was intent on extending its dominion southward, but the real spark that ignited the conflict was the assassination of Diego Portales in 1837. Portales was the strongman in the Chilean government of President José Joaquín Prieto (1831–1836; 1836–1841), and his high-handed measures made him an unpopular figure. Given his advocacy of a war against the Confederation, a rumor that he had been assassinated by agents of the Confederation stirred a wave of patriotic emotions. For the first time Chileans fought an external enemy: the war of independence had been, in fact, mostly a civil war. Chile's military victory over Peru and Bolivia led to a national reconciliation, including a restitution of pensions and ranks for the defeated forces of the 1829–1830 civil war. It also led to the election of the leader of the Chilean war effort, General Manuel Bulnes, to the presidency in 1841. A Chilean defeat in the war would have magnified factional disputes and threatened the stability of its institutions. The clear-cut victory created common symbols and a new sense of unity, and led to the inauguration of a government elected with overwhelming support.

Another important factor in the consolidation of Chile's institutions was the decisive control of the military by civilian authorities. Bulnes was a general, but his was a thoroughly civilian form of rule. He deliberately reduced the size of the regular army. By the end of Bulnes's two governments (1841–1846; 1846–1851) there were far fewer regular soldiers than at the beginning. Instead, Bulnes further encouraged the development of the national guard. Led by loyal government supporters, the part-time guard was composed mainly of civilians such as artisans, shopkeepers, and small proprietors. It numbered ten to twenty-five times the size of the peacetime army. A revolt against the government in 1851 partly reflected the discontent of regular army officers based in Concepción with military policy. Bulnes led national guard forces to suppress the uprising, which was aimed at preventing his elected successor, Manuel Montt, a civilian, from taking office. He then assisted Montt in putting down another revolt in 1859 with loyal army and guard forces.

Bulnes was deliberatively supportive of the fledgling institutional system. As head of the victorious army, he was in a position to ignore the constitution and

suspend electoral contests to institute personal rule, but he did not do so. He relied on a collegial body, the cabinet, to carry out the main tasks of government,
drawing his ministers from different sectors of public opinion and changing them
periodically to reflect new pressures and interests. He also respected a Supreme
Court decision that went against the wishes of one of his most important ministers, firing him in the process. Though the executive most often took the initiative,
congress had to approve all legislation. The legislature gradually became more as-
sertive and a platform for dissenting views. As early as the 1840s the congress resorted to delaying approval of the budget law in order to extract government
concessions. Rather than defying this challenge to his authority, Bulnes sought
compromises with it. Throughout the nineteenth century all relevant political factions gained representation in the legislature as well as in the cabinet, and had to
learn to collaborate within the shared institutional framework to further their interests. Every nineteenth-century head of state, with the exception of Jorge Montt,
who became president after the 1891 civil war, had extensive prior experience as an
elected representative in congress. Moreover, the five presidents who succeeded
Bulnes until 1886 began government service in his administration.

Yet another factor contributing to regime consolidation was economic growth,
even if such growth was itself facilitated in what was a virtuous circle by the nation's
political stability. The break with the colonial trade limitations opened the country
to the international market, and Chilean exports thrived. Newly discovered silver
deposits complemented copper exports, and shipments of wheat increased sharply
with the development of the new California market. The state played an important
role in encouraging development. It obtained foreign credit, opened new ports or
improved old ones, built railway lines, and established a merchant marine. Foreign
creditors were quick to take note as Chilean issues brought higher prices on the
London market than those of any other Latin American country.

There was a broad elite consensus on the merits of an outward-oriented development policy. Landowners in the central valley, miners in the north, and merchants in Santiago and in port cities all benefited from and promoted an economy
based on the export of primary goods in the production of which the country had
a decisive advantage. Most manufactured products were imported. There was no
protectionism for domestic industry and no effective political force to press for it.
The potential internal market for Chilean industry was small, and many obstacles,
including the long distances from Europe and the United States and the latter's tariff barriers, discouraged manufacturing for export. However, an incipient industrialization did begin around textiles, leather goods, iron works, and ship building. It
supplied the military and produced materials used in mining, construction, and
railways. By the end of the nineteenth-century Chilean industries made hundreds
of cannons, cauldrons, locomotives, wagons, and rails.

In sum, by midcentury, Chile had laid the foundations for constitutional republican rule. Victory in an international war, the control of the military by the constitutionally established authorities who respected the legal strictures, and economic
growth contributed to this result. The congress had taken its place as a basic arena
for political accommodation, compromise, overview of the executive, and opposition. And although the franchise was limited and subject to intervention, it became the only mechanism for selecting political officeholders.

State Expansion and Elite Reaction (1850–1890)

The sharpest political differences among nineteenth-century elites stemmed from the reaction of local and national notables, particularly those close to the Church, to the expansion of the state. When state institutions began to expand into the local level, rationalize taxes and duties, invest in public works projects, and reduce Church influence over national life, they generated bitter opposition. Some historians have interpreted nineteenth-century controversies as a struggle between a conservative rural "aristocracy" with a firm grip on the state and a rising group of miners, bankers, merchants, and professionals seeking political control. That view presupposes that political differences were the product of a fundamental, economically based cleavage among the elite. In fact, there was broad consensus on the merits of free trade policies and on the pursuit of a development model based on primary goods exports. Moreover, socioeconomic divisions among the dominant sectors were not so clear-cut: the wealthiest families often had cross-investments in all areas of the economy.

Moreover, by midcentury the state was not simply a tool of economic elites but had a considerable degree of autonomy. An entirely new profession of urban-based government officials and politicians had appeared on the political scene. Like President Manuel Montt (1851–1856; 1856–1861), they relied on the state for their positions and had a stake in the expansion of governmental authority. By 1860 over 2,500 persons worked for the state, not counting thousands of workers hired by municipalities and government-financed public works projects or the many individuals associated with the national guard and the armed forces.

State autonomy was in part a function of growing governmental institutionalization and of the ability of state officials to manipulate the verdict of the electorate. But it was also the product of a system of revenue collection tied to an export economy. Reliance on customs revenues in a time of export expansion meant an incremental and automatic infusion of larger sums of money into state coffers without imposing large-scale domestic taxation. From 1830 to 1860 government revenues from customs duties, representing about 60 percent of all revenue, increased seven times. State revenues enabled the construction of numerous public works projects, including the second railroad system of Latin America and the first to be operated by a government. In the fifteen years between 1845 and 1860, expenditures on education alone quadrupled.

Given the encroachment of the state on the localities and its increasing secularization, control of the state and its expenditures became the most important political issue of the time. Were urban or rural areas to be favored by state resources? Which port facilities should be improved? Where were the railroad lines to be built? Should local officials remain subordinated to the national government's decisions and largess, or should they be autonomous from it? And most importantly, should the state or the Church control the expanding educational system, civil registry, cemeteries, and hospitals?

The Conservative Party became the foremost expression of discontent over the state's challenge to the Church's monopoly over educational, cultural, and family life. The party was originally formed by a group that split away from the Montt government as he pressed to enhance further the role of the state. Once in opposition, the Conservatives soon made alliances of convenience with some ideological Liberals who, while supporting the concept of a secular state, wanted more decentralization of political authority and an expansion of electoral participation. The unsuccessful 1859 uprising reflected the seriousness of the political controversies as a few Liberal, Conservative, and regional elements attempted to prevent Manuel Montt's closest associate from succeeding him to the presidency. Though the government forces, known as the Nationals, controlled the rebellion, Montt's associate withdrew his candidacy. The new National president, José Joaquín Pérez (1861–1866; 1866–1871), saw the political wisdom of granting amnesty to the rebels and, following the Bulnes precedents, of incorporating both Conservatives and Liberals into cabinets of national unity in what became known as the Liberal-Conservative fusion.

A few measures were adopted during the Pérez administrations to curb the power of executive authority. The president was restricted to one term, armed personnel were barred from voting booths, and other minor electoral reforms were made. However, the basic character of the state remained unchanged. With Pérez's support, the Liberals outmaneuvered their Conservative allies and continued the basic policies of the preceding National governments. State power transformed the Liberals, not vice versa. State authority expanded further and the secularization of public institutions continued.

By the midpoint of the administration of Liberal president Federico Errázuriz (1871–1876), the Conservatives had had enough. They left the cabinet and, once again, made an alliance of convenience with another opposition group, the Radical Party, even though it was, ironically, even more extreme in its anticlerical and secularizing positions than the Liberals controlling the government. This unlikely alliance held a majority in congress. The Conservatives took advantage of it to press for a liberalization of the electoral system in 1874 by eliminating the requirement for voters to show proof that they had the requisite income to vote. The income levels that were demanded of voters were not high, but they helped the government prevent opposition voters from registering to vote. The new rule simply limited voting to all men who knew how to read and write, a point that opposition voters could prove with relative ease before voter registration boards. As a result the electorate tripled from 50,000 to 150,000 by 1878.

The 1874 reforms were not sufficient to counteract the strong intervention of local agents of the executive in the electoral process, an intervention that became more blatant and violent as the government's control over the electorate diminished. Hence in 1890 the Conservatives presented a new electoral law regulating the way in which voting was supposed to be conducted. It created a secret voting booth to which all voters had to retire to place their ballots in an officially stamped envelope given to them at polling places. This change strengthened the secrecy provisions in Chile's electoral tradition, and antedated similar reforms in Argentina (1912) and France (1913).

All opposition groups stood to gain from these reforms. Given the failure of armed conspiracies in 1851 and 1859, their only hope of gaining control of the government lay in reducing the executive's power to manipulate the voting process. The key role played by the Conservative Party in suffrage expansion (which, surprisingly, has been attributed to the Liberals and Radicals by most historians) meant that a key party of the Chilean right remained committed to expressing its power capabilities through the electoral system, not, as in other countries, through conspiracies with the armed forces. Given the proximity of the Conservative Party to the Church, it also meant that Church opposition to republican democracy, typical of Latin Europe, never developed in Chile. On the contrary, its main political ally was the driving force in the nation's nineteenth-century democratization.

The stakes involved in the control of the executive increased dramatically with the Chilean victory in the War of the Pacific (1879–1883), again against Peru and Bolivia. In the 1860s and 1870s customs duties as a percentage of government revenue had declined to as low as 40 percent. After the war, with the incorporation of Peruvian and Bolivian land with the only natural nitrate deposits in the world into Chilean territory, customs duties once again climbed to over 70 percent of government income. Chile acquired the monopoly of nitrate production, used as a fertilizer and for gunpowder. Though a majority of the nitrate fields fell into the hands of foreign interests, the Chilean state was able to retain close to 50 percent of all profits through taxation. From 1870 to 1890 government revenues climbed over 150 percent, leading to a new wave of public works projects and other government expenditures. The boom in nitrate exports helped the Chilean economy match that of the United States for the record of the two top performing economies in the world during the nineteenth century, although Chile's per capita income was about half of that of the United States.

The struggle over the state's role in society resulted in the civil war of 1891 during the closing months of José Manuel Balmaceda's government (1886–1891). Opposition to Balmaceda crystallized over the most contentious issue of the nineteenth century: whether or not the president could name his successor and intervene in the elections to impose him on the country. Balmaceda's defeat permitted the unfettered application of the 1890 electoral reforms, which finally generated the free expression of the citizens' options between the various candidates presented by the parties. This opened the way for the Chilean regime to finally become, at least in a minimal sense, a democratic one.

Transformation of the Party System with Democratization (1891–1925)

After 1891 the center of gravity in the Chilean political system shifted away from the office of the president. A new law of municipal autonomy and the 1890 electoral reform finally freed local party leaders from national government interference to compete for votes. A parliamentary interpretation of the constitution gave legislators the right to approve all cabinet ministers, further democratizing the political system.

Politics in the parliamentary republic (1891–1925) became a logrolling game as legislative factions jockeyed for influence. Budget laws were carved up to please local supporters. The state expanded as it developed new agencies and functions. Civil servants, excluding all teachers, railway workers and health professionals in public employment, increased from 3,048 in 1880 to 13,119 in 1900 and 27,479 in 1919. Despite considerable ministerial instability during this period given shifts in political coalitions and complex electoral pacts, there was a bedrock of stability in the leadership of the growing state by a professional civil service.

A key organization of twentieth-century politics, the political party with extensive local bases, developed principally during this period. Abstention rates during elections often reached more than 50 percent, and ensuring that a party's electorate actually did come to the polls became a complex job. Attempts to buy votes were not infrequent. Much of the day-to-day party activities shifted from the hands of notables to those of professional politicians and local activists.

These political changes coincided with the profound socioeconomic transformations set in motion by nitrate production, which soon employed 10 to 15 percent of the active population. It in turn stimulated the national market for industrial goods, construction, and transportation services. Rural areas and their commercial networks also experienced changes, as agriculture and agro-industry sought to meet the demand for food in the arid north where the nitrate mining operations were located. The urban population increased from 26 percent of the total in 1875 to about 45 percent by 1925. Literacy also increased to about half the population by the early 1920s, as new schools for boys and girls dotted every town. Public high schools were built in major cities. The new urban landscape benefitted the Radical Party as well as the Democrats, a party with social democratic leanings connected to the labor movement. In addition, a Socialist Workers Party and anarcho-syndicalists also developed their presence among workers.

Unions mushroomed everywhere as nitrate, dock, railway, and industrial workers and artisans sought to improve their lot. However, many government and business elites thought that labor militancy threatened the nation's progress. Since nitrate revenues were the lifeline of the state and the economy, any cut in export revenues because of strikes had considerable repercussions. The army was repeatedly used to put down strikes, often with great brutality, as in the Iquique massacre of 1907, when up to several hundred people were killed. Repression of labor union activities created a leftist union leadership, as radical workers were more likely to assume the great personal risks involved. And yet the openness of the political system meant that repression of labor union activity at the point of production was not accompanied systematically by political repression. Working-class leaders were allowed to publish newspapers, create cultural associations, lobby congress, and create political parties. Despite their radical outlook, they realized that their cause could best be advanced politically through alliances of convenience with traditional parties eager to maximize their electoral fortunes. Thus in 1921 Luís Emilio Recabarren, a founding figure of the labor movement and the Socialist Workers Party, and one of his comrades were elected to congress through an electoral pact with the Radical Party. This repeated earlier successes in local elections in which pacts had been forged with either Radicals or Democrats. The repression of organized workers therefore contributed to the formation of a leftist labor union and party leadership, and the relatively open and representative character of the political system meant that they were able to build their political organizations.

Chilean political leaders were under great pressure to solve what was called the "social question." Liberal president Arturo Alessandri (1920–1924) promised to do so by passing a sweeping package of labor and welfare laws, including the legalization of unions and the right to strike. His Conservative Party opponents also proposed their own alternative projects. Congressional discussions of these measures dragged on. In September 1924 young army officers gathered in the congressional galleries and demanded that the legislators pass the reforms; they obliged by approving both the Liberal and the Conservative projects. The army's unprecedented intervention in the legislative process led to the president's resignation and to the formation of a governing military junta. Higher-ranking officers in January 1925 toppled it and called for the president's return. In reassuming power, Alessandri proposed a new, once again fully presidentialist constitution. It was approved in a plebiscite, after which presidential and parliamentary elections were held.

And yet political irregularities continued. The newly elected president was forced to resign, given that his minister of defense, Colonel Carlos Ibáñez, organized a plebiscite to justify his own assumption of the presidency. During his government (1927–1931) congress and the parties lost influence. Ibáñez also tried to reduce the strength of the communist-controlled labor federations, which represented a majority of organized workers. Interpreting the labor laws approved in 1924 to suit his own ends, Ibáñez established legal unionism only where his agents could find leaders who agreed to support his government. This manipulation of the laws delayed their full and correct implementation until the late 1930s. With the catastrophic effects of the Great Depression (with Chilean exports dropping to less than 20 percent of their value by 1931), a political crisis forced Ibáñez to resign. After an uncertain year of further instability, Arturo Alessandri was reelected president in 1932 by a large margin.

Polarization and Mass Participation (1925–1970)

Chile's reliance on lucrative nitrate exports came to an end when Germany developed a synthetic nitrate just before World War I. The decline of the Chilean nitrate industry took over a decade to unfold, but with the world economic collapse of the early 1930s it came to a complete halt. The Chilean economy took nearly a decade to recover from this shock. Greatly expanded copper production replaced nitrate as the nation's principal export. By the late 1930s copper represented roughly 55 percent of export earnings, increasing to about 80 percent by the 1970s.

The constitution of 1925 strengthened the presidency and established the separation of Church and state. However, the most important political change of the 1920s was the rise of the left. The Communist Party was officially founded when the Socialist Workers Party voted in December 1921 to adhere to the Third International. By the end of the decade, a Trotskyite splinter had been expelled from the party, and various socialist groups had been created. After Ibáñez's resignation, all these organizations emerged from their underground work to produce a confusing array of political groups on the left. However, in April 1933 a core of highly popular leaders formed the Socialist Party of Chile by uniting most of the preexisting socialist and Trotskyite organizations. The new Socialist Party quickly gained a significant working-class base by attracting the support of the country's legal unions, with which the Communists had refused to collaborate, given their origins. Thus by the early 1930s two major parties claiming to represent the workers had emerged, leading to a complex relationship of competition and/or cooperation between them that continues to this day. And with the rise of the Marxist left, the party system became highly polarized, covering the full range of the ideological spectrum.

In 1934 the Third International adopted a "popular front" strategy of seeking alliances with like-minded parties to stop the spread of fascism. As a result, the Chilean Communist Party agreed to socialist initiatives designed to unite the labor movement and coordinate political strategies. With an eye on the next presidential elections, the Radical Party withdrew its support for the conservative second Alessandri administration (1932–1938) and joined with the left. The resulting Popular Front coalition elected the Radical Pedro Aguirre Cerda to the presidency in December 1938. This electoral victory marked the success of a center-to-Marxist left coalition which would govern the country until the onset of the Cold War in 1947. It encouraged the incorporation of the communist-led unions within the framework of the 1924 labor laws that shaped Chile's industrial relations system. And it created the State Development Corporation (CORFO) in order to plan and direct an industrialization process aimed at substituting imported consumer goods with locally produced articles.

The creation of CORFO was symptomatic of a change of direction in Chilean economic policy. With the drastic decline of the capacity to import in the early 1930s, policymakers thought that the nation should not rely on imports to satisfy most of its needs. They therefore encouraged national industrial growth by establishing new lines of credit, protectionism, direct and indirect subsidies, price controls, as well as state investments in key areas such as steel and energy. As a result, by the late 1960s Chile produced a broad range of consumer goods, if not always at internationally competitive levels of efficiency.

One of the Popular Front governments' objectives in fostering industrialization was the creation of jobs in urban areas in order to absorb the influx of new rural migrants into the cities. By 1940, 53 percent of the population lived in urban areas, a figure that increased to 76 percent by 1970. The population in cities with more than 20,000 people increased at an even faster rate. The new industrialization in the long run, however, did not generate employment at a faster rate than the increase in urban population. The secondary sector (including for present purposes mining, construction, transport, and particularly manufacturing) absorbed roughly the same proportion of the economically active population in 1970 as it had in 1940, even though its proportion of the gross domestic product increased from 38 percent in 1940 to 48 percent in 1970. It was the service sector that absorbed increasing shares of total employment while contributing a smaller share of the GDP, while the primary sector (agriculture, forestry, and fishing) declined on both counts.

The Popular Front coalition broke down in part because of internecine squabbles among Socialists and between Socialists and Communists, and in part because of the fear of both Socialists and Radicals (particularly after the 1947 municipal election) that the Communists were gaining votes at their expense. The onset of the Cold War and US pressure also played a role in the Radicals' decision not only to expel the Communists from the cabinet but also to declare the party illegal in 1948. The disarray of the left and a distrust of the Radicals after so many years of bargaining with both the left and the right finally led the electorate to turn, once again, to Carlos Ibáñez (1952–1958) and his promises to govern above party politics. Chilean women, who were granted the right to vote in national elections in 1949, finally voted for the first time ever in the 1952 presidential election.

Ibáñez's term was marked by the initiation of broad-ranging social reforms (prepared by the previous Radical administration of Gabriel González Videla, 1946–1952). They effectively initiated, for the first time ever, old age pensions and began to offer all children school breakfasts and lunches. This measure initiated a process by which Chile reached full coverage in primary school enrollments.

The Ibáñez administration ended with a sense of failure, given its inability to control inflation, which reached 86 percent in 1955. The disintegration of the Ibáñez movement might have allowed the Radicals to move once again to fill the center of Chilean politics, but they were challenged in that role by the emerging Christian Democratic party led by Eduardo Frei, who fused various Social Christian groups together, including major portions of the old Conservative Party. But the real surprise of the 1958 presidential election was the showing by Salvador Allende, the candidate of the Communist and Socialist parties. With 28.9 percent of the vote in the sharply divided contest, he narrowly failed (2.7 percent) to defeat the winner, Jorge Alessandri.

In office, Alessandri (1958–1964), a businessman supported by the right and occasionally by the peripatetic Radicals, applied a new set of austerity measures and obtained increased foreign aid to attempt economic stabilization. In the wake of the Cuban revolution, the United States became determined to prevent a growth of leftist influence in the rest of the hemisphere. Chile, with its large Marxist parties, became a priority of the Kennedy and Johnson administrations' foreign aid programs and covert intelligence operations.

During the 1964 presidential election, the Chilean center and right, as well as the US government, sought to prevent what almost occurred in 1958—an Allende victory. As a result the right decided to support the centrist Frei candidacy, which promised a "revolution in liberty." The CIA contributed $1.20 per Chilean voter to the antileft propaganda effort, over twice as much as the $0.54 per US voter that Lyndon Johnson and Barry Goldwater jointly spent in their own presidential campaigns that year. Frei was elected with an absolute majority of the votes. His government, that of his successor—the Socialists Party leader Salvador Allende—and the breakdown of democracy will be discussed after a review of the principal aspects and actors of the political game of twentieth-century Chilean politics.

POLITICAL GROUPS AND THE STATE: THE POLITICAL SYSTEM AT MIDCENTURY

By midcentury the Chilean state absorbed about 24 percent of the GDP. The state also generated over 55 percent of gross investment and roughly 50 percent of all available credit. About 13 percent of the active population worked for the state, not counting the employees of the thirty-nine key corporations in which CORFO owned majority shares or the forty-one other enterprises where its participation was substantial. Government agencies distributed most health care and social security benefits, regulated prices and wages, and settled labor disputes. Indeed, the dominant role of government in regulatory, distributive, and redistributive policies meant that private groups were constantly turning to state agencies and to the legislature, at times through elected local government officials, to gain favorable rulings and dispensations.

Chilean society had numerous civil organizations. They included professional societies, student unions, trade and pensioners' associations, youth and church groups, mothers' clubs, and neighborhood councils. Workers were represented by industrial, craft, and peasant unions (the latter legalized only in 1967), which were subjected to a series of state regulations and restrictions, although their leadership was democratically chosen by the rank and file. Civil servants were organized into associations that acted as unions but were never officially recognized as such. Most groups sought to maximize their political clout before the state by organizing national associations with national headquarters. Large industrial, agricultural, and commercial interests were respectively organized into the Society for Industrial Advancement, the National Agricultural Society, and the Central Chamber of Commerce, all of which were affiliated with the Confederation of Commerce and Production. Professional societies were grouped in the Confederation of Professional Associations. Roughly 60 percent of all unionists were affiliated directly or indirectly with the Central Labor Federation (CUT). Some specialized workers, small industrialists and retail merchants, truck owners, and so on, also had national organizations.

Following the 1925 constitution, the president—elected for a six-year term—was the source of major initiatives in the political process. Yet the president was far from an all-powerful figure. The most important checks on executive authority came from the competitive party system. But presidential authority was also checked by the differentiation of governmental institutions and the marked autonomy of agencies even within the executive chain of command.

The legislature did not have the same power that it had under the parliamentary republic. Nevertheless, the Chilean congress remained the most powerful in Latin America, with the ability to modify and reject executive proposals. The congress was the main arena for discussion and approval of budgetary matters as well as for the all-important issue of wage readjustments for public and even private employees.

In the final analysis, legislative politics was party politics, and presidents could cajole and bargain with allied as well as with adversary political groups for mutual advantage. By contrast the two other branches of government, the judicial system and the comptroller general, were well insulated from both presidential and legislative scrutiny. Judicial promotions were determined by seniority and merit, and though the president retained some power of appointment, his candidates had to come from lists prepared by the judges themselves. Equally independent was the comptroller general. His agency was charged with auditing public accounts and ruling on the legality of all executive decrees. The comptroller's rulings on financial matters were final; on other matters, the president could, with the concurrence of his cabinet, overrule the comptroller. However, because of the prestige of the latter's office, this could be done only at the risk of considerable controversy.

Even within the executive branch presidential authority was circumscribed. Forty percent of public employees worked for over fifty semiautonomous agencies that, though nominally under government ministries, enjoyed significant managerial and even budgetary autonomy. As elsewhere, the web of private interests affected by a particular agency soon learned to develop more or less workable relationships of mutual benefit with it. Vested interests often made it difficult for a new administration to abolish old programs and bureaus, and innovations often required the creation of new agencies to administer the new projects, thus contributing to the progressive expansion of the state apparatus. Civil service organizations and professional associations anxious to place their members in the state sector further complicated the picture. Some state agencies became virtual fiefdoms of architects, civil engineers, lawyers, or doctors.

Though many agencies actually had formal interest-group representation on managing councils, such representation never became as important as the more informal and fluid constituency ties. Chilean politics never became corporative politics. Most private groups did obtain legal recognition. But that was a routine procedure and hardly meant that the government was officially sanctioning particular associations with exclusive rights to represent functional segments of society before the state. Indeed, most claims on the state were made by highly competitive groups, often representing interests drawn from the same horizontal or class lines.

If Chilean politics was not corporative, neither was it praetorian. Despite the vast and disarticulated state apparatus and the claims of a multiplicity of interests jockeying for advantage, Chilean politics did not involve the naked confrontation of political forces each seeking to maximize its interests through direct action in the face of weak or transitory authority structures. The key to the Chilean system, which discouraged both corporatist and praetorian tendencies, was the continuing importance of political parties and a party system tied to the legislature, the principal arena for political give-and-take. From the turn of the century on, the norm in Chile was not the direct link between government agencies and interest associations or the unmediated clash of organized social forces. Rather, party structures, permeating all levels of society, served as crucial linkage mechanisms binding organizations, institutions, groups, and individuals to the political center. Local units of competing parties were active within each level of the bureaucracy, each labor union, and each student federation. Parties often succeeded in capturing particular organizations or in setting up rival ones. Once an issue affecting the organization arose, party structures were instrumental in conveying the organization's demands to the nucleus of the policymaking process or in acting as brokers before the ubiquitous bureaucracy.

As noted above, the Chilean party system was fragmented and competitive. With the exception of the Christian Democrats in the mid-1960s, no single party received more than 30 percent of the votes in congressional or municipal elections from 1925 to 1973. The party system was also highly polarized. During the 1937–1973 period, the vote for the left (Socialists and Communists) averaged 21.5 percent (or 25.7 percent if one excludes the 1949, 1953, and 1957 elections in which the Communists were banned from participation), and the vote for the right averaged 30.1 percent. Since neither the right nor the left could obtain an effective majority on its own, center groups, especially the Radical Party, played an important if little appreciated role in the polarized system. By dealing with both extremes, they were essential elements in most legislative majorities or in winning presidential coalitions—all of which permitted the political system to muddle through despite the sharp ideological divergences. And yet the center movements could not succeed in establishing themselves as a majority force, although they occasionally eroded the strength of either the left or the right. For example, sup-

ported by voters on the right, the Christian Democrats scored a dramatic gain in
the 1965 congressional election, obtaining 42.3 percent of the vote. But the Liberals
and Conservatives, having merged to form the National Party in 1966, regained
much of their historical strength by 1969, and their candidate outpolled
the Christian Democratic nominee in the 1970 presidential election.

Given the fact that no single party or tendency could capture the presidency
alone, coalitions were necessary. These were either formed before the election and
resulted in winning an absolute majority, as was the case in 1964, or they had to
be put together after the election in order to obtain the constitutionally mandated
congressional approval of a candidate receiving only a plurality of the vote, as occurred
in most cases. But, invariably, coalitions tended to disintegrate shortly after
the election. The president could not succeed himself, and party leaders scrambled
to disassociate themselves from the difficulties of incumbency in order to maximize
electoral fortunes in succeeding contests. This meant that presidents had to
compromise often with new supporters in the legislature, to salvage part of their
programs and to govern.

Despite the polarization of the party system, politics did not revolve around
only ideological and programmatic discussions. Obtaining benefits for groups and
even favors for individuals continued to be an important part of party activities. In
fact, officials from all parties spent most of their time acting as political brokers—
processing pensions for widows, helping Protestant ministers qualify for the white-collar
social security fund, interviewing the labor minister on behalf of a union
leadership, seeking a job for a young schoolteacher, obtaining bridges and sewer
systems for communities, and so forth. Legislators had access to state agencies because
of congressional influence over purse strings, promotions, and programs affecting
the bureaucracy.

An important political issue that led to extended bargaining in the legislature
and to a flurry of demands and pressures from organized groups was the yearly discussion
of the wage readjustment law. The law was intimately related to the budgetary
approval process and gave the legislators (and therefore the parties) an input
into the economic policy planning process. The state-controlled wage scales in the
public sector were used as guidelines for the private sector, and therefore the readjustment
laws, which also regulated social security benefits, were of great concern
to the broader public. In an economy averaging over 25 percent inflation with
sharp yearly variations, a fundamental demand would be readjustments that would
exceed, or at least match, the rate of inflation. Occasionally, amendments favoring
specific groups or unions, but not all in the same category, would be approved as
the legislators in the majority group sought to pay off political debts or favor their
party comrades in positions of leadership. And yet the political ramifications of
class cleavages in the society would become apparent as the left would normally
press for higher wages and benefits for working-class sectors, and the right would
often favor restrictive readjustments to meet fiscal and inflationary targets.

There were no giants in the Chilean political system. No single group could win
a complete majority or totally impose its will on the others. In fact, since there was
no ideological or programmatic consensus among the polarized political forces, the
Chilean polity was in many respects a stalemated one, in which each decision led
to extensive debates and long processes of political accommodation—or to lengthy

protests by the dissatisfied groups. In such a setting, change could only be incremental, not revolutionary. Though upper-class sectors were favored by existing arrangements, an intricate stalemate reflected a situation in which each group derived benefits. There was a strong consensus over procedure, and over the expression of power capabilities through elections. But as the left gained positions of power, the right and the sectors it represented began to question the validity of the process itself.

THE BREAKDOWN OF DEMOCRACY

Chile Under Eduardo Frei

The election of Eduardo Frei to the presidency in 1964 marked a significant shift in the center of Chilean politics. Unlike the Radical Party or the Ibáñez movement, the Christian Democrats (DC) claimed to be a new and cohesive ideological center, intent on breaking the political stalemate. They argued that their reformist strategy would lead to genuine economic and social progress and that it represented a viable third way between the right and the Marxist left. The Christian Democrats therefore ignored the fact that they had achieved the presidency with the endorsement of the rightist parties, and that their unprecedented 1965 majority in the chamber of deputies was obtained with the support of traditionally right-wing portions of the electorate. They tried to govern as if they had become a majority party that would monopolize the presidency without coalition support for decades to come.

The Radicals, rather than being cultivated as a potential ally in the political center, were maligned as pragmatic opportunists and were forced to relinquish some of their hold over the state bureaucracy. With the exercise of rigid party discipline in the chamber of deputies, which prevented the legislature from overruling presidential initiatives, the Christian Democrats used their lower house majority as rubber stamp.

The animosities created by the Christian Democrats' disdain for coalition politics were compounded by the reforms they set in motion. These were ostensibly designed to raise the living standards and political participation of lower-class sectors as well as modernize the social and economic systems. Two new groups were mobilized as never before: the urban shantytown dwellers and the peasants. The former were encouraged to set up neighborhood councils and a variety of self-help organizations with cultural and community development ends. The latter rapidly became unionized once the peasant unionization law was approved in 1967, or they were included in the peasant cooperatives that were set up in the lands expropriated under the government's new agrarian reform program. Small landholding peasants were also encouraged to form cooperatives. As a result, roughly half the peasant labor force had become organized one way or another by 1970. Many new (particularly craft) unions were also formed among urban workers. Training programs were begun for both workers and peasants to increase their skills.

The reforms in the countryside engendered great opposition on the right, which traditionally had a strong political base among the landowners who were threatened with expropriations and peasant unionization. The reforms also caused resentment and bitterness on the left. As the many young Christian Democrats in charge of the new programs spread throughout the country using modern techniques and displaying new equipment, it became clear that the DC was attempting to build a strong political base among popular sectors, precisely those sectors that Communists and Socialists considered their own natural base of support. This led to an intense effort by the left to compete with the DC in the creation of the new popular organizations. As a result sharp party conflicts were extended to broader sections of the population, creating sectarian divisions and feelings at the grass roots as never before. The threat to the left and the overall party competition for popular support were enhanced by the rise of an extreme left movement that also sought to organize its following.

The popular mobilization of the 1960s should therefore be seen as the result of party competition, with primarily political consequences. It cannot be said that the process got out of hand, either in terms of the capacity of party elites to control it or in terms of its having overburdened the nation's economy. In fact, during the Frei administration the general economic situation improved and state income increased, thereby generating greater economic capacity to increase the income of the newly mobilized popular sectors as well as a larger government capability to finance new programs. Though state income rose with better tax collection, the economic and fiscal improvements of the period were largely due to a rise in the price of copper during the Vietnam War and to foreign credit, mainly from US government and private sources. The latter caused an increase in Chilean external debt by the end of Frei's term with debt service payments equivalent to roughly a third of export earnings.

Despite all its efforts, the DC vote in the 1969 congressional elections was reduced to 29.8 percent. And given the events of the previous six years, it proved impossible to have anything but a three-way race in the 1970 presidential elections. The right would have nothing to do with the Christian Democrats and decided to rally behind the candidacy of former president Jorge Alessandri. The Radicals and other small centrist and leftist groups joined the Socialists and Communists in forming the Popular Unity (UP) coalition, which presented Salvador Allende as candidate.

Allende obtained 36.2 percent of the vote, Alessandri came in a close second with 34.9 percent, and the DC nominee Radomiro Tomic trailed with 27.8 percent. This result was not the expression of heightened electoral radicalism. Allende, in fact, received a smaller percentage of the vote than in 1964, when he was supported by only Socialists and Communists. Moreover, although Tomic ran on a leftist platform, it is clear from survey and electoral data that his voters would have gone to the right rather than the left.

Following constitutional procedure, the congress had to elect the president from the two front-runners, since none of the candidates received an absolute majority of the vote. In the most flagrant foreign intervention in Chilean history, US president Richard Nixon ordered the CIA to do everything necessary to prevent Allende from coming to power, including economic sabotage and a military coup. The Christian Democrats, unable to vote for their own candidate, held the key swing votes in the legislature, and President Frei and his colleagues were subjected to internal and external pressure to vote for Alessandri. When it appeared that they would reluctantly honor tradition by selecting the front-runner, the CIA helped organize an attempt to kidnap the chief of staff of the armed forces to provoke a military coup. General René Schneider was killed and the coup attempt backfired. It was the first assassination of a major Chilean leader since Portales was killed in 1837.

The Allende Years

Allende's inauguration as president represented the first time that a coalition dominated by the Socialist and Communist parties took control of the executive. The coalition had campaigned on a program designed to initiate a transition to socialism while preserving Chile's traditional democratic freedoms and constitutional procedures. With the unanimous consent of the congress, US interests in the copper mines were nationalized. Resorting to executive powers, some of which were based on admittedly obscure though never repealed legal statutes, the government purchased or took over a broad range of industries as well as the private banking sector and, using Frei's agrarian reform law, accelerated expropriations of farmland. Some industry and land takeovers were instigated by workers or peasants, led in most cases by leftist or extreme leftist militants, who began sit-in strikes demanding the expropriations. This phenomenon was aided by the overall political climate created by the Allende inauguration, which favored working-class actions, even when they contradicted government policies.

The government also set in motion a plan to raise wages, salaries, and benefits, particularly for the lowest-paid workers, and to increase social services in poor communities. These measures were taken to stimulate the economy by increasing demand and to strengthen the government's electoral support. For the left's working-class constituents, socialism principally meant a better standard of living. The policies were apparently successful, as economic growth in 1971 was the best in decades, and the Popular Unity got about 50 percent of the vote in that year's municipal elections.

The initially favorable economic trends were, however, quickly reversed. Reflecting the needs of poor people, rising demand was disproportionately channeled to a greater consumption of basic consumer items such as food and clothing, areas of the economy that were least able to respond with rapid production increases. Inflationary pressures were therefore strengthened, particularly since government spending increased without a proportional rise in tax receipts. By the end of 1972 inflation had reached 164 percent and currency emissions accounted for over 40 percent of the fiscal budget. Moreover, the economy was clearly hurt by politically motivated cutbacks in credits and spare parts from the usual US private or governmental sources. Foreign-exchange reserves dwindled rapidly as Chile imported more food and equipment with less recourse to credit and as it sought to meet payments, though partly rescheduled, on the foreign debt. The price of copper dropped to record lows, adding to the difficulties.

Early political success also proved short-lived. In 1972 the UP suffered reverses in key by-elections as well as in important institutional elections, such as the University of Chile or labor federations. The courts, the comptroller general, and congress objected increasingly to government initiatives. And most importantly, the early tacit support of the Christian Democrats turned into active opposition, leading to congressional censorship of ministers and to attempts to limit presidential authority.

   The process that led to the brutal 1973 military coup that ended the Allende experiment is highly complex, multidimensional, and dialectical. It cannot be reduced to a simple set of causes that are easily construed with the benefits of hindsight. Surely the government made many unwise decisions or proved indecisive at important turning points; the sabotage and conspiracies of foreign and domestic interests seeking to preserve privilege at all costs helped to create an acute economic and political crisis; the actions of revolutionary groups both within and without the government coalition contributed to the exacerbation of an atmosphere of extreme confrontation that strengthened the disloyal and reactionary opposition; elements in the armed forces proved to be less than totally committed to the constitution and the democratic system; the state's capacity to control and direct civil society disintegrated; and in the long run the dependency of the economy made the Allende experiment excessively vulnerable. All these factors are important, but they are not sufficient to explain the final result if viewed apart from a historical process in which contingent events played an important role. The breakdown of the regime was not preordained. It is a mistake to view the middle sectors as hopelessly reactionary, the workers as so radicalized that they would not stop short of total revolution, the army so antidemocratic that it was only waiting for its opportunity, the economy so dependent and the United States so single-handedly powerful and intransigent that the only possible denouement was full-fledged authoritarianism. There was room for choice, but with each unfolding event in the historical process that choice was markedly reduced.

   If a single factor must be highlighted, the breakdown of Chilean democracy should be viewed as the result of the inability and unwillingness of moderate forces on both sides of the political dividing line to forge center agreements on programs and policies as well as on regime-saving compromises. The UP could not obtain a workable majority on its own, and the option of arming the workers as demanded by revolutionary groups only undermined the government's legitimacy and credibility. The Chilean left had won an election and had promised to retain its commitment to the country's long democratic tradition. But without support from centrist forces, principally from the Christian Democrats who had made Allende's election possible in the first place, the UP would not have sufficient power to carry out its programs.

   The failure of center agreements resulted from political pressures originating in the extremes of both sides of the polarized party system. The government coalition was in fact sharply divided, the basic disagreements being those separating the Communists from the majority faction in the Socialist party. The latter wanted to press as fast as possible to institute the UP program and felt that support for the government would increase only insofar as it took decisive action to implement a socialist system. Compromise with the DC would, in the Socialists' view, only divert revolutionary objectives and confuse the working class. They therefore sought to undermine UP-DC collaboration and agreements. The Communists were more willing to moderate the course of government policies in order to consolidate a narrower range of changes and broaden the government's legislative base by resolving differences with the Christian Democrats. Both Socialists and Communists were pressured by the non-UP extreme left, which sought to accelerate changes through direct action outside constitutional procedures. Their influence in the UP coalition was magnified by the proximity of their positions with those of elements in the Socialist Party majority; therefore, the extreme left was not marginalized at the fringe of the political process.

Allende shared the Communists' position but did not wish to break with his own Socialist Party. He therefore projected an ambivalent image and at times failed to take decisive action—for fear of alienating his party—without the certainty of receiving consistent support from the center forces in exchange. These political differences affected the daily operation of government agencies; employees, for example, often would not take orders from superiors belonging to other parties. The president and the ministers were so involved in tending to these daily crises that they had little time to structure long-term policies, analyze the consequences of short-term ones, or develop a coherent strategy to deal with the moderate opposition.

The Christian Democrats were also torn by internal differences. The party was divided into left- and right-leaning factions of approximately equal strength. The 1971 party leadership came from the left-leaning group, and it sought to maintain a working relationship with the government, while the right-wing faction pressed for a tougher opposition stand. However, the party leadership was at first rebuffed by an overly confident UP government exhibiting the same arrogance the DC had shown previously, a situation that only strengthened the position of the right-wing sector within the party. Ironically, constitutional reforms adopted in 1970 by the DC and the right had diminished the role of the legislature, thus reducing the executive's need to reach agreements with the opposition. The right-wing faction was also strengthened by the vehement attacks on prominent DC leaders in the leftist media and by the assassination of a former Frei cabinet minister. Though this killing was the action of a small leftist fringe, the DC blamed the government for tolerating a climate of violence that, it argued, led to such incidents.

As a centrist opposition force, the DC was vulnerable to pressures from the right of the party system. If the DC leadership could not show that its tacit support for the government had resulted in moderating UP policies, the party stood to lose the anti-UP vote to the right without gaining greater support from the left. Therefore the DC was soon forced to work with the right in opposition. The turning point came in mid-1971 with the first special by-election to fill a vacant congressional seat in which, given the winner-take-all nature of the contest, a UP victory was certain if the opposition fielded separate candidates. Consequently the DC approached the government suggesting an agreement that would have led to a joint UP-DC candidacy, an offer that Allende accepted but the Socialist Party vetoed. In view of this rejection, the DC turned to the right, and the joint opposition candidate won decisively. As a result of this experience, a leftist splinter group decided to leave the Christian Democratic Party, which strengthened further the rightist faction within it. The DC alliance with the right-wing National Party continued in future elections, adding to the polarization of forces.

In February 1972 the DC obtained congressional approval of legislation severely limiting the president's ability to intervene in the economy, thereby challenging the essence of the government's program and marking the beginning of a fundamental constitutional confrontation between the president and the congress. Interpreting 1970 constitutional amendments differently from the president, the opposition argued that congress required only a simple majority to override a presidential veto of the new legislation, while the UP maintained (more correctly) that a two-thirds majority was needed. It then became clear to moderates on both sides that accommodation was essential. On two separate occasions government and DC representatives met in an attempt to reach a compromise that would have allowed the government to keep a substantial public sector of the economy while giving the private sector certain guarantees. But the talks collapsed. The rightist Nationals suggested a DC sellout, while the Socialists and other leftist groups stepped up factory expropriations in order to present the DC with a fait accompli. They thus undermined the negotiating position of a moderate Radical splinter group entrusted by Allende with conducting the discussion, and as a result this group left the UP coalition to join the opposition. This further polarized the political forces, reducing the potential success of a center agreement.

By mid-1972, the critical situation of the economy and the growing aggressiveness of the opposition led the government to try once again to hold talks with the Christian Democrats. This time Allende was strongly committed to reaching a compromise, and the UP made substantial concessions leading to agreement on a broad range of issues. However, the more conservative faction within the Christian Democratic Party maneuvered successfully to prevent negotiators from finishing their work. By that point, most sectors within the DC felt that the government was clearly on the defensive and thought that by concluding an agreement with it the party would lose support among the increasingly discontented middle sectors, thereby running the risk of being routed by the Nationals in the March 1973 congressional elections. Considerations of short-term party interest thus carried the day.

Toward the end of 1972, qualitative changes had begun to take place in Chilean politics. The parties had repeatedly called the mass rallies that characterized the Allende years not only to increase their bargaining stakes but also to prove actual power capabilities. Nonetheless, the nature of this mobilization soon changed. Business and professional associations increasingly took matters into their own hands, and before long the DC and the Nationals were falling over each other not to direct but to pledge support for the independent action of a whole range of groups. These demonstrations culminated in the massive October 1972 strike and lockout by hundreds of truck owners, merchants, industrialists, and professionals. The government parties countered by mobilizing their supporters, also initiating a significant organizational infrastructure that could operate at the margin of party leadership directives. These demonstrations and counterdemonstrations by a vast array of groups, which had continued to increase during the Allende years, were partly stimulated by a vitriolic mass media giving at least two totally different interpretations of every event, generating a dynamic in which the symbolic became the real, falsehoods turned into hysterically believed truths, and perceived threats were taken as imminent. The climate of agitation was also increased by CIA funds that flowed to opposition groups, strengthening them significantly as political actors independent of party control. The decreased capacity of party elites to control group mobilization and confrontation was more serious for government leaders than for the opposition. It meant that the government lost an important measure of authority over society, that the state itself would be bypassed as the central arena for political confrontation, and that the legitimacy of regular bargaining processes was undermined. In this crisis atmosphere, Allende turned to a presumably neutral referee who would ensure institutional order until the March 1973 congressional elections could clear the political air. Military men were brought into the cabinet, and the chief of staff was made the minister of the interior.

The incorporation of the military into the government ended the strikes of October 1972 and freed the political forces to concentrate on the congressional elections, which party leaders saw as the decisive confrontation. But in serving as a buffer between contending forces, the military itself became the object of intense political pressures. The left within the UP criticized it for slowing down government programs and initiatives, while the more strident elements on the right accused it of helping a government that would otherwise fall. Other sectors went out of their way to praise the military, a tacit recognition that they were the only force with real power. These pressures politicized an institution that had largely remained at the margin of political events. Though it was hardly perceived at the time, a cleavage began to appear within the military between officers supporting the government because they saw it as the constitutional government and those more receptive to the increasingly louder voices of opposition elements calling for the government's downfall.

The March 1973 elections symbolized the final polarization of Chilean politics as the government and the opposition faced each other as two electoral blocs. But the elections did not help resolve the political crisis. The opposition failed to gain the two-thirds majority it needed to impeach Allende, and the government failed to obtain majority control in either house of congress. Given the massive inflation and serious shortages of basic goods, as well as the climate of political uncertainty, the government's showing was commendable since it managed to win seats at the expense of the opposition. And yet the final results were not dramatically different from those that the two blocs had obtained as separate parties in the previous congressional contest. The electorate did not provide the magic solution. Its task done, the military left the cabinet.

Soon a decisive event initiated the final stage in the breakdown of the regime. On June 29, 1973, a military garrison revolted. Though the uprising was quickly put down, President Allende and his advisers realized that it was only a matter of time before the *golpista* (pro-coup) faction of the armed forces consolidated its strength. They again dismissed the far left's counsel to arm the workers, arguing that the creation of a parallel army would only accelerate the coup. Ironically, military officers were quicker to believe, or to make believe, not only that the workers could be a potent force but that sectors of the left had already structured a viable military capability. And yet the well-publicized efforts of military commanders to find secret arms caches uncovered nothing of importance, although they attempted to convey the impression that they had.

To the consternation of the leadership of his own Socialist Party, Allende once again called for talks with the Christian Democrats. And despite the vocal opposition of many of their followers, the Christian Democratic leaders, urged to do so by the cardinal, agreed to the new negotiations. However, an agreement at that point was unlikely. The hard-line faction of the Christian Democrats had replaced the more moderate leadership, and Allende was thus obliged to deal with the group most hostile to his government and policies. Moreover, the country was once again in the throes of massive lockouts, strikes, and civil disobedience campaigns led by business and professional associations (with considerable CIA funding), all demanding the president's resignation. By that time significant working-class groups, such as the copper miners, had also staged strikes to express their discontent with specific government policies, which encouraged the opposition. Any form of support for the government by the Christian Democrats would therefore have been seen as a sellout by the opposition. The political arena had been reduced to a few men attempting to negotiate a settlement. Even though these men no longer had the kind of control over social forces they once had, a dramatic announcement from the talks would have placed the nation's largest parties and most respected leaders on the side of a peaceful solution and would have undermined the subversive plans of military officers.

But agreement was not forthcoming. The Christian Democrats did not take Allende at his word that he really wanted a settlement, believing instead that he was buying time in order to force an armed confrontation. However, it is clear from the president's actions that he sought an agreement. He kept moderate leaders in his cabinets, even though they were severely attacked by the left within and outside the UP, and he virtually broke with his own party. Furthermore, Allende finally agreed to the Christian Democratic demand of bringing the military back into the government. In combating to the end the dubious prospect of "Marxist totalitarianism" and in constantly increasing bargaining demands, the DC leaders failed to realize how much stake they had in the political order they thought they were defending. By not moving forcefully to structure a political solution, they undermined the fragile position of the president and his advisers, who were seeking accommodation. Instead, the DC supported a chamber of deputies declaration calling on the military to safeguard the constitution and declaring that the government had lost its legitimacy.

Two weeks later, the top military leadership led the brutal revolt against the government, prominently displaying the chamber's resolution as evidence of the legality and broad-based support for their action. Air force jets bombed and strafed the presidential palace with Allende inside. After offering resistance, he committed suicide. Thousands of government supporters, or presumed government supporters, were arrested, mistreated, tortured, or killed in the months that followed.

Some prominent Christian Democrats condemned the coup in the initial moments. But others, including the leadership, welcomed it as inevitable and blamed the government for all that had transpired. Little did they realize what the "saving" action of the military would mean for the country's future and their own.

The Military in Government

The September 11, 1973, coup marked the most dramatic political change in Chilean history. A military junta headed by the commanders of each of the services and the national police took power and argued that they had overthrown the Allende government in order to protect democracy and restore constitutional government. But the new authorities soon defined the Chilean crisis as one of regime rather than of government. They blamed the breakdown of Chile's institutions not only on the Popular Unity government but also on liberal democracy itself.

Democracy had permitted divisive party competition and the rise of Marxist political leaders intent on defining the nation's politics in class terms. It had also generated demagogic politicians who contributed to economic mismanagement. Government was best left, in their view, in the hands of technicians who could formulate the best policy choices with administrative efficiency until the people had the necessary maturity to exercise better judgment.

The goal of the new junta thus was to transform the country, creating a new democracy and a new citizenry devoid of the vices of the past. The congress was closed, local governments disbanded, and elections banned. Newspapers, radio stations, and magazines were shut down, and those allowed to publish were subjected to varying degrees of censorship. Officials and leaders of the Popular Unity government and parties were arrested and exiled; some were killed. Within months of the coup, Christian Democratic leaders, unwilling to accept an indefinite military regime, saw their activities severely curbed as well. The parties of the right willingly declared themselves in recess. Unlike the fascist regimes of the 1930s, the military opted for political demobilization and rebuffed its right-wing supporters who wanted to create a new party or "civic-military movement" to organize popular allegiance to the dictatorship.

Despite a declaration of principles that drew inspiration from conservative Catholic social doctrine, the dictatorship had no intention of developing a corporative sort of regime. All of the country's major interest groups, including employers and professional associations and trade organizations (many of which had supported the coup with enthusiasm), saw their influence markedly diminished. The new authorities were not interested in bringing into the decision-making process any expression of societal interests. They were convinced that with disciplined administrative management and expert advice, they would modernize the country without the interference of special interests or partisan groups.

The dictatorship simply mimicked the hierarchical administrative style of the military. As a result, General Pinochet concentrated extraordinary power in his own hands. He commanded the largest and most important service, the army, and his fellow officers named him the first president of the junta. Subsequently they never insisted on pursuing early suggestions that called for the rotation of this position among the junta's four members.

While both executive and legislative power rested in the junta, within a year Pinochet had acquired the reins of executive power and relegated his colleagues to a vaguely defined legislature as heads of commissions specializing in different areas of policy. Under the provisions of a Statute of the Military Junta, a proto-constitutional document, Pinochet declared himself the "Supreme Chief of the Nation," although the junta still had to approve all cabinet and ambassadorial nominations. A subsequent constitutional decree named Pinochet "President of the Republic of Chile" in addition to preserving his prior titles of "President of the Governmental Junta" and "Supreme Chief of the Nation." General Pinochet's position as "president of the republic," and the junta's as the "legislative power," was reaffirmed once again in the so-called transitory articles of the constitution adopted in 1980. Pinochet also changed his military title in order to emphasize a position of preeminence over his colleagues in the other services, who then became his subordinates in rank. In 1979 he adopted the designation "Generalissimo of the Armed Forces" and later "Captain General." He positioned himself to control all military promotions and retirements, and not only those in his own service.

This concentration of power had no parallel in other military regimes in Latin America. Pinochet was not a retired military officer, unlike most of his Argentine counterparts, nor did he serve at the behest of the corps of generals, unlike Brazilian military presidents. Policy decisions never originated among high-ranking officers and were never reviewed by them. Pinochet stressed repeatedly that the armed forces were not to deliberate political matters. In this sense, their relation to the executive power was one of subordination just as it had been, in the past, to the Chilean presidents. Military officers occupied a majority of all positions in the government, but they reported to their superiors, military or civilian, within the government. General Pinochet led a military government, but it was not, strictly speaking, of the military. His regime is best described as a dictatorship of the commander in chief. As such, it was a curiously personalized regime in which power derived from occupancy of the top office of a military bureaucracy.

This type of dictatorship was facilitated by the highly professional, obedient, and hierarchical nature of the Chilean military. Paradoxically, these were qualities that stemmed from Chile's democratic past. The military was not involved in politics, and Chilean politicians did not expect it to be the source of political instability or coups. It is highly symptomatic that the coup against President Allende did not break the military line of command. The president had appointed General Pinochet to the top position in the army shortly before.

Policy Initiatives of the Military Government

The Pinochet government undertook more far-reaching changes than any that preceded it over the past fifty years. The repressive apparatus of the state increased enormously, as did the jurisdiction of military courts over offenses by civilians. But in other respects the size of the state and its role in national life were drastically reduced.

The government pursued an aggressive policy of privatization. All land held under the agrarian reform program was turned over to individual property holders. Only a handful of industries remained in the public sector (aside from the railways and utilities, the most important of these was the copper company initiated by Allende's nationalization of US-owned assets; and yet new investments in copper have come from the private sector, mainly in the form of foreign/Chilean joint ventures). The rest of the government-controlled industries were sold to national and foreign private investors, often at bargain prices. As part of debt-for-equity swaps to reduce an external debt that increased to $20 billion by 1986, many formerly Chilean firms were denationalized.

The authorities put in place a radical program of privatizing state services in social security and health, which meant curtailing the traditional publicly funded institutions. The public housing development program was also turned over to the private sector. Labor legislation was extensively revamped, making it more difficult for workers to pressure employers through collective action. The size of the unionized workforce declined by about 60 percent compared to its highest membership point in the last two years of the Allende government. Wages and salaries declined in real terms by as much as 50 percent with respect to their levels in 1970, and did not recover fully—even during years of strong growth—during the whole period of military government. This led to a significant regression in the distribution of income.

The government also undertook educational reforms. Public, primary, and secondary schools were turned over to municipal administrations (led by mayors appointed by the government), and new legislation encouraged the formation of private schools and universities.

The economy was opened up to external competition by drastic cuts in import duties, resulting in numerous bankruptcies as industries were unable to adjust to the shock. Except for a few years in the late 1970s and early 1980s in which the government's economic team greatly overvalued the national currency with catastrophic results, economic policies generally sought to stimulate growth through the development of new exports. These policies were successful and reduced the reliance on copper exports to about 45 percent in the late 1980s.

Economic growth rates were very spotty during the sixteen and a half years of military government. There were severe recessions in 1975 and in 1982 (in each of those years the economy declined by about 14 percent) and periods of significant growth (or recovery). Overall, the per capita income of Chile by the end of the 1980s was only slightly higher than its 1970 level measured in constant dollars. And yet the military government prided itself on its economic management, given the fact that the economy registered strong growth in the last three years of its rule. Moreover, inflation was low, the external debt shrank by $3 billion, and unemployment dropped significantly. Chilean businessmen also developed a new confidence in their ability and in the economic future of the country, which they associated with the free market and open economy policies of the regime. This sense of success was magnified by the disastrous economic performance of Latin America as a whole during the 1980s.

Economic and social policy initiatives were in the hands of a team of young economists known as the Chicago Boys, due to their free market and monetarist approaches. Pinochet felt comfortable with them because of their technical competence and their lack of direct connections with any of the prior Chilean parties. Their belief that Chilean underdevelopment could be attributed to an overbloated state that restricted private initiative corresponded well with the effort to drastically restrict state institutions in favor of privatization in all domains of national life.

Opposition to the Military Regime

Many dictatorships think they can reduce support for the opposition by combining repression with political, social, and economic changes. This goal proves to be elusive in countries like Chile with strong party systems. Citizens by and large retain their political predilections, which are passed on from one generation to the next supported by family and community ties creating a collective political memory. Party militants also retain at least the rudiments of their organization, and they often remain active as leaders in social groups and associations whose activities are allowed by the regime.

Chile was no exception to this rule. The parties retained their organization despite severe repression, which was directed especially at the left. Many party militants remained in positions of leadership in the same social groups where they found an audience before, be it the labor movement, student federations, or community associations. Supporters of the military government rarely won the internal elections of these groups when they were held freely. The Catholic Church assumed a very important role in the overall opposition to the regime. It continually called for national reconciliation and for a return to liberal democracy. The Church also confronted the regime for its many abuses of human rights and protected the lawyers and other professionals who actively documented such abuses and defended their victims in court. Moreover, the Church gave legal cover and other forms of support to many groups, such as social science researchers, journalists, unions, and popular community associations through which opposition views were expressed and organizing took place. It was through such Church-sponsored activities that the Christian Democrats and the left gradually came together during the dictatorship, leaving behind their bitter divisions from the Allende period.

Through a combination of social mobilization, calls for negotiations, and international pressures, the opposition continually tried to force the military to abdicate and accept a transition to democracy. Militants on the extreme left, some associated with the Communist Party, attempted to organize armed resistance to the regime. All actions undertaken by such groups, including a failed attempt to assassinate Pinochet, were sharply criticized by the rest of the opposition on grounds of both morality and expediency. The bulk of the opposition condemned all forms of violence, and such incidents—some of which were of dubious origins—seemed to play into the hands of the dictatorship by lending credence to its claims that the country, suffering terrorist threats, was not ready for democracy.

Some opposition attempts to mobilize people against the regime were enormously successful in the major cities. Massive protests took place for several years beginning in May 1983. The movement, initially called by labor leaders, consisted of banging pots at a certain hour in the evening, boycotting classes, staging work slowdowns, and refraining from using public transportation and shopping. The military regime eventually met such protests, which were held monthly at first, with massive displays of force and random, brutal repression by the army and police. The protests increasingly led to violence, which the government tried, with characteristic aplomb, to blame on the opposition. Labor and political leaders were arrested and tried under security laws, some in military courts.

The moderate opposition eventually called off the protest movement in order to break the increasing cycle of violence. And yet the movement served an important function. It demonstrated both to the government and to the opposition that after ten years of military rule, in which the government, controlling television and most of the rest of the mass media, relentlessly diffused a single interpretation of all events, the opposition could still generate a massive demonstration against the authorities. This emboldened the parties to seek new forms of exercising political leadership, and it convinced many civilian politicians on the right that the military government's long-term project was not entirely viable. Such politicians, whose concerns were dismissed high-handedly by Pinochet, began to organize a new political party of the right, taking some distance from the military regime. This eventually generated a bitter split on the right of the Chilean party spectrum between those who identified closely with the military regime and those who did not.

While the moderate opposition continually expressed willingness to negotiate with the military regime over forms of transition to democracy, Pinochet steadfastly refused to entertain any such discussions. The personalized Chilean military regime had a narrow inner circle of power, allowing no space for the development of moderate but influential segments of political leadership within the ruling circles. If such segments had existed, the opposition could conceivably have found a willing partner in the regime to search for a suitable transition formula. But dissenters who emerged within the regime were simply excluded from it, and the opposition's attempts to press the government and the armed forces to negotiate came to nothing.

Throughout the military regime, the opposition enjoyed many expressions of international solidarity. The international community repeatedly condemned the government's violations of human rights. When the AFL-CIO threatened to boycott the unloading of Chilean exports in the United States in 1978, the government prepared labor legislation that allowed a significant reactivation of Chile's unions. And arms sales to the Chilean military from major American and European manufacturers were significantly curtailed. Given the orthodoxy of its economic management and commitment to its debt obligations, the Chilean government was well received only in international financial circles.

THE TRANSITION TO DEMOCRATIC GOVERNMENT

The opposition was finally able to force the military government into a transition to democracy by using the procedures Pinochet himself had put into the 1980 constitution. The origins of this document go back to the immediate postcoup period. The new military authorities were in a juridically untenable position. They justified their seizure of power in part by noting that the Allende coalition had violated the 1925 constitution, but they themselves were violating it daily. The junta therefore argued that the existing constitution was inadequate to protect democracy and announced that a new one would be written. A committee of rightist civilians was charged in 1974 with the task of preparing the draft of a new charter.

The committee soon ran into disagreements between extremist and moderate members. Eventually, as head of the Council of State, former president Jorge Alessandri took a leading role in drafting the document, which he presented to General Pinochet in 1978 for his approval. It adhered quite closely to Chilean constitutional traditions. It also called for a transition period of five years in which General Pinochet would continue to govern as president but would share legislative responsibilities with a congress whose members would initially be designated.

Pinochet changed the draft, strengthening the power of nonelected and military officials and extending the presidential term of office to eight years. Moreover, he added twenty-nine "transitory articles" that suspended the application of the bulk of the constitutional provisions until the beginning of a second presidential term after the enactment of the constitution. One of these articles named Pinochet to the presidency for a first term to begin on March 11, 1981, and others assigned the legislative power to the junta. The transitory articles therefore permitted Pinochet to extend his personalistic regime for another eight years.

What was to prove decisive for the transition to democratic government were the stipulations Pinochet added to the transitory articles for the presidential succession at the end of the first term. At that point the commanders in chief of the armed services (including Pinochet himself) would select a new presidential candidate, whose name would be submitted to the voters in a plebiscite. If that individual won the plebiscite, congressional elections would be held within a year, and the constitution would be fully applied. If the candidate lost the plebiscite, within a year there would be open presidential as well as congressional elections. Pinochet had every intention of running for a second term of office, and he had no difficulty, when the time came, in obtaining the nomination from his colleagues. Pinochet felt confident of his ability to win plebiscites. He did so by a large margin in 1978, and he obtained what was announced as 65 percent approval in the plebiscite held on September 11, 1980, to approve the 1980 constitution and his own "first presidential term" along with it.

But both of these plebiscites were highly irregular, and the opposition had little difficulty in contesting their validity. This rejection of the plebiscites' legitimacy, especially of the one that presumably had approved the constitution and Pinochet's own presidential term along with it, struck a raw nerve in ruling circles. Hence Pinochet and his supporters took pains continually to stress the "constitutionality" of the government. Moreover, adherence to the 1980 constitution became the centerpiece of the government's political program, replacing the earlier emphasis on building a new Chile that became untenable in the context of the severe economic crisis of 1982–1983 and the rise of the protest movement. The authorities also turned the defense of the "institutionality" enshrined in the constitution into one of the principal missions of the armed forces.

By late 1986 the opposition had exhausted its efforts to force the government into a transition through social mobilization and other forms of pressure, and it began to look forward to the 1988 plebiscite as a possible mechanism to defeat the government. Recalling its criticisms of the prior plebiscites, the opposition stipulated a series of conditions that would have to be met for the new plebiscite to be considered a valid expression of the voters' will. These included the reestablishment of a proper electoral registry (the previous one had been burned by the military), sufficient time for the registration process to ensure that large numbers of citizens actually registered, television access for advocates of the "no" ("no" to another term for Pinochet), the necessary voting procedures to ensure secrecy, and assurances that opposition delegates would be able to observe the balloting and vote-counting processes. The US ambassador in Santiago, Harry Barnes, made it clear to the members of the military junta that the United States agreed with these conditions and would not consider the plebiscite valid unless they were all met. Surprisingly, the new constitutional court set up by the 1980 constitution also agreed with these conditions, and Pinochet had no recourse but to accept them.

As the campaign preparations began, the opposition organized a broad coalition for the "no" that included all groups except the Communist Party, whose leaders only belatedly saw any value in the process. The opposition used the time segment the authorities gave it on television very cleverly, with a message focused on future happiness and reconciliation that was developed by social scientists using political marketing techniques. It also organized poll watchers in every single locality of the country and an alternative vote-counting system that would give it the possibility of checking the veracity of official figures. Citizens were to vote yes or no to

Pinochet's continuing in the presidency, and when the votes were counted on the night of October 5, 1988, 54.7 percent had voted no, and 43 percent yes. Over 90 percent of registered voters cast ballots, and over 90 percent of those eligible to register had done so.

Pinochet was shocked, yet there was little he could do to ignore the result. The plebiscite was a procedure that he himself had introduced into the constitution, and he could not easily turn against the "institutionality" he had for years urged the armed forces and his civilian supporters to uphold. The opposition also gave the regime no excuses to suspend the plebiscite or the vote count. From beginning to end, it conducted an orderly campaign, refraining from staging demonstrations that might be construed as provocations, especially on the day of the plebiscite. The night of the vote count some government officials did seek to tamper with the results. But while this effort was under way, the commander in chief of the air force freely admitted to a journalist that the figures released by the opposition were correct.

The outcome of the plebiscite meant that open presidential and congressional elections would be held within a year. The opposition parties agreed to support a single presidential candidate, Christian Democrat Patricio Aylwin, and to present basically a single list (with a parallel list including some Communist and other leftist candidates running in a few districts) for the senate and the lower house. The opposition demanded that the constitution be revised, and in subsequent negotiations the government agreed to significant changes. The amended constitution was submitted to ratification by a new plebiscite, and the opposition had to agree to respect the new constitutional framework.

Presidential and congressional elections were held on December 14, 1989. Aylwin won 55.2 percent of the validly cast vote, defeating two candidates on the right, and his coalition obtained 56.5 percent of the vote for seats in the lower house of congress.

Rebuilding Chilean Democracy

President Aylwin's term in office was shortened to four years as part of the agreement with the dictatorship that altered the constitution in mid-1989. Pinochet probably thought that he would return to power after four years, because he and his supporters assumed that the incoming opposition would prove to be incompetent in office. They expected heightened labor conflicts, leftist insurgencies and terrorism, tension connected with demands for an accounting of human rights violations, a breakup of the Concertation coalition of Christian Democrats, Socialists, Radicals, and a new Party for Democracy (PPD); and a shaky economy, which had already become overheated when the military government overspent for electoral purposes. Pinochet also remained following the transitory articles of the 1980 constitution as army commander for another eight years. He even created a shadow cabinet to monitor developments.

All these predictions proved to be incorrect. In March 1994, President Aylwin turned the government over to Eduardo Frei Ruiz-Tagle, another Christian Democrat and the son of the former president, for a six-year term. In 2000 Socialist and PPD leader Ricardo Lagos won the next six year term, and in 2006 Socialist

Michelle Bachelet was inaugurated for a four-year term as the first woman to serve as president in Chile. The Concertation of Parties for Democracy has led Chile for twenty years, becoming the longest running and most successful governing coalition in Chilean history.

The Economy

From 1990 to 2008 the Chilean economy more than doubled in size, reaching a per capita income of $14,900 in purchasing power parity terms. The economic crisis of 2009 created a recession, but annual growth of about 4 percent is expected to resume in 2010. Since 1990 the yearly rate of investment has oscillated between 24 and 27 percent of GNP. Large amounts of foreign investment have flowed into the country since the return to democracy. During the four years of Bachelet's presidency about $17 billion came in, while the total stock of such investment then totaled about $110 billion.

The dictatorship reoriented the Chilean economy toward export-led growth. This has continued since 1990, and presently Chile exports roughly 40 percent of its GNP. Copper accounts for less than half of all exports given the diversification of the products the country now places in international markets, which include paper and pulp, fish, fruit, wine, chemicals, and transport equipment. The Concertation governments have concluded 57 trade agreements with countries all over the world, establishing free trade with the European Union, the United States, China, South Korea, and Mexico. As a result its trading partners are very broadly diversified, and the country normally has a positive balance between exports and imports—including with China. Chilean businesses have also invested about $26 billion abroad, mainly in neighboring countries.

The Concertation governments have paid careful attention to keeping macroeconomic stability. Fiscal accounts have been kept in balance when measured on an average over several years. Central Bank reserves have averaged about $16 to $20 billion year after year, and a new sovereign fund, invested abroad, contains another $20 billion. Inflation has been kept under double digits for two decades, a Chilean record since the 1870s. Chilean sovereign bonds have the highest investment grade ratings.

The country has made enormous investments in infrastructure. Ports, airports, roads, and superhighways have been built, increasing the overall efficiency of the economy. Very few urban agglomerations remain that cannot be reached by a paved road.

Enormous challenges remain for future Chilean economic growth. The country must enhance its productivity, invest more in research and development, and improve the value added as well as the technological acumen of its products. It must also tackle high levels of youth unemployment. And yet public opinion surveys consistently indicate that Chileans have a moderately optimistic view of their own future economic circumstances.

Social Policies and Achievements

Social spending on education, health, and housing has increased by about 8 percent per year since 1990. The country now has full coverage of educational enrollments through high school, and about 35 percent of its eighteen- to twenty-four-year-olds have matriculated in some form of higher education. All primary schools, even in the most remote rural locations, are connected to the Education Ministry's computer network, and all children learn digital literacy from a young age. Primary schools use their computer facilities to offer evening classes for adults, and about half the total population uses the Internet. The major challenge in education lies in improving its quality, as Chilean students have mediocre scores on international tests. There is also a considerable gap between achievement levels of students in private and in public schools that must be addressed. A major effort has been made to increase preschool education and day care centers, especially under President Bachelet, with the aim of providing universal coverage for all families who demand such placements.

Health indicators in Chile show considerable improvement. Life expectancy at birth is seventy-eight years (81 for women), and infant mortality is about seven per thousand births. All pensioners, children, and poor people have access to free medical care, including medicines, at public expense. Others must make a copayment, depending on their level of income. However, the state health system provides free care to those who require organ transplants or are afflicted with any of fifty-six illnesses, including cancer, diabetes, and cardiovascular pathologies. People who have private health insurance are also covered by this health guarantee once they have paid all their deductibles. The government of President Lagos instituted these policies, which represent a substantial reversal of the privatization of health care pursued single-mindedly by the dictatorship.

The military regime drew international attention by privatizing the Chilean social security system. Everyone with a formal labor contract had to contribute a monthly amount to a private pension fund that was invested in various instruments. However, this left people who did not have a continuous formal employment history lacking adequate pensions, and up to 84 percent of retirees drawing pensions from the private system have required some state subsidies in order to reach even minimal pension levels. Moreover, the private pension funds have had very high administrative costs. The Concertation governments have long considered the privatization of the social security system to be a failure. Instead of reverting fully to a public system, however, President Bachelet decided to institute a new universal pension system paid out of general revenues. It provides a minimum pension (currently of about $220 at PPP exchange rates) to every person who reaches the age of sixty-five and whose income is below the sixtieth percentile of all national incomes, regardless of his or her employment history. The new reform also establishes a sliding scale of state subsidies for pensions drawn from the private funds that raise them above the minimal pension levels on a gradated basis. Again, this is a step away from the privatized pension system. Both the health and pension reforms constitute no less than the creation of a veritable welfare state, much like those in Europe, in the Americas.

The Concertation government housing policies have been designed to eliminate urban shantytowns in the country. Close to 90 percent of the Chilean population now lives in urban areas, and this has been a major challenge. Through a program of state subsidies, all poor families are given title to a small house in a new development after paying a minimum deposit of about $300. Subsequently, they must pay a monthly amount that is adjusted to their income. The objectives of this program are nearly complete, and this has dramatically transformed the urban land-scapes of the country. The next challenge is to increase the size of the dwellings. However, with the decline of the birth rate (currently the Chilean population is at replacement level), the average size of the nation's households is 3.7 persons.

Antipoverty programs put into place over the past twenty years have made ma-jor inroads in reducing the numbers of the poor. Whereas about 45 percent of Chileans lived under the poverty line in 1990, the 2009 estimate indicated only 13 percent. The antipoverty programs have targeted the most vulnerable households with intense monitoring and assistance. The income distribution in Chile as mea-sured conventionally continues to be very regressive, with a Gini index of about .54. However, economists estimate that about 46 percent of the income of the poorest 20 percent of households comes from cash and in-kind transfers to them from state programs. Recalculating the Gini coefficient with such figures reduces the income disparities to about .44.

Human Rights Policies

President Patricio Aylwin himself handled the difficult issue of human rights vio-lations during the military regime. He first reviewed the cases of 384 political pris-oners who were in jail when he took office, rapidly releasing most of them. A last handful of prisoners who participated in violent incidents resulting in death had their sentences changed to exile abroad. Aylwin also appointed a Truth and Rec-onciliation Commission (TRC) with representatives of all segments of opinion that documented some 3,200 disappearances after arrest by agents of the dictator-ship. The TRC also produced a report that gave the country a balanced interpreta-tion of its recent and very conflicted past. Only the military hierarchy, led by Pinochet, objected to that interpretation. The parents, widows, or widowers of dis-appeared persons were compensated by the state with lifelong pensions. Their chil-dren were given stipends and scholarships until age 35 as long as they were enrolled in postsecondary education. The Chilean state has spent about $1.2 bil-lion on such reparations since 1991.

The evidence gathered by the TRC was released and made available to the fam-ilies to initiate prosecutions of the perpetrators of human rights violations. To as-sist this process, the government argued for a new interpretation of Pinochet's 1978 amnesty law: it stated that unless the body of a disappeared person was found, the amnesty could not be applied. Without a body, the crime would be considered a case of kidnapping instead of a homicide, and it would therefore not fall under the purview of the 1978 amnesty because the crime would not have con-cluded before that year. An appellate court justice first accepted this interpretation in 1993 in the case of peasants who had disappeared in Paine, and this turned the amnesty law into a tool for judicial investigations of human rights violations. Sub-sequently the appellate courts determined that Chile's signature to international human rights conventions rendered human rights violations unprescribable, and the 1978 amnesty law inapplicable.

Both of these decisions were ratified by the Supreme Court before General Pinochet, who had just left his position as head of the army, was arrested in Lon-don. Several high-ranking officers of the dictatorship's security services were al-ready serving long jail sentences for human rights violations, and about 400 others were being prosecuted or investigated for such crimes. Hence, it is not true, as is commonly asserted, that human rights prosecutions in Chile started *after* Pinochet's arrest. The judicial processes began soon after the TRC produced its report and took longer than expected, given the difficulty of securing information which Pinochet, as head of the army, could easily conceal but his successor as army chief did not. At present, there are about 120 persons serving time in jail for human rights violations in Chile, about 20 of whom have been condemned to life-long terms.

Prosecuting Pinochet was impossible while he kept his position as head of the army. As soon as he left it, swearing in as "senator for life" under the provisions of the 1980 constitution, the families of the victims of disappearances and other crimes initiated judicial processes against him. Judge Juan Guzmán was put in charge of investigating the cases, and he was about to initiate Pinochet's interrogation—a necessary step in following due process—when the general was arrested in London. Far from aiding the prosecution of Pinochet, the arrest had the opposite effect. Guzmán could interrogate Pinochet only after he returned to Chile, but by then the general had suffered several strokes that cast doubt on his ability to understand the charges against him. The judge ruled that Pinochet's immunity from prosecution by virtue of his position in the senate had to be lifted, and he ordered Pinochet's house arrest under the human rights charges. But Pinochet's prosecution in the criminal cases that were presented repeatedly against him, both for human rights violations and for corruption, never concluded because of the same medical reasons related to his mental condition. Nonetheless, he spent the rest of his days under house arrest as numerous cases were initiated against him.

The Frei government convened a roundtable of military and human rights lawyers to discuss human rights violations. It ended with a report in which the military services admitted to engaging in such violations and promised to never again do so. Subsequently the Lagos government named a commission to investigate torture under Pinochet. It issued a report showing that 28,000 Chileans had been subjected to torture in nearly 100 clandestine detention centers. Such persons were also offered state reparations, including medical benefits. In addition, the government assisted the return of about 40,000 political exiles who applied for repatriation.

In sum, of all recent cases of transition out of dictatorial rule, Chile is the country that has done the most to discover the truth and to grant universal reparations to victims of human rights violations. Its approach is a worthy model because it is predicated on the notion that the judiciary should deal with such cases without political interference. This has the effect of helping reconstitute judicial institutions tainted by the workings of the previous dictatorial regime and reaffirming judicial independence and rule of law. It also helps consolidate a newly restored or newly created democracy.

Constitutional Reforms

The 1980 constitution dictated by Pinochet was never applied as originally written. Major reforms were introduced in 1989 that diminished the influence and changed the membership (adding civilian authorities) of the National Security

Council and lifted the prohibition on Marxist political groups. Soon after the initiation of the Aylwin government a constitutional reform permitted a return to elected municipal governments.

The rightist parties in the legislature opposed further major changes to the constitution. They benefited from having nine "designated senators" because they had all been appointed at the end of the dictatorship and were all aligned with the right. They also supported having former presidents join the senate "for life," a provision curiously applied to Pinochet but denied to Aylwin due to a technicality. They resisted further reducing the National Security Council to an advisory body. And they insisted on retaining an article defining the armed forces as the "guarantors" of Chilean constitutional and institutional integrity. Presidents Aylwin, Frei, and Lagos all presented bills to change these elements of the constitution.

These undemocratic features of 1980 constitution began to lose their political sting as time went by. When the eight-year terms for the designated senators ended, the Frei government replaced half of them with its supporters, and Frei himself joined the ranks of the senate as a former president while Pinochet was removed from it. As a result, President Lagos was finally able to pass constitutional reforms that eliminated all of these undemocratic elements from the constitution in 2005. The new document corresponds fully with democratic constitutional doctrine and symbolizes the consolidation of Chile's renewed democracy.

Political Evolution

The municipal elections of 1992 were conducted with a proportional representation system that was similar to the one that was used prior to 1973. This was the first normal multiparty election in the country after the dictatorship. Chilean voters were still split into right, center, and left tendencies in about the same proportions as before. Since the presidential elections now call for a second round of voting if no candidate reaches an absolute majority, the electorate is forced to choose between a representative of the Concertation or the rightist Alliance. Similarly, all parliamentary elections are conducted with a binomial formula. Each party list can present only two candidates per district, and the list that obtains the most votes can win both seats only if it has more than double the number of votes as the runner-up list. This system also tends to force the electorate to consider a choice of candidates structured around the two main opposing coalitions. The past two decades have shown that the Chilean electorate is about evenly divided, with a slight advantage for the center-left, when it has to opt between either left- or right-leaning candidacies. Until 2009 this has allowed the Concertation to win all presidential contests and more votes—but not necessarily a proportionate number of more seats—in legislative elections.

A small shift in the electorate then produced overall electoral victory for the rightist Alliance, formed by the Union of Independent Democrats (UDI) and National Renewal (RN). The UDI was created by close supporters of the Pinochet dictatorship, while RN was more distant from it and represents a greater degree of continuity to the pre-1973 Chilean right. Nonetheless, both parties are presently committed to supporting Chilean democracy, and both have condemned the human rights violations and corruption of the Pinochet years. In this sense too the Chilean democratic transition has gone a long way. The rightist candidate for the presidency in the elections of 2009, Sebastián Piñera, actually voted for the "no" with the parties of the Concertation in the plebiscite that defeated Pinochet.

CONCLUSION

As Chileans celebrate the bicentennial of their independence from Spain, they can take pride in their nation's recovery of its deep democratic roots. In joining the OECD, the country can also point to its significant achievements in creating a welfare state and in generating rapid economic growth over the past two decades. Chileans have also confronted, with a combination of clear-headed analysis as well as retribution and punitive justice, the negative legacies of the greatest political crisis in their history. The nation's political leaders have learned from the mistakes of the recent past. The main lesson is that it is always best to search for pragmatic solutions to the country's problems through consensus-forming negotiations, rather than to succumb to divisive rhetorical excesses. It is through careful reform mongering that the Concertation has fulfilled the prediction that Salvador Allende made just before his death, that one day, sooner rather than later, the broad, poplar-lined avenues would open the way to a better life for the Chilean people.

SUGGESTED READINGS

Angell, Alan. *Politics and the Labour Movement in Chile.* London: Oxford University Press, 1972.

Arriagada, Genaro. *Pinochet: The Politics of Power.* Winchester, MA: Unwin Hyman, 1988.

Bauer, Robert J. *Chilean Rural Society from the Spanish Conquest to 1930.* Cambridge: Cambridge University Press, 1975.

Blakemore, Harold. *British Nitrates and Chilean Politics, 1886–1896: Balmaceda and North.* London: Athlone, 1974.

Boorstein, Edward. *Allende's Chile: An Inside View.* New York: International, 1977.

DeShazo, Peter. *Urban Workers and Labor Unions in Chile, 1902–1927.* Madison: University of Wisconsin Press, 1983.

De Vylder, Stefan. *Allende's Chile: The Political Economy of the Rise and Fall of the Unidad Popular.* Cambridge: Cambridge University Press, 1974.

Drake, Paul W. *Socialism and Populism in Chile, 1932–52.* Champaign-Urbana: University of Illinois Press, 1978.

Foxley, Alejandro. *Latin American Experiments in Neoconservative Economics.* Berkeley: University of California Press, 1983.

Galdames, Luis. *A History of Chile.* Translated and edited by Isaac J. Cox. Chapel Hill: University of North Carolina Press, 1941.

Gil, Federico. *The Political System of Chile.* Boston: Houghton Mifflin, 1966.

Gil, Federico, Ricardo Lagos, and H. A. Landsberger, eds. *Chile at the Turning Point: Lessons of the Socialist Years, 1970–73.* Philadelphia: Institute for the Study of Human Issues, 1979.

Huneeus, Carlos. *The Pinochet Regime.* Boulder: Lynne Rienner, 2007.

Infante, Ricardo B., and Osvaldo Sunkel. "Chile: Towards Inclusive Development." *CEPAL Review,* April 2009.

Kaufman, Robert R. *The Politics of Land Reform in Chile 1950–1970: Public Policy, Political Institutions, and Social Change.* Cambridge: Harvard University Press, 1972.

Kornbluh, Peter, ed. *The Pinochet File: A Declassified Dossier on Atrocity and Accountability.* National Security Archive/New Press, 2003.

Loveman, Brian. *Chile: The Legacy of Hispanic Capitalism.* New York: Oxford University Press, 1979.

Mamalakis, Markos J. *The Growth and Structure of the Chilean Economy: From Independence to Allende.* New Haven: Yale University Press, 1976.

Pike, Fredrick. *Chile and the United States.* Notre Dame, IN: University of Notre Dame Press, 1963.

Roxborough, Ian, Philip O'Brien, and Jackie Roddick. *Chile: The State and Revolution.* New York: Holmes & Meier, 1977.

Scully, Timothy R. *Rethinking the Center: Party Politics in Nineteenth- and Twentieth-Century Chile.* Stanford: Stanford University Press, 1992.

Sigmund, Paul E. *The Overthrow of Allende and the Politics of Chile, 1964–76.* Pittsburgh: University of Pittsburgh Press, 1977.

———. *The United States and Democracy in Chile.* Baltimore: Johns Hopkins University Press, 1993.

Smith, Brian H. *The Church and Politics in Chile: Challenges to Modern Catholicism.* Princeton: Princeton University Press, 1982.

Soifer, Hillel David. "The Sources of Infrastructural Power: Evidence from Nineteenth-Century Chilean Education." *Latin American Research Review* 44, no. 2 (2009).

Spooner, Mary Helen. *Soldiers in a Narrow Land: The Pinochet Regime in Chile.* Berkeley: University of California Press, 1999.

Stallings, Barbara. *Class Conflict and Economic Development in Chile, 1958–1973.* Stanford: Stanford University Press, 1978.

Valenzuela, Arturo. *Political Brokers in Chile: Local Politics in a Centralized Polity.* Durhan, NC: Duke University Press, 1977.

———. *The Breakdown of Democratic Regimes: Chile.* Baltimore: Johns Hopkins University Press, 1978.

Valenzuela, J. Samuel. *From Town Assemblies to Representative Democracy: The Contested Building of Electoral Institutions in Post-Colonial Chile.* Kellogg Institute Working Paper. Forthcoming.

Valenzuela, J. Samuel, and Arturo Valenzuela, eds. *Military Rule in Chile: Dictatorship and Oppositions.* Baltimore: Johns Hopkins University Press, 1986.

Valenzuela, J. Samuel, Eugenio Tironi, and Timothy R. Scully, eds. *El eslabón perdido: Familia, modernización y bienestar en Chile.* Santiago: Taurus, 2006.

Winn, Peter. *Weavers of Revolution: The Yarur Workers and Chile's Road to Socialism.* New York: Oxford University Press, 1986.

Chapter 27

ARGENTINA

Decline and Revival

PETER CALVERT

ARGENTINA, THE FIFTEENTH largest country in the world, presents many paradoxes. With an area of some 2,767,000 square kilometers, it had a population of only 40.9 million in July 2009, ranking thirty-second in the world. It is incredibly rich in agricultural land: the vast pampa, stretching westward between Buenos Aires and the Andes, makes Argentina one of the world's few grain-exporting nations and the only one in the Southern Hemisphere. Yet some three-fifths of the population live and work in the sophisticated urban environment of greater Buenos Aires. Argentina is also self-sufficient in oil and natural gas and wealthy in mineral resources. Although comparable in size to Australia, it has failed to develop along the same lines; in 1930 it entered a long period of decline. In 1930, in fact, Argentina was the seventh richest country in the world. By 1980 it was seventy-seventh, and its rulers seemed resigned to permanent membership in the Third World. A literate, sophisticated people had been subjected to an exceptionally brutal military dictatorship. "Argentina," people said, "is the land of the future, always has been and always will be."

BUENOS AIRES VERSUS THE PROVINCES

In colonial times, Argentina lay on the farthest edges of the Spanish Empire. The first Spanish settlers in what is now Argentina came from Peru, and until 1776 the region remained backward and neglected. A fine natural port founded in 1580, Buenos Aires stagnated while trade was channeled through Lima. Direct trade between Buenos Aires and Spain (notably in hides and in silver from what is now Bolivia) only later stimulated the growth of the town. In 1776 the viceroyalty of the River Plate (Río de la Plata) was established. Buenos Aires began to grow rapidly. In 1807 the doomed attempt of Sir Home Popham to seize the city for the British Empire taught its inhabitants that they could defend themselves. It went on to free itself from Spanish rule in 1810, its *cabildo* (town council) governing on behalf of the Spanish king, Ferdinand VII, though he was at the time a captive of the French emperor Napoleon Bonaparte. In 1816, when the Spanish moved to recapture

Buenos Aires, the independence of what was then called the United Provinces of South America was declared at Tucumán.

Buenos Aires in 1810 was already bigger by far than the other main towns scattered along the River Plate and in the west and northwest, in the lee of the Andes. The colony was underpopulated for its size, although the vast and largely treeless plains, the hinterland of Buenos Aires known as the pampas, still contained a substantial native American population. In the vast, flat rural plain of the province (as opposed to the city) of Buenos Aires roamed the Argentine cowboy, the gaucho, who opened up the interior and gave Argentina its national myth.

Argentina remained disunited for much of the nineteenth century, owing to the rivalry between Buenos Aires and the other provinces. The former favored a centralized structure with Buenos Aires dominant, whereas the latter wanted a federal structure with provincial autonomy. Buenos Aires derived its revenues from the port, whereas the prices of provincial manufactures, such as textiles, were undercut by cheaper foreign imports. Buenos Aires did not share its wealth with the other provinces and, moreover, grew more European in its outlook and amenities; the provinces remained backward, dominated by autocratic, often savage leaders (caudillos). The struggle between federalists and centralists was overshadowed after 1835 by the dictatorship of Juan Manuel de Rosas, caudillo of Buenos Aires. He ignored the national problem, giving the provincial rulers complete freedom of action in return for recognizing him as national leader. Paradoxically, this helped create the national unity he opposed. In 1852 he was deposed by a coalition of his political opponents and died in exile on his farm just outside Southampton, England, in 1877.

In 1853 a federal constitution was created for the new Argentine Republic. Buenos Aires seceded from the federation but in 1859 was defeated in a military confrontation with the other provinces. In 1861 its forces were victorious and it joined the union in order to dominate it. In 1880, three centuries after its founding, the city of Buenos Aires replaced Rosario as the federal capital. A new capital for the old province of Buenos Aires—still the country's largest—was built at La Plata. The provincial caudillos made the transition to being more conventional politicians, though it was the great landowners, the *estancieros,* who dominated national life.

The next four decades were years of economic transformation as the combined impact of British investment, European immigration, railway expansion, and the beef, grain, and wool of the pampas made Argentina rich. These developments first benefited the cattle barons and big landowners who dominated politics, but two new classes emerged to challenge their hold on power: professionals such as bankers, brokers, and lawyers and an urban working class composed largely of recent immigrants. In any one decade from 1880 to 1950, there were proportionately three times as many immigrants to Argentina as to the United States.

MODERN PARTIES AND AN OLD-FASHIONED MILITARY

The first challenge came in the 1890s with the foundation of the Radical and Socialist parties, but fraudulent elections kept the oligarchy of landowners, merchants, and bankers in power. In 1912, however, President Roque Sáenz Peña, though a conservative, insisted on the adoption of a law introducing secret ballots to reduce electoral corruption. As a result, in 1916 Hipólito Yrigoyen, nephew of the founder of the Radical Party, the Unión Cívica Radical (UCR), became Argentina's first popularly elected president. The economy was still growing strongly in 1922, and manufacturing industry developed under Yrigoyen's Radical successor, Marcelo T. de Alvear. In 1928 Yrigoyen was elected to a second term, causing a split in the party in opposition to Yrigoyen's personalism. Before the effects of the 1929 depression were felt, Yrigoyen's reclusiveness and society's failure to perceive the threat of a military takeover made it possible in 1930 for a small band of cadets to seize power, armed with wooden rifles and led by a retired general, José E. Uriburu.

From 1932 to 1943, a period known as the Infamous Decade, the oligarchy resumed power in the form of a loose coalition (the Concordancia) of Conservatives and antipersonalist Radicals, supported by the armed forces. Their friends and supporters benefited from the economic recovery and from Argentina's role in supplying the Allies with meat and grain during World War II. But the war divided Argentine society further. Some leaders were strongly pro-Allies, but a suspicious isolationism had become the norm, and important elements in the armed forces, admiring German military prowess, were openly pro-Axis. When in 1943 it seemed that the civilian politicians would install a pro-Allies president, the army intervened again.

The year 1943 was a turning point. Colonel Juan Domingo Perón, secretary of the army lodge that planned and executed the coup, became minister of war and secretary for labor and social welfare in the military government. He promoted labor reforms and encouraged unionization, becoming immensely popular with the masses, though not with the oligarchy. In 1946, in a free election, he won the presidency decisively. In 1949 he amended the constitution to permit his reelection in 1951 and held power until 1955.

Perón's populist and personalist regime had many of the marks of a dictatorship: control of the media, suppression of dissent, establishment of a single ruling party, the cult of personality. However, his rule was based on an alliance with the trade unions and mobilized the popular support of the urban underprivileged, the *descamisados* (shirtless ones). Large welfare programs brought Perón a devoted following and yielded real benefits to the poor, dramatized from the Ministry of Social Welfare by Perón's charismatic wife, Eva Duarte de Perón (Evita), who came to be regarded virtually as a saint, and for many still is.

A staunch nationalist, Perón bought out the British-owned railways, greatly accelerated industrialization under strong government control, and increased the role of the state in the economy. In his foreign policy he sought a "third position," later to be termed nonalignment, and the leadership of South America. However, he neglected the agricultural sector, formerly the basis of Argentina's export trade. Rural migration increased, and serious economic imbalances developed. As inflation rose and agricultural output fell, the economy's growth slowed down. Evita Perón died in July 1952, depriving her husband of his strongest ally with the masses.

During his second term from 1951, after surviving an attempted military coup, Perón tempered his policies. He resisted workers' wage demands, supported the farmers, and as of 1954 welcomed foreign capital in the petroleum industry. Such changes alienated many former supporters. Discontent grew with both the repressive nature of the regime and the large bureaucracy. Attacks by overzealous supporters on the Roman Catholic Church compounded Perón's problems. Finally, in September 1955 the armed forces intervened, and Perón went into exile in Spain. However, his legacy and his political movement survived to form the fundamental divide in Argentine politics for the next four decades.

The Peronists, the Military, and the Guerrillas

The armed forces sought in vain to exclude both Perón and his supporters from national politics. The leader of the coup of 1955, General Eduardo Lonardi, was prepared to work with the Peronists but was soon deposed by the more intransigent General Pedro Aramburu. For three years (1955–1958), Aramburu attempted to suppress all vestiges of Peronism. Elections from which the Peronists were barred installed a left-wing Radical, Arturo Frondizi (1958–1962), under whom economic development accelerated. Promising fifty years of development in five years, he delivered forty years of inflation in four. When Frondizi proposed allowing the Peronists (though not Perón himself) to stand for election, he too was deposed by the army.

New elections were held in 1963, and Arturo Illia, another Radical, was elected. However, in 1966 the military ousted him as well, claiming that he had been ineffective. The new military government headed by Juan Carlos Onganía (1966–1970) made it clear that it intended to stay in power as long as necessary to revive the economy. Supported by authoritarian controls, his minister of economy and labor, Adalberto Krieger Vasena, produced a viable but austere recovery plan. But Krieger Vasena was forced to resign in May 1969 in the wake of a massive demonstration in the city of Córdoba (the Cordobazo). Further strikes and protests followed.

Meanwhile, under the influence of the Cuban revolution and its aftermath, two main urban guerrilla movements emerged, a pro-Cuban organization called the Revolutionary Army of the People (ERP) and a Peronist group known as the Montoneros. The Montoneros kidnapped and murdered former president Aramburu, thereby undermining Onganía, whose colleagues deposed him in June 1970. An unknown general, Roberto Levingston, was appointed to head the government but was replaced in March 1971 by General Alejandro Lanusse, the organizer of the 1970 coup, who took over the presidency himself.

Lanusse inherited an impossible situation and took the ultimate gamble of holding fresh elections in March 1973 and allowing the Peronists to take part for the first time in twenty years. Perón's candidacy was disallowed (he had now been in exile for eighteen years), but his proxy, Héctor Cámpora, was allowed to stand and was duly elected. Cámpora's presidency lasted only a few weeks. Having offered freedom to captured guerrillas, he resigned in order to force Perón's return. The military, internally divided, yielded. Perón's return to the country in June 1973 was marred by violence at Ezeiza Airport in which many died. In September, nevertheless, he was returned to the presidency, with his third wife, María Estela (Isabelita) Martínez de Perón, as vice president.

However, the hopes of Perón's supporters were soon dashed. Perón, by then a sick man of seventy-eight, was unable to meet the many conflicting demands made on him during his short third term as president. He tried to distance himself from the leftist fringe that had infiltrated the movement during the last years of military proscription, only to find that the two major insurgent movements, the Peronist Montoneros and the Marxist ERP, battled openly for power with kidnappings, bombings, and assassinations.

At Perón's death on July 1, 1974, his widow, Isabelita, became, by an irony of history, Latin America's (and indeed the world's) first woman executive president. Not only was the Peronist movement divided, but its extreme wings were at war. As chaos spread rightist death squads appeared, controlled by Isabel Perón's chief confidant, the influential minister of social welfare, José López Rega (El Brujo, or the Sorcerer). The country slid into anarchy. Violence increased, inflation rose to 364 percent in 1976, and the government did little to stop it. In March 1976 the armed forces again seized power.

The Junta and the Dirty War

The governing junta of service chiefs chose the commander of the army, General Jorge Videla, as the new president. Under their leadership, the government began what was euphemistically known as the "process of national reorganization." The period has since become better known abroad as the dirty war (*la guerra sucia*).

The process was a concerted attempt to eradicate terrorism by the use of terror. Tens of thousands of "suspects" were arrested, tortured, and murdered. People were arrested simply to fulfill the quotas imposed on provincial agencies. The most conservative estimates put the number of people killed, or "disappeared," at over 15,000. Such a wholesale purge inevitably included some genuine terrorists, and by 1978 the disruptive capacity of the Montoneros and the ERP had been drastically reduced by the death, exile, or imprisonment of their known leaders.

Meanwhile, massive borrowing and the overvaluation of the currency led to a rapid growth in consumer spending, giving the middle classes a false sense of prosperity. Videla, who had retired from the army and junta in August 1978, was succeeded as president in a quasi-constitutional fashion by General Roberto Viola in March 1981, at the start of a new economic recession. Ill health and the opposition of military conservatives to his relatively conciliatory policies forced Viola out of office in November. A right-wing nationalist, General Leopoldo Fortunato Galtieri, took over in December as president and head of the junta.

The Falklands/Malvinas War

At the beginning of 1982, there was a series of labor demonstrations and strikes, culminating on March 30 in a violent confrontation between demonstrators and government forces in Buenos Aires. Galtieri, however, had seized power with a plan that he believed would guarantee his position. On April 2, Argentine forces seized the British-ruled Falkland Islands (Islas Malvinas) in the South Atlantic, title to which had been disputed by Argentina since British occupation in 1833. The eighty-seven-man British garrison was rapidly overwhelmed by 10,000 Argentine soldiers, and Argentine sovereignty was proclaimed. Initially the seizure of the is-lands was a resounding success for the government; the Peronists had always sup-ported it. However, the final defeat of the Argentine forces by a small British naval task force on June 14 was a catastrophe and a national humiliation. The military government of Galtieri, inept politically and economically, had failed in combat—the professional field in which it claimed national preeminence. Galtieri was abruptly replaced and a retired general, Reynaldo Bignone, was selected to head an interim government under which the military could retreat from power without paying the penalty for its misdeeds.

Bignone, having established a dialogue with the political parties, called elections for October 30, 1983, in an atmosphere of deep economic crisis and national con-fusion, fueled by growing civilian demands for the investigation of human rights abuses committed by the services. The UCR (Radicals) and the Partido Justicial-ista (Peronists), the two main parties, chose Raúl Alfonsín and Italo Luder as their respective presidential candidates. The former, a fifty-seven-year-old lawyer who had courageously opposed the war and had a record of defending human rights, obtained a massive victory over Luder, who lacked charisma and whose party was deeply divided.

A Halting Redemocratization

Inaugurated as president in December 1983, Alfonsín faced massive problems. Of a foreign debt of $40 billion left by the military government, one-quarter had been wasted and another quarter was never traced. Meanwhile, hyperinflation and eco-nomic stagnation combined to frustrate the hopes that Alfonsín's victory had aroused; for fifteen consecutive years, Argentina had triple-digit inflation, a world record. During the first year of Alfonsín's presidency, after very protracted negoti-ations, he managed to renegotiate the foreign debt, maintain political stability, and reach some accord with the Peronists. Abroad, he finalized with Chile a long-standing dispute over possession of three islets in the Beagle channel at the extreme south of Tierra del Fuego, which had almost brought the two countries to war in 1978.

Two issues dominated Alfonsín's government: relations with the military and the resuscitation of the economy. In theory committed to eradicating the military from Argentine politics and establishing a working democratic system, Alfonsín soon had to temper his policies with reality. The public was demanding that ser-vice personnel be tried for gross human rights abuses during the "dirty war." Os-tensibly an asset to Alfonsín, public pressure on this issue was in fact a two-edged weapon. Alfonsín was sensitive to the dangers of isolating the armed forces from civilian society and sought to maintain national unity. Few objected—even within the reconstituted services—to the 1985 court-martial of the first three military juntas to rule Argentina after the 1976 coup, for offenses that included abduction, torture, and murder. (In December four of the accused were acquitted, but sen-tences were passed on the remaining five, including sentences of life imprisonment for General Videla and Admiral Eduardo Massera.) Nor did many complain about the prosecution of the high command that had held office during the South At-lantic conflict.

However, as evidence of military atrocities increased, so too did military claims that the dirty war was a just war and that a general amnesty should be enacted. Alfonsín attempted to resolve this conflict in December 1986, when congress approved a law, known popularly as the Punto Final (Full Stop) Law, which established a sixty-day deadline for new indictments. The government had expected that only seventy such cases might be presented. But by the deadline, over 250 indictments had been accepted. Moreover, for the first time, serving officers as well as retired ones were accused.

In April 1987, military rebellions broke out in Córdoba and later at the Campo de Mayo. There the rebels included veterans of the Falklands campaign in full service camouflage and painted faces (*carapintadas*). Despite popular demonstrations in support of democracy, the military was granted concessions, sparking controversy. A new army chief of staff was appointed, and Alfonsín submitted to congress legislative proposals that came to be known as the Obediencia Debida (Due Obedience) Law, absolving most junior military officers. Out of some 370 members of the armed forces due to be tried for human rights offenses, only between thirty and fifty were left to face charges. Even this number was too many for some sectors of the military, and there were minor insurrections in January and December 1988. Then in January 1989 the army claimed to have successfully defeated an attack by forty left-wing activists on a military base at La Tablada, 25 kilometers west of Buenos Aires. The alleged guerrillas, thirty-nine of whom were already dead, were said to have been members of a hitherto unknown organization, All for the Country Movement (MTP), which has since been confirmed as a real, if doomed, attempt to resuscitate the guerrilla conflict, led by Enrique Gorriarán Merlo and a small group of former members of the ERP.

Economic Crisis

What defeated Alfonsín was the Argentine economy. After pursuing gradualist policies to reactivate it in 1984–1985, the government turned in June 1985 to the fashionable doctrine of the "heterodox shock." The Austral Plan was named after the new currency that was to end inflation, by then running at an estimated annual rate of 1,129 percent. But the accompanying freeze on wages led to labor unrest, with the Peronist-dominated trade unions holding a series of one-day strikes. Hence, despite its initial promise, the plan was effectively abandoned while the midterm elections took place.

With the elections out of the way and inflation again soaring, in February 1987 a second Austral Plan (the Australito) was announced. Older devices such as devaluation, pegging (or linking) wage increases to price rises, and lower interest rates were tried again—unsuccessfully. The deficit on the public sector account worsened, and inflation continued to spiral upward. These problems led to deteriorating relations with foreign creditors and pushed the currency to the edge of collapse. In early 1989 the World Bank, which until that time had broadly supported Alfonsín, suspended all financing in Argentina. Negotiations with international creditors were deferred indefinitely. Despite the efforts of two new finance ministers in as many months, no credible economic strategy emerged, and control over inflation was abandoned while the elections of May 1989 were held.

A New Kind of Peronist

With his economic policy in ruins, Alfonsín's sole remaining aim at the end of his presidency was to be succeeded by another democratically elected president. Despite the crisis the elections were both peaceful and orderly. The UCR candidate, Eduardo César Angeloz, proposed widespread privatization and economic austerity in order to combat the economic crisis but was saddled with the burden of Alfonsín's failure. Victory went to the Peronist candidate, Carlos Saúl Menem, the flamboyant former governor of the inland province of La Rioja. In his campaign, Menem captured the popular vote and a Peronist majority in the senate with the promise of a "production revolution" based on wage increases and significant aid to industry. Yet long before he was due to take office, food riots, looting, and bombings in several Argentine cities forced Alfonsín to impose a state of siege and to hand over presidential power to Menem five months early, on July 8, in order to avoid a total breakdown of public authority.

When Menem succeeded Alfonsín, it was the first time since 1928 that an elected president had handed over the office to his successor without military pressure. Democracy, even in the midst of the greatest economic crisis of the century, was still immensely popular. It was immediately clear, moreover, that Menem's economic strategy, to turn Argentina into what he called a "popular market-capitalist country," was much closer to that of the Radicals than his campaign had suggested. The results too were much the same—the collapse of the currency and a second hyperinflationary wave. Menem's relaxed use of presidential authority, divisions in the cabinet, and reluctant support for policies so different from traditional Peronism increased the difficulty in reducing state expenditures and selling state-owned enterprises. The government's troubles were further exacerbated by the public airing of the president's marital problems.

With regard to the military, Menem, who had spent the entire period of the military regime under house arrest, advocated conciliation, despite strong resistance from his own supporters. After weeks of rumors, a series of pardons affecting 277 individuals, including guerrillas but, more importantly, members of the military junta responsible for the Falklands debacle, was issued in October 1989. At the end of 1990, however, military discontent reemerged. The government was taken by surprise when supporters of Colonel Mohammed Ali Seneildín, leader of the December 1988 revolt, rebelled on December 3 and seized the military headquarters, with the loss of at least three lives. Negotiations were rejected; the headquarters were stormed, and the leaders were charged with insurrection. They were sentenced to indefinite imprisonment and discharge from the service. The price was Menem's irreversible decision on December 29 to pardon General Jorge Videla and all others convicted for human rights crimes during the dirty war.

From then on, though, the relative strength of the armed forces continued to decline. In February 1990, Menem decided to resume diplomatic relations with the United Kingdom, keeping the issue of the sovereignty of the disputed islands, as he put it, "under an umbrella." In June 1991 the government announced that the armed forces would be reduced from 75,000 to 55,000 and the period of conscription reduced from one year to six months.

Meanwhile, in January 1991 a series of ministerial changes were to transform the country's economic prospects. The new minister of the economy, Domingo Cavallo, proceeded to implement his Convertibility Plan. This had three main planks. The first was the so-called dollarization of the economy, whereby the Argentine economy was linked to the US economy by the establishment of a fixed exchange rate of 10,000 australes (or one new peso) to the US dollar. This brought inflation down into low single figures in a few weeks and some US$20 billion of "hot money" back into the country. The second was a program of privatization that would reverse forty years of Peronist policy and buy time to fulfill the third, a plan to improve government finances by collecting taxes that had been widely evaded. By the time Menem visited the United States in November, he was celebrated as Latin America's leading free market reformer and US ally. As a result, in March 1992 Menem secured a promise of debt reduction under the Brady Initiative. Argentina's accumulated debt was reduced from over $60 billion to some $48 billion.

At the same time, support for the ruling Peronist Party strengthened. In the provincial elections, the Peronists won fifteen of the twenty-one governorships at stake, including that of the key province of Buenos Aires, where Vice President Eduardo Duhalde won 47 percent of the votes cast. Although their opponents were in disarray, the Peronists were not free of problems, notably the persistent accusations of corruption leveled against them and their inability to agree on a successor to President Menem. Thus in February 1993 Peronists began to campaign for a constitutional amendment to permit Menem's reelection.

In legislative elections held on October 3, 1993, the Peronists won 42.3 percent of the votes cast, giving them 123 seats of the 254-seat chamber of deputies, less than the two-thirds majority necessary in the lower house to approve a constitutional amendment. But anxious to avoid another humiliating defeat for his party in a national referendum on the question of constitutional reform, former president Alfonsín, who was reelected as UCR leader in November 1993, entered into a dialogue with President Menem. The terms of their agreement were endorsed by a UCR national convention in early December. The main proposals detailed in the agreement were allowing a president to seek a consecutive term in office; the creation of the post of coordinating minister to fulfill a prime-ministerial function; an increase in the number of seats in the senate and a reduction in the length of mandate of all senators; and reform of the procedure for judicial appointments. This last proposal was important in securing UCR support, as the Supreme Court was Peronist dominated. No action was taken, however, to correct the problem that had helped bring down Alfonsín—the ability of the provinces to run up debts that the federal government then had to meet. President Menem immediately declared his intention to seek reelection in 1995.

Constitutional Reform

Elections to a 305-seat constituent assembly, which was to draft and approve the proposed constitution, took place on April 10, 1994. The Peronists won 37.7 percent of the votes cast and the UCR only 19.9 percent—the party's worst election result since Argentina's return to democracy in 1983. The Frente Grande, a loose left-wing coalition formed in mid-1993 to oppose the proposed reforms, came in third, receiving an unexpected 12.5 percent of the ballot. However, on August 22 the assembly approved the new constitution, which came into force on the following day. Concessions included the reduction of the presidential mandate from six years to four; the creation of the post of chief of cabinet; a runoff election for presidential and vice presidential candidates when neither obtained 45 percent of the votes cast, or 40 percent when the nearest candidate gained less than 30 percent of the ballot; the establishment of an autonomous government in the city of Buenos Aires with a directly elected mayor; the extension of congressional sessions to nine months; an increase in the number of senators from two to three from each province; the creation of a Council of Magistrates and other judicial reforms.

In the event, the presidential elections of 1995 were overshadowed by the economic impact of the Mexican economic crisis (the tequila effect). President Menem won reelection decisively, gaining 49.8 percent of the votes cast in the only round of balloting. The president had carried every province, and his party, the Peronists, gained an overall majority of three seats in the 257-seat chamber of deputies.

In the aftermath of his victory, President Menem confirmed his intention to retain Cavallo as economy minister. But later in the year tension grew between the two as Cavallo complained publicly of resistance to free market reform among entrenched interests in government. Eventually, in 1996, Cavallo was dismissed, but his plan had been so successful that even after the 1997 recession set in, the government was reluctant to contemplate devaluation. At the same time, falling revenues and the inability to control expenditures by the provincial governments created a widening fiscal gap that could be filled only by increased borrowing. Meanwhile, though Menem was able to see out his second term, his efforts to prevent Governor Duhalde from succeeding him further split the Peronists, while Cavallo formed a new party, Action for the Republic, and attracted some support. Hence during the 1999 elections, the conservative UCR mayor of Buenos Aires, Fernando de la Rúa Bruno, heading an Alliance between UCR and Frepaso (center-left dissident Peronists), won the presidency decisively. The Peronists lost control of the chamber of deputies but retained a majority in the senate.

Unfortunately, by the time de la Rúa took office, the country was already deep in recession. Unemployment was reaching record levels. In March 2001, therefore, he brought Cavallo back for a second spell as economy minister. The appointment stabilized the situation briefly. However, the government was so weak that when Cavallo announced his plan to reduce the budget deficit in 2001 by $3 billion, it was to be achieved by tax increases rather than by spending cuts, which would have involved dismissing public sector workers, cutting their salaries, or reducing state retirement benefits. Confidence was further undermined by Cavallo's frenetic activity, constantly unveiling new measures and holding press conferences three times a day. In July, after a deal with fourteen powerful provincial governors, the senate was finally persuaded to pass the zero deficit law. With this as an excuse, the IMF in August reluctantly agreed to disburse $1.2 billion due in September and even lend a further $8 billion, despite clear signs that the situation was out of control and the strong reservations of the Bush administration in the United States, who wanted to make an example of Argentina to other states.

THE 2001 CRISIS AND ITS AFTERMATH

During the midterm elections on October 14, the electorate showed its anger by giving the opposition Peronists a majority in both houses of Congress. From there they watched as Cavallo made a desperate effort to avoid default. In response to a massive run on the banks, the government on November 30 imposed limits on both cash withdrawals (the *corralito*) and capital movements, effectively ending peso convertibility. Throwing gasoline on the flames, the IMF in response held back the $1.3 billion due to be paid in December. At the weekend of December 15–16, public order began to break down as desperate people started to loot supermarkets. Others banged empty pots (*cacerolazo*) and hammered on the shutters of the banks in frustration. Huge crowds collected in the Plaza de Mayo shouting for the government to go. Heavy-handed police intervention claimed twenty-five lives, injured hundreds, and led to thousands of arrests, which only made matters worse. Finally on December 20, President de la Rúa asked the Peronists to join a government of national unity. They prudently refused. He resigned and was lifted off the roof of the Casa Rosada by helicopter, while Cavallo fled to Patagonia in fear of his life. Over the next two weeks, five people served consecutively as interim president. When on January 1, 2002, the Peronist-dominated congress chose Eduardo Duhalde to serve out de la Rúa's term, the country had already defaulted on its debt. Congress granted the new president emergency powers, and the peso was devalued on January 7. But the peso's new value could not be sustained. On January 17 the stock market reopened sharply down, and violent demonstrations continued across the country against the shortage of cash brought about by the *corralito*. When on February 9 the government unveiled plans to cut the already spartan federal budget by $370 million, some 3,000 demonstrators again filled the Plaza de Mayo for a *cacerolazo*. In response the government restored convertibility and agreed to allow people to cash their pay checks in full.

Fresh rioting followed. Even so, at the beginning of April, Argentina was given the uncompromising message by the IMF that no further help would be available unless even more drastic cuts were forthcoming. On Monday, April 22, therefore, the banks were again closed by government decree. The following day, after failing to win support for an emergency plan to exchange frozen bank deposits for government bonds, the economy minister resigned together with most of the rest of the cabinet. At that point the peso had fallen to US$3.50, having lost just under 69 percent of its value since the beginning of the year. Inflation had risen to 20 percent, millions had effectively lost their savings, public sector workers were rioting, and half the population was said to be living below the national poverty line. In consequence there had been a steep rise in robberies, kidnappings, and other crimes, which the underpaid police were either unable or unwilling to combat. Thieves who stole nearly 3,000 miles of copper wire between January and September seriously disrupted the telephone service, and utility workers were physically attacked when they tried to carry out repairs.

To his credit, President Duhalde remained calm and avoided inflammatory language, and constitutional processes were maintained. By the time elections came around in March 2003, the economy had fallen so far that it was beginning to pick up. With Duhalde ruled out, the Peronists chose as their candidate fifty-three-year-old Néstor Carlos Kirchner Ostoic, the charismatic governor of the remote southern province of Santa Cruz. He obtained only 22.24 percent of the vote on the first round, against 24.45 percent for Menem, who soon realized that he could not win and ungraciously withdrew.

Consequently Kirchner won with the smallest proportion of the vote in Argentine history. Taking office on May 25, with the country in economic crisis, he kept on Roberto Lavagna as economy minister. After difficult negotiations with the IMF Kirchner rescheduled US$84 billion of the foreign debt and exchanged 76 percent of the internal debt for bonds at a rate of approximately one-third of its nominal value. With economic growth picking up to exceed 7 percent in 2005 and 2006, on December 15, 2005, he paid off Argentina's debt to the IMF in full. At the same time he retired dozens of senior officers from the armed forces and several senior judges before moving to overturn the notorious Full Stop and Due Obedience laws. The PJ remained split, but in the 2005 congressional elections Kirchner's Frente para la Victoria (FPV) obtained over 40 percent of the vote and subsequently gained the support of other factions. Moves to reduce the stranglehold of the utility companies were also popular, though the imposition of price controls in 2002 had stifled investment. In 2004 a new state-owned energy company, Energía Argentina (ENARSA), was founded. More than sixty contracts with privatized utilities were renegotiated, and that of Aguas Argentinas (a subsidiary of the French conglomerate Suez) to supply water to the capital was cancelled. Before Kirchner's term ended, however, new accusations of corruption surfaced. Kirchner had a falling out with Lavagna, and the new economy minister, Felisa Miceli, was forced to resign after more than $60,000 was found in a bag in her office bathroom.

On July 2, 2007, Kirchner announced that he would not seek reelection. His wife, Senator Cristina Fernández de Kirchner, who in 2005 had beaten Hilda González, wife of former president Duhalde, to become a senator for the province of Buenos Aires, won the presidency with 45.3 percent of the vote in the first round, taking office on December 10, 2007. In March 2008, however, Kirchner's government attempted to introduce new taxes on agricultural exports, effectively raising the export tax on soybeans from 35 percent to 44 percent, and provoked a furious response from the farmers. Meanwhile, wheat farmers suffering from prolonged drought and historically low world prices faced the prospect of a harvest down by almost half and worth 40 percent less than the previous year. In a self-defeating move they were forbidden to export grain needed for home consumption, sharply reducing Argentina's ability to earn foreign exchange. Beef exports in 2008 for the first time were exceeded by those of Uruguay. In the end the tax project failed in the senate when Vice President Julio Cobos voted against it. By this time the economy was moving into recession and unemployment rose to 19.8 percent in May 2009. In November 2008 congress accepted a proposal to transfer some $30 billion in private pension funds to the state social security system in an effort to balance the books.

As the economy continued to deteriorate, the midterm elections were brought forward to June 28, 2009, when ex-president Néstor Kirchner set a new precedent in running for a seat as a deputy in the province of Buenos Aires to rally support for his party list. The gamble failed. The Kirchner faction won just 29.6 percent of the poll, losing control of congress, the major provinces, the Peronist Party and even its native state, Santa Cruz. Néstor Kirchner was defeated by Francisco de Narváez of the anti-Kirchner Unión Pro-alliance and resigned as party leader, being replaced by Daniel Scioli, governor of Buenos Aires.

FOREIGN RELATIONS

Relations between Argentina and the United States continued to improve into the 1990s under US president Bill Clinton's administration. In late August 1994, Argentine-British relations became strained after the new constitution reiterated Argentina's claim to sovereignty over the Falkland Islands. However, Argentine and British troops together patrolled the "green line" in Cyprus. By signing the Treaty of Tlatelolco, sending a naval force to the Persian Gulf in 1990, and supporting UN operations in Bosnia-Herzegovina and Haiti, President Menem signaled his country's intention of playing a new and wider role in the "new world order" and actively participating in UN peacekeeping operations. Meanwhile, with the excuse of economic constraint, the military budget was cut; the army's strength was reduced by a further 15 percent, to 23,000, in 1995; and conscription officially ended. With the issue of sovereignty still "under an umbrella," talks led to an agreement signed in New York on September 27, 1995, on joint exploitation of the Malvinas basin, which enabled oil companies to bid for licenses in the disputed area without incurring penalties. Had the area been as rich as many believed, Argentina stood to gain handsomely from rising world prices, but in 2010 the government went back on its agreement with Britain and tried hard to block access to the basin instead. Menem decisively rejected the Radical Party's policy of seeking leadership of the Third World and took Argentina out of the nonaligned movement. Reemerging as a candidate member of the First World, Argentina rejected its traditional posture of suspicious isolationism to come out as a strong ally of the United States and an example to the world of the success—fleeting as it turned out—of the free market.

Argentina's economic collapse at the outset of 2002 left a residue of popular distrust of neoliberal policy and of political leaders subject to guidance by public and private creditors, including the United States and the IMF. Public frustration and the widespread grassroots organization to which it gave rise thus provided a base for a major policy shift. With the inauguration of Nestor Kirchner in 2003, Argentina aligned itself with Brazil, then governed by the Workers Party, in seeking to strengthen Mercosur and, with Latin America and other Third World countries, in challenging First World blueprints for the World Health Organization (WTO) and the Free Trade Agreement of the Americas (FTAA). Relations with the United States deteriorated when US prosecutors alleged that the Cristina Kirchner campaign had received illegal subventions from Venezuela, which was regarded with great suspicion by the US government.

SUGGESTED READINGS

Alexander, Robert J. *Juan Domingo Perón: A History.* Boulder: Westview, 1979.

Argentina, Republic of. Comisión Nacional sobre la Desaparición de Personas. *Nunca mas: Informe de la Comisión Nacional sobre la Desaparición de Personas.* Buenos Aires: Editorial Universitaria de Buenos Aires, 1986.

Calvert, Susan, and Peter Calvert. *Argentina: Political Culture and Instability.* London: Macmillan, 1988.

Crawley, Eduardo. *A House Divided: Argentina, 1880–1980.* London: Hurst, 1984.

Di Tella, Guido. *Argentina Under Perón, 1973–76: The Nation's Experience with a Labour-based Government.* London: Macmillan, 1983.

Falcoff, Mark, and Dolkart, Ronald H., eds. *Prologue to Perón: Argentina in Depression and War, 1930–1943.* Berkeley: University of California Press, 1975.

Fraser, Nicholas, and Marysa Navarro. *Eva Perón.* London: André Deutsch, 1980.

Graham-Yooll, Andrew. *A State of Fear: Memories of Argentina's Nightmare.* London: Eland, 1986.

Imaz, José Luís de. *Los que mandan.* Buenos Aires: Editorial Universitaria de Buenos Aires, 1964.

Kirkpatrick, Jeane. *Leader and Vanguard in Mass Society: A Study of Peronist Argentina.* Cambridge: Massachusetts Institute of Technology, 1971.

Mallon, Richard D., and Juan V. Sourrouille. *Economic Policymaking in a Conflict Society: The Argentine Case.* Cambridge: Harvard University Press, 1975.

Martínez Estrada, Ezequiel. *X-ray of the Pampa.* Trans. Alain Swietlicki. Austin: University of Texas Press, 1971.

Milenky, Edward S. *Argentina's Foreign Policies.* Boulder: Westview, 1978.

O'Donnell, Guillermo. *Modernization and Bureaucratic-Authoritarianism: Studies in South American Politics.* Berkeley: University of California Press, 1973.

Page, Joseph A. *Perón: A Biography.* New York: Random House, 1983.

Platt, D. C. M., and Guido di Tella, eds. *Argentina, Australia, and Canada: Studies in Comparative Development, 1870–1965.* London: Macmillan, 1985.

Potash, Robert A. *The Army and Politics in Argentina, 1928–1945: Yrigoyen to Perón.* Stanford, California: Stanford University Press, 1969.

———. *The Army and Politics in Argentina, 1945–1962: Perón to Frondizi.* London: Athlone, 1980.

Rock, David. *Argentina 1516–1982: From Spanish Colonization to the Falklands War.* Berkeley: University of California Press, 1985.

Schoultz, Lars. *The Populist Challenge: Argentine Electoral Behavior in the Postwar Era.* Chapel Hill: University of North Carolina Press, 1983.

Scobie, James R. *Argentina: A City and a Nation.* New York: Oxford University Press, 1971.

———. *Buenos Aires: Plaza to Suburb, 1870–1910.* New York: Oxford University Press, 1974.

Snow, Peter G. *Political Forces in Argentina.* Boston: Allyn & Bacon, 1971.

Tamarin, David. *The Argentine Labor Movement, 1930–1945: A Study in the Origins of Peronism.* Albuquerque: University of New Mexico Press, 1985.

Timmerman, Jacobo. *Prisoner Without a Name, Cell Without a Number.* Trans. Tony Talbot. Harmondsworth, UK: Penguin, 1982.

Turner, Frederick C., and José Enrique Miguens, eds. *Juan Perón and the Reshaping of Argentina.* Pittsburgh: University of Pittsburgh Press, 1983.

Wynia, Gary W. *Argentina in the Postwar Era: Politics and Economic Policy Making in a Divided Society.* Albuquerque: University of New Mexico Press, 1978.

Chapter 28

URUGUAY AND PARAGUAY

An Arduous Transition

DIEGO ABENTE BRUN
WITH MICHAEL DANIELSON

URUGUAY AND PARAGUAY, two of the smallest nations of South America, are often confused with each other because their names are so similar. However, their differences are probably among the greatest between any two single countries in Latin America and can be traced back as far as the beginning of the Spanish conquest in 1536.

Both countries developed around a city; Asunción in Paraguay, Montevideo in Uruguay. The former, established in 1537, is the oldest city in the Rio de la Plata basin. It remained the center of the Spanish domain in the area until the end of the seventeenth century, when it lost its supremacy to the port city of Buenos Aires due to the administrative partition of the province of Paraguay. Yet it was not until 1680 that the Portuguese established the first settlement, the Colonia del Santísimo Sacramento, in what is now Uruguayan territory. Some forty-five years later, the Spaniards expelled the Portuguese and in 1726 established the city of Montevideo.

Asunción was a very suitable center for the Spanish domain. It was located on a bay overlooked by the hills of Lambare and therefore easy to defend from nearby Indian populations. Furthermore, the Spaniards formed a political alliance with the Indians living in that particular area, which gave rise to some of the unique features of the Paraguayan nation. For example, the Indians gave the Spaniards women, whose brothers were consequently obliged to work certain days a week for their *cuñados* (brothers-in-law). This hastened the process of racial integration, or *mestizaje,* and made Paraguay one of the most homogeneous mestizo countries in Latin America. The practice also contributed to the preservation of the Indian language, Guaraní, because the mestizos learned the Indian tongue from their mothers and Spanish from their fathers. Although carrying heavy racial overtones, this bilingualism persists into the present day.

In the area surrounding Montevideo, by contrast, there were few Indians, and they did not have close contact with the Spanish settlers, who were mostly cattle ranchers. As a result, the country was populated by mostly *criollos* (Hispanic Creoles), and *mestizaje* was almost unknown. In addition, the waves of European, especially

538

Italian and Spanish immigrants in the second half of the nineteenth century and the first decades of the twentieth, ultimately made Uruguay a racially European country.

During the colonial years Paraguay acquired its own cultural, linguistic, and economic identity and proclaimed its independence from Spain in 1811. At the same time it rejected the domination of Buenos Aires, the city to which it had been administratively linked before the breakdown of the Spanish Empire in the Americas. In 1814 José Gaspar Rodríguez de Francia was made dictator in a truly Roman fashion—first for a two-year term and then for life. Ruling until his death in 1840, he succeeded in isolating the country and in defeating the pro–Buenos Aires tendencies. He tolerated no political activity and instituted an all-embracing repressive state.

Uruguay, meanwhile, was invaded and annexed by the Portuguese-Brazilian empire in 1816 and existed as the Cisplatine province until 1828. It became an independent republic in 1830, probably the first buffer state in Latin America, created after long negotiations between Brazilians (Portuguese) and Argentineans with the intermediation of the British envoy, Lord Ponsonby.

In Paraguay, Francia was succeeded by Carlos Antonio López, who followed some of Francia's policies but opened the door to greater commerce and allowed limited political liberalization. Nevertheless, he secured total power for himself and his family, particularly for his son Francisco Solano, who was made brigadier general of the Paraguayan army at the age of eighteen. In quasi-monarchic fashion, Francisco Solano López succeeded his father, who died in 1862. Solano López had been in Europe in 1852–1853 and was heavily influenced by the France of Napoleon III as well as by European geopolitical doctrines. Thus in 1864, arguing that a partial invasion of Uruguayan territory by Brazilian troops constituted a threat to the equilibrium of the nations of the Río de la Plata, he declared war on Brazil. He later declared war on Argentina when it refused to let Paraguayan troops cross Argentine territory to engage the Brazilian army. Finally Uruguay declared war on Paraguay, although its participation was minor. The war ended five years later with the destruction of Paraguay and the death of Marshal López, who, true to his previous statements, heroically accepted death but not surrender.

URUGUAY

Democracy: Practice and Tradition of Coparticipation

Until 1973, Uruguay was considered one of the most stable democracies of Latin America, a model of freedom and progress. Although such claims may be exaggerated, it is true that until the late 1960s Uruguay had a relatively stable polity and ranked among the most democratic regimes in Latin America. Let us therefore examine how this situation came into being.[1]

Early in the nineteenth century, the Uruguayan caudillos (later the political elites) decided that institutionalized compromises were necessary. Thus the history of Uruguay since 1830 has been characterized by compromises among caudillos—broken from time to time and then replaced by other compromises. This process led to the institutionalization of a practice known as coparticipation, a constant in Uruguayan history and the ideological and practical framework in which Uruguayan politics evolved until the late 1960s. Hence, regardless of which of the two traditional parties, the Blancos (whites, conservatives) or the Colorados (reds, liberals), was in power, there was always room, a coparticipative role, for the opposition.

The first half of the twentieth century was dominated by the Colorado populist leader José Batlle y Ordóñez. Batlle, president from 1903 to 1907 and from 1911 to 1915, represented the most progressive wing of the Colorado Party, and his influence in Uruguayan politics had far-reaching consequences. Under his leadership, Uruguay underwent a rapid process of modernization financed, in part, by rising export revenues. Batlle's influence was most prominent in economic and social reforms. Among other things, he nationalized foreign banks and the public utility companies, enacted a pension law, established provisions for rest days and workmen's compensation for industrial accidents, and legalized the eight-hour workday. His policies also opened the door for the newly mobilized social and political forces of Montevideo, most of them immigrants or sons of immigrants, to enter the political arena. These new citizens, representing the middle and working classes, tended to support the party and faction that implemented such reforms. By the turn of the century the population of the capital city, Montevideo, already represented 30 percent of the population of the country, and 47 percent of that population was composed of immigrants. Considering this, it is evident how deeply Batlle's policies changed the map of the country. In electoral terms, his reforms meant that the total number of voters jumped from 31,262 in 1910 to 299,017 in 1928.[2]

Under Batlle's influence, the situation in Uruguay changed during the 1920s and 1930s in two important ways. First, the power and role of the state were greatly enhanced through state intervention in the economy. Public and semipublic corporations (*entes autónomos*) were created, necessitating expansion of the state bureaucracy. By the 1930s, the budget of the state *entes* represented 62 percent of total national expenses, and the total number of public employees had reached 52,000—approximately 5 percent of the national population.[3] Second, through the reforms promulgated by Batlle, the middle and working classes of Montevideo gained participation in the political system. This gain was also facilitated by the expansion of the industrial sector. For example, the number of industrial establishments increased from 714 to 7,403 between 1901 and 1930.[4]

This new situation did not supersede coparticipation, the old and resilient political tradition; in fact, a new collegial system (*colegiado*) was introduced for the exercise of executive power. The first *colegiado* (1917–1933), a personal triumph for Batlle, consisted of a dual executive power. On the one hand, the president was in charge of foreign affairs and defense, political, and police matters, while on the other, the National Council of Administration, composed of six members representing the majority party and three from the largest minority party, was in charge of all other administrative matters. The second *colegiado* (1952–1966) eliminated the president and vested all power in the council, which, like previous ones, had one-third of its seats reserved for the first minority party.[5]

Two factors are of particular importance in explaining the long-lasting success of coparticipation. The first is the country's steady rate of economic growth in the first half of the twentieth century. That growth allowed the political system to accommodate increasing political and economic demands from different social sectors and to foot the bill for a semiwelfare state. The years between 1900 and 1930, the period of *crecimiento hacia afuera* (outward-looking growth), were characterized by an export boom based on meat, wool, and hides. The total value of exports increased from 29.4 million pesos in 1900 to 73.3 million pesos in 1915 and 100.9 million pesos in 1930. By the 1930s, that model of growth had been replaced by a model of *crecimiento hacia adentro* (inward-looking growth), though exports, particularly wool, continued to provide the hard currency that financed the model. The internal dynamic of growth, however, was provided by an industrial process of import substitution. The number of industrial establishments increased from 6,750 in 1930 to 23,080 in 1952, and the number of jobs provided by them jumped from 54,000 to 141,000 in the same period.[6] The proportion contributed by industrial production to the GDP grew from 12.5 percent in 1930 to 20.3 percent in 1950.[7] The fact is that the rate of growth increased steadily, either through exports or through import substitution, and provided the government with the necessary resources to accommodate social, economic, and political demands and therefore maintain its political efficacy.

A second important factor explaining Uruguay's democratic stability until the late 1960s is its peculiar legal-constitutional framework. By accepting the political reality of a highly fragmented political scene and a machine-type political party system, Uruguay institutionalized a stable and mutually accepted formula for resolving political disputes. An important part of this framework of practical and legalized coparticipation was the electoral law, passed in 1910, whereby parties were able to withstand fractionalization without losing electoral strength. The law, known as the *ley de lemas* (law of party designations), established a system in which voters in national elections chose simultaneously the party of preference and, within that party, the preferred candidate. In US terms, that would be tantamount to holding the primaries and the national elections on the same day, the winner being the most popular candidate of the most popular party.

BREAKDOWN OF DEMOCRACY AND EMERGENCE OF THE MILITARY DICTATORSHIP

The decade of the 1950s signaled the beginning of the end of the economic bonanza and the political model that this bonanza helped to sustain. Excessive dependence on exports, particularly on a few products, and an industrialization process that relied too heavily on protectionist measures and foreign currency generated by a depressed export sector brought about crises of increasing gravity. Total exports dropped from US$254.3 million in 1950 to US$129.4 million in 1960. Recurrent balance of payments problems forced the continuing devaluation of the peso, from 1.90 to the dollar in 1950 to 11.30 to the dollar in 1960 to 250 in 1971.[8] The average annual rate of growth declined from 4.8 percent between 1945 and 1955 to 0.9 percent between 1955 and 1970, while the per capita rate of growth for the last period was 0.3 percent.

The industrial sector lost the dynamism of the earlier period. The number of people employed by industry dropped from 200,642 in 1960 to 197,400 in 1968.

The annual rate of growth of the industrial sector decreased from 6 percent between 1945 and 1954 and to 1.6 percent between 1960 and 1970.[9] The inflation rate, which had been 9.8 percent in 1955 and had never before surpassed 15 percent, reached a record high of 125.4 percent in 1968.[10] There was also a dramatic decline in real wages, especially after 1970. The index of real wages dropped from a base of 100 in 1957 to 76.5 in 1967,[11] and from an index of base 100 in 1968 to 66.2 in 1979.[12] The second figure means that in 1979 workers earned an average of 33.8 percent less than in 1968.

This economic stagnation, combined with high rates of inflation and continued balance of payments deficits, provoked strong reactions from all economic sectors, particularly the landed upper classes. In the 1958 elections, the landowning elites supported the conservative Blanco Party, which won its first national election in the twentieth century. In order to reverse what the landed elites considered a virtual confiscation of their export earnings through the mechanism of multiple exchange rates, in 1959 the Blanco government passed the Exchange Reform Law. The government was also forced into a number of agreements with the International Monetary Fund (IMF) to regularize the constant balance of payments deficits. The crisis, however, continued to deepen. The *colegiado* system of government, created by the 1952 constitution, was blamed for many of the difficulties, and in 1966, concurrent with the national election, a new constitution that restored the presidential system was approved.

Retired general Oscar Gestido of the Colorado Party won the election, but he died less than a year after taking office and was replaced by his vice president, Jorge Pacheco Areco. By the time Pacheco replaced Gestido, the Tupamaro National Liberation Movement, an urban guerrilla group, had become very active. The Tupamaros, who aimed to overthrow the capitalist regime, were mainly young intellectuals, students, and salaried members of the middle class. They established a highly efficient organization and carried out some spectacular *coups de main*, including the kidnapping of the British ambassador, the Brazilian consul, and the US police adviser, Dan Mitrione. Mitrione was later killed when the government refused to accept the Tupamaros' conditions for his release. Pacheco was thus forced to employ increasing force, and the level of repression gradually rose.

The 1971 elections took place in a tense climate. The Uruguayan left coalesced in the Broad Front (FA), composed of Christian Democrats, Socialists, Communists, and independent leftists. Its presidential candidate was retired general Liber Seregni, a prestigious and widely respected military man. The Broad Front, as expected, did well in Montevideo, where it captured 30 percent of the votes, but it fared poorly in the countryside. Colorado candidate Juan M. Bordaberry, with the support of his party's conservative *pachequista* faction, became the new president. Whereas Pacheco was from the upper classes of Montevideo, Bordaberry was closely associated with the even more conservative landowning classes.

The truce declared by the Tupamaros during the preelectoral and electoral periods, designed to help the Broad Front, was soon over, and a dialectic of increasing repression and rising guerrilla activities began to escalate. The army, which had been called in September 1971 to lead the antisubversive campaign, prepared a full-scale offensive. The killings of a frigate captain and an army colonel (the brother of General Gregorio Alvarez, who became president in 1981) enraged the military, and by September 1972 it had almost completely wiped out the Tupamaro movement. Simultaneously, a whole array of right-wing counterguerrilla movements—death squad types of organizations—mounted a general antileftist persecution. The army's success was based not only on its military superiority but also on the extensive and undiscriminating use of torture against anybody suspected of being connected with the Tupamaros.

Once the process of overt military intervention in the political life of the country was set in motion, it became increasingly difficult, and ultimately impossible, for civilian political leaders to reverse it. Thus, although the antiguerrilla campaign was almost completely successful by the end of 1972, the military gradually assumed a larger role in the decision-making process. With documents seized from the Tupamaros, the military launched a campaign against "corruption" and demanded a greater role in the management of state corporations and other state agencies. President Bordaberry caved in to virtually every demand, and by early 1973 he was a puppet of the military.

The first stage of the final crisis began in February 1973, when the army and the air force resisted Bordaberry's designation of a new defense minister. They further demanded the establishment of a National Security Council (COSENA) composed of officers and civilians to deal with security and economic matters.

Parliament, trying to stop the military from completely taking over the government, conducted a series of investigations into the use of torture in army detention centers. On June 27, 1973, the generals retaliated by closing Parliament and replacing it with the Council of State, composed of forty-six members handpicked by the military. Political parties and activities were banned, the National University closed, and workers' organizations outlawed as the most terrible political persecution in Uruguayan history was unleashed. From that time on, the only significant changes were in the degree and scope of repression. In 1976 Bordaberry was forced to resign and was replaced by a civilian handpicked by the military, Aparicio Méndez, who was never more than a figurehead.

Early in the 1980s, the military institutionalized the dictatorship. Following the Brazilian model of changing presidents without changing the regime, the National Security Council elected a new president, General Gregorio Alvarez, in 1981. Soon after assuming power, Alvarez called a national referendum to approve a new constitution greatly restricting political activities—particularly those of the nontraditional parties—and perpetuating a growing role for the military. The plebiscite was a crushing defeat for the military, as 54 percent of the voters, ignoring official intimidation, rejected the constitution. The process of controlled liberalization continued, however, and the military promised to hold free presidential and congressional elections in November 1984. Late in 1982, the Colorado and Blanco parties were allowed to organize internal elections, and the antigovernment factions scored a major victory, winning over 70 percent of the votes. In mid-1983, the government-opposition talks regarding the transition collapsed, due to the intransigence of the military in its attempt to secure control over the decision-making process even after the elections. The government responded by increasing the levels of political repression and press censorship, but the result was a series of mass rallies (the first public gatherings in Montevideo in years) demanding an immediate return to democracy.[13]

Finally, after prolonged negotiations, the military retreated to the barracks in 1984, and Colorado candidate Julio María Sanguinetti was elected president. The elections were marred, to say the least, when the candidacy of two popular anti-military leaders, Wilson Ferreira Aldunate of the Nationalist (Blanco) Party and General Liber Seregni of the FA, was prohibited.[14] Sanguinetti led the first post-military government through rough waters, particularly because of the military's adamant refusal to allow officers to stand trial for human rights violations and po-litical crimes. Sanguinetti, however, managed to consolidate the restored demo-cratic system. In the elections of November 1989, Luis A. Lacalle Herrera of the Blanco Party won the presidency.

Meanwhile, the economic situation improved in some respects in the late 1970s. In the early 1980s, however, Uruguay plummeted into one of its worst recessions up to that point (the 2002 recession was even worse; see below) with negative growth rates of -1.3 percent in 1981, -10.0 percent in 1982, and -8.5 percent in 1983. Inflation, on the other hand, returned to a high of 57.5 percent in 1983 and hovered around 60 percent thereafter.

The sectors that benefited most from the policies of the military dictatorship were precisely those linked to the export of nontraditional goods, and bankers. The landowning classes benefited to the extent that they provided the raw mate-rials for most of the nontraditional export industries, such as tanning and leather goods. The sectors that suffered most were industrialists producing for domestic consumption—because of the contraction of the market—and salaried workers and employees—because real wages and salaries declined 35 percent between 1972 and 1979. Labor unions were all but destroyed, and workers were absolutely de-fenseless against the military dictatorship.

The US Role

US private investment in Uruguay has never been substantial. In 1960 it totaled only $47 million.[15] By 1980 total US investment in Latin America was more than $38 billion, but Uruguay, Paraguay, and Bolivia shared less than 2 percent of that amount. Nor has US economic aid been significant. US loans and grants (exclud-ing military programs) grew from $10.1 million in 1972 to $13 million in 1975 but declined sharply thereafter to $0.2 million in 1978, reflecting the general de-terioration of US-Uruguayan relations between 1977 and 1980. This deterioration was due to the Carter administration's human rights policy and the failure of the Uruguayan dictatorship to take positive steps toward stopping the systematic vio-lation of human rights and civil liberties.

US military aid, however, has been a different matter. The total extended to Uruguay between 1950 and 1966 was $33.2 million. The figure for 1969 was $1.6 million, increasing to $5.2 million in 1971. It decreased somewhat until 1973 and then jumped to a high of $8.2 million in 1975.[16] In 1977 secretary of state Cyrus Vance announced that because of the pattern of gross violations of human rights by the Uruguayan government, the United States was suspending all military aid to that country. That policy was reversed by President Reagan in 1981.

Regardless of how much money the United States appropriated for military aid to Uruguay each year, there was some sort of US involvement during the heyday of the repression between 1970 and 1975. The role of US police adviser Dan Mitrione, for example, killed by the Tupamaros on charges of training Uruguayan policemen in torture methods, has never been adequately explained.

From Democracy to Dictatorship: A Reassessment

The history of the rise and fall of democracy in Uruguay permits us to draw some interesting conclusions. The uninterrupted economic growth from 1900 to 1950 allowed the political process to become relatively autonomous from the pressures of the dominant classes. The extent to which these classes were able to function normally and make a satisfactory profit was related to their willingness to maintain a low profile in the political arena and give a free rein to the politicians. The landowning elites, for example, may have felt that their earnings were being confiscated by exchange laws, but the rising prices they charged for the products they sold allowed them to prosper anyway. In fact, it was not until almost a decade after the crisis in the export sector began that they became directly involved in purely political matters.

The relative autonomy of the political process from economic pressure by the dominant classes was also favored by the development of a system of political machines that promoted the development of a welfare state. Hence, whereas the economically active population represented some 39 percent of the total population, the number of people on the government payroll plus the passive groups (i.e., retirees and pensioners) represented, in 1969, almost 20 percent of the total population.[17] The state thus became a tremendous source of patronage, and the parties developed increasingly larger political machines to control it.

When the crisis emerged in the late 1950s, due to depression of the export sector and decline in the growth rate of the domestic industrial sector, it became increasingly difficult for any government to respond to the contradictory demands of various classes and economic sectors. The emergence of an armed challenge to the regime, the Tupamaros, aggravated the situation. Both the dominant classes and the military felt that their interests were threatened.

An external factor that may have heavily influenced the Uruguayan process is the involvement of more powerful neighboring states in internal power struggles. The three most powerful countries in the area—Brazil, Argentina, and Chile— were also suffering military dictatorships (except for the 1973–1976 Peronist parenthesis in Argentina) at the time of the military drive in Uruguay. The influence of Brazil, especially, appears to have been quite strong. Likewise, when the winds of liberalization began to blow in the Southern Cone countries, it became increasingly difficult for the military to continue refusing the domestic demand for democratization.

Uruguay in the 1990s: A Rebirth

As elsewhere in Latin America in the 1980s and 1990s, the retreat of the military has been halting and incomplete, and the return of elections did not immediately lead to full-blown class- or sector-interest competition or to constituency representation and accountability. Even so, the vitality of the born-again democratic system in the 1990s was impressive in light of the repression suffered in the 1970s and the constraints on resource allocation in the 1990s.

The economy, by all counts a disaster as transition to civilian rule got under way in the 1980s, made something of a comeback in the 1990s. Offshore-style banking confidentiality and beachfront resort development, among other things, attracted major investments in the late 1980s and early 1990s. GDP growth registered an impressive 7.5 percent in 1992, dropping to 1.7 percent in 1993 and leveling off at about 4 percent in 1994. From 1990 to 1999, per capita GDP increased by an annual average rate of 2.8 percent from $4,802 to $6,173.[18] This per capita growth rate was twice as high as the 1.4 percent increase for the Latin American region as a whole over the same period.[19] The foreign debt to GDP ratio fell over the first half of the 1990s, but by 1999 had begun to increase again to reach 39.5 percent of GDP.[20] Although inflation and poverty fell significantly over the period, the unemployment rate increased from 8.5 percent in 1990 to 11.3 percent in 1999, despite notable growth in per capita GDP. At the beginning of 1995, the country confirmed its commitment to the Southern Cone common market (Mercosur) by implementing the custom union's common external tariff on most tradable goods.

Military restiveness on a lesser scale continued into the early 1990s, but it was popular opposition to the austerity measures on which foreign credit was conditioned that forced the major traditional parties into a National Accord. That accord carried over with respect to economic strategy from the tenure of the Colorado Party's Sanguinetti to the Blanco Party government of Luis Alberto Lacalle, elected in 1989, and to the subsequent government of Sanguinetti, returned to office in 1994.

The fact that the traditional parties had moved right and become almost indistinguishable opened political space to the left. Occupying the space on the political spectrum where factions of the Colorado Party were found in midcentury is the FA, led by former mayor of Montevideo Tabaré Vázquez. In the 1994 elections, the traditional parties and the FA essentially divided the electorate into thirds. Although the Colorado Party won the 1994 elections, the FA had been improving its electoral performance consistently since the return of democracy, having won 21 percent of the vote in 1984 and 1989 and 31 percent in 1994.[21]

In response to the increasing electoral success of the left, in 1996 the Blanco and Colorado parties worked together to push through a significant electoral reform. Among other changes, they eliminated the *ley de lemas* for selecting the president and replaced it with a system of primary elections.[22] It was argued that eliminating this system would ensure the election of stronger presidents and more stable coalitions.[23] Perhaps the most crucial aspect of the 1996 reform is requiring runoff elections when no party wins a majority of the votes in the first round, opening up the possibility for the Blanco and Colorado parties to form a second-round coalition to defeat the FA.[24]

In the elections of late 1999, the reforms seemed to work well for the traditional parties, as Colorado Party patriarch Jorge Batlle became president, but only after a runoff election against FA candidate Tabaré Vázquez.[25] In the first round the FA was victorious, winning 40.1 percent of the vote, but was narrowly defeated by Batlle, with the help of the Blanco Party endorsement, in the runoff election.[26]

RETURN OF ECONOMIC CRISIS AND THE
DECLINE OF THE TRADITIONAL PARTIES

With a minority in congress, President Batlle invited the Blancos to join a coalition government of short duration. Brazil's devaluation of its currency in 1999 and Argentina's economic meltdown in 2001 had a devastating impact on the economy of Uruguay, and soon emergency measures were adopted; they included tax increases and a one-week bank holiday to prevent a massive withdrawal of deposits. By his last year in office, despite the beginnings of an economic recovery, President Batlle had approval ratings in the single digits.[27]

Though there may be room for debate about Uruguay's economic performance during the 1990s, the economic and social indicators during the administration of President Batlle were unequivocally poor. Beginning with the devaluation of the Brazilian real in 1999, which damaged the competitiveness of the export sector, and intensifying with the economic collapse of neighboring Argentina at the end of 2001, the Uruguayan economy slipped into a deep crisis. From 1999, when President Batlle was elected, until his final year in office in 2004, the poverty rate more than doubled from 9.4 percent to 20.9 percent.[28] Near the end of his five-year term in 2003, the debt-to-GDP ratio hit a staggering 98.4 percent. Per capita GDP fell 14 percent between 1999 and 2003 and remained well below its 1999 level during the 2004 election year. Though some indicators were beginning to improve by 2004, the economy was in significantly worse shape than in 1999 and the political damage to the traditional parties had already been done, particularly to President Batlle and his Colorado Party.

As the 2004 elections neared and popular disillusionment with the traditional parties and the status quo mounted, the prospects of Tabaré Vázquez and his coalition of parties from the left were stronger than ever.

A DECISIVE VICTORY FOR THE LEFT

Joining its counterparts throughout Latin America, the Uruguayan electorate delivered a strong rebuke to the traditional parties and the status quo of neoliberal economic policies of the previous decade and handed a decisive electoral victory to the left. Founded in 1971, the FA enjoyed uninterrupted growth in the national vote, culminating in a decisive victory in 2004. Tabaré Vázquez, leader of the Encuentro Progresista–Frente Amplio–Nueva Mayoría coalition (FA), was elected president in the first round, winning 51.7 percent of the valid votes.[29] The Blanco Party ran a distant second with 35.1 percent, and the long dominant Colorado Party suffered a devastating defeat with 10.6 percent of the vote. The FA also secured control over both houses of the legislature, as well, with fifty-two out of ninety-nine House of Deputies seats and sixteen out of thirty Senate seats, bringing about the formation of the first majority government in almost forty years.[30]

President Vázquez strategically nominated the leaders of the coalition's internal factions to the most important cabinet posts. He named Senator-elect Danilo Astori as finance minister and Senator-elect José "Pepe" Mújica as secretary of agriculture. Astori, a Vázquez rival within FA and leader of the Uruguay Assembly

(AU), represents the center-left side of the FA. In addition to its role in Vázquez's domestic governing strategy, the naming of Astori to this important cabinet post sent a clear signal to international financial markets that the FA government would not stray radically from the economic orthodoxy of its predecessors. By contrast, Mújica, a former Tupamaro guerrilla and political prisoner, and his Movement for Popular Participation (MPP), along with the Communist and Socialist parties, represented the left side of the coalition.[31] Out of fourteen cabinet posts, six of the ministers were factional leaders securing 88 percent of FA legislative seats, helping to ensure party discipline in the legislature. Seven posts were reserved for Vázquez's most trusted allies, and an additional post was given to the MPP, the FA faction that received the most votes.[32]

Vázquez entered the government with a 68 percent approval rating and only 7 percent disapproval.[33] This level of approval is especially striking when contrasted with the historically low approval of outgoing President Batlle. Hence, though these approval ratings moderated over time and tensions would eventually emerge within the FA coalition—particularly over the question of trade agreements with the United States—the Vázquez government came into office with a strong mandate and enjoyed several early policy successes. Human rights took center stage during the first year of FA government, as the remains of victims of the military dictatorship were exhumed. In 2006 ex-President Juán María Bordaberry and his foreign minister were tried and convicted for crimes against humanity.[34] These trials and convictions were made possible by the Vázquez government's reinterpretation of the 1986 law that had given amnesty to members of the outgoing military regime.[35]

Beyond these historic convictions, the social policy successes of the FA government included the passage of PANES (Plan de Atención Nacional de Emergencia Social), a welfare program that provides cash benefits to poor families on the condition that their children enroll in school and obtain health services.[36] Labor law reform led to the reinstatement of collective bargaining rights for labor unions (which had been eliminated under 2009 Blanco Party presidential candidate and then-president Lacalle in 1992), and the tax code was reformed with the objective of achieving a more equitable distribution of income.[37]

ELECTIONS OF 2009

As Vázquez's term as president progressed, two clear leaders emerged within the FA coalition as potential successors. In FA internal elections in November 2006, José Mújica's MPP won the largest share of the vote with 31 percent, followed by economics minister and AU leader Danilo Astori with 13 percent.[38] These two factional leaders faced off in the FA primary elections of 2009. Mújica was victorious in these elections, winning 52.4 percent of the FA votes compared to Astori's 39.7 percent, but in the general elections Astori joined the ticket as candidate for vice president as Mújica's running mate.[39] In the primary election for the principal opposition Blanco Party, former president Luis Alberto Lacalle won 57 percent of the vote and similarly incorporated the second-place finisher, Jorge Larrañaga, as his vice presidential running mate. Finally, the Colorado party primary was won easily by Pedro Bordaberry.

The general election was held on October 25, and although its overall percentage of the vote (and legislative seats) declined, the FA and the Mújica-Astori ticket emerged with a strong plurality of the vote. Nevertheless, the FA won only 48.1 percent of the vote, thus forcing a runoff election that was held on November 29. Though the Colorado Party and Bordaberry finished in third place, the party increased its percentage of the vote by six points and went from three Senate seats and ten House of Delegates seats to five and seventeen seats, respectively. Though the FA held on to its absolute parliamentary majority, the coalition lost seats in both chambers, as did the Blanco Party.[40]

Similar to the situation a decade earlier in 1999, the Blanco and Colorado parties formed a second-round electoral coalition in an attempt to defeat the FA. Key differences include the fact that in 2009 Lacalle of the Blanco Party was at the head of the ticket and the FA was the incumbent party. In the end, the history of 1999 did not repeat. Pepe Mújica and Danilo Astori won 52.4 percent, defeating the Blanco-Colorado second-round alliance by close to 9 percent and firmly establishing the FA as Uruguay's new dominant political party.[41] The Mújica government is likely to be a continuation of the highly successful Vázquez administration. The one area where changes are likely, ironically, is in the relation between government and opposition. Mújica has indeed announced the return to the interparty coparticipation tradition of yesteryear, abandoned since the 1990s.

PARAGUAY

A Society in Conflict: 1870–1940

The War of the Triple Alliance (1864–1870) left Paraguay in ruins, the economy in bankruptcy, the physical infrastructure destroyed, the population decimated, the national territory reduced by some 60,000 square miles. In 1870 a liberal constitution was approved, but it was a dead letter. The two traditional parties, the Conservative, or Colorado (Red), and the Liberal, or Azul (Blue), were founded in 1887, but the former remained in power until 1904, not precisely through democratic means. Widespread corruption among government officials made things even worse. The enactment in 1883 and 1885 of the Laws of Sale of Public Land and Yerbales (maté plantations) brought about not only the beginnings of the great *latifundio* but also the eviction of poor peasants who had occupied those lands for generations. One Spanish Argentine capitalist alone bought 14 million acres (5.7 million hectares) of land in the Chaco. In general, most of the 74.1 million acres (30 million hectares) of public lands were absorbed by private claimants.[42]

At the end of the nineteenth century, the situation could not have been worse. A few *estancieros* (ranchers) owned most of the land. A few foreign enterprises had a quasi-monopoly of tannin and yerba maté, two of the main export products. Poverty and backwardness were widespread. Political and civil rights were routinely violated, and the political elite was unresponsive. With public indignation aroused by this situation, the Liberal Party organized a successful revolt that won widespread popular support. The 1904 revolution, however, promised much but accomplished little. The main sources of wealth, including the newly developed *frigoríficos* (meatpacking and processing plants), continued to be in foreign hands.[43]

By the 1920s, tension with Bolivia regarding the territory of the Chaco esca-lated to a point of no return, and war broke out in 1932. The Paraguayan victory heightened social and economic mobilization, generating demands that existing institutions could not meet. On February 17, 1936, President Eusebio Ayala was overthrown and replaced by Colonel Rafael Franco, a Chaco War hero. Although the *febrerista* (after the month of the revolution) movement was quite heteroge-neous, its ranks filled by Nazis and fascists, social democrats, and Marxists alike, it set in motion some of the major social and economic reforms in Paraguayan history.

In August 1937, a military uprising toppled the *febreristas*. The provisional gov-ernment held elections in 1939, and the candidate of the Liberal Party, another Chaco War hero, General José F. Estigarribia, ran unopposed. In 1940 Estigarribia assumed dictatorial powers and replaced the 1870 constitution, but he died shortly thereafter in an airplane crash.

THE RISE OF MILITARISM

The army, which between 1936 and 1939 had been playing the role of arbiter, slowly moved toward assuming permanent and direct control. When Estigarribia died in 1940, his successor, General Higínio Morínigo, was selected by the mili-tary with little—if any—civilian influence. He assumed dictatorial powers and be-came the first strictly military dictator in Paraguayan history.

Morínigo found his military support in a fascist lodge known as the Frente de Guerra (War Front) and, among civilians, in a group known as the *tiempistas* (af-ter their newspaper *El Tiempo*), which had an ambiguous, conservative Christian-corporatist ideology. Fortunately for him, World War II helped keep exports at high levels and increased foreign exchange reserves. Although Morínigo never con-cealed his sympathies for the Axis powers, he astutely managed to sell his hemi-spheric loyalty to the United States, thus securing a US offer of some $11 million in lend-lease military aid as well as $3 million in economic aid.[44]

Morínigo's economic policies were characterized by increasing state intervention—a trend that started in the early 1930s and led to the creation of public corpora-tions. Among them were COPAL (now APAL) in the field of alcohol production and sale, COPACAR in meat commercialization, and FLOMERES, the state mer-chant fleet. The cost of living increased dramatically from an index of 110 in 1940 (base: 1938 = 100) to 432 in 1948, an average annual increase of 41.5 percent.[45]

Morínigo's regime was far more repressive than his predecessors'. His corporatist and authoritarian views were well expressed in the motto of his revolution: Disci-pline, Hierarchy, Order. In 1942 he dissolved the Liberal Party. With a Colorado-military coalition, Morínigo returned to harshly repressive policies, which prompted the rebellion of the Concepción military garrison in March 1947 and, with it, the outbreak of a bloody five-month civil war. With the majority of the army and the officer corps opposing the dictator, the Colorados turned to the United States for help. They needed assistance, they claimed, "to protect hemi-spheric security from the bloody designs of Stalinist imperialism." But the US State Department, after sending a CIA man to check on the claim, concluded that the rebellion was "far from being communist-dominated," and the request of the Colorados was turned down.[46] The Argentine president, Juan D. Perón, though, viewed a similar petition sympathetically and secretly provided the weaponry that permitted the Paraguayan government to defeat the rebels on the outskirts of Asunción. Morínigo's victory, however, was a Pyrrhic one, for the Colorados grew stronger and, fearing that Morínigo would not turn over power to their presidential candidate, Natalicio González, overthrew him in February 1948.

THE ERA OF STROESSNER

The period that followed the 1947 government victory was marked by the increasing "Coloradization" of the country. Civil service positions and access to and promotion within the army were contingent on having a proven Colorado background. Meanwhile, the Korean War helped keep exports at high levels from 1949 to 1953. Monetary reserves, which had dropped from $11 million in 1946 to $3.1 million in 1949, jumped to $17.7 million at the end of 1953. In spite of that, the internal economic situation deteriorated rapidly. Inflation grew at an annual average rate of 67 percent between 1947 and 1953 and reached a record high of 157 percent in 1952. The value of the local currency, the guaraní, fell by more than 700 percent between 1946 and 1954.[47]

The worsening internal economic situation, coupled with the intense conspiratorial activities of almost every *presidenciable* politician, submerged the country into one of the most unstable periods of its history. There was a brief but full-scale return to praetorianism as the Colorados engaged in bitter factional struggles, each faction seeking the support of key army officers to advance its particular goals. As a result, the public mood—which in 1936 had favored change—in 1954 called for peace and order.

On May 4, 1954, taking advantage of the situation, forty-two-year-old General Alfredo Stroessner staged a coup that overthrew the Colorado president, Federico Chávez. Three months later, replacing a provisional president, Stroessner assumed power as the victorious candidate in a one-man presidential election. Although he was considered a transitional figure, Stroessner skillfully played military and civilian sectors against each other, and in 1959, after almost a year of increasing labor and student unrest, he consolidated his position by closing the Colorado parliament and expelling half of its members from the country. By the beginning of the 1960s, he had become the unquestionable leader; few *políticos* (politicians) or military men dared to challenge him.

THE SOCIOECONOMIC STRUCTURE

Between 1954 and the early 1970s, the Paraguayan economy was characterized by very low rates of growth within the framework of a traditional social structure with widespread precapitalist forms of production in the countryside. Vast sectors of the peasantry were virtually excluded from the monetary economy and were devoted to subsistence crops on land they did not own. By the end of the 1950s, for example, 1,549 landowners controlled some 85 percent of the land, and only 0.9 percent of the territory was dedicated to agriculture.[48] In addition, Paraguay did not undertake import substitution, unlike most other Latin American countries, and consequently the industrial sector was quite underdeveloped. By 1963, for example, out of a population of some 1.9 million, only 35,000 were employed by industry, and nearly half of them, 17,482, worked in plants employing fewer than ten workers; there were only thirty-one industrial firms that employed more than 100 persons each.[49] Foreign investment, mostly British and Argentine, was concentrated in a few relatively dynamic sectors, particularly the meatpacking and processing industry, lumber, banking, and, more recently, cottonseed oil production.

The economic situation in general was one of quasi-stagnation. The GDP increased between 1954 and 1969 at an annual rate of 3.7 percent, while the GDP per capita increased at an annual rate of only 1.3 percent.[50] The government, nevertheless, achieved two goals—controlling inflation and developing infrastructure—the former through a tight monetary policy, the latter through foreign loans and grants. The government also achieved some equilibrium in the balance of payments thanks to standby agreements signed with the IMF and to US economic aid, especially the US PL-480 program that allowed Paraguay to import wheat with credit granted on favorable terms.

Economic stagnation was accompanied by highly unequal income distribution. Although there are no reliable studies for that period, economist Henry D. Ceuppens estimated that 5 percent of the population had an income share of 50 percent of GNP; 15 percent, an income share of 20 percent; 80 percent of the population shared the remaining 30 percent of GNP.[51]

The 1970s witnessed the most rapid modernization in recent Paraguayan history. Two basic factors account for the dynamics and characteristics of this process. First is the Itaipú hydroelectric dam, a project jointly undertaken by Paraguay and Brazil at a cost of $15 billion—almost five times the GNP of Paraguay in 1980. In full operation, the dam is the greatest in the world, producing 12.6 million kilowatts per hour.

The second factor was an agricultural boom associated with a shift to commercial export agriculture, particularly soybeans. The construction of the Itaipú dam and the agribusiness boom brought about a massive influx of foreign capital. As a result, foreign exchange reserves increased dramatically from $18 million in 1970 (the same level as 1953) to $781 million at the end of 1981. The process was also marked by a decline in the importance of Anglo-Argentine investments in relation to Brazilian, US, European, and Japanese investments. Meanwhile, a powerful commercial agricultural sector dominated by multinational companies emerged, which dramatically transformed the countryside.

The rate of GNP growth increased from an average of 6.4 percent for the 1970–1975 period to an average of 10.2 percent for the 1976–1978 period. In 1979, the rate was 10.7 percent and in 1980, it reached a record high of 11.4 percent. In 1981 it dropped to a more modest 8.5 percent, and 1982 and 1983 witnessed a deep recession and negative growth rates.[52] The commercial deficit increased dangerously and reached a record high of $545 million. Moreover, the factor allowing substantial balance of payments surpluses in spite of increasing commercial deficits over the previous five years—the influx of foreign capital, mostly related to the Itaipú project—started to decline in 1981. The foreign debt, on the other hand, increased from $98 million (16.7 percent of the GNP) in 1970 to $2.2 billion (52 percent of the GNP) in 1988.[53]

The modernization process has had other negative consequences too. Inflation reached a high of 28.1 percent in 1979. It decreased to 22.4 percent in 1980 and to 13 percent in 1981, but the real rate may have been much higher than these official figures. The government reacted with tough monetary restrictions, so tight that the country was thrown into a severe recession. The real minimum wage fell by some 17 percent between 1964 and 1980. The GNP per capita in 1980 was $1,131, but 62 percent of the urban population had an income of between $150 and $440.[54] In Asunción, the capital city, 13 percent of the population, or 68,000 people, live in eighty-nine *villas miserias* (shantytowns) scattered around the city.[55]

The most important consequence of the rapid process of economic modernization, however, is the parallel process of social mobilization that is, in turn, greatly increasing social and economic demands on the political system.

The completion of the Itaipú project and the loss of the capital influx associated with it placed a considerable strain on the government. The approximately 12,000 Paraguayan workers employed by the project were gradually laid off in the early 1990s, and with continual delays in the start-up of the Paraguayan-Argentinean Yacyreta hydroelectric project, there was no new project big enough to absorb them.

The Political Process

By the early 1960s, Stroessner consolidated a power structure based on three pillars: Stroessner himself, the army, and the Colorado Party. He demonstrated his ability to remain in power against all odds by harshly repressing his opponents and coopting the rest, particularly army officers and members of the Colorado Party. Corruption and contraband for the benefit of a small clique became widespread and were part of the arsenal of payoffs at the regime's disposal. Officially, it was considered *el precio de la paz* (the price of peace).

The dominant economic classes readily and happily "exchanged the right to rule for the right to make money," to borrow Barrington Moore's phrase. In actuality, they had never governed, and therefore the transaction was acceptable. The pressure groups, chronically weak, were satisfied with the "peace" that few other rulers had been able to deliver over such an extended period of time. Important sectors of the population, discouraged by the high level of political repression, also accepted the situation as an unchallengeable fait accompli.

Between 1954 and 1962, the regime relied heavily on massive repression and coercion. That approach gradually gave way to an authoritarian model that emphasized limited cooptation without renouncing repression as an occasional necessity. Cooptation in Paraguay, however, did not involve access to public offices. Because of the rigid power structure, it implied the absence of politically motivated harassment or repression of individuals as long as they stayed away from the political arena. However, the regime continued to unleash periodic waves of repression to remind the real and potential opposition, as well as its own followers, that attempts to change the status quo would involve a very heavy price. The elements of psychological terror and latent threat proved very effective.

The turning point in the transition from a naked dictatorship to an authoritarian regime was the legal recognition, in 1962, of a splinter Liberal group. In exchange, the group participated in the 1963 presidential "elections," thus providing a token opposition. Soon afterward, the participationist groups within the opposition prevailed over those proposing an insurrectionary strategy. In 1964 the Febrerista Party was legally recognized, and most of the exiled Liberal leaders were allowed to return. The municipal elections of 1965 witnessed the participation of the Lista Abierta (Open List) registered by the Febreristas but headed by a distinguished independent physician and supported by mainstream Liberals. The elections, as usual, were plagued by widespread official fraud, but they demonstrated that the majority of the Liberals did not support the Liberal minority splinter group recognized in 1962. That helped the leaders of the majority to win legal recognition as the Liberal Radical Party, the word "radical" being added to distinguish the group from the one legalized in 1962. In 1962 and again in 1967, as well as in the 1964 recognition of the Febrerista Party, US pressure for liberalization played a significant role.

In 1967, with the participation of four opposition parties, a national convention was held to amend the 1940 constitution. In reality, the only important issue was the addition of an article allowing Stroessner to run for reelection two more times. He did so in 1968 and 1973, winning easily in elections characterized by widespread fraud.

Participation, however, proved to be a one-way street, with all benefits accruing to the government. Legal opposition parties, though not openly repressed, had their activities restricted to such an extent that they gained very little political ground. An office-seeking elite within the parties remained satisfied to have access to some thirty seats in the senate and chamber of deputies, with the corresponding salaries and benefits. Soon, however, it became clear that there were too many politicians and too few sinecures. Politicians began to fight fiercely for the spoils that the regime put at their disposal. Such party infighting further debilitated the legal opposition, already perceived by the public as a highly ineffectual ornamental device.

Within this context—the debilitation of the legal opposition—student and peasant movements rose to prominence in the late 1960s and early and middle 1970s. Both groups had become disenchanted with the legal opposition, not only because of its chronic inefficacy but also because it failed to provide a real ideological alternative to the right-wing regime. In a few years, they succeeded in organizing some of the largest mass movements in recent Paraguayan history. As a result, peasants and students were harshly repressed. The ferocious persecutions unleashed between 1975 and 1980 badly crippled the mass movements.

Other sources of opposition to the regime were the Catholic Church and allied groups. Since the late 1960s, the Catholic hierarchy had steadfastly opposed and denounced regime abuses as a matter of public posture. The Church, however, did not perceive itself as being an opposition force and therefore did not have a clear political strategy.

Hence the 1970s were characterized by the increasing strength of the government vis-à-vis the opposition. The general improvement in economic conditions and the Itaipú-related boom of the late 1970s further reduced the ability of the opposition to draw support from wide sectors of the population. In 1977 the government further divided the legal opposition by isolating the sectors that refused to go along with a 1977 constitutional amendment devised to allow Stroessner to run for reelection indefinitely. Splinter groups of the Liberal Party took advantage of the government search for potential opposition parties. At one time, there were five Liberal parties, four of them bidding for recognition from the government to participate in the 1978 elections. Two of them were finally selected, thus assuring for themselves the highly contested parliamentary seats and for the government the continuation of the democratic façade.

Strengthened by its political and economic success, the regime continued to harass the nonparticipationist opposition. In the late 1970s, these sectors succeeded in articulating a joint opposition front, the Acuerdo Nacional (National Accord), uniting the Liberal Radical Authentic Party, the Febrerista Party, the Christian Democratic Party, and the Popular Colorado Movement (MOPOCO), a Colorado group expelled from the country by Stroessner in 1959. The Acuerdo was born under and encouraged by international and US pressure against the Stroessner regime for its violation of human rights. It grew stronger as pressure increased during the Carter administration years. But as international pressure decreased, particularly after the election of Ronald Reagan in November 1980, the importance of the Acuerdo gradually diminished. Its activities, in any case, had been confined to public condemnation of the regime, but it attained high visibility and had significant public impact.

For the government, nevertheless, there were problems. International criticism of its human rights violations was translated into actual sanctions when the US government almost terminated its military assistance program and greatly reduced its economic aid. Moreover, the country was unable to obtain loans from international institutions on the preferential terms it was accustomed to because of the US refusal to vote favorably on those credits. Internally, the government faced some of its most severe domestic problems since the late 1950s. Within the Colorado Party, there were numerous confrontations among sectors competing for control of the party organization, particularly local branches or sections (*seccionales*) and student organizations. Furthermore, discontent among the youth whose potential role was being postponed while the ruling old guard refused to leave them room for upward mobility increased significantly. Moreover, the growing politicization of student and labor sectors resulted in mounting pressure for liberalization. The transition to democracy in neighboring Argentina and Brazil further undermined the Stroessner regime.[56]

The final blow to the thirty-five-year-old Stroessner dictatorship came as a result of a major split in the ruling Colorado Party. In August 1987, an aging Stroessner moved virtually to expel from the party a sizable part of its leadership. That group became known as the traditionalists and was believed to be considering ending the automatic endorsement of the Stroessner candidacy for president. The attack on the traditionalists was led by a group of extreme right-wing zealots and diehard Stroessner loyalists known as militants.

After seizing control of the party, the militants moved to secure their position in the state apparatus and the military. When Stroessner underwent major surgery in late August 1988 and his health became increasingly worrisome, the militants sped up their moves and sought to position Stroessner's eldest son, a recently promoted air force colonel, next in the line of military succession. To do so, a large number of generals and colonels had to be retired or reassigned, a move that began in early

January 1989. But on February 2, when Stroessner sought to retire General Andrés Rodríguez, his major military rival and First Army Corps commander, Rodríguez struck back and with widespread support from all units overthrew Stroessner on the morning of February 3, 1989, after ten hours of bloody battles.

General Rodríguez became provisional president and called for elections within ninety days as the first step in a transition to democracy. He ran as the candidate of the Colorado Party. Adopting a strong pro-democracy message, Rodríguez won the elections of May 1 by a landslide; he captured slightly more than 70 percent of the votes, against 20 percent for his closest competitor, PLRA leader Domingo Laíno. Opposition parties complained that they could not organize for elections in such a short period of time after three decades of repression. While the preelectoral campaign allowed parties full political freedom, and although General Rodríguez became a very popular candidate who would have won anyway, the elections were marred by irregularities and systematic, widespread, although not massive, fraud.[57]

Upon assuming the presidency, General Rodríguez moved decisively in the direction of greater liberalization and the incorporation of opposition or independent leaders into positions of leadership, including the Supreme Court and some ambassadorships. Nevertheless, much remained to be done before a true democratic system could emerge.

THE TRANSITION

In 1989 few believed that Paraguay could experience a transition to a democratic system along the lines followed by other countries in the region. Guided by deterministic and historic dogmas, many could understand the present only as the endless repetition of the past. Yet neither the historic legacy of Paraguay nor the specific nature of the Stroessner regime constituted insurmountable obstacles to a transition to democracy. The coup of February 3, 1989, began a process of transition from above and within that gradually assumed a dynamic of its own and is now approaching a successful conclusion.

In the early stages of the process, General Rodríguez sought the support of the international community by committing himself to democratize the country but without jeopardizing the old basis of political power of the Colorado Party: its privileged and incestuous relation with the armed forces, its unlimited and exclusive access to state patronage, and its thorough manipulation and control of the electoral process. Democratization thus in reality meant liberalization. To legitimize this, elections were called for May 1, when Rodríguez was elected president and a Colorado-controlled congress was installed.

The process of liberalization, though, strengthened the opposition and allowed it to gain bargaining power. Simultaneously, it fostered the fragmentation of the Colorado Party, as different factions vied for control of the party. Consequently political power became more dispersed and major political decisions began to require the give-and-take that characterizes coalition building. As power became less centralized and concentrated, the chances for furthering the process of liberalization and acceleration—democratization—improved.

It was in this context that a convention to write a new constitution to replace Stroessner's 1967 chart met in 1992. The new document neatly reflected the political reality. A presidential system with a very strong congress was adopted as its framework. Important principles such as decentralization and many programmatic statements about agrarian reform, social justice, and workers rights were also incorporated. But the most far-reaching clauses were those concerning the transfer of power.

To begin with, the constitution banned all forms of reelection and included, in its transitory part, an article tailor-made to impede a possible Rodríguez bid for reelection. This caused considerable tension, and generals loyal to him subtly threatened a coup. Rodríguez refused to swear allegiance to the new constitution, but the ceremony was held nonetheless before congress and the document entered into effect on June 20, 1992.

Within a year, on May 9, 1993, the first relatively competitive elections were held. Three candidates—Juan Carlos Wasmosy for the Colorado Party, Domingo Laíno for the Authentic Radical Liberal Party, and Guillermo Caballero Vargas for the newly formed Encuentro Nacional—competed, and Wasmosy won with some 39 percent of the vote.

The elections brought into sharp relief both what had been achieved in terms of democratization and what remained to be done. On the one hand, the hotly contested primary elections within the Colorado Party threw a shadow of doubt over the legitimacy of Wasmosy's candidacy, as most observers believed his opponent, Luis María Argaña, won the election only to be deprived of it by manipulation of the vote-counting process. On the other hand, the failure of both opposition candidates to join forces reflected the inability of political actors to develop effective mechanisms of coalition building. But perhaps more importantly, extensive political manipulation occurred throughout the electoral process. The Colorado-run Electoral Board controlled the process and excluded the opposition from meaningful oversight of registration rolls, distribution of polling places, and appointment of electoral officers, not to speak of the thorough utilization of the state apparatus and resources to support the campaign of the official candidate. Furthermore, a sector of the military establishment, led by Major General Lino Oviedo, openly intervened in support of Wasmosy's candidacy.

Considering all these problems part and parcel of the transition process, and taking into account that the opposition parties, combined, nevertheless won a majority in congress, both the Authentic Radical Liberal Party and the Encuentro Nacional formally recognized the results as valid and lent legitimacy to the Wasmosy government.

Wasmosy's term was characterized by his inability to obtain the support of his own party for his program. The opposition parties mustered much of the backing needed to weather the difficulties in the belief that it was fundamental for the success of the transition process that Wasmosy complete his term without interruption. In exchange, the opposition won some important concessions, including the reorganization of the judiciary and the appointment of a more balanced nine-member Supreme Court. Of equally fundamental importance was the establishment of a three-member Supreme Electoral Tribunal, which promises a true reform of the electoral process.

A major military crisis erupted in April 1996 when Wasmosy dismissed the commander of the army, General Lino Oviedo, and he refused to step down.

Oviedo had become a sort of power behind the throne, and there was a general perception that Wasmosy could not adopt major decisions without his agreement. Thanks to the prompt reaction of the congress, youth, political parties, the international community, and the institutionalist sector of the armed forces, Wasmosy stood firm, and within twenty-four hours Oviedo resigned. He was subsequently tried and sentenced to ten years in prison. This outcome represented the removal of the last obstacle to the complete subordination of the military to the constitution and civilian control.

Wasmosy's mishandling of the aftermath of the 1996 military crisis, however, permitted Oviedo to run for president in the Colorado primary elections previous to the general elections of 1998. In a three-way race the former general won by a razor-thin margin, but the Supreme Court finally ruled him ineligible and ratified a ten-year prison term. His vice presidential candidate, Raúl Cubas, led the Colorado ticket with Argaña, who came in second, as vice presidential candidate.

The opposition united behind Liberal Party (PLRA) leader Domingo Laíno as presidential candidate accompanied by Carlos Filizzola, of the Encuentro Nacional, as the vice presidential nominee. The result was a disaster for the opposition, as the Colorado ticket won 54 percent of the votes against some 42 percent for the opposition.

Soon, however, the political crisis reemerged in full force as Cubas bent legal and constitutional rules to facilitate Oviedo's assumption of power. The crisis led to the impeachment of Cubas. As the process unfolded, Vice President Argaña was assassinated. Massive demonstrations against Cubas were violently suppressed, and at least eight students were killed in the plaza of the congress. Cubas resigned and fled to Brazil, while Oviedo escaped to Argentina.

Following constitutional procedures, the president of the congress, Luis González Macchi, assumed the presidency to complete the term. He invited opposition parties to join a government of national unity, but his lack of leadership and the constant infighting within his coalition left a government that was weak and marred by corruption and inefficiency.

The elections of 2003 presented yet a new scenario. The Colorado Party ran with the candidacy of Nicanor Duarte Frutos, a former minister of education. The Liberal Party put up Julio C. Franco, who had been elected vice president after González Macchi assumed the presidency. A new political party, Patria Querida, emerged around the candidacy of businessman Pedro Fadul and displaced the Encuentro Nacional, whose participation in the government of González Macchi made it lose credibility. The Oviedistas ran with the caudillo's own party, UNACE. Duarte Frutos won with 37 percent, followed by Franco with 23 percent and Fadul with 21 percent. UNACE won 13 percent of the votes and the Encuentro Nacional was relegated to a distant fourth with around 2 percent of the votes.

The government of Duarte Frutos began its tenure auspiciously. It reversed a severe economic crisis thanks to the appointment of a respected independent economist as finance minister. The economy sailed along relatively well, as Paraguay, like other Latin American countries, benefited from the commodity boom. Yet Duarte Frutos's political ambition and his attempts to modify the constitution to allow him to run for reelection led his government astray. His administration was tainted by widespread corruption and marred by his use of the state apparatus to punish opponents and Colorado Party dissidents alike. He seemed intent on re-constituting a regime along the lines of the Stroessner dictatorship, with himself at the helm. Yet he ended up furthering the division of the Colorado Party and even-tually its downfall.

The presidential election in April 2008 ended sixty-one years of hegemonic Col-orado Party rule. Fernando Lugo, a former Roman Catholic bishop, was elected president with 41 percent of the vote and the support of the Liberal Party, a num-ber of center-leftist parties, and a recently formed leftist party.

In spite of the momentous changes it produced, the electoral outcome did more to *rearrange* the electoral map than to *transform* it. Indeed, in 2008 the combined op-position gathered 43.3 percent of the votes, while the Colorado Party and UNACE together added 52.5 percent, almost the same distribution as the 2003 election. What changed in 2008 was, first, the distribution of votes among the Colorados and UNACE—the Colorados lost seven percentage points and UNACE picked up eight—and, second, the uniting of the opposition behind Lugo.

In his first year in office, Lugo scored some important successes in fighting cor-ruption, especially in the police, renegotiating the Itaipú treaty with Brazil (thus ensuring Paraguay a bigger slice of the pie), promoting economic reforms and an ambitious public works program, and, after much vacillation, beginning an ambi-tious antipoverty program. On the other hand, Lugo made no serious attempt at securing a solid support in congress, not even from the PLRA that makes up more than 80 percent of the theoretically pro-government legislators, and stumbled po-litically several times. As a result he has faced recurrent political difficulties.

Lugo, a political outsider, has inherited the heavy burden of more than a half century of one-party rule. Furthermore, opposition from vested political and eco-nomic interests has been entrenched and strong. Unfortunately, these difficulties were compounded by frequent political blunders. Paraguayans are yearning for real change. It remains to be seen whether Lugo rises to the challenge and delivers what they seek.

Notes

1. For an elaboration on the theme of coparticipation as a framework to study Uruguayan politics, see Martin Weinstein, *Uruguay: The Politics of Failure* (Westport, Conn.: Greenwood, 1975). This section generally follows Weinstein's approach.

2. Juan E. Pivel Devoto, "Uruguay independiente," in Antonio Ballesteros, ed., *Historia de América y de los pueblos Americanos* (Barcelona: Salvat Editores, 1949), 21: 628–632; and Martin H.J. Fynch, *A Political Economy of Uruguay Since 1970* (New York: St. Martin's, 1981), pp. 11–13.

3. Weinstein, *Uruguay,* p. 69.

4. Luis Macadar, Nicolas Reig, and José E. Santías, "Una economía Latinoamericana," in Luis Benvenuto et al., *Uruguay hoy* (Buenos Aires: Siglo 21, 1971), pp. 50–52.

5. Víctor Pastorino, *Itinerario del colegiado* (Montevideo: Agencia Periodística Inter-americana, 1956).

6. Wálter Luisiardo, *Reflexiones sobre aspectos de la historia económica del Uruguay: Período 1900–1979* (Montevideo: Comisión Coordinadora para el Desarrollo Económico, 1979), pp. 12–24.

7. Fynch, *Political Economy of Uruguay*, p. 171.

8. Luisiardo, *Reflexiones*, pp. 44–48, 69.

9. Fynch, *Political Economy of Uruguay*, pp. 220–223; Luisiardo, *Reflexiones*, p. 68.

10. James W. Wilkie and Peter Reich, *Statistical Abstract of Latin America* (Los Angeles: University of California Press, 1979), p. 332.

11. Weinstein, *Uruguay*, p. 119.

12. Luisiardo, *Reflexiones*, p. 95.

13. For an excellent analysis of this complex process, see Charles G. Gillespie, "Uruguay: Transition from Collegial-Technocratic Rule," in *Transitions from Authoritarian Rule*, ed. Guillermo O'Donnell, Philippe Schmitter, and Laurence Whitehead (Baltimore: Johns Hopkins University Press, 1986), 2:173–195.

14. For the sake of brevity, I refer to the coalition of left and center-left parties as the Frente Amplio, although in the 2005 elections it was officially known as the Encuentro Progresista–Frente Amplio–Nueva Mayoria (EP–FA–NM).

15. Fynch, *Political Economy of Uruguay*, pp. 183–184, 264.

16. Wilkie and Reich, *Statistical Abstract*, pp. 144, 518.

17. Macadar, Reig, and Santías, "Una economía Latinoamericana," p. 102. The estimation goes as follows: 213,000 public employees + 346,000 pensioners = 559,000, which is 19.96 percent of a population of around 2.8 million.

18. Economic Commission for Latin America and the Caribbean, "Cuadro 1: Evolución de algunos indicadores económicos, 1990–2007," *Panorama Social de America Latina: Anexo 2008*, www.eclac.org/estadisticas/publicaciones (October 14, 2009).

19. Ibid.

20. Economic Commission for Latin America and the Caribbean, Table 2.2.4.6, "Latin America and the Caribbean: Total External Debt as Percentage of GDP," *Statistical Yearbook 2008*, http://websie.eclac.cl/anuario_estadistico/anuario_2008/eng/index.asp (November 8, 2009).

21. Elaboración del Área Política y de Relaciones Internacionales del Banco de Datos de la FCS en base a datos de la Corte Electoral.

22. David Altman, Rossana Castiglioni, and Juan Pablo Luna, "Uruguay: A Role Model for the Left?" in Jorge G. Castañeda and Marco A. Morales, eds., *Leftovers: Tales of the Latin American Left* (London: Routledge, 2008), p. 157.

23. Gerardo Caetano, "Del triunfo electoral a los desafíos del gobierno del Frente Amplio (2004–2006)," p. 1. Text in the possession of the author.

24. Ibid. Mario Toer, *De Moctezuma a Chávez: Repensando la historia de América Latina* (Buenos Aires: Ediciones Cooperativas, 2007), p. 206.

25. Altman et al., "Uruguay," p. 157.

26. Elaboración del Área Política y de Relaciones Internacionales del Banco de Datos de la FCS en base a datos de la Corte Electoral.

27. Facultad de Ciencias Sociales, Universidad de la República–Uruguay, Area Política y Relaciones Internacionales, Banco de Datos, "Evaluación de gestión," www.fcs.edu.uy/pri/opinion.html (November 13, 2009). The tables are based on periodic public opinion surveys conducted by Equipos-Mori. Net approval rating calculations by the author.

28. Economic Commission for Latin America and the Caribbean, "Cuadro 4: Magnitud de la pobreza y la indigencia, 1990–2007," *Panorama Social de América Latina: Anexo 2008*.

29. Corte Electoral, Uruguay, www.corteelectoral.gub.uy/nacionales20041031.

30. Daniel Buquet and Daniel Chasquetti, "Elecciones Uruguay 2004: Descifrando el cambio," *Revista de Ciencia Política* 25, no. 2 (2005): 143.

31. Daniel Chasquetti, "Uruguay 2006: Éxitos y dilemas del gobierno de izquierda," *Revista de Ciencia Política* 27 (2007): 249–263.

32. Buquet and Chasquetti, "Elecciones Uruguay 2004."

33. Facultad de Ciencias Sociales, Universidad de la Republica–Uruguay, 2009.

34. Casquetti, "Uruguay 2006," p. 250; BBC News. "Time-Line Uruguay," http://news.bbc.co.uk/2/hi/americas/country_profiles/1229362.stm (November 14, 2009).

35. Casquetti, "Uruguay 2006," p. 250.

36. Altman et al., "Uruguay," p. 164.

37. Liliana DeRiz, "Uruguay: La política del compromiso," in *Cultural Political y Alternancia en América Latina* (Editorial Pablo Iglesias, 2008), p. 226. Also see discussion in Altman et al., "Uruguay," pp. 164–165.

38. Chasquetti, "Uruguay 2006."

39. Corte Electoral, "Elecciones internas para los partidos políticos, 2009," www.corte electoral.gub.uy (November 15, 2009).

40. Corte Electoral, "Elecciones nacionales Uruguay 2009," www.elecciones uruguay2009.com.

41. "Corte electoral uruguaya proclama triunfador al Frente Amplio," *La Prensa Latina: Agencia Informativa Latinoamericana,* www.prensa-latina.cu/index.php?option =com_content&task=view&id=143390&Itemid=1 (December 4, 2009).

42. Domingo Laíno, *Paraguay: De la independencia a la dependencia* (Asunción: Ediciones Cerro Corá, 1976), p. 171; Harris G. Warren, *Paraguay and the Triple Alliance: The Post-War Decade, 1869–1878* (Austin: Institute of Latin American Studies, University of Texas Press, 1978), p. 286.

43. US Department of Commerce, *Commerce Yearbook* (Washington, D.C.: Government Printing Office, 1928–1932); *Foreign Commerce Yearbook* (Washington, D.C.: Government Printing Office, 1932–1950).

44. Michael Grow, *The Good Neighbor Policy and Authoritarianism in Paraguay* (Lawrence: Regents Press of Kansas, 1981), p. 115.

45. US Department of Commerce, *Investment in Paraguay: Conditions and Outlook for United States Investors* (Washington, D.C.: Government Printing Office, 1954), pp. 15–17, 84.

46. Grow, *Good Neighbor Policy,* pp. 63, 118, 146–147 n. 27.

47. US Department of Commerce, *Investment in Paraguay,* pp. 84–85.

48. Carlos Pastore, *La lucha por la tierra en el Paraguay* (Montevideo: Editorial Antequera, 1972), p. 422.

49. Censo Industrial 1963; cited in Henry D. Ceuppens, *Paraguay año 2,000* (Asunción: Editorial Gráfica Zamphirópolos, 1971), p. 61.

50. Wilkie and Reich, *Statistical Abstract,* p. 262.

51. Ceuppens, *Paraguay año 2,000,* pp. 37, 124–126.

52. Banco Interamericano de Desarrollo, *Progreso económico social en America Latina: Informe 1980–1981* (Washington, D.C., 1981), pp. 358–360; *ABC Color,* "Suplemento económico," July 25, 1982, pp. 4–5.

53. Ricardo Rodríguez Silvero, "Paraguay: El endeudamiento externo," *Revista Paraguaya de Sociología* 17, no. 50 (January–May 1980): 81; *Ultima Hora,* February 26, 1989, p. 12.

54. Fernando L. Masi, "Paraguay: Analysis of the Socio-Economic Evolution" (manuscript at the American University, 1982), p. 21.

55. Study done by the Comité de Iglesias, cited in *ABC Color,* "Actualidad profesional," March 5, 1982, pp. 2–3.

56. An extended discussion of these issues can be found in Diego Abente, *Stronismo, Post-Stronismo, and the Prospects for Democratization in Paraguay,* Working Paper 119, Kellogg Institute, University of Notre Dame, 1989; and "Constraints and Opportunities: External Factors, Authoritarianism, and the Prospects for Democratization in Paraguay," *Journal of Interamerican Studies and World Affairs* 30, no. 1 (Spring 1988): 73–104.

57. For a discussion of the elections, see Latin American Studies Association International Commission to Observe the Paraguayan Elections, "The May 1, 1989, Elections in Paraguay: Toward a New Era of Democracy?" *LASA Forum* 20, no. 3 (Fall 1989): 39–48.

Suggested Readings

Uruguay

Benvenuto, Luis, et al. *Uruguay Hoy.* Buenos Aires: Siglo 21, 1971. Uruguay as seen by the Uruguayans; interesting perspectives.

Fynch, Martin H.J. *A Political Economy of Uruguay Since 1970.* New York: St. Martin's, 1981. An excellent analysis of the Uruguayan economic process until the late 1970s; a must-read.

Handelman, Howard. *Military Authoritarianism and Political Change in Uruguay.* AUFS Report. Hanover, N.H.: American Universities Field Staff, 1978. A good short analysis of contemporary trends and events.

————. *Economic Policy and Elite Pressures in Uruguay.* AUFS Report. Hanover, N.H.: American Universities Field Staff, 1979. A good short study on recent changes in the decision-making process.

Kaufman, Edy. *Uruguay in Transition.* New Brunswick, N.J.: Transaction, 1979. An interesting, up-to-date work on Uruguayan politics.

Pivel Devoto, Juan E. "Uruguay independiente." In Antonio Ballesteros, ed., *Historia de América y de los Pueblos Americanos,* 21: 405–638. Barcelona: Salvat Editores, 1949. A good short introduction to the history of Uruguay.

Quijana, José M., and Guillermo Waksman. "Las Relaciones Uruguay–Estados Unidos en 1977–1979." *Cuadernos semestrales* 6 (1979): 310–343. A good study on recent trends in US-Uruguayan relations with a useful statistical appendix.

Verdisco, Aimee E. "Between Accountability and 'Reivindicación': Development and Intranational Differentiation in Uruguay." Ph.D. diss., State University of New York, 1996.

Weinstein, Martin. *Uruguay: The Politics of Failure.* Westport, Conn.: Greenwood, 1975. A comprehensive analysis of Uruguayan politics; especially good for the years between 1900 and 1960.

Paraguay

Abente, Diego. *Stronismo, Post-Stronismo, and the Prospects for Democratization in Paraguay.* Working Paper 119. Kellogg Institute, University of Notre Dame, 1989.

Bouvier, Virginia M. *Decline of the Dictator: Paraguay at a Crossroads.* Washington, D.C.: WOLA, 1988.

Cardozo, Efraim. *Breve historia del Paraguay.* Buenos Aires: EUDEBA, 1965. A good short introduction to Paraguayan history.

Grow, Michael. *The Good Neighbor Policy and Authoritarianism in Paraguay.* Lawrence: Regents Press of Kansas, 1981. A well documented study of the 1939–1949 period.

Hicks, Frederick. "Interpersonal Relationships and Caudillismo in Paraguay." *Journal of Inter-American Studies and World Affairs* 13 (January 1971): 89–111. An interesting if dated study of Paraguayan politics.

Lewis, Paul H. *The Politics of Exile: Paraguay's Febrerista Party.* Chapel Hill: University of North Carolina Press, 1968. An in-depth study of the Febrerista Party.

———. *Paraguay Under Stroessner.* Chapel Hill: University of North Carolina Press, 1980.

Pastore, Carlos. *La lucha por la tierra en el Paraguay.* Montevideo: Editorial Antequera, 1972. A very good social history of Paraguay with emphasis on the agrarian process.

Warren, Harris G. *Paraguay and the Triple Alliance: The Post-War Decade 1869–1878.* Austin: Institute of Latin American Studies, University of Texas Press, 1978. The best analysis of the first postwar decade.

Chapter 29

CONCLUSION

A New Kind of Togetherness

JAN KNIPPERS BLACK

LATIN AMERICA HAS never been far removed from the moods and manias of its ambitious northern neighbor. Like a long-suffering and not necessarily willing spouse, Latin America has been courted occasionally with false promises, but more often taken for granted when the United States was feeling confident and battered when the United States was suffering from insecurity or delusions of invincibility. It is not entirely clear, as we enter the second decade of the twenty-first century, whether the United States is feeling confident or insecure. For the time being, however, it appears to have overcome its delusions of invincibility. If there is anything that Americans north and south of the Rio Grande share at this juncture, it is hope for change. And if, as seems to be the case at street level, it is hope for the same kind of change, then change in the nature of north/south relations might be a good place to start.

A measure of the pace and direction of social change in the Americas, as elsewhere, is how long it takes a word or phrase that carries a positive connotation to come to mean the opposite of what it once did. When the first edition of this book came off the press a quarter century ago, in 1984, the word "reform" still meant change in the direction of greater equity, that is, change favoring the have-nots. Before the end of the 1980s it had come to refer more often to change favoring the haves, particularly foreign creditors and investors. And the demand from below for structural change—legal and institutional change to lock in enhanced equity in income and opportunity—had given way to demand from above for "structural adjustment" to push costs and responsibility downward in the social pyramid and benefits up and out. No far-reaching and powerful, or seemingly sustainable, turnaround is as yet under way in either Anglo or Latin portions of America. But, as we have seen in the preceding chapters, there are many cautious and some bold beginnings and intensifying countercurrents on many sides.

We have indeed seen dramatic change—for good and ill—in the hemisphere over the last quarter century, beginning with a shift in elite attention from muddled Cold War concerns to more straightforward commercial ones, and thus a shift in watchdogs from military and intelligence operatives to international financial institutions. Since 9/11, 2001, however, while the once "hidden hand" of the global money movers hides in plain sight, the new all-purpose rationale of antiterrorism and the widespread popular movements in protest against unmet need and corporate greed are generating now more attention of the cloak-and-dagger kind. As these developments, along with the spread of modern conveniences and inconveniences, are felt from north to south, one wonders how Anglo-Americans could fail to note the convergence of interests and concerns. Still, much of what Anglo-Americans are inclined to see as change in Latin America actually represents change in their perceptions of Latin America, as well as in their perceptions of their own society.

Getting to Know the Neighbors

Latin America is more familiar to us now. That is due only in part to the enormously increased volume of academic studies inspired by the birth of a multidisciplinary field. It is also due to increased travel and investment by US citizens and to expanded US public and private programs of exchange, propaganda, proselytizing, relief, and development. The perspectives of diplomats and others, whose writings provided our images in decades past, derived almost exclusively from contacts with the political and economic elites. But thousands of Peace Corps volunteers and other Americans coming of age since the 1960s have come to know Latin America's peasants and workers and marginalized would-be workers as real people—friends.

Can it be that Latin America's poor, stereotyped in the not-so-distant past as ignorant and passive, have only recently become clever, energetic, and enterprising? Or is it that we are only beginning to learn of the courage required to overcome official intimidation and of the ingenuity required to survive on the edge? Is it possible that Latin America's middle classes, traditionally hedonistic and lackadaisical, have only recently become entrepreneurial? Or can it be that we have only recently realized that the professional who seems never to be in his office actually juggles three offices: his bureaucratic post, his chair at the university, and his private practice?

A student of mine once commented that "Brazilian women don't work; they have maids." No doubt there are still women in the Americas who are pampered and cloistered. But now that we know the maids as well as the mistresses, we know that the issue of whether "to work or not to work" is even phonier for most Latin American women than for their Anglo-American counterparts. In fact, we have now seen that the greater the economic or political threat to survival, the more central will be the role of women in combating that threat. Women have long been the economic and organizational mainstays of the poorest urban shantytowns. More recently, the large-scale involvement of women in danger-fraught human rights networks and in revolutionary movements has been particularly striking. To declare that Latin Americans, for reasons of work roles or sex roles, intellect or temperament, are unequal to the task of their own development on their own terms is to declare our ignorance of them.

While Latin America has been overrun in the past half century with US slogans, products, and advisers, there has also been movement in the other direction. Latin

American scholars have set the tone for studies by US academic specialists in Latin American affairs. Some of the best US novelists have experimented with literary styles pioneered by Latin American novelists. Latin American graphic arts, music, and cinematography have gained in popularity with US audiences. US churches have been influenced by the liberation theology that swept first, like a firestorm, through Latin America's religious communities. Some of Latin America's "best and brightest," driven from their own countries by dictatorial regimes supported by the US government, have settled in the United States and have deepened our own national debates about domestic and foreign policy.

Of course, Anglo-America and Latin America share the shame of past and present mistreatment of native American and Afro-American populations. Furthermore, much of the United States shares with much of Latin America the heritage of Spanish conquest and settlement and 300 years of Spanish colonialism. Indian and Spanish cultures, never quite suppressed in the southwestern United States, are now being revitalized by the annual influx of Mexican and Central American workers, estimated to be in the millions, seeking the employment that eludes them at home. Miami, of course, has become an outpost of Cuba, and the northeastern part of the United States has absorbed great numbers of Caribbean immigrants. As these workers, refugees, and immigrants, documented or otherwise, move from state to state and city to city in search of work, no part of the United States is immune from the process of Latinoization.

There were some 30 million Hispanics in the United States in 1996. That number had increased to some 42 million, or about 14 percent of the population, by 2010, surpassing blacks in numbers to become the largest ethnic minority in the United States. Although some people lament the trend, I lament only its causes. There is no denying that Latin Americans, like past waves of immigrants, are enriching our culture and our national life.

Finally, we are getting to know Latin Americans as a consequence of our government's incessant meddling in their affairs. Despite the wonders of technology and imaginative methods for intimidating whistleblowers, government secrets have become ever harder to keep. The media sooner or later catches up with our boys in camouflage. Their exploits in Central America in the 1980s, along with the images of peasants on the receiving end of bombs and bullets and of leaders pleading, in flawless English, for arms or for reason, were brought into our homes nightly in living color. In the decades since, the plight of Colombian peasants being sprayed, in their fields of corn as well as of coca, with US biochemical toxins has attracted little media attention in the United States, despite the displacement of 2–3 million Colombians. But the ramifications of that long-running "low-intensity conflict" and the expanding US military presence are not lost on Latin American leaders and publics. If that conflict—and US involvement in it—continue to escalate, the story cannot be kept much longer from the attention of the US public, or from impacting the general tone of US-Latin American relations.

A CONVERGENCE OF IMPACTS AND ISSUES

US presidents always begin their speeches before the assembled dignitaries of Western Hemisphere summits with the assertion that America is one—one society and one market. Then follows rhetorical fluff about individualism, democracy, godliness, private enterprise, and the security threat. But there is a growing unacknowledged reality to the oneness of America. Latin America is increasingly sharing not only the blessings of US-style modernization but its demons as well. And many of the problems that have long plagued Latin America are more and more apparent and bedeviling in the United States itself. The clearest trend in the Americas is a trend toward convergence—if not of interests, at least of problems.

Latin America, now the world's most urbanized region, boasts or frets of several of the world's largest cities. To Latin America, as to the United States, urbanization has brought both advantages and disadvantages. It has led to new, more effective forms of political organization and has facilitated the extension of services—electricity, running water, health care, public schools—to a greater proportion of the population. It has extended the reach of the communications media, enhancing their ability to disseminate information, misinformation, and disinformation. In Latin America, as in the United States, urbanization has weakened the constraints, but also the socialization and the security, that flowed from extended family systems. To Latin America, more recently than to the United States, it has also meant traffic congestion, pollution, and anonymous, impersonal street crime.

Latin American economies have long suffered from fluctuations in world prices for a limited number of minerals or agricultural products and from deterioration in the terms of trade for such primary products. Before World War II, agriculture contributed twice as much to regional gross product as manufacturing did. Although most Latin American countries still depend on the export of one or two primary products, manufacturing's share of gross regional product, by the late 1960s, was well above that of agriculture. In the 1970s, Brazil began to earn more from the export of manufactures than from that of primary products. By the 1990s, more than half of Latin America's exports were at least processed. At the same time, however, the importation of capital goods and, in the case of most countries, of energy to fuel the industrialization process led to soaring debts and other problems.

While Latin America has been industrializing, or at least expanding export processing, the United States has been moving in the other direction. Spurred by incentives offered by both US and foreign governments and lured by cheap labor, US-based corporations have shifted capital—and jobs—to the Third World, including Latin America. Thus the United States, for several decades the virtually unchallenged provider of manufactured goods to Latin America, has itself become increasingly dependent on foreign investment, the importation of manufactured goods, and the export of primary products, particularly wheat.

In most Latin American countries, as in the United States, the idea of stimulating the economy from the bottom up—of expanding the domestic market and producing to meet effective mass demand—has been abandoned in favor of producing for export and/or for the relatively affluent. Modernization, in Latin America as in the United States, has meant increasingly capital-intensive—as opposed to labor-intensive—industry, resulting in chronic unemployment. In the absence of stunningly innovative policy, the unemployment problem in both Americas promises to get worse.

Since the Iberian conquest of the New World, the concentration of landowner-ship has been among Latin America's most obstinate problems. Conquistadores and others favored by the Iberian monarchs carved out for themselves enormous estates complete with resident native American populations or imported African slaves to do the work. But the land grabs of the colonial period pale by compari-son to those inspired since the mid-nineteenth century by the growth of export markets for primary products. Effective and enduring land reform has been rare in the twentieth century, and in some countries the ongoing seizure of peasant lands leaves an ever increasing proportion of the rural population dependent on seasonal work for large landholders. As semifeudal estates are transformed into agribusi-nesses and machines replace workers, displaced peasants are left with neither land nor wages. The displaced indigenous may be left also with individual and collec-tive identity crises, as well as with charges of "terrorism" against them for trying to defend their homelands.

FREE MARKETS AND COSTLY POLITICS

In the 1970s, many Latin American governments, recognizing that their agricul-tural sectors had been neglected or milked while import substitution industrializa-tion was being promoted, turned their attention to the modernization of agricultural production and offered new incentives for the export of agricultural products. One consequence was that lands that had been used to produce staples for domestic consumption were converted into production for export. Export earnings, not usually redistributed in any form to the general population, have risen. Meanwhile, increasingly, basic foodstuffs must be imported, resulting in higher prices for the consumer and rising foreign debt.

As is often pointed out in comparisons of Anglo-America and Latin America, Anglo-America was early blessed with a land tenure pattern of small holdings, or family farms. However, while the US government spoke in the 1960s of the need for land reform in Latin America, the concentration of landholdings, favoring agribusiness conglomerates, assumed a dizzying pace in the United States. By the end of the century, the family farm was clearly an endangered species.

Denationalization, the process whereby ownership or control of resources passes from national to foreign hands, has long been a major problem for Latin America. For the first century or so of independence, it was primarily the land and mineral resources that attracted foreign investors, with the diplomatic—and sometimes military—backing of their governments. Transportation, public utilities, and other infrastructure projects also were often undertaken and controlled by foreigners. By the mid-twentieth century, foreign firms and multinational corporations had be-gun to capture, or recapture, domestic markets for durable consumer goods and to buy out or squeeze out local industries. More recently, foreign firms have com-peted successfully for control of retailing and services as well. Even seemingly un-alienable resources, like water, were falling under the control of foreign firms in the early twenty-first century.

For most of the century in Mesoamerica and for several decades in South America, the denationalizers have been predominantly US-based corporations. Since the 1970s, however, firms based in West Europe and East Asia have been gaining rapidly in the competition for Latin American markets and for the fruits of Latin American land and labor. The same European and Asian companies, joined more recently by those of Middle Eastern oil potentates, have also been increasing their shares of US consumer markets at the expense of US-based companies, as well as their shares of ownership of US farmland and urban real estate, banks, and industries.

A kindred and more insidious problem in the United States, which has received less attention even though it is far more serious, is that of "delocalization." The same multinational banks, conglomerates, and chains that have displaced Latin American businesses and rendered Latin American economies dependent have also bought out or squeezed out local businesses in Tennessee and Michigan and New Mexico. Such companies, which pay campaign debts in Washington and taxes in the Bahamas, have no national or local allegiances. When they see greater profits to be made in São Paulo or Shanghai, they leave Nashville or Albuquerque jobless with no regrets; they were never a part of the community. Many of the companies that moved to Mexico in the early years of NAFTA have since relocated to China for even cheaper labor, even as Chinese operations are beginning to be outsourced to Cambodia or Burma.

Several Latin American countries made headway in the 1960s and 1970s toward gaining control over their resources and their economies. Expropriation of mineral resources was particularly common, and was so popular that even the most *entreguista* right-wing military dictators rarely dared to try to reverse it openly and straightforwardly. The doctrine that subsoil resources are national domain was inherited by most of the Latin American countries from the Spanish crown. Mexico, in 1917, declared its petroleum and other subsoil resources social property, to be owned and exploited by and for the people as a whole; it made the claim an economic reality with the nationalization of those resources in 1938. Most other Latin American countries subsequently established public corporations to manage the production, importation, or distribution of petroleum and other energy products. Meanwhile, in the United States an ever smaller number of companies make ever larger profits, while consumers undergo ever more frequent price-gouging energy crises that leave them disposed to accept foreign military adventures obliquely excused as pursuit of energy sources.

Attempts by Latin American nationalists to regain control of their economies have often been undertaken at great cost. Such attempts generally have the effect of adding the great weight of the multinational corporate community and the US government to the ubiquitous schemes against popular governments. And foreign creditors and multilateral financial institutions weighed in heavily in the 1980s and 1990s with pressure for privatization and debt-for-equity swaps. Nevertheless, the extension of national control over the economy is central to the agenda of popular movements in Latin America. Political leaders were forced at the turn of the twenty-first century, by the globalized control of credit conditionality, to backtrack on the issue. But the issue has since been revisited, particularly where multinational corporations have overreached, privatizing or polluting such essentials as water, and angry peasants have risen up in response. Access to resources is among the issues of global corporate encroachment now seen as challenging regional as well as national interests. In the United States, the ideas of public control over national or local resources and, in general, of placing public interest over private profit are edging at a snail's pace from the category of heresy to that of dissidence.

For Latin America, the 1980s was a decade of turmoil. Civilian rule was restored in Argentina only after the military regime instigated and then suffered humiliating defeat in a war with Great Britain over the Falklands/Malvinas Islands. Military regimes held on in Chile and Paraguay until the end of the decade. In Central America, following on the success in 1979 of the Nicaraguan revolution, insurgency and counterinsurgency raged throughout the 1980s in El Salvador and Guatemala. Reagan administration efforts to reestablish US hegemony in the region swept Honduras, Costa Rica, and even Panama into the turmoil. Such conflict exacerbated debt exposure and other economic disasters, resulting in what came to be known throughout Latin America as the "lost decade." After having grown since midcentury at rates averaging 4 to 6 percent annually, Latin American economies in the 1980s experienced a negative per capita growth rate of -8 percent, along with inflation levels ranging to more than 10,000 percent and high levels of unemployment and underemployment.[1] In 1990 an estimated three-quarters of the population was suffering from some degree or manifestation of malnutrition.

Economic growth resumed in the 1990s in several countries, especially Mexico, Chile, Argentina, and finally Brazil, spurred largely by massive privatization of public assets and services. But growth spurts were often followed by prolonged recession—in the case of Argentina in 2001–2002 all-out economic meltdown. Moreover, new wealth did not trickle down. Overall income levels at the turn of the twenty-first century remained below those of 1980. The gap between rich and poor countries in Latin America, already the world region of greatest inequality, continues to grow. Likewise in the United States since the 1970s, the gap has been growing—generally the outcome not of policy failures but of policy decisions. Between 1983 and 1998, while the household net worth of the richest 1 percent of the US population increased by 42 percent, that of the poorest 40 percent dropped by 76 percent, and the trend has since continued. By 2007, the top 1 percent of US households claimed more wealth than the bottom 90 percent.[2]

Meanwhile, the debt trap that is bankrupting so many Latin Americans is thereby destroying markets for US manufacturers and wiping out jobs for US workers. It is sadly ironic that even as the United States struggles against the encroachment of East Asia, the European Union, and the newly industrializing countries on traditional markets, it continues, through unqualified support for the global creditor cartel, to weaken economies in the one area where it had the greatest trade advantages and to leave those countries with few profitable exports save the two least welcome, officially, in the United States: drugs and people. In fact, one of the largest sources of foreign exchange for Latin America over the past decade has been remittances from emigrant workers.

Moreover, like Third World debts in general, Latin American debts are increasingly owed to private banks. To many of the same banks, and particularly to banks in China, the United States now owes much of its national debt of more than $10 trillion. The US debt tripled in the 1980s, and, though the annual deficit dropped in the 1990s, both the debt itself and its proportional claim on the budget mushroomed after 2000. To an even greater extent than is true of most Latin American countries, the rising US debt may be attributed to unproductive military spending.

Between 2006 and 2008 in most of Latin America, as a consequence at least in part of policy decisions propelled by popular activism, poverty levels began to diminish. In the United States, however, a rising tide of hope for change over the same period has yet to slow the steep decline for working and would-be working classes in standard of living. Indexes of health, education, services, and infrastructure suggest that the quality of life gap between the United States and Latin America has been narrowing steadily since World War II. Even discounting the limitations of statistics and of index making, this indicates promising long-term progress for Latin America. In the shorter term, however—since the 1970s, for example—it also suggests slowed progress or even regression on the part of the United States.

Since the 1980s, US public budgets—from federal to local levels—have been steadily eroded and public responsibilities steadily privatized, exacting a terrible toll on what we euphemistically call the development of human resources. Mushrooming public outlays for privatized prisons are balanced almost dollar for dollar by cuts in public budgets for higher education. In 2009 Americans were spending more per capita on health care than any other people in the world; yet some 44 million lacked any kind of medical insurance, and few of the insured had full coverage. Immunization programs for children were shrinking, along with prenatal care, and while life expectancy for non-Hispanic whites continued to rise, for minorities it had begun to drop.

The proportion of American children in low-income families rose in the 1980s, dropped in the 1990s, and has risen again since 2000. According to a survey conducted by Columbia University's National Center for Children in Poverty, more than one-third of America's children were in low-income households in 2004. In 2009, 14 percent of US households who had mortgages were facing foreclosure, and 20 percent of US citizens had no reliable source of potable water. Such circumstances did not reflect policy failure, but rather policy decisions with respect to allocation of cost and benefit. Changes in US tax laws since the late 1970s, according to the Congressional Budget Office, left 90 percent of Americans paying more while the richest 10 percent paid up to a third less.

While the gap between Latin America and the United States has been narrowing, the gap between the United States and the more prosperous and egalitarian states of Western Europe has been widening. As Latin America, in aggregate, becomes more nearly a part of the "developed" world, the United States becomes more nearly a part of America. Whether or not Latin America is perceived to have been developing in the late twentieth century depends on which countries, which years, and which indexes are emphasized. What is more readily apparent, however, is that the United States has been underdeveloping.

Even if Latin America and Anglo-America increasingly share the blessings and the curses of modernization—along with such problems as competition from stronger economies, excessive dependence on the export of primary products, concentration of landownership, the undermining of local businesses by multinational corporations, staggering debts, chronic unemployment, and a growing gap between rich and poor—is it not obvious that the two Americas are centuries apart in matters of government and politics? Perhaps. But there too similarities and convergences can be found.

From Anticommunism to Antiterrorism

In the 1960s and 1970s, much of Latin America experienced the rise of a new and very modern kind of military dictatorship—institutional, technocratic, self-confident, and ruthless. In demobilizing civilian political organizations and imposing their new order, these military establishments were assisted by paramilitary, intelligence, and police networks with expertise in surveillance, torture, and assassination. This development is not unrelated to the economic problems mentioned above. Those who are left on the margin by modernization, who are needed neither as workers nor as consumers, and who are written off by the economic planners cannot simply be ignored. They are the ill-fed, ill-clothed, ill-housed masses who are presumed to constitute a threat to the established order. The greater their numbers and the greater their sophistication and potential for political organization, the more elaborate will be the apparatus of repression required to contain them.

But there are limits to the efficacy of rule by brute force. Those who wield economic power—domestic and foreign—finally rediscovered the fact that a civilian government that is uninterested in acting upon or unable to act upon a popular mandate, and unwilling or unable to control military and paramilitary forces, is often a better hedge against social change than a repressive military government. The 1980s witnessed withdrawal of the generals from Latin America's presidential palaces and a process of "redemocratization." But the withdrawal was initially only partial—not to a safe enough distance to allow democracy a free rein—and the new democracies, to a large extent, represented the victory of form over substance.

Politics in Latin America has often been associated, in the minds of Anglo-Americans, with violence and petty corruption. But political assassination has been no stranger to the United States, and in the aftermath of Watergate, the Iran-Contra affair, and so many other scandals in the heart of the US government—more recently, a war launched on the basis of pre-misinterpreted intelligence and revelations of US torture of prisoners in Iraq, Afghanistan, and elsewhere—Anglo-Americans should at least be learning humility.

It should not go unnoticed in the United States that the Latin American states with the highest levels of political development suffered the cruelest fate during the era of militocracy. Many of the same antiegalitarian economic policies that were imposed on Brazil in the 1960s and the Southern Cone countries in the 1970s by counterrevolutionary military regimes have since been adopted in the United States without an open rupture in democratic processes. Perhaps the majority in the United States has been saved—by the myth of a classless society and the alienation of almost half of the eligible electorate—from a fate worse than economic deprivation.

But not all US citizens are spared the kind of official violence that is commonly employed in Latin America and elsewhere to contain a growing sector of marginalized would-be workers. Such containment in the politically decentralized United States is carried out by increasingly autonomous local police forces. Police brutality, particularly against minority groups, is common from coast to coast. Amnesty

International has called attention to the use of such brutality by New York City police, and Human Rights Watch has cited the abuse of female prisoners in several state institutions. The US federal prison population doubled in the 1980s and again in the 1990s. At some 2.3 million in 2009, it was the largest prison population in the world, accounting for one-fourth of all the world's prisoners.

Except for such brief skirmishes, as those in response to the inner-city riots following the assassination of Dr. Martin Luther King and to Vietnam War protests, the United States has been spared the spectacle of troops on the streets. But it has not been spared the general trend toward militarism. The enhanced power of the US military establishment since the Cold War has been expressed primarily in the increasing militarization of the US foreign policymaking apparatus and in the military's ever increasing peacetime share of the national budget.

The role of military establishments in the two Americas proceeded in tandem. The incorporation of Central America and the Caribbean into the US sphere of influence in the early twentieth century, through military intervention and, in some cases, direct military occupation, left a more modern form of militarism firmly entrenched. In the 1950s and 1960s, the US military, on the premise of the need for a global strategy in the face of a permanent global war, undertook the organizational and technological modernization of the South American military establishments as well. An aspect of the Cold War worldview, inculcated or reinforced through US training, was the idea that the political arena was the battleground of the Cold War, and, as such, too important to be left to civilians. It is not surprising, then, that the US intelligence technicians and techniques employed to ferret out "subversives" in Latin America came to be unleashed on US citizens as well. The people of the United States have reaped at home what they allowed the US government to sow abroad. As the late US senator Hubert H. Humphrey commented in 1973:

> With Watergate we have seen officials of our government commit criminal acts that strongly resemble the practices and methods directed against foreign governments and other peoples. Counterespionage, cover-ups, infiltration, wiretapping, political surveillance, all done in the name of national security in faraway places, have come home to haunt us. The spirit and the purpose of domestic policy is said to condition our foreign policy. The reverse is also true.[3]

The end of the 1980s also marked the end of the Cold War. Soviet leader Mikhail Gorbachev had simply opted out. But as the Christmas season 1989 US invasion of Panama demonstrated with great clarity, the end of the Cold War did not mean the end of US intervention. The Cold War was never the reason for such intervention; it was only the rationale, and new rationales, including the war on drugs and the war on terrorism were already on the drawing board. After the 9/11, 2001, attacks by Muslim terrorists on New York City and Washington, D.C., most Latin American leaders and groups considered troublesome by the Bush administration were relabeled terrorists, and anti-terrorism became the all-purpose rationale for intervention.

Like Watergate the more effectively suppressed Iran-Contra scandal of the 1980s, the extraconstitutional modalities of the "war on terror" in the 2000s offer mounting evidence that a democracy cannot maintain an empire without detriment to the essentials of its democratic character.

LEARNING TO LIVE WITHOUT EMPIRE

Some seventy-five years ago, in times not so different from these, when in the United States the lines outside soup kitchens were lengthening and the ranks of the homeless swelling, and when the United States had fallen into disrepute beyond its own borders for such practices as gunboat diplomacy, a newly elected Democratic president, Franklin Delano Roosevelt, pledged nonintervention and ushered in a period of good neighborliness toward Latin America. Under cover of the Cold War, and more recently of the wars on drugs and on terrorism, subsequent US presidents have failed to honor that pledge. But the gunboat diplomacy of the late twentieth and early twenty-first centuries has proved as subversive to the spirit of American democracy as did that of the last century's youth, and a renewed pledge of nonintervention is overdue.

Such a pledge must be understood to cover not only interventions undertaken for straightforwardly strategic or political motives covered previously by the now defunct Cold War. It must subsume any and all substitute rationales for the ongoing pursuit of indefensible objectives. Given the recent history of military abuse of civil liberties and human rights in Latin America and given our professed intent to support fledgling democracies, there can be no excuse for continuing to extend aid in any form to Latin American military or paramilitary forces or for promoting arms sales—and thus arms races.

Little wonder that Latin America's democratic leaders—threatened at the least with trade disruption and credit freezes and all too often with military conspiracy or even US military intervention if they moved to reward their own constituencies with a measure of economic democracy—have been skeptical of official US protestations of common economic interests. The fact is, however, that the ordinary people of the United States and of Latin America, as opposed to the high-rollers who place their bets in a global game, occupy the same hemisphere. Now more than ever, as economic communities are roped off in Europe and Asia, Americans of North and South are destined to share either prosperity or destitution.

The economic troubles felt throughout the hemisphere in the 1980s have generally abated, at least in terms of the figures and purposes that matter most to economists, investors, and creditors. But policy continues to favor the private sector over the public sector, capital over labor, global enterprise over national and local business, financial sleight of hand over production and consumption for internal mass markets, and exploitation and depletion over conservation and regeneration. The same policies that have stripped Latin America of internally generated capital, obliterated social services, suppressed local markets, and kept labor cheap have served to draw US capital—and jobs—abroad.

Having contributed, through unqualified support for a set of policies now known as "structural adjustment," to the impoverishment of the only area where the United States had a traditional trade advantage, the US government proceeded to place already shortchanged US workers in the position of competing for jobs with even more desperate Latin American workers. It cannot be said that this system has failed—every system works for somebody—but it has failed the people of the Americas, all of the Americas, and for the sake of us all it must be reversed.

The bureaucracies and mind-sets generated by the Cold War and by an exploitative boom-and-bust approach to development are inappropriate for the challenges of the twenty-first century. To the extent that the Obama administration and the Democratic legislative majority seek seriously to promote economic democracy in the United States, we would find that goal to be furthered by promoting economic democracy in Latin America as well. Even though the economies of South America are becoming increasingly diversified, NAFTA and other US-propelled integrative initiatives are likely to survive; thus the economies of Anglo- and Ibero-America will remain to some degree intertwined and the well-being of their peoples interdependent.

Though wiser policy might have delayed it, the passing of Pax Americana is not a matter of choice. The "American Century" presaged by the inner circle of the George W. Bush administration, and clearly intended to be the American century all over the world, was a dangerous illusion. In the commercially driven new world order, the world's mightiest military machine is a devalued currency—just so much Confederate money. For half a century, the Cold War provided cover for the pursuit of private and bureaucratic interests in Latin America and for the use of Latin America in posturing and saber-rattling for domestic political advantage. Stripping away that cover—and subsequent substitute covers—should make it possible and even necessary, at last, to base policy on the legitimate interests of Americans and on a profound understanding of the common interests of the peoples of the Western Hemisphere.

PAYING ATTENTION TO LATIN AMERICA

The question about Latin America raised most frequently by US journalists and pundits at the end of the first decade of the twenty-first century has been, Where is Latin America headed? The answer, it seems to me would have to be "out of the US backyard." The tortured generation now in office is trying, albeit cautiously, to undo some of the political and economic damage of the past several decades. Being in office is not the same, of course, as being in power; but such leaders are beginning to acquire economic options, as the emergence of China as a new superpower means also a new supermarket, and political options extended by collaborating among themselves. Political leverage was enhanced over the past decade as revulsion against the policies and posturings of the Bush administration became such as to build bridges across the great gulfs between Latin American nations, parties, and classes.

That administration wanted its constituents to worry about terrorist threats emanating from Latin America as well as about the prospect that US-based companies might lose access to Latin American resources. A more benign motive, but one nonetheless reflecting an imperial mind-set, has been the prospect that Latin Americans might ask us to stop helping them. It may be that what Latin America needs most now from the United States is inattention, and what the United States needs most from Latin America is advice.

If the US electorate is serious now about "change," as the electoral outcomes of 2006 and 2008 suggest, there are important lessons we should be learning from Latin America. Pursuit of the legitimate interests of US citizens would be well served by attention to the strategies and means whereby Latin Americans have dealt with—and begun to solve—many of the problems that bedevil us as well.

Trickling Up from Meltdown

It used to be said that Brazil was the country of the future—and always would be. That is said no more. Brazil appears to have reached out and grasped that future. While the United States borrows from foreign governments and banks to replenish its own failed banks, Brazil holds foreign reserves that exceed the sum of its foreign debt. And under the Workers Party government of Luiz Inacio (Lula) da Silva, the benefits of a thriving economy reach well beyond the elite. His *bolsa família,* or family allowance, program, for example, offers low-income families material incentive to keep their children in school. The program has markedly enhanced school attendance as well as the president's popularity.

The US government, accustomed to a trickle-down approach to all economic challenges, might have done well in 2008–2009 to look to the experience of the Argentines, who pulled out of their 2001–2002 meltdown by building from the bottom up. A serious rescue plan for the US financial sector has further enriched the bailed-out bankers, but unemployment and homelessness continue to climb. In Argentina, cash-free communities began early on to barter goods and services, and then to create their own local currencies. As the practice spread, communities converted currencies, trading among themselves in a broad-based movement. Workers began to reopen factories owners had abandoned and to produce for local markets. And others began to produce and offer whatever they could, including food from urban gardens and sidewalk tango lessons.

Self-Help for Lack of Options

All well-meaning US development agencies employ the rhetoric of self-help promotion; but how much do pampered US bureaucrats really know about self-help? Shouldn't we be learning from those who turned to self-help because it was the only help available? Cubans, who have had to build back from scratch again and again, as their market systems were yanked out from under them, have become masters of self-help. From alternative energy and transport to urban gardens and commercially viable organic substitutes for pesticides to a surfeit of well-trained doctors and celebrated artists and athletes, Cubans have continually turned lemons into lemonade.

As the US Congress struggles to wrench from the world's most expensive private medical industry a glimmer of acceptance of the notion of a public right to affordable health care, Cubans enjoy cradle-to-grave care that is accessible, preventive, holistic, integrated, and free; its outcomes have been highly praised by international organizations, particularly the World Health Organization. The

United States might have profited also from accepting the assistance offered by Cuba to the Gulf Coast in the wake of Hurricane Katrina. Cuba regularly entertains major hurricanes and rarely suffers casualties.

RESURRECTING THE RULE OF LAW

Latin America's transitions from authoritarianism—in several cases brutal systems of state-sponsored terror—have not been easy. Shredded constitutions cannot be adequately patched up so long as the perpetrators of great crimes remained unpunished, unrepentant, or even officially unidentified, protected by state secrets claims and amnesty decrees and by military and intelligence agencies still exercising inordinate power. Even where the truth about abuse of power was generally known, moving against the abusers proved difficult. Until widely experienced truth becomes "official truth" and then "official history," abused populations cannot, and abusers need not, assume that it really is history, that is, that such patterns of abuse will not be allowed to return.

A return to elections and civilian government has been only the first step toward resurrection of the rule of law. Serious pursuit of such resurrection carries great risk, greater risk than most who have fortunes or prominent positions or even forums to lose are willing to take. Judge Juan Guzman Tapia, who vigorously pursued the prosecution of Chilean dictator, General Augusto Pinochet, maintains that he was only doing his job; but most in positions of authority shrank from undertaking any such job.

There were nevertheless individuals and human rights organizations throughout Latin America who persisted, and while there remain some categories of citizens—unorganized urban workers and indigenous peasants, for example—who still lack protections or full exercise of their rights, vigorous processes of investigation and prosecution were finally launched in most countries. By 2009, governments in Brazil and around the Southern Cone had passed into the hands of leaders who had opposed the tyrants and had themselves suffered abuse. Twenty-two Western Hemisphere countries had ratified the 1969 American Convention on Human Rights and accepted the jurisdiction of the Inter-American Court for Human Rights; and the court's rulings in one country were being cited in rulings elsewhere in Latin America.

Meanwhile, the United States continues to shrink even from investigation, never mind prosecution, of official perpetrators of torture and other forms of civil and human rights abuse and violation of international law over the past decade. The best we've been able to do has been the perjury conviction of a vice presidential aide, whose sentence was at any rate soon to be commuted by the outgoing president. The passing of the highest offices of government in a landslide election seems to have been enough to quiet the anxieties of most who understood that the rule of law had been badly breached.

CHALLENGING ELECTIONS AS IF OUTCOMES MATTERED

A popular landslide is certainly a feat to be celebrated; but we have yet to learn to reject the idea that we are not entitled to a victory *unless* it is a landslide. In that regard also, as in so many others relating to "free and fair" and creditable elections, we have a great deal to learn from Latin Americans. When electoral politics loses appeal in much of Latin America, as it does about every other decade, US leaders and opinion-makers begin to talk about the unpreparedness of Latin Americans and their preference for anarchy or authoritarianism. It may be, though, that those Latin Americans simply have a lower threshold of intolerance for sham.

Experience on both sides of the Rio Grande, including experience with elections, has clearly shown that the impact of empire does not start at the Mexican border, but rather at the Washington, DC, beltway. The US electorate, like Latin American ones before it, has experienced elections that were exclusive and reversible, for profit and for show. Along with get-out-the-vote campaigns, we have seen campaigns to throw-out-the-vote, keep-out-the-vote, turn-back-the-vote, and get-out-the-vote-on-the-wrong-day-or-in-the-wrong-place.

We have seen voters excluded for reasons of race, ethnicity, or class, reasons partisan or otherwise indefensible. We have seen election results reversed by timely breakouts of rioting and breakdowns of electronic voting and counting machinery and by questionable resort to recount, recall, impeachment, and indictment. We have seen candidates and elected representatives purchased wholesale by corporations, and, in general, the commercialization of electoral process. And we have seen straightforwardly partisan supervision of elections at the highest levels, indicating that control of the levers of power was not intended actually to be put at risk.

All broad-based Latin American parties or popular movements have at some point faced the dilemma of whether or not to stage an open-ended challenge to a fraudulently determined electoral outcome—risking further polarization and perhaps even a violent crackdown on the opposition—or simply to concede. Unqualified concession, however, also carries risk; it means risking irrelevance not only of opposition parties or coalitions, but of the electoral process. Democracy has come to Latin America at great cost, and the unarmed and unrich are learning to defend it.

SECURITY AS FREEDOM FROM DEBT AND FEAR

US citizens will not find security at home or abroad so long as US foreign policy continues to make the world more dangerous. We have always been led to believe that national prosperity (that will surely trickle down sooner or later) depends on US dominance abroad. This year, 2010, may well be the most promising one since the Great Depression for exploding that myth. But any government that, on behalf of its citizens, would seek to back away from pursuit, or acceptance, of empire may be in need of guidance. That guidance might well be sought from Latin Americans who, on matters of US imperial design, have always been ahead of the learning curve.

The spin that passes for policy has always been about God's plan and the national interest, freedom and security, democracy and development, trade and aid, and more recently, human rights. Such spin, mainly for domestic consumption, continually reinforces public misperceptions about the ways of the world and the US role in it. The strategy, or practice, of empire maintenance is something else entirely—always to some degree about pillage, though the nature of the loot, the actors in the game, and the powers in the play-offs are subject to change. The up-shot of this stew of spin and strategy is well expressed by a character in Graham Green's classic novel, *Our Man in Havana*. He allows that this world of "intelli-gence" and intrigue is a fantasy world, but that out of it come real bullets that kill real people. Over the past century Latin Americans have taken more than their share of the real bullets.

The twenty-first century, however, has seen an important transformation in the Western Hemisphere. Survivors of the worst of times—the 1970s in South Amer-ica and the 1980s in Central America—have taken the reins and are proving less vulnerable than their predecessors either to intimidation or to bribery. Moreover, they appear to be more confidently nationalistic than most of their predecessors and at the same time more open to collective consultation among Latin American leaders and to collective solutions to common problems.

While the abundant natural wealth, and until 2000 the current account surplus, of the United States has been drained off into foreign wars, into domestic security programs, and into the pockets of megacorporate CEOs, and the country has be-come deeply indebted to others, especially China, Latin American economies have become increasingly diversified and thus less dependent on any single trading part-ner. If the United States is now to begin to build more cordial and productive re-lations with Latin American countries, it must understand and acknowledge that Latin America is no longer its dependent and obedient client.

With stronger economies and more democratic governments than ever before, and with organizations and institutions (like MERCOSUR, the South American common market, and UNASUR, the union of South American nations) that allow those countries to consult, coordinate, and collaborate without US intrusion, Latin American leaders and countries will continue to exercise a larger role in world politics and world markets, whether the United States likes it or not. The United States would thus be better served by a policy that recognizes their inde-pendence and offers them the respect they deserve.

NOTES

1. *The IDB*, September-October 1989, pp. 6–9.
2. Bill Moyers, "A New Story for America," *The Nation*, January 22, 2007.
3. Hubert H. Humphrey, "The Threat to the Presidency," *Washington Post*, May 6, 1973.

Acknowledgments

In preparing this fifth edition, I benefited from the financial assistance of the Joseph and Sheila Mark Fund. I am grateful for that assistance and, as always, for the all-purpose assistance of my husband, Martin C. Needler.

About the Book, Editor, and Contributors

This textbook, extensively revised and updated in this new fifth edition, introduces the student to what is most basic and most interesting about Latin America. The authors—each widely recognized in his or her own discipline, as well as among Latin Americanists—analyze both the enduring features of the area and the pace and direction of change. The book conveys the unifying aspects of Latin American culture and society, together with the distinct characteristics of major subregions and countries.

Highlights of the fifth edition include the traumatic impact of drugs and debt and the interventions they elicit throughout the hemisphere. Contributors also examine turn of the century trends, including emphasis on the export sector, pressure to privatize, general retrenchment with regard to social welfare programs, spurts of economic growth, steady growth in income gaps, and new threats to distinctive ecological zones. The burgeoning of new populist political parties and social movements in response to economic crises and extreme deprivation is also addressed here.

Jan Knippers Black is professor of international policy studies at the Monterey Institute of International Studies, where she has served as president of the faculty senate. She has also had teaching, research, or administrative appointments at several other institutions, including the University of New Mexico, American University in Washington, DC, St. Antony's College, Oxford, and the University of Pittsburgh's Semester at Sea. A former Peace Corps volunteer in Chile, she holds a PhD in international studies from American University in Washington, DC. Black has served on more than two dozen editorial, advisory, or governing boards, and she has visited more than 175 countries, lecturing or conducting research in most of them. She has authored or edited and coauthored more than a dozen books, coauthored another dozen, and published more than two hundred chapters and articles in reference books, anthologies, journals, magazines, and newspapers. Recent publications include *Development in Theory and Practice: Paradigms and Paradoxes* (2nd ed., 1999); *Inequity in the Global Village: Recycled Rhetoric and Disposable People* (1999); and *The Politics of Human Rights Protection* (2009).

ABOUT THE CONTRIBUTORS

Diego Abente Brun, a fellow at the US National Endowment for Democracy, has previously served as Paraguay's minister of justice and labor and senior adviser to the minister of finance, as ambassador to the Organization of American States, as vice president of the Senate of the Republic of Paraguay, and as president of his political party, Encuentro Nacional. He was elected to the senate after about a decade as assistant and associate professor of political science at Miami University, Ohio. He is the author of several articles on the politics of Paraguay, Uruguay, and Venezuela that have appeared in scholarly journals, including *Comparative Politics, Latin American Research Review, Journal of Latin American Studies, Journal of Interamerican Studies,* and *The Americas.* He is currently working on a book on the politics of Paraguay.

Pablo Andrade is a professor at the Universidad Andina Simón Bolívar in Quito, where he is also the academic coordinator of the master's program in Latin American Studies. He wrote his PhD dissertation on democratization processes in Ecuador at the graduate program in social and political thought at York University in Canada and has been a Fulbright visiting scholar at UCLA and senior associate member at St. Antony's College, Oxford. His research and publications have dealt with Latin American political thought, constitutional reform in Ecuador, Ecuador's foreign policy, and Ecuador's relations with the United States and with other countries of the Andean region.

Peter Bakewell holds the Edmund and Louise Kahn Chair in History at Southern Methodist University in Dallas. He has previously taught at Cambridge University, the University of New Mexico (where he also served as associate editor of the *Hispanic American Historical Review*), and Emory University in Atlanta. Among his many publications are definitive studies of colonial era silver mining in Mexico and Bolivia. His recent books include *A History of Latin America: Empires and Sequels, 1450–1930* (1997; 2nd ed., 2003).

Jan Knippers Black is a professor in the Graduate School of International Policy and Management at the Monterey Institute of International Studies in California, a Middlebury College affiliate. Previously she has been senior associate member at Saint Antony's College, Oxford; faculty on the University of Pittsburgh's Semester at Sea; research professor of public administration at the University of New Mexico; and senior research scientist and chair of the Latin American Research Team in the Foreign Area Studies Division of American University in Washington, D.C. Her many publications include textbooks on the market in 2010 in five distinct subfields of political science.

Peter Calvert is professor emeritus of comparative and international politics at the University of Southampton, England. He was educated at Campbell College, Belfast; Queens' College, Cambridge; and the University of Michigan, Ann Arbor. He took his doctorate at Cambridge. In 1964 he was appointed lecturer in politics at Southampton and in 1984 was appointed to a personal chair there. He retired in 2002 but continues to work on the politics and international relations of the Western Hemisphere and coedits the journal *Democratization.* Among his recent publications are *Politics and Society in the Third World,* with Susan Calvert (2nd ed., 2001), *Comparative Politics: an Introduction* (2002), and *A Political and Economic Dictionary of Latin America* (2004).

Michael L. Conniff is director of the global studies program at San Jose State University in California. Previously he directed the Center for Latin American and Caribbean Studies and taught history at the University of South Florida in Tampa. He has published books on Brazil—*Urban Politics in Brazil* (1982), and Panama—*Black Labor on a White Canal* (1985) and *Panama and the United States* (1992). He has also worked extensively on populism and in 1999 published *Populism in Latin America.* He has edited several other books, including *Modern Brazil* (1991; with Frank McCann) and *Africans in the Americas* (2002; with T. J. Davis). His survey *A History of Modern Latin America* (with Larry Clayton) came out in 2005. He also served as a Peace Corps volunteer and as executive secretary of the Conference on Latin American History.

Michael S. Danielson is a PhD candidate in political science at American University. He holds an Masters in International Policy Studies from the Monterey Institute of International Studies, Spanish and Philosophy degrees from Santa Clara University, and has worked as a policy analyst at the Children's Defense Fund in Washington, DC, and the Center on Policy Initiatives in San Diego, California. His dissertation research, supported by Fulbright-García Robles and Gill Family Foundation grants, examines the role of transnational migrants as political actors in their Mexican hometowns. His article "Walking Together, but in Which Direction? Gender Discrimination and Multicultural Practices in Oaxaca, Mexico" (with Todd A. Eisenstadt) was published in *Politics & Gender* in 2009, and his chapter "All Immigration Politics Is Local: The Day Labor Ordinance in Vista, CA" is forthcoming (2010) in *Taking Local Control: Immigration Policy Activism in U.S. Cities and States*, edited by Monica Varsanyi (Stanford University Press and the UCSD Center for Comparative Immigration Studies). He has studied in Argentina as well at the University of Buenos Aires and the Latin American Faculty of Social Sciences (FLACSO).

Steve Ellner earned his PhD in Latin American history at the University of New Mexico and has taught at the Universidad del Oriente in Puerto La Cruz, Venezuela, since 1977. His most recent book is *Rethinking Venezuelan Politics: Class Conflict and the Chavez Phenomenon* (2008). He is also the author of *Organized Labor in Venezuela, 1958–1991: Behavior and Concerns in a Democratic Setting* (1993) and *Venezuela's Movimiento al Socialismo: From Guerrilla Defeat to Innovative Politics* (1988). He is coeditor of *Venezuela: Hugo Chávez and the Decline of an "Exceptional Democracy"* (2007), *Venezuelan Politics in the Chavez Era: Class Polarization and Conflict* (2003), and *The Latin American Left: From the Fall of Allende to Perestroika* (1993). He is a frequent contributor to several US magazines, including *In These Times* and *NACLA: Report on the Americas*.

David Fleischer received his PhD in political science from the University of Florida and has taught at the University of Brasilia since 1972. He was visiting professor at George Washington University, the Federal University of Minas Gerais (UFMG), the State University of New York at Albany, and the University of Florida. He was a Peace Corps volunteer in Brazil (1962–1964). He is the author of ten books, including *Corruption in Brazil* (2002) and *Las consecuencias políticas del sistema electoral brasileño* (1995), and coauthor of *Brazil in Transition* (1983) and *Da distensão à abertura* (1988). He has contributed chapters to forty-eight books, including *Reforming Brazil* (2004), *Corruption and Political Reform in Brazil* (1999), and *Brazil: A Country Study* (1998). He has conducted research on legislatures, election and party systems, and corruption in South and Central America and Africa.

José Z. Garcia is professor of political science and former director of the Latin American Institute at New Mexico State University in Las Cruces. He has lived in Ecuador and Peru and has done extensive research on military factionalism in Peru. More recently, he has done extensive research on the military in Central America, including preparation of a book on the Salvadoran military. Professor Garcia is experienced in practical politics as well; he served for several years as chair of the Democratic Party of New Mexico's Dona Ana County. He is currently serving on the governor's New Mexico-Mexico Border Commission.

William P. Glade is professor of economics at the University of Texas-Austin and director of the Mexican Center at the university's Institute of Latin American Studies. He has also served as senior scholar and acting secretary of the Latin American Program in the Woodrow Wilson International Center for Scholars, Smithsonian Institution, Washington, DC. From 1989 to 1992, he was associate director in charge of educational and cultural affairs at the United States Information Agency. Recent publications include articles on systemic transformation in Latin America and the former centrally planned economies and two edited volumes—*The Privatization of Public Enterprises in*

Latin America (1991) and *Bigger Economies, Smaller Governments: Privatization in Latin America* (1996)—and, with Charles Reilly, *Inquiry at the Grassroots: An Inter-American Foundation Fellowship Reader* (1993).

William Godnick is program coordinator for the United Nations Regional Center for Peace, Disarmament, and Development in Latin America and the Caribbean and a PhD candidate at the University of Bradford's Department of Peace Studies in the UK, specializing in issues of human security and social capital in Latin America. He holds an MA in international policy studies from the Monterey Institute of International Studies. Previously he was senior adviser for Latin America for the London-based NGO International Alert. He has lived and worked extensively in the Bahamas, Bolivia, Chile, Colombia, El Salvador, Honduras, and Peru.

Alfonso Gonzalez is professor emeritus of geography at the University of Calgary in Alberta. Since receiving his PhD from the University of Texas-Austin, he has been on the faculty at San Diego State College, Northeast Louisiana State College, Southern Illinois University, and the University of South Florida, where he served as chair of the Department of Geography. Professor Gonzalez specializes in Third World and Latin American geography, with particular attention to population, settlement, and socioeconomic development. He has performed field and archival research in several areas of Hispanic America and Spain and has presented and published numerous papers and book chapters. He has coedited (with Jim Norwine) two editions of a book: *The Third World* (1988) and *The New Third World* (1998).

Fred R. Harris, a former member of the US Senate (D-Oklahoma, 1964–1972), is a professor of political science at the University of New Mexico and a member of the board of directors of the North American Institute. He has been a Fulbright scholar in Mexico, a visiting professor at the Universidad Nacional Autonoma de Mexico, and a Distinguished Fulbright Lecturer in Uruguay, and he has taught and lectured extensively in Mexico and Latin America. He has produced sixteen nonfiction books (nine as author, seven as coauthor or editor), including, with Lynn A. Curtis, *Locked in the Poorhouse: Cities, Race, and Poverty in the United States* (1998) and, with David Cooper, *Estudios sobre los Estados Unidos y su relacion bilateral con Mexico* (1986). He is also an award-winning author of three novels.

Jane S. Jaquette is a teaching professor emerita of politics and diplomacy and world affairs at Occidental College in Los Angeles. She received her BA from Swarthmore College and her PhD from Cornell University. A Latin Americanist who specializes in the comparative study of women's political participation and women in development, she is a past president of both the Latin American Studies Association and the Association for Women in Development. She has edited and contributed to several books on women and development and on women's movements and democracy in Latin America, most recently *Women and Gender Equity in Development Theory and Practice* (2006) and *Feminist Agendas and Democracy in Latin America* (2009). She is finishing a book on power and citizenship in the work of Machiavelli and Hobbes.

Shane Lewis holds a master's degree in applied geography at Texas State University. He received an astronomy degree from the University of Texas in 1991 and stayed on to develop a human subject research management system for the UT vice president for research. Since 1999, he has served as software developer for an international network of nongovernmental organizations seeking to document the ecological and human impacts of mining in the developing world. Current research projects focus on the complex ecological and economic trade-offs implicit in all attempts at sustainable development. These efforts have been supported by a fellowship from the prestigious Mexico-Norte research network.

Anthony P. Maingot is professor emeritus of sociology at Florida International University in Miami. He has previously taught at Yale University and at the University of the West Indies in Trinidad and served as acting dean of international affairs at Florida International. Born in Trinidad, Professor Maingot studied at the University of Puerto Rico and the University of California, Los Angeles, before receiving his PhD from the University of Florida. He was a member of the Constitutional Reform Commission of Trinidad and Tobago from 1971 to 1974 and president of the Caribbean Studies Association from 1982 to 1983.

Cynthia McClintock is professor of political science and international affairs and former director of the Latin American studies program at George Washington University in Washington, DC. She is also a former president of the Latin American Studies Association. Her BA is from Harvard and her PhD from the Massachusetts Institute of Technology. Professor McClintock is the author of many books, chapters, and articles, particularly on Peruvian domestic and international politics, including *Peasant Cooperatives and Political Change in Peru* (1981); *Revolutionary Movements in Latin America: El Salvador's FMLN and Peru's Shining Path* (1998); and, with Fabian Vallas, *The United States and Peru: Cooperation—at a Cost* (2003). She also coedited, with Abraham Lowenthal, *The Peruvian Experiment Reconsidered,* (1983). She has also served on the Council of the American Political Science Association and currently chairs its comparative democratization section.

Martin C. Needler is a former dean of the School of International Studies at the University of the Pacific and trustee of Saint Antony's College, Oxford. He has previously held teaching positions at Dartmouth College, the University of Michigan, and the University of New Mexico and postdoctoral fellowships or research positions at UCLA, Harvard, and the University of Southampton. He has published thirteen books, principally on Latin American politics and US foreign policy, including *Political Development in Latin America* (1968), *Politics and Society in Mexico* (1971), *The Problem of Democracy in Latin America* (1987), and *Mexican Politics: The Containment of Conflict* (3d ed., 1995). His *Identity, Interest, and Ideology: An Introduction to Politics* came out in 1996. Professor Needler holds a PhD in political science from Harvard University.

Jorge Nef is professor of government and international affairs and former director of the Center for Latin American, Caribbean, and Latino Studies at the University of Southern Florida in Tampa. He is also professor emeritus at the University of Guelph. He graduated from the University of Chile and has studied at Vanderbilt University, the Facultad Latinoamericana de Ciencias Sociales, and the University of California. A past president of the Canadian Association of Latin American and Caribbean Studies (CALACS) and editor of its journal, and past president of the Canadian Association for the Study of International Development (CASID), he is a fellow of the Centers for Research on Latin America and the Caribbean (CERLAC) and for Refugee Studies (CRS), both at York University. *Human Security and Mutual Vulnerability* (1995), *Managing Development* (2007), *Capital, Power, and Inequality* (2008), and *The Democratic Challenge* (2009) are among his numerous books, monographs, and articles. He has been a consultant for national and international agencies in international development, a participant in the expert groups of the South Commission in Geneva (1989) and in Team Canada during the prime minister's 1995 visit to Chile, and an expert witness for the US Senate's Committee on Foreign Affairs.

Liisa L. North is professor emerita of political science at York University and a fellow of York's Center for Research on Latin America and the Caribbean (CERLAC), where she has headed several international cooperation programs organized with the Latin American Faculty of Social Sciences (FLASCO) and various Andean NGOs. She has published monographs, book chapters, and articles on party politics, civil-military relations, and development processes in Chile, Peru, and Ecuador; on the civil wars, United Nations peacekeeping missions, and human rights and refugee crises in El Salvador and Guatemala; on Canadian-Latin American relations; and on rural development issues. She is coeditor, with John D. Cameron, of *Desarrollo rural y neoliberalismo: Ecuador desde una perspectiva comparativa* (2008). Her articles have appeared in *Studies in Political Economy, Latin American Perspectives, Third World Quarterly, Ecuador Debate*, and *World Development.*

James Petras is professor emeritus of sociology at the State University of New York at Binghamton. He is the author of forty books, published by leading US and British presses and translated into twenty-eight languages. He also has over four hundred scholarly articles in refereed journals. His publications span a broad range of topics on Latin American and global developments, among them, *US Hegemony Under Siege: Class, Politics, and Development in Latin America* (1990); *Democracy and Poverty in Chile* (1994); *La continuacíon de la historia* (1996), and, with Henry Veltmeyer, *Globalization Unmasked: Imperialism in the 21st Century* (2001). He is currently working as a freelance writer and an adviser to the landless workers' movement in Brazil.

James Lee Ray is professor of political science at Vanderbilt. He previously served on the faculties of State University College at Fredonia (New York), the University of New Mexico, and Florida State University. Professor Ray is author of *Global Politics* (8th ed., 2005) and has published articles in a number of journals, including the *British Journal of Political Science, International Interactions, International Organization, International Studies Quarterly*, and the *Journal of Theoretical Politics*. He has recently contributed chapters to *Progress in International Relations Theory (2003)* and *The Scourge of War* (2004). He is currently working on a book with a working title of *American Foreign Policy and Political Ambition.*

Steve C. Ropp is professor of political science at the University of Wyoming. He is the author of *Panamanian Politics: From Guarded Nation to National Guard* (1982); coeditor (with James A. Morris) of *Central America: Crisis and Adaptation* (1984); and coeditor (with Thomas Risse and Kathryn Sikkink) of *The Power of Human Rights: International Norms and Domestic Change* (1999). Professor Ropp has taught courses on Latin American politics, US foreign policy and international relations in Latin America, Asia, and Europe. At present, he is conducting research on various forces shaping and reshaping Panama, as well as on populism in the Americas and Europe.

Karl H. Schwerin is professor of anthropology at the University of New Mexico. Throughout his career he conducted fieldwork in several Latin American countries, with particular emphasis on economic and subsistence patterns, adaptive strategies, and processes of culture change. Professor Schwerin has served as president of the American Society for Ethnohistory and the University of New Mexico chapter of the scientific research society Sigma Xi. From 1987 to 1993, he chaired the Department of Anthropology at the University of New Mexico. He has published four books and numerous papers on a broad range of topics relating to Latin America and tropical societies worldwide. To mark the occasion of the seventy-fifth anniversary of the Department of Anthropology at the University of New Mexico, he has been writing a history of the department. A substantive and theoretical study of Carib warfare in Venezuela will appear shortly. Professor Schwerin also continues his long-term study on the ethnographic researches of the French explorer Alcide d'Orbigny.

Wendy Muse Sinek is a doctoral student at the University of California-Berkeley, specializing in Latin American politics. She holds an MA in international policy studies from the Monterey Institute of International Studies and has lived and worked extensively in Ecuador, Nicaragua, and the Dominican Republic. More recently, she has conducted fieldwork in Cuba and Brazil, with particular attention to the dynamics of social movements that emerge in response to economic crises.

Wayne S. Smith, an adjunct professor of Latin American Studies at the Johns Hopkins University in Baltimore and a senior fellow at the Center for International Policy in Washington, DC, was a US Foreign Service officer for over twenty-five years. When he left the service in 1982 because of profound disagreements with the Reagan administration's policies, he was chief of mission at the US Interests Section in Havana and was recognized as the State Department's leading expert on Cuba. Smith holds three master's degrees, and his PhD is from George Washington University in Washington, DC. His published works include *The Closest of Enemies: A Personal and Diplomatic Account of US-Cuban Relations Since 1957* (1987); *Portrait of Cuba* (1991); and *Toward Resolution: The Falklands/Malvinas Dispute* (1991), which he edited.

David Stea is emeritus professor of geography and former director of the Center for Texas-Mexico Applied Research at Texas State University-San Marcos. For almost two decades he was professor of architecture and planning at UCLA and the University of Wisconsin. He is also a past president of the Association for Borderland Studies and one of the founders of environmental psychology. A student also of aeronautical engineering and architecture, he has a doctorate in psychology from Stanford University. He has made his home in Mexico since 2006 and has previously spent extended periods there and elsewhere in Latin America. as well as in Indonesia and New Zealand. Stea was nominated for the Right Livelihood Prize (the "alternative Nobel") in 1987. He received an honorary doctorate from the University of A Corunna, Galicia, Spain in 2003 and was named Distinguished Visitor by the city of Veracruz, Mexico, in 2008. He is coauthor of *Image and Environment, Maps in Minds,* and *Peacemaking,* and of numerous book chapters and articles on Latin America.

Nelson P. Valdés is professor of sociology at the University of New Mexico and visiting professor and director of the Fundacion Amistad at Duke University. Born in Cuba, he came to the United States in 1961. Since 1977 he has traveled to Cuba on more than a dozen occasions. Professor Valdes holds a PhD in history from the University of New Mexico and has published five books and numerous articles on Cuba. He founded and served as director from 1986 to 1996 of the Latin America Database, a computerized database that produced two electronic newsletters: the *Central America Update* and the *Latin American Debt Chronicle.* Professor Valdes has been a board member of the Center for Cuban Studies (New York) and the Instituto de Estudios Cubanos (Miami), and he has served as the Latin American analyst for the Pacific News Service. He is now a member of the editorial board of the leading social science journal in Cuba, *Temas.* He is also project director of Cuba-L Project, a news and analysis distribution service of materials on Cuba, a spin-off of Latin America Database. In 1998 he established the Cuba Research and Analysis Group, a nonprofit organization.

Arturo Valenzuela was appointed in 2009 by President Barack Obama and confirmed by the United States Senate as US Assistant Secretary of State for Western Hemisphere Affairs. He is on leave from his long-term positions as Professor of Government and Director of the Center for Latin American Studies at Georgetown University. He served as Deputy Assistant Secretary of State for Inter-American Affairs in the first Clinton Administration and as Senior Director at the National Security Council in Clinton's second term. He has been a member of the Council on Foreign Relations and Board Member of the National Democratic Institute for International Affairs, the National Council of La Raza, Drew University, Le Institut des Ameriques, and of America's Watch. He has served on the editorial boards of *The Journal of Democracy, Third World Quarterly, Latin American Research Review, Foreign Policy Bulletin,* and *Current History.* The author or co-author of six books on Chilean politics, he is the co-editor and co-author with Juan Linz of *The Failure of Presidential Democracy* (1995). Professor Valenzuela previously taught at Duke University and has been a Visiting Scholar at Oxford University, the University of Sussex, the University of Florence, the University of Chile, and the Catholic University of Chile.

J. Samuel Valenzuela is professor and former chair of the Department of Sociology at the University of Notre Dame. He was formerly on the faculties at Yale and Harvard Universities and has been senior associate member at Saint Antony's College, Oxford University. He is the author of *Democratización via reforma: La expansión del sufragio en Chile*, coauthor of *Chile, A Country Study*, and coeditor of *Military Rule in Chile: Dictatorship and Oppositions* and of *Chile: Politics and Society*. He has also written numerous articles on the intersection between labor and politics and on democratization and electoral politics.

Henry Veltmeyer is professor of sociology and international development studies at Saint Mary's University, Halifax, Nova Scotia. He also has a faculty appointment in the doctoral program in development studies at the Autonomous University of Zacatecas in Mexico. He has written and contributed to the publication of a wide range of articles and books on the dynamics of global development and Canadian political economy as well as the sociology of Latin American development. His publications include *Rethinking Development: Caribbean Perspectives, Canadian Corporate Power*, and, with James Petras, *Neoliberalism and Class Conflict in Latin America*. His most recent books are, with James Petras, *System in Crisis* (2003) and *Globalización en America Latina* (2004); and edited, *Globalization/Antiglobalization* (2004) and *Nongovernmental Organizations and Development* (forthcoming).

Christine J. Wade is an associate professor of political science and international studies at Washington College in Chestertown, Maryland. She holds a PhD in political science from Boston University. She is the coauthor, with John Booth and Thomas Walker, of *Understanding Central America* (5th ed., 2009) and coauthor, with Tommie Sue Montgomery, of *A revolução salvadorenha* (2006). Her current research focuses on postwar politics and peace building in El Salvador and Nicaragua.

Thomas W. Walker is professor emeritus of political science and director emeritus of Latin American studies at Ohio University. He holds a PhD in political science from the University of New Mexico. He has been doing research in Central America for more than three decades and has served on international electoral observation teams in Nicaragua in 1984, 1990, and 1996. Walker is the author, editor/coauthor, or coeditor of ten books on the politics of Central America, including *Understanding Central America* (2d ed., 1993), *Nicaragua: Living in the Shadow of the Eagle* (4th ed., 1991), and *Nicaragua Without Illusions: Regime Transition and Structural Adjustment in the 1990s* (1997).

Index